THE
Pruning
BOOK

THE
Pruning
BOOK

LEE REICH

The Taunton Press

Publisher: Suzanne La Rosa
Associate publisher: Helen Albert
Editorial assistant: Cherilyn DeVries

Editor: Ruth Dobsevage
Designer: Joan Lockhart
Layout artist: Lynne Phillips
Illustrator: Dolores R. Santoliquido
Indexer: Harriet Hodges

Typeface: Minion
Paper: 70-lb. Patina
Printer: Quebecor Printing/Hawkins, New Canton, Tennessee

Taunton
BOOKS & VIDEOS
for fellow enthusiasts

First printing: 1997
Printed in the United States of America

The Taunton Press, 63 South Main Street,
PO Box 5506, Newtown, CT 06470-5506

Library of Congress Cataloging-in-Publication Data

Reich, Lee.
      The pruning book / Lee Reich.
          p.   cm.
      Includes index.
      ISBN 1-56158-160-7 (alk. paper)
        1. Pruning.   I. Title.
    SB125.R38   1997
    635.9'1542 — dc20   96-34301
                                        CIP

ACKNOWLEDGMENTS

A number of people helped bring
The Pruning Book to fruition. Thanks,
first of all, to *Horticulture* magazine's
Tom Cooper for sowing the seed of the
idea. At The Taunton Press, associate
publisher Helen Albert and editorial
assistant Cherilyn DeVries nourished that
seed as it developed and grew into the
book you now hold in your hands. And
thanks to my editor, Ruth Dobsevage, for
her thoroughness and humor. Also for
her pruning—of words—where needed.

I appreciate commentary provided by
the following people on selected portions
of the draft: Dr. John Barden of Virginia
Polytechnic Institute and State University,
Dr. Richard Harris of the University of
California at Davis, and Dr. William
Welch of Texas A & M University. And
thanks goes to my father, Joseph Reich,
for his part in reading and providing
insightful criticism on the draft from
beginning to end.

CONTENTS

PART
3
SPECIALIZED
PRUNING
TECHNIQUES

Plant Lists

INTRODUCTION

Do you wince with pain, as if amputating without anesthetic, when pruning a plant? Or do you ruthlessly attack? Either approach can have good results—provided your cuts are well reasoned, well timed, and well made. These are the three keys to successful pruning, and my aim in writing this book is put them into your hands.

I have attempted to include here nearly every plant that might benefit from pruning. And I use the word "prune" quite literally: "to remove dead or living parts from (a plant) so as to increase fruit or flower production or improve the form" (*Webster's New Twentieth Century Dictionary of the English Language, 1962*). To this end, you will find between these two covers information on how to prune a lilac bush, an apple tree or a maple tree, a hibiscus hedge, a bougainvillea, strawberries, tomato vines, a weeping fig, a wisteria vine, chrysanthemums…as I said, any plant that benefits from pruning. The last section of this book guides you through such specialized pruning techniques as bonsai, espalier, even lawn mowing. (I did say that this book was meant to be comprehensive and fully embrace the word "prune.")

This book is intended for readers as diverse in their interests and skills as the range of plants covered. Too often, directions for pruning are unduly complicated, even for seasoned pruners. I have drawn on my own experiences, in research and in the field, as well as what has been previously written about pruning, to put together a text that is, I hope, both practical and readable.

Information is arranged so that both novices and experts can easily sift out what they need.

This book parts company with other books about pruning in two ways. First of all, I have had no qualms about debunking or at least questioning the value of certain long-held and well-entrenched pruning practices. Cutting back the tops of woody plants when transplanting, flush-cutting limbs from shade trees, and applying wound dressings are all examples of traditional practices that, on the basis of recent research, should no longer be universally recommended (but are still recommended in too many "modern" publications). Let careful and rigorous observation, rather than tradition, be our guides in pruning. The plants will be thankful, and show it.

This book also distinguishes itself in being a book only about pruning. While writing this book, I was often tempted to describe flowers and fruits, to mention site selection, fertilization, and other considerations attendant to growing particular plants listed. But I resisted temptation. Presumably you have done your homework in these matters—now you are ready to prune. What these pages lack in incidentals about plants, I hope they make up for with thoroughness about pruning those plants.

But enough words. As Thackeray observed, approvingly, "One sees him clipping his apricots and pruning his essays." Here, here, and on with both.

New Paltz, New York
May, 1994

2

HOW TO USE THIS BOOK

Ideally, you will curl up with this book some winter evening—not to prune, of course, but just to read about pruning. The dead of winter is a perfect time to imprint firmly in your mind why a plant might benefit from pruning, what tools you should use, where and when to make the cuts, and how you can generally expect a plant to respond. All this information is offered in Part 1 of this book, "The Basics." With your homework done, you then will be prepared when a break in the weather gives you an urge to prune. All you'll need is a glance at Part 2, "The Plants," for specific information on your particular plant—or plants.

Such a scenario may be wishful thinking, so I've also done my best to accommodate those of you whose initial contact with this book will be as you grab a pair of pruning shears and run out into the garden the first balmy day of the season. A little box entitled "The Bare Bones" at the beginning of each chapter in Part 2 provides you with the essentials for pruning all the plants in that chapter. These instructions will not make you an expert pruner, but will offer sufficient guidance to keep you and your plants reasonably happy.

Part 2, "The Plants," forms the bulk of this book, with each chapter consisting of plants grouped in the categories for which we value them: deciduous ornamental bushes, evergreens, fruits, houseplants, etc. Roses are such a large, popular group that they earn their own subcategory—in the chapter on deciduous ornamental shrubs, of course. These chapters offer detailed pruning instructions in addition to "The Bare Bones" at the beginning.

Use the information in Part 2 by first looking up the appropriate chapter for the plant that you want to prune, then reading over the instructions in that chapter, or a heading within the chapter. Next, check the chapter's Plant List for specifics on the particular plant. If you have trouble assigning a plant to a chapter, look the plant up in the Index.

An advantage of grouping plants the way they have been grouped in Part 2 is that it allows you to prune a plant even if you do not know its name. Or even if the plant has not been included in this book! All you need to do is to decide what sort of plant it is. Even a beginning gardener can differentiate between a deciduous and an evergreen plant—just wait for winter. A year of observation may be needed before you can pigeonhole an unknown plant into an appropriate category, and perhaps subcategory (spring- versus summer-flowering shrub, for example).

Part 3 of this book, "Specialized Pruning Techniques," broadens your pruning skills. Here you will learn about pollarding, pleaching, and topiary; you will find out how to grow a fuchsia as a small tree, how to prune...er, mow... your lawn, how to create a bonsai, and how to espalier an apple tree.

Notwithstanding all the guidance, both general and specific, offered in this book, one caution is in order: No matter how or what you are pruning, couple use of your pruning tool with a keen eye. Plants do not always obey all the rules. Close observation of how a plant grows, and how it responds to your cuts, makes for better—and the most satisfying—results.

PART 1

1

THE

BASICS

CHAPTER ONE

WHY PRUNE?

There are undoubtedly gardeners who shudder at the thought of putting a blade to a plant. After all, look within the forest and the field at wild plants, their stems untouched by pruning saws and clippers. These plants seem happy enough, living their lives unpruned.

In fact, wild plants are pruned. Large tree limbs on the ground following a wind or ice storm are a dramatic demonstration of "natural" pruning; less obvious are the smaller twigs and branches that litter the ground beneath trees and shrubs. How much natural pruning occurs depends not only upon wind and weather, but also on the plant species. Silver maple and boxelder are frowned upon as landscape trees because of their notorious habit of dropping branches of various sizes. My American persimmon trees save me some pruning work by naturally shedding some of their twiggy branches after they bear fruit.

Animals also contribute to natural pruning. Not only do deer shorten branches, but they also enjoy nibbling along the length of a branch, which results in bare regions of "blind wood." If only deer would browse yews in a more artistic fashion! Rabbits take care of natural pruning near ground level.

Lower limbs of crowded plants also are naturally pruned, dropping off as they weaken and die from lack of light. Foresters encourage this natural pruning by planting timber trees close together, to produce straight, branchless (hence knot-free) trunks.

Whether wild plants, pruned one way or another, suffer or benefit from such pruning becomes a philosophical question. The ragged scar left where wind ripped a large limb off a tree is going to be subject to infection, which is obviously of no benefit to the plant. On the other hand, small plants might benefit from the increased light they receive after a large limb drops from a nearby tree. With natural pruning, individuals may suffer, but the population—the collection of plants in the forest or field—benefits, or at least changes in a natural progression.

Cultivated plants are another story. We prune our cultivated plants both for ourselves and for the plants. Each one has aesthetic, sentimental, even monetary, value, so pruning cannot be left to the vagaries of nature. Deliberate pruning may be necessary.

Most important, before pruning any plant, is to have a clear objective in mind, as well as an understanding of how the plant is likely to respond to whatever cuts are made. Done correctly, pruning will not harm a plant, and may actually help it. Later we will delve into how plants respond to pruning, as well as how to prune without causing them harm.

For now, let's consider the reasons for pruning: to keep a plant healthy; to keep a plant from growing too large; to make a plant more beautiful; to improve the quality or quantity of flowers, leaves, or fruits.

Prune for plant health

Peer into the center of an old, unpruned tree or shrub, and you'll see a jumble of branches rubbing together, many of them weak and dying, some already dead. The wood is weak from lack of light, which, along with poor air circulation, creates the dank conditions favored by disease-causing organisms. This problem is not limited to woody plants. Such conditions might develop within a couple of months even on an herbaceous plant—witness the average tomato plant, carefully pruned early in the season to grow up a stake, then becoming a tangle of stems once summer's heat spurs growth beyond a gardener's enthusiasm for pruning.

Pruning away some branches within that tangled mass of vegetation lets in light and air. The light itself inhibits the growth of certain disease-producing microorganisms, and the combination of light and air circulation promotes more

Natural pruning is fine in the forest, but undesirable in a backyard.

A tangle of branches leads to dead, weak, or diseased wood.

rapid drying of leaves, shoots, and fruits, further reducing the chances of disease. Removing crossing limbs also prevents wounds created by rubbing, another possible entryway for disease.

Let's turn now to a large maple tree, "pruned" naturally by a windstorm. That windstorm does not lop off branches cleanly, or necessarily at a point where the plant can best heal the wound. The

Neglect, or the wrong choice of plants, and a house is swallowed in greenery.

ragged, misplaced cut will heal poorly, leaving a large scar through which disease can gain a foothold. Touching up natural pruning with a sharp saw keeps such a plant healthy.

As you look over a plant, no matter what kind of plant it is, be ready to cut away portions attacked by disease or insects. On a dormant plant, look for such problems as bark cankers, which are dark, sunken areas where diseases spend the winter, or tarry, black growths on *Prunus* species, which are indicative of black knot disease (see the photo below). In summer, timely pruning away of stems whose leaves have been blackened by fire blight disease can prevent future infections. Cutting off a raspberry or currant cane below the swollen spot where a borer has entered can stop further damage.

Pruning to promote and maintain plant health begins as soon as you set a new plant in the ground. This is the first and last time you get to view the roots, so take the opportunity to cut off any diseased parts and cut cleanly—for better healing—any ragged ends. Remember that bare-root plants, whether vegetable transplants, shrubs, or trees, are stressed

Pruning helps keep certain diseases, such as black knot of plum, in check.

by root loss. Pruning the stems of trees and shrubs, or cutting off some or a portion of the leaves of vegetable transplants, may help these plants recover from the shock of transplanting under dry conditions. With good growing conditions, however, such pruning is unnecessary and results in less growth than if the plant is left unpruned.

Pruning also keeps trees healthy by directing growth while the tree is young, so that limbs are firmly anchored to the trunk, and not apt to break in high winds or under their own weight or when loaded down with fruits.

Prune to keep a plant from growing too large

Pruning dwarfs plants, and is thus a way to control their size. That said, there is a better, or at least an easier, way than pruning to keep plants from growing out of bounds. You need not search far to see homes whose entrances, windows, whose very walls are being gobbled up by the somber yews and junipers planted along their foundation walls. Perhaps the homeowners ignored the plants for a few years, not realizing that the neglected plants would grow into such large, billowing masses of greenery.

Rather than fighting a plant back every year with metal blades, just plant a tree, shrub, or vine that naturally will keep within its allotted space. Dwarf forms exist for many plants, and these eliminate or at least reduce the need for pruning. 'Aurea Nana' arborvitae, for example, never grows higher than 5 ft., as compared with 20 ft. or more for the species. With some plants, most notably fruit trees, size control can be achieved by grafting a stem onto a dwarfing rootstock. Apple rootstocks have been the most studied, and are available for a

Pruning and good plant choice make a well-proportioned landscape.

range of tree sizes, from a full-size tree 30 ft. high down to a 6-ft. dwarf.

For people willing to commit themselves to an annual pruning regime, or in those situations where dwarf plants are not available, pruning is the answer. Many houseplants, for example, are by nature large tropical trees that cannot be allowed to express their full vigor within the confines of a home. Street trees beneath power lines need occasional cutting to keep the lines clear. Peach trees are not naturally very large trees, yet are large enough to put the fruits beyond convenient reach. Left to its own devices, a cultivated grape vine is likely to clamber up a pole or nearby tree to bear much of its fruit at an inaccessible height, as do wild grapes. In all these cases, controlling plant size by pruning does not mean wantonly hacking back branches. Each cut must take into account the plant's needs as well as its response to various types of pruning

This topiary brings another meaning to the phrase 'bear hug.'

cuts. Pruning roots as well as branches may be called for to keep a plant to size.

For many gardeners, and I count myself among such souls, pruning to keep a plant small is not drudgery, but enjoyable and interesting. With only 4 ft. between trees, my apples require dwarf rootstocks *and* diligent pruning to prevent overcrowding—all the while maintaining fruitfulness, of course. Pruning to dwarf a plant is carried to its extreme with the art of bonsai, by which meticulous pruning of both the branches and roots of trees and shrubs creates a picturesque landscape in miniature.

Prune to make a plant more beautiful

When you prune a plant for beauty, your goals may run the gamut. You may want to knit together a view with a uniform hedge or a pleached tunnel of trees. At the other extreme, you may want to shape a plant in a whimsical manner. Topiary animals, carved from shrubs and "scurrying" across an expanse of lawn, are certain to cause a pleasant surprise the first time they come into view. A uniform hedge with "end posts" of shrubs sheared in ornate geometric forms similarly draws your eye. Used on too many plants in a given scene, either extreme in pruning—that which creates harmony or that which creates interest—is unpleasant. The first becomes boring and the second becomes disturbing.

To achieve either effect, a plant's growth can be merely coaxed along in its natural form, or growth can be more radically redirected in a formal manner. No matter how much you prune any plant, however, it will attempt to resume its natural growth habit. And this growth habit will change somewhat as the plant ages. Young plants tend to grow more upright, with longer branches and larger leaves than older plants. A formal shape, being farther from a plant's natural growth habit than a natural shape, usually requires more diligent pruning. So the cordon apple tree—consisting of a single stem—might require pruning two, three, or even more times each year, some in winter and some in summer. A standard apple tree, in contrast, gets along fine with its once-a-year pruning in late winter.

Not all plants trained in a naturalistic way require little pruning: Remember those bonsai plants mentioned a few sentences ago? Their "natural" appearance is actually the result of meticulous pruning of both roots and shoots—all to keep them looking, in miniature, just like their full-size brothers and sisters.

Prune to improve the quality or quantity of flowers, leaves, or fruits

A plant's appeal comes not only from its shape, but also from the individual size or sheer mass of its blooms, its leafy raiment, or its luscious fruits—perhaps all three! Pruning can help coax the best from a plant in any of these respects.

How can pruning have such an effect? Removing stems from a plant removes buds that would potentially have grown into shoots, so more energy gets

Fruit thinning, a type of pruning, results in large and luscious peaches.

The craggy trunk of this bonsai captures the venerability of an ancient tree.

channeled into those buds and shoots that remain. Vigorous new shoots stimulated by pruning are those that are most fiery red on a red-osier dogwood and are what give a pollarded tree—cut back each winter to a mere stump a few feet high—its characteristic headdress of lanky shoots and oversized leaves. (Oversized leaves are often associated with overly vigorous growth.) The more new growth you can stimulate on a woody plant that flowers only on new shoots, the greater the show of flowers each summer. Drastically cutting back such plants in late winter or early spring stimulates an abundance of new shoots.

Some of the buds removed when you lop a branch off a fruit tree are flower buds. Fewer flowers results in fewer fruits, but those fruits that remain get an increased share of the plant's energy. The result is that the remaining fruits are larger and sweeter. An additional benefit of reducing the number of fruits is that a plant might bear moderate crops every season, rather than having alternating seasons of feast and famine. Because of hormones produced in developing fruits, a large crop one year suppresses flower-bud initiation, and, hence, fruiting, in plants whose flowers open a year after the first traces of flower buds are laid down.

Light has a dramatic effect on plant performance, and by cutting off branches to change the form of a plant, you also affect the amount of light reaching the remaining branches. Hedges look their best fully clothed with leaves from head to toe, so they are always sheared at least slightly narrower at their heads than at their feet to allow leaf-nourishing light to reach all surfaces. Fruiting demands abundant sunlight—transformed within plants into sugars—so fruit trees are trained and maintained in such a way that each part of the plant gets as much sun as possible.

Stems are not the only parts of a plant that you can prune to improve plant performance. Removing all but a few flower buds on a dahlia pumps the flowers that do remain into show-quality "dinnerplate" blooms. Similarly, pinching some flowers off a peach tree—yet another form of pruning—redirects the plant's energies to fewer peaches, making them sweeter and larger. (Pinching off flower buds supplements fruit thinning that results from earlier pruning of branches that had flower buds and subsequent pinching off of excess small fruits.)

And one more reason to prune...

Upon coming to the end of this list of reasons to prune, I suddenly realized that there is one more reason, for better or worse, why we prune plants—because we are human. Plants offer us more than mere aesthetic or utilitarian pleasure; they also are outlets for our creativity. We enjoy watching plants respond to our care, reacting to our pinching, snipping, watering, and fertilizing. By this, I do not mean merely watching a plant shrink as we lop off its branches, but, rather, how the plant regrows in response to just how and when it was cut back.

Pruning is just one of many gardening practices, yet it is among the most effective and interesting in terms of what it can accomplish. Depending on how and when you prune, the influence may be evident in a few weeks, in a year, or over the course of years. This book, I hope, will help you to get a response to pruning your plants that both pleases you and keeps your plants happy.

CHAPTER TWO

TOOLS OF THE TRADE

A bowsaw with a sharp blade makes easy work of thick limbs.

Soon after the first human deliberately pruned a plant, ideas for designs of specialized pruning tools may have taken shape. As long ago as the first century A.D., a Roman named Columella wrote of the *vinitoria falx*, a grape-pruning tool with six different functions. Today, you will not find one pruning tool to do six different jobs; depending on your plants and horticultural aspirations, you may not even need six different tools. But if you grow plants, you probably will need at least one pruning tool—in all likelihood a pair of hand-held pruning shears.

More on what tool or tools you will need in a bit; first, a comment on pur-chasing a pruning tool. Better-quality tools cost more and are, in my opinion, well worth the extra money. But be fore-warned that when it comes to pruning tools, "better quality" can have more than one meaning. It may mean a tool manufactured from higher-quality materials, or a tool designed to cut more effectively, or a tool that is more comfortable to use. I have cut branches using stainless-steel pruning shears that were shiny and expensive, but not particularly comfortable to hold or especially effective at cutting, despite the high-quality materials they were made from. If possible, try out a pruning tool once you find one in your price range.

The thumbnail is a useful—and convenient—pruning tool.

Always use a pruning tool appropriate to the size of the pruning cut. Too many gardeners attempt to shimmy and wiggle hand-held pruning shears through branches that are too thick to cut effectively with this tool. Using the wrong size tool makes pruning more difficult—even impossible—and leaves a forlorn-looking plant with ragged stubs. Before purchasing a pruning tool, think about what you will be cutting.

It is sometimes stated, especially in older gardening books, that all pruning should be done with a knife, or with just your thumbnail. The implication is that timely pruning removes any growth before it is beyond the size that can be handled by either of these "tools." (The quotation marks are for the thumbnail.) Perhaps so, in an ideal world, or for a person growing only a half-dozen houseplants in an apartment. But

pruning a gardenful of plants with your knife and thumbnail is not practical. And even if it were practical, some limbs do not display their character at an early enough age to signal their need for removal. And how about that wrist-thick limb, dead from disease and now needing removal?

That said, the thumbnail is a fine and convenient pruning tool, ideal for such tasks as pinching out the tips of outdoor chrysanthemums and indoor avocado trees. Do not overlook the rest of your hand as a useful pruning implement. Prune suckers from a tomato plant by just grabbing them, then snapping them off with a downward jerk. Snap off unwanted watersprouts from a tree in the same way way, the minute you notice them. There is no need to trek to the garden shed for any other equipment.

(If you never considered your hand as a pruning tool, stretch your mind and also consider these other specialized "tools:" a shovel, for root pruning; a stream of water from your hose or a broom handle with a piece of hose attached, to thin blossoms from a fruit tree.)

The pruning knife comes highly recommended by those gardeners with the expertise to use it. This knife differs from other knives in having a curved blade, which helps it keep contact with the branch as you cut. If you choose to use a pruning knife, buy one with a folding blade (for safety in carrying it) and a thick handle that is easy to hold without causing blisters.

Personally, I have never been able see the advantage of a pruning knife over a good pair of hand shears, what the British call secateurs. The hand shears will never slip and nick nearby stems, and will cut through wood up to ½ in. thick, which is more than you could ask from a pruning knife. As mentioned previously, this tool is probably the one you will need if you own but one pruning tool.

Because a pair of hand shears is such a useful tool—one which I often drop into my back pocket before I walk out into the garden—check out the style (see the sidebar below), the weight, the hand fit, and the balance of several models before you settle on one. You can buy special shears tailored to fit small hands or left hands. Make sure any pair of shears has a convenient safety catch that does not slip into the "open" position when you want it closed, or vice versa; otherwise, if you carry them as I do, you could end up

ANVIL VS. BYPASS HAND SHEARS

H and shears fall into one of two categories: anvil and bypass (the latter sometimes called "scissors"). The business end of the anvil-type shears consists of a sharp blade that comes down on top of an opposing blade having a flat edge. The flat edge is made of a soft metal so as not to dull the sharp edge. Bypass pruners work more like scissors, with two sharpened blades sliding past each other.

Anvil shears generally are cheaper than bypass shears—and the price difference is reflected in the resulting cut! Often, the anvil pruner will crush part of the stem. And if the two blades do not mate perfectly, the cut will be incomplete, leaving the two pieces of the stem attached by threads of tissue. That wide, flattened blade also makes it more difficult to get the tool right up against the base of the stem you want to remove.

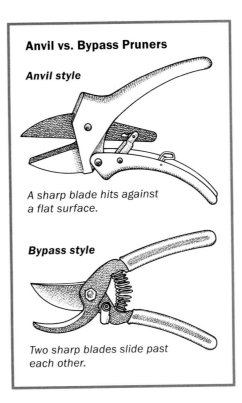

Anvil vs. Bypass Pruners

Anvil style

A sharp blade hits against a flat surface.

Bypass style

Two sharp blades slide past each other.

with a hole in your back pocket. Also take note of how easily the blades of a particular pair of hand shears can be sharpened; some shears have replaceable blades. A bypass pruner should have an adjustable tension screw, so that the blades can be made to close easily, yet be tight enough so as not to bind onto a stem. I particularly like the hooked end of my Pica shears, which prevents stems from slipping free of the jaws as I cut. And for the professional landscaper or orchardist, who is confronted with hours of pruning at a stretch, pneumatic or electrically operated hand shears are available.

For pruning branches larger than ½ in. across, up to about 1½ in. in diameter, you need lopping shears, usually just called a "lopper." This tool is essentially the same as hand shears, except that the blades are heavier and the handle is a couple of feet long. Like hand shears, the lopper's business end may be either of the anvil or bypass type. The long handles of the lopper give you leverage to cut through those larger stems, and allow you to reach into the base of an over-grown rose or gooseberry bush without being attacked by thorns. Some loppers gain extra cutting power with a gear or a ratchet mechanism that allows the blades

The lopping shears slices through stems up to about 1½ in. across.

to sever wood even 2 in. thick. Those extra mechanisms do add weight to the end of the tool, which, with its long handles, may become unwieldy after a few hours of use. Of all the loppers that I have used, I prefer an old pair I bought at a farm sale. The long wooden handles absorb shock and are smoothed from decades of use, and the small bypass blades make a clean cut in spite of the chipped beak on one of the blades. This tool slices through wood up to 1½ in. thick.

If more cutting power is needed than lopping shears can provide, I can always run to the shed and grab a pruning saw. Saws are the next step up in necessary tools as you progress to thicker wood. Do not try to use a saw from your woodworking shop to remove a limb, because such a saw works effectively only on dry wood. The teeth on pruning saws are designed to cope with green wood without clogging or gumming. Larger teeth generally cut quickest, leaving a rougher edge, but the new, so-called Japanese blades (sometimes called "turbo" or "frictionless" blades) cut quickly despite their small teeth. A nice saw for making fast work of limbs up to 3 in. in diameter is a "Grecian" pruning saw, with a curved blade and teeth set to cut on the pull stroke. These small saws squeeze their way into tight places among branches, and, if designed so that the blade folds into the handle, will even squeeze into your back pocket. Where space is not quite so restricted (on the plant, not your pocket), my preference is for the narrow-nosed bowsaw (photo, p. 13), which has a thin, easily replaceable blade that cuts on both the push and the pull strokes. Heavier-bladed, straight-bladed pruning saws look much like carpenter's saws, but with a different set of dentures. Avoid those that are reversible, having a row of coarse teeth

on one edge of the blade and narrow teeth on the other. Such saws inevitably make unwanted cuts on wood near the side of the blade that you are *not* using! Purchase two separate saws instead.

A 'Grecian' pruning saw cuts through moderately thick limbs in tight places, then folds up into your back pocket.

Use a hand shears (the bypass type is shown here) to slice through stems up to ½ in. in diameter.

Manual (top) and electric (above) hedge shears are essential for keeping hedges at their best.

for the job, or, even better, hire a professional with a chainsaw to do the job for you. Experience with chainsaws breeds respect for this useful, albeit dangerous, pruning tool. If you feel the need to own a chainsaw, purchase one scaled to the thickness of wood you will be cutting. And when you make your purchase, also buy a pair of goggles and, along with a gasoline-powered saw, a set of ear protectors.

If you have formal hedges to take care of, you also need some sort of hedge shears to keep them shapely. Manual shears look like giant scissors with straight handles. Shearing a long hedge of privet by hand can be tiring, so choose hedge shears with care. Recognize that longer blades and handles—which allow you to bite off more and reach farther with each cut—also add to the weight of the tool. Because you constantly bang the handles together as you cut, pay attention to how the handles feel and what kind of shock absorption they have as they come together. My Sandvik shears have padded rubber handles and enough bounce from a rubber shock absorber to make the handles spring apart after banging together, ready for the next cut. Many hedge shears have a notch near the base of the blade for lopping off an occasional, overly vigorous stem that you might come across as you progress down the length of a hedge. Wavy blades on a pair of shears reputedly do a better job by keeping stems from sliding out the mouth of the shears without being cut. I have not experienced that problem because I keep the straight-edged blades on my hedge shears sharp.

Of all power pruning tools used by the average homeowner, probably none is more popular than the electric hedge clipper. The straight bar of this tool, with its oscillating blade, makes it easy to put a

We cannot leave the subject of pruning saws without mention of the chainsaw. These gasoline or electric saws make relatively short work of large limbs—even whole trees (but that can hardly be called "pruning")! A chainsaw is overkill where you have only a backyard full of plants to prune. If the size of a cut dictates the need for such a tool, rent one

flat top on a hedge. Nonetheless, I still prefer a good pair of manual hedge shears because they are easier to sharpen and require no long extension cord. I can run out and prune a little bit of the hedge at a time, without investing any time or effort in coiling and uncoiling the extension cord. The manual shears, especially if they have high-quality blades, makes a rhythmical and pleasant sound as the honed metal blades slice against each other. If noise does not concern you and extension cords are too much trouble, gasoline-powered hedge clippers are available, but these are mostly heavy-duty models for professional landscapers.

Now we enter the realm of specialized pruning tools, which you may or may not ever require. The first is a shearing knife, useful for keeping a Christmas tree or a large hedge shapely and dense as it grows. This knife has a long handle and a blade that is thin, sharp, and also long. Because it is used samurai fashion, also consider purchasing leg guards along with a shearing knife.

Growers of red raspberries constantly have to remove wayward suckers, and a tool that facilitates this job is a bush hook, which consists of a sharpened hook at the end of a long handle. With this tool, you can walk along the row, hook the blade under a sucker, and jerk it out cleanly without even stooping. I stoop. (Anyway, I have only seen this tool pictured in old gardening books, so if you want one, you probably will have to make it yourself or have it made.)

A lawnmower is, of course, also a specialized pruning tool, one with which everyone is familiar. Reel mowers can be human-, gasoline-, or electric-powered and cut more cleanly than rotary mowers, which must be powered by either gasoline or electricity.

Do not overlook a scythe for "pruning" high grass. The so-called European-style scythe has a straight snath and a light-weight blade that is hammered, then honed, to a razor-sharp edge—all in all a pleasure to use and not to be confused with the heavy, American-type scythe that has a curved snath.

A European-style scythe cuts high grass quietly and efficiently.

**Saw or slice high limbs
from the ground with
a pole pruner.**

And then there is the highly specialized strawberry pruner, described in Liberty Hyde Bailey's *The Pruning Book* (1912), for cutting all the runners off a strawberry plant all at once. The tool consists of a 10-in. diameter metal cylinder with one edge sharpened and the other attached to a handle that can be banged with a hammer or stomped upon with your foot. You place the cylinder around a plant, then apply the downward force to cut off the runners.

Of all the pruning tools available, the one that has the least to recommend it is the high-limb chain saw. The chain part of this tool is attached at either end to a rope. You throw the device over a high limb, grasp onto each end of the rope, centering the toothed chain over the limb, then alternately pull down on the ropes. The results can be disastrous: The worst-case scenario has the limb toppling on top of you, tearing a long strip of bark off the trunk on the way down.

A saner way to deal with high limbs is with a pole pruner, an effective pruning tool that admittedly does not reach as high as the high-limb chain saw. With a shearing head seated atop the pole and activated by a handle or rope at the bottom, the tool performs the same job as hand shears, many feet up in the tree. You could also attach a curved Grecian saw on the head of a pole. If you stand slightly to the side when using it, both the curve of the blade and gravity will help you along with your sawing.

Very useful is the pole pruner at whose head is attached *both* shearing blades and a saw. Once you have managed to work this tool up through the tree to the branches that you want to cut, you have a choice of cutting devices. Still, the two-headed pole pruner is not quite as versatile as Columella's six-in-one tool for pruning grapes.

Caring for pruning tools

A pruning tool that you treat with affection will return the favor with years of good service. If the expense of a tool will induce you to give it greater care, then this is one more reason to pay as much as you can afford for it.

Pruning tools do not need to be babied, just cleaned, sharpened, and oiled. Dirt on the blades of a tool may nick or dull its edges, so give the blade—no matter what kind of pruning tool it is—a wipe with a rag each time you finish using it. (I leave a rag hanging conveniently on a nail in my garage near where I keep my tools so that I have no excuse not to use it.) Clean sap off blades with a rag dipped in a solvent such as kerosene. Periodically apply a few drops of oil to the bolt that joins the blades of hand shears, lopping shears, and hedge shears, as well as to the spring that spreads the hand shears' handles. Also oil the wooden handles of tools, unless they are coated with varnish.

You will find it easier and quicker to cut if your tool is sharp. Less immediately obvious will be the beneficial effect on the plant. Plants like sharp pruning tools because clean cuts heal fastest.

You need a whetstone and perhaps a file to sharpen the blades of your pruning tools. (The file is needed for quickly removing metal when a blade has been nicked, not for sharpening.) Before using a whetstone, make sure it is thoroughly wet by soaking it in either lightweight oil or water. Then, when you use the whetstone, keep it wet by applying a few drops of oil or water (whichever you soaked the stone in) to its surface as you use it for sharpening. The liquid floats away particles that you grind off. Hold the blade against the whetstone, or vice versa, maintaining the existing angle on the edge of the blade, then move the blade or whetstone in a motion as if you were shaving a thin slice from the whetstone.

Know your tool before you attempt to sharpen it. On an anvil-type pruner, you need to sharpen only one blade, and you sharpen this blade on both sides. As you sharpen, avoid putting a curve on the edge of the blade. Unless the edge is perfectly straight, it will not rest true against the flat opposing anvil, and stems will cling together with a few threads of plant tissue after each of your cuts. On hedge shears, bypass hand shears, or bypass lopping shears, do sharpen both blades. Because these blades cut as they slide past each other, sharpen each blade only on its outside edge.

Pruning saws need special treatment, depending on the type of saw. Use a special jig and round file to sharpen the blade of a chainsaw. Blades of handsaws are tedious to file, so I would pay to have one of these sharpened. Fortunately, the only saw that I use frequently enough to require sharpening is my bowsaw. When its blade dulls, I just throw it out and snap in a new one. Other types of pruning tools sometimes also have replaceable blades.

When you are not using a pruning tool, store it in a place that is dry and beyond the reach of inquisitive children. An especially good time to go thoroughly over your pruning tools, drying, sharpening, and oiling them, is when you are ready to put them away for the season. Then again, as we shall soon see, there is no season when the avid gardener cannot find something to prune.

Plants usually respond in a predictable way to pruning. Depending on which part of the plant (stems, flowers, fruits, roots, bark, or leaves) you prune and the degree of pruning, you might get effects on the plant as a whole, as well as right where you make the cut. By understanding how a plant responds, you can get the desired results. Wherever you cut, you wound the plant; therefore you want to prune in a way that facilitates healing.

Overall effects of pruning

Let's get one fact straight: Pruning dwarfs plants. Leaves are what make food for a plant, and the stems are one place in which plants squirrel away food for later use. Cut away a stem or leaf, and you have left the plant with less food. Root pruning decreases the amount of water and minerals a plant can take up. Less food, minerals, or water results in less growth.

The only situations where pruning might not have a dwarfing effect on a plant are when you prune off a dead stem and when you prune off fruits or fruit buds. A plant obviously grows better when removal of a dead stem prevents spread of diseases or insects to healthy limbs. And removing fruits redirects energy that would have nourished fruits into nourishing shoots.

Barring the above two exceptions, many gardeners might take issue with my assertion that "pruning dwarfs plants." Who has not drastically cut back a tree or branch in late winter, only to watch new shoots grow defiantly as compared with more sedate, unpruned counterparts? And the more severely the tree or branch was cut back, the more energetic the response of remaining buds. If you observed even more closely, you would have noticed that new shoots from wood that was pruned back also began to grow earlier in the season, and continued to do so later in the season.

So pruning has stimulated growth, right? Wrong—at least if you consider the plant as a whole. What has happened is that pruning has caused "local" stimulation, that is, stimulation of the buds just below the point where pruning occurred. If you were to tally together the weight of stems pruned off plus the weight of new growth that the tree would have made if it had not been pruned, you would find this total to be significantly greater than the weight of new growth on a pruned tree.

Whether or not you use pruning to dwarf a plant, the local effects of pruning cuts are going to influence plant form as well as the production of fruits and flowers. Often, we may accept some amount of dwarfing as a necessary evil just because we want to prune for other effects. All plants respond to pruning in qualitatively the same manner. By understanding how a plant will respond to your cuts, you can achieve the desired result, whether or not a general dwarfing of the plant is one of your aims.

Localized effects of pruning stems

Pruning a stem can strengthen it, induce flower buds, and/or cause branching, but the effect depends on both the degree and the timing of your cut.

Effect of degree of cutting

Plants show some differences in how they react when their stems are pruned, but such differences are quantitative rather than qualitative, so general rules are useful. For example, picture a young shoot, less than a year old, be it the main stem of a tomato plant or a branch growing off a limb on an apple tree. Unpruned, such a stem will continue to grow from its tip, and side branches may or may not grow out farther down along the stem. The number and the vigor of side branches depend on the vigor of the plant. Those on a tomato plant, for example, may be numerous and strong enough to match or overtake the growth of the main stem. On the apple tree, though, side branches might push out only a few inches of new growth.

Pinching For the least pruning possible on a stem, pinch out the growing point of a shoot with your thumbnail. This pinch causes growth to falter briefly, but also has another effect. The tip of any stem releases a hormone, called auxin, that moves down that stem, inhibiting the growth of lower buds. Remove that stem tip and you stop auxin flow, so lateral buds that were dormant are awakened into growth and existing side shoots now grow more vigorously. Pinching generally is useful for slowing stem growth, to direct the energies of a tomato plant in late summer to ripening fruits, for example. Pinching also is useful when you want to encourage branching (see the drawing on p. 24), as on a potted avocado tree whose single, lanky stem looks ungainly.

Heading You can prune a stem by shortening it with pruning shears or a knife. This type of cut is called a heading cut, and plant response depends on the

Effect of Pinching

Pinching out the tip of a stem encourages branching.

degree of heading. If you cut a young stem back by one-third, buds that might have stayed dormant on the remaining part of that stem will now be prompted to grow, and they will do so more enthusiastically than if the stem were left alone. Shorten that same stem by two-thirds, and the resulting new growth will be even more vigorous (see the drawing at right on the facing page). (Remember: all this stimulation applies only to the cut stem; the plant as a whole is dwarfed by pruning.) Those buds nearest a heading cut are the ones that make the most vigorous upright shoots; lower down, buds will push out growth that is less vigorous and comes out at wider angles to the cut branch.

The more vigorous a young stem is before it is headed back, the more

vigorous the response to such pruning. As a general rule, the more vertical the orientation of a stem, the greater its vigor. And a heading cut into one-year-old wood elicits a greater response than does a cut into older wood.

Too many gardeners irreverently hack back their plants in an effort to get rid of unwanted growth, then bemoan the dense and vigorous regrowth from these heading cuts. Nonetheless, in the right situation, a heading cut is a useful pruning technique. There are times when vigorous new growth is needed: to make a strong trunk on a young tree; to create new, bearing wood, if needed, for fruits or flowers; for a decorative effect; to invigorate a frail stem. A heading cut also is the cut of choice where you want branching, such as on a newly planted tree consisting of only a single upright stem. Or when you shear a hedge—making, essentially, hundreds of heading cuts—to create a densely branching visual and physical barrier.

Thinning   What happens if, instead of cutting off only part of a stem, you remove it completely, or cut it back to a larger branch? This type of pruning cut is called a thinning cut, and the plant response is: nothing, near the cut. Or, at least, very little. (Remaining shoots on the plant will grow more than they otherwise would have, though.)

So use thinning cuts when you want to remove unwanted growth, such as in the center of a tree or bush, where growth is too dense; reserve heading cuts for situations where you want lush regrowth or branching.

Effect of time of year
"Prune when the knife is sharp" goes the old saying. Not true. (But don't ever prune if the knife—or shears—is not

sharp.) How a plant responds to pruning depends not only on *how much* you cut off a stem, but also on *when* you do it.

As each growing season draws to a close in temperate climates, trees, shrubs, and vines lay away a certain amount of food in their above- and below-ground parts. This food keeps the plants alive through winter, when they cannot use sunlight to make food because of lack of leaves (on deciduous plants) or cold temperatures. This stored food also fuels the growth of the following season's new shoots and leaves, which, as they mature, start manufacturing their own food and pumping the excess back into the plant for use in the coming winter.

When you prune a dormant plant, you remove buds that would have grown into shoots or flowers. Because food reserves within a pruned plant are reapportioned amongst fewer buds and the roots are all prepared to support growth of more buds, shoots growing from those buds that remain grow with increased vigor.

As the growing season progresses, response to pruning changes, because shoot growth of woody plants generally grinds to a halt well before leaves fall in autumn. In fact, growth commonly ceases by midsummer. So the later in the growing season that you prune, the less inclined a woody plant is to regrow—the year of pruning, at least.

Traditional theory holds that summer pruning is more dwarfing than dormant

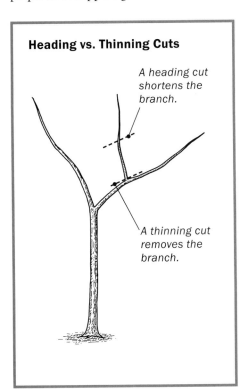

Heading vs. Thinning Cuts

A heading cut shortens the branch.

A thinning cut removes the branch.

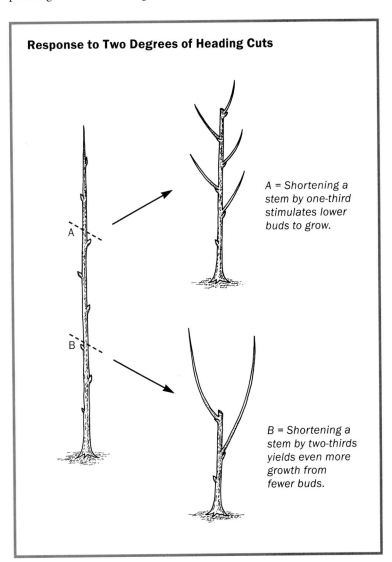

Response to Two Degrees of Heading Cuts

A

B

A = Shortening a stem by one-third stimulates lower buds to grow.

B = Shortening a stem by two-thirds yields even more growth from fewer buds.

pruning, but recent research puts this theory on shaky footing. True, if you shorten a stem while it is dormant, in February, for example, buds that remain will begin to grow into shoots by March and April, whereas if you cut back a shoot in midsummer, no regrowth might occur. Ah, but what about next spring? That's when the summer-pruned shoot, according to this recent research, waits to respond. (Plants have an amazing capacity to act however they please no matter what we do to them.)

What are the practical implications of all this? First of all, if you want to stimulate bud growth, prune a stem when it is dormant. On the other hand, summer is the time to remove a stem to let light in among the branches (to color up ripening apples or peaches, for example), or to remove a stem that is vigorous and in the wrong place. Upright watersprouts, for example, are less likely to regrow if snapped off before they become woody at their bases. Under certain conditions, summer pruning *can* be more dwarfing than dormant pruning, because regrowth following summer pruning can be pruned again. Under certain conditions, summer pruning also can prompt the formation of flower buds rather than new shoots—just what you want for solidly clothing the limbs of a pear espalier with fruits or the branches of a wisteria vine with flowers.

The response to summer pruning depends on the condition of the plant as well as the weather. A weak plant may be killed by summer pruning. A late summer wet spell, especially if it follows weeks of dry weather, might awaken buds that without pruning would have stayed dormant until the following spring. And these responses interact with plant response to various degrees of pruning.

Regrowth and flowering are the dramatic responses to pruning; you also must consider plant health when deciding when to prune. Although immediate regrowth rarely occurs after late summer or autumn pruning, cells right at the cut come alive to close off the wound. Active cells are liable to be injured by cold weather, which is a reason to avoid pruning in late summer or autumn except in climates with mild winters or with plants that are very hardy to cold. Dormant pruning just before growth begins leaves a wound exposed for the minimum amount of time before healing begins. Some plants—peach and its relatives, for example—are so susceptible to infections at wounds that they are best pruned while in blossom. On the other hand, the correct time to prune a diseased or damaged branch is whenever you notice it.

Also consider your own health (your equanimity and your energy) when timing your pruning. Depending on the number of plants you have to prune, as well as other commitments, you may not be able to prune all your plants at each one's optimum moment. I prune my gooseberries in autumn (they never suffer winter damage), my apples just after the most bitter winter cold has reliably passed, and my plums (a peach relative) while they are blossoming.

Plants such as maples, birches, grapes, and kiwis bleed sap profusely if pruned just as their buds are swelling in spring. The way to avoid this loss of sap is to prune either in winter, when the plants are fully dormant, or in spring, after growth is underway. The sap loss actually does no harm to the plants, so rushing or delaying pruning on this account is not for your plant's health, but so that you can rest easy.

Root pruning is a way to keep potted plants small.

Effects of pruning parts other than stems

Stems are not the only parts of a plant you might have cause to remove. You might get a desired response by removing flower buds, flowers, young fruits, or even by cutting back plant roots. Less common pruning practices involve cutting into the bark or removing leaves. Let's see how a plant responds to having each of these parts pruned off.

Pruning flowers and fruits

Ripening fruit demands lots of energy from a plant. Flower buds are potential draws for this energy, and whenever you cut, pinch, or otherwise remove either flowers or fruits, you leave the plant with fewer sinks among which to distribute the remaining food. The result is straightforward: bigger flowers and fruits.

In woody plants, the removal of fruits one year has an effect that carries over to the following year. Seeds within fruits produce hormones that inhibit flower-bud formation. Because many plants initiate flower buds a year before the flowers actually open, the hormones from a large crop of fruit one season result in light flowering and a light crop of fruit the following season. Removing some fruits—or flowers or flower buds—each year evens out the production from year to year, eliminating alternating years of feast and famine.

Obviously, to reap benefits from flower bud, flower, or fruit removal, such pruning must be done early in the season. How early depends on how soon a particular plant initiates flower buds. And such pruning must be in the right degree. You won't get the desired effect from inadequate pruning, while excessive pruning of this type reduces the current year's crop too much and results in too heavy a crop the following year.

Ringing the bark, by peeling away a section from between two parallel cuts, can stimulate flowering.

Pruning roots

Root pruning is a centuries-old practice that can reduce water uptake, mineral uptake, and/or the production of certain hormones. Whatever the precise mechanism, root pruning dwarfs any plant. The technique reaches its extreme in bonsai, where, in conjunction with shoot pruning, it keeps a plant that would have otherwise grown to a full-size forest tree small enough to spend centuries in a miniature pot. Less dramatic, but equally useful, is pruning roots to keep a houseplant, or other potted plant, to a manageable size.

Because root pruning temporarily cuts down on a plant's water supply, this pruning should be accompanied by shoot pruning—to remove transpiring leaves—if performed on plants in full leaf. A dormant, leafless plant that has been root-pruned may automatically adjust the number of leaves it grows, when awakening in spring, to the amount of root loss suffered, so it does not necessarily also need its branches pruned.

You don't have to confine your root pruning to potted plants. In the middle of the 19th century, root pruning was used as a way to dwarf fruit trees planted in open ground. In his book, *The Miniature Fruit Garden* (1866), Thomas Rivers described how he root-pruned his trees by either digging them up and replanting them, or by digging trenches around them, then backfilling with new soil. Great judgment, of course, was needed as to how much root pruning a tree could tolerate without excessively enfeebling or killing it. Because of the great labor involved, as well as the somewhat unpredictable response, root pruning fell out of favor. More recently, however, tractor-pulled blades have taken the backache out of root pruning, and there is renewed interest in this technique in commercial orchards.

Besides dwarfing a tree, root pruning also has been used to hasten fruiting; this is another traditional practice that recently has been shown to be of dubious, or no, value. And Mr. Rivers was not the first to recommend root pruning for this effect. Three hundred years previous, Estienne and Liebault (in *Maisons Rustiques*) recommended that young apple trees "loveth to be digged twice," presumably to keep them small and get them to bear fruit. Wisteria vines are notably tardy to flower, and one traditional recommendation for coaxing them along in this direction is to root-prune them. Personally, I'll put my money on summer pruning rather than root pruning to bring any plant to flower. (And, of course, time—every plant must attain a certain age before it can flower.)

Another bona-fide use for root pruning is to lessen the transplant shock of woody plants. An individual root responds to being pruned by growing new lateral roots near the cut. The response is similar to a plant's response to a heading cut on a stem, and, like a heading cut, root pruning is dwarfing even though growth in the region of the cut is stimulated. But if you are going to move a tree or shrub, root pruning a year or more ahead of time reduces transplant shock by inducing the plant to grow masses of roots near enough to the plant to be taken up with the root ball.

Despite the proven uses for root pruning, this practice is somewhat a shot in the dark as compared to the relatively straightforward response of plants to the removal of flower buds, flowers, or fruits. Still, some plants tolerate it and respond more predictably than others. I easily keep my potted fig manageable and fruitful by hacking away of a portion of its root ball each autumn. Response of plants growing in the ground to root pruning depends not only on how much and when you prune, but also on whether or not they receive adequate water during the subsequent growing season. Practice root pruning with moderation and do not forget an important function of roots: to anchor a plant to the ground. Depending on its size and how much you prune, a plant might need a supporting stake until new roots grow.

Removing bark

Removing a piece of bark is a traditional pruning practice that can, in fact, be used to stimulate shoot growth or flowering. Taking out a whole ring of bark—a practice known as bark ringing or girdling—about the time a tree should be in flower often induces the tree to flower the following season. The ring is made by peeling away bark between two cuts scored ¼ in. to ½ in. apart, depending on the severity of the effect desired. For a lesser effect, just make a single cut around the bark, a technique called scoring. The effect also can be further attenuated by not ringing or scoring completely around a trunk or stem, or by doing either in a spiral fashion, rather than in a closed circle. Cutting out a notch of bark just above or below a bud, a technique called notching, affects only the bud. A notch below a bud slows or prevents its growth; a notch above stimulates the bud to grow. Scoring, ringing, and notching all elicit their responses by perturbing the flow of water, minerals, and hormones within a stem or trunk.

Removing leaves

Leaf removal is rarely practiced, but is another way to induce growth from a bud. Like stem tips, leaves produce the hormone auxin, which inhibits bud growth lower on a stem. Between any leaf and stem is a bud, and auxin produced

Depending on where you make it, a notch can suppress or stimulate growth from a bud.

by that leaf inhibits growth of that bud. So if you want a shoot at a particular place along a growing stem, just pull off the leaf at that point. You could even just cut off the leaf blade—that's where the hormone is made, and the leaf stalk will fall off by itself shortly.

Wound healing: how to cut

Pruning, of necessity, wounds a plant. But this injury need not compromise the plant's health if proper techniques are used.

Plants have an uncanny ability to deal with wounds. Immediately following any wound, whether from the effects of high wind or from the sharp edge of your pruning saw or shears, cells in the vicinity of the wound burst into activity. Their goal: to prevent the spread of infection and seal off the wound. Unless the weather is frigid, rapid respiration ("breathing") and cell division occur, during which time natural antimicrobial chemicals are released and new cells grow to seal off the wound. With little or no microbial growth in frigid weather, the plant can wait to begin repair.

Your job, as a pruner, is to pinch, snip, lop, or saw in such a way as to facilitate your plants' natural healing processes. (To the stickler on terminology, the damaged tissue never actually "heals," but, rather, the damage is overgrown and contained by healthy tissue.) First and foremost in facilitating healing (I've said my bit, so henceforth will dispense with the quotation marks) is to make all cuts clean. Ragged edges leave more damaged cells and more surface area to close over. Sharp prunings tool are a must.

Smaller cuts leave smaller wounds. Try to prune off that tomato sucker when it is 1 in. long rather than when it has shot out to 2 ft. Prune away that misplaced

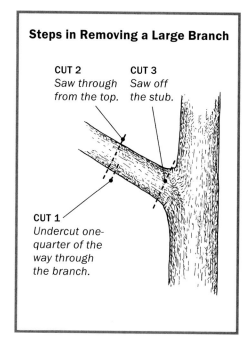

Steps in Removing a Large Branch

CUT 2
Saw through from the top.

CUT 3
Saw off the stub.

CUT 1
Undercut one-quarter of the way through the branch.

maple limb when you can do it with hand shears rather than a chainsaw. Not only will a larger wound take longer to heal over, but new shoots are more likely to sprout up around a larger cut. Pruning away small stems, rather than large ones, also removes less stored food and food-producing tissue of a plant, which is desirable unless you are deliberately attempting to dwarf your plant.

Removing a large branch

Removing a large branch with a single pruning cut can pull off long shreds of bark from a tree as the branch comes toppling down. Avoid this by making three separate cuts. First undercut the branch one-quarter of the way through about 12 in. farther out than your eventual cut. Next, saw through from the top, near the first cut but a couple of inches farther out on the branch. After the branch falls (without tearing any bark), saw off the easily held stub that remains.

Pruning to eliminate disease or insects

Pruning away a diseased or insect-infested part of a plant is pointless unless the whole problem is removed. For this reason, always cut branches back about 6 in. in from where you see the problem. On a large limb that you do not want to cut back, pare away diseased portions of wood back to healthy portions. In either case, healthy wood is evident by its light color and absence of borings. Once you have cut off a diseased or insect-infested portion of a plant, do not just leave it lying on the ground. Disease spores may waft back up into your plant, or insects may make their way back onto your plant or into the soil to complete their life cycle. Thoroughly compost, burn, or otherwise destroy any pest-ridden plant parts that you remove.

Clean tools can be important when cutting away diseased portions of a plant, because some diseases can be transmitted from plant to plant in this way at some point in their life cycle. This is the case, for instance, with fire blight disease, which attacks many members of the rose family during the growing season, but not while an infected plant is dormant in winter. When disease transmission is a hazard, sterilize your pruning tool between cuts by dipping it in alcohol or 10% bleach solution.

Pinching a stem

Young, actively growing tissue heals easiest and quickest, which makes pinching out a growing point between thumbnail and forefinger the least damaging method of pruning. No special instructions here, except perhaps to do this pruning without dirt under your fingernails. (Just kidding. What true gardener has clean fingernails?)

Pruning stems and branches

Shortening a woody stem—a heading cut—must be done with care. Always cut a stem back to a bud, which is where a leaf is growing, or grew the previous season. Most new growth originates from buds, so if you leave an inch of stem beyond the last bud, that inch of stem will eventually die, leaving a stub that will rot away and provide possible entryway for disease. (A few plants—yew and some rhododendrons, for example—can sprout new buds anywhere along their stems; stubs on such plants will not

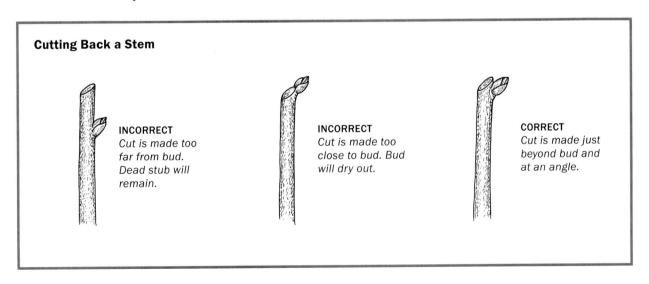

Cutting Back a Stem

INCORRECT
Cut is made too far from bud. Dead stub will remain.

INCORRECT
Cut is made too close to bud. Bud will dry out.

CORRECT
Cut is made just beyond bud and at an angle.

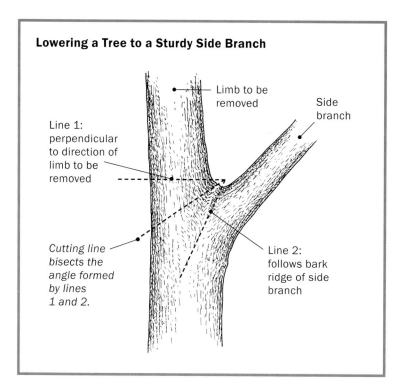

Lowering a Tree to a Sturdy Side Branch

Limb to be removed

Side branch

Line 1: perpendicular to direction of limb to be removed

Cutting line bisects the angle formed by lines 1 and 2.

Line 2: follows bark ridge of side branch

die back.) On the other hand, if you cut a stem too close to a bud, you might damage the bud or cause it to dry out. The way to shorten a stem is to cut it back a little beyond a bud, at an angle, so that the cut slopes down ever so slightly behind the bud.

If you are shortening part of a tree back to one of its sturdy side branches, begin your cut just above the ridge of bark between the limb to be removed and that branch. Make the angle of your cut midway between a line perpendicular to the limb to be removed and a line that follows that ridge of bark back from the crotch. The resulting cut will angle down slightly, but leave enough wood for continued strong attachment of the branch.

Rather than shortening part of a tree to a branch, you might have occasion, instead, to cut off the branch. Do not cut the branch back flush with the trunk or limb to which it is attached. Look, again,

near the origin of a branch for that ridge of bark above the point of attachment, and for a raised collar beneath the point of attachment. Cut the branch just beyond a line from that ridge to that collar. That ridge and that collar will form a natural protection zone, preventing the spread of infection into the trunk when the branch is removed. Removing or damaging the protection zone also can cause sprouts to grow in the vicinity of the wound—just what you don't want when you make a thinning cut!

Avoid erring in the opposite direction and leaving a stub when you remove a branch. The stub will die and decay. Even if decay does not spread into the tree, the dead stub will delay the healing over of the wound and be incorporated within the new growth. If a tree already has a dead stub, do not try to dig out the dead portion from within the branch collar. Just cut the dead branch back to the collar, which will heal by enveloping the stub.

If no branch collar is obvious, as happens with birch and alder trees, you can make an intelligent guess as to its

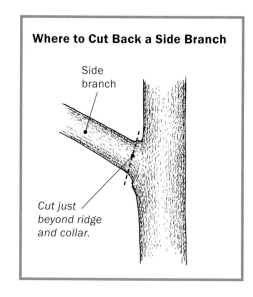

Where to Cut Back a Side Branch

Side branch

Cut just beyond ridge and collar.

location with the help of the ridge of bark between a branch and the limb to which it is attached. The angle that the bark ridge makes with the axis of the branch is about equal to the angle that the bark ridge makes with the branch collar.

Pruning codominant stems

You will not find a branch collar where two stems or limbs are vying to become the "leader," or main trunk of a tree. That's because neither one really is a branch; each is one of two co-dominant stems. Both stems are merely extensions of the main stem below. Maples, especially Norway and silver maples, have a strong tendency to de-velop codominant stems.

Terminology and anatomy aside, what is one to do with such codominant stems? One of them must be removed. The two, nearly parallel stems are weakly attached to each other because of the dead bark that accumulates in the narrow space between them, and because neither is strongly embraced by a branch collar. Although neither stem has a collar, each

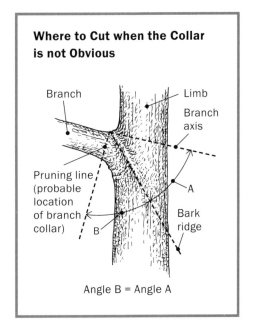

Where to Cut when the Collar is not Obvious

Branch
Limb
Branch axis
Pruning line (probable location of branch collar)
A
B
Bark ridge

Angle B = Angle A

does have a ridge of bark on its upper and lower side. Remove one of the stems with a cut from its upper bark ridge to its lower bark ridge. The wound heals best if you make this cut while the stem is still young (and especially if the ridge is formed with the confluent barks turning out, rather than in, on each other—but you can't do anything about this).

DO WOUNDS NEED DRESSING?

Whether you've cut off a true branch or a codominant stem, do nothing to the bare wound now staring you in the face. Marketing or, perhaps, an innate desire for nurturing has induced humans for centuries to cover wounds with dressings ranging from clay to manure to tar. Such dressings, for the most part, keep the wound moist, maintaining a hospitable environ-ment for disease-causing microorganisms. (Exceptions exist: a particular dressing might be useful because it contains hormones to prevent resprouting, or insecticides to fend off borer attack on susceptible plants such as elm and pecan.) Because of the way codominant stems are attached, removal of a large one eventually results in a hole in the trunk. No need to fill this gaping hole, either, unless you want to fill it with something merely to keep out water. The water may bother you, but it won't bother the plant.

A good pruning cut—not a poultice—allows a woody plant to seal off the wound and prevent the spread of infection. Take care in how you cut, and appreciate the plant's natural ability to heal itself.

PART 2

THE

PLANTS

CHAPTER FOUR

DECIDUOUS ORNAMENTAL BUSHES

**These deutzia bushes
(Deutzia gracilis and
D. × Rosea) maintain
their individuality,
yet blend into this
shrub border.**

A bush is a bushy, woody plant. (Now, that's profound.) Numerous shoots originating at or near ground level are what make a plant bushy. None of these stems ever gets the upper hand over other stems, at least not permanently, so the plant never has a single trunk. Each stem of a bush typically lives just a few years, then dies, its place taken by another stem. On many bushes, stems also branch profusely, clothing the plant from top to bottom with leaves, and perhaps flowers and fruits.

Among bushes, growth habits vary. New shoots on red-osier dogwood, for example, arise from buds on spreading roots and underground stems, making for an ever-widening clump that can fill in an area. At the other extreme is a witch hazel bush, which typically is very reluctant to grow vigorous new shoots. As compensation for this restraint, an individual stem of witch hazel lives for a relatively long time—for a bush.

Because they typically grow densely and not to great height, bushes serve two purposes in the landscape. A bush might be grown as an individual specimen plant, standing alone as a focal point in the landscape, or nestled among other, dissimilar plants, perhaps trees, other bushes, and even herbaceous flowering plants. In either case, bushes grown so that each can express its individuality are commonly—and in this book—called shrubs.

Bushes grown as a hedge, on the other hand, do not stand out as individuals, but meld together into a more or less uniform swathe of greenery (or red-ery, in the case of red-leaved plants), a living wall. Living walls, like those of brick or wood, define spaces and screen out unwanted views or unwanted stares. (Hedges also are cheaper than some built walls, even though they are slower to "erect.")

The natural growth habit of a bush influences its shape. Many short branches clothed throughout with small leaves make billowing mounds of boxwoods. Lanky stems, originating each year mostly from ground level, make forsythia

Whether it is grown as a small tree or large shrub, Kousa dogwood requires little pruning.

a fountain of yellow flowers in spring, green leaves in summer, and tan stems in winter. True, the boxwood can be trained to the shape of a vase, and forsythia can be made more formal. As a rule, however, it's best to use your pruning tools to coax a bush along in the direction of its natural inclinations.

Deciduous bushes grown as shrubs

How you should prune a bush depends on when it flowers and what age stems provide the most ornamental effect. Does the shrub flower early in the spring, or later in the summer? Does it flower on old stems, on those that grew last year, or on new shoots? With shrubs grown for their colorful dormant stems, it is often the younger stems that are most dramatic. In the sections that follow, general guidelines for each category are followed by Plant Lists that give specifics. Roses get their own discussion because of the special enthusiasm people have for

Even in winter, this beech hedge defines the landscape with its twigs and dead leaves.

them, and because there are so many types. If you are unsure which category your plant falls into, look it up in the Index, which begins on p. 228. Or, if you do not know the plant's name, categorize it by just watching when and on what age stems flowers are borne.

Pruning at planting time

A shrub may or may not need pruning when you plant it. Bare-root shrubs unavoidably lose roots during transplanting, and the traditional recommendation for such plants is to "cut back the tops to balance the root loss." Over the decades, this recommendation has periodically been challenged with rigorous experiments whose results have been almost universally ignored. Cutting back the top always seemed like the "right thing to do." Of course, none of this applies to balled-and-burlapped or potted shrubs, which lose few or no roots in transplanting.

In fact, if you can ensure a bare-root plant of ideal growing conditions after transplanting, and this mostly means timely watering, then that plant will repay your efforts with better growth the less that you prune it. Cutting back the top of a shrub removes some stored food as well as buds, and buds have been shown to produce hormones that stimulate root growth.

With good growing conditions, prune any new shrub—whether bare root, balled-and-burlapped, or potted—as little as possible. Remove any diseased or dead stems, as well as those that are crossing and rubbing together. Prune away any wayward stems that jut off awkwardly and alone into space, giving the plant an an unbalanced posture. If you plant in autumn, remove some of the top to prevent wind from blowing the

as-yet poorly anchored plant out of the ground.

If you cannot give a newly transplanted, bare-root shrub ideal growing conditions its first season, then go ahead and prune it to put the tops and roots back in balance. Use mostly thinning, rather than heading, cuts.

Maintenance pruning of shrubs that make few suckers

Included within this category are bushes that naturally build up a permanent framework of branches, only rarely sending up new suckers at or near ground level. These shrubs flower directly on older wood, or from shoots that grow from older wood.

The purpose in pruning these plants is twofold. First, build up a picturesque framework. This should require no more than occasional pruning on your part. And second, prune to keep the plant within its allotted bounds.

Grouping plants always entails a certain degree of arbitrariness, and because of their disinclination to sucker, a few plants in this category could also be considered "trees," especially if deliberately trained to one or a few trunks. So if a "shrublike tree" is not listed here, look in the Plant List of deciduous ornamental trees, which begins on p. 80.

When training these young plants, take care to build up an artistic framework of more or less permanent stems. Look at how the stems reach out of the ground, and try to envision them, longer and thicker, years hence. Cut them back if doing so suits your artistic fancy. The nature of any bush is to send up new stems at or near ground level, so if you do not like the stems dealt to you when you planted the shrub, feel free to cut them all down and start all over (at the expense of some growth, of course).

Plant List

DECIDUOUS SHRUBS THAT MAKE FEW SUCKERS

Acer palmatum (Japanese Maple)

Aesculus parviflora (Bottlebrush Buckeye)

Berberis Thunbergii (Japanese Barberry)

Cephalanthus occidentalis (Buttonbush)

Chaenomeles **spp.** (Flowering Quince): Prune when dormant or right after flowering.

Chimonanthus praecox (Wintersweet)

Colutea arborescens (Common Bladder Senna)

Comptonia peregrina (Sweet Fern)

Cornus alternifolia (Pagoda Dogwood)

Corylopsis **spp.** (Winter Hazel)

Corylus Avellana (European Filbert): These plants also can be trained to trees.

Cotinus Coggygria (Smokebush): If you grow this plant for its purple leaves rather than for its flowers, prune severely in winter to stimulate vigorous new growth each spring.

Cotoneaster **spp.** (Cotoneaster)

Cyrilla racemiflora (Swamp Cyrilla, Leatherwood): This bush flowers in whorls at the bases of the current season's growth, but the woody framework grows quite beautiful with age. To enjoy both the framework and the flowers, prune younger shoots back to within a few buds of the framework each spring.

Daphne **spp.** (Daphne): Do not prune.

Dirca palustris (Leatherwood)

Elaeagnus multiflora (Cherry Elaeagnus, Gumi)

Elaeagnus umbellata (Autumn Olive)

Enkianthus **spp.** (Enkianthus): The plants need little pruning, but will sprout readily wherever stems are cut back.

Euonymus alata (Winged Euonymus, Winged Spindle Tree)

Fothergilla Gardenii (Dwarf Witch Alder)

Fothergilla major (Large Fothergilla)

Hamamelis **spp.** (Witch Hazel): When the plant grows as high as you want it to, thin out vigorous stems to keep it at that height. You also can train witch hazel as a tree.

Hibiscus syriacus (Rose-of-Sharon)

Hippophae rhamnoides (Common Seabuckthorn)

Hydrangea paniculata 'Grandiflora' (PeeGee Hydrangea): Prune in spring. Flowers form on current shoots, so cut back young shoots to ground level or almost to a permanent framework of older limbs, leaving just a few young buds per shoot.

Ilex decidua (Possum Haw)

Ilex verticillata (Winterberry)

Itea virginica (Virginia Sweetspire)

Ligustrum **spp.** (Privet): Privets are usually hedged, but an individual bush does make a nice informal shrub. Prune whenever you want, but if you like the flowers and want as

Good pruning develops the artistic and permanent branching pattern of Japanese maples, whether dwarf or full size.

(continued on page 40)

Once plants in this category mature, they are the easiest shrubs to prune: just don't!

That's the general rule, but admittedly a little pruning may be in order. Remove any dead, crossing, or otherwise poorly placed stems. These plants are hesitant to grow numerous lanky new shoots, but for the plant that does become too crowded, cut away twiggy growth or completely remove one or more older stems. The best approach depends on the growth habit of the particular plant. On those few shrubs that are propagated by grafting, remove any sprouts originating below the graft, preferably with a sharp yank rather than with pruning shears, to reduce the chances for regrowth. Use your shears artistically, to help a Japanese maple develop its signature, neat, mounded habit, or to help promote the naturally layered appearance of a pagoda dogwood.

Pruning also can rejuvenate an old plant. This is more often needed with flowering shrubs than with shrubs grown mostly for their form or for their leaves. Lightly heading back some branches every few years might be enough to rejuvenate certain plants. On others, rejuvenation will involve occasionally cutting away a major stem completely, allowing it to be replaced by a sucker originating low in the bush. Watch your plants closely to determine their pruning needs, if any.

DECIDUOUS SHRUBS THAT MAKE FEW SUCKERS   *(continued)*

many as possible of them (I don't—they have a rank smell), wait until right after flowering to prune.

Lindera Benzoin (Spicebush)

Loropetalum chinense (Loropetalum)

Magnolia spp. (Magnolia): Carefully train plants when they are young so that you can avoid having to make large cuts, which heal poorly, on older plants. Prune *M. Soulangiana* (Saucer Magnolia) and *M. stellata* (Star Magnolia) just before growth begins or right after flowering finishes. Deadhead by cutting flowers off rather than by snapping them off, so that you do not injure the growing point just below each blossom.

Paeonia suffruticosa (Tree Peony): Little pruning is needed, just enough to keep the plant tidy and to remove disease.

Paliurus Spina-Christi (Christmas Thorn, Jerusalem Thorn Tree)

Parrotiopsis Jacquemontiana

Poncirus trifoliata (Hardy Orange)

Rhamnus spp. (Buckthorn)

Spiraea bullata (Crispleaf Spiraea)

Stachyurus praecox: Occasionally cut away old stems after they flower.

Viburnum acerifolium (Mapleleaf Viburnum)

Viburnum alnifolium (Hobblebush)

Viburnum betulifolium

Viburnum Carlesii (Koreanspice Viburnum)

Viburnum cassinoides (Withe-rod Viburnum)

Viburnum dilatatum (Linden Viburnum)

Viburnum × Juddii (Judd Viburnum)

Viburnum Lantana (Wayfaringtree)

Viburnum macrocephalum (Chinese Snowball Viburnum)

Viburnum plicatum (Doublefile Viburnum)

Viburnum rhytidophylloides (Lantanaphyllum Viburnum)

Zenobia pulverulenta (Dusty Zenobia): Remove spent flowers, with short stems attached.

Maintenance pruning of shrubs that flower on one-year-old wood

You will find many familiar flowering shrubs in this category. Because they all flower only on wood that grew the previous season, as a rule these shrubs require annual pruning to stimulate new growth, each year, for the following year's flowers. Left unpruned, any of these shrubs becomes a crowded mess, with old branches coughing forth few flowers that, in the case of those plants that can grow tall, are beyond nose level and almost out of sight.

The one-year-old shoots on which flowers are borne may grow mainly from older stems up in the shrub, or else mostly from ground level. The location of these flowering shoots determines pruning technique, so I have subgrouped plants accordingly, and follow with instructions for each.

In their youth, the only pruning these plants require is to have some of their youngest stems thinned out during the dormant season. Although I have divided shrubs that flower on one-year-old wood into two subgroups (depending on whether flowering wood grows mostly from ground level or from older branches up in the shrub), three general rules apply to pruning mature plants of both types.

1. On shrubs with variegated leaves, be sure to remove any shoots that have nonvariegated leaves. Such shoots are the most vigorous ones, and will, if unchecked, eventually take over the plant.

2. Prune those shrubs that flower early in the season right after their blossoms fade; prune those shrubs that flower from summer onward just before growth begins for the season. Pruning early-flowering shrubs after they bloom allows you to enjoy their blossoms, but still

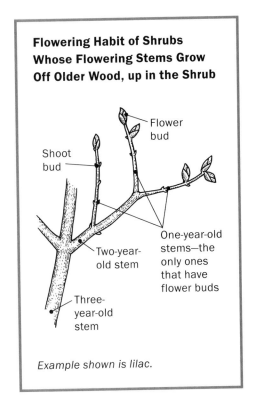

Flowering Habit of Shrubs Whose Flowering Stems Grow Off Older Wood, up in the Shrub

Flower bud

Shoot bud

One-year-old stems—the only ones that have flower buds

Two-year-old stem

Three-year-old stem

Example shown is lilac.

leaves enough time for shoots to grow and ripen wood sufficiently for next season's blooms. Of course, the stems of some of these early-flowering shrubs, cut and plunked into a vase of water indoors, provide cheery blooms to carry you through late-winter garden doldrums—don't hesitate to cut a few for this purpose. The later-flowering shrubs usually bloom on new shoots (that grow off year-old stems), so cutting before growth begins has little effect on the season's flower show. In the following two Plant Lists, I have indicated the flowering season for each shrub.

3. Prune every year, in such a way that the whole shrub is renewed over time. New wood that originates low in the shrub should eventually and annually replace older wood, keeping the plant low, neat, and abundantly flowering.

Now for a few specifics for each subcategory.

Shrubs that flower off older wood up in the shrub can be left for a few years before any wood is removed. Peer in at the base of a mature plant and you will notice wood of various ages growing up from ground level. Begin pruning by cutting away, within 1 ft. of the ground, some of the oldest stems. Those oldest stems are also the tallest ones, so these first cuts quickly lower the plant. If the clump that makes the base of the bush has grown too wide, selectively cut the oldest stems from around the edge of the clump. With early-flowering shrubs, this pruning also has the advantage of removing many spent flowers all at once. The energy that would have gone into seed formation can now be channeled into flowers for next year.

After cutting away some of the oldest stems, move on to detail work. Lower some of the older stems that remain, keeping an eye on the form of the plant and cutting back to a vigorous branch any stem that is too tall or that droops too much. To prevent overcrowding, each year also remove at ground level a portion of the youngest stems. Thin out those within the main clump as well as those that might be spreading, if you want to keep the shrub contained. Finally, higher up in the shrub, head back those stems that have flowered.

It is impossible to give a prescription for how long to leave an older stem, or for how many new stems to leave each year. Such details depend on the nature of the plant as well as how high and how wide you want the plant to grow.

Shrubs that flower on young stems originating at ground level need more drastic pruning. With these shrubs, every year cut away all wood more than one year old, either right to ground level or else to a vigorous branch originating low on the plant. You can tell the age of a stem by its thickness and, on many plants, by the color or texture of the bark.

One of the worst things you can do to shrubs in either subcategory is not to prune it at all. Even worse is to butcher any of these individual plants with a hedge shears.

Maintenance pruning of shrubs valued for their current growth

Here we have shrubs valued only for their new growth. Older stems either detract from the appearance of the plant or else do not survive winter. It is the new shoots that carry the flowers or particularly ornamental leaves that we are after. And yes, in some cases—the young, red stems of red-osier dogwood, for example—we value the plant for the young stems themselves.

This group of shrubs is the easiest of all to prune: simply lop the whole plant down to the ground just as buds are swelling. This annual lopping keeps these shrubs from becoming twiggy at their centers and stimulates vigorous regrowth. For a plant that flowers only on new shoots, the greater the vigor of those new shoots, the more the flowers. With nonflowering shrubs valued for their foliage, very vigorous shoots often bear leaves that are both larger and have a different shape than those that would be borne on more sedate shoots.

When you prune these plants, you do not have to obliterate all above-ground

(continued on page 47)

Plant List

Abeliophyllum distichum (Korean Abelialeaf):
Early blossoming. Right after flowering,
shorten one-third of the branches so they are
about 18 in. long.

Acanthopanax Sieboldianus (Fiveleaf Aralia):
Late blossoming, but the flowers are not all
that showy. If you want this shrub to have an
upright habit, shorten stems as they age and
begin to arch to the ground. Also prune away
excess suckers.

***Amelanchier* spp.** (Saskatoon, Juneberry,
Serviceberry, Shadbush): Early blossoming.

Amorpha fruticosa (False Indigo):
Late blossoming.

Aralia spinosa (Devil's Walkingstick, Hercules'
Club): Late blossoming. This plant can
spread underground. If disciplined, it can be
trained to a tree.

Aronia arbutifolia (Red Chokeberry): Early
blossoming. You can train this plant to several trunks, which are permanent unless a
borer attacks one. If that occurs, cut back the
attacked trunk and let a new one grow.

Aronia melanocarpa (Black Chokeberry):
Early blossoming.

Baccharis halimifolia (Groundsel Bush):
Late blossoming.

Buddleia alternifolia (Garland Butterfly Bush,
Alternate Leaf Butterfly Bush): Early blossoming.

Calycanthus floridus (Common Sweetshrub,
Carolina Allspice): Blossoms sporadically
from spring into summer, but prune it right
after its spring flush of blossoms.

Clethra acuminata (Cinnamon Clethra):
Late blossoming.

Clethra alnifolia (Summersweet Clethra, Sweet
Pepperbush): Late blossoming.

Clethra barbinervis (Japanese Clethra):
Late blossoming.

Clethra tomentosa (Woolly Summersweet):
Late blossoming.

Colutea arborescens (Common Bladder-
senna): Blooms in early summer, but on new
wood, so prune this bush back to older wood
while it is still dormant in late winter.

Cytisus scoparius (Broom): Early blossoming.
Broom does not regrow from old, leafless
wood, so it will die if the bush is cut back
heavily. The bush does need pruning, though,
or it becomes top-heavy. Prune right after
flowering, back to just beyond where old
growth ends.

***Deutzia* spp.** (Deutzia): Early blossoming.
What little pruning these plants need should
be done right after flowering.

Dirca palustris (Leatherwood):
Early blossoming.

Edgeworthia papyrifera (Paperbush,
Mitsuma): Early blossoming.

Exochorda racemosa (Pearlbush):
Early blossoming.

***Forsythia* spp.** (Forsythia): Early blossoming.
(photo, p. 44)

***Genista* spp.** (Woadwaxens): Flowering times
vary, depending on the species, so follow the
general rule about when to prune. Avoid
severe pruning, though, or you will excessively weaken these shrubs.

Holodiscus discolor (Creambush, Ocean-
spray): Late blossoming.

Hydrangea macrophylla (Bigleaf Hydrangea):
This plant blossoms late, but the flower buds
are formed the previous growing season at or
near the ends of branches. Leave old, dry
flowers on the plant for winter interest and to
protect the coming season's flower buds from
winter cold. Prune in spring, cutting stems
that have flowered back to the fat flower

(continued on page 44)

buds. Also thin excess twiggy growth to let light and air into the bush.

Hydrangea quercifolia (Oak-leafed Hydrangea): Late blossoming. Prune the same way as Bigleaf Hydrangea (p. 43), unless you are more interested in the decorative leaves than the flowers. For leafy shoots rather than flowers, cut stems back by one-quarter in late spring. Where winters are cold, you may have no choice, because the flowers buds winterkill.

Jasminum nudiflorum (Winter Jasmine): Early blossoming. If you are willing to prune this shrub annually, shorten flowering stems right after they finish flowering each year, occasionally cutting older stems back to the ground. Otherwise, rejuvenate the shrub every few years by lopping the whole thing almost to the ground.

Kolkwitzia amabilis (Beautybush): Early blossoming.

Lagerstroemia indica (Common Crape Myrtle): Late blossoming. Wherever this plant is not reliably winter hardy, cut off winterkilled wood or cut the whole plant to the ground in early spring. Drastic pruning keeps the plant in bounds and results in larger flowers. Where Crape Myrtle is hardy, it requires little pruning, and eventually holds its leaves and flowers high above the ground, showing its attractive bark.

***Lonicera* spp.** (Bush Honeysuckle): Early blossoming. When the bush grows large enough, you can thin out the interior and make a vaulted, natural playhouse for a child.

Myrica Gale (Sweet Gale, Bog Myrtle, Meadow Fern): Sweet gale is grown for its fragrant leaves, not flowers, so prune it while it is still dormant.

***Neillia* spp.** (Neillia): Early blossoming.

Nevusia alabamensis (Snow-wreath): Early blossoming.

Forsythia in bloom.

Notospartium Carmichaeliae (Pink Broom): Late blossoming. Give this bush little annual pruning, but when the whole plant becomes old and weak, cut everything to near ground level and let it start growing afresh.

Oemleria cerasiformis (Indian Plum, Osoberry): Early blossoming.

Philadelphus coronarius (Mock Orange): Early blossoming.

Philadelphus pubescens: Early blossoming. In addition to cutting away some of the oldest stems, each year also pinch out shoot tips to promote branching. Otherwise, the bush becomes too gawky.

Potentilla fruticosa (Bush Cinquefoil): Late blossoming. There are many ways to approach this bush with pruning shears. Some people suggest removing one-third of the stems in winter, others suggest cutting away weak wood and shortening the strong wood by one-half. I cut everything down to 6 in. above ground each spring, which keeps the bushes short and tidy, although blossoming is slightly delayed.

Prinsepia sinensis (Cherry Prinsepia): Early blossoming.

Prunus glandulosa (Dwarf Flowering Almond): Early blossoming.

Prunus triloba (Flowering Almond): Early blossoming.

Rhododendron spp. (Deciduous Azaleas): Early blossoming. The deciduous species require little pruning other than removal of spent flowers and dead wood. Periodically rejuvenate by thinning out older wood on large plants. Buds form freely along stems, so you can cut them back to wherever you want. Some azaleas tend to grow long, unbranched stems that need to be pinched or cut back to promote bushiness.

Rhus aromatica (Fragrant Sumac): Early blossoming.

Rhus typhina (Staghorn Sumac): Early blossoming. If you are not interested in the flowers and fruits, but want vigorous growth to highlight the leaves, cut the bush back severely every spring.

Ribes alpinum (Alpine Currant): Prune anytime, because this shrub is grown only for its foliage and form.

Sambucus nigra (European Elder): Early blossoming.

Spiraea cantoniensis (Double Reeves Spiraea): Early blossoming.

Spiraea nipponica (Nippon Spiraea): Early blossoming.

Spiraea prunifolia (Bridlewreath Spiraea): Early blossoming.

Spiraea Thunbergii (Thunberg Spiraea): Early blossoming.

Spiraea Vanhouttei (Van Hout Spiraea): Early blossoming.

Staphylea spp. (Bladder Nut): Early blossoming, but blossoms are not spectacular enough to warrant delaying pruning until after they are past.

Stephanandra incisa (Cutleaf Stephanandra): Early blossoming, but flowers are inconspicuous, so there is no need to delay pruning until after they have faded. Prune just enough to maintain a pleasing shape. Watch out for tip rooting of stems that arch to the ground.

Syringa spp. (Lilac): Early blossoming. In addition to following the general pruning guidelines, each year clip or break off spent flowers. *S. Meyeri* (Meyer Lilac) requires little pruning.

Tamarix parviflora (Small-flowered Tamarix): Late blossoming.

Viburnum × Burkwoodii (Burkwood Viburnum): Early blossoming.

Viburnum dentatum (Arrowwood Viburnum): Early blossoming.

Viburnum opulus (European Cranberry Bush Viburnum): Early blossoming.

Viburnum setigerum (Tea Viburnum): Early blossoming.

Viburnum trilobum (American Cranberry Bush Viburnum): Early blossoming.

Weigela florida (Old-fashioned Weigela): Early blossoming. Prune weigela heavily to keep it neat.

ANNUAL PRUNING OF LILAC

1. After the flowers fade, start pruning lilac by cutting some of the oldest stems nearly or right to the ground.

2. Next, shorten any very tall stems to a strong branch.

3. Decongest the base of the plant by cutting away some of the youngest stems.

4. Direct the plant's energy into growth, rather than seeds, by snapping off spent flower heads right after bloom.

5. The finished shrub, shapely and ready to prepare for next year's show.

Plant List

Abelia × grandiflora (Abelia): Abelia can be grown a number of ways, because it flowers on new wood arising anywhere on the shrub. Where winter cold cuts back the plant, prune it below where wood was killed or to within a few inches of the ground. Where all the stems survive winter cold, merely remove some of the oldest wood at ground level. If you want to limit the plant's height or promote branching, pinch the tips of new growth in spring.

Kerria japonica (Japanese Rose, Kerria): Early blossoming. Wood that has flowered often dies, and that old brown wood also puts on a poor show against the young stems, which stay a vibrant green in winter. Therefore, drastic pruning is needed annually. Cut away wood that has borne flowers.

Physocarpus opulifolius (Common Ninebark, Eastern Ninebark): Early blossoming. Cut out the oldest and weakest wood.

Prunus tenella (Dwarf Russian Almond): Early blossoming. Cut the whole plant to the ground in spring, right after blossoms fade.

Rhodotypos scandens (Jetbead, White Kerria): Early blossoming. Cut oldest stems to the ground and shorten others by about one-half.

Salix spp. (Willow): Early blossoming. Bushy willows require little or no pruning unless you are growing them for their catkins, in which case prune them back hard right after they flower. Of course, also prune in winter—to cut off some stems to bring indoors for forcing. Species grown for their catkins include *S. Elaeagnos* (Rosemary Willow, Hoary Willow), *S. gracilistyla* (Rosegold Pussy Willow), *S. discolor, S. caprea,* and *S. melanostachys* (Black Pussy Willow).

Spiraea × arguta (Garland Spiraea): Early blossoming.

Spiraea × Bumalda (Bumald Spiraea): Depending on the particular variety, flowers appear either on new or old wood. Time your pruning accordingly.

Symphoricarpos albus (Common Snowberry): Late blossoming. Occasionally cut the oldest stems to the ground.

---

traces of them. But if you do leave a short, woody framework (assuming the plant does not winterkill), this framework will become overcrowded after a few years. Cut off and back some of this wood when that happens, to leave space for new shoots to emerge. For those plants that do winterkill, cut them down to just below the point of winterkill.

Maintenance pruning of roses

Pruning roses need not be complicated. The rose, after all, is just another flowering shrub, albeit one that inspires poets and painters, the formation of societies, and an undue amount of verbiage on "special" pruning needs. Despite the fanfare, roses respond to pruning as do any other shrubs.

Most roses need annual pruning to keep them healthy and shapely,

PRUNING A BUTTERFLY BUSH

1. A butterfly bush in spring, just before growth begins.

2. Lop all the branches to the ground.

3. All that remain are some stubs with new growth starting to poke out.

floriferous, and within bounds. To this end, always cut away misplaced wood on any rose bush, which includes stems that are trailing on the ground if you want the bush growing upright, stems that are rubbing together, and stems that are overcrowded. As you shape your plant, prune to an outside bud where you want a branch to be spreading. Prune to an inside bud where you need to fill in the center of the bush. Also cut away excessively twiggy stems. And cut back any stem that is either diseased or winterkilled until you see white pith, which indicates that you have reached healthy wood.

On any grafted rose, keep on the lookout for sprouts from below the graft union. The leaves, thorns, or, if you let a sprout grow long enough, the flowers, on such sprouts will be different from those of the grafted variety. Remove these sprouts, which are from the rootstock, as soon as you notice them.

You might prune your rose bush in one, two, or all of three different seasons. The first time is in the spring, just as buds are swelling and growth is about to begin. You could have done this pruning while your bush was fully dormant, but differences between healthy and diseased or dead wood are more evident as growth begins. It is also easier to see where to cut to improve the form of a bush while it is still leafless.

Summer pruning usually entails cutting off the flowers, either in their full glory for vases, or after they are spent. Pruning spent flowers saves the plant the stress of forming fruits, called hips. Do not cut spent flowers from roses such as the rugosa rose, the dog rose, and *Rosa Moyesii* because these roses have prominent and ornamental hips. In climates with very long growing seasons, you can cut any everblooming type of

Plant List

DECIDUOUS SHRUBS VALUED FOR THEIR CURRENT GROWTH

Buddleia Davidii, B. Fallowiana, and their hybrids (Butterfly Bush)

Callicarpa japonica (Japanese Beautyberry)

Caryopteris × clandonensis (Bluebeard, Blue-spiraea, Blue-mist Shrub): Cut the previous year's stem growth in late winter to within 1 ft. or so of the permanent framework of branches.

Caryopteris incana (Common Bluebeard)

Ceanothus americanus (New Jersey Tea, Wild Snowball, Mountainsweet) and other decidu-ous species and hybrids.

Ceratostigma plumbaginoides

Ceratostigma Willmottianum (Chinese Plumbago): Cut back in spring to a point below where stems have been winterkilled.

Clematis heracleifolia var. Davidiana

Clematis integrifolia: Late blossoming

Cornus alba (Tartarian Dogwood): To promote new growth of bright-red stems, prune hard every spring, completely removing one-third or more of the stems. Alternatively, prune less severely and allow the bush to grow larger, with red twigs mostly at its periphery.

Cornus Amomum (Silky Dogwood): Late blos-soming. Prune as for *C. alba*, but less severely because the young stems are not as attractive.

Cornus racemosa (Gray Dogwood): The gray color of wood a few years old contrasts nicely with the reddish-brown young wood. Each spring cut away some of the oldest stems and thin out some of the youngest stems to keep the bush open and to stimulate new shoot growth.

Cornus sanguinea (Bloodtwig Dogwood): The young shoots are, unfortunately, not all that "bloody." The bush is by nature unkempt so needs regular pruning to keep it neat rather than to stimulate new growth.

Cornus sericea (Red-osier Dogwood): This species is closely related to *C. alba* and needs the same pruning.

Cotinus Coggygria (Smokebush): If you grow this plant only for its purple leaves, prune it severely each spring. Otherwise, little pruning is required.

Diervilla sessifolia (Southern Bush-honeysuckle)

Elsholtzia Stauntonii (Mint Shrub): Late blossoming.

Eucalyptus Gunnii (Cider Gum, Cider Tree): Grow this plant as a shrub for its juvenile foliage, maintained each year by severe pruning.

Pruning Tartarian dogwood produces an annual show of young stems with the brightest color.

Fuchsia magellanica (Hardy Fuchsia): If grown where winters are mild, above-ground por-tions of the plant survive and can make a permanent framework. In this case, prune the plant back to the permanent framework each spring. Otherwise, prune to ground level.

Hydrangea arborescens 'Grandiflora' (Hills-of-snow)

Hypericum spp. (St.-John's-Wort)

Leycesteria formosa (Himalaya Honeysuckle)

Perovskia atriplicifolia (Russian Sage)

Rhus typhina (Staghorn Sumac): Prune back severely each spring if you are growing this plant mostly for its leaves, rather than for its woody form or fruits.

(continued on page 50)

***Salix* spp.** (Willow): Bushy willows to prune back hard are *S. irrorata*, to stimulate an annual flush of white, young stems, and *S. purpurea* (Purple Osier Willow), whose young stems are used for baskets. If you are not growing a bushy willow for its decorative young stems or for its catkins (see *Salix* in the Plant List on p. 47), little or no pruning is required.

Sambucus nigra (European Elder): Prune elder back hard each spring if you value it mainly for its leaves, which is undoubtedly the case if you planted one of the varieties with fancy yellow or incised leaves.

***Sorbaria* spp.** (False Spiraea): Late blossoming.

Spartium junceum (Spanish Broom, Weavers' Broom): Prune just before growth begins, cutting back almost, but not quite, into old wood. Eventually try to renovate the whole bush by cutting it down to the ground. Have a new plant ready, though, because this severe cutting sometimes kills an old bush.

Spiraea albiflora (Japanese White Spiraea): This spiraea blooms relatively early, but on growing shoots, so prune while the plant is dormant.

Spiraea* × *Billiardii (Billiard Spiraea)

Spiraea* × *Bumalda (Bumald Spiraea): Depending on the particular variety, Bumald Spiraea flowers on new or old stems. Time your pruning accordingly.

Spiraea japonica (Japanese Spiraea)

Tamarix ramosissima (Tamarisk, Salt Cedar)

Vitex Agnus-castus (Chaste Tree, Hemp Tree): Prune the plant back to where it winterkilled or to within a few inches of the ground.

Vitex Negundo: Prune the same as *Vitex Agnus-castus.*

rose back by about one-third in the middle of August to encourage a good show of autumn blooms.

The third season when you might prune a rose is in autumn. Where winter winds may batter the stems of your bush, perhaps rocking the plant loose in the soil, shorten some stems. And if winter temperatures in your area drop lower than your rose bush can tolerate, you have to bundle up your plant to carry it through the cold weather. In this case, autumn prune to reduce the size of the bush so that it fits into the blanket of straw, Styrofoam "rose cone," or whatever other winter protection you provide.

The growth habit of your bush, and, to a lesser extent, your taste in flowers, dictate pruning from here on. Put simply, an individual rose stem grows, flowers, then gets so old that it flowers little or no more. Prune a rose bush so that the whole shrub is continuously renewed over time. New wood, originating low in the plant, replaces old wood, which you periodically cut away. The number of

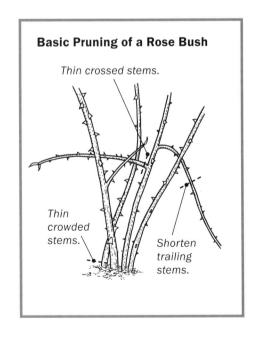

Basic Pruning of a Rose Bush

Thin crossed stems.

Thin crowded stems.

Shorten trailing stems.

young stems might also need to be reduced if they are overcrowded.

The duration of this renewal cycle depends on the growth habit of your rose bush. At one extreme are roses such as the Hybrid Teas, which flower on the current season's shoots. If you cut these plants low every year, you still get flowers—on the new growth. At the other extreme are Climbing Roses, which flower only on old wood, and need little or no annual pruning.

By observing the growth and flowering habits of your rose bush over time, you can apply the general principles above and do a professional pruning job—even if you do not know your rose's name or what type it is. If the plant flowers only on older wood, you will want to leave enough older wood for this year's flowers. Where a bush is overburdened with old wood, remove just some of it to stimulate the growth of, and make way for, new wood. Preserve the graceful, arching growth habit of a bush that is naturally inclined to grow this way by doing most of your cutting at the base, perhaps shortening an occasional gawky stem, just as you would with any other shrub.

More specific recommendations for the various categories of roses are listed in Plant List, which begins on p. 53. But be forewarned: centuries of breeding within and between rose species have made rose nomenclature complicated and inexact. Consequently, there is some variation in growth and flowering habits of roses even within a given category. Also note that the same variety name might be attached to roses in more than one category. For example, 'Lutea' is the variety name for a Climbing Rose and for a Scotch Rose; 'Versicolor' is the name for a Gallica Rose and a Damask Rose. Always couple the information that follows with your own observations.

'Albertine' climbing rose flowers on laterals that grow from older canes.

Renovating an overgrown shrub

You perhaps have inherited, with your property, a neglected, old shrub. This plant presents you with a tangled mass of stems, an awkward posture, and few flowers: not a pretty sight. Can this shrub be brought back to its former glory? Probably.

You have two options in renovating this shrub. The first is the drastic one: you merely lop the whole plant to within 1 ft.

Pruning a Climbing Rose

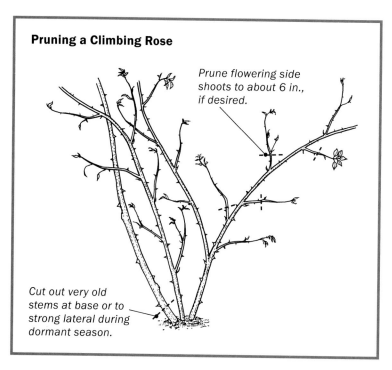

Prune flowering side shoots to about 6 in., if desired.

Cut out very old stems at base or to strong lateral during dormant season.

Pruning a Mature Floribunda Rose Bush

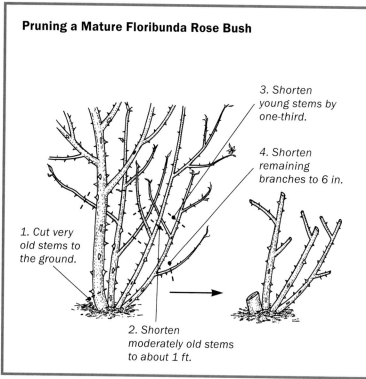

3. Shorten young stems by one-third.

4. Shorten remaining branches to 6 in.

1. Cut very old stems to the ground.

2. Shorten moderately old stems to about 1 ft.

of the ground just before growth begins for the season. Then cut away any twiggy stems still remaining. Be careful not to cut below the graft union with those few shrubs that are grafted onto a rootstock. Otherwise, the whole renovated plant will grow to become whatever the rootstock is.

Your renovated bush will hardly be worth looking at for a year, perhaps two years. A few very vigorous shoots will grow that first season. The next dormant season, thin out some of these stems, and you're on your way to a "new," shrub, full of blossoms and with a graceful growth habit. You will soon have what amounts to a whole new plant from the ground up.

Your second option is to renovate the shrub over a period of four or five years (see the drawing on p. 60). Although this takes more time, the plant will look decent throughout the recovery period. Each year, just before growth begins in spring, cut out two or three of the oldest stems to ground level or to vigorous branches low on the plant. Also thin out some of the youngest stems, making sure to leave a few as replacement shoots for the old wood you are removing. After a few years—how many depends on how long the shrub has been neglected—you will have cut away all the old wood and replaced it with new wood.

Rather than renovation, you might instead consider capitalizing on your overgrown shrub's age and venerability by transforming the plant into a picturesque small tree. Select as trunks two or three of the oldest stems having pleasant form and growing from ground level to as high as the proposed crown of your tree-to-be. Remove all other growth

(continued on page 60)

Plant List

ROSES

Climbing Roses: Climbing Roses have a mostly permanent framework of older canes on which flowers are borne. Some varieties flower only once per season, while others produce a more modest second bloom. Less vigorous Climbers are sometimes called Pillar Roses.

Climbing Roses require little pruning. If you can reach high enough, right after the flowers have faded cut back flowering branches growing off the canes to about 6 in. Do this immediately if the variety is able to bloom again that season; otherwise, you can wait to prune, if you desire, until the following spring, just before growth begins. Especially on those varieties that flower only once a season, pruning branches is not obligatory.

When a cane becomes very old, cut it away at its base to stimulate the growth of a young replacement. You will have to watch your plant to gauge how long to wait before replacing an old cane.

Some Climbers require even less pruning. Very vigorous varieties, such as 'Kiftsgate', 'Mermaid', and 'Cerise Bouquet', grow so large that there is no hope—and fortunately no need—for pruning them. Bush roses that have mutated to become climbers, such as 'Climbing Queen Elizabeth', 'Gloire de Dijon', and 'Mme. Alfred Carrière', require nothing more than the cutting out of dead wood and heading back of weak wood. (A myth has been promulgated that cautions against severe pruning of the latter varieties for fear that such pruning will cause them to revert to their bush forms. Not so! An equally chance mutation would be needed for a climber to revert back to a bush form, and this is unlikely. A more plausible explanation for the response of such plants to severe pruning is that growing conditions were less than ideal, and severe pruning further weakened already weak plants.)

English Roses: See Shrub Roses

Floribunda Roses: These roses produce clusters of flowers. Individual flowers resemble those of Hybrid Teas, but are smaller.

Floribundas need annual pruning to prevent them from becoming overgrown masses of twigs. Flowers are borne on both new shoots and on old stems, with the old stems bearing the first flowers of the season and the young shoots bearing the later flowers.

Prune to preserve some new and some old stems. While a plant is dormant, shorten older stems to about 1 ft., occasionally removing some of the very oldest ones completely. Prune young stems moderately, shortening them by about one-third. Cut back any remaining branches to 6 in.

To deadhead spent blossoms of Floribundas, cut off the whole cluster rather than individual flowers. Cut back to a leaf with a bud between it and the stem so that you do not leave a dead stub.

Grandiflora Roses: Grandifloras lie somewhere between Hybrid Teas and Floribundas in the size of individual flowers and clusters of blos-

'American Pillar' brings rustic charm to this arbor.

'Impatient', like other floribunda roses, makes up for smaller size blossoms with sheer abundance.

(continued on page 54)

soms. In Great Britain, Grandifloras are considered part of the Floribunda spectrum—which seems reasonable. Floribundas and Grandifloras are pruned in the same way, so refer to Floribunda (p. 53) for details.

Hybrid Perpetual Roses: These old roses are the forerunners of Hybrid Teas, and by comparison are more vigorous and flower twice each season, rather than continuously. Because they flower on growing shoots rather than on older wood, Hybrid Perpetuals can take the same hard pruning as Hybrid Teas. While the plant is dormant, shorten strong stems to about 1 ft., weak ones to about 6 in. Every few years, cut one of the oldest stems to the ground to encourage a young replacement.

'Chicago Peace', a hybrid tea rose.

'Scarlet Meidiland' is a carefree landscape rose.

Some varieties, such as 'Frau Karl Druschki', produce extremely long stems in one season of growth. If you have enough space around such a plant, deal with that lanky growth by pegging it down to the ground. The recumbent posture induces shoots to grow sprout all along the long stem, giving you flowers all over the place. Each spring cut away enough of the old stems to make room for new ones, and shorten branches growing off remaining stems to about 6 in.

Hybrid Tea Roses: Hybrid Tea roses produce long-stemmed, large blossoms, singly or in small clusters, throughout the growing season. The degree of dormant pruning required depends on how much, if any, of the old stems winterkilled, as well as the size of plant, and the number and size of blossoms you desire. To a point, the more drastically you prune, the fewer, the larger, and the later the blossoms, and the smaller the plant.

Begin pruning just before growth begins. Shorten the weakest stems the most, to 6 in. if you want your bush small. Shorten strong stems to 1 ft. or more. Occasionally cut away a stem at its base to stimulate and make room for a young replacement shoot.

Prune away spent blossoms during the growing season. Generally cut back to a bud where the stem meets the stalk of a leaf having five leaflets. If you want especially large blossoms, remove lateral flower buds from a shoot before they open, forcing the shoot to channel all its energy into the remaining central flower bud (drawing, p. 57).

Landscape Roses: This relatively new category of roses consists of low-growing plants that bear masses of small flowers and are used as groundcovers or low shrubs. Pruning a slope covered with established plants is well-nigh impossible—and unnecessary. If you really must, put on some heavy boots so that you can walk right into the planting, and cut back any lanky, vertical stems and dead wood.

Miniature Roses: These roses are low growing, with commensurately diminutive leaves and flowers. Pruning is simple—or is it just that the plants are so small and manageable? Shorten strong growth, thin out weak growth, and occasionally cut away an old stem completely. Keep the plant shapely.

Old-Fashioned Roses: See Shrub Roses

Pillar Roses: See Climbing Roses

(continued on page 56)

Pruning a Pegged Hybrid Perpetual Rose

A pegged rose flowers on laterals of the pegged-down shoots.

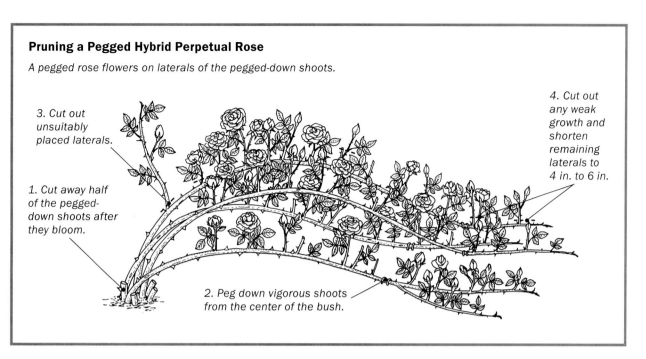

3. Cut out unsuitably placed laterals.

4. Cut out any weak growth and shorten remaining laterals to 4 in. to 6 in.

1. Cut away half of the pegged-down shoots after they bloom.

2. Peg down vigorous shoots from the center of the bush.

Pruning a Hybrid Tea Rose

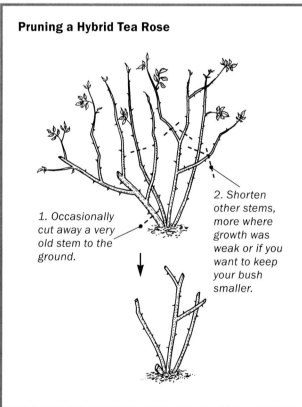

1. Occasionally cut away a very old stem to the ground.

2. Shorten other stems, more where growth was weak or if you want to keep your bush smaller.

Cutting Spent Hybrid Tea Rose Blossoms

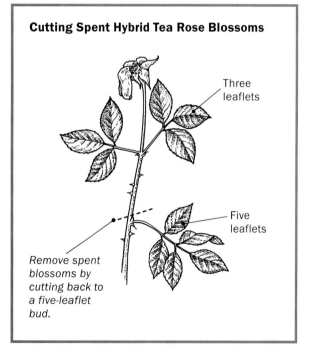

Three leaflets

Five leaflets

Remove spent blossoms by cutting back to a five-leaflet bud.

PRUNING A POLYANTHA ROSE

1. This polyantha rose needs to be pruned before growth gets underway.

2. Stems have been shortened and some old stems cut away.

3. In just a few weeks, the rose again looks glorious.

Polyantha Roses: These old-fashioned dwarfs bear dense clusters of small flowers. Many new stems grow from the base of the plant. Shorten older stems, occasionally removing some of the oldest ones completely to ground level, and cut back younger stems only slightly. Alternatively, prune the whole plant almost to ground level every spring.

Rambling Roses: Ramblers usually flower only once per season, mostly on short branches growing off long stems produced the previous season. Branches on older canes also can bear some flowers.

Prune mostly by cutting away stems that have flowered. The easiest time to do this is right after flowers fade, because then new growth is not yet entangled with old growth, and you can see most easily what has flowered.

In one type of Rambler, typified by 'Dorothy Perkins' and other varieties derived from Rosa Wichuraiana, most new growth arises at the base of the plant, near ground level. If the number of such shoots seems excessive, remove some when you prune. On the other hand, if an insufficient number of replacement shoots is growing from the base, leave some stems that have flowered, but shorten their branches to about 4 in. after the flowers fade. These stems will flower again next year.

On another type of Rambler—'New Dawn' and 'Paul's Scarlet Climber' are examples—new shoots originate higher up along old canes, rather than from the base of the plant. Prune these Ramblers by cutting away stems that have flowered back to new stems growing off along older wood. If there are insufficient new stems, retain some of those that have flowered, but shorten their flowered branches after the flowers fade. Occasionally stimulate new growth near ground level by cutting old wood to within 1 ft. of the ground.

Shrub Roses: Aren't all roses "shrubs," you ask? Yes and no. Yes, they are (even the climbers can be coerced into a more typically shrubby habit); but no, there is actually a specific group of roses commonly called "Shrub Roses."

For the purposes of this book, I have thrown a few other shrubby roses into this category, because of their similar origins and shrubby habits. This mixed bag thus includes Shrub Roses (some of the newer of these are called English Roses), Old-fashioned Roses (sometimes called Old Garden Roses), and Species Roses. For specifics, see the sidebar on pp. 58-59.

Species Roses: See Shrub Roses

Standard Roses: A Standard Rose is a rose grown in the form of a small tree—a straight trunk capped by a mop of flowers. Nurseries make these roses by grafting any one of various types of roses atop a trunk grown from a vigorous rootstock (typically a rugosa or briar rose).

Prune a standard rose according to what type of rose is grafted atop the trunk. Just before growth begins, stub all the branches on a Standard Hybrid Tea back to 6 in., and thin out or shorten any weak or crowded wood that remains. With a Standard Floribunda, also prune just before growth begins, shortening one-year-old wood to 2 ft. and two-year-old wood to 6 in. Drastically shorten any older wood.

Weeping standards are made by grafting Rambling Roses atop a trunk. If the grafted Rambler is the type that sends out most new growth from the base of the plant (now high atop the trunk) rather than along older stems, cut stems that have flowered back to their bases right after flowers fade. If too few new shoots are growing to replace those old stems, leave some stems that have flowered, but shorten their branches to 6 in. right after flowering. If the grafted Rambler is the type that sends out new growth along older stems, just shorten branches to 6 in. right after flowering, and cut away surplus old wood.

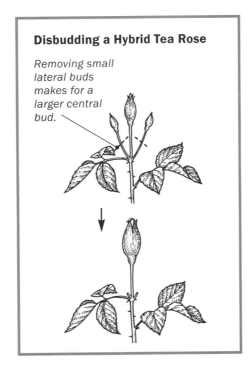

Disbudding a Hybrid Tea Rose

Removing small lateral buds makes for a larger central bud.

Cut away flowering canes from this rambling rose following bloom to make way for canes that will flower next year.

SHRUB ROSES: A Pruner's Guide

The roses listed here are all shrubby, but they vary in their vigor and their tendency to send up new sprouts from ground level, as well as in their flowering habits. At one extreme in shrubby roses are those that make few new shoots and flower mostly on older wood (Group 1). Other shrubby roses that flower on older wood send up many vigorous shoots from ground level each season (Group 2). Another type of shrub rose blooms reliably on both new and old wood (Group 3).

GROUP 1

Shrubby roses in this group shrubs need little pruning: only occasional removal of old wood and thinning out of crowded stems just before growth begins or just after flowers fade.

The following roses are representative of this extreme:

Rosa gallica, French or Apothecary Rose, represented by 'Pumila', 'Rosa Mundi', 'Belle 'Isis'
Rosa Hugonis, Father Hugo's Rose
Rosa moschata, Musk Rose, represented by 'Plena'; 'Pax', 'Buff Beauty', and 'Penelope' are varieties or parents of Hybrid Musk Roses
Rosa spinosissima, Scotch or Burnet Rose, with 'Andrewsii', 'Fulgens', 'Lutea', 'Sulphurea', and 'Frühlingsgold' as representative varieties

GROUP 2

Shrubby roses in this group require moderate pruning just before growth begins. Each year take out, at ground level, some of the oldest wood. Also shorten lanky stems that are arching to the ground, or that will arch to the ground once weighted down with blossoms. Do not shorten those stems so much that you ruin the fountainlike growth habit, though. Where branches have grown very long, shorten them to about 6 in.

This category includes:

Burgundy Rose, represented by 'Parviflora' Modern Shrub Roses that bloom only once
Moss Rose, represented by 'Muscosa' and 'William Lobb'
R. × alba, represented by varieties 'Incarnata' and 'Suaveolens'
R. centifolia, Cabbage Rose, represented by 'Cristata'
R. damascena, Damask Rose, including varieties such as 'Celsiana', 'Trigintipetala', and 'Mme. Hardy' (these sometimes bloom repeatedly during the growing season, in which case pruning spent blossoms helps stimulate vigorous regrowth for return bloom)
R. Moyesii
R. rugosa, Japanese Rose, represented by 'Magnifica', 'Rosea', 'Rubra' (these will flower on new shoots growing from ground level, but such blossoms are few and late)

GROUP 3

Shrubby roses in this group get pruned most severely, to induce vigorous shoots for blooms throughout the season. Just before growth begins, shorten vigorous wood originating near ground level by one-third, and branches to 1 ft. Thin out twiggy growth. And, of course, deadhead religiously to stimulate new growth and to prevent fruit formation.

Some of the shrubby roses that require this treatment include:

Modern Shrub Roses that bloom throughout the growing season
R. × borboniana, Bourbon Rose, represented by 'Boule de Neige' and 'Souvenir de la Malmaison'
R. chinensis, China Rose, represented by 'Minima'; Fairy Rose, represented by 'Viridiflora'

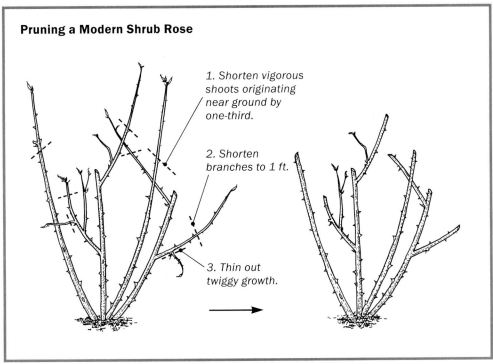

1. 'William Lobb', a moss rose, looks intimidating before pruning.

2. Cutting away some of the oldest wood, at its base, opens the bush quickly.

3. Detail work on stems that remain is shortening laterals and lanky stems.

4. 'William Lobb' now looks healthier and happier.

Pruning a Modern Shrub Rose

1. Shorten vigorous shoots originating near ground by one-third.

2. Shorten branches to 1 ft.

3. Thin out twiggy growth.

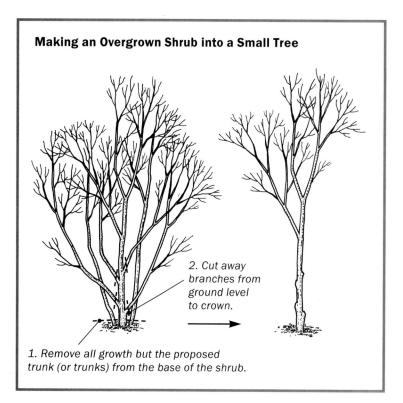

Making an Overgrown Shrub into a Small Tree

2. Cut away branches from ground level to crown.

1. Remove all growth but the proposed trunk (or trunks) from the base of the shrub.

from the base of the plant. Also cut away any branches growing off those new trunks between the ground and a few feet above the ground—high enough so the plant looks like a tree. Finally, make some heading and thinning cuts to shape the crown.

In subsequent years, new sprouts will grow from ground level and off the trunks; after all, the plant was once a bush. Remove these diligently. With time, the plant will become less rebellious, making fewer such sprouts, and will take the form of a venerable tree.

Sometimes you must consider merely grubbing out an old, neglected shrub rather than renovating it. Surely there is no reason to hesitate with your shovel and saw if you do not like having the plant, perhaps any plant, at the particular location. With a few shrubs, such as woodwaxens and brooms, you

Gradual Renovation of a Shrub

FIRST YEAR
Thin the youngest stems and cut away some of the oldest stems.

SECOND AND SUBSEQUENT YEARS
Repeat the first-year sequence.

New wood gradually replaces old wood, and growth fills in at the base of the plant.

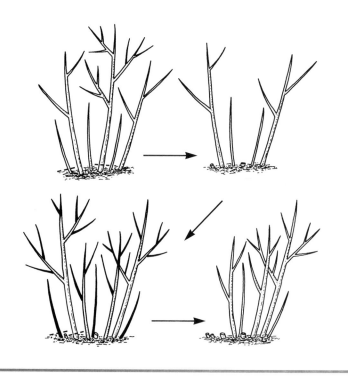

PRUNING A NEGLECTED SHRUB

1. How to begin pruning this neglected lilac bush?

2. First remove any wayward old stems right to the ground.

3. Also cut away some old stems in the center of the bush.

4. Thin younger stems to make room for those that remain.

5. Shorten any branches that droop too much.

Lilac makes a nice hedge, but only if pruned informally.

have to grub them out when they become overgrown. They rarely regrow from old wood, so often die when cut back severely.

If your shrub is a particularly rare species or variety, propagate a new plant before taking any drastic measures at renovation.

Deciduous bushes grown together as a hedge

In order for a hedge to do its job of providing a physical, psychological, and/or visual barrier, each plant making it up must be fully clothed in leaves from head to foot. To create dense and uniform growth, you have to choose appropriate species, plant them correctly, and—just as important—prune the plants soon after you set them in the ground.

Pruning the young plants

The first pruning is simple but brutal: Cut the whole plant down to within a few inches of the ground. This drastic pruning encourages both vigorous regrowth and low branching.

If the new plants already are well branched right to ground level, it is unnecessary to prune so severely. (The severe pruning recommended is a necessary evil: It temporarily stunts the plant, but does give it the desired growth habit.) Some plants, such as beech, hornbeam, and Nanking cherry, are naturally furnished with branches throughout. Any plants that have been grown in containers may be similarly well furnished if they are old enough and already were pruned correctly as hedge plants in their youth. On these already well-branched plants, head back the main stem and laterals just enough so that they continue to branch further as they grow.

Once you give your hedge plants their first pruning, let them grow unmolested for the rest of their first season.

The second season is as important as the first, with regard to pruning, in the development of a shapely, dense, formal hedge. (Let an informal hedge just grow its second season.) While the plant is still dormant, shorten main stems by about half their length, and branches to just a few inches. Again the goal is to promote dense branching. And again, only a slight

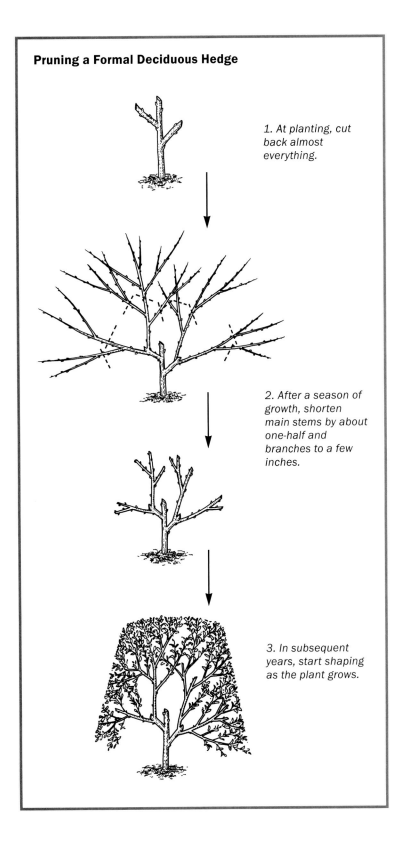

Pruning a Formal Deciduous Hedge

1. At planting, cut back almost everything.

2. After a season of growth, shorten main stems by about one-half and branches to a few inches.

3. In subsequent years, start shaping as the plant grows.

Prune this spiraea hedge, which looks best grown informally, just as you would the individual shrubs. Avoid using hedge shears.

shortening of stems is needed on those plants that already are twiggy from top to bottom.

If your hedge is going to be formal, also start bringing the whole hedge to its desired shape as you shorten growth for this second season. Do this even though the hedge has not yet reached its final size. A formal hedge may take many forms, but whatever the shape, the top should be narrower than the bottom. If the top is wider than the bottom, the bottom will become shaded. Over time,

the shaded portions will die out, leaving gaps in the hedge.

Maintenance pruning

Once a hedge has reached the size and shape that you want, your job is to keep the hedge in that condition. If your hedge is informal—and many bushes (see the Plant List on p. 66) look uncomfortable in formal attire—prune the plants as you would individual shrubs. To wit: prune early-blossoming bushes right after their blossoms fade, late bloomers while they

Shearing a Rigidly Geometric Hedge

are still dormant. Prune by cutting out the oldest stems to ground level or to vigorous young branches, and by shortening stems that are too lanky. The aim is to make the line of arching stems look like a breaking wave advancing across the landscape.

Other plant species will try to invade a hedge, and are easily overlooked amongst the more tangled branches of an informal hedge. As you prune, also cut away—or grub out—unwanted invaders.

Prune the formal hedge with a hedge shears. To maintain its crisp form, a formal hedge needs shearing at least once a year. The frequency of shearing needed depends on just how crisp you want the lines of your hedge, as well as the vigor of the plants. Do your first shearing of the season while the plant is in full leaf,

preferably after the initial growth flush has subsided so that regrowth is minimized. Where winters are very cold or with hedge plants of questionable hardiness, avoid shearing after midsummer, lest you stimulate soft new growth that can be damaged by low temperatures.

When you shear, hold the cutting blades parallel to the surface that you are creating. Shear back almost to the point where you previously sheared. I start low on the hedge and work my way upward, which makes it easier to reach across the top and leaves me less inclined to let the upper portions spread increasingly outward over time. If the hedge is rigidly geometric, especially if its shape inter-locks with other forms in the nearby landscape, stretch a taut line a few inches above the desired cutting line as a guide.

If you want flowers on your formal hedge, you have to accept a more ragged look. With a hedge that flowers early in the season, shear right after the flowers have faded. Depending on the plant species, you may get one more shearing in, but you have to allow sufficient time for regrowth—and raggedness—on plants that flower on stems that grew the previous season. Of course, you can keep shearing back growth on a plant like flowering quince, which flowers on older wood. In this case, though, all the flowers will be buried within the branches. And

that's only if those branches get sufficient light to make flower buds.

With a formal hedge that flowers later in the season, you can cut to your heart's content before growth begins in spring. But soon after growth begins, don't touch those new stems or you won't have flowers.

When you finish shearing any hedge, sweep off the bulk of the clippings, then rake them up. Those few that remain on top or fall within the hedge become inconspicuous within a day or two as they dry and shrivel.

Plant List

DECIDUOUS HEDGES

Abelia × *grandiflora* (Abelia)

Acanthopanax Sieboldianus (Fiveleaf Aralia)

Berberis Thunbergii (Japanese Barberry)

Carpinus Betulus (European Hornbeam)

Chaenomeles spp. (Flowering Quinces)

Corylus spp. (Filbert): Best as an informal hedge, pruned by selectively removing the oldest stems, rather than by shearing.

Crataegus spp. (Hawthorn)

Deutzia gracilis (Slender Deutzia)

Euonymus alata (Winged Euonymus, Winged Spindle Tree)

Fagus sylvatica (European Beech)

Forsythia spp. (Forsythia): Best as an informal hedge, pruned by selectively removing the oldest stems, rather than by shearing.

Hibiscus syriacus (Rose-of-Sharon): With a coarse texture yet upright growth habit, this bush makes an informal hedge that needs little pruning, except perhaps to restrict its height.

Hippophae rhamnoides (Sea Buckthorn)

Lagerstroemia indica (Common Crape Myrtle): Best as an informal hedge, pruned

by selectively removing the oldest stems, rather than by shearing. Where the tops of the plant are only marginally cold hardy, cut away any winterkilled stems each year before growth begins. If you train the plants as trees, with more or less permanent trunks, cutting the ends of some branches back 1 ft. to 2 ft. will help flowering.

Ligustrum spp. (Privet): As a hedge, privet usually needs two or three shearings each year. Prune anytime.

Potentilla fruticosa (Bush Cinquefoil): Best as an informal hedge, pruned by selectively removing the oldest stems, rather than by shearing.

Ribes alpinum (Alpine Currant)

Rosa rugosa (Japanese Rose): Best as an informal hedge, pruned by selectively removing the oldest stems, rather than by shearing.

Spiraea Vanhouttei (Van Hout Spiraea): Best as an informal hedge, pruned by selectively removing the oldest stems, rather than by shearing.

Symphoricarpos albus (Common Snowberry)

Syringa vulgaris (Common Lilac): Best as an informal hedge, pruned by selectively removing the oldest stems, rather than by shearing.

Renovating a deciduous hedge

With neglect, an informal hedge becomes overgrown, a mass of plants spreading too wide with their bases becoming overcrowded and bare. Renovate such a hedge by crawling inside, to the base of the plants, and cutting away some of the oldest wood near ground level. After you finish that, shorten any overly long stems that remain in order to narrow the hedge.

An alternative, if you have the energy or machinery, is to cut all growth to within 1 ft. of the ground, then go back over the plants and remove any twiggy stems that remain. The hedge will look young, spry, and full within a couple of years.

A formal hedge also can suffer from neglect, and even if you you shear the hedge diligently, it is still going to need periodic renovation. The reason is that when you shear, you always shear *almost* back to where you last sheared so that bare stems are not staring out at you. As a result, the hedge is always slowly enlarging.

A formal hedge with bare areas near ground level probably was improperly pruned when it was very young. Unfortunately, there is little you can do to fill in those bare spots, short of cutting the whole hedge almost to ground level, then pruning the resulting stems as if they were a newly planted hedge. That is, head back the stems to make them branch before they begin their second season of growth. In the third season, start shearing the plant to the desired form, even though it is not yet full size.

To renovate the formal hedge that has grown too tall and wide, but is otherwise full from top to bottom, prune all growth back so that the hedge is 6 in. narrower and shorter than you want for its final width and height. Do this just before growth begins in spring, so that the hedge is soon clothed and presentable. Depending on the thickness of the branches, you might need pruning shears rather than hedge shears for this job. The task is not as tedious as it may seem, because a single cut within the hedge will remove a stem with all its attached twiggy growth. As the new shoots grow, shear them back with your hedge shears, at first keeping the hedge a bit smaller than its desired, final size. You now have a "new" hedge.

If you don't like the idea of your hedge being so loose and open—even temporarily—then initially prune back the branches on one side only. Also lower the hedge, if necessary. The following year, prune back the branches on the other side.

A hedge of burning bush adds a ribbon of color to the autumn landscape.

Neatly formed, dark branches complement the beauty of these cherry blossoms.

In this section we will admire deciduous trees, and prune them for beauty, strength, and long life. For a clear and simple definition of a tree, I consulted my six-year-old daughter. She told me that a tree is big, woody, and has a trunk. I'll add that most new growth on trees arises up in the crown, not near ground level, and that's the difference between a tree and a bush. Both are woody, and some bushes—autumn olive, for example—can grow quite large. After a few years, though, the archetypal tree puts its energy only into new branches up in the crown, which rises atop a permanent trunk.

Trees vary in their shapes, but all have potentially the same basic parts. There is a trunk, of course, that woody, lower portion of the tree clear of branches. And perhaps leaders, which are extensions of the trunk within the plant. If a tree has one leader, it is called a central leader, and off it grow scaffold limbs, the main side branches of the tree. And then there may be some very vigorous, upright shoots, often growing many feet in a single season. Those that originate up in the plant are called watersprouts; those originating at the base of the plant are called root suckers or root sprouts. The vigor, upright position, and location of watersprouts and suckers generally detract from the beauty of a tree. What's more, such shoots are weakly attached.

Crowns of deciduous trees range from round-headed to spirelike. The spirelike tree—typified by pin oak, sweet gum, and tulip tree—has a single, dominant central leader, which each year pushes higher with new branches growing off it. Although a round-headed tree may have had a dominant leader when young, this leader was soon overtaken by branches, each, in turn, soon overtaken by their side branches.The result (see the photo on p. 70) is the large, spreading crown typical of white oak and sugar maple. Not all trees fit neatly into one or the other category of tree shape, and these shapes can also be influenced by the richness of the soil and the amount of shade in which the tree grows.

Nonetheless, keep in mind the two basic tree forms in the ensuing discussion. They have an important influence on how to handle trees in their formative years. And, as with most pruning, your goal usually is merely to help the tree along. This means building a strong framework on the young tree, maintaining the health and shape of the mature tree, and rejuvenating, when necessary, the neglected, old tree—all the while retaining a natural growth habit.

A note about timing when pruning deciduous trees…with few exceptions, the ideal time is late winter or early spring, just before growth begins. If you cannot bring yourself to sacrifice any

A single dominant leader gives this dawn redwood a spirelike crown.

blossoms from an early-flowering tree, then prune just after the flowers fade, which is not much after growth begins. Pruning while a plant is leafless, or nearly so, offers you an unobstructed view of the branches, making it easier to see what to cut and actually to make the cuts. Wounds also heal most quickly just as growth is getting underway. Some trees, such as maples and birch, bleed sap when cut in spring. Bleeding does the plant no harm, but if it makes you queasy, prune

DECIDUOUS ORNAMENTAL TREES

EXCEPT FOR small trees that develop multiple trunks, allow only one vertical shoot to become the trunk, then central leader. Bend down, cut back, or cut off any competitors.

SELECT scaffold limbs that are thinner than the leader and spaced 1 ft. to 2 ft. apart along the trunk. The height of the lowest one depends on how high a head you want (on your tree!). Keep in mind that scaffold limbs will grow thicker, but their height above ground never changes.

ALLOW weak, temporary branches to remain along the developing trunk and central leader to help thicken and protect them from sunburn. Remove these temporary branches after a couple of years.

PRUNE the developing tree as little as possible!

USE mostly thinning cuts to reduce or maintain size and let light and air into the crown of a mature or overgrown tree.

Lack of a dominant leader gives this oak a rounded crown.

earlier in winter or later in spring, when the plant will not bleed. If you dormant-prune in winter, try to avoid pruning until the coldest part of winter is past.

Definitely avoid pruning late in summer or in autumn. Pruning late in summer is apt to stimulate succulent growth that cannot harden before cold weather arrives. Wounds made in autumn heal poorly, and many fungi are then spreading their disease-producing spores.

Pruning at planting time

Early tree care—and pruning is part of this care—is all-important to the future health and beauty of a tree. When it comes to training the young branches, some pruning may be necessary. But keep this in mind: the less pruning the better.

Let's start with the roots. Little or no root pruning is necessary on a plant whose roots were balled and burlapped after it was dug from the field. If a few lanky roots were tucked in around the ball when the plant was dug, either dig a hole large enough to accommodate those roots as they stretch naturally outward, or else cut them back. It's your choice. Do not just stuff them into the planting hole, or the tree may eventually strangle itself. If your new tree was growing in a pot, slide it out of the pot and then take a knife and slit the root ball in a few places. Tease out the roots at the surface of the root ball with a stick to make sure they grow outwards, into the surrounding soil.

If the tree you receive from a nursery is dormant and bare root, take this last opportunity, before you put the tree into the ground, to inspect the roots. Cut off any that are dead, diseased, or broken. (Be aware that healthy roots of all plants do not look clean and white—healthy persimmon roots, for example, are black.) Cutting frayed ends cleanly reduces the surface area of wounds, so that healing is quicker, reducing the risk of root diseases. As with a balled and burlapped tree, shorten any roots that are too long to splay out into the planting hole—or dig the hole larger.

Slitting the Root Ball of a Potted Tree

Trimming the Roots of a Bare-Root Tree

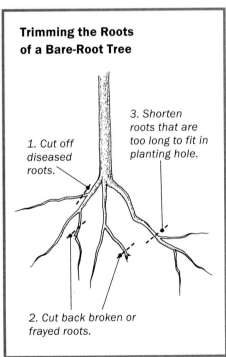

1. Cut off diseased roots.

3. Shorten roots that are too long to fit in planting hole.

2. Cut back broken or frayed roots.

Now, let's turn to the above-ground portions of the tree. Most important is to promote the development of a single central leader, the lower portion of which will be the future trunk. (Some trees naturally develop a few main trunks, all originating at ground level, and look quite handsome that way. These plants are usually small trees that never grow large, so developing a strong framework is not as critical as with a massive tree.) If several shoots are competing to become the central leader of your new tree, completely cut away all but one of them. Otherwise, the similar size of such shoots and the dead bark that builds up in the narrow-angled crotch between them creates a weak joint that may well split apart as the shoots and their branches grow heavy. Pruning to a single leader is particularly important on trees whose crowns are round-headed, because of the natural tendency, especially with age, for their leaders to be overtaken by other shoots. Shoots on trees with naturally spirelike growth habits less often misbehave in this way.

If your tree has two central leaders of equal girth and with a narrow crotch between them, cut away one of them. If a side branch has decided to turn its tip upward with loftier aspirations, either shorten that branch or quell its desires by bending it to a more horizontal position with a weight or with a string tied to the trunk or a stake. Or simply remove the offending branch.

Keep to a minimum any other pruning of the above-ground portion of the tree at planting time, and make mostly thinning, rather than heading, cuts (see the drawing at left on p. 25). Cut or pull off any suckers. Cut away any dead, diseased, or broken branches, and remove enough branches along the future trunk so that those that remain are well separated. You

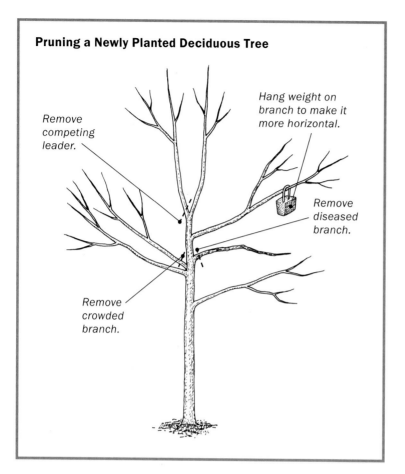

Pruning a Newly Planted Deciduous Tree

Remove competing leader.

Hang weight on branch to make it more horizontal.

Remove diseased branch.

Remove crowded branch.

reducing the number of growing points and hence the number of leaves, which transpire water. The traditional recommendation to cut back the top of a tree when you set it in the ground makes sense only for trees that might be expected to suffer from water stress. But do not expect such a tree to grow as much as an unpruned tree getting sufficient water. More leaves mean more photosynthesis, which means more growth. Also, buds awakening at the tips of new shoots produce hormones that stimulate root growth; the more of those buds that remain, the more the roots grow. This is another reason to make mostly thinning, rather than heading, cuts on a new tree—fewer terminal buds are removed.

In summary, if you want maximum growth on your newly planted tree, keep pruning to a minimum, using mostly thinning cuts. Rather than pruning to reduce leaf area, help your young tree along with a stake against wind and with water in times of need.

Pruning while training

The first years that your tree is in the ground, while it is developing branches that will become its main framework, are important to its future strength and beauty. Pruning is one way to direct growth. This pruning is best done while the tree is young, because the small cuts you make on a small tree leave correspondingly small wounds and are less debilitating than the large corrective cuts that are necessary on a large tree. Still, any pruning slows growth, so do only what is absolutely necessary. (In the case of a very windy site, however, pruning specifically to slow growth is beneficial.)

will eventually cut off most, if not all, of these branches, but leave them for now. They help feed the young tree and thicken its trunk.

Two special conditions may necessitate more severe pruning of your newly planted tree. The first is a windy site. In this case, remove enough branches to prevent the crown from acting like a sail and catching enough wind to loosen the tree or even wrench it out of the ground. Use thinning rather than heading cuts.

The second condition that calls for more severe initial pruning is when the tree may experience drought in its first season, either through lack of rain or insufficient watering. Pruning increases the chances for surviving drought by

Your first goal as you train a young tree is to develop a sturdy trunk. You began this process when you pruned the tree at planting time, by selecting a single leader and pruning away, or bending down, any competitors. Continue this process, strictly disciplining the tree to have only a single leader. The trees to watch most closely are those that are naturally round-headed, because their leaders tend to lose their dominance sooner than we would like on a landscape tree.

If you plan to use pruning to restrict the height of your tree, begin such pruning before the tree reaches its desired height. Stop upward progress of the leader by cutting it back to a weak branch. Done early on, not only are the resulting cuts smaller, but the crown's appearance also retains a natural upward flow to gradually smaller branches rather than looking as if it has been stubbed back. Best of all, of course, is to plant a tree that will mature at the desired height.

Your second goal in training a young tree is to build up a framework of permanent scaffold limbs that are strong, well connected, and, of course, good-looking. Depending on the height of clear trunk that you want, some of these scaffolds may actually be semi-permanent—even an old tree with its first scaffold limb 8 ft. above ground needs to retain lower branches when it is young, for nourishment. Do not select permanent or semi-permanent scaffolds starting too low on the trunk, because the distance of any of these limbs from the ground never changes. (Actually, the distance decreases slightly as a limb thickens.)

Gaze up along the trunk to select scaffold limbs, keeping in mind three criteria: The limbs must have adequate spacing along the trunk; the points of

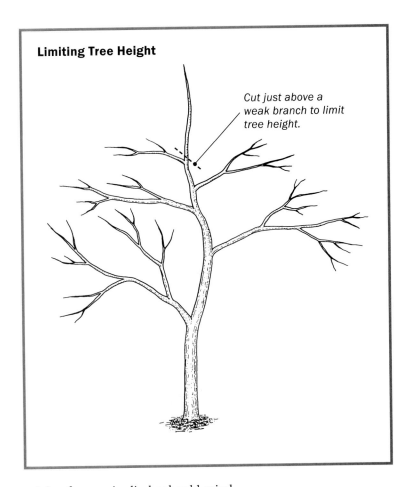

Limiting Tree Height

Cut just above a weak branch to limit tree height.

origin of successive limbs should spiral upward around the trunk; and each limb must make a strong union with the trunk. Just as the distance of a limb from the ground never changes, neither will the distance between limbs. And as the limbs thicken, they will crowd even closer. Select as permanent scaffold limbs side branches that are spaced from 6 in. to 18 in. apart along the trunk (see the top drawing on p. 74), with the smaller distances reserved for trees whose ultimate size is the least.

Choosing for scaffold limbs branches that originate in a spiral up the trunk makes for a prettier tree and allows each limb to be adequately nourished by water and minerals moving up from the roots. For a large tree, no branch should be closer than 3 ft. to the next one directly above it. This way, each scaffold limb will have plenty of space in which to develop.

As you look over branches that are potential scaffold limbs, how do you know which are strongly attached? The most important indicator of a strong union is that the branch is thinner than the leader. This way, the leader will envelop the base of the branch as they both grow. If a particularly well-positioned branch is too thick in comparison to the leader, you can retain that branch as a scaffold limb by suppressing its rate of growth. Do this by pruning part of the branch off or by bending it to a more horizontal position. If the branch has laterals growing from it, thin some of these, especially those out near the end.

A wide crotch angle between a scaffold limb and the trunk is another sign of a strong union. The problem with a narrow crotch angle is that an increasing amount of dead bark builds up in it over time. Being dead, this bark does not help hold the limb to the trunk. More important, a narrow angle means that the branch is growing more nearly vertical, and the more upright a branch, the greater its vigor. It may be thicker than the leader, or on its way to becoming so. If a narrow-angled branch is particularly well positioned, cut it all the way back when it is only a few inches long, and a wide-angled shoot will often grow in its place (from a latent bud at that node).

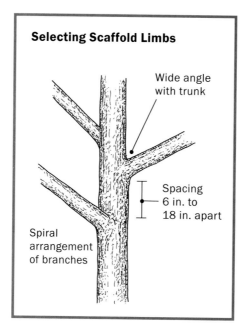

Selecting Scaffold Limbs

Wide angle with trunk

Spacing 6 in. to 18 in. apart

Spiral arrangement of branches

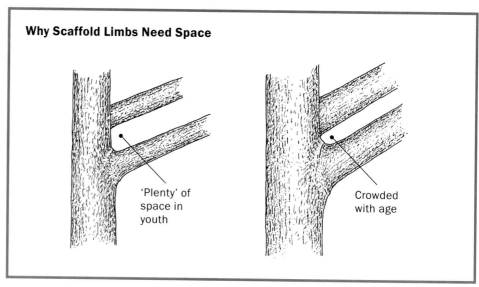

Why Scaffold Limbs Need Space

'Plenty' of space in youth

Crowded with age

Continue to select scaffold limbs over the first few years as your young tree develops. As the main scaffold limbs grow, they will develop their own side branches. For side branches that are strongly attached and have sufficient room to develop, choose those that are thinner than the scaffold limbs themselves and at least 2 ft. away from where the scaffold limb attaches to the central leader. If side branches are well placed but overly vigorous, suppress their growth by bending them down or by pruning them a little. Rarely does a scaffold limb need encouragement to send out branches, but in case it does, use heading cuts. To induce branching on scaffold limbs of deciduous conifers such as larch, dawn redwood, and bald cypress, pinch back shoots as they are expanding.

Some young trees, especially those that eventually become round-headed, develop a lanky leader that is reluctant to make side branches. (Side branches won't grow during the season that the developing leader is growing, that is; the following growing season, the shoot loses control and is overtaken by one or more branches—hence, the round head.) Coax such a lanky leader to branch by heading it back a few inches during the growing season, when it has grown a few inches above where you want a scaffold limb (see the top drawing on p. 76). A shoot from the top bud usually continues growing nearly vertically, as a continuation of the leader, while one, perhaps two, lower buds push out new growth at a wide angle. If necessary, repeat this procedure at each level that you want a new scaffold limb. In contrast to round-headed trees, leaders of trees having a spirelike growth habit are as a rule naturally well supplied with potential scaffold limbs from head to foot.

Above: With dead bark rather than living tissue between them, these two upright limbs are liable to split apart.

Left: A branch that is thinner than the leader and growing out at a wide angle indicates a strong union.

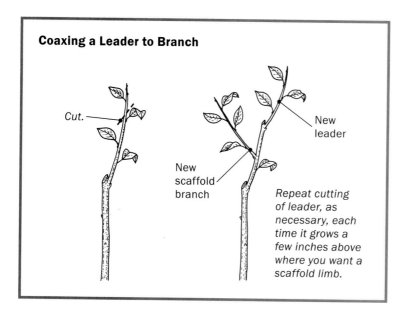

Coaxing a Leader to Branch

Cut.

New scaffold branch

New leader

Repeat cutting of leader, as necessary, each time it grows a few inches above where you want a scaffold limb.

Your young tree will undoubtedly grow many other branches in addition to those that you have selected to become permanent, or semi-permanent, scaffold limbs. Leave most of these for the time being, especially those that are weak or only moderately vigorous. They help feed and thicken the trunk and guard the thin new bark against sunburn. (In the northern hemisphere, this is likely to occur on unshaded south and west sides.) If any temporary branches are growing too vigorously, suppress their growth by pruning them back when they are dormant or by pinching them back in summer, repeatedly if necessary. In any case, do not let any temporary branch

A NOTE ON PRE-PRUNED TREES

I must interject here a short note on pre-pruned trees, as received from nurseries—certain nurseries, at least. Small trees, consisting of only a single whip, are commonly already headed back. Your only recourse, in this case, is to provide good growing conditions and train the tree as described in the text.

Larger trees, already with scaffold branches, also are commonly pre-pruned, giving them what at first appears to be the ideal shape: a length of trunk capped by a nice, full head of branches. But such a tree is really a well-proportioned tree only in miniature. After you plant it out in the landscape, you want a clear trunk longer than 3 ft. And while scaffold limbs 2 in. apart may look nice and full on a miniature tree, they are going to be overcrowded and poorly anchored when each limb is 1 ft. thick. Your recourse with a nursery-butchered tree is to provide good growing conditions and do what pruning is necessary to remove competing leaders and to thin excess scaffold limbs so each has adequate space to develop along the trunk. The real solution, of course, is to avoid purchasing poorly pre-pruned trees in the first place—or you could give the nursery owner a copy of this book.

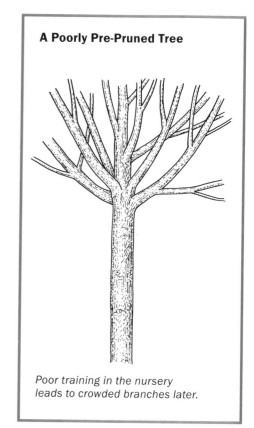

A Poorly Pre-Pruned Tree

Poor training in the nursery leads to crowded branches later.

grow more than 1 ft. in one season. Do not leave any branches—even temporary ones—originating within 6 in. of a scaffold limb.

Remember that those temporary branches are temporary. Never let them grow so vigorously as to overtake either the leader or the scaffold limbs. After a few years, begin removing temporary branches, starting with those that are largest. Do not allow any to grow to the point where their removal leaves a large wound.

Not all trees fall into such neat categories typified by the round-headed white oak or spirelike pin oak. Some trees, such as white birch and alder, naturally form multiple trunks. As you train a tree, you may not always find scaffold branches that are strong, well connected, and well positioned. This is where judgment and ingenuity are needed on your part, which is what makes pruning both an art and a science.

Maintenance pruning

If you did a good job training your tree when it was young, little maintenance pruning is necessary. The grown-up, well-trained tree has large scaffold limbs that are strong and well placed, allowing sufficient light to fall within the canopy to nourish all parts. And the tree looks nice.

Nonetheless, even a mature tree needs periodic pruning. Except in those rare instances where you need to induce branching, limit your pruning to thinning cuts. Remove any limbs that are diseased, dead, or nearly so, as well as one of any two limbs that cross or rub against each other. Remove watersprouts and suckers. These vigorous vertical stems sometimes have the annoying habit of resprouting, even if you—correctly—cut them completely away at their bases.

Red maple welcomes fall with fiery foliage and good form.

Above: Flowering dogwood develops a naturally layered look with little or no coaxing from your pruning shears.

Right: Prune magnolia when young to avoid the need for larger cuts, which heal poorly.

There are two ways to quell this habit. The first way, for the sprout that is still young and tender, is to grab hold of it and rip it off with a sharp tug. The second way, for the shoot that has become woody, is to prune with shears, then paint the wound with a commercial growth regulator (such as Tree-Hold, or other product containing naphthalene-acetic acid).

As any tree ages, it may grow top-heavy and/or develop drooping branches. Limbs higher up in the crown become proportionately more vigorous and increasingly shade those lower down, so the latter grow weak and die. Counteract this tendency by pruning so that the foliage is most dense in the lower half of the tree. Thinning cuts in the crown also help keep the tree open to light and air. Reserve heading cuts for younger branches lower down, to invigorate a faltering stem or shorten a drooping branch.

Not every mature tree received good training in its youth; perhaps you have inherited a misguided tree. Typically, such a tree, besides having poorly selected scaffold limbs, has been butchered by heading cuts. Rampant but crowded and weakly attached shoots sprout from the ends of these limbs. Begin pruning such a tree by dealing with the main scaffold limbs, removing those that are overcrowded or poorly placed (if possible—admittedly, there are trees that are beyond repair). Then thin out the stems growing from the ends of the previously headed limbs, leaving only one if you want to extend that limb. Otherwise, cut the headed limb back to a weaker lateral.

Occasionally, high wind, perhaps in conjunction with snow, ice, or rain, breaks limbs off trees, even trees with sturdy limbs. Repairing such damage may be a job for a professional arborist. Damaged branches need to be cut off cleanly, either at their point of origin or back to a lateral limb. Restore the symmetry of the crown using mostly thinning cuts.

Renovating a deciduous ornamental tree

Eventually, a tree may need renovation because of a combination of age and neglect. Perhaps a tree has grown too large, either in height or width, and the weight of the branches bends the lower limbs too close to the ground. Perhaps a tree is too dense with foliage, creating so much interior shade that inside branches are weakened and humans made gloomy. Letting more air pass through the crown also lessens the stress of wind on the trunk and major limbs.

Lower an old tree by shortening major limbs to vigorous side branches that are at least one-third the diameter of your cut. Stare at the limb structure within your tree before you begin, because you might even be able to pick out a natural lower tier of branches to cut to. Such cuts will suffer less regrowth, and also will preserve the natural form of a round-headed tree even when you remove a lot of wood. Merely lopping off the ends of limbs is a no-no: It looks bad and does little as far as lowering the tree.

Reducing the height of a tree that has a naturally spirelike growth habit usually changes its form. When you lop back that single, stalwart leader, the top of the tree becomes round-headed. Don't feel bad about this. Many spirelike trees undergo this transformation naturally with age. (This is what put the "bald" in bald cypress.)

On trees that have grown too wide, the heavy branches often arch downward. The way to narrow such trees and leave more head space beneath them is by shortening the horizontal limbs to upward-growing side branches.

Open up the crown of a tree to more light and air using thinning cuts, mostly in the top and around the periphery of the crown. The renovated tree will then have most of its foliage in the lower parts and the interior of the crown, giving a well-proportioned appearance to the tree and decreasing the chance that the interior bark, which was previously most shaded, will sunburn.

Be aware that some trees do not tolerate severe pruning, and could die from such treatment. The chart below, from the British Arboricultural Association, lists the tolerance of some trees to severe pruning. When many severe cuts are needed on any tree, spread the job of renovation over a period of two or three years.

TOLERANCE OF TREES TO SEVERE PRUNING

High	Intermediate	Low
Elm	Ailanthus	Beech
Horse chestnut	Alder	Birch
Linden	Ash	Hornbeam
Mulberry	Catalpa	Walnut
Oak	Cherry	
Poplar	Maple	
	Sycamore	

Plant List

DECIDUOUS ORNAMENTAL TREES

***Acer* spp.** (Maple): Young maple bark is susceptible to sunburn, so make sure to leave those temporary branches for shade, even if the tree will eventually be high-headed. You can train some of the smaller maples—*A. Ginnala* (Amur Maple), for example—as large shrubs, but do not cut back old stems because new ones rarely grow up from ground level. As trees, some species require more pruning than others. The weak wood of fast-growing *A. Negundo* (Box Elder) and *A. saccharinum* (Silver Maple) needs frequent pruning to keep limbs strong and to remove dead and broken branches.

***Aesculus* spp.** (Horse Chestnut)

Ailanthus altissima (Tree-of-Heaven): The wood is brittle, so make sure you prune to a strong framework. Pull off root suckers.

Albizia Julibrissin (Silk Tree): The silk tree naturally develops multiple trunks.

***Alnus* spp.** (Alder)

***Amelanchier* spp.** (Juneberry, Shadblow, Serviceberry): The juneberry naturally grows multiple trunks, but can be trained to a single trunk.

***Betula* spp.** (Birch): Grow plants as single trees or as clumps. To create a clump, either plant a few trees together in one planting hole, or cut an established tree to ground level and let a few shoots develop into trunks. Keep an eye out for codominant stems on young plants, and cut away one of them as soon as you notice it. Do what pruning is needed when a stem is small, and keep pruning to a minimum.

***Carpinus* spp.** (Hornbeam)

***Catalpa* spp.** (Catalpa)

***Celtis* spp.** (Hackberry)

Cercidiphyllum japonicum (Katsura Tree)

***Cercis* spp.** (Redbud): Prune as little as possible so that the plant can develop its natural shape.

***Chionanthus* spp.** (Fringe Tree): Grow this plant as either a tree or a shrub. In either case, prune after flowering so that you can enjoy the show first.

Cladrastis lutea (Yellowwood)

***Cornus* spp.:** These plants grow as small trees or large shrubs. In either case, they require little regular pruning, especially if allowed to express their natural growth habit. *C. florida* (Flowering Dogwood) usually grows as a small tree, eventually developing a few feet of clear trunk below its layered branches. *C. mas* (Cornelian Cherry) develops multiple trunks,

Pruning is just part of what might be required in tree renovation. Cabling and bracing, for example, might also be needed, but these techniques are outside the realm of pruning, so they warrant no discussion here. Sometimes you can substitute pruning for cabling or bracing—rather than strengthening a weak limb, you can decrease the weight on it by cutting it back.

Renovating an old, neglected tree can be hazardous. Much of the work takes place high above ground, and involves the removal of large limbs. If you have any doubts about your agility, your bravery, your equipment, or your skills (even if you know where to cut, you also have to know where a limb will drop and, perhaps, how to lower it with ropes), call a professional arborist. Offer your knowledgeable suggestions with your feet firmly planted on terra firma. (For a list of arborists in your area who have passed the certification examination of the International Society of Arborists, call 217-355-9411.)

although you can easily train it to a single trunk. *C. Kousa* (Kousa Dogwood) often develops a single trunk, but that trunk remains furnished with branches all the way down to the ground.

Crataegus **spp.** (Hawthorn): Hawthorn is a twiggy tree that also can be planted in masses to shear as a hedge.

Davidia involucrata (Dove Tree): Train the tree carefully when young—with one or more trunks—to avoid later on having to make large cuts, which heal poorly. Prune after flowering.

Delonix regia (Royal Poinciana)

Erythrina **spp.** (Coral Tree): Erythrina includes deciduous, evergreen, and semi-evergreen trees, all of which require little beyond standard maintenance pruning. Some plants have particularly picturesque branching patterns, most evident in winter; prune these to bring out their best form.

Fagus **spp.** (Beech)

Franklinia Alatamaha (Franklinia)

Fraxinus **spp.** (Ash): Ashes are fast growing with brittle wood, narrow crotches, and often few branches. Counteract potential problems by maintaining a single leader, using heading cuts to induce branching, and selecting scaffold limbs with care. With species having two pairs of buds at each node *(F. Uhdei* and *F. velutina),* the upper pair produces upright growing shoots and the lower pair produces wide-angled shoots. Allow one of the upper buds to to grow when you need to extend a leader or scaffold branch; cut back a shoot from the upper bud to induce a lower bud to grow where you want a wide-angled side branch.

Fremontodendron **spp.** (Fremontia, Flannel Bush): Fremontia does not require pruning. But you can prune to control size, create a single-trunked tree, promote bushiness, and so forth. If you do prune, do so after flowering, and wear long gloves because the hairs on the seed capsules are irritating.

Ginkgo biloba (Ginkgo, Maidenhair Tree): Give this tree time, rather than pruning, to develop an attractive natural form.

Gleditsia triacanthos (Honey Locust)

Gymnocladus dioica (Kentucky Coffee Tree)

Halesia **spp.** (Silver-bell Tree, Snowdrop Tree)

Kalopanax pictus

Koelreuteria **spp.** (Golden-rain Tree)

Laburnum anagyroides (Goldenchain Tree): Train this plant either as a large shrub or as a single-trunked tree. Avoid large cuts, because they heal slowly. Besides regular maintenance pruning, done after flowering, also remove developing seed pods, which are poisonous, messy, and sap the plant's energy.

Larix **spp.** (Larch): To promote bushier growth, pinch the developing shoots in spring. When making heading cuts on older branches, cut back to where the branch still has leaves, or to a side branch.

Liquidambar **spp.** (Sweet Gum)

Liriodendron Tulipifera (Tulip Tree): The wood is brittle but the tree naturally develops a good, strong form. Shorten branches that threaten to break under their own weight, preferably while the tree is young so you can avoid making large cuts. These heal slowly.

Maclura pomifera (Osage Orange): This dense-growing tree can be trained as a thick hedge,

The fan-shaped leaves of ginkgo are both unique and beautiful.

Ginkgo develops good form with a minimum of pruning.

(continued on page 82)

which is an especially good barrier because of its thorns, or as a tree with a single trunk.

***Magnolia* spp.** (Magnolia): Do what little pruning a magnolia requires while stems are small, because large cuts heal slowly.

***Malus* spp.** (Crabapple)

Melia Azedarach (Chinaberry)

Metasequoia glyptostroboides (Dawn Redwood): To promote bushier growth, pinch developing shoots in spring. When making heading cuts on older branches, cut back to where the branch still has leaves or to a side branch.

***Nothofagus* spp.**

Nyssa sylvatica (Sour Gum, Tupelo)

***Ostrya* spp.** (Hop Hornbeam)

Oxydendrum arboreum (Sourwood, Sorrel Tree)

Parrotia persica (Persian Parrotia)

Paulownia tomentosa (Empress Tree)

Phellodendron amurense (Cork Tree)

***Platanus* spp.** (Plane Tree, Sycamore)

Poncirus trifoliata (Trifoliate Orange, Hardy Orange)

***Populus* spp.** (Poplar, Aspen, Cottonwood): Columnar types, such as *P. alba* 'Pyramidalis' and *P. nigra* 'Italica' (Lombardy Poplar) look best branching from the base, so head back young trees after planting and then as shoots grow. No need for anything more than basic pruning on round-headed trees such as *P. deltoides* (Cottonwood). *P. tremuloides* (Quaking Aspen) is commonly grown in groves of several trees, which need no pruning beyond cutting away dead or diseased wood and removing lower branches to expose the attractive bark.

***Prunus* spp.** (Flowering Cherries and Plums)

Pseudolarix Kaempferi (Golden Larch): To promote bushier growth, pinch developing shoots in spring. When making heading cuts

on older branches, cut back to where the branch still has leaves, or to a side branch.

Ptelea trifoliata (Stinking Ash, Water Ash): Grow this plant as a large shrub or as a small tree.

***Pyrus* spp.** (Pear): Many ornamental pears tend to develop upright, crowded branches. Take special care to train trees with adequate branch spacing, and spread branches for wide crotch angles. Watch for evidence of fire blight disease, pruning it out whenever noted. Avoid too severe pruning on healthy trees or you will stimulate overly succulent shoots, which are especially susceptible to fire blight.

***Quercus* spp.** (Oak)

***Robinia* spp.** (Locust)

Sapium sebiferum (Chinese Tallow Tree)

Sassafras albidum (Sassafras)

Sophora japonica (Chinese Scholar Tree)

***Sorbus* spp.** (Mountain Ash)

***Stewartia* spp.** (Stewartia): Train as either a tree or a shrub.

***Styrax* spp.** (Snowbell): Snowbells tend to be shrubby trees that need periodic thinning out of weak or crowded branches.

Tamarix aphylla (Athel Tree)

Taxodium distichum (Bald Cypress): To promote bushier growth, pinch developing shoots in spring. When making heading cuts on older branches, cut back to where the branch still has leaves, or to a side branch.

***Tilia* spp.** (Linden, Basswood, Lime Tree)

Tipuana Tipu (Tipu Tree)

***Ulmus* spp.** (Elm)

Zelkova serrata (Japanese Zelkova): Zelkova makes repeated efforts at multiple leaders, so be diligent in pruning out competitors if you want to maintain a single trunk. Even if you allow multiple leaders, still thin out excess stems so that the crown does not become overcrowded.

Stewartia summer flowers are followed by colorful leaves in autumn, then interesting bark in winter.

CHAPTER SIX

EVERGREEN TREES AND BUSHES

'America' rhododendron in all its glory.

Evergreens provide welcome greenery for northern winters; and even in climates mild enough where almost all woody plants are evergreen, these plants still can provide a verdant backdrop or a focal point in the landscape. We seem to enjoy the view of evergreens more than their use. They are not plants we typically gravitate to for shade or for playing under or climbing in. Form is all-important with evergreens. This emphasis on form and year-round greenery should not diminish the other qualities of evergreens—the texture and glossiness of their leaves, and perhaps their show of flowers.

Trees and bushes are lumped together in this section because with many evergreens the distinction between a tree and a bush is hazy—at least when you stand back and look at the plant. It's often a question merely of size, since trees and bushes are both commonly clothed with leafy branches right down to ground level, hiding a single trunk even if it is present. In this chapter I have divided evergreens into functional rather than botanical groupings: conifers, broadleaf evergreens, palm trees, and bamboo.

As a general rule, evergreens require little pruning—unless you insist that a plant conform to your desires rather than to its natural growth habit. In that case, it's better to choose a plant that will mature to the size and shape that you want. Otherwise, you create unnecessary work for yourself. And although plants never give up trying to grow, you may slowly lose the enthusiasm to keep a plant in check. You do not have to look

Just a bit of pruning and this bird's nest spruce rises to the occasion.

far to find a home whose doorways or windows are engulfed by evergreens that were once small but grew beyond the energy of the homeowner. To reiterate: Form is all-important. And if the plant naturally adopts the desired form, so much the better.

A couple of other generalities apply to this very diverse group of plants. First of all, they need no special pruning at planting time. Because they are usually sold either balled and burlapped or potted, evergreens do not suffer transplant shock. (Unless they are very small and quickly moved, evergreens cannot be transplanted bare root, because they continually lose water through their leaves.) Prune as needed when transplanting, only to develop strength and beauty.

Many evergreens can be grown as either informal or formal hedges. For a formal hedge, the plant should have small leaves, or at least small in proportion to the size of the hedge, and be able to tolerate shearing. The more rigid the form, the more shearings that are required (for more on hedges, see pp. 60-65).

Coniferous trees and bushes

Cones are the giveaway for conifers ("cone-ifers"), but are not always all that obvious. The cones of yew, which look like small brown seeds peeking out of their scarlet, fleshy covering, are hardly cone-y, but are botanical cones nonetheless. Conifers also have narrow or needlelike leaves. But "narrow" is a matter of degree, and the leaves of a conifer such as podocarpus are actually broader than those of a "broadleaf" evergreen such as heather. Still, you identify most conifers by their cones and narrow leaves.

CONIFEROUS TREES AND BUSHES

TO CONTAIN GROWTH or make a plant smaller, prune just before growth begins, cutting stems back to side branches within the plant. Conifers vary in their ability to regrow from old wood, so be careful.

TO MAKE A PLANT DENSER, shorten new growth in spring as it is expanding.

ON TREES, maintain a single central leader with well-placed, weaker scaffold branches growing off it.

GENERALLY, coniferous evergreens need little pruning when being trained or after they mature, especially if you plant one suited to the site.

Growth habits and timing of pruning

Conifers have two types of growth habits; random branching and whorled branching. Recognizing them is a matter of importance when it comes to pruning.

Branches on random-branching conifers arise anywhere along the trunk and branches. Typically, random-branching conifers grow in spurts through the season. These plants vary in their capacity to resprout when cut back into older wood. Shear any of these conifers to make growth more dense. How much you can shear depends on whether the particular species can sprout new growth from either old or young wood, or just from young wood.

Branches on whorled-branching conifers arise in whorls at discrete intervals along the trunk or stems. Whorled-branching conifers generally have few latent buds or dormant growing points on the leafless parts of stems, so the stems do not regrow when cut back. And, as growth begins, each bud is already programmed for all the growth

Growth Habit of Conifers

*Random branching pattern
(e.g., juniper)*

*Whorled branching pattern
(e.g., pine, spruce)*

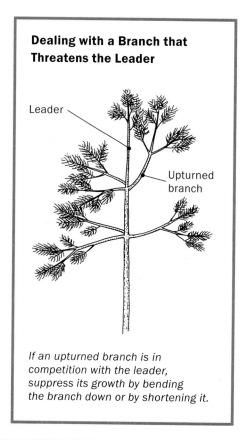

Dealing with a Branch that Threatens the Leader

Leader

Upturned branch

If an upturned branch is in competition with the leader, suppress its growth by bending the branch down or by shortening it.

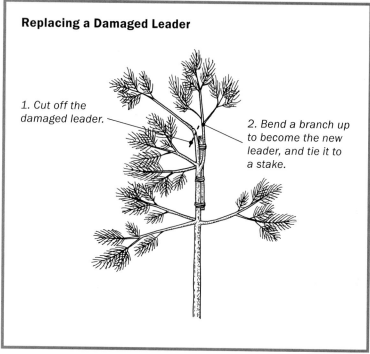

Replacing a Damaged Leader

1. Cut off the damaged leader.

2. Bend a branch up to become the new leader, and tie it to a stake.

for that season. To make a whorled-branching conifer bushier or to slow its growth, pinch back new growth in spring just as the buds are expanding, but before they are fully expanded. The best time to remove branches, however, is just before growth begins, so that new foliage hides the cuts.

Pruning while training

Most coniferous trees have a naturally spirelike habit, at least when young, so they need little pruning beyond that necessary to maintain a single central leader, or extension of the trunk within the plant. Rarely do any shoots compete with the developing leader, but if they do, cut them off completely as soon as you notice them. Otherwise, you will have two shoots developing into leaders, with a narrow angle between them. Not only will this upset the symmetry of the tree, but old, dead bark will build up in that narrow-angled crotch, and, with no living tissue to join them, the two leaders may split apart with age.

All branches growing off the central leader should be subordinate to it in position and in growth rate. As long as the diameter of the branches remains less than the diameter of the central leader, wood of the central leader can envelop the branches where they meet, leading to strong unions. In the rare instances where a branch is growing too fast in comparison with the leader, slow its growth by shortening it. Do this by cutting one or more laterals on this side branch back to other laterals, thereby preserving the natural beauty of the plant and avoiding dead stubs.

If by chance the developing leader is damaged or broken off, replace it with another leader. In whorled conifers, one or more of the topmost branches will bend upward of their own accord to attempt leadership. Select one of these as the leader, and help it along by temporarily tying it to a stake either set in the ground or lashed to the remaining portion of the previous leader. The other branches will droop back to their subordinate position. If a stub was left where the old leader was lost, a latent bud at the base of that stub may grow into an upright shoot. This shoot will be more vigorous and in a better position to serve as a leader than any side branch, so give it preference. In any case, do select and encourage a new leader, or else vigorous new shoots will poke up along the tops of the upper branches—not a pretty sight!

A central leader may not be forever or for all conifers. Conifers that grow as low or sprawling shrubs do not naturally form central leaders—nor are they supposed to! And with age, some conifers that were spirelike in their youth develop a rounded head. Prune the major branches that form the rounded head of such a conifer so that they are unequal in vigor. This makes the top both stronger and prettier.

Direct growth on young plants of whorled conifers by shortening or removing elongating shoots as they are expanding. Because growth for the season is preordained and contained in the expanding shoots on these conifers, you generally cannot prompt the growth of side branches by heading back existing branches. You can control the size of a pine tree or make it denser by shortening the "candles."

Random-branching conifers are more accommodating when it comes to pruning, because the location of their buds and the time of their growth are not so rigidly programmed. Train these plants by cutting wayward branches off or back to side branches, and promote

denser growth and branching with heading cuts. Limit plant size by shortening branches before growth begins each season. To reduce the size of a random-branching conifer more drastically, shorten branches back to side branches within the plant, so that pruning cuts are hidden from sight.

Conifers have fine-textured leaves and are clothed with leafy branches from top to bottom, so they make ideal hedges. Depending on the natural size of the particular conifer and the desired size of the hedge, an informal coniferous hedge may need little pruning beyond the removal of occasional wayward limbs.

Below: Make growth more bushy on whorled conifers by pinching back new growth just as it is expanding.

Left: Shorten pine 'candles' by breaking off a portion—cutting would leave ragged ends on the leaves.

1. How can you deal with this branch jutting out of place?

2. If you shorten it just as much as needed, you'll be left with an ugly stub staring you in the face.

3. Instead, prune off the branch with a cut well down within the bush.

4. The offending branch is gone without a trace.

The amount of cutting back tolerated depends on the ability of the particular plants to send out new growth from old wood. No matter what kind of evergreen is involved, shape the hedge correctly from the start, giving it a slightly wider base than top. If the hedge's sides are vertical or, even worse, if the hedge is top-heavy, the lower branches will become shaded, lose their leaves, and die.

Maintenance pruning

Despite the preceding verbiage, conifers chosen to suit their site require only minimum pruning. Keep an eye out for overcrowded limbs, which can lead to the shading and death of light-starved branches. Periodically thin out laterals where they are overcrowded. Also prune away any dead or diseased wood.

As a conifer ages, its lower limbs may start to die, the amount depending on the degree of shading and the plant's tolerance for shade. Even if they don't

die, you may want to remove lower limbs as a plant ages. An old tree might look nicer with its crown up off the ground (although many conifers do not) or, in the case of a plant such as lacebark pine, with its decorative old bark in full view. Perhaps you want to be able to sit or walk beneath the canopy. If you are going to remove older limbs, spread this job over a period of years, rather than stressing a tree by doing it all at once.

Your aim with a mature coniferous hedge is to keep the plants full and within bounds. Shape whorled conifers, and make growth dense, by clipping back new growth (the candles, in the case of pines) before it is fully expanded. You can use hedge shears on whorled-branching

conifers like firs because of their naturally dense growth. Hedge shears also work fine on random-branching conifers—they will send out new growth from branch tips as well as from random points along branches. Shear just before growth begins for the season so that new growth will hide the cuts. If necessary, shear again later in the season, but less severely. Later cuts are less likely to be hidden by new growth (definitely not with a whorled-branching conifer), and you should avoid shearing severely enough or late enough in the season to stimulate soft, new growth that may not harden off before winter. Where more radical shaping on either type conifer is necessary, use hand shears or a lopper to shorten branches to their point of origin or to side branches within the plant.

There is one basic problem with shearing conifers to size. (Actually two, the first being that the practice is too pervasive.) Inevitably, when you cut back branch tips you always leave at least a little of the earlier growth. The result is that a sheared plant keeps growing larger and larger. Eventually, such a plant outgrows its bounds, and then the choices are limited to digging out the plant—or the whole hedge—or to renovating by drastic pruning of all the wood. Few conifers regrow when severely cut back. The way to avoid this problem and produce a more natural-looking hedge (admittedly not always desirable) is to shorten branches selectively each year with pruning shears. Better yet, choose the right size and shape of plant at the outset.

Plant List

CONIFERS

Abies spp. (Fir): Firs have a whorled branching pattern with few dormant buds. Because they have such short spaces between leaves along a stem, firs are dense and need little pruning. If necessary, pinch developing shoots in spring for more bushiness, and cut wayward branches back to laterals. Unless you want to restrict height, do not pinch the topmost whorl, because regrowth from there is usually poor. For hedging, shear after growth hardens in midsummer.

Agathis robusta (Queensland Kauri): This whorled-branched conifer develops a naturally symmetrical shape so it needs little help from you. Occasionally these trees try to develop two leaders; remove the weaker one when you notice it.

Araucaria heterophylla (Norfolk Island Pine): This symmetrical tree with whorled branches rarely needs pruning. Laterals never turn upward, so protect the leader—it is irreplaceable. Pinch side shoots if you want more branching.

Calocedrus decurrens (California Incense Cedar): This tree needs little pruning. Let it grow naturally or shear it as a hedge.

Cedrus spp. (True Cedar): True cedars have a random branching habit. Short growths, called spurs, form on branches, and these have some latent buds. To control size, cut branches back to laterals, although sometimes this will cause a vigorous new shoot to grow from a spur. To make the plant fuller, pinch back developing shoots. Generally, these plants require little pruning. You can shear *C. Deodara* (Deodar Cedar) as a hedge.

Cephalotaxus spp. (Plum Yew): These random-branching trees and shrubs need little pruning beyond the removal of dead, diseased, and misplaced wood. Old wood will make new growth if cut back, so you can grow this plant as a tree or a shrub, sheared or clipped informally.

Chamaecyparis spp. (False Cypress): To shorten a branch of this random-branching conifer, cut it back to wherever it still has leaves, and new growth will push out. Redirect growth by cutting a branch back to a lateral. Prune the ends of branches to make the plant grow more densely. False cypress is a good plant for hedging.

Cryptomeria japonica (Japanese Cedar): Cryptomeria has a random branching habit. To shorten a branch, cut it back to a live lateral shoot (some naturally die and fall off) or to a tuft of foliage. Make growth more dense by pinching back expanding foliage.

Cunninghamia lanceolata (China Fir): China fir has a whorled branch arrangement. Remove misplaced, dead, and diseased branches as well as suckers growing from the roots.

× **Cupressocyparis Leylandii** (Leyland Cypress): This randomly branched conifer rarely needs pruning unless you want to shear it as a hedge, and even that is rarely necessary except to control size.

Cupressus spp. (Cypress): Cypresses are randomly branched conifers that can push out new growth wherever there are leaves. So if you want to shorten a branch, cut it back either to a lateral or a point where leaves persist. Cypresses tolerate being sheared for hedging. To make a specimen tree denser, prune back the tips of the branches. Following pruning, cypresses are slow to begin growth.

Juniperus spp. (Juniper): Junipers have a random branching pattern, with some growing points even where there is no foliage. Therefore, these plants can be cut back more severely than many other conifers. Plants have either needlelike or scalelike leaves. Species with scalelike leaves, such as *J. chinensis* (except when juvenile), *J. horizontalis* (Creeping Juniper), *J. occidentalis* (California Juniper), and *J. virginiana*

(Red Cedar), regrow following pruning better than do those with needlelike leaves, such as *J. Sabina* (Savin Juniper) and *J. squamata*.

Cutting back the stem tips makes the plants denser. Junipers take well to shearing, for hedging. Two or three shearings a year might be needed for a tight, formal hedge.

To remove larger branches without leaving a mangled look, shorten them to weaker laterals within the plant. This pruning is a way to make a plant smaller and to open up the interior to light, where shaded branches often die out. Shortening individual limbs in this manner is also the way to contain the growth of a prostrate form of juniper while preserving the natural form of the plant.

Libocedrus spp. (Incense Cedar): Prune stems on this randomly branched conifer back to wherever leaves persist, or back to laterals. Promote dense branching by pruning back the stems tips. Incense cedar tolerates shearing as a hedge.

Picea spp. (Spruce): Spruces have a whorled branching pattern with a few dormant buds. To make a plant smaller or to shape it, prune back to side branches or to visible dormant buds. To make a plant denser, pinch lateral shoots when they are about half-grown in spring. Or shear just before growth begins, shearing a second time, if necessary, in late spring or early summer. Generally, spruces need little regular pruning. Even old plants look best with their oldest branches retained, gracefully sweeping the ground.

Pinus spp. (Pine): Pines have a whorled branching pattern and, with few exceptions, almost no latent buds or dormant growing points. Exceptions include *P. nigra* (Austrian Pine), *P. resinosa* (Red Pine), and *P. sylvestris* (Scotch Pine), which are capable of resprouting from buds on two-year-old wood where needles are retained.

Make a pine tree smaller by cutting branches back to secondary branches within the canopy while the plant is dormant. Pruning the "candles," which are expanding new growths, can keep a tree from growing large or make a tree fuller and bushier. New shoots generally arise only from buds within candles.

Completely breaking off a candle discourages further elongation at that point. Shortening a candle, instead, decreases the distance at which the next whorl of branches develops, making for a denser tree. Snap the end of a candle off with your fingers rather than cutting it back with pruning shears to avoid also cutting off expanding leaves, which would then brown at their tips.

(continued on page 92)

This Norfolk Island pine has naturally good form. It requires little or no pruning.

A couple of tricks sometimes fool mature pine stems to grow side branches. The first trick is is to cut away a ring of bark ⅛ in. wide around the stem where you want branching to occur. The other trick is to remove needles 1 in. to 2 in. beyond where you want branching to occur. Both tricks are most successful the younger the tree and the closer to the end of the stem you can cut bark or remove needles.

Platycladus orientalis (Oriental Arborvitae): This randomly branching conifer can regrow wherever there is foliage, so you can cut wood back either to side branches or to where foliage persists. To make the plant denser, cut back the tips of the stems.

Podocarpus macrophyllus (Southern Yew, Japanese Yew, Buddhist Pine): This randomly branching conifer resprouts even if cut back into old wood, so shape the plant with heading and thinning cuts. To make the plant denser, pinch or shear the tips of growing shoots during any of its growth flushes through the season.

Pseudotsuga menziesii (Douglas Fir): Douglas fir rarely requires pruning. The tree has a whorled branching habit with few dormant buds, so limit pruning to shortening to side branches, for size control and cutting back new growth as it expands for a denser tree. You can shear Douglas firs as a hedge plant. Do not cut out the top of an old tree or it will decline.

Sciadopitys verticillata (Umbrella Pine, Japanese Umbrella Pine): This whorled conifer has an attractive natural symmetry so it needs little pruning. Watch for, and eliminate, any competitors with the central leader.

***Sequoia* spp.** (Redwood and Sequoia): *S. sempervirens* (Redwood) is randomly branched and well supplied with latent buds throughout. Head or thin stems to shape a tree and control its size. Promote denser growth by pruning branch tips. Allow only a single leader to grow. *S. Wellingtonia* (Giant Sequoia) is also random-branching, but has few live buds on leafless wood. Shorten a branch either to a live lateral (some naturally die and drop) or to where there is a tuft of foliage. Promote branching by pinching back expanding shoots.

Sequoiadendron giganteum (Giant Redwood): This random-branching giant has such a pleasing natural growth habit that it rarely requires any pruning. That's good, because it grows to a height of 250 ft. or more!

***Taxus* spp.** (Yew): Yew is random branching and well supplied with dormant growing points, so will return to life even if cut back brutally. Control size and shape the plant with heading or thinning cuts. Pruning the ends of stems makes growth denser. For a formal hedge or bush, shear yew as needed just before growth begins for the season, then shear again one or two times during the season. Training yew as a tree shows off its beautiful reddish bark.

***Thuja* spp.** (Arborvitae): This randomly branching conifer can regrow wherever there is foliage, so cut wood back either to side branches or to where foliage persists. To make the plant denser, cut back the tips of the stems, or shear.

***Tsuga* spp.** (Hemlock): Hemlocks are randomly branched conifers that are full and graceful without any pruning. Grow hemlocks as trees or hedge plants. Clip or shear hedges just before growth begins, repeating, if necessary, in midsummer. Hemlock will resprout from bare wood, so you can rejuvenate a plant by cutting it back severely.

Broadleaf evergreen trees and bushes

Generally, do what little pruning is necessary to bring out the natural form of a broadleaf evergreen. The right plant in the right place needs minimal pruning. Techniques for pruning evergreen trees and shrubs are similar to techniques for pruning their deciduous counterparts (see chapters 4 and 5). Because evergreens are clothed in year-round greenery, though, the arrangement of their branches is never prominent, so we prune these plants for pleasing three-dimensional form, as well as for plant health, strength (in the case of trees), and perhaps flowers.

When needed, direct growth just as you would on any other plant. To remove a wayward stem without causing regrowth, cut it away at its point of origin or back to one of its side branches. Where you want denser growth, shorten a stem while the plant is dormant or pinch a shoot as it is growing. Wait to prune early-flowering plants until after their blossoms fade if you do not want to miss their show. Other specifics with respect to timing of pruning are noted in the Plant List, which begins on p. 96.

Except where otherwise indicated, do most pruning of these plants around the time that growth is beginning. Dormant pruning can be done anytime that a plant is dormant, but if you wait until just before growth commences, new growth will quickly hide the pruning cuts. Also, winter damage is more evident once new growth begins, and it is less likely to occur with marginally cold-hardy plants pruned at this time.

Just a little pinching and thinning keeps this Mexican orange shrub shapely and florific.

Training

Prune a bush to give a pleasing form and sufficiently dense growth.

Most important with a broadleaf evergreen tree is to train the branches to a sturdy framework when the plant is young. Begin as soon as you plant by allowing only a single main stem, which will become the future trunk and central leader of the tree. If two or more shoots are competing for the role of central leader, cut away all but one. If a branch is turning upward and threatening the leader's dominance, slow growth on that branch by pruning it back partially or by bending it down, with weights or string, to a more horizontal position (see the top drawing on p. 86). Throughout the early development of your tree, keep that central leader upright and dominant.

This single-leader "rule" is not hard and fast. Because the distinction between trees and shrubs is vague with evergreens, many plants that are naturally bushy can be trained to small trees (and many of the trees can be bushlike). Small trees are not threatened by collapse, and many of them look attractive with multiple trunks originating from ground level. Develop this form by selecting two or three trunks as the plant grows; alternatively, let the plant grow as a bush, then reduce the number of stems growing from ground level and trim off branches from the stems that remain to make them into trunks.

Small branches growing off the central leader of a developing tree will, in time, become main scaffold limbs of that tree. Begin selecting future scaffold limbs when you put the tree in the ground. Choose branches that are spaced far enough apart along the developing leader so that they will not be crowded even when the tree reaches old age. A distance of 6 in. to 18 in. is adequate, with the closer distances reserved for smaller trees. Successively higher branches should arise in a spiral fashion up the trunk so that each has adequate space to develop and is not being starved by another branch directly and closely beneath it. So that the trunk can envelop and firmly hold the base of a branch, that branch must be thinner than the trunk. If a well-placed branch is too thick in proportion to the trunk, slow its growth by pruning part of it away, especially near the end of the branch. Strength that comes from good scaffold-limb choice and development becomes increasingly important with larger trees.

Selecting Scaffold Limbs

Future scaffold limbs should be spaced 6 in. to 18 in. apart and should spiral upward in an uncrowded pattern.

Leave any other branches growing off the leader as temporary branches. These branches will help strengthen the developing leader and trunk. Only remove those branches that are crowding the permanent scaffolds. Leave temporary branches only for about three years, and prune them back in the meantime if they start getting too big.

Choose side branches growing off scaffold limbs in a similar way as you chose the scaffolds themselves. Retain side branches that are not crowding each other or growing too near the central leader, then prune to suppress the growth of any that threaten to grow thicker than the limb from which they spring.

Maintenance pruning

With good early training, neither trees nor bushes in this category require much pruning. As with any plant, remove dead, diseased, and misplaced wood. Some of the plants look nicer if their faded flowers are removed. A few of the bushes require heavy annual pruning for a good show of flowers or to keep the plants from growing scraggly. Aside from consulting the Plant List, which begins on p. 96, another way to tell how much pruning is needed to keep your bush happily flowering is to watch the plant for a season or two and note how old the wood is when it bears flowers. The younger the flowering wood, the more severe the annual pruning required.

Renovation

Major renovation of any broadleaf evergreen must be done with caution, because some of these plants do not regrow from old wood and some do not heal large wounds well. Consult the Plant List that follows for specific directions. Or determine how well your plant resprouts from old wood by heading back a branch to an older, leafless portion and watching its response. Merely shearing the top of a plant is not a good way to lower it—the plant will look horrendous right after pruning and even worse when it sends out new sprouts along the tops of the branches. Instead, cut an individual tall limb back either to its point of origin or to a branch low within the canopy. Do not make too many major cuts in a single year, or you will overly stress the plant. Only certain bushes tolerate severe cutting back in the name of renovation. To make a renovated plant less of an initial eyesore, spread the job over a few years, shortening some of the decrepit, old wood to the ground or to low, vigorous branches each year.

Plant List

Abutilon **spp.** (Flowering Maple): Regular pruning is needed to stimulate shoots, on which blossoms form. Either cut the whole plant back in late winter or, in mild climates, cut a different portion of stems back periodically throughout the year.

Acacia **spp.:** Little pruning is needed, whether these plants are grown as bushes or as trees. Beyond training, just cut away dead wood and twigs.

Acalypha **spp.** (Copperleaf): Prune as needed, to shape plants. If you grow copperleaf as a hedge, shorten stems with pruning shears and pinch shoot tips. Using hedge shears mutilates the large, decorative leaves.

Aralia japonica. See *Fatsia japonica.*

Arbutus **spp.** (Manzanita, Strawberry Tree): The strawberry tree tolerates severe pruning.

Arctostaphylos **spp.** (Bearberry, Manzanita): Prune to make these shrubs shapely, removing stems completely or shortening them to side branches. Do not cut back to bare wood, because it may not send out new growth. Pinch back shoots to make them grow more bushy. These plants normally need little pruning.

Aucuba japonica (Japanese Laurel): This plant will tolerate severe pruning needed to rejuvenate or shape it. Cut stems to the ground or back to leaves or buds. Pinch shoots to promote bushiness.

Azara microphylla (Boxleaf Azara): Pinch and shorten shoots on young plants to promote bushiness. Cut off stems that have flowered after the flowers fade. Provide for renewal by occasionally cutting away the oldest stems at ground level.

Berberis **spp.** (Barberry): Prune evergreen species right after flowers fade in spring.

Bougainvillea **spp.** (Bougainvillea): Prune in summer and early autumn, depending on how vigorously the plant is growing and how firm you want to be about controlling that growth. Thin crowded wood and shorten lanky stems just before growth begins. If you want to, you also can limit the number of main trunks sprouting up from the ground. Grown with one or just a few stems, bougainvillea becomes a nonclinging vine.

Brachychiton **spp.** (Bottle Tree): This tree needs little pruning beyond basic training.

Brassaia actinophylla (Australian Umbrella Tree, Queensland Umbrella Tree): Prune mostly to make a plant full, by heading back stems and pinching new growth. The plant will resprout if cut to the ground for renovation.

Brugmansia **spp.** (Angel's-trumpet): Prune back stems to a couple of buds to stimulate new flowering shoots. Do this periodically through the growing season or, where winter weather is cool or cold, just before growth begins for the season.

Buxus **spp.** (Box): Box requires little pruning, unless clipped as a formal hedge. Prune whenever needed, but where winters are cold, do the job at least a month before the average date of the first autumn frost. To renovate, cut the plant to ground level just before new growth begins.

Caesalpinia **spp.:** Prune or don't prune *C. Gilliesii* (Bird-of-paradise Shrub), as you like, to make the plant shrublike or treelike, or to reduce its height if it has grown too tall. *C. pulcherrima* (Barbados-pride, Dwarf Poinciana) needs no regular pruning. Cut it to the ground every year if it is damaged by frost or if you want to keep it small.

Callistemon **spp.** (Bottlebrush): Follow general pruning directions, but do not cut back to leafless parts of stems because they will not send out new sprouts. Direct the shape and size of the plant with small cuts; cuts over 1 in. in diameter do not heal well.

Calluna **spp.** (Heather): Older wood does not resprout readily, so shorten the previous season's growth by one-half to keep heather compact. If you shorten stems with hedge shears, vary the angle at which you hold the shears so that the finished surface is rolling rather than flat-topped.

Calothamnus **spp.** (Net Bush): Cut older stems back right after flowering to keep the plant invigorated.

Camellia **spp.** (Camellia): Little pruning is required beyond that needed to shape a plant. Thin flower buds on young plants to channel energy into growth, and on older plants if you want to increase the size of remaining flowers. The best time to prune stems is just after the flowers fade.

Camellias vary in their growth habits. If your plant is too spreading when young, cut back some side branches to divert energy into vertical growth. Similarly, if your plant is too gangly, head some stems to the bases of previous years' growth to induce branching. (Only one bud will break from cuts on the youngest wood.) With camellias such as *C. reticulata,* which are reluctant to sprout from older wood, promote bushiness by merely pinching the growing tips.

Renovate an overgrown camellia by cutting the whole bush to bare stems, either all at once or over the course of a couple of seasons. You cannot do this with *C. reticulata,* because it may not regrow.

Cantua buxifolia (Magic Flower, Sacred-flower-of-the-Incas): Prune this sprawling shrub, which grows almost like a vine, by removing or shortening misplaced stems after the flowers fade. For a neat plant, tie the stems to a trellis or a post.

Carpenteria californica (Tree Anemone): Despite the common name, this plant is bushy—and requires little regular pruning.

Casuarina equisetifolia (Horsetail Tree, South Sea Ironwood): This tree needs little pruning. Shear, if desired.

Ceanothus **spp.** (Redroot): As soon as the flowers fade, prune the flowering shoots of evergreen species so that they are only two or three buds long.

Chamelaucium uncinatum (Geraldton Wax Plant): Train this plant as a tree or shrub.

Prune the mature plant after the flowers fade, but do not cut back into leafless wood.

Choisya ternata (Mexican Orange): Pinch growing tips to control plant size and thin out older stems to stimulate new growth.

Chorisia **spp.** (Floss-silk Tree): These plants require little pruning.

Cinnamomum Camphora (Camphor Tree): Little pruning is necessary.

Camellia in bloom.

Cistus **spp.** (Rock Rose): Rock rose does not take kindly to pruning, but looks unkempt if left alone. New shoots do not break from older wood, so keep a plant low and bushy by pinching or lightly shearing new growth as it develops. Periodically cut back the oldest stems right after the flowers fade, either to the ground or to branches. Cuttings root readily, so it is easy to have a replacement ready in case of disastrous response to pruning.

Clerodendrum **spp.** (Glory-bower, Kashmir-bouquet): *C. Bungei* and *C. philippinum* are vigorous and spreading. Keep them in check by cutting them back severely in spring, pinching back new growth, and cutting off or digging up suckers from wandering roots. The lanky stems of *C. Thomsoniae* (Bleeding Glory-bower, Tropical Bleeding-heart) could

(continued on page 98)

make this shrub a vine. Prune it lightly right after blossoms fade, shortening some stems and disentangling and removing some others.

Clethra arborea (Summersweet, Sweet Alder): This tree needs little pruning.

Cleyera japonica: This shrub needs little pruning.

Clianthus puniceus (Glory Pea, Parrot's-beak, Red Kowhai): After flowering, completely cut away some of the oldest and most spindly stems. Then head back some of the stems that remain. Vigorous new growth will blossom the following year.

Codiaeum variegatum (Croton): Prune mostly to keep the plant thick with leaves. Head back leggy stems, then pinch growing shoot tips. If the whole plant is overgrown, first cut back one part of the plant, then cut back the other part after growth is well underway on the first part.

***Coprosma* spp.:** *C. × Kirkii* grows low and spreading; keep it dense by shearing it back in spring or summer. *C. repens* (mirror plant, looking-glass plant) grows larger and needs periodic pruning, whenever you wish, to keep it from becoming straggly.

***Cordyline* spp.** (Dracaena): These plants are closely related to dracaena (the plant with this botanical name), even to the point of sharing their common name. Both plants need little pruning. If a stem grows too tall, lop it back and it will send out one, perhaps two, new shoots—probably. Or cut an old stem completely to the ground to make room for younger replacements. Prune while the plant is actively growing.

Corokia cotoneaster: Prune as needed with an eye to accentuating the picturesque form of the branches.

***Correa* spp.:** Pinch shoots to promote branching, then shorten stems right after the flowers fade. But do not cut back to the leafless parts of stems or you may not get regrowth.

Corynocarpus laevigata: Once trained as a shrub or small tree, this plant needs little pruning.

***Cotoneaster* spp.** (Cotoneaster): Like the deciduous species, the evergreen species require little pruning. Do what little pruning is necessary in winter, or wait until old leaves are falling and new buds are just beginning to grow. Keep an eye out for branches blackened by fire blight and cut them back 1 ft. into healthy wood.

Crassula argentea (Jade Tree): Prune just before growth begins. The plant resprouts readily from old nodes.

Crinodendron Patagua: Little pruning is needed for this plant, which can be grown as either a shrub or small tree.

***Daphne* spp.:** For these evergreen species, prune back flowering shoots right after the flowers fade.

Dendromecon rigida (Tree Poppy): Prune back ungainly shoots after flowering ceases, but avoid cutting back to wood more than 1 in. thick.

Diosma ericoides (Breath-of-Heaven): Keep this shrub compact by shearing branches back right after the flowers fade. Thin out excessive growth. Do not, however, cut the whole branch back severely, because it may not recover.

Dodonaea viscosa (Hop Bush): This versatile plant can take on many guises. You can leave the upright stems to grow into a billowy mass or you can shear them into a formal hedge. Remove most of the stems and the plant will grow into a small tree with single or multiple trunks.

***Dombeya* spp.:** No special pruning is needed to keep these trees and shrubs neat and healthy. Prune in early spring or, in tropical areas, in summer.

Cotoneaster berries add a touch of color in fall.

Dracaena spp. (Dracaena): Dracaenas need little pruning. If a stem grows too tall, lop it back and it will send out one, perhaps two, new shoots—probably. Or cut it completely to the ground to make room for younger replacements. Prune while the plant is actively growing.

Drimys Winteri (Winter's-Bark): Train to a single trunk or to multiple trunks. From then on, just basic pruning is needed, which can be done at any time.

Duranta repens (Pigeon Berry, Skyflower): Prune away stems that have borne berries, cutting them either to the ground or to low side branches that have not yet flowered. Prune enough to prompt a good supply of new shoots, which will flower the following year.

Elaeagnus spp.: Evergreen species need only basic pruning in late spring.

Eranthemum pulchellum (Blue Sage): Pinch shoot tips to make this sprawling shrub more compact. Lop all stems down to the ground in spring to get an overgrown plant back in order quickly.

Erica spp. (Heath): Clip back spring-flowering heaths to the bases of flower stalks right after flowers fade. Prune summer-, fall-, and winter-flowering heaths the same way, except wait until just before growth begins in spring. Do not prune into old wood, which will not resprout. And if you use a hedge shears, vary the angle of cut so that you leave a wavy, rather than a flat-topped, surface. *E. arborea* (Tree Heath) needs no pruning except to shape the plant and remove damaged wood.

Eriogonum spp. (Wild Buckwheat, Umbrella Plant): Encourage dense growth on young plants by pinching shoot tips.

Escallonia spp.: Prune escallonias annually, either shearing them as hedge plants or keeping them shrubby by cutting away the oldest stems at ground level. Also cut back wayward branches.

Eucalyptus spp.: Eucalyptus trees and shrubs require little pruning. When a bushy type gets too gangly, cut the plant to the ground and allow a few of the new sprouts to grow for a new framework. The small and large tree types of eucalyptus need little or no pruning beyond their training stage. To make multiple trunks on a small tree, cut it down to within 2 ft. of the ground and select new trunks from the sprouts at the base. Bending a small trunk to the ground, and holding it down with rope, will stimulate new sprouts near ground level if none are already there. Some types of eucalyptus are grown for their juvenile leaves. On these plants, cut the stems back heavily each year to stimulate vigorous regrowth of juvenile wood.

Euonymus spp.: The evergreen species need little more than corrective pruning, or you can shear them as hedge plants.

Euphorbia pulcherrima (Poinsettia): Prune poinsettia in spring, after blossoming finishes. The more severely you cut back the plant, the more spectacular the flower display—this is not necessarily all-important if you also want leafy mass from a poinsettia nestled among other plants in a shrub border. Shoots allowed to grow unchecked on severely pruned bushes will have lanky stems with large flowers at their ends. For a bushier plant, and more, albeit smaller, flowers, head back the stems every two months until September. As a houseplant, cut back poinsettia stems to 6 in. in April or May. Depending on the particular variety, pinching may or may not be needed to promote bushiness. At any rate, cease pinching in September; a period of long nights is then needed in order to induce flower buds that will open by Christmas.

Eurya emarginata: This relative of camellia needs little pruning.

✕ *Fatshedera Lizei* (Aralia Ivy, Tree Ivy): This plant displays its hybrid heritage of a bush and a vine as its vertical stems collapse under their own weight. Train the plant either as a loose bush or as a bushy vine. If you need to start again, just cut the stems to the ground and the plant will regrow.

Fatsia japonica (Japanese Fatsia, Paper Plant): Fatsia (sometimes listed botanically as *Aralia japonica*) typically sends up new shoots from

(continued on page 100)

ground level. Thin them out if they are too numerous, and when a stem grows too tall or too old, cut it back to a branch or to the ground, to be replaced by a young sprout. Prune in spring or summer.

Ficus **spp.** (Ornamental Figs): No special techniques are required for pruning ornamental figs. Prune in spring and summer; where winters are frost free, prune anytime.

Fuchsia **spp.** (Fuchsia): Pruning stimulates the growth of new shoots, which, after six to ten weeks of growth (and cool night temperatures), bear flowers. Prune according to how large you want your bush to grow; the more severe the pruning, the smaller the bush. Where winters are cold, wait to prune until just before growth begins. Pinch the tips of the stems as they grow to promote more bushiness.

Galphimia glauca: This shrub tends to get leggy, so pinch out the tips of growing shoots to promote bushiness, or clip with hedge shears.

Gamolepis chrysanthemoides: Unpruned, this vigorous shrub has most of its leaves out near the ends of the stems. For a fuller look, regularly pinch back growing shoots, beginning after the flowers fade. For a quick renovation, cut the whole bush back severely, either in late winter or during the growing season.

Gardenia **spp.** (Gardenia): Outdoor shrubs need little pruning. Just before growth begins, shorten some stems and thin out twigs. To promote further branching, pinch the tips of growing shoots, but not later than August. Stems will regrow if you have to cut them back severely to renovate the bush. Prune a potted gardenia the same way as an outdoor shrub, except more frequently and severely, to keep it pot size.

Garrya **spp.** (Silk-tassel Bush): These bushes need little pruning, whether grown as shrubs or as informal hedges.

Grevillea robusta (Silk Oak): Because of its inherently weak wood, silk oak needs to be trained to an especially sturdy framework. Shorten lanky stems and thin out dense wood enough to allow wind to pass through the canopy. Avoid leaving large pruning wounds, which heal poorly.

Grewia occidentalis (often sold as *G. caffra):* This shrub is adaptable in the landscape. Shear it as a hedge, pinch it to promote bushiness, or let it grow with abandon as a fountain of green. For maximum flowers, reserve major pruning for autumn, after flowering stops.

Hakea **spp.** (Pincushion Tree): These plants need little pruning and can be trained either as bushes or as small trees.

Hebe **spp.:** These vigorous shrubs tolerate heavy pruning. To promote bushiness, shorten stems that have flowered by half their length. To renovate a bush, cut away the oldest stems to the ground, then shorten those that remain so they are each 1 ft. or so long.

Heteromeles arbutifolia (Toyon, Christmas Berry): Toyon tolerates various types and degrees of pruning, so do what is necessary to grow it as a shrub, an informal hedge, or a small tree, or to renovate it. Prune just before growth begins.

Hibbertia **spp.** (Button Flower, Guinea Gold Vine): Prune *H. cuneiformis* in spring, after blossoms fade. *H. scandens* stems are more trailing, like those of a vine, and the flowers appear throughout the growing season. Prune before growth begins, untangling and cutting back stems that are congested or too old.

Hibiscus Rosa-sinensis (Chinese Hibiscus): Blossoms form on new growth. Stimulate new growth on mature plants by shortening stems, before growth begins, by about one-third. If needed, pinch the growing tips of young plants to promote branching. Renovate overgrown shrubs by periodically cutting back the oldest stems to well-placed side branches lower down. Do this periodically through the growing season until August. Do not shear hibiscus if you grow it as a hedge. Prune branches selectively instead.

Hoya carnosa (Wax Plant): Prune this trailing shrub as needed. The only caution is not to disturb the stalks of old flowers, because new flowers will also be borne on them.

Hymenosporum flavum: This tree naturally makes few branches, but you can change its ways by pinching growing shoots. On isolated plants, shorten long, weak stems if they need strengthening. Trees planted together in groves do not need pruning.

Hypericum calycinum (Rose-of-Sharon, Aaron's Beard): This low shrub gets straggly unless you prune it back severely almost every spring.

Ilex spp. (Holly): Prune as needed for good structure and form, but avoid cutting back into leafless portions of the plant if you want regrowth. Prune while the plant is dormant.

Illicium spp. (Anise Tree): These plants need little pruning and can be grown as shrubs, hedges, or small trees.

Ixora coccinea (Jungle-of-the-woods, Jungle-flame): This bush needs only occasional basic pruning.

Jacaranda mimosifolia (Green Ebony): Train this tree to a single trunk or to multiple trunks. Little pruning is needed beyond training. New sprouts grow readily from near ground level, and are useful for changing the form of the plant or for replacing wood damaged by cold.

Jasminum spp. (Jasmine): All jasmines flower on growth that is one year old, so prune them just after they finish flowering. Shorten scraggly stems, thin out overcrowded and old stems, and pinch growing tips where you want branching.

Justicia spp. (Water Willow): Pinch stem tips of *J. Brandegeana* (Shrimp Plant) as they grow to encourage branching. Once the plant is sufficiently bushy, stop pinching and let flowers form at the ends of branches. After the flowers fade, cut back the flowering stems. Severely cut back stems of *J. carnea*

(Brazilian-plume) in spring every two or three years, then pinch the stems as growth progresses to encourage bushiness. Just cut away the oldest wood at ground level on *J. californica* (Chuparosa), *J. Leonardii,* and *J. spicigera.* Also pinch new shoots a couple of times during the growing season on the latter two species.

Kalmia latifolia (Mountain Laurel): Mountain laurel needs little pruning beyond what is necessary to keep the plant shapely and remove dead or diseased wood. Prune right after flowers fade. If necessary, make drastic cuts to promote young growth to replace a leggy branch, or even to renovate a whole, overgrown shrub.

Lantana spp. (Shrub Verbena): Prune these shrubs regularly to remove old wood and keep them tidy. Cut just before growth begins, as much as you like, because flowers form on new wood. If you have the time and the inclination, also pinch out the tips of developing shoots to promote bushiness.

Be careful not to damage the flowering spurs of hoya, because they also bear next year's flowers.

Laurus nobilis (Laurel, Sweet Bay): Prune in spring and, as needed, through the growing season to shape the plant any way you like — as a formal or informal hedge, or a tree.

Lavandula angustifolia (Common or English Lavender): Prune in spring to keep the plant neat and to remove winterkilled wood. Later in the growing season, clip off spent flower heads as they form. Lavender is not usually long-lived.

(continued on page 102)

Leptospermum spp. (Tea Tree): Prune these shrubs right after the flowers fade. Grow the plants as informal or formal shrubs, or as small trees. Because old wood will not send out new growth, cut back stems to side shoots.

Leucophyllum frutescens (Ceniza, Barometer Bush): Prune ceniza while it is dormant. Little pruning is needed, but if you want to renovate an unkempt plant, just cut it back almost to the ground.

Leucothoe spp. (Fetterbush): Prune fetterbush just before growth begins in spring, cutting away the oldest stems and shortening lanky stems. If you prune off spent flower heads after blossoming ceases on *L. Davisiae* (Sierra Laurel), the bush may bloom again in autumn.

Ligustrum spp. (Privet): Privets are adaptable plants. Prune as much or as little as needed, and whenever you want, all depending on what you want the bush to look like.

Lithocarpus densiflorus (Tanbark Oak): This tree needs little pruning.

Loropetalum chinense: This shrub needs little pruning.

Lyonothamnus floribundus (Catalina Ironwood): This tree needs little pruning beyond the removal of unsightly spent flowers.

Magnolia spp.: Magnolias need little pruning beyond that necessary to develop good form and remove diseased, dead, and misplaced wood. Wounds are slow to heal and susceptible to disease, so make cuts in summer, completely removing some stems or shortening others to branches. Avoid creating large wounds.

× **Mahoberberis spp.:** These bushes need little pruning. Shorten scraggly stems, or cut old ones to the ground, as necessary.

Mahonia spp. (Oregon Grape Holly): The species vary in their growth habits and pruning needs. Generally, prune right after

the flowers fade. Upright stems of *M. Bealei* and *M. Fortunei* have a bold visual effect, which should not be disrupted with heading cuts. When a stem grows too old or too tall, just cut it away at ground level to make room for new stems. Bushier species such as *M. Aquifolium* and *M. pinnata* benefit from having their stems shortened to give the plants more fullness and better shape. Periodically cut away the oldest stems. Maintain colonies of plants that spread by underground stems *(M. Aquifolium* 'Compacta', *M. nervosa,* and *M. repens)* by shortening the stems to whatever height you desire.

Malvaviscus arboreus (Wax Mallow, Turk's-cap): Prune anytime during the growing season to keep this vigorous bush tidy and contained. You can also clip wax mallow as a formal hedge.

Maytenus Boaria (Mayten): Prune just before growth begins. Train mayten as a tree with a single trunk or with multiple trunks. Remove suckers at the base of the tree, and thin branches to keep the crown open.

Melaleuca spp. (Honey Myrtle, Bottlebrush): Prune honey myrtle anytime, bringing out its character as a shrub, developing a single trunk as a tree, or, in the case of *M. hypericifolia* and *M. nesophylla,* shearing the plant as a hedge. Do not expect regrowth from cuts back into old wood.

Michelia spp.: These plants need only corrective pruning to develop a desirable shape. *M. Figo* (Banana Shrub) is happy as a shrub, a clipped hedge, or a tree with multiple trunks. *M. Doltsopa* grows to become a large tree, but is content to look like a shrub in its youth.

Murraya paniculata (Orange Jasmine): Orange jasmine requires no special pruning, and you can grow it as an informal shrub, as a tree, or as a clipped hedge.

Myoporum spp.: These bushy plants, some species of which grow to tree size, need little pruning other than removal of wayward stems and, if trained to trees, lower limbs.

Myrica **spp.:** These plants are adaptable. Let them grow unrestrained, except for occasional tidying, as informal bushes. Or shear regularly for a formal look. Or prune away lower branches to make a small tree with multiple trunks. Apart from regular shearing as a hedge, prune just before growth begins.

Myrsine africana (Cape Myrtle, African Boxwood): Shear this dense shrub for a formal appearance, or selectively clip wayward stems for a more billowy, informal look.

Myrtus communis (Myrtle, Greek Myrtle): Myrtle is a naturally dense plant even without pruning. Shear for a formal look, or selectively remove branches for an informal look. You can also remove branches to bare the trunk and make a small tree. Selective removal of some upper branches gives the plant a more open look.

Nandina domestica (Heavenly Bamboo): Clean up and make way for new growth by cutting away old, ragged stems at ground level.

Neopanax arboreus (Five-fingers): This tree needs no special pruning beyond the removal of wayward or unhealthy stems.

Nerium Oleander (Common Oleander, Rosebay): This large bush sprouts freely from its base. Prune just before growth begins, limiting plant size by cutting the oldest wood at ground level and shortening overly long stems to side branches. Pinch shoot tips to promote bushiness. You can cut a long-neglected shrub to the ground and it will send up new shoots. By removing lower branches and root suckers, you can train oleander to be a small tree. Be careful of how you dispose of prunings. All parts of the plant are extremely poisonous, and even burning produces an irritating smoke.

Nothofagus **spp.:** No special directions are needed to prune this genus.

Olmediella Betschlerana (Costa Rican Holly, Puerto Rican Holly, Manzanote): This versatile plant needs little pruning, and can be trained as a shrub or tree, or grown as either a formal or informal hedge.

Osmanthus **spp.** (Osmanthus, Devil-weed): These plants require little pruning.

Paxistima **spp.:** *P. Canbyi* (cliff-green) and *P. Myrsinites* (Oregon Boxwood) both are trailing shrubs that require little pruning.

Pernettya mucronata (Pernettya): Pernettya requires little pruning other than removing wayward stems, and occasionally shortening old stems to stimulate new growth. It can be pruned anytime.

Phillyrea decora: This bush has a dense and neat growth habit, so requires no pruning beyond cutting back occasional wayward stems just before growth begins in spring.

Phlomis fruticosa (Jerusalem Sage): To keep this bush from becoming ragged, each year prune stems back by about one-third. Also cut away any thin stems. Plants bloom through spring and summer, and will keep up the pace better if you shorten flowering stems after each flush of flowers.

Photinia **spp.:** Train the young plant to a few stems. On mature plants, cut stems frequently to stimulate the growth of new red leaves.

Pieris **spp.** (sometimes mistakenly called Andromeda): Pieris requires little pruning. If necessary, shorten a stem to shape a bush. Cutting back to a group of leaves results in several new sprouts; cutting back into bare wood usually produces only one. Prune right after flowering.

Pittosporum **spp.:** Pittosporums are adaptable and can be trained as trees, shrubs, or hedges. Cut back wayward stems for an informal look, or shear as needed for a more formal appearance. These plants withstand the heavy pruning needed to remove excess old stems and to bring a plant back into bounds. The species *P. floribundum* grows neither large enough for a tree nor dense enough for a hedge; grow it as a specimen shrub.

Plumbago auriculata (Cape Leadwort): Grow cape leadwort as an informal mound or as a compact bush. Prune after flowering. On informal plants, just cut back lanky stems. For a more compact plant, shorten the youngest stems by about one-third each year; occasionally cut away old stems completely.

(continued on page 104)

Below: The rhododendron bud at right is a terminal growth bud; pinch it off just before growth begins to encourage branching. The fat bud at left is a flower bud.

Prunus **spp.:** Evergreen species grow as trees or as bushes, with no special pruning needs.

Pyracantha **spp.** (Firethorn): Unpruned, firethorn bushes grow a bit too wild, with their light-starved interiors bearing few berries. Firethorn does tolerate severe pruning, except to leafless stubs, so always prune back to a side branch or to a leaf, or remove a branch completely. Regular pruning, done after the berries drop in winter, consists of shortening wayward stems and thinning dense growth. If you want a more compact bush, pinch the tips of new shoots. If renovation of the whole plant is needed, cut the oldest wood right down to the ground in late winter.

Pyrus Kawakamii (Evergreen Pear): Prune this tree when young to develop a strong framework of branches. Mature trees need periodic pruning to remove dead, diseased, crowded, and old wood.

Quercus **spp.** (Oak): Tree species that develop round heads with age need help in getting their heads up off the ground. Maintain a single, central leader and a framework of subordinate scaffold limbs. Eventually, the leader will lose dominance and the head will spread, high above the ground. From then on, the tree needs little pruning.

Quillaja Saponaria (Soap-bark Tree): A mature soap-bark tree needs little pruning. Branches clothe the trunk all the way to the ground; remove them if you want a clear trunk. In exposed sites, thin branches to let the wind pass through the crown.

Rhododendron **spp.** (Azalea and Rhododendron): Young rhododendrons tend to be leggy. Encourage branching by pinching off terminal growth buds just before growth begins and by pinching growing shoots before their leaves fully expand. (You can recognize terminal growth buds by their slenderness, in contrast to the fat stubbiness of flower buds.) On younger or smaller plants and, where practical, on older plants, remove spent flower heads by bending the stalks over until they break away from the stems. Be careful not to damage the growth buds at the base of each flower stalk.

Mature rhododendrons need little pruning beyond that necessary to shape or renovate the plant, as well as to remove diseased and dead wood. Generally, prune right after flowering. An exception would be *R. maximum* (Rosebay), which flowers late, after shoots have begun growth.

If a rhododendron overgrows its bounds, you can cut the whole bush back drastically as soon as it finishes flowering. Ideally, prepare

Right: Branching can also be encouraged by pinching young rhododendron shoots before their leaves fully expand.

the bush a year or two before such surgery with mulch and a good supply of moisture and food. Select new main stems from among those that grow after you prune. Rhododendrons do not always push out new growth from old stubs, so play it safe with gradual renovation, cutting back a few old branches each year. Rhododendrons that are particularly reluctant to sprout from old wood include the Falconeri and the Thomsonii series, "tree" rhododendrons, and those with smooth bark. Train these plants by pinching their shoots while the plants are young so that they never need renovation.

In contrast to rhododendrons, azaleas are well supplied with leaves and growth buds all along their stems. Shape and renew azaleas by shortening and removing stems, and promote bushiness by pinching growing tips. If you grow azaleas in a greenhouse, stop pruning by June if you want early flowers. Flower buds usually take eight to ten weeks to develop with temperatures greater than 65°F. The buds then are ready by September (although sometimes plants need to be exposed to long nights also).

***Rhus* spp.** (Sumac): The evergreen sumacs are bushes or bushy trees that need little pruning other than that necessary to shape the plants. Prune them in spring.

***Ribes* spp.** (Currants and Gooseberries): Little pruning is need on either *R. speciosum* (Fuchsia-flowered Gooseberry) or *R. viburnifolium*. Occasionally cut away the oldest stems on the former species.

***Rondeletia* spp.:** Pinch growing tips and shorten stems, right after flowering, to promote bushiness.

Rosmarinus officinalis (Rosemary): Upright varieties such as 'Tuscan Blue' need more pruning than do prostrate varieties such as 'Prostratus' and 'Lockwood de Forest'—but only for the sake of appearance. Rosemary does not sprout new growth from the bare parts of stems, and old wood eventually becomes bare, so you cannot head back an old plant to renovate it. Instead, train the plant when it is young, shortening leafy

young stems right after the flowers fade and pinching the growing tips to promote bushiness.

***Salvia* spp.** (Sage): To keep these bushes neat, cut stems back by half and thin out twigs, or just let the plants grow willy-nilly.

Santolina Chamaecyparissus (Lavender Cotton): This bush is apt to become scraggly, so prune it—severely, if necessary—right after it finishes flowering. If grown as a hedge, prune early in the season, then again after a flush of blooms.

***Sarcococca* spp.** (Sweet Box): Prune these shrubs anytime, occasionally cutting the oldest stems to the ground. *S. Hookerana* and *S. saligna* (Willow-leaf Sarcococca) spread slowly underground, so also remove stems growing out of bounds. You can renovate the shrub by cutting all the stems to the ground.

***Schinus* spp.:** Train both *S. Molle* (California Pepper Tree) and *S. terebinthifolius* (Brazilian Pepper Tree) carefully to a sturdy framework of branches when the trees are young. This is important for *S. Molle* in order to avoid large pruning cuts later, which heal poorly. The wood of *S. terebinthifolius* is brittle, so shorten rangy branches and thin the crown to let wind through the branches. You can also grow *S. Molle* as a sheared hedge.

Severinia buxifolia (Chinese Box Orange): Do any pruning needed in spring to grow this plant as a small tree. Otherwise, shear during the growing season for a hedge.

Simmondsia chinensis (Jojoba): As a specimen shrub, this plant needs little pruning. Shear regularly for a more formal hedge.

***Skimmia* spp.:** Skimmias are naturally slow-growing and dense, so they need little regular pruning.

Sparmannia africana (African Hemp): To tidy up this plant, prune out the oldest stems at ground level and shorten those that are overly long. Another approach is to remove almost all of the stems and grow the plant as a small tree.

(continued on page 106)

Spathodea campanulata (African Tulip Tree, Flame-of-the-forest): When mature, this tree needs little pruning. The wood is brittle, so train a young tree to a strong framework.

Stenocarpus sinuatus (Firewheel Tree): Give this tree good basic training when young, and only occasional maintenance pruning will be needed when it matures.

Stransvaesia Davidiana: Prune Stransvaesia while it is dormant, emphasizing the plant's natural lines and growth habit.

Streptosolen Jamesonii (Fire Bush, Orange Browallia, Marmalade Bush): Prune heavily to contain the plant and to stimulate new growth on which blossoms are borne throughout the growing season. Do this pruning right after flowering ceases or just after frosty weather ends.

Syzygium **spp.** Neither *S. Jambos* (Rose Apple, Malabar Plum) nor *S. paniculatum* (Australian Brush Cherry) needs extensive or frequent pruning. Just shorten misplaced stems in spring. You can shear or clip Australian brush cherry as a formal or informal hedge.

Tecoma stans (Yellow Bells, Yellow Elder): Yellow bells is a bush that needs only basic maintenance pruning just before growth begins in spring. You can also train the plant as a small tree with one or more trunks. Remove faded blossoms to prolong the flowering period.

Tecomaria capensis (Cape Honeysuckle): Unchecked, cape honeysuckle turns into a sprawling bush. If this is the form that you want, just remove wayward branches right after blossoms fade. To grow it more like a vine, allow the plant to grow only a few stems; cut all others to the ground.

Tetrapanax papyriferus (Rice-paper Plant): Each stem of this plant is capped by flowers, with two shoots angling up and out from beneath each flower like the letter Y. Periodically thin out the stems, at ground level, to restrict their number, or remove all but one trunk. Also shape the plant by shortening stems up in the plant. Side branches will grow when you cut back to the middle of a stem, but regrowth rarely occurs when you cut back to a side branch. Avoid touching new growth to bare skin, because it is highly irritating.

Teucrium **spp.** (Germander): Prune regularly only if you want your plant to look neater. Do so by shortening shoots in late winter, then again one or two times during the summer. To renovate the whole plant, cut it almost to the ground in late winter, and thin out any remaining twiggy growth.

Thevetia peruviana (Yellow Oleander): This large bush sprouts freely from its base. Prune just before growth begins, limiting plant size by cutting the oldest wood to the ground and shortening overly long stems to side shoots. Pinch shoot tips during the growing season to promote bushiness. You can cut a long-neglected shrub to the ground and it will send up new shoots. By removing lower branches and diligently removing root suckers, you can train the plant as a small tree. If you do so, thin out the crown to keep it open or else wind is liable to topple over this shallow-rooted plant.

Tibouchina Urvilleana (Glory Bush, Lasiandra, Pleroma): Pinching shoots and shortening lanky stems keep this plant bushy and compact. Quickly revitalize an overgrown bush by lopping everything to the ground. New shoots will sprout.

Trichostema lanatum (Romero, Woolly Blue-curls): Pinch shoot tips to promote branching. Also cut back stems after they flower to promote additional flowering and branching.

Triphasia trifolia (Limeberry): Little pruning is needed.

Tristania **spp.:** None of the commonly cultivated species needs much pruning.

Pruning *Tetrapanax* (Rice-paper Plant)

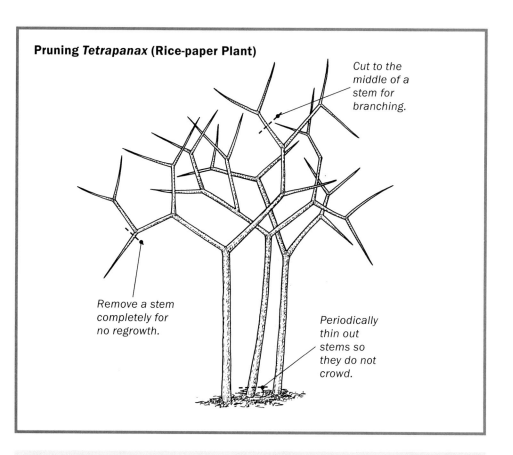

Cut to the middle of a stem for branching.

Remove a stem completely for no regrowth.

Periodically thin out stems so they do not crowd.

Turraea obtusifolia (South African Honeysuckle): Prune this bush anytime that suits your needs.

Umbellularia californica (California Bay, California Laurel, Pepperwood): California bay needs little pruning beyond initial training if allowed to develop as a tree. You can grow this plant as a hedge, in which case prune in spring and again, if necessary, in summer. If you want to renovate or dramatically reshape this plant, cut it back severely.

***Viburnum* spp.:** Prune an evergreen viburnum just before growth begins only as needed to give the plant a pleasant shape.

Vitex lucens (Pururi): Train pururi when young to have either a single trunk or multiple trunks. Subsequent pruning needs are minimal, just the removal of misplaced, dead, and twiggy wood.

Xylosma congestum: Xylosma is a most adaptable plant—you can prune it to be a single or multi-trunked small tree, an espalier, a creeping ground cover, a formal or informal hedge, even a living sculpture. Whatever your goal, prune as severely as necessary just before growth begins. Or don't prune xylosma at all, and let it grow as an informal shrub.

***Yucca* spp.:** Prune flower stalks back to the whorl of leaves after flowering ceases. At that time, also thin out offshoots to prevent overcrowding. On treelike species, cut out-of-place branches back to where they meet other branches or the trunk.

Palm trees

Palm trees, although broadleaf evergreens, warrant a special section because there are so many genera and species, and they can all be pruned in essentially the same manner. Palm trees grow from their tips, rarely branching, so there is little that you can do to shape a plant. (*Hyphaene thebaica*, Gingerbread

As this palm grows taller, its older leaves should be pruned off.

Palm, is a notable exception.) Some palms grow new trunks at ground level. If a cluster of various-aged trunks becomes overcrowded or too wide, cut unwanted trunks down to the ground. With some species, old trunks die after fruiting—remove the dead trunk at ground level. Still other palms have one major trunk, but occasionally send up one or more new ones from the ground. These palms look best with single trunks, so remove upstarts when they appear.

Beyond trunk removal, other pruning of palms consists of removing old flower clusters, fruits, and dead fronds, mostly to clean up the trees. A heavy fruit such as a coconut does not look bad, but is a hazard if it drops onto someone's head. Dead fronds can similarly present a hazard of dropping on an unsuspecting passerby, or can harbor rodents. Fronds with spiny leaflets can cut skin, and dry fronds present a fire hazard. And anyway, dead fronds spoil the look of a plant.

Remove dead fronds in two stages. First hack back the leaf stalk almost to its base, using a machete to make two cuts that leave an upside-down V. A year later, the remaining base of the dead stalk will be easy to pull off, or the base will have fallen off by itself.

Prune fruits, fronds, and stems from palm trees whenever needed.

Bamboo

Bamboos warrant their own section here because, although they represent many genera and species, their pruning needs are essentially uniform. Pruning bamboo consists of cutting away old canes to the ground. Do no cutting for the first three years after the plants are set in the ground, to allow the planting to establish itself. After that, a general rule is to remove canes that are three years old (or

older, if you have been remiss) to make room for new canes. Thin out two-year-old canes also if you want new canes to grow thicker, but avoid excessive thinning of a grove or plants will not be able to create the shade they need.

To emphasize the vertical look of a clump or a grove of bamboo, cut off lower side branches if they appear.

Also prune to control growth, if needed. For hedging, lop off the tops of the plants when they reach the desired height. Never cut off the top of a bamboo cane below where it has leafed out or that cane is liable to die. Limit the underground spread of "running" bamboos by cutting down all canes at the boundary of the grove. A lawnmower is effective against young shoots. Sinking a barrier of metal, concrete, or other impenetrable material 2 ft. into the soil will keep the roots from spreading.

A grove of yellow-groove bamboo is mysteriously inviting.

THE BARE BONES

BAMBOO

CUT to the ground canes that are three years old, or older.

KEEP running types of bamboo from spreading beyond their allotted space.

CHAPTER SEVEN

ORNAMENTAL VINES

Honeysuckle festoons a wall.

Vines are long-stemmed plants that grow skyward, but only if they get help. To get themselves up off the ground, they borrow the support of nearby trees or bushes, walls, posts, pergolas, wires, fences, even (unfortunately) downspouts and gutters.

The mere proximity of a plant with long stems to a support does not get those stems skyward. The vine needs a way to grip. Along the stems of English ivy are aerial rootlets that insinuate themselves into tiny holes in mortar and bricks and hold the plant as it grows upward. Grape tendrils are actually modified leaves that quickly close around whatever they touch, pulling the plant upward hand over hand (tendril over tendril). It is the leaf stalks themselves of clematis that twine, in a similar manner, around any available support. At the tips of the tendrils of a vine such as Virginia creeper grow little discs, called holdfasts, that both look and act like suction cups. And finally there are those vines that whose stems simply flail around in space until they touch a suitable object thin enough to twine around. Each twining vine's upward mobility starts with an innate twist. Japanese wisteria, for

ORNAMENTAL VINES

CUT newly planted vines almost to the ground in order to force new growth into just one or a few shoots.

PRUNE OUT tangled or dead stems.

TO CONTROL SIZE, cut the oldest stems back to their bases or to low, healthy side shoots.

PINCH OR CUT BACK unruly growth in summer.

DO the bulk of pruning on early-flowering vines right after flowers fade. With vines flowering from summer onwards, or with vines whose flowers and fruits are inconsequential, prune just before growth begins for the season.

example, is a clockwise twiner, while Chinese wisteria twines counterclockwise.

The long stems of a few plants have no means for clinging to a support. Such plants—bougainvillea, aralia ivy, and *Forsythia suspensa*, for example—are perhaps best considered as sprawling bushes, and are treated as bushes in this book. Planted against a wall, they may press upward for a distance, lacking anywhere else to go. These plants can be grown like bona-fide vines if they are restricted to only a few stems, and those stems are tied to some support. Then again, some of the self-climbing vines included in this chapter could be grown as sprawling bushes if their stems were headed and pinched to encourage low branching and discourage lanky growth. With even stricter pruning, a clinging vine such as wisteria can even be trained as a tree, with a trunk that eventually supports the head.

Pruning while training

All perennial vines need pruning as soon as they are planted. Channel the plant's energy into one or a few stems to induce a rapid climb up the support. Do this by cutting away extraneous shoots or by pinching their tips to slow their growth.

Depending on the plant's growth habit and the plant's support, you may opt for a single permanent stem, a few permanent stems, or a permanent stem with permanent side arms growing from it (see the drawing on p. 112). The permanent stems to which a vine is cut back to each year are called cordons. A plant such as silver lace vine or a late-flowering clematis, which grows vigorously and flowers only on new

'Heavenly Blue' is the variety name and color of this morning-glory; no pruning is needed.

Three Ways to Train a Woody Vine

Single permanent stem

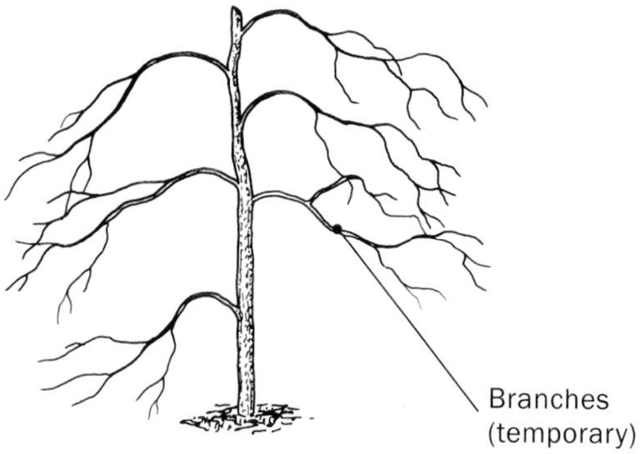

Branches
(temporary)

A few permanent stems

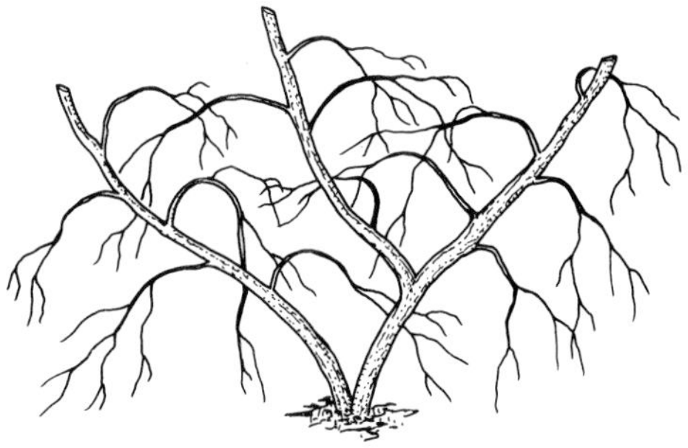

One permanent stem and cordons

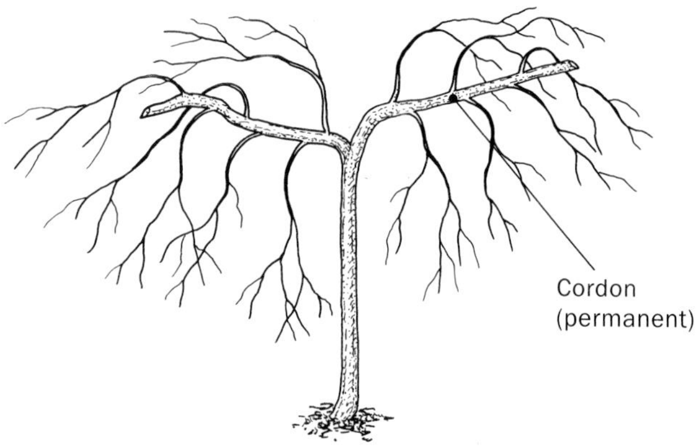

Cordon
(permanent)

growth, does not need any permanent stems or cordons, because you prune each year by lopping all growth nearly back to the ground.

Maintenance pruning

A few kinds of vines need little or no regular pruning. Examples are annual vines, such as morning-glory and cardinal climber, on which you want maximum growth from the start to the end of the growing season. Other examples include some vines that are allowed to ramble over the ground, like bittersweet, which is naturally unruly and looks right at home billowing over low mounds of earth and enveloping old tree stumps. (Even so, a vine used as groundcover may need drastic mowing every few years to prevent the buildup of an increasingly thick mat of old stems.) And yet another example is any vigorous vine permitted to express its full vigor using a living tree as support. *Clematis montana* or climbing hydrangeas are sometimes grown this way, unfettered. But the tree and the vine must be well matched, or one will suffocate the other.

Aside from the above exceptions, most vines, once they have climbed their support, need at least a little annual pruning—and some vines will need more than a little. Cut away dead and diseased stems, as well as those that are spindly. Depending on what the vine is climbing on, annual pruning may be necessary to control growth. In the wild, many ornamental vines clamber into trees, so that eventually only birds can appreciate the parts of the vine with leaves and flowers. For most ornamental uses, we want leaves and flowers in sight and, in the case of fragrant flowers, near nose level; periodic removal of old stems keeps leafy and florific younger stems low on the plant.

Pruning is also needed to keep an ornamental vine looking ornamental. Periodically cutting away old stems low in the plant not only brings leaves and flowers low, but also disentangles stems. Without pruning, the plant eventually becomes an unsightly mass of dead, diseased, and weak stems because of shading and crowding.

Regular pruning also helps those vines that are grown for flowers to put on their best show. Plants whose blooms appear on vigorous growth of the current season benefit most from the stimulation of new growth by pruning, and such vines can be lopped clear down to the ground just before growth begins each season. These vines also can be allowed to use a nearby shrub for support (a late-flowering clematis returning the favor on an early-blooming lilac, for example), because a yearly lopping back prevents the vine from engulfing the shrub. Pruning has less effect on the flowering of vines whose blooms appear on shoots growing from older wood.

Generally, the time for pruning a vine is just before growth begins, while the plant is still dormant. With vines that flower early in the season, you can wait to prune until after flowers fade so that you do not sacrifice any of the show. Summer pruning, in addition to dormant pruning, helps keep an overly rampant vine in check, and results in tighter growth on other vines when a more formal effect is desired.

Renovation

A vine whose growth is out of hand—or an inherited monster—is easy to renovate. Just cut the whole plant almost to the ground. Then, from among the new sprouts, select one or a few stems with which to rebuild the plant anew.

Left: An oak tree provides support for a wisteria vine.

Below: Bittersweet can be trained, but also looks good left to its own whims.

Plant List

Akebia quinata (Five-leaf Akebia): Control growth by thinning out stems just before growth begins or just after flowering. Remove stems that are spindly or tangled, and, if you prune after flowering, stems that have flowered.

Allamanda cathartica (Allamand, Golden-trumpet): Prune lightly just before growth begins.

Ampelopsis spp.: The twining stems of some species are very vigorous (*A. brevipedunculata* var. *Maximowiczii*, for example) and can be left to climb up trees without restraint. On an arbor or pergola, keep growth in check by shortening some stems each year. Or, even neater, train one or more stems as permanent cordons, then cut back the stems each year to within a few buds of the cordons while the plants are dormant. Over the years, pictu-resque knobby stubs will build up where you keep shortening the stems. Other species, including *A. arborea* (Pepper Vine) and *A. humulifolia,* similarly need their stems shortened and thinned out. In addition, dig out unwanted suckers from spreading roots of *A. arborea.*

Anemopaegma Chamberlaynii: Prune this tendriled vine lightly in spring to keep it in bounds, then again after the flowers fade, removing spindly stems and overly rampant growth.

Antigonon leptopus (Coral Vine): Shorten and remove stems, when and as needed, to control growth and avoid a dense tangle of living and dead stems.

Aristolochia spp.: Prune these vigorous twiners to keep them in bounds. They flower early and on one-year-old wood, so cut out excess growth right after the flowers fade.

Beaumontia grandiflora (Herald's-trumpet, Easter-lily Vine): Depending on where this plant is grown, flowers appear either on current shoots (in Florida) or on shoots two years old and older (in California). Prune severely in the latter case, lightly in the former.

Berberidopsis corallina: Prune this twining vine lightly just before growth begins.

Bignonia capreolata (Cross Vine, Trumpet Flower): Just before growth begins, remove suckers and shorten shoots that flowered previously to a few buds. If more growth control is needed, cut back stems as they grow.

Celastrus scandens (Bittersweet): When the plant is dormant, cut off tangled branches and those that have fruits—they are decorative indoors. Also shorten the previous season's growth. Pinch shoot tips in summer to promote branching.

Cissus spp. (Grape Ivy, Treebine): These vines require little pruning. Prune only to control growth, disentangle stems, and remove weak, diseased, or dead stems.

Clematis spp.: Cut all clematis vines to within a few inches of the ground when you plant them in order to force new shoots from the base of the plant and from below ground. From then on, the pruning method depends on the growth and flowering habit of the particular plant (see the sidebar on pp. 118-121).

Clytostoma callistegioides (Argentine Trumpet Vine, Love-charm): Tendrils of this rampant grower cling to almost anything. Cut the plant back whenever needed to keep growth in check.

Cryptostegia spp. (Rubber Vine): Prune after the flowers fade.

Distictis spp.: Depending on the vigor of the vine and the space allotted, prune as needed to control growth. Species vary in their vigor, from the weak-growing *D. laxi-flora* to the stronger-growing *D. buccinatoria* (Blood-trumpet) to the strongest grower, *D. × Riversii.*

Euonymus Fortunei: Varieties of this plant run the spectrum, from those that are shrubby to those that are vining, climbing with aerial roots. Prune vining plants as needed to keep them in bounds. Do most of the pruning early in the season, then prune more lightly, as needed, as the plant grows. When grown as a groundcover, the vines need to be severely cut back every few years to prevent the buildup of an increasingly thick mat of old stems.

Ficus pumila (Creeping Fig, Climbing Fig): Prune whenever and to whatever degree necessary to control growth. Eventually, the ends of stems become mature, producing larger leaves and bearing fruit. Periodically shear the plant back if you want to retain its smaller leaves and prevent its maturing.

Gelsemium sempervirens (Yellow Jessamine, Carolina Jasmine; Trumpet Flower): Prune after flowering to get rid of dead and broken stems, then shear back remaining growth.

Hardenbergia **spp.:** Prune these twining vines after flowering to control growth and to remove tangled and old or weak stems.

Hedera Helix (English Ivy): Prune English ivy as needed to keep the vine within bounds. Do major pruning in the spring, then follow up through the season. Severely cut down English ivy used as a groundcover every few years to prevent a mat of old stems from building up. With time, ivy may take on a mature growth habit. It then grows as a bush rather than a vine, has unlobed leaves, and bears flowers followed by berries. You can prevent your plant from becoming mature by pruning it severely. The basal portion of even a mature plant always remains juvenile.

Hibbertia scandens (Snake Vine, Gold Guinea Plant): Prune early in the season, before flowers open, removing overcrowded and tangled stems.

Holboellia **spp.:** Prune lightly, as needed, to get rid of weak stems and contain rampant ones.

Hydrangea anomala petiolaris (Climbing Hydrangea): Prune just before growth begins by cutting back overly vigorous stems and shortening flowering stems that are growing too far out from the wall or other support. Pruning also stimulates the growth of new shoots, on which flowers are borne.

Ipomoea **spp.** (Morning-glory): Cut perennial species of this twining vine to the ground before growth begins for the season. Annual species require no pruning.

Jasminum **spp.** (Jasmine): Jasmine is a twining vine that flowers on old stems. Each year, right after flowering, cut back one-third of the old stems to make way for, and stimulate the growth of, new ones that will flower the following year.

Lapageria rosea (Chilean Bellflower, Chile-bells): This twining vine needs little pruning, which can be done whenever necessary.

Lonicera **spp.** (Honeysuckle): Depending on the species, flowers are produced early in the season on short branches growing off previous year's stems, or later in the season on longer, current growth. Prune those plants that flower early—which include *L. Pericly-menum* (Woodbine), *L.* × *Tellmanniana*, and *L. tragophylla*— right after flowering. Cut back some flowering wood and thin out weak growth. Prune late-flowering vines just before growth begins, shortening old stems and removing those that are overcrowded. More vigorous species, such as *L. japonica* (Japanese Honeysuckle) need more ruthless cutting back than moderate growers, such as *L. Hildebrandiana* (Giant Burmese Honeysuckle, the "giant" being the leaves and flowers) and *L. sempervirens* (Trumpet Honeysuckle).

Macfadyena Unguis-cati (Cat's-claw, Funnel Creeper): Just before growth begins remove suckers and stems that flowered previously. Cut low in the plant to keep it full from the ground up.

Mandevilla **spp.:** Prune just before growth begins, removing enough twining stems so that they are not too tangled. Mandevilla blooms on new growth so you can lop the whole plant back severely if necessary. Pinch shoot tips if you want to promote further branching.

Mandevilla in all its tropical splendor.

(continued on page 116)

***Muehlenbeckia* spp.** (Wire Plant): Masses of wiry stems give wire plant its common name. Prune them back as much as needed whenever they grow out of bounds.

Oxera pulchella (Royal Climber): Prune to contain growth and remove dead stems, right after the flowers fade. Unpruned, the stems pile together to form a shrublike plant.

***Pandorea* spp.:** Prune as needed to retain healthy growth and to keep the plant within bounds.

***Parthenocissus* spp.** (Woodbine): All woodbines require similar pruning. Just before growth begins, cut away stems growing out of bounds. With *P. quinquefolia* (Virginia Creeper) and *P. tricuspidata* (Boston Ivy), which cling to surfaces by holdfasts, also cut away stems whose holdfasts have come loose—they cannot grip a surface again. Cut back wayward stems on all species throughout the growing season.

Pileostegia viburnoides: This vine, which clings by aerial roots, needs little pruning apart from shortening the flowering branches in spring if they become so long and heavy that they threaten to pull the plant off its support.

Polygonum Aubertii (Silver Lace Vine): Just before growth begins each season, heavy pruning will stimulate an abundance of new shoots, on which flowers are borne. You can even prune the plant down to the ground each year to get it started.

Pyrostegia venusta (Flame Vine, Golden-shower): Flame vine is a rampant grower that flowers on new shoots, so prune heavily in winter to keep the vine in bounds and to stimulate new growth.

Rhoicissus capensis (Cape Grape, Evergreen Grape): Pinch growing tips and cut away stems as needed during the growing season.

Schizophragma hydrangeoides (Hydrangea Vine): Prune just before growth begins by cutting back overly vigorous extension shoots. Shorten flowering shoots where they grow out too far out from their supporting wall or fence. Pruning also stimulates the growth of new shoots, on which flowers are borne. Plants allowed to ramble over the ground or to climb naturally up trees need no pruning.

Solandra guttata (Goldcup, Trumpet Plant): Promote new growth and branching by heading stems severely and pinching the growing shoots. The stems are thick for a vine, and if you prune severely and frequently enough through the season, you have a goldcup shrub—somewhat wild—rather than a goldcup vine.

***Solanum* spp.:** Prune these vines just before growth begins to untangle their stems, limit size, and stimulate new flowering shoots. Through the growing season, cut back wayward shoots. Species vary in vigor, so different species require different degrees of pruning. With more severe and frequent pruning, many species become shrubby.

Sollya heterophylla (Bluebell Creeper, Australian Bluebells): Prune early in the season to direct and control growth.

Stauntonia hexaphylla: Flowers are borne in the axils of new shoots, so prune the stems almost to the ground or to a permanent framework each year, just before growth begins.

Tetrastigma Voinieranum (Chestnut Vine, Lizard Plant): Cut back the vining stems whenever necessary.

Trachelospermum jasminoides (Star Jasmine, Confederate Jasmine): Lightly prune this vine, which clings by means of aerial roots, just before growth begins.

***Wisteria* spp.:** Wisteria is a naturally twining vine that can take many forms—a two-dimensional covering against a wall, a three-dimensional blanket over an arbor, or a freestanding (with the initial help of a stake) tree or shrub. Whatever the form, in new plants encourage the strong growth of shoots that will comprise the main framework of the "finished" plant. This framework consists of a trunk and one or more main arms. To encourage side shoots in the developing plant, head back stems intended to become the permanent framework to about 3 ft. each winter until they have grown as long as you want them to. Subsequently, head them back each year, in midsummer, to where they started growing for that season.

Wisteria often is reluctant to settle down and flower. Sometimes this is the fault of the gardener, and sometimes it's only a matter of time (especially if plants have been grown from seed). Flowers are borne near the bases of growing shoots, but not if a plant is growing too vigorously. Avoid severe annual pruning, which stimulates excessively vigorous growth. If a plant continues to grow too vigorously despite your non-efforts, try root pruning too slow it down.

An even better way to slow growth and coax the maximum number of blossoms from wisteria is with a combination of summer and winter pruning of side shoots. About midsummer, prune each side shoot back to it about 6 in. long. This will only temporarily check growth; the plant soon will grow new shoots. Go over each of these branches again in winter, shortening them to two or three buds. This is also a good time to remove any stems that are too tangled.

There are other variations on pruning wisteria: pinching out the tips of all side shoots a few times during the growing season; cutting side shoots monthly to two or three buds; or shortening side shoots to 6 in. every two weeks throughout the summer. Any of these methods is especially useful when you want the tighter and more florific habit needed for a tree wisteria or more formal espaliered wisteria. Nonetheless, many people are disinclined to pay any attention to their wisteria vine once bloom is past, and are willing to sacrifice some bloom. They can follow the advice of Liberty Hyde Bailey, writing in 1927 in his *Standard Cyclopaedia of Horticulture:* "There are several ideas about training wisteria. A good way is to let it alone. This produces rugged, twisted, and picturesque branches and gives a certain oriental effect, but is not the best method for covering a wall-space solidly or for making the best display of bloom."

Left: Detail pruning puts the dripping lavender-colored wisteria blossoms where you want them.

Below: Minimum pruning produces a rugged old wisteria.

CLEMATIS: A Pruner's Guide

The numerous species and hybrids of clematis can be lumped into one of three pruning groups based on whether flowers form on new wood, (Group 1) on old wood (Group 2), or on a little of both (Group 3). Plants within each group can be pruned similarly. If you are not sure which group a plant belongs to, let the plant grow freely for a year or two, and watch how it flowers.

Following the description of each group and instructions for pruning is an alphabetical listing of species and varieties in the group. (Varieties may represent a species or hybrids of two or more species— hence the separate listings of species, then varieties.) Where a variety name is assigned to more than one species, or hybrids of species, the species or hybrid origin is listed in parentheses after the variety name.

PRUNING A
GROUP 1
CLEMATIS

1. *Clematis paniculata*, a Group 1 clematis, in late winter.

2. Begin by cutting the stems loose from the building.

3. Next start pulling the vine down.

4. A quick tug gets most of the vine all at once.

5. Thin out stems near ground, leaving about 1 ft. of growth.

6. The completed pruning job.

Clematis in this group bear their flowers late in the season, from summer through autumn, toward the end of new shoots.

Group 1 is the easiest to prune. Just before growth begins for the season, lop all stems back to strong buds within 1 ft. or so of the ground. There is no need to cut back so severely if you are going to let the plant ramble high into a tree. Certain plants in this category, such as *C. orientalis* and *C. tangutica*, start blooming earlier and then continue longer if they are not cut back so hard.

The following species and varieties are included in this group:

C. Addisonii
C. aethusifolia
C. akebioides
C. apiifolia
C. × *aromatica*
C. brachiata
C. Buchananiana
C. campaniflora
C. chiisanensis
C. chinensis
C. connata
C. crispa
C. × *cylindrica*
C. Douglasii
C. Drummondii
C. × *Durandii*
C. × *eriostemon*
C. Fargesii souliei
C. finetiana
C. Flammula

C. fusca
C. gentianoides
C. glauca
C. heracleifolia
C. × *huldine*
C. integrifolia
C. × *Jouiniana*
C. ladakhiana
C. ochotensis
C. ochroleuca
C. orientalis
C. paniculata
C. Pitcheri
C. recta
C. Rehderana
C. serratifolia
C. songarica
C. speciosa
C. stans
C. tangutica
C. tangutica var. obtusiuscula
C. ternifolia
C. texensis
C. thibetana
C. tosaensis
C. triternata
C. uncinata
C. versicolor
C. Viorna
C. Vitalba
C. Viticella

'Abundance'
'Alba' (*C. integrifolia*)
'Alba Luxurians'
'Allanah'
'Anna'
'Ascotiensis'
'Bill MacKenzie'
'Blue Boy'
'Campanile'
'Cardinal Wyszynski'
'Carmencita'
'Comtesse de Bouchaud'
'Davidiana'
'Drake's Form'
'Duchess of Albany'
'Edward Pritchard'
'Elvan'
'Étoile Rose'
'Gipsy Queen'
'Gravetye Beauty'
'Hendersonii'
'John Huxtable'
'Kermesina'

'King George V'
'Lady Betty Balfour'
'Ladybird Johnson'
'Little Nell'
'Mme. Baron Veillard'
'Mme. Édouard André'
'Mme. Grangé'
'Mme. Julia Correvon'
'Margaret Hunt'
'Margot Koster'
'Mary Rose'
'Minuet'
'Mrs. Robert Brydon'
'Olgae'
'Pagoda'
'Pastel Pink'
'Perle d'Azur'
'Peveril'
'Pink Fantasy'
'Prince Charles'
'Purpurea'
'Purpurea Plena Élegans'
'Rosea' (*C. douglasii and C. crispa*)
'Rouge Cardinal'
'Royal Velours'
'Rubra' (*C. viticella*)
'Rubro-marginata'
'Sir Trevor Lawrence'
'Star of India'
'Tango'
'Tapestry'
'Princess of Wales'
'Twilight'
'Venosa Violacea'
'Victoria'
'Volluceau'
'Warsaw Nike'
'Wyevale'

Clematis in this group bear their flowers early in the season, in the leaf axils of the previous year's stems.

Group 2 is also relatively easy to prune. Prune severely as soon as the flowers fade, cutting the whole plant to within 1 ft. or so of the ground. You have to be a little careful, because very old stems may not resprout following severe cutting. Either do not cut the plant back into very old wood (in which case the plant gets larger and larger each year), or at least do not cut back all of the stems, or have a young replacement stem ready in case the plant dies. You can also train these plants to cordons. Then, each year right after flowering, cut back stems that bore flowers to within a few inches of the cordon.

No matter which way you grow plants in this group, the new shoots that appear following pruning are those that will bear flowers the following season. To some degree, the less you shorten stems one season, the earlier the blossoms appear the following season.

Also, because members of this group vary in their vigor, they likewise vary in the amount of pruning they need to control their size. *C. montana* and *C. Armandii*, for example, are extremely vigorous, while little wood needs to be removed from weak growers such as *C. alpina* and *C. macropetala*. You may even have to pinch and shorten shoots of vigorous growers in summer to keep growth in check.

The following species and varieties are included in this group:

C. afoliata
C. alpina
C. alpina sibirica
C. Armandii
C. australis
C. chrysocoma
C. cirrhosa
C. cirrhosa var. balearica
C. columbiana
C. foetida
C. Forsteri
C. gentianoides
C. hexasepala
C. hookeriana
C. indivisa
C. × *jeuneana*
C. macropetala
C. marata
C. marmoraria
C. Meyeniana
C. montana
C. nepalensis
C. ochotensis
C. parviflora
C. petriei
C. phlebantha
C. quinquefoliata

Bud on 'Crimson Star', a Group 2 clematis.

GROUP 3

Clematis in this group flower more or less throughout the season on both new shoots and older stems, with the bulk of the flowers usually appearing during the summer. Some of these plants bear a profusion of early flowers on short shoots, and then another crop of flowers later in the season. Those plants with large flowers typically bear them on the ends of longer shoots.

Pruning this group is a little trickier than pruning the other groups. If you cut a plant back sharply before growth begins, you miss the earliest flowers. But if you prune severely after the first flush of blooms, you miss the later ones. No wonder that the recommendation is often made not to prune at all. But then the plant becomes a tangled mess.

In fact, Group 3 clematis can be contained by pruning without undue sacrifice of flowers. One option is to cut back the whole plant drastically every few years just before growth begins, with little or no pruning in the intervening time; in this case you give up only the earliest blossoms of one season. Or divide the plant in half, and severely prune each half in alternate years. The most refined approach is to thin out lightly and disentangle stems before growth begins, then go over the plants again after the earliest flowers fade, severely shortening the stems that have borne those flowers.

The following plants are included in this group:

C. florida
C. fusca
C. × Jackmanii
C. japonica
C. × phlebantha
C. Potaninii

'Alba (C. × Jackmanii)'
'Alba Plena'
'Alice Fisk'
'Andrew'
'Annabel'
'Asao'
'Barbara Dibley'
'Barbara Jackman'
'Bees Jubilee'
'Belle Nantaise'
'Belle of Woking'
'Blue Diamond'
'Bracebridge Star'
'Capitaine Thuilleaux'
'Carnaby'
'Cassiopeia'
'Chalcedony'
'Charissima'
'Corona'
'Countess of Lovelace'
'Crimson King'

'C. W. Dowman'
'Daniel Deronda'
'Dawn'
'Dr. Ruppel'
'Duchess of Edinburgh'
'Edith'
'Edouard Desfossé'
'Elizabeth Foster'
'Elsa Späth'
'Empress of India'
'Étoile de Malicorne'
'Étoile de Paris'
'Fair Rosamond'
'Fairy Queen'
'Fireworks'
'Four Star'
'General Sikorski'
'Gillian Blades'
'Gladys Picard'
'Gokonosho '
'Guiding Star'
'Haku Ookan'
'Henryi'
'Herbert Johnson'
'H.F. Young'
'Hidcote Purple'
'Horn of Plenty'
'Imperial'
'Ishobel'
'James Mason'
'Jim Hollis'
'Joan Picton'
'Joan Wilcox'
'John Paul II'
'Kacper'
'Karin'
'Kathleen Dunford'
'Kathleen Wheeler'
'Keith Richardson'
'Ken Donson'
'King Edward VII'
'Kiri Te Kanawa'
'Lady Londesborough'
'Lasurstern'
'Lawsonia'
'Lincoln Star'
'Lord Nevill'
'Louise Rowe'
'Mammut'
'Marcel Moser'
'Miriam Markham'
'Miss Bateman'
'Miss Crawshay'
'Moonlight'
'Mrs. Bush'

C. Spooneri
C. uncinata
C. × vedrariensis
C. verticillaris

'Alexander'
'Apple Blossom'
'Blue Bird'
'Burford White'
'Candy'
'Columbine'
'Continuity'
'Crimson Star'
'Elizabeth'
'Francis Rivis'
'Frankie'
'Grandiflora'
'Highdown'
'Jacqueline du Pré'
'Louise'
'Madeleine'
'Maidwell Hall'
'Markham's Pink'

'Pamela Jackman'
'Peveril'
'Picton's Variety'
'Rosy O'Grady '
'Rosy Pagoda'
'Rubens'
'Ruby'
'Snowbird'
'Snowdrift'
'Tetrarose'
'White Columbine'
'White Moth'
'Willy'
'Wilsonii'
'Wisley'

'Mrs. George
  Jackman'
'Mrs. James Mason'
'Mrs. N. Thompson'
'Mrs. Oud'
'Mrs. P.B. Truax'
'Mrs. Spencer Castle'
'Myojo'
'Nelly Moser'
'Pennell's Purity'
'Percy Lake'
'Percy Picton'
'Peveril Pearl'
'Phoenix'
'Prince of Wales'
'Prins Hendrik'
'Proteus'
'Rouge Cardinal'
'Royalty'
'Rubra (C. ×
  Jackmanii)'
'Saturn'
'Scartho Gem'
'Sealand Gem'
'Sir Garnet Wolseley'
'Snow Queen'
'Superba'
'Susan Allsop'
'Syliva Denny'
'The President'
'Titania'
'Veronica's Choice'
'Violet Elizabeth'
'Vyvyan Pennell'
'Wada's Primrose'
'Walter Pennell'
'Wilhemina Tull'
'Will Goodwin'
'William Kennett'

GROUP 4

Uh oh, another group? Clematis do not fall as neatly as one would hope into the three flowering groups, and a few varieties choose to straddle the fence between Groups 1 and 3.

Prune these plants heavily before growth begins, and you get a profusion of blossoms late in the season. Just prune lightly and you get larger blossoms that are borne early and then repeat occasionally through the summer — but the plants also keep growing larger and larger. The dilemma is similar to that faced with Group 3, except more so. So prune Group 4 clematis severely every other year, or else divide the plant in half and severely prune each half in alternate years, in each case, just before growth begins.

The following plants are included in this group:

C. fargesii var. souliei

'Beauty of Richmond'
'Beauty of Worcester'
'Blue Gem'
'Corona'
'Daniel Deronda'

'Duchess of
  Sutherland'
Ernest Markham'
'Hagley Hybrid'
'John Warren'
'Lady Caroline Nevill'
'Lady Northcliffe'
'Marie Boisselot'
'Maureen'
'Mrs. Cholmondeley'
'Mrs. Hope'
'Niobe'
'Richard Pennell'
'Serenata'
'Sieboldii'
'Silver Moon'
'Venus Victrix'
'Ville de Lyon'
'Violet Charm'
'W.E. Gladstone'

Flowering Habit of Group 3 Clematis

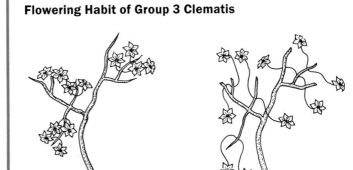

(Leaves not shown)

Early flowers are borne on one-year-old wood, or from short shoots growing off one-year-old wood.

Later flowers are borne on long shoots of current season's growth.

CHAPTER EIGHT

EDIBLE FRUITS AND NUTS

This luscious bounty is the result of regular—and correct—pruning.

Think of the sweetness of a perfectly ripe pear or strawberry: That sweetness comes from sugar, a carbohydrate, the fuel that energizes cells in plants. Producing luscious fruits demands lots of energy from a plant, so your aim in pruning fruits is first to ensure that the plant has enough energy to make the fruits, and then to direct a good portion of that energy to the fruits themselves.

Since sunlight is the ultimate source of energy, allowing the plant to combine carbon dioxide and water to make stored energy, or carbohydrates, you will use your pruning tools to help the plant—tree, bush, or vine—drink in as much sunshine as possible. Left to their own devices, most fruit plants eventually shade themselves to the point of bearing relatively few fruits for the size of the plant, and poor-quality fruits at that.

Keeping the canopy of branches open has two other benefits specific to fruit plants. An open canopy allows sprays to penetrate those plants that require spraying. And good air circulation and sunlight speed the drying of leaves and fruits, decreasing the incidence of disease.

You are also going to use pruning to apportion energy within your fruit plant, balancing the amount of leaf and shoot growth with the amount of fruits ripened. Leaves are needed to capture the sun's energy and shoots are needed on which to hang fruits. But beyond what is needed for these purposes, what we demand of these plants is fruit! (I am getting a little carried away here—fruit

Most fruit and nut plants require regular pruning. Even those plants that bear reasonable crops without such care will usually bear more or better fruits if pruned. (Nuts are fruits, so I will herewith dispense with repeating "and nuts" every time I write "fruits.")

plants do gratify also with their beauty, and some make great climbing trees.)

Have you ever noticed a wild apple tree, blueberry bush, or grape vine, never pruned (except by wind, ice, and pests) yet apparently loaded with fruit? Look more closely next time—for the amount of space the plant occupies, is it really bearing a large crop? Probably not. And look at the fruit, and taste it. It is small and not especially sweet. Cultivated fruits are—or should be—large and luscious, and they get that way by breeding or selecting the best from wild plants, by being well fed and watered, and by being pruned to balance growth among leaves, shoots, and fruits.

Tree fruits

A good crop of large fruits puts a heavy weight on branches, so special attention must be paid to training a fruit tree to a sturdy framework. This may even mean pruning back part of a branch just to keep it from breaking under a potentially heavy load of fruit—what sweet work!

Pruning the young fruit tree

The first years a fruit tree is in the ground are important to its future performance—in terms of luscious fruits and even its beauty as a plant. These are the years that the tree lays down what will be, for better or for worse, its permanent framework of branches. Your goal is to help that tree develop branches that are strong enough to support their load of fruit, and to do so without shading each other. (Strength is not a consideration if the branches of your fruit tree are going to be physically supported for their whole life, as is the case for trellised or espaliered plants.) You also want the tree to grow rapidly, to fill the space you have allotted it. And, of course, you want to pick your first fruits

---

THE BARE BONES

TREES, BUSHES, AND VINES THAT PRODUCE EDIBLE FRUIT

WITH FEW EXCEPTIONS, prune fruit plants while they are dormant.

WITH A YOUNG FRUIT TREE, choose as scaffold limbs branches that are 6 in. apart and leaving the trunk at wide angles. If the tree is initially a single stem, cut back that stem at planting to 2 ft. to 3 ft. above ground level, then select side branches as the plant grows. If the tree already has branches, save those that are wide angled and in good position, and remove all others. Shorten those that you save to a few inches. Do no more pruning on a young tree than is absolutely necessary or you will delay fruiting.

MATURE FRUIT TREES need annual pruning. The amount of wood to remove to reduce the fruit load and to stimulate new shoot growth depends on the size of the particular fruit and the bearing habit of the particular tree.

PRUNE FRUIT BUSHES little or not at all when young, then annually remove the oldest wood and thin out the youngest wood. The younger the wood on which most fruits are borne and the more new shoots that grow each year from ground level, the more severe the annual pruning that is needed.

AT PLANTING, CUT VINES back to a few buds to channel energy into growth of a single (sometimes two) stems. From then on, training depends on the fruit and the kind of trellis or arbor you provide. For details about specific fruits, see the Plant List, which begins on p. 141. Renewal wood is provided by cutting back growth to within few buds of permanent cordons or the trunk.

as soon as possible. Whatever you do to your young tree, keep in mind these goals: good form, rapid growth, and early fruiting.

Your pruning shears is only one of the tools you'll employ to train your tree. You will also use your fingernails to pinch growing points, perhaps a knife to notch or ring bark, and strings or weights to bend branches downward. You will not need a saw during the training period; if you do, you have neglected your tree too long.

A fruit tree, as you receive it from a nursery, is either a whip, which is just a single stem, or a feathered tree, which is a young tree that already has side branches. The feathered tree, being more developed, is more desirable and more expensive. Fruit trees usually are dug from the nursery field while they are dormant, to be sold bare root. Occasionally, the trees are dug with a ball of soil and sold balled and burlapped, with their roots more or less intact, or are grown and sold in pots, in which case their roots are not disturbed at all.

Take a look at the roots of your plant before you set it in the ground—after all, this is the last look you should ever get at them! With a potted plant, tease out the roots around the outside of the root ball to encourage them to grow into the surrounding soil. Use a stick or a fork, and if some of the roots have circled around inside the pot so tightly that you cannot tease them outward, make some vertical slits in the root ball with a knife. (Circling roots are "pot bound" from spending too much time in the pot. Avoid purchasing a tree that is excessively pot bound, because it will eventually strangle itself.)

Treat the roots of a balled and burlapped tree the same as those of a potted tree. If any long roots were

Slitting the Root Ball of a Potted Tree

wrapped around the root ball when the tree was packed up, spread them out or, if you do not want to dig a hole big enough to accommodate them, cut them back. Do not fold them into the planting hole.

Look closely at all the roots of a bare-root tree. Cut back any that are too long to fit into the planting hole, or dig a larger hole. Also cut back into healthy tissue any roots that are dead or diseased. Some roots may have had their ends frayed as the plant was lifted out of the soil. Trim these roots back cleanly so that, with less surface area to the wound, healing will occur more rapidly.

Now plant the tree.

Next, turn your attention to the top of the young plant. Keep in mind the shape that you want for your tree when it grows up. In contrast to many ornamental trees, which are "high-headed," you probably want the first side branch on a fruit tree to originate fairly low, because then you have more fruit within reach, or more fruit, plain and simple, especially if the tree is a dwarf that will never grow higher than 7 ft. anyway. On the other hand, you do not want that first limb to be so low that it droops to the ground under its weight of fruit, or makes it difficult for you to mow, mulch, or cultivate beneath the tree.

Although many different tree forms have been spawned over centuries of training and pruning fruit trees, three forms predominate: the central leader, the open center, and the modified central leader. The leader referred to here is the main stem of the tree, a continuation of the trunk. The central-leader tree has a single, dominant leader off which grow branches of decreasing length as you move up the tree. (A compact central-leader tree is sometimes called a "dwarf pyramid.") These branches will become the scaffold limbs, or main branches, of the tree. The open-center tree has a vase shape, with three or four leaders growing off the trunk in an outward and upward direction. Branches grow off these leaders. The modified central-leader tree is a hybrid of the first two systems. The tree starts out as a central leader, and at a height of about 7 ft., growth of the leader is stopped as it is bent over or headed back to a weak side branch. The ideal form for a particular tree will depend not only on your whims, but also on the plant's natural growth habit.

For any of the three basic tree forms, branch selection begins the first season. In the case of the open-center tree, once you have selected three or four side branches, cut the central stem off just above the topmost side branch. The tree then continues upward and outward growth along these side branches, now officially leaders (but not central leaders). In the case of the central-leader or young modified central-leader tree, select side branches growing off the central leader.

Side-branch selection determines the future shape and strength of the tree, so

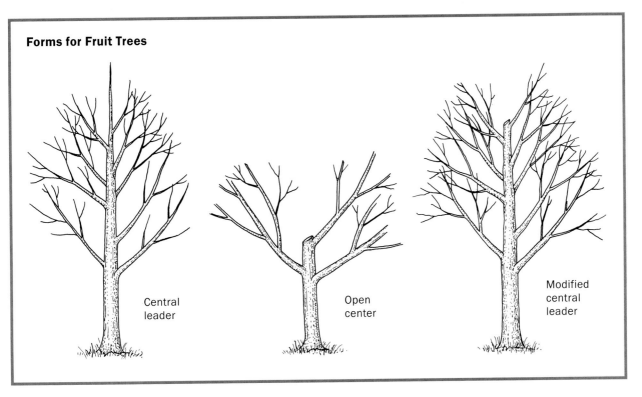

Forms for Fruit Trees

Central leader

Open center

Modified central leader

select with care. Each side branch needs adequate space in which to develop. Start with the first branch about 2 ft. from the ground, then space subsequent ones about 6 in. to 18 in. apart as you move up the trunk, the spacing depending on the eventual size of the tree (larger tree, larger spacing). Ideally, branches should originate in a spiral arrangement up the trunk so that each branch has space to spread and does not rob minerals and water coming up from the roots from another branch that is close and directly above.

As you select new side branches during the first few years of growth, your tree will look admittedly sparse. But do not be tempted to space branches closer together or closer to the ground. Throughout the life of the tree, the location of those branches will never change. In fact, they will crowd somewhat closer with age as they thicken.

Besides adequate spacing, each side branch needs to be firmly anchored to the leader, or, in the case of the open-center tree, leaders. A strong union is possible only when a leader envelops the base of the attached branch, and this is possible only when a branch is thinner than the leader off which it grows. Such a side branch typically grows out at a wide angle to the leader, and this also makes for a strong union. A branch emerging at a narrow angle tends to accumulate dead bark, which weakens the union, in the crotch between the branch and the leader.

Do not neglect the development of the central leader on a tree trained either as a central-leader tree or modified central-leader form. This leader should be truly a central leader, at all times the most dominant and upright stem of the tree—the horticultural top dog. If the leader branches to make two equally vigorous leaders, remove one completely and immediately. Do not let premature fruiting of the developing central leader rob it of strength or cause it to bend over.

So there's the ideal: a strong, central leader with well-spaced, firmly anchored branches; or, in the case of the open-center tree, a short trunk capped by three of four strong and firmly anchored leaders off which grow side branches. Trees rarely conform to this ideal if allowed to grow naturally. (If toying with natural growth makes you uneasy, take comfort in the fact that no wild peach tree ever bore a 3-in. diameter fruit practically bursting with ambrosial juice.)

How do we coax a newly planted tree into having good form? First, the easy stuff… prune dead or diseased wood

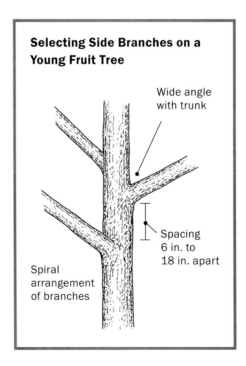

Selecting Side Branches on a Young Fruit Tree

Wide angle with trunk

Spacing 6 in. to 18 in. apart

Spiral arrangement of branches

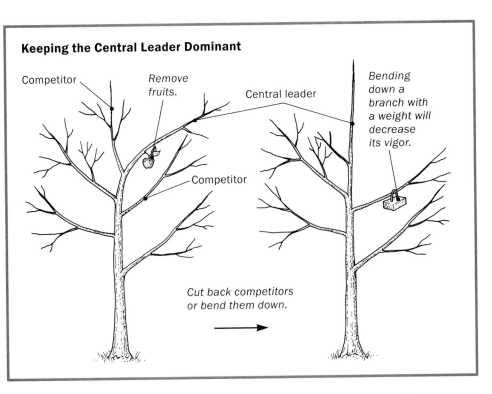

Keeping the Central Leader Dominant

Competitor

Remove fruits.

Central leader

Bending down a branch with a weight will decrease its vigor.

Competitor

Cut back competitors or bend them down.

back into healthy tissue, and also prune back broken stems. If your new tree is a whip, head it back to promote low branching. How low you head the whip will determine the height of the lowest branches as well as their vigor. Commercial growers generally head whips back to 2 ft. or 3 ft. above ground level. Lower heading results in fewer, but longer, branches; higher heading, the opposite (see the drawing on p. 128). Expect a more vigorous response from a more vigorous (thicker) whip. Prune for lower branching if the site is windy.

A feathered tree already has side branches, so save those worth saving, and remove the others. Whether or not you shorten a well-placed branch that you save depends on how you are growing the tree. If the tree is a dwarf, perhaps trellised, and you want the earliest possible fruiting, do not shorten any branches except those that are drooping. If you are growing a large, freestanding

tree, shorten branches to stubs to stimulate vigorous regrowth and delay fruiting so that energy is channeled into shoot growth. In this latter case, shorten most severely those branches that are spindly. If the tree is to have a central leader and the leader on your feathered tree continues, unbranched, far above the bottom tier of branches, also head back the leader to promote the next tier of branching.

Only two other conditions necessitate further pruning of the tops immediately following planting. The first is with a bare-root tree that may suffer from lack of water its first season in the ground. Traditional reasoning has held that the tops of bare-root trees need pruning in order to balance the inevitable loss of roots that occurred when the tree was dug from the nursery. In fact, such pruning is needed only when water is short, to avoid water loss through leaves. Moreover, if a plant receives good care

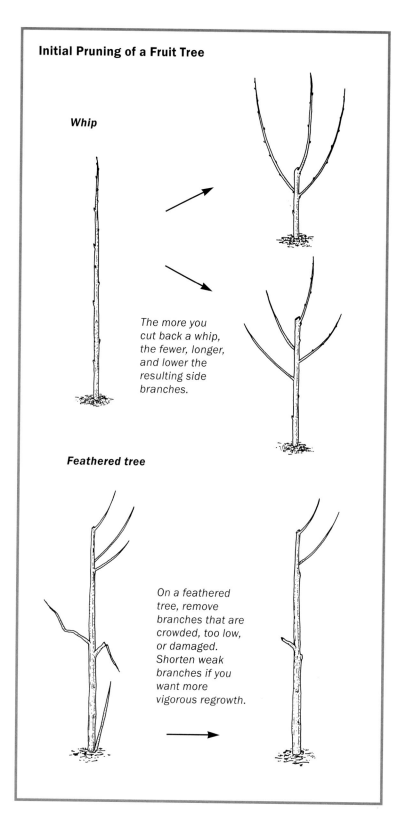

Initial Pruning of a Fruit Tree

Whip

The more you cut back a whip, the fewer, longer, and lower the resulting side branches.

Feathered tree

On a feathered tree, remove branches that are crowded, too low, or damaged. Shorten weak branches if you want more vigorous regrowth.

once in the ground, natural hormones produced in the buds, especially terminal buds, stimulate root growth. Why not water instead?

The other condition possibly requiring top pruning in the first season is if the tree is heavily branched and the site is windy. In that case, thin out branches to keep the tree from sailing in the wind. Or stake the tree—trees on certain rootstocks need staking anyway, when young or throughout their life.

As the central leader grows, induce it to keep sending out side branches by heading it back from time to time. As a general rule of thumb, each year cut off about one-third of the previous season's growth while the plant is dormant. Alternatively, cut back the leader by a few inches during the growing season each time it grows a few inches above the point where you want a side branch. The uppermost bud that remains after heading the leader usually sends out a vertical shoot that becomes a continuation of the leader, and lower buds push out side branches. If the top few buds push out vigorous upright shoots, cut away all but the top one. Select new side branches that are well spaced along the leader and firmly anchored to it.

Branches generally need little additional pruning. Usually they branch further and stay subordinate to the leader. (Leaders need coaxing to make side branches because upright growth promotes apical dominance, the result of a hormone produced in the topmost bud suppressing growth of buds farther down the stem.) If a side branch is not branching or is threatening the leader with overly exuberant growth, shorten it or, better still, bend it to a more horizontal position with weights or string. Also shorten any side branch that is too lanky back to where it turns downward if it is drooping. The largest side branches should be those lowest along the central leader, so that the tree is wider at the bottom than at the top.

With the open-center tree, head back the three or four leaders so that each is well furnished with branches. But make sure no branches originate so low that they interfere with each other. The aim is for growth that is upward and outward, like a vase. What needs to be pruned to achieve this goal depends on the plant's natural growth habit. More upright trees need more vertical shoots removed, and naturally drooping trees need more "hangers" removed.

A few neat tricks can help your tree along in its development. Suppose a sprout is emerging in a perfect position to become a scaffold limb, except that it makes a narrow angle with a leader. Widen the angle by inserting a clothespin or toothpick between it and the leader (see the photo on p. 130). Another way to get wide-angled branches is to head back a whip when it is dormant, then cut back the central stem again when the new

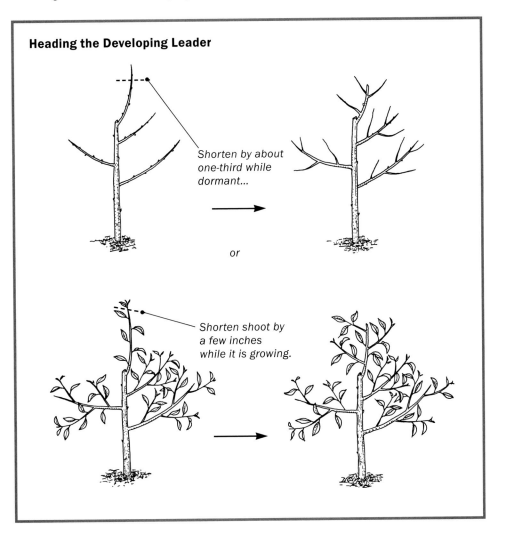

Heading the Developing Leader

Shorten by about one-third while dormant...

or

Shorten shoot by a few inches while it is growing.

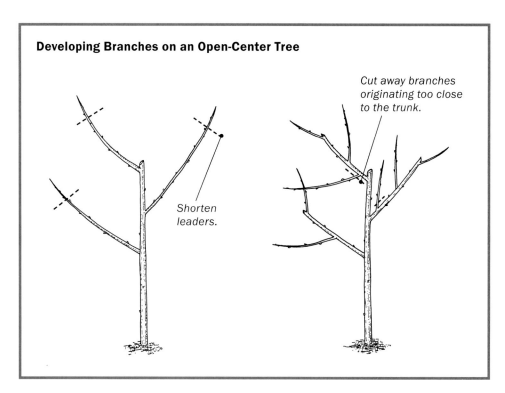

Developing Branches on an Open-Center Tree

Cut away branches originating too close to the trunk.

Shorten leaders.

A toothpick is a convenient tool for spreading young stems.

topmost shoot is about 6 in. long, removing all the upper upright shoots. What remains will be wide-angled, new shoots, perfect for three or four leaders of an open-center tree. And what if no side branch is growing where you want it to? Sometimes—only sometimes—cutting a notch into the bark above a bud will induce that bud to grow out into a shoot. Removing a leaf on an actively growing shoot also can cause the bud where the leaf was attached to send out a shoot. What if the leader made only feeble growth for the season? Head it back severely to stimulate vigorous regrowth.

A few more pruning cuts complete those necessary to train your young fruit tree. Perhaps hardest (psychologically, not physically) to remove are flowers or fruits. Your young tree should be channeling its energy into growth, not fruit, so be judicious about when to start allowing fruits, and how many to allow. Otherwise, your plant may never become more than a mere runt. And do not forget to keep fruits off a developing central leader, because they not only sap the leader's strength, but also can weigh it down, pulling it over so that it loses apical dominance.

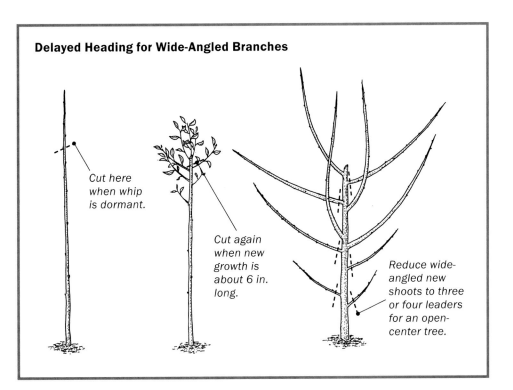

Delayed Heading for Wide-Angled Branches

Cut here when whip is dormant.

Cut again when new growth is about 6 in. long.

Reduce wide-angled new shoots to three or four leaders for an open-center tree.

Your tree likely will grow more branches than those you are going to retain as scaffold limbs. Smaller secondary branches may even crowd too closely on larger branches. In hot, sunny climates, save a few temporary branches on the trunk to avoid sunburn of young bark. Otherwise, remove excess branches on your tree.

Also keep on the lookout for very vigorous vertical shoots—called watersprouts or suckers—arising from the tops of branches or from down near the ground. Those high in the tree ruin its form and create excessive shade. Those arising near ground level may be growing from the rootstock of a grafted tree, and so would grow on to produce useless fruit. Remove any watersprout or sucker

Notching the bark above a bud will sometimes cause that bud to form a shoot, creating a side branch just where you want it.

The quickest and most effective way to get rid of a watersprout is just to grab it and snap it off while it is still succulent.

right at its base as soon as you notice it. Ripping it off with a quick jerk of your hand rather than cutting it reduces the chances of new sprouts growing from the same point.

Finally, remember the third goal in training a tree: minimum delay before the plant begins fruiting. A young fruit tree needs some pruning, but excessive pruning stimulates too much vigorous shoot growth, and most young trees already have plenty of that. Despite all that has been said here, minimize delay in reaping your edible rewards by pruning no more than is absolutely necessary!

Pruning the mature fruit tree

Don't stop pruning any tree bearing good crops. The tree still needs annual pruning, just as it did when it was young, although for different reasons. Prune the mature tree to keep it healthy, to keep it within its allotted space, and to keep it bearing regular crops of the best fruit possible. True, some tree fruits seem to bear well with little pruning, but these are mostly uncommon fruits that have yet to be studied in rigorous detail. They too may turn out to do better with annual pruning.

Pruning keeps a tree healthy by ridding it of diseased and dead wood, and by creating conditions unfriendly to disease-causing microorganisms. Whenever you see a diseased stem on a tree, cut it off back into healthy, lighter-colored wood. Under certain conditions, such as when pruning fire-blighted stems from a pear tree in summer, you could spread disease on your pruning shears, so sterilize the tool between cuts with a dip in alcohol or 10% bleach solution. (Winter pruning does not present this hazard, so no sterilization is necessary.) Also cut away dead wood in such a way as to promote

most rapid and thorough healing (for details, see pp. 30-33).

Most fungi and bacteria that cause disease thrive in dark, dank conditions. If you prune to keep the tree canopy open to light and air, then leaves, twigs, and fruits dry quickly. Stems bathed in light also are able to grow more vigorously and better resist diseases. Generally, do such pruning while a plant is dormant, though in some cases, you might do it during the growing season to allow better air circulation around ripening fruits. Keeping an open canopy also reduces branch rubbing, another possible entryway for disease.

The greatest skill involved in pruning fruit trees is striking a good balance between some naturally opposing tendencies of these plants. You want to balance shoot growth throughout the plant, counteracting the natural tendency of a tree to pump most of its energy into shoots at the top of the canopy. On a top-heavy tree, the lower branches are shaded and the fruit is mostly high up, out of reach. Avoid this situation by making mostly thinning cuts on upper branches and heading cuts on lower ones.

You also want to balance shoot growth and fruiting. Shoot growth is needed for leaves, to make sugars, and for branches on which to hang fruits; yet the fruits are what we are really after. You want to balance high yields with high quality. The more fruits a tree bears, the less energy doled out to each fruit, so the fruits are smaller and less tasty. This is of little consequence with a naturally small fruit like a sweet cherry, but can spell the difference between a drippy "wow" and a mealy "ho-hum" for a naturally large fruit like a peach.

Finally, you want to balance this year's crop with next year's. Developing fruits produce hormones that suppress flower-bud initiation, so a large crop one year results in a light crop the next. Dormant pruning of stems to remove potential flowers, and pinching or knocking off excess flowers or fruitlets, can avoid cycles of feast and famine.

How much pruning is needed to balance all these opposing forces depends on where the particular plant bears its flowers, and on how big its fruits are. The peach tree bears fruit only on stems that grew the previous season, so it needs fairly severe annual pruning to stimulate an annual flush of vigorous new shoots for the following year's crop. An apple tree, which bears fruits on short, knobby branches as aged as ten years old, needs little such stimulus. Both fruits are large, so the trees do need pruning of branches, flowers, or fruits to reduce the current crop, increasing its quality and ensuring a good return bloom the following season.

Even after dormant branch-pruning has removed potential fruits, you may have to go over the trees to thin individual fruitlets by hand. The sooner after fruits initially form that you do this, the greater the effect on fruit quality and next year's crop. However, delay spring fruit thinning until the risk of frost, which will damage fruitlets, has safely past. A few weeks after bloom, most fruit trees suddenly shed weaker or damaged fruitlets—the so-called "June drop." You may want to hand thin in two installments, the first right after bloom and the second after June drop.

Whenever you thin, selectively remove smaller fruitlets and any damaged ones, just as the tree naturally does. Generally, leave space between fruitlets equal to two or three times the mature size of the fruit. Pinch off fruitlets one by one or, if you have many trees, knock them off in quantity with a blast of water or by batting them with a piece of hose attached to the end of a broom handle.

(Commercially, apples and some other fruits are thinned with chemicals.)

Except where you need a replacement shoot, always remove, right at its base, any watersprout or root sucker, just as you did when training the tree. These vigorous shoots create shade and upset the form of the plant.

Although fruit trees are generally pruned while they are dormant, there also is a place for for pruning them during the summer. Response to summer pruning depends on when during the growing season you prune, what you cut, the particular variety of fruit, and the weather. No wonder generalizations are hard to make about summer pruning! Summer pruning can promote the formation of fruit buds, at its best smothering branches with flowers and then fruits, exactly the type of growth sought after on an espalier. And "Espalier" (pp. 212-225) is the chapter in which the details of summer pruning are covered. At the very least, summer pruning can open up the canopy as fruits are ripening, limiting diseases and, for those fruits that need direct light to color up (not all do), increasing fruit color. Do

Thinning fruits increases the quality of those that remain.

such pruning around midsummer, when there is less chance of regrowth because lateral buds have probably already become dormant for the season.

Ideally, no fruit tree would ever grow larger than you want it to. Either you have enough space to accommodate its natural size, or else you choose a specific rootstock that keeps the plant small. In the real world (a suburban yard, for example), a dwarfing rootstock does not exist for most fruits and space may not be available for a fruit or nut tree 30 ft. high and wide. And who wants to climb a high ladder to bring in the harvest? Fortunately, you can limit the size of any fruit tree with judicious pruning; the sidebar on the facing page tells how.

Renovating a neglected fruit tree

A neglected large and craggy fruit tree may have a certain rustic charm, but that tree is a sorry tree indeed, in terms of producing tasty fruits. How sorry depends on the fruit and the environment—some nut trees get along well despite neglect, and I have known a nearly neglected, old cherry tree to bear plenty of fruit of good quality.

But an old fruit tree usually has plenty of problems: The fruits may be too high, too few, and too small; pests are likely rampant; and the shaded interior of the tree will probably consist of nothing but wood (which still must be fed by the plant), not fruit or leaves.

Renovating a tree can bring it back to its former glory, but before you even pick up your pruning tools, ask yourself whether your efforts will be justified. Is the tree of a particularly good variety? Do you really want a tree where that tree is? Some trees do not live long enough to justify drastic renovation, which should be spread over two or three years; and then another two years might be required

before the tree is bearing a full crop. Peach trees, for instance, are not long-lived and recover poorly from wounds, especially the large wounds needed for renovation. Some young trees could already be cropping in that time, so before beginning renovative pruning, consider "pruning" the tree with a saw—at ground level.

If you do decide to renovate the old tree, start while your tree is dormant. First make some large cuts low in the crown to thin it out and, if you want, to lower it and limit its spread. Cut one or two major limbs back to their origin or to sturdy side branches. If more major limbs need cutting back, wait a year, and if still more must go, hold off for yet another year. If you cut too much in one year, there is risk of sunburn on once-shaded bark.

New sprouts may grow near some of your pruning cuts. Some of these sprouts, especially those of moderate vigor, might be in good positions to make permanent new limbs. Save those, and cut away the others, especially when many are clustered near a pruning cut.

With major cuts out of the way for now, progress to more detailed pruning, using a small pruning saw and lopper. Look over the stems and cut back to sound wood any that are diseased, dead, or broken. Also remove stems that are overcrowded or weak. Cut back any drooping stem to a branch near the place where the stem starts drooping. As always, take into account the kind of tree you are working with—American persimmon, for example, has a naturally drooping growth habit.

Finally, stand back and admire your work. Cleaned up, an old fruit tree looks even more charming than it did when it was neglected and overgrown. Now give your tree a hug.

Pruning to keep any tree within bounds should consist mostly of thinning cuts. Remove an offending stem by cutting it back to its origin, to a sturdy side branch within the canopy, or to a weak side branch farther out. Less regrowth is likely to occur from such cuts than from merely heading back smaller stems that are too high or too wide around the periphery of the crown. Making fewer large cuts lower in the tree also is less work than making many small cuts high in the tree. Start pruning your tree to limit its size before it becomes full size. For example, top the leader, or bend it over, before it grows as high as you want your tree to grow. Prune to limit tree size while a tree is dormant or while it is actively growing.

Root pruning also can dwarf a fruit tree. Root prune by pushing a shovel into the ground in a ring around the plant, 2 ft. to 4 ft. from the trunk, sometime between late fall and early spring. (Mechanical cutter bars pulled by tractor have been designed for this job in orchards.)

Fruiting itself can slow down shoot growth, and if your tree is reluctant to start fruiting, you can coerce it into puberty by bark ringing. This technique involves making a cut around the trunk, or two cuts, $\frac{1}{4}$ in. to $\frac{1}{2}$ in. apart, with the bark between the cuts removed. By the end of the season the ring will have healed. You can even ring individual branches, rather than the trunk.

Good judgment is needed for root pruning or bark ringing. Either technique, done too severely or too frequently, done on a weakened tree, or done just before a summer of drought, could kill the tree. Both techniques have been applied mostly to apple trees, so be cautious about applying them to other fruits. Never ring stone fruits (*Prunus* species) because wounded bark heals poorly and is especially attractive to pests. At their best, though, either technique decreases shoot growth and, in the case of ringing, increases fruiting.

Judiciously applied, bark ringing may encourage a tree to start fruiting. Make parallel cuts a short distance apart, then remove the bark between the cuts.

PRUNING A NEGLECTED FRUIT TREE

1. This apple tree has not been pruned for years.

2. Cutting away some vertical limbs quickly lowers the tree and lets more light in.

3. Drooping branches, which bear poor fruit, are lopped off.

4. Renovation is finished for this year, but must be continued over a period of a few years.

Bush fruits

It is in the nature of a bush that its stems are short-lived, as they are always being replaced by new ones thrown up from ground level. (What did you think made a bush bushy?) So pruning the young fruit bush is important only in terms of its survival and health, and so that you get to pick your first crop as soon as possible. No sturdy framework of permanent stems is necessary.

Pruning the young fruit bush

A bush that has been grown in a pot, or that has been dug from a nursery field with its roots more or less intact, then balled and burlapped, needs little or no pruning when it is planted. Knock the potted plant out of its pot, then use a stick or a fork to tease out the roots at the outside of the root ball. If the plant has started to become pot bound, with roots circling around the outside edge of the root ball, loosen the roots from the root ball so that they radiate outward when you set the ball in its planting hole. Slicing a little way into the root ball from top to bottom with a knife deals with congestion within the root ball. A balled and burlapped bush needs nothing done to its roots, except the cutting back of any lanky roots that might have been tucked in around the root ball when the plant was packed up.

With the bare-root bush, inspect the roots carefully before you plant. Cut off any dead roots, and cut roots that are diseased or have frayed ends back to healthy, light-colored tissue.

With just a few exceptions, the stems of your new bush do not need pruning right after you set the plant in the ground. Of course, you should check for stems that are dead, diseased, or broken, and remove them. Also, if the site is very windy, thin out stems to prevent wind from rocking the plant or yanking it out of the ground before the roots have grabbed hold of the soil. The tops do not need pruning just because it was bare root ("to balance the inevitable root loss that occurred during transplanting" said the old books) so long as you provide the plant with sufficient moisture throughout its first season. Minimizing pruning and using mostly thinning cuts helps get your bush off to a good start because shoot buds, especially terminal buds, produce hormones that promote root growth.

A few fruit bushes (noted in the Plant List on pp. 141-176) benefit from being cut clear to the ground right after they are planted. The benefits are threefold: First, removing all wood eliminates possibly diseased stems that could spread infection to new shoots. Second, with all stems removed, the young plant can put its initial efforts into growing shoots and roots rather than bearing any fruits on older stems. And third, the decapitated plant will send up many vigorous, young shoots near ground level, which—in the

Pruning is part of the prescription for an abundant harvest—in this case, of blueberries.

cases of plants that bear on one-year-old wood—will bear a respectable crop the next season.

After any initial pruning, the frequency and degree of subsequent pruning needed by a young fruit bush depends on the particular fruit. Bushes mature quickly, so this quickly moves us into the realm of maintenance pruning.

Maintenance pruning

Most fruit bushes demand annual pruning for sustained, high-quality harvests. This keeps a bush open to air and light, limiting diseases by promoting quick drying of the stems, leaves, and fruits. And abundant light improves quality of the fruit.

Annual pruning also renews the plant, as you cut away the old stems to stimulate growth of young stems and make room for them. How long before you cut away an old stem from a bush depends on the particular fruit. Bush fruits that bear *only* on vigorous stems of the previous season must have all of these stems cleared out after they finish fruiting. Other bushes produce stems that can bear for a few years before they peter out and need replacement. In any case, lop the old stem back to ground level, or back to a young, vigorous side branch originating low in the plant.

Most maintenance pruning for fruit bushes takes place while the plant is dormant, preferably in late winter. Timing is less critical for plants that are cold hardy, because pruning wounds on these plants are less likely to be damaged by cold, and there are few or no cold-damaged stems to prune from these plants at winter's end. In addition to pruning to keep a bush open and replace old stems, also cut away dead, diseased, and damaged stems, and shorten any that droop to the ground.

A few months after you finish your annual dormant pruning on a fruit bush, you will discover a pleasant by-product of your efforts: The fruit is now wonderfully easy to harvest! No more squirming through a tangle of stems—with some plants a thorny tangle—to reach the fruits, or jumping up in the air grasp at a cluster out of reach. The fruits are just splayed out before you, within easy reach.

Renovating a fruit bush

Neglected, a fruit bush may grow too high and too wide, and probably too dense. Because bushes so readily send up new shoots at or near ground level, an easy way to renovate is merely to lop the whole works down to the ground when the plant is dormant. Following this drastic pruning, the plant will put out many vigorous sprouts. Thin them out so that they are not crowded, and the bush is up and running again. The one problem with lopping the whole plant to the ground is that you sacrifice at least one year of fruit.

There is a less drastic approach to renovation, one that is more trouble but keeps the plant bearing fruit without an intermission. This involves gradually renewing the bush over a period of two or three years. Cut away only a portion of the oldest stems at or near ground level each year, when the plant is dormant. At the same time, thin out some of the youngest stems. After a few years, all the old, decrepit stems will be gone, and the bush will consist of various ages of healthy, bearing stems. How many new stems to leave after each year's thinning as well as how long to leave an older stem before cutting it away depends, of course on the particular plant's bearing habit, which is detailed in the Plant List (which begins on p. 141) for each fruit.

Vine fruits

A fruiting vine generally consists of a permanent trunk, perhaps some cordons (which are permanent branches or, if only one, a continuation of the trunk), and non-permanent fruiting arms. With the young plant, your goal is to induce development of the trunk, and, if planned, one or more cordons as quickly as possible. Achieve this goal by providing good growing conditions and by pruning.

Pruning the young fruiting vine

Most fruiting vines are sold bare root. Inspect the roots before you put the plant in the ground, and cut off any that are diseased or dead. To promote healing, cut back to healthy tissue damaged roots or roots with frayed ends. Also cut back any roots that are too long to fit in the hole that you have provided for the plant—or make the hole bigger.

A potted vine, or one that is balled and burlapped, requires little or no pruning of its roots. Just tease out the roots from the outside of the root ball to encourage their growth into the surrounding soil. And if roots are circling the outside of the root ball of the potted vine, pull them loose or slit the root ball. This prevents the roots from continuing to grow around and around, eventually strangling the plant.

Now for the top of the plant. Cut it back to within 1 ft. of the ground to stimulate vigorous growth of a single shoot. If the plant has more than one stem, cut back the sturdiest of them and remove all the others.

In some cases, fruiting vines are deliberately trained to develop more than one permanent trunk. If that is your plan, cut off any spindly stems, then leave two or three sturdy ones and head them back to about 1 ft. Don't worry if a plant destined to have a multiple trunk starts with a single stem. Even after you head back that single stem, buds near ground level will push out other shoots.

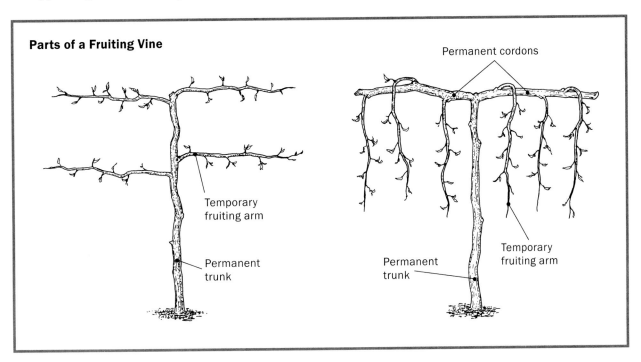

Parts of a Fruiting Vine

Permanent cordons

Temporary fruiting arm

Permanent trunk

Permanent trunk

Temporary fruiting arm

Help your vine get up off the ground during its first season by tying the trunk-to-be to a stake or, in the case of twiners, by twisting the shoot around the stake. This lending hand does more than just make a tidy plant. Keeping the growing shoot vertically oriented invigorates it by stimulating production of a hormone in the shoot tip that keeps the tip growing and suppresses the growth of side shoots. Side shoots would steal energy from the growing trunk and are superfluous, anyway. Throughout the growing season, rub out any young, green side shoots that do try to grow. If you are remiss about this task, cut them away when the plant is dormant. Keep an eye out for sprouts growing near the ground also.

Suppose your young vine does not act as planned its first season, and grows just a few spindly shoots? In that case, begin again, with drastic heading back of the dormant plant. (Also try to pinpoint and correct any deficiencies in growing conditions.)

Maintenance pruning

You have only to look at a wild grape vine to recognize the need for regular pruning of any fruiting vine. Wild grapes clamber high into trees, putting their fruits well out of reach. And the grapes that you can get to are hardly of the highest quality (genetics is admittedly also a factor here), because the vine's primary aim is to make as many seeds as possible, not luscious fruits. Wild vines also use up energy that could go to the fruits in feeding all that wood that carries the plant high into the trees. And a free-growing vine tangles around itself, creating dark and dank conditions with many dead and diseased branches.

Convinced that your fruiting vine needs pruning? Fruiting vines vary in their bearing habits as well as the quantity of fruit they can ripen to highest quality, so maintenance pruning for each plant is detailed in the Plant List. The one common thread is that they all do need annual pruning in order to bear good yields of savory fruits, to remain healthy, and to keep the fruit easily accessible.

Renovating a fruiting vine

Fruiting vines are easy to renovate. The simplest way to do it is to lop the whole plant, while it is dormant, down to the ground. (With evergreen vines, lop in winter, when the plant is resting.) Treat new growth just as you would on a young plant—a very vigorous "young" plant, with that grown-up root system now fueling fewer buds.

Because you miss out on a year or more of fruit when you lop the whole plant to the ground, you might opt for a less drastic method of renovation. In this case, peer among the stems and select a new trunk, then side arms or cordons, whatever is needed. Cut away everything else. As with the more drastic renovation, prune while the plant is dormant, both for its sake and because if the vine is deciduous, you can more easily see its stems when they are leafless.

Even with the latter renovation, you will be surprised at how much wood you remove from the plant. Renovating a vine will seem ruthless, but don't worry—the plants recover well and quickly.

Plant List

Acerola cherry *(Malpighia glabra):* Prune this evergreen shrub only as needed to shape it.

Almond *(Prunus dulcis* var. *dulcis):* Train the young tree to an open-center form. Once you have selected your tree's main branches and eliminated others, only a minimum amount of pruning is needed. Nuts are borne mostly on spurs on older wood, although some varieties also bear laterally on one-year-old wood. As your tree ages, prune to keep the interior of the crown open and to stimulate some growth for new fruiting wood. Pruning, fertilization, and watering should result in 6 in. to 10 in. of new growth each year. Rather than pruning every year, you can instead make larger cuts and prune every two or three years.

Apple *(Malus sylvestris):* Which of the three common methods of training—central leader, modified central leader, or open center—is most suitable for a particular tree will depend on the variety. Train an upright grower such as 'Red Delicious' or 'Jonathan', especially if grown on a vigorous rootstock, as a central leader, because that is its natural inclination. 'Golden Delicious' has a naturally spreading habit, so can be trained to an open-center form.

Keep pruning to a minimum during the formative period, or you will unduly delay fruiting. The "dwarf pyramid," as promoted in many British publications, is a small, central-leader tree whose scaffold limbs are repeatedly headed in order to develop a dense pyramid—unfortunately at the expense of early fruiting. Nonetheless, your tree may need an occasional heading cut to invigorate a stem or to promote branching, especially if the plant is a weak grower such as 'Empire' or a so-called "spur-type" variety. A weak tree on a dwarfing rootstock needs rather severe heading to prevent its becoming a runt bearing too many fruits too early in its life. On a tree that is growing moderately or vigorously, bend stems toward a horizontal position when you want to promote branching. This technique will also slow growth and promote early fruiting.

Apples have been grown so extensively and for so long (even the Latin word for "apple," *pomum*, also meant "fruit") that many training systems have been developed. Apples are ideal for the centuries-old practice of espalier, a method of growing treated in a separate section of this book (pp. 219-222). In the last few decades, a number of training systems have been developed to capitalize on the ability of dwarf trees to yield prodigious quantities of fruit (for the amount of space they occupy), and to do so early in their life. I'll discuss one of these systems, the slender spindle, a few paragraphs hence, on p. 142.

Once an apple tree matures, it requires only moderate pruning. Most varieties bear their fruits on spurs, which are stubby branches elongating only about ½ in. per year. (If a branch on an apple tree mutates to become especially spurry and new trees are propagated from this branch, then you have a "spur-type" variety, such as 'Macspur' and 'Sturdeespur Delicious'.) Because spurs grow off wood that is more than two years old, an apple tree needs little new growth to keep fruitful. Some varieties—'Gala' is one example—also flower on one-year-old wood, but fruit set is poor and fruits are small from such flowers.

(continued on page 142)

Apple spurs, on which fruits are borne, eventually need to be thinned to prevent overcrowding and to make way for new growth.

Prune your mature tree mostly when it is dormant. Completely cut away overly vigorous stems, most common high in the tree, as well as weak twigs, which often hang from the undersides of limbs. Shorten stems that become too droopy, especially those low in the tree. After about ten years, those fruiting spurs become overcrowded and decrepit, so thin out and shorten them to invigorate them and give them more room. When a whole limb of fruiting spurs declines with age, cut it back to make room for a younger replacement.

Slender spindle is a productive way to grow apple trees.

A few apple varieties—'Cortland' and 'Idared', for example—do not bear fruits on spurs, but at the ends of willowy stems about 6 in. long. Train these so-called tip bearers to open-center or modified-central-leader form. Avoid shortening too many stems on mature trees or you will end up cutting off too much of your potential crop. Leave stems of moderate length, and encourage compactness and branching by shortening very long stems instead.

Pruning apple trees in summer can have some benefits. In some cases, summer-pruning promotes fruit-bud formation. This approach is used mostly with apples grown as espaliers, so is dealt with in that section of the book (pp. 219-222). Summer pruning also can enhance the red color of red apples. Cutting away some shoots just before the fruits begin to ripen lets them bathe in light, which is needed to make them rosy red.

The slender spindle system is a relatively new way to train and prune an apple tree, bringing with it the advantages of high yields and early fruiting—usually in the tree's second season! The essence of this system is to begin with a branched young tree, if possible, then do an absolute minimum of pruning and keep bending branches towards the horizontal. Dwarf rootstocks are a must, and the tree must be supported by a sturdy post throughout its life.

Begin training your slender spindle its first season. As soon as you plant, cut off any branches within 1 ft. of the ground, and head back the leader 10 in. above the highest branch. Also cut off any upright branches on the upper portion of the tree, any that are more than half as thick as the leader, and any that are crowding. If your tree is merely a whip, head it back to 2½ ft. to 3 ft. above ground level. Varieties that make many spurs are shy to branch, so head these varieties more severely. As the season progresses, branches will grow. About midsummer, bend them almost to a horizontal position with weights or with strings tied to stakes in the ground. To maintain a moderate amount of vigor in spur-type varieties, do not bend their branches too low.

Continue the following seasons as you did the first season. Head the leader, select new branches, and bend the branches. To dampen the increasing vigor of branches higher up in the tree, bend them increasingly lower. If any branches grow too long, shorten them early

(continued on page 144)

Training a Slender Spindle

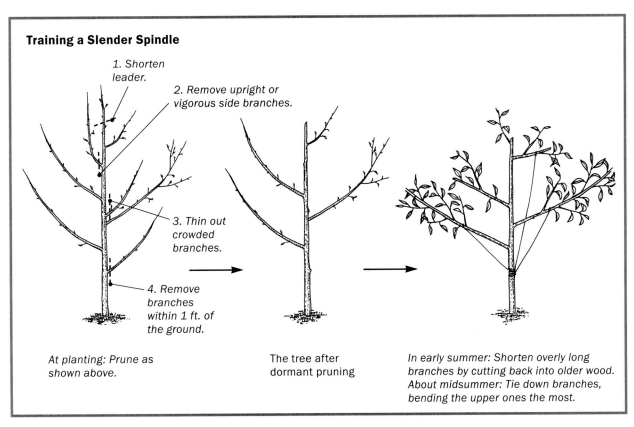

1. Shorten leader.

2. Remove upright or vigorous side branches.

3. Thin out crowded branches.

4. Remove branches within 1 ft. of the ground.

At planting: Prune as shown above.

The tree after dormant pruning

In early summer: Shorten overly long branches by cutting back into older wood. About midsummer: Tie down branches, bending the upper ones the most.

Maintenance Pruning of a Slender Spindle

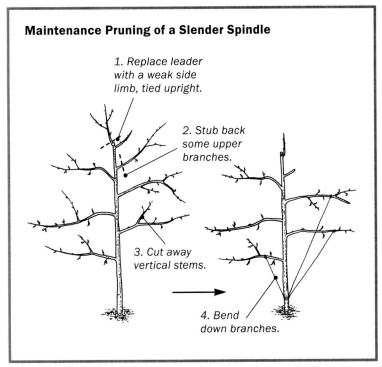

1. Replace leader with a weak side limb, tied upright.

2. Stub back some upper branches.

3. Cut away vertical stems.

4. Bend down branches.

Thinning Old Apple Spurs

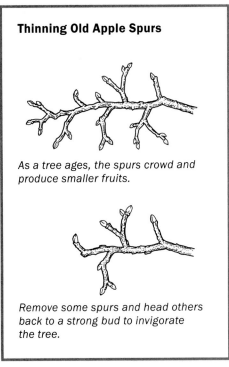

As a tree ages, the spurs crowd and produce smaller fruits.

Remove some spurs and head others back to a strong bud to invigorate the tree.

in the season, when new growth is a few inches long, back into older wood. Do not shorten branches the same year that you bend them; wait a year or two. Prune and regulate growth so that branches make your tree taper out from top to bottom.

Maintenance pruning of a slender spindle begins when the tree reaches a height of 6 ft. or 7 ft. Each year, cut back the leader, while it is dormant, to a weak lateral, then tie the lateral in an upright position to the pole—that's your tree's "safety valve," to take up excess vigor. Periodically cut old branches high in the tree back to stubs, from which will grow renewal branches, or to fruit buds. Remove excess vertical shoots and bend down those you retain. If the lower limbs grow too wide, cut them back into older wood (see the drawing at top right on p. 143).

No matter what training and pruning system you use for apple trees, if you do it correctly, you will eventually be rewarded with a snowball of bloom in spring. That leaves you one more pruning job: fruit thinning. Apples respond thankfully to a 5-in. spacing, with no more that one fruit per flower cluster. Don't worry, only about 5% fruit set constitutes a full crop following a snowball bloom. (And each fruit needs the work of 40 leaves for nourishment.)

Apricot *(Prunus Armeniaca):* Apricot is susceptible to a number of diseases that infect the wood, so prune just before growth begins in spring. Where springs are wet, summers are dry, and there is ample time for wood to harden off before cold weather, you can even wait until summer to prune.

Train the young tree to an open-center or modified-central-leader form. Trained against a wall as a fan-shaped espalier, the blossoms, which open very early in spring, can be easily protected from frost. (See p. 222 for information on training and pruning an apricot espalier.)

Because an apricot tree bears fruit on wood from one to three years old, prune enough to stimulate a moderate amount of new growth

each year. Using a combination of heading and thinning cuts, strive for new-shoot growth of 12 in. to 18 in. and plenty of light bathing all the branches. Cut away older wood, as well as diseased or dead wood. More severe pruning will reduce your crop, but the fruits will be larger. Fruit thinning is unnecessary unless the crop is very heavy, in which case thin the fruits so that they are about 2 in. apart.

Avocado *(Persea americana):* Prune avocado after the particular variety's normal harvest season. The time varies: June for the variety 'Fuerte', autumn for 'Haas', and so forth.

Although avocado wood is weak, the branches are firmly anchored, so that little pruning is needed in developing a tree's framework. Just make sure that the trunk is sturdy enough to hold up the tree. At a windy site, slow upward growth of a young tree to give the trunk a chance to thicken. With an upright variety such as 'Zutano', pinch terminals as the tree grows to promote low branching. Otherwise, you will have to climb high in a ladder to pick most of the fruit when the tree is mature.

Even the mature avocado tree needs little pruning beyond the removal of diseased, dead, or misplaced wood. You can use pruning to control the tree's size. Severe pruning does not stop this tree from flowering with abandon (although fruit set is reduced), but watch for sunburn on once-shaded bark. If your pruning does suddenly expose the bark, paint it with diluted white latex paint. Rather than pruning to keep a tree small, consider planting a naturally dwarf variety such as 'Gwenn' or 'Whitsell'.

Banana *(Musa acuminata):* Although a banana plant might grow to a height of 20 ft. or more, the true stem of the plant is the rhizome, the thickened, underground stem at the base of the plant. The above-ground portion of the plant is herbaceous, a tightly wound sheath of leaves—a pseudostem—with new leaves, and, finally, a cluster of fruits, pushing up from below. After fruiting, a particular pseudostem dies (but not the whole rhizome), at which point you should cut it down.

A single rhizome produces more than one pseudostem, and your other pruning task is to reduce the number of pseudostems to prevent excessive shading and competition for water and nutrients. As a general rule, allow three pseudostems per plant: one fruiting, one ready to follow, and one just peeking up from below. Pseudostems that you save should be spaced out around the rhizome. If you have a choice, remove pseudostems originating high on the rhizome, because they are poorly anchored and apt to topple from wind. Also remove short pseudostems having very broad leaves, which indicate some problems during emergence. Remove a pseudostem by forcing a machete downward between the pseudostem and the rhizome.

A bulbous male flower precedes the female flowers, which become the bananas you eat. The females do not need to be fertilized to make fruits, so you can cut off the male flower, possibly diverting more energy into the developing fruits—whether or not it does, you can eat the male flower.

Blackberry (*Rubus* spp.): Cultivated blackberries may be erect, semi-erect, or trailing. All types have perennial roots but biennial stems—called "canes"—which fruit their second season, then die. Annual pruning is a must.

Plants are usually sold bare root and dormant, and if this is the case with your plants, cut all canes to ground level right after you plant. This prevents disease carryover on old canes as well as premature fruiting, and stimulates the growth of buds below ground. To keep fruit off the ground and make harvesting easier, train plants to a trellis, which can be as simple as two wires—one at 3 ft. and the other at 5 ft. above ground level—strung between sturdy posts. Trellising is not absolutely necessary with erect blackberries.

After this banana pseudostem bears fruit, it will be replaced by a younger pseudostem.

Prune erect and semi-erect blackberries twice each year (see the top drawing on p. 146). In summer, pinch out the tips of new canes just as they reach a height of 3 ft. Pinching induces the growth of lateral branches, which will bear fruit the following season. All canes do not reach this height simultaneously, so go over the planting a few times during the summer. Prune again while the plants are dormant, first removing, at ground level, all canes that fruited the previous season. (You could, instead, have cut them away during the summer, right after harvest.) Also remove any young canes that are crowded, spindly, or diseased. Finally, shorten the fruiting laterals to a length of 12 in. to 18 in., allowing more growth on the sturdier laterals because they can bear more fruit.

Prune trailing blackberries by first cutting away any canes that have fruited. Do this right after harvest or when the plants are dormant. While the plants are dormant, also thin out new canes to the most vigorous eight to ten per plant. Shorten overly long canes to 7 ft. and laterals to between 12 in. and 18 in.

(continued on page 147)

Pruning Erect and Semi-Erect Blackberries

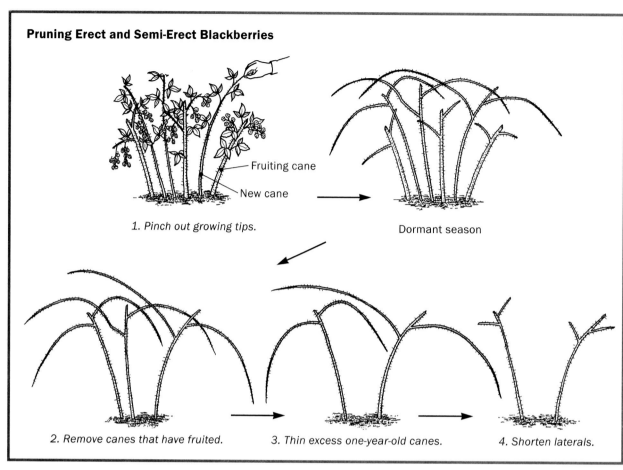

Fruiting cane

New cane

1. Pinch out growing tips.

Dormant season

2. Remove canes that have fruited.

3. Thin excess one-year-old canes.

4. Shorten laterals.

Pruning Trailing Blackberries (Dormant Season)

1. Cut away canes that have fruited.

2. Thin new canes to about 10 per plant.

3. Shorten new canes to about 7 ft.

4. Shorten laterals to 12 in. to 18 in.

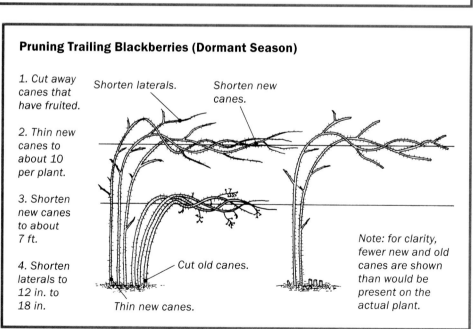

Shorten laterals.

Shorten new canes.

Cut old canes.

Thin new canes.

Note: for clarity, fewer new and old canes are shown than would be present on the actual plant.

After you dormant-prune trailing black-berries, weave or tie the canes up to the trellis. You can just let each season's new canes trail along the ground, where they will be out of the way of the fruiting canes. Or train new canes on one wire or in one direction along the trellis, and fruiting canes along the other wire or in the other direction.

Blueberry *(Vaccinium* spp.): The three species of cultivated blueberries—highbush (*V. corymbosum*), rabbiteye *(V. asheii),* and lowbush *(V. angustifolium)*—bear fruits on one-year-old wood, but their pruning needs vary because of their widely differing growth habits. They are all bushy, with lowbush plants growing only about 1 ft. high, highbush plants growing about 6 ft. high, and rabbiteye plants soaring to 15 ft. or more. The only pruning these species need the first three years is removal of dead and diseased stems. If you can bring yourself to do it, remove flowers the first few years to divert energy into shoot growth rather than fruits.

A highbush blueberry stem typically remains productive for about four years, so the first step in annual dormant pruning of these plants is to cut away, near ground level, stems more than four years old. After that, head back young, weak stems less than ¼ in. thick to strong branches or buds, and remove older twiggy growth. Thin out stems in the center of the bush if they are crowded and shorten or remove stems that droop to the ground. Certain varieties, such as 'Cabot' and 'Pioneer', produce an excessive number of fruit buds on fruitful shoots. With such vari-eties, shorten each fruiting stem so that it has only three to five fruit buds. These are plump as compared to the pointy vegetative buds.

Prune rabbiteye blueberries in a manner similar to highbush blueberries, but less heavily because of the rabbiteye's inherent vigor. Be careful not to prune so much that you stimulate excessive shoot growth at the expense of fruiting, but prune enough to keep the interior of the bush from becoming too shaded, and to keep the plants from growing too tall. Prune a mature bush mostly by selectively cutting the oldest and largest stems to the ground.

Lowbush blueberries spread beneath the ground with underground stems, called rhizomes, and new shoots originate directly from these rhizomes as well as from buds on stems above ground. The best fruits are borne on the youngest stems, especially those that grow directly from the rhizomes. Therefore, prune lowbush blueberries severely, cutting the plants completely to the ground every second or third winter. The plants do not bear at all the season following pruning, so if you do not want to miss a year of fruit, divide the planting into halves and prune an alternate half of the bed each year. Or divide the planting into thirds and prune a different third each year—the reduced production of second-year stems will be offset by the increased proportion of the bed bearing fruit each year.

Buffalo berry *(Shepherdia* spp.): Buffalo berry bushes require little or no pruning.

Butternut *(Juglans cinerea):* Male flowers appear on one-year-old wood and female flowers appear on growing shoots. Despite the young growth needed for flowers, butternut requires little pruning beyond that needed to train it to a sturdy framework when young, and to remove diseased, broken, or misplaced wood as the tree ages.

Carambola *(Averrhoa Carambola):* See Starfruit

Cashew *(Anacardium occidentale):* Cashew is a sprawling tree that never gets tall and bears plenty of new flowers at the ends of new shoots. The plant needs little pruning.

Cherimoya *(Annona Cherimola):* Prune cherimoya during the brief period just before growth begins, when the plant is leafless. Because the wood is brittle, train the tree to a sturdy framework. Cherimoya has several buds at each leaf, and if a scaffold branch is growing out at too narrow an angle, you can stub it back and a new branch will grow—at

(continued on page 148)

Shortening a blueberry stem leaves fewer plump fruit buds, but the berries will be larger.

a wider angle—from one of the other buds. A cherimoya tree grows rapidly in its youth, then slows down and never becomes very large. Keep the tree even smaller than its natural size if you plan to hand-pollinate, which is often necessary in dry climates.

Fruit is borne mostly on growing shoots, with some fruit also produced at old leaf scars on older wood. Severe pruning reduces flowering on young shoots, as well as fruit set; on the other hand, the trees bear fairly well without any pruning. Nonetheless, moderate pruning is the best course to follow for good fruit size and to minimize breakage of limbs weighed down with fruits at their ends.

Cherry *(Prunus* spp.): A sweet cherry tree *(P. avium)* can grow quite large, and if you want to let it grow to full height, train it as a central leader. To limit height, lop the leader back to a weak branch for a modified central-leader form. Sweet cherry trees have a natural tendency to develop bare stems, devoid of branches. Counteract this tendency by heading the developing leader about 12 in. above the point where you want each tier of scaffold limbs, and similarly head scaffold limbs for secondary branching. Once mature, the tree requires little pruning, because fruits form both on young wood and on spurs on older wood, and because the potential crop does not respond to fruit thinning. Prune just as growth begins in spring.

In contrast to the sweet cherry tree, the tart cherry tree *(P. Cerasus)* is naturally small and spreading. Train tart cherry trees to either open-center or modified central-leader form. Like sweet cherries, tart cherry fruits are borne on young wood and on spurs on older wood. Beyond basic annual pruning, prune tart cherry trees a moderate amount to keep them invigorated. Prune more severely where winters are bitterly cold. Severe pruning will stimulate more vigorous, but less fruitful, young stems, so that most of the fruiting is taken up by flowers on spurs. Flowers on spurs are more cold hardy than those growing laterally on young stems.

Duke cherries *(P. × effusus)* are thought to be natural hybrids of sweet and tart cherries. The fruits, growth habits, and pruning needs of duke cherries lie intermediate between those of the sweets and the tarts.

Nanking cherry *(Prunus tomentosa)* and sand cherry *(P. Besseyi)* are two bush species occasionally grown for their fruits and as ornamentals. Both species fruit well with little or no pruning. During the dormant season, occasionally cut away old stems at ground level, thin out the center of a bush for light and air, and cut away dead or diseased wood.

Cherry-of-the-Rio-Grande *(Eugenia aggregata):* Prune this evergreen shrub only as needed to shape it. Fruits are borne at the bases of new shoots.

Chestnut *(Castanea* spp.): Chestnut needs minimal pruning. Train the young tree to a sturdy framework with a single trunk. Prune the mature tree, which bears flowers on growing shoots (the male catkins toward the ends and bisexual catkins lower down), only to remove crossing, dead, or diseased wood.

Citrus *(Citrus* spp.): Citrus grow as bushy evergreen trees that need little or no pruning—just as well, given the capricious response of citrus to pruning cuts. Do most of what little pruning is necessary just before the spring flush of growth where winters are cold, or anytime in perpetually hot climates. With 'Valencia' oranges or other citrus having some fruit on the branches year round, prune when there is the least fruit on the tree (late summer with 'Valencia').

On the young tree, prune mostly to space branches and to remove suckers growing below the graft. The plant is naturally so bushy that little specific training is needed, or possible. Because it is often hard to force stems into the roles you select for them, wait until a plant is a few years old, and older stems have calmed down in growth, before selecting scaffold limbs. Or just leave the plant to its own whims.

Prune a mature tree just enough to keep it from growing too large and to thin out the interior if it becomes too shaded. Flowers form on older wood as well as in the leaf axils of growing shoots, with the best fruit set on the latter flowers. The bark is susceptible to sunscald, so paint bark with a 50:50 mixture of white latex paint and water whenever your pruning suddenly exposes the bark to the sun. Where brown rot is a problem, prune back low hanging stems so that spores from the soil cannot reach the fruits. Even where brown rot is not a problem, the lower "skirt" of a citrus tree eventually becomes dense with old wood that is not only unproductive, but also interferes with getting at the tree. Fight your way under such a tree, and lop off some of those branches from below to let in light and air.

Lemon trees have a particularly gawky growth habit, naturally making long stems that are easily broken under their weight of fruit. Stems also interlace to make harvesting difficult. Prune a lemon tree frequently and lightly, thinning and shortening stems.

Because citrus wood has many dormant buds, older trees that are healthy but not fruiting satisfactorily can be rejuvenated with drastic pruning. "Skeletonize" a tree by removing all wood thicker than 1 in. to 1½ in. in diameter. "Buckhorning" is a more drastic way of rejuvenating a tree by dramatically lowering it (but also delaying fruiting). Saw all major limbs to 1-ft. long stubs, then remove any remaining twiggy growth. Thin out some of the vigorous shoots that follow buckhorning. With any drastic pruning, remember to paint all newly exposed bark white to prevent sunscald.

In spite of their capricious nature with regard to pruning, citrus can be sheared as hedges or trained as espaliers.

Cranberry *(Vaccinium macrocarpon):* Cranberries are low evergreens whose lanky stems sprawl along the ground. Along the length of the trailing stems grow short, upright fruiting stems. And wherever a

Above: A buckhorned citrus will soon resprout, then become productive again.

Left: This Eureka lemon hedge screens a steep yard from the street.

trailing stem touches moist earth, roots develop. With time, the fruiting stems become overcrowded, and the sprawling stems begin to pile high. Prune cranberries in winter by thinning out fruiting uprights and cutting away some of the sprawling stems.

(continued on page 151)

Pruning Red Currant as a Stool (Dormant Season)

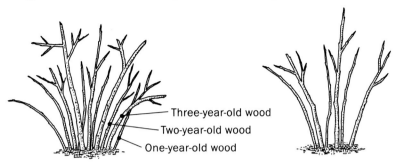

Three-year-old wood
Two-year-old wood
One-year-old wood

1. Cut away all three-year-old wood.

2. Thin out one-year-old wood to about six vigorous upright shoots.

Note: for clarity, three rather than six of each age of shoot are shown.

Pruning Red Currant to a Leg

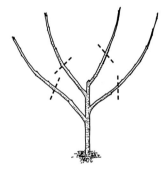

Train three to four stems as a permanent framework, then head them back to promote branching.

Each winter, shorten branches to a few inches. Also remove suckers or shoots originating low on a stem.

If you want especially neat growth, also shorten side shoots to 6 in. in summer...

then to a couple of buds in winter.

Currant *(Ribes* spp.): Red and white currants (various combinations of *R. rubrum, R. sativum,* and *R. petraeum)* are essentially all the same fruit, differing only in color. They bear mostly on two-year-old and three-year old wood, and a little toward the bases of vigorous, year-old shoots. Prune while the plants are dormant. Currants can be pruned as a bush, or "stool," or to a more upright form, or "leg."

To grow a bush as a stool, with new stems originating at or below ground level, prune any shoot right down to the ground after its third season. To prevent overcrowding, also thin out one-year-old stems by cutting to the ground all except a half-dozen of those that are the sturdiest and the most upright.

Especially in Great Britain, red and white currants are sometimes grown with a permanent framework of branches on a "leg," which is a trunk only a few inches long. Train the young bush so that three or four stems grow outward and upward, without crowding, from the leg. Build up a more or less permanent framework of branches by heading these stems to promote branching. Each winter, shorten new stems that grew off the permanent framework branches to a few inches in length. For tighter growth, such as when you espalier a red currant, prune back side shoots in summer to about 6 in. just as the fruit starts to color, then go over those shoots again in winter, shortening them to no more than a couple of buds.

Black currants *(R. nigrum)* bear their best fruits on stems that grew previous season. Each year, while the plants are dormant, cut either to the ground or to a low, vigorous branch any wood that has borne fruit. As an alternative, prune black currants at harvest time, cutting off the fruiting stems (which can then be stripped of their fruits). In either case, go back over the plants while they are dormant, thinning out crowded young stems and removing stems drooping to the ground.

(continued on page 152)

PRUNING BLACK CURRANT

1. 'Consort' black currant, before pruning, has two-year-old stems and one-year-old stems. Black currants bear fruit on one-year-old stems.

2. Prune away, or to vigorous side shoots, all two-year-old stems.

3. After pruning, only the one-year-old fruit-bearing stems remain.

Clove currant *(R. odoratum,* although sometimes called Missouri currant or buffalo currant, and sometimes confused with *R. aureum)* fruits in the same way as red and white currants. With stems arching to the ground, and new suckers popping up even a few feet from the mother plant, clove currant is naturally unkempt. Besides removing old stems and thinning young stems, tidy up the plant by shortening stems arching to the ground. Remove a sucker by grabbing it and jerking upward. Then trace the attached underground stem back to the mother plant, where you can cut it off.

Date *(Phoenix dactylifera):* Like other palms, the date palm has a single growing point at the top of its trunk. At its base, the plant produces offshoots, which can be used for making new plants. To propagate from an offshoot, dig soil away from it, taking care not to injure the roots. Then sever the offshoot from the main plant with a wide chisel or sharp shovel. To reduce water loss, cut off all but a dozen leaves from the offshoot, then keep the leaves wrapped in burlap, with only their tips exposed, for a year after transplanting.

Although more leaves generally mean more and better fruits from a bearing palm tree, there are circumstances that warrant pruning off some leaves. You may have to remove some foliage to make room for positioning bags, if you use them to protect the fruit clusters from rain. Leaf removal also decreases the humidity around the fruits, reducing the incidence of fruit checking and blacknose. Therefore, cut off enough leaves so that the lower ends of the fruit bunches are exposed. Do this in early summer. When this pruning results in the loss of many leaves, as happens with varieties such as 'Halawy' and 'Khadrawy', which have short fruit clusters, you also have to reduce the crop in proportion to the leaf loss.

As your plant ages, remove old and dying leaves. The leaves die after three to seven years, but do not fall off naturally. It is easier to cut the leaves off before their bases become hard and dry. If healthy leaves are damaged by cold, do not cut them off; a good part of each leaf may still be functioning.

Thinning the fruits results in more consistent harvests of higher-quality dates, even when no healthy leaves need to be pruned off. Remove half to three-quarters of the flowers within each bunch by cutting off the ends of all fruit strands, and then completely removing some individual strands. Where strands are numerous and short, as with 'Halawy' and 'Khadrawy', mostly remove whole strands, rather than shorten them. For high-quality, large dates such as 'Medjool', you can reduce the number of fruits by selectively removing flowers on a strand.

Reducing the number of bunches is yet another way to thin the crop. Remove all bunches the first three years that an offset is in the ground, then gradually increase the fruit load each year. A mature 'Deglet Noor', for example, can mature about a dozen bunches, each weighing about 20 lb. Do not overthin date fruits, though, or puffiness, blistering, and blacknose can result. The bearing capacity of a particular date palm depends on growing conditions, plant age, plant vigor, and variety.

Elderberry *(Sambucus canadensis):* Elderberry is a suckering shrub that fruits reasonably well even when neglected. Annual pruning will, however, bring out the best from the plant in terms of beauty and fruit production. Prune when the plant is dormant, thinning out new suckers where they crowd or spread too far, and cutting away wood older than three years old. When you thin suckers, remove first those that are diseased, broken, or most spindly.

Feijoa *(Feijoa Sellowiana):* See Guava

Fig *(Ficus carica):* The fig is an adaptable plant that you can train either as a bush or as a tree. The bush form is preferable where figs are marginally cold hardy; a cold winter might kill back a single trunk of a fig tree, but perhaps not all stems of a fig bush. If you grow fig as a tree, train it to an open-center form or, where sunlight is intense, to a modified open-center form (not a modified central leader!), with stems eventually filling in the center to prevent sunburn. With most varieties, branching is usually sufficient so that few or no heading cuts are needed during training. A notable exception is 'Calimyrna' ('Smyrna'). Training the plant to a sturdy framework is especially important with 'Mission', because of the tendency for this variety's limbs to split under the weight of the crop. With any variety trained as a tree, remove suckers growing near the ground.

A fig plant is capable of bearing fruits laterally toward the end of last year's wood—this early crop is called the "breba" crop—as well as on the current season's growth. Many varieties set fruit without pollination, but some require the assistance of a special wasp (*Blastophaga psenes*) and a nonedible fig (caprifig) to set fruit. With varieties that set both breba and main crops, the breba fruit can be different from the main crop fruit. 'Mission' brebas, for example, are few and small, while the main crop fruits are large, round, and abundant. The variety 'King' needs pollination for the main crop, but not for the breba crop.

How a variety bears its fruit influences pruning technique. 'Beall', 'Flanders', 'King', 'Mission', 'Osborne', 'Pasquale', 'Tena', 'Ventura', and 'Verte' produce good breba crops, so the dormant plants should not be pruned heavily or you will cut off the previous year's wood, which will bear that crop. Prune 'Adriatic' ('Grosse Verte'), 'Alma', 'Blanche', 'Brown Turkey', 'Calimyrna', 'Celeste', 'DiRedo', 'Everbearing', 'Excel', 'Magnolia', and 'Osborne' more heavily, because they yield only light breba crops. Prune 'Kadota' ('Dottato') and 'Panachee' most heavily, for the late crop only. Stems on these last two varieties are commonly stubbed to 3 in. to 4 in., stimulating vigorous new growth that will be loaded all along its length with an especially uniform crop of fruit.

Allowing for varietal differences, prune mature fig plants enough to stimulate new growth (about 1 ft.) each year and to prevent overcrowding of branches. Even varieties grown for their breba crop need pruning to stimulate enough new growth for the next year's crop. Thin out crowded wood and head back long stems, but try to avoid making too many heading cuts, especially on varieties yielding good breba crops. 'Mission' tends to develop large drooping stems from scaffold limbs; cut these off. 'Calimyrna' and 'Kadota' tend to grow long, unbranched stems that eventually bend over and sunburn; shorten or remove them before they age. You can promote an earlier and heavier breba crop on 'Brown Turkey' by cutting off the very tips of the stems just before growth begins for the season.

Because the fruit is such a delicacy and the plants do not mind having their roots confined, figs have long been grown in greenhouses and in pots where the climate is too cold for outdoor figs. (The minimum temperature tolerated depends to a large extent on the variety, but the stems of figs are generally cold hardy to about 15°F.) Root restriction and root pruning of potted figs help check rampant growth and keep the plants fruitful. Summer pruning, by pinching out the growing tip after every foot or so of growth early in the season, is frequently employed to promote profuse branching for a heavier breba crop.

In cold climates, you also could bend the stems to the ground and cover them with soil, dirt, leaves, or other insulating material for protection from cold. To maintain a supply of flexible, fruiting wood, prune such a plant by a renewal system. In autumn, cut to the ground any wood that is two years old (or older, if the plants have not previously been pruned like this), then reduce the number of one-year-old stems. Bend the stems that remain down to the ground slowly, so that they do not break (see the drawing on p. 154). Forcing a spade into the ground to cut the roots on one side of the plant makes it easier to bend the whole top to the ground in the opposite direction. Wait until the weather is sufficiently cold before covering the plant, or else the buried wood will rot. In spring, uncover the plant and pull it upright before growth begins.

(continued on page 154)

Do not prune a fig variety that bears on one-year-old wood too heavily or you will remove the crop.

Filbert *(Corylus* spp.): Filbert grows as a small tree or a large shrub. If you choose to grow the plant as a tree, train it to an open-center form. Prune the mature plant moderately every year, enough to stimulate new growth on which the following year's nuts will be borne, and to reduce the tendency to alternate years of heavy and light cropping. The more one-year-old stems you see when you dormant prune, the greater the present year's potential crop and the more severely you should prune. The combined effects of pruning, fertilization, and water should result in new shoots that grow 6 in. to 10 in. in a season in order to give you consistent crops of large nuts.

Commercial filbert orchards are sometimes pruned by cutting three-quarters of all the wood out of every fifth tree on every fifth year. Pruned trees yield no crop the season following pruning, but very good yields of large nuts for the next couple of years.

British gardeners employ a kind of summer pruning called "brutting" to subdue overly vigorous growth on a filbert tree. To brut, you grab a vigorous stem when it is about 12 in. long, then bend it over enough to break it but leave it hanging on the plant. Brutting allegedly also helps ripen nuts and induce shoots to carry female flowers.

Gooseberry *(Ribes* spp.): A gooseberry bush bears some of its fruits laterally on one-year-old wood, but most fruit is borne on spurs on wood that is two and three years old. Annual pruning improves fruit quality, and makes it easier to reach within the thorny bushes to pluck the berries.

Usually the plant is grown as a "stool," which, after pruning, consists of a half-dozen shoots each of one-, two-, and three-year-old wood, all originating at ground level. Prune a stooled plant when it is dormant, by cutting to the ground some of the one-year-old stems and all those that are more than three years

(continued on page 156)

Overwintering a Fig

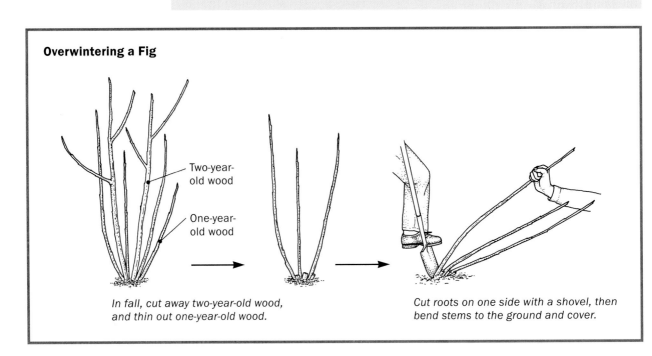

In fall, cut away two-year-old wood, and thin out one-year-old wood.

Two-year-old wood

One-year-old wood

Cut roots on one side with a shovel, then bend stems to the ground and cover.

PRUNING GOOSEBERRIES

1. This 'Welcome' gooseberry bush is awaiting its annual pruning.

2. After cutting to the ground stems that are more than three years old, thin out the youngest stems.

3. Shorten lanky stems because they would lie on the ground once laden with fruit.

4. Thinning some of the remaining stems lets air circulate and makes harvesting easier.

5. Here is 'Welcome' ready for another season.

Pruning a Gooseberry 'Tree'

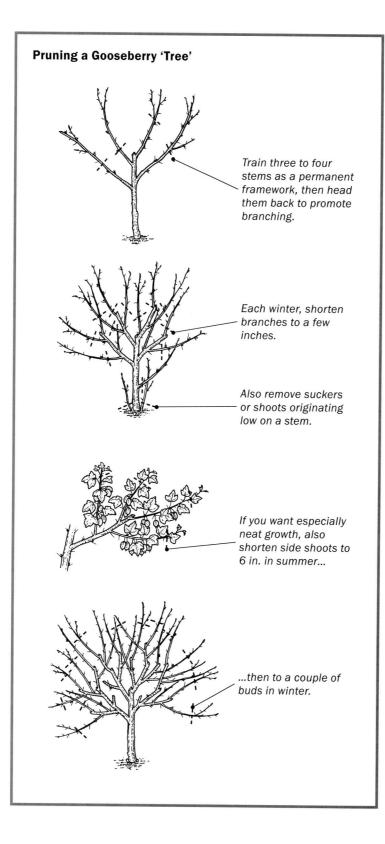

Train three to four stems as a permanent framework, then head them back to promote branching.

Each winter, shorten branches to a few inches.

Also remove suckers or shoots originating low on a stem.

If you want especially neat growth, also shorten side shoots to 6 in. in summer...

...then to a couple of buds in winter.

old. Darkening and peeling bark on older stems helps you distinguish them from younger stems. Also shorten lanky stems that otherwise would droop to the ground under their load of fruit.

Another way to grow gooseberry is as a small tree, on a "leg," with a trunk only a few inches long, or grafted atop a longer trunk of *R. odoratum*, *R. aureum*, *R. divaricatum*, *R. nidigrolaria*, or *R. sanguineum*. For tree forms, train the head of a young plant to a permanent framework of three or four branches pointing upward and outward. Shorten these stems each winter for a couple of years to induce further branching and create a permanent framework.

Side shoots will grow off the permanent framework. Prune these side shoots according to how neat you like your plants and how large you like your gooseberries. More severe pruning gives a neater bush with fewer, yet larger, fruits. At the very least, each winter cut away any side shoots that are crossing, drooping, or otherwise

Bearing Habit of Grape

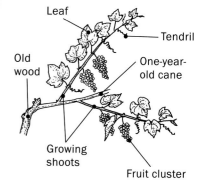

Leaf

Tendril

Old wood

One-year-old cane

Growing shoots

Fruit cluster

Grapes are borne near the bases of growing shoots originating on one-year-old canes.

misplaced. Very vigorous side shoots can be left to fruit if they are not overcrowding the bush, or they can be cut away entirely.

If your goal is really tidy plants and really large gooseberries, shorten all side shoots in early July to about 5 in. Then, during the winter, cut them back again, to about 2 in. Summer pruning also has the benefit of incidentally removing tips of stems infected with powdery mildew, and this may help limit the spread of disease.

Grape (*Vitis* spp.): Grapes are borne, of course, on vines, and these vines are capable of prodigious growth. The three types of grapes cultivated for their fruit are the European wine grape (*V. vinifera*, also known as the vinifera grape), the American grape (mostly *V. labrusca*, also known as the fox grape), and the muscadine grape (*V. rotundifolia*). Annual dormant pruning is necessary for any grape vine to remain healthy and bear the best-tasting fruits, with all those fruits conveniently within reach. Be ready to prune off quite a bit from your vine—over three-quarters of the previous year's growth!

Grapes bear fruits mostly near the bases of shoots growing from canes, which are one-year-old stems. You can easily distinguish a cane from older wood because the bark on a cane is smooth and tan, whereas that on older wood is dark and peeling. Not all canes are equally fruitful. Those that are most fruitful are moderately vigorous, about pencil thick, with 6 in. to 12 in. of space from node to node. Generally, it is the first few buds on a vinifera or a muscadine cane that give rise to fruitful shoots; therefore, these varieties are "spur pruned," with their fruitful canes shortened drastically. On American grapes, those fruitful shoots arise from buds farther out along the canes, so these varieties are "cane pruned," leaving fewer but longer canes; see the sidebar on p. 158 for one cane-pruned system. (The so-called French-American hybrids bear similarly to American grapes, as do the following vinifera varieties: 'Thompson Seedless', 'Chardonnay', 'Sauvignon Blanc', 'White Riesling', 'Barbera',

'Cabernet Sauvignon', 'Grenache', and 'Salvador'. Cane-prune all of these.)

With a spur-pruned vine, all of the previous season's growth is cut back to one to four buds—these shortened canes are now "fruiting spurs." (Do not count the cluster of buds at the very base of a cane.)

Below: This grape vine consists of a trunk topped by two horizontal cordons off which are growing last year's fruiting canes.

Left: The vine has been spur pruned by shortening all canes back to about two buds and thinning some out where overcrowded.

The fatter canes, which are capable of bearing more fruit, can be left longest. Adjust the total number of buds that you leave on the plant according to its vigor, allowing more buds when the previous season's growth was more vigorous. When you finish pruning, the spur-pruned vine will look like a small tree, with a 6-ft. trunk capped by a cluster of fruiting spurs and, soon, growing shoots.

(continued on page 159)

The Kniffin System for Training Grape Vines

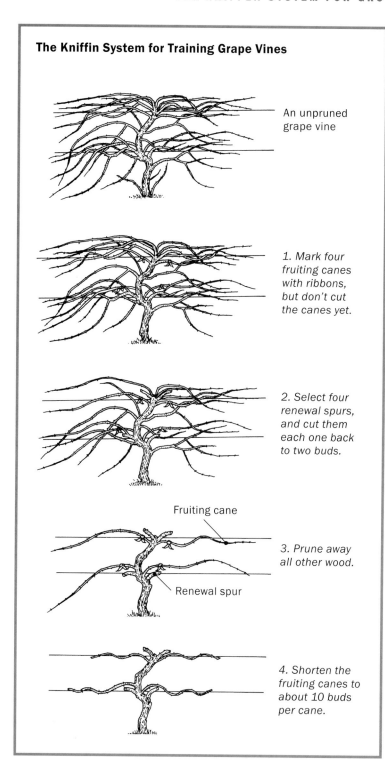

An unpruned grape vine

1. Mark four fruiting canes with ribbons, but don't cut the canes yet.

2. Select four renewal spurs, and cut them each one back to two buds.

Fruiting cane

3. Prune away all other wood.

Renewal spur

4. Shorten the fruiting canes to about 10 buds per cane.

T he Four-arm Kniffin System is a common method of growing a cane-pruned vine, using, for support, a two-wire trellis, with one wire 6 ft. and the other wire 3 ft. above ground. The mature plant consists of a trunk with four canes growing from it, two trained in opposite directions along the upper wire and two similarly trained along the lower wire. Prune while the vine is dormant, beginning by selecting four canes to carry the season's fruits. These canes should be moderately vigorous and originate close to the trunk and near the wires. You are going to save these canes, so mark them with ribbons so that you do not accidentally cut them off. With this year's fruiting canes selected, plan for the following season's crop by forcing new shoots (which will become fruiting canes in a year) to grow from well-placed short branches, called renewal spurs. Select four branches, two near the upper wire and two near the lower wire, that have plump buds near their bases. The age of the wood to be saved for renewal spurs is unimportant, just as long as the wood has healthy buds near its base. Form the renewal spurs by cutting each of these well-placed branches back to two to four buds. Next, cut away all growth except for the renewal spurs and the canes you saved. Finally, shorten each of the canes to about 6 ft. in length, leaving about 10 buds per cane. The more vigorously the cane grew the last season, the less you need to shorten it.

Spur-pruned or cane-pruned vines can also be grown as cordons. A cordon is a permanent arm from which grow fruiting canes and renewal spurs, or, in the case of a spur-pruned vine, only fruiting spurs. A cordon is ideal for covering an arbor. With a cane-pruned variety, select canes and renewal spurs that are well spaced along the cordon, then cut away all other wood. With a spur-pruned variety, just stub all growth to within a few buds of the cordon. In either case, prune enough so that there is about 1 ft. of space between canes or fruiting spurs along the cordon. Because muscadine grapes can support such large crops, the plants are commonly grown as large single or multiple cordons.

As might be expected of a plant that has been cultivated for thousands of years, many ways have been devised for training grapes.

Different methods of training influence the amount of heat, air, and sunlight the growing vine is exposed to, all of which can influence fruit quality and ripening. In very cold climates, consider training a vine to multiple trunks—in case of winter damage to one—or to a low trunk that grows from ground level at an angle so that canes can be laid on the ground and mulched for winter protection. With the latter method, tie the canes along a low wire just before growth begins. Then, as the growing season progresses, tie fruiting shoots growing from these canes to an upper wire, to bathe in sunlight and air. Old trunks are most susceptible to winter cold damage, so periodically replace an old trunk with a young one, not even sacrificing one season's harvest if you trained your vine to multiple trunks.

(continued on page 160)

Pruning Cordon-Trained Grapes

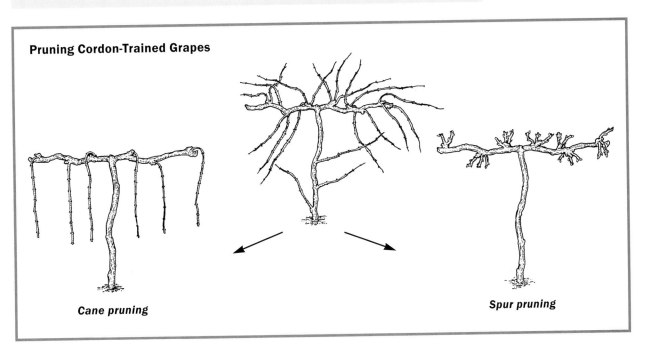

Cane pruning

Spur pruning

Special techniques have evolved to increase fruit quality. Removing some clusters or berries within clusters increases the size and quality of fruits that remain. Thin fruits early in the season, and when thinning excess clusters, selectively remove those toward the end of a shoot. On spur-pruned varieties, generally allow only one cluster per shoot. In cold climates, fruit thinning also hastens ripening and leaves the vine more hardy going into winter. Clipping off leaves around a cluster can increase air circulation and decrease diseases. And girdling the bark of a healthy vine as fruits are setting can increase berry size, while girdling as ripening begins can hasten ripening.

Thinning grapes within a cluster decreases disease and makes the remaining berries tastier and larger.

For centuries, vinifera grapes have been grown in greenhouses—and some of those vines are centuries old! Because of limited space, the size of the vine must be restricted by a combination of winter and summer pruning. Where space permits, grapes can be trellised and grown the same as outdoor grapes, always balancing the number of fruits left with the amount of light available and the amount of foliage that space allows.

The traditional method for growing greenhouse grapes is to train a single shoot from the outside wall up along the ridge to the peak of the house. (Where climate permits, the roots can be planted just outside the greenhouse and the vine threaded in through a hole low in the wall. This practice has been used to force grapes out of season or to make possible growing them where summers are not warm enough.) As the single shoot is trained up to the peak, any laterals that appear are pinched as soon as they have four leaves; sublaterals are completely removed. In winter, shorten the single shoot and cut off the laterals.

That single shoot becomes the permanent cordon of the established vine. Once the vine is fruiting, each winter shorten all laterals to single bud spurs. Two flowering shoots typically grow from each spur, and once flowers show, remove the weaker of the two shoots. Tie the remaining shoot to a crosswire support and pinch out its growing tip, three leaves past the last bunch to show. Remove lateral shoots as they appear and when flowers open, remove all but one flowering cluster per flowering shoot. Mmmmmmm.

Grumichama *(Eugenia brasiliensis):* Prune this evergreen shrub only as needed to shape it.

Guava *(Psidium* spp. and *Feijoa Sellowiana):* Guavas are represented by two botanical genera, both of which are in the Myrtle family. The plants are similar in that they both become medium-sized shrubs or small trees, depending on how you want to train them. Both also are ornamental and can be grown as informal bushes, or, with some sacrifice of fruit, can be sheared for a formal effect.

The common guava *(P. Guajava)* and the strawberry guava *(P. littorale* var. *longipes)* bear their fruits in leaf axils of growing shoots. For best fruiting, prune heavily to stimulate new fruiting shoots and to prevent limb breakage by fruits borne far out on the periphery of the plant.

Feijoa, sometimes called pineapple guava (*Feijoa Sellowiana*), bears fruit towards the base of the previous season's wood. So that you can enjoy both the flowers and the taste of the fruits, do what little pruning is necessary after flowers fade in spring. The fleshy petals, purple tinged white, are as tasty as they are pretty.

Hazelnut (*Corylus* spp.): See Filbert

Jaboticaba (*Myrciaria cauliflora):* Jaboticaba is a slow-growing, evergreen tree with the unusual habit of bearing single fruits or clusters of fruit right on the bark and large limbs and on out to the tips of small branches. No pruning is needed.

Jackfruit (*Artocarpus heterophyllus):* This odd tree bears fruits right on the trunk and larger limbs—and a good thing, too, because each fruit can weight 40 lb. or more! The tree itself can grow large, so prune it when you want to control its size.

Jostaberry (*Ribes nidigrolaria):* Jostaberry is a relatively new fruit, a hybrid of gooseberry, European black currant, and Worcesterberry. Fruits develop laterally on one-year-old wood as well as on spurs of older wood. This robust bush needs annual dormant pruning to keep it from growing too large and to thin the fruits. Each year cut away at ground level one or two of the oldest stems, and thin out any overcrowded young stems.

Jujube (*Ziziphus Jujuba):* Jujube is a small to medium-sized tree that requires little or no regular pruning by you. One reason is that many of the branches that grow at each node are deciduous, falling from the plant at the end of the growing season. The roots tend to sucker, often sending up shoots many feet from the mother plant, and an appropriate tool for removing the suckers is a lawn-mower. In China, where jujubes are very popular, fruit yield on mature trees is increased by girdling right after the blossoms fade. But before you go at your tree with your girdling knife, be aware that the crop is increased at some sacrifice of sweetness.

Juneberry (*Amelanchier* spp.): Both tree and bush species of juneberries are grown for their fruits. The tree species require little pruning, and even at that, not every year. The bush species most commonly grown for its fruit is the saskatoon (*A. alnifolia*). On this plant, stems that are between one and four years old bear the best fruit. Older stems bear fruits that tend to be small and dryish. Therefore, cut to the ground any stems more than four years old and thin out, again at ground level, stems that grew the previous season, leaving only a half-dozen of the most vigorous ones.

Kiwifruit (*Actinidia* spp.): Besides the fuzzy kiwifruit (*A. deliciosa*), other *Actinidia* species are cultivated for their equally delicious fruit. Most notable among these are the so-called "hardy kiwifruits," *A. arguta* and *A. Kolomikta*. All the plants are rampant vines that need to be pruned twice a year.

Although they can casually and decoratively clothe arbors and pergolas, train kiwi plants to a trellis if you want the maximum amount of fruit and if you want that fruit to be easy to pick. A single wire strung between posts could have a cordon trained along it with fruiting arms drooping down. Better, though, is a trellis consisting of T-shaped supports, 6 ft. high with 6-ft. crossarms, and three to five 12-gauge wires strung between crossarms (see the drawing at left on p. 162).

No matter what kind of support you provide, initially restrict the vine to a single shoot and get it up off the ground by tying it, as it grows, to a post. Pinch off any other shoots that attempt to grow off the primary shoot or from the ground. When the trunk-to-be reaches the height of the middle wire of the T-trellis (or the wire of the single-wire trellis), pinch out the tip to make two new shoots, which you can train as permanent cordons along the wire in either direction.

Lateral shoots, which will be the fruiting arms, will grow off this cordon and either drape over the outside wires or directly down. Stimulate the growth of these fruiting arms by shortening the developing cordon every year, during the dormant season, to within 2 ft. of where it began growth the previous season. If the tip of the cordon ever stops growing or makes tight, thin curls around the wire, cut it back to a strong bud to jump-start

(continued on page 162)

Jackfruit is enormous and odd-looking, but delectable.

vigorous growth again. Thin out fruiting arms so that they are 1 ft. apart along the cordon, then tie the arms to the outside wire of the T-trellis so that wind cannot whip them around.

Once each cordon is about 7 ft. long, your plant has filled its trellis. After that, annual dormant pruning is as follows: First, shorten each cordon to the point where it began growth the previous season. Next, stimulate shoot growth for next year's fruit, because fruits are borne toward the bases of currently growing shoots arising from wood that grew the previous season. The fruiting arms give rise to laterals that fruit at their bases, and during each dormant season, shorten each lateral so that it is 18 in. long. Buds on these laterals will likewise grow into shoots that fruit at their bases in the subsequent season. In winter, shorten these sublaterals to 18 in., and remove those that are crossing or spindly. Following winter pruning, retain only a single strong fruiting cane, either the original arm or one of its laterals or sublaterals. When a fruiting arm with its lateral, sublateral, and subsublateral is two or three years old, cut it away to make the room for a new fruiting arm.

Did you notice how similar the fruiting habit of kiwifruit is to grape? As expected, you also could treat them in a similar fashion, each year cutting back fruiting arms to replacement arms near their point of origin.

Kiwifruit vines are strong growers that also need summer pruning to keep them in bounds. Keep the main trunk clear of shoots by cutting them away any time you notice them. Shorten excessively rampant shoots growing from the cordons to short stubs, leaving buds for future replacement arms. Cut away tangled shoots before the vine starts to strangle itself. And finally, shorten fruiting arms and their laterals if they get too long.

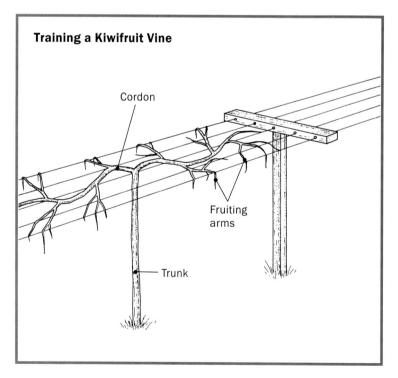

Training a Kiwifruit Vine

Cordon

Fruiting arms

Trunk

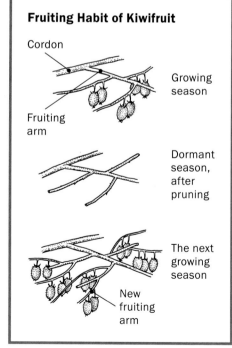

Fruiting Habit of Kiwifruit

Cordon

Fruiting arm

Growing season

Dormant season, after pruning

The next growing season

New fruiting arm

Because male plants are needed only for their bloom, prune them severely right after they bloom, removing about 70% of the previous year's growth. Cut back any flowering shoot to a new shoot, which will flower the following year. Male vines do not need to put any energy into fruit production, so they generally are more vigorous than female vines.

Litchi *(Litchi chinensis):* Litchi grows to be a round-topped evergreen tree that is ornamental in its own right, and made more so when loaded with the red fruits that form at the ends of stems. The tree can be reluctant to flower (making it only a handsome ornamental) because flowering requires just enough cold (or drought) to induce dormancy, but not so much as to damage this somewhat cold-tender tree. Careful management is thus required to keep a tree fruitful wherever the climate is less than ideal. Litchi is a native of China, where the traditional advice is that you should "keep the tree calm" for fruitfulness. Prune when the fruit is ripe, cutting off the last foot or so of stems as you harvest clumps of fruit. In summer, pinch new growth. To control tree size, cut away upright stems. In climates where winters are too warm or wet to induce the natural dormancy needed for flowering, try girdling selected stems in autumn.

Fruit set is usually good when a plant does flower. Although rarely practiced, fruit thinning can increase fruit size.

Longan *(Euphoria Longan):* Longan requires regular pruning so that the plant has good form and produces regular crops of good-sized fruits. Large panicles of flowers form at the ends of stems, and if fruit set is good, the resulting fruits will be undersized and next year's crop will be reduced. Avoid this by thinning the fruits, cutting back whole stems that terminate in fruiting panicles. Longan stems also have a natural tendency to be bare except toward their ends. Head these stems back to stimulate the growth of laterals.

Loquat *(Eriobotrya japonica):* Loquat is a small evergreen tree growing in flushes through the year, with the largest flush in spring. Prune the young tree so that its stems are well spaced. On the mature tree, flowers form at the ends of some shoots as they cease elongating. Even though only a dozen or fewer flowers are likely to set fruit from clusters of 50 or more, further fruit thinning is often necessary. Clip off whole clusters or individual fruitlets at any time through winter until early spring. The tree needs little other pruning beyond occasional shortening of stems (which incidentally thins fruit) to let light within the canopy. Remove wood infected with fire blight.

Macadamia *(Macadamia integrifolia, M. tetraphylla):* Train young trees to a central leader. Leaves form in whorls, with three buds above each leaf. The uppermost bud gives rise to an upright shoot, which is fine for extending the leader of a young tree, but makes a weak scaffold limb. Strive to space branches about 1 ft. apart along the leader, heading the leader if no branches are growing where you want them. If one of the upper of the three buds starts growing to become an upright scaffold limb, cut it back and a lower bud will grow into a wide-angled scaffold limb. Reduce the number of branches where they crowd on a scaffold limb.

Macadamia bears racemes consisting of up to 100 flowers in the axils where leaves are or were attached, but usually sets only about a dozen nuts on each raceme. With heavy flowering and natural thinning, the mature trees need little pruning.

(continued on page 164)

Loquat flowers form at the end of shoots.

Mango *(Mangifera indica):* Train the young mango tree to a sturdy framework, heading back gangly shoots that sometimes develop in order to induce branching. These evergreen trees grow in flushes through the season, with extension growth initially from terminal buds. Hundreds or even thousands of flowers form in panicles at the ends of some stems, and when this happens, further extension is from branches on those stems. If a flower panicle is damaged or does not set any fruit, a new panicle may form laterally on the stem.

Mature mango trees require little pruning, mostly to get rid of dead and crowded wood and to keep the trees from growing too large. Shortening a stem in late summer or fall brings fruit production back within the crown on lateral flower panicles lower on the stem. Control tree height by selectively removing vigorous upright stems. (Commercial growers sometimes hedge mangos—nonselectively cutting all stems growing beyond a certain point—to keep the trees in bounds.) The trees tend to alternate heavy and light crops, and pruning, by removing stems with flower clusters, might help even out yields. Bark girdling in late summer, following harvest, can also help improve yields and decrease vigor, but should be done with caution. One method is to ring individual branches that would be pruned off anyway after harvest.

Mangosteen *(Garcinia Mangostana):* Mangosteen is a small evergreen tree bearing fruits at the ends of shoots. Little pruning is needed beyond the thinning of inner stems.

Medlar *(Mespilus germanica):* A medlar tree needs training in its early years to build up an attractive and sturdy framework. Beyond that, what little pruning is needed is confined to the removal of dead and crossing stems and the thinning out of spindly stems to admit light and air into the canopy. Blossoms are borne singly on the ends of short shoots that grow from lateral buds on one-year-old wood and from spurs on older wood. Be careful not to prune off the extremities of too many branches, for this is where many of the flowering shoots arise. Where winter cold damages the plant, the year-old stems bear more of the fruits than the less hardy spurs. Prune accordingly.

Mulberry *(Morus spp.):* Once you have trained your mulberry tree to a sturdy framework, no special pruning techniques are required. Fruits are abundant, appearing from axillary buds of growing shoots and on spurs on older wood. Prune only as needed to remove dead, exhausted, and overcrowded wood. To train a mulberry to a tidy form, develop a set of main limbs, then prune branches growing off these limbs to six leaves in July in order to make short, fruiting spurs.

Natal Plum *(Carissa grandiflora):* Prune this evergreen shrub only as needed to shape it.

Nectarine *(Prunus Persica var. nucipersica):* The nectarine is nothing but a fuzzless peach, differing from the peach only in the gene that makes fuzz. Refer to "Peach" (p. 166) for specific pruning guidelines.

Olive *(Olea europaea):* Olive can grow to be an ancient tree, with strong yet limber wood. Unpruned, the plant grows dense with twigs and sends up many basal sprouts, making it more of a shrub than a tree in its youth. Train the young plant to an open-center form with three scaffold limbs, thinning out overcrowded wood and watersprouts, and heading back drooping wood. Rub off buds near ground level that threaten to become suckers; once a sucker takes hold, pull it off rather than cut it back, to reduce the possibility of resprouting. To hasten fruiting, keep your pruning to the absolute minimum. Wait until the tree has been in the ground for three to five years and is bearing fruit before pruning to develop good secondary branching. Even then, avoid making severe cuts.

Prune the mature tree mostly to keep it from growing too large, to let light bathe all branches, and to encourage a continual supply of new fruiting wood. Fruits form in leaf axils along, but not to the end, of the previous year's stems (and sometimes from dormant buds in one- or two-year-old wood). Many flowers make up each panicle but only three to five fruits per foot is sufficient for a full crop. When fruit set is heavy, fruit thinning will increase fruit size and oil content, hasten fruit maturity, and allow a good crop the following year. The most effective way to thin fruits is by hand, in late spring or early summer. Thinning fruits by pruning stems is effective only with stems bearing heavy loads of fruit, or else too many leaves are proportionately removed. In years of heavy crops, cut some of these stems right after fruit set.

When pruning stems, avoid severe cuts. Where summers are dry and little or no irrigation is available, prune the stems in summer to reduce the number of leaves competing with the fruit for water. If olive knot disease is a threat, prune in summer or, if you prune in winter, sterilize your pruning tools between cuts. Cut away galls produced by this disease. If frost has damaged your tree, wait until early summer to prune.

To rejuvenate an old olive tree, cut back some large limbs, whitewash the newly exposed trunk to prevent sunburn, and thin out new shoots that develop.

Papaya *(Carica Papaya, C. pubescens):* The papaya is hardly a tree, with its short life and weak, hollow stem (except at the leaf nodes). Plants are usually grown from seed, and start fruiting within a year or two of sowing. Male, female, or hermaphroditic flowers form in leaf axils. (Sprouts on what was a male tree sometimes start to bear female flowers, but not reliably.) Usually the plant grows as a single stem, unless the growing point is damaged naturally or by pruning. But no pruning at all is necessary.

After about three years, a papaya plant begins to bear fewer and smaller fruits. The increasingly tall plant also becomes more liable to topple. You could rejuvenate it by cutting it down to within 18 in. of the ground, making the cut at a slant and just slightly above a node so that water does not collect in the stump. The stump would send out new sprouts, which might fruit sooner than if you started a new seedling. On the other hand, sprouts from an old stump may

not yield well, and older trees commonly become infected with a virus. Given the speed with which seedlings bear fruits and the potential drawbacks of old plants, the best pruning option is to cut your papaya all the way to the ground—i.e., kill it—and sow some new seeds.

Passionfruit *(Passiflora spp.):* Tasty passionfruits follow beautiful passionflowers. The flowers form in the leaf axils of growing shoots. Annual pruning is not a necessity, but does keep the vine—which clings to everything, including itself, with strong tendrils—from becoming too tangled. Pruning also keeps the fruit within easy reach, although you can simply let ripe fruits just drop to the ground. As a minimum, thin out tangled growth and shorten stems in mid-winter. For more tidiness and productivity, train the vine up to a trellis consisting of T-shaped end posts with three wires strung between them. Form a permanent cordon along the middle wire and let branches drape over the outside wires. Each winter, cut every branch to a stub just a few inches long, or at least thin the branches out and shorten them. Go over the vines in summer to thin tangled growth, but leave some shade in hot climates or the fruit will sunburn.

Easiest of all to prune is the temperate species, *P. incarnata,* commonly known as maypop. Maypop dies to the ground each year, but then resprouts each spring with vigor, also sending up suckers from its rapidly spreading roots. Just jerk excess suckers out of the ground with a little tug, or grow the plant in a bed surrounded by grass and let your lawnmower do the pruning. No stem pruning is needed.

Pawpaw *(Asimina triloba):* Pawpaw grows to become a small tree that needs little pruning beyond the training stage. The roots sucker, throwing up shoots at some distance from the trunk, so remove these shoots or else you will end up with a pawpaw thicket such as forms in the wild. (If your tree is grafted, its root suckers will bear fruit that is different from those on the mother tree.) Fruits are produced on stems that grew the previous

(continued on page 166)

season, so prune occasionally while the plant is dormant to stimulate growth for the following year's fruit. Not much stimulation is needed, though. Each flower contains several separate ovaries, so can give rise to a cluster of fruits.

Peach *(Prunus Persica):* The ideal time to prune either the young or the mature tree is during blossoming. Peach is very susceptible to bark diseases, and wounds heal quickest as growth is beginning. This delayed dormant pruning also makes it easy for you to recognize and selectively remove winterkilled wood.

Peach is a naturally spreading tree, so has been traditionally trained to an open-center form. (For greater productivity, commercial growers now also train peaches to central-leaders or even trellised V's.) Most important with the young tree is to use the minimum number of cuts in training, in order to minimize the delay before you taste your first fruits. If possible, train the tree with the lowest limb pointing southwest so that it shades the trunk and lessens the chance of sunburn. (White latex paint on the trunk also helps.) As you train your young tree, take into account its natural growth habit. Dwarf varieties such as 'Compact Redhaven' naturally form more side branches than do full-size varieties, so require fewer heading cuts. For an espalier, train your peach to a fan, whose pruning is covered in more detail on pp. 224-225.

A young tree typically grows very vigorously, shading the interior of the canopy even after careful dormant pruning. To keep the interior of the tree fruitful, prevent shading by thinning some of the very vigorous upright shoots early in the growing season. As the tree matures, it will produce fewer and fewer such sprouts.

Although the young peach tree should be pruned as little as possible, the mature tree needs more severe pruning than most other fruit trees. Having large fruits, the peach responds well to fruit thinning—one result of pruning. Another reason for severe pruning is that fruits are borne only on one-year-old stems. Use mostly thinning cuts because these serve to keep the canopy open for maximum fruit yield and color. Remove vigorous upright growth, thin remaining stems, and occasionally cut back into two- or three-year-old wood. Cut back drooping stems as well as any very short stems—both types typically produce small fruits for lack of sufficient leaves. More heading cuts, in contrast, increase fruit size, but at the expense of yield and color. Strive for 18 in. to 24 in. of new growth each year in response to pruning (in combination with watering and feeding). When you are finished pruning a peach tree, the branches should be open enough to let a bird fly right through the crown.

Make adjustments in your pruning for differences in growing conditions. Where summers are dry and trees are not irrigated, make severe heading cuts to stimulate rapid growth early in the season, before good growing conditions cease. Where water and nutrients are available throughout the growing season, thinning cuts are sufficient.

When fruit set is good, branch pruning alone does not remove a sufficient number of fruits. Hand thin the fruits. If you are pressed for time, you can thin with a forceful stream of water or by banging off excess fruitlets with a piece of hose attached to the end of a stick. The sooner that you thin the fruits, or even the blossoms, the greater the effect on fruit size, the earlier the fruits ripen, and the greater the benefit to next year's crop. Of course, with early thinning you also run the risk of too few fruits; a late frost or an insect such as the plum curculio might provide an unfortunate supplement to your thinning. The best course to follow is to do a light early thinning, then to go over the trees again about six weeks later, after the natural period of shedding fruitlets ("June drop") is over. Final fruit spacing should be about 8 in., unless fruits are concentrated only on some stems, in which case fruits can be closer. (About 35 leaves are needed to nourish each fruit. Do you want to count?)

Pear (*Pyrus* spp.): Pears are naturally upright trees that bear most of their fruits on long-lived spurs, stubby branches that grow only a fraction of an inch each year. The young trees grow vigorous shoots that sometimes are tardy in settling down to fruit. Old trees go to the other extreme, often becoming overburdened with too many fruiting spurs and insufficient new growth. Counteract these tendencies with minimal pruning of the young tree, and more aggressive pruning of the old tree.

Train the young pear tree as a central leader or as modified central leader. Use any of the techniques described in the general section on training fruit trees (pp. 123-132) to create wide-angled scaffold limbs. With their long-lived spurs, pears also make very neat espaliers (see pp. 219-222 for more information on pruning a pear espalier).

As the tree matures, the weight of the fruit will keep branches down, and then you can begin pruning for fruit rather than for limb positioning. Thin out stems where growth is too dense, mostly high in the tree. Pull off watersprouts as soon as you notice them. Also cut away weak wood, such as spindly stems hanging from the undersides of limbs.

Such stems are not very fruitful and the fruits they do bear are poor quality. If a long limb is drooping downward, cut it back to a strong side branch or to a point where it is not drooping. When fruiting spurs become too old and crowded to bear well, head and thin them to give them room and to stimulate new growth.

Vigorous shoots are particularly susceptible to fire blight disease, so avoid severe pruning, which stimulates such growth. If you do see evidence of fire blight, prune it out. Throughout the growing season, prune stems whose leaves have been blackened by this disease at least 6 in. back into healthy wood. (Don't confuse fire blight with sooty mold, which also blackens leaves. Sooty mold is superficial and can be rubbed off the surface of leaves. In addition to blackened leaves, a fire-blighted stem curls around at its tip in a characteristic shepherd's crook.) Sterilize your pruning tools between cuts to avoid spreading the disease to healthy stems. In winter, again prune back blighted stems and also cut out dark, sunken cankers in major limbs. You don't have to sterilize the pruning tools between cuts made in winter.

(continued on page 168)

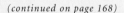

As the name implies, fire blight blackens a pear branch as if it had been singed by fire.

As pear spurs age, they need to be thinned out to stimulate and make room for growth of younger spurs.

Thinning Old Pear Spurs

On old trees, crowded spurs produce smaller fruits.

Remove some spurs and head others back to a strong bud to invigorate the tree.

Pineapple Side Shoots

Slip (along fruit stalk)

Sucker (along stem)

Ground sucker (from ground)

Pruning pear stems also thins the fruit—but not enough. Go over the tree after fruit set and hand thin so that fruits are spaced 5 in. apart. Because the beginnings of next year's flower buds don't form until some 60 days after the current year's blossoms appear, there is no need to rush fruit thinning for good return bloom in the year following a bumper crop.

Pecan *(Carya illinoinensis):* Male flowers appear on one-year-old wood, and female flowers appear on growing shoots. Nonetheless, pecan requires little pruning beyond that needed to train it to a sturdy framework when young and to remove diseased, broken, or out-of-place wood as the tree ages.

Persimmon *(Diospyros spp.):* Persimmons grow to become large trees with drooping branches. That drooping habit is sometimes expressed in young trees by their long, willowy shoots. While training a tree, shorten such shoots or support them with stakes. Only a few terminal buds normally extend the growth of a stem, so head or bend any stem where you want it to branch lower down. Create an open-center or modified-central-leader form for the plant. Avoid the open-center form in hot, dry climates or else the bark and fruit might sunburn. No matter what the form, a strong framework is important since persimmon wood is brittle.

Persimmon fruits are formed in the leaf axils of new shoots that grow from last year's wood, especially those shoots growing near the end of one-year-old wood. Some pruning is thus needed to stimulate new growth each year. Prune during the dormant season, heading back some one-year-old stems to decrease fruit load the upcoming season, and to keep bearing wood near the main branches. Be careful not to cut off the ends of too many one-year-old stems or you will harvest too few fruits. The American persimmon *(D. virginiana)* needs little pruning, because it naturally drops some stems that have borne fruits.

Except where fruit set is low, hand thin Oriental persimmon *(D. Kaki)* fruits if you want them to grow large. The presence of a male tree is likely to cause overbearing on Oriental persimmon varieties capable of setting fruit without pollination. American persimmons are naturally small, so don't expect them to get bigger as the result of hand thinning.

Pineapple *(Ananas comosus):* A pineapple plant is a compressed stem, a whorl of leaves whose growing point eventually becomes a stalk capped by the pineapple fruit. Side shoots grow from this compressed stem. Those arising at ground level are called ground suckers and those along the stem are simply called suckers. Side shoots that originate on the fruit stalk are called slips, while those that originate where the plant stem and the fruit stalk meet are called hapas.

Unpruned, a pineapple plant sprawls along the ground as side shoots jut out and the plant bows under its own weight. Pruning keeps the plant neater and gives better fruits. Prune a month or two after you harvest the fruit, cutting off slips and hapas. Ground suckers ripen quickest but also give the smallest fruits, so you may want to remove them. If, after removing slips, hapas, and ground suckers, the number of remaining suckers still seems excessive, thin them out.

Pistachio *(Pistacia vera):* Pistachio is a naturally bushy tree, rarely growing higher than 20 ft. Whether grown with multiple trunks or as a modified central leader, training is very important for the first four or five years. Terminal buds are vegetative with strong apical dominance that suppresses the growth of buds farther down the stem. As a result, stems grow mostly from their tips, eventually becoming so long that they arch down to the ground and sunburn. Make as many heading cuts as are necessary into old or young stems in order to get branching every 30 in., then head branches to induce further branching.

Most of the lateral buds on one-year-old wood of pistachio are flower buds only. (On many other fruits, buds are mixed vegetative and flower buds.) This flowering habit makes for a lot of flowers, but, again, few branches. On the mature tree, even heading cuts may not induce branching, which is why training the young tree is so important. The properly brought-up mature tree probably needs only light annual pruning consisting of many heading cuts into both young and old wood. Why "probably?" Because the pruning needs of pistachio have not yet been clearly established.

Pitanga *(Eugenia uniflora):* This evergreen can be grown as a shrub or small tree. Flowers are borne at the juncture of new and old growth. Prune to encourage some new growth as well as to thin out wood that is crowded or decrepit.

Pitomba *(Eugenia Luschnathiana):* Prune this evergreen shrub only as needed to shape it.

Plum *(Prunus* spp.): Plums represent several species, differing dramatically in fruit size, color, and flavor, and less so in growth and fruiting habit. Plants range from bushes to trees, the latter of which are trained to open-center or modified central-leader form. European plums *(P. domestica)* include varieties such as 'Lombard' and 'Yellow Egg', as well as prune plums such as 'Italian' and 'Stanley', and gages such as 'Reine Claude' and 'Jefferson'. Japanese plums *(P. salicina)* are represented by such varieties as 'Abundance', 'Burbank', and 'Satsuma', and American plums *(P. americana* and other species) by the varieties 'De Soto' and 'Hawkeye'. Broadening the palette (and your palate)—and further confusing the nomenclature—are the many hybrids between plum species: For example, 'Ember' and 'Monitor' are hybrids of American and Japanese plums, and 'Kaga' and 'Hanska' are hybrids of American and another oriental species *(P. Simonii)*. Plums also have been hybridized with sand cherries and with apricots, the latter cross producing "plumcots," "pluots," and "apriums."

Pruning plums is easier than categorizing them. Beyond training, which is unnecessary for many of the bushy hybrids, plums require little pruning. The plants fruit abundantly on spurs and, in the case of the Japanese plums, on one-year-old stems as well. Prune mostly to let light into the center of the tree, and for a moderate amount of new growth for next year's fruit. Occasionally remove the oldest wood at ground level from bushy plants of the American species. Generally, there is no need to thin plum fruits. Go ahead and prune more heavily if you want to keep the plant smaller—a plum tree can tolerate it. And you will have to prune even more if you grow a plum as an espalier (see p. 225).

Japanese plums are large fruits, and the crop can be heavy enough to break limbs. Prune these plums more severely than the others so that the tree does not have long, breakable branches of fruit, and because you need to stimulate abundant new growth for next year's fruit. If fruit set is heavy, hand thin the fruits to 5 in. apart.

There is one more type of plum, the Damson plum *(P. insititia)*, usually used for jam and pastry filling, but pretty good eaten fresh. This wildish tree needs the bare minimum of pruning.

Pomegranate *(Punica Granatum):* Train the young pomegranate to either a single trunk or to five or six trunks. In areas where pomegranate is not reliably cold hardy, multiple trunks provide insurance that the whole plant does not die to the ground in winter. Flowers are borne on spurs of two- and three-year-old wood, so the mature plant plant requires only light annual pruning, just enough to stimulate some new growth each year and to thin out excess fruits. Also cut suckers to the ground, unless any are needed to replace a damaged trunk.

Prickly Pear *(Opuntia* spp.): These mostly thornless cacti require no pruning.

(continued on page 170)

Quince can be trained as a handsome small tree, shown here, or as a bush.

Quince *(Cydonia oblonga):* Quince is a small tree or large bush that flowers at the ends of short shoots growing from one-year-old wood. Train your quince as a bush, or as a tree with one or a few trunks. The mature plant needs little pruning. Use a combination of heading and thinning cuts to keep the plant open to air and light, and to stimulate a foot or two of new growth each season. Do not confuse this quince with the pink-flowered flowering quince *(Chaenomeles* spp.), whose fruits may be edible, but are unpalatable.

Raspberry *(Rubus* spp.): Raspberries may be red or yellow (both *R. idaeus* or *R. idaeus* var. *strigosus),* purple *(R. × neglectus),* or black *(R. occidentalis)*—and some black raspberries, also called blackcaps, produce nearly white fruit. Red and yellow raspberries spread as new canes grow up from wandering roots, while black and purple raspberries hopscotch along as the tips of their canes arch to the ground to root and form new plants. No matter what their color, all raspberries

have perennial roots but biennial canes. Summerbearing red and yellow raspberries canes just grow their first year, then begin to die after they have fruited in their second season. Everbearing, sometimes called fallbearing, red and yellow raspberries begin to fruit at the ends of first-year canes in late summer and autumn, then fruit lower down on those same canes the next summer before those canes die. Black raspberries and purple raspberries fruit just like summerbearing red and yellow raspberries, except that fruits form on laterals of second-year canes. The one constant in pruning all these raspberries is to cut all old canes completely to the ground right after you plant, if the plant is dormant.

Prune summerbearing red and yellow raspberries in three steps. First, cut to the ground any canes that have fruited. Do this anytime from immediately after harvest until just before growth begins the following spring. Second, while the plants are dormant, thin out canes that grew the previous season

(continued on page 173)

Fruiting Habit of Raspberries

Summerbearing red and yellow raspberries

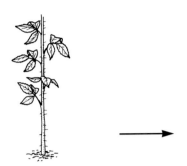

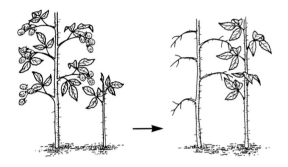

First season:
Plant produces only stems and leaves.

Second season:
Last year's canes bear fruit, then die; new canes will fruit the following year.

Everbearing red and yellow raspberries

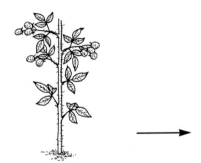

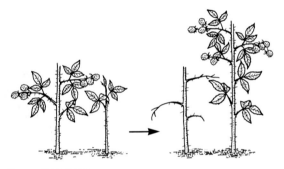

First season:
Fruits are borne at tops of new shoots in late summer and fall.

Second season:
Early-summer fruits are borne lower down on last year's canes, which then die; new canes bear in late summer and fall.

Black and purple raspberries

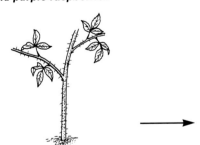

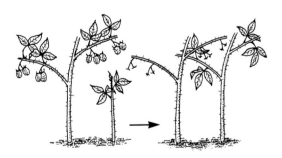

First season:
Plant produces only stems and leaves.

Second season:
Last year's canes bear fruit, then die; new canes will fruit the following year.

Pruning Summerbearing Red and Yellow Raspberries

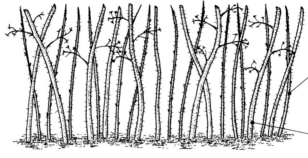

One-year-old cane

Two-year-old cane

Dormant plants

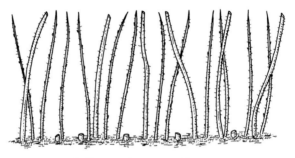

1. Remove two-year-old canes.

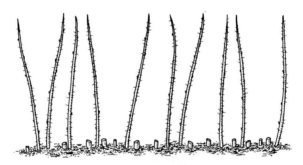

2. Thin excess one-year-old canes.

3. Shorten remaining canes.

so that the row is no wider than 12 in., with 6 in. or more between canes. You could have done some of this pruning while the canes were first growing, and this would cause less weakening and crowding of plants, and leave you less to thin during the dormant season. No matter when you do your thinning, selectively remove those canes that are thinnest, diseased, or broken.

The third step in pruning summerbearing red and yellow raspberries is to shorten the remaining canes. How much to shorten them depends on how you trellis your raspberries, because the only reason to shorten them is for convenience and to prevent the canes from flopping around in the wind. The longer the canes, the more fruit you will harvest. If you tie the canes to two wires, one 2 ft. and one 5 ft. off the ground, shorten the canes to about 6 ft. With this same trellis, you can leave the canes nearly full length if you bend them along and weave them around the upper wire.

Prune everbearing red and yellow raspberries the same way as the summerbearers, with one slight difference. The canes you save, pruned in the third step, will have started fruiting at their ends late the previous season, and will "finish" fruiting lower down. Therefore, shorten those canes to just below where they stopped fruiting the previous season. The old fruit stalks still hanging on the canes will tell you where to cut.

A simpler way to prune everbearing red and yellow raspberries is just to mow the whole planting down each autumn. Do this and you do not need a trellis or have to worry about cold damage or deer browsing in the winter. Diseases are less of a problem because they cannot be harbored on old canes over winter. By following this system, however, you only

(continued on page 175)

PRUNING RED RASPBERRIES

1. Unpruned red raspberry canes are unkempt and crowded.

2. Old canes must be cut away, then young ones thinned out.

3. Long canes can be kept neat by weaving them into the upper wire.

4. Pruning complete, these neatly trellised raspberries will yield a good crop, easily picked.

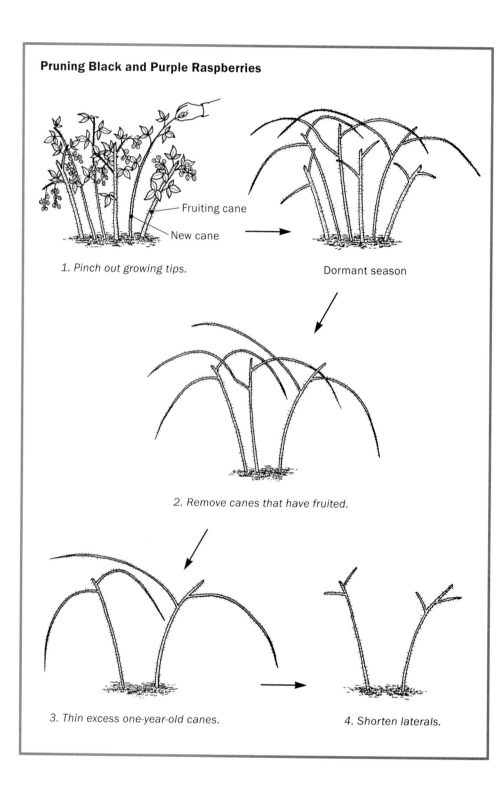

Pruning Black and Purple Raspberries

Fruiting cane

New cane

1. Pinch out growing tips.

Dormant season

2. Remove canes that have fruited.

3. Thin excess one-year-old canes.

4. Shorten laterals.

get to harvest berries borne on new shoots at the end of the season, so you sacrifice the summer crop.

Prune black raspberries and purple raspberries in four easy steps. The first step is to prune away any canes that have fruited, anytime from right after harvest until growth begins the following spring. The next step, in summer, is to prune off the top 2 in. of each growing cane as it reaches a height of 18 in. This summer topping stimulates the growth of branches, which will fruit the following growing season. If you are willing to trellis your plants, either by tying all canes to a pole at each hill or to a single wire strung between posts, your bramble patch will be neater; you will also harvest more berries because you can wait to top each cane until it is 3 ft. high. Whether you top at 18 in. or at 3 ft., go over the plants a few times during the summer, as often as new canes reach pruning height.

Do the last two steps in pruning while the plants are dormant, preferably just before growth begins in spring. Cut any diseased, damaged or spindly canes to the ground. And finally, shorten branches that resulted from your summer pruning so that they are 4 in. to 18 in. long, leaving those that are fattest the longest.

Rose Apple *(Syzygium Jambos):* Prune this evergreen shrub only as needed to shape it.

Salal *(Gaultheria Shallon):* Prune only as needed to shape the plant.

Sapodilla *(Manilkara Zapota):* This compact evergreen bears fruits in leaf axils toward the ends of small, young stems. Little pruning is needed beyond the removal of vigorous uprights.

Starfruit *(Averrhoa Carambola):* Starfruit, also called carambola, is a medium-sized evergreen tree that bears its star-shaped fruit on old wood. It needs little pruning beyond removal of vigorous uprights to prevent shading and crowding.

Strawberry *(Fragaria* spp.): Most pruning of strawberry plants is of runners, the long stems that that grow out from the crown to crawl atop the ground, producing new plants at nodes. Left alone, the mother, daughter, and granddaughter plants strew about, creating shade that results in fewer fruits and more diseases.

'Earliglow' strawberry, awaiting harvest.

For best health and fruiting, each strawberry plant needs about 1 square foot of space all to itself. Plants grown in the "hill" system are originally planted 1 ft. apart, so must have all their runners removed. Plants grown as a "matted row" are planted a few feet apart, with runners allowed to fill in between mother plants. With "spaced row" plants, an intermediate training system, you allow just some of the runners to form, usually four per plant.

All newly planted strawberries need their flower buds pinched off until the plants are established. Do this for about two months after planting.

Renovation of a June-bearing strawberry bed is an annual affair that forestalls the bed's eventual decline. (Not forever, though. After

A net keeps birds away from the ripening fruit.

(continued on page 176)

five or ten years, replant a new bed elsewhere.) The time to renovate is right after harvest. Begin by cutting off all the leaves with hand shears or with a mower set high, then raking them away. Next, dig out excess plants where they are crowded, selectively removing those that are oldest. Fertilize, then water, and the plants, after their short rest, will send out new leaves. (Replant, rather than renovate, a bed of everbearing or day-neutral strawberries when it declines.)

As with other herbaceous perennials, the crown of a strawberry plant does branch and become decrepit with age, at which time it can be divided. This method of revitalizing a plant is used only with strawberries that make few or no runners, such as alpine strawberries. To divide the crown, dig up the plant, then cut off young branch crowns—with attached roots—from the outer edge of the crown and plant them. But alpine strawberries reproduce reliably from seed, which is just as easy as dividing crowns and avoids the risk of propagating a disease-infected plant.

Surinam Cherry *(Eugenia uniflora):* See Pitanga

Tree Tomato *(Cyphomandra betacea):* Encourage branching of the developing tree by pinching out the growing point of the trunk at between 3 ft. and 8 ft., depending on how high you want the head. The mature tree flowers on growing shoots. Prune stems back to within the crown each year to encourage new growth and to prevent fruit from being borne only at the periphery of the crown, subjecting limbs to breakage. There is no need to thin the fruits.

Walnut *(Juglans* spp.): Both English walnuts *(J. regia,* and sometimes called Persian walnuts) and black walnuts *(J. nigra)* are grown for their nuts. Male flowers form in catkins that grow off year-old wood and female flowers form on the current season's shoots.

Train English walnut to open-center, central-leader, or modified central-leader form, but if you expect the tree to grow large, the latter two forms make sturdier trees. If a shoot destined to become a scaffold limb is too upright, rub it off and a new one, with a wider crotch angle, will grow from a secondary bud. Also, varieties differ in their natural growth habit. For example, 'Placentia' and 'Payne' are naturally spreading, and 'Eureka' and 'Franquette' are naturally upright.

Prune mature English walnut trees annually to keep them invigorated and to prevent the interior of the crown from becoming shaded. On older varieties, such as 'Franquette' and 'Hartley', only terminal buds and those just below where nuts were borne the previous season grow out to become new flowering shoots. More modern varieties grow flowering shoots from many lateral buds when the plants are young. These fecund varieties need more severe pruning in order to prevent overbearing, especially on young trees which would otherwise never become more than runts. Head back young stems on these trees by one-quarter to one-half, and regularly thin fruiting branches to let light into the canopy.

For nut production, black walnut rarely needs pruning once the tree has been trained to a sturdy, central-leader framework. Modify your pruning, though, if your eventual goal is also to harvest the trees for their beautiful wood. In this case, you want a straight, knot-free trunk, which you get by removing branches before they grow too large. As soon as the base of the first branch is 1 in. in diameter, remove all branches from the trunk halfway up the tree. As the tree grows, continue to remove branches until you have at least 9 ft. of clear trunk.

White Sapote *(Casimiroa edulis):* The tree tends to grow long, unbranched stems, so head the leader when it is 3 ft. high and head the branches when they have grown 1 ft. to 2 ft. Prune the mature tree to control its size.

CHAPTER NINE

HOUSEPLANTS

Houseplants are either herbaceous plants or merely diminutive versions of woody trees, shrubs, or vines that grow outdoors. The woody houseplants generally are tropical or subtropical evergreens—after all, who would want a deciduous houseplant?

For instruction on how to prune any houseplant, just look up the plant in its category—conifer, palm, broadleaf evergreen, vine, etc.—elsewhere in this book. Then prune the houseplant version just as you would the full-size version, pruning more heavily to keep it smaller, and taking into consideration the fact that the plant will never experience cool or cold weather.

The only special pruning a plant needs when grown as a houseplant is root pruning. Once a plant has grown as large as you want it to, the soil must be periodically renewed around its roots. The only way to accomplish this without increasing the size of the pot is to cut off some roots.

Depending on the vigor of the plant, root pruning may be needed once a year or every few years. The best way to tell when root pruning is needed is to knock

Houseplants need occasional pruning. Leave the ladder outside.

This potted plant is rootbound.

a plant out of its pot and look at the roots. If they are going around and around in a thick mat at the surface of the root ball, root pruning is needed. Or the plant might call out by itself for root pruning, with a mass of roots sneaking out of the drainage hole in the bottom of a pot, futilely searching for new soil.

When you root-prune, either tease long roots out of the root ball and shorten them with your pruning shears, or else slice pieces of soil and roots off the edge of the root ball with a sharp knife. (Don't expect the knife to be sharp when you're done!) Then tease out the remaining roots at the outside of the root ball. Return the plant to its pot and pack fresh soil in around the root ball.

Once the plant is back in its pot, the stems also will need some pruning in order to keep the top of the plant in proportion to the size of the container while retaining a pleasing shape. The goal here is beauty, not growth. After all, you're not seeking maximum growth from a houseplant that already is full size—full size for your house, that is.

Every technique recommended for full-size plants can be applied to houseplants. Head stems and pinch shoots for bushiness, and thin out wood to prevent regrowth. To lower an indoor tree, shorten major limbs to side branches within the crown, just as you would on an outdoor tree. The difference between working on the dwarf and the full-size tree is that with the dwarf the work is more intimate—and your feet are on the ground!

PRUNING A HOUSEPLANT

1. To keep it from growing larger, this potted kumquat needs annual root and shoot pruning.

2. Slice off the outside layer of roots and soil.

3. Teasing roots at the outside of the root ball will get them growing quickly out into the new soil.

4. Just cut back occasional larger roots.

5. Pack new soil in around the old root ball.

6. After shoot pruning to keep the top of the plant in bounds, the potted kumquat is ready to grow.

CHAPTER TEN HERBACEOUS PLANTS

Even herbaceous perennials benefit from judicious pinching, snipping, and dividing.

Herbaceous plants are the ephemerals of the garden, vanishing with hardly a trace at the end of each season. To get them on with their show as quickly as possible, allow most herbaceous plants just to grow like all getout, unrestrained. Remember, any leaves that you remove slow a plant down, in growth and in flowering. Nonetheless, for form, flowers, or fruits, herbaceous plants are sometimes pruned—and that is the subject of this chapter.

Note that many plants grown as herbaceous annuals in temperate gardens are woody perennials in warm-winter climates. For instructions on pruning them as woody perennials, see the appropriate section elsewhere in this book.

Pinching to promote bushiness

Pinching out the tip of the stem of an herbaceous plant stops that stem's growth and causes the lower buds, in the leaf axils, to grow out into shoots. As a result, the plant becomes bushier. Therefore, while not absolutely necessary, pinching the tips of plants such as lavatera, marigold, and zinnia makes them fuller.

Early in the growing season, when any and every flower is still to be cherished, you may find that the top bud on, for example, a marigold seedling is a flower bud, or even an already opened flower! Grit your teeth and pinch it off. Not only will doing so make the plant bushier, but it will also channel energy destined for that flower into the growth of new shoots. Allowing a small seedling to flower prematurely saps its strength, so the plant is likely to remain a runt. Defer your pleasure. (As consolation, read the tongue-in-cheek words that Charles Dudley Warner wrote in 1888 in *My Summer in a Garden:* "The principal value of a private garden is…to teach patience and philosophy, and the higher virtues—hope deferred, and expectations blighted, leading directly to resignation, and sometimes to alienation. The garden thus becomes a moral agent, a test of character, as it was in the beginning.")

But do not carry pinching to excess—it does delay flowering. And, not that large flowers are always better than small flowers, but the more flowering shoots on a plant, the more flowers but the smaller the size of each flower. A single pinch is usually sufficient for marigolds and other naturally bushy flowers. Certain chrysanthemums look best with repeated pinching (but see the Plant List, which begins on p. 185). With snapdragon and some other spiky flowers, you have a choice: Do you want a single large spike, or several smaller ones?

Pruning for extra-large flowers or fruits

Just as pinching the tips of stems makes bushier plants with more, but smaller, flowers, limiting the number of shoots or flowers has the opposite effect. This is how you grow a "football" 'mum, a "dinnerplate" dahlia, or a giant tomato. (Again, see the Plant List for special information on pruning 'mums, dahlias, and tomatoes.)

Channel any plant's energy into fewer growing points by pinching off side shoots, pinching off lateral flower buds, or limiting the number of stems growing from the crown of a perennial plant. Remove a side shoot or lateral flower bud while either is still young enough to be succulent and pinched off. At that stage, removing the side shoot hardly affects overall plant growth because the side shoot is not yet contributing to the energies of the plant. And a young flower bud has not yet drawn too much energy from the plant. *Aster novi-belgii,*

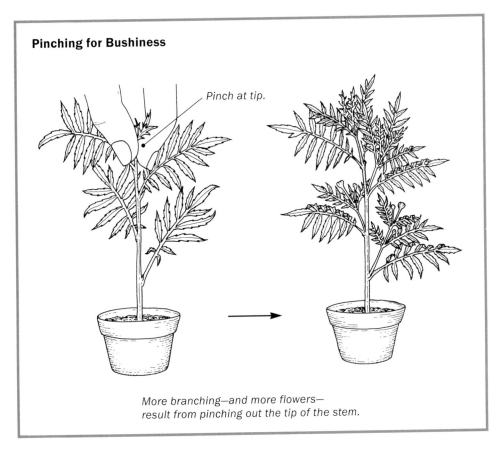

Pinching for Bushiness

Pinch at tip.

More branching—and more flowers—result from pinching out the tip of the stem.

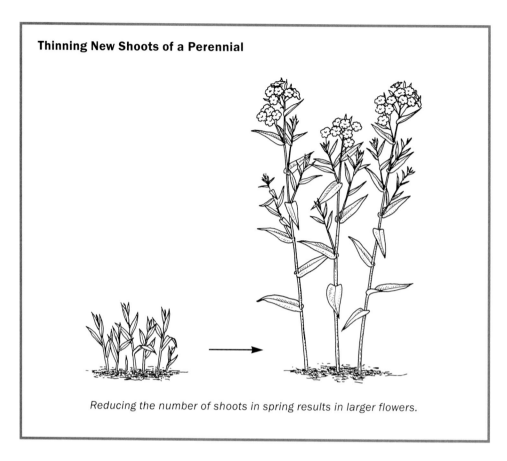

Thinning New Shoots of a Perennial

Reducing the number of shoots in spring results in larger flowers.

perennial phlox *(Phlox paniculata)*, and thick-leaf phlox *(P. carolina)* are examples of perennial flowers that perform better if you reduce the number of shoots they send up from ground level. When shoots are 2 in. high, remove all but three per plant.

Deadheading for neatness and continued bloom

Removing spent flowers from an herbaceous plant—called deadheading—keeps things tidy and allows the plant to channel its energy into more flowers rather than producing seeds. The raison d'être for annual plants, from their perspective, is to make seeds. Once that occurs, they are apt to slacken their efforts at making more flowers. Deadheading keeps annuals energetic.

Even some perennial flowers, such as delphinium *(Delphinium* hybrids) and Canterbury-bells *(Campanula Medium)*, put on a second show later in the season if their spent flowers are cut back after their first show of the season.

You would have quite a time trying to cut off individual flower stalks of a plant such as sweet alyssum *(Lobularia maritima)*, which forms a low-growing mound completely showered with blossoms. Deadhead this plant by shearing the whole mound back with either grass or hedge shears after a flush of bloom. This plant sprawls out of bounds, and shearing also puts the plant back in place. Other annuals that benefit from this treatment (it's really not the plant, but we gardeners who benefit) include nasturtium *(Tropaeolum* spp.)

and petunia (*Petunia × hybrida*), although in some sites, any of these trailing plants look best completely unrestrained. Perennials that benefit from shearing include basket-of-gold (*Aurinia saxatilis*), cottage pink (*Dianthus plumarius*), sea pink (*Armeria maritima*), edging candytuft (*Iberis sempervirens*), spike speedwell (*Veronica spicata*), and horned viola (*Viola cornuta*). Sheared plants appear stunned for a couple of days after the operation, but good growing conditions soon have them happily lumbering along the ground and, in some cases, flowering again that same season.

Deadheading also keeps a planting tidy by preventing unwanted self-seeding. Especially fecund plants include feverfew (*Chrysanthemum Parthenium*), perennial phlox (*Phlox paniculata*), thick-leaf phlox (*P. carolina*), and, with a common and botanical name to scare any fastidious gardener, giant hogweed (*Heracleum Mantegazzianum*).

Crown division to rejuvenate a perennial

Although an attraction of perennial flowers is their perennial nature, "perennial" does not mean that the plants never need any care. With time, these plants suffer from age as their clumps spread outward, the old centers dying out, or inch upward and then weaken from exposure. Crown division keeps a plant young.

As soon as you see the first green shoots of an aged perennial poking through the ground in the spring, run to the garage, grab a shovel, and lift the clump out of the earth. Shake some soil from the roots so that you can see what you are doing, then start cutting apart the crown. Depending on how the crown grows and its age, use your bare hands, a shovel, a sharp knife, or hand pruning shears.

The pieces that you want to save for replanting are the youngest ones, typically those at the outer edge of the

Periodically shearing alyssum after each flush of blossoms sets the stage for repeat shows.

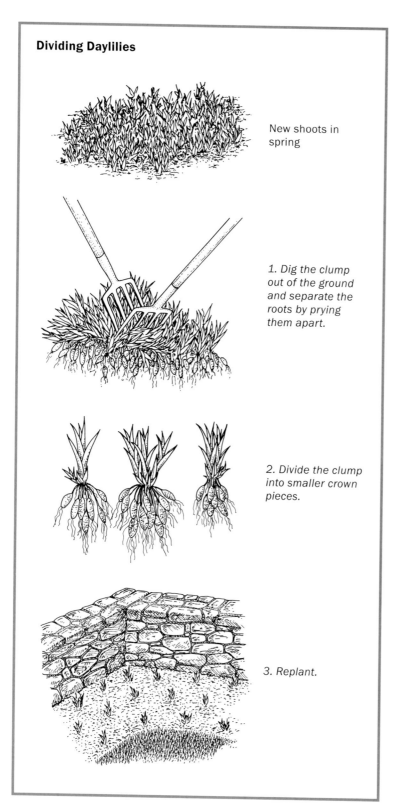

Dividing Daylilies

New shoots in spring

1. Dig the clump out of the ground and separate the roots by prying them apart.

2. Divide the clump into smaller crown pieces.

3. Replant.

crown and having some roots attached. Replant only the most vigorous young crown pieces, first enriching the soil, if necessary, with humus, fertilizers, and other amendments.

Perennials vary in the frequency with which they need division. To look their best, asters and hardy chrysanthemums require division every year. The same goes for bee balm *(Monarda didyma)*, tansy *(Tanacetum vulgare)*, goldenrod *(Solidago* spp.), and artemisia *(Artemisia* spp.), not for the sake of appearances, but to keep them from spreading. Division every three or four years is sufficient for sea pink *(Armeria maritima)*, phlox *(Phlox* spp.), coralbells *(Heuchera sanguinea)*, Canterbury-bells *(Campanula Medium)*, snow-in-summer *(Cerastium tomentosum)*, Siberian and Japanese irises *(Iris siberica* and *I. kaempferi)*, veronica *(Veronica* spp.), yarrow *(Achillea Millefolium)*, and Shasta daisies *(Chrysanthemum × superbum)*.

Don't be too eager to divide certain perennials. Bridle your spring-induced enthusiasm and wait until after blossoms fade to divide Oriental poppies *(Papaver orientale)*, bleeding heart *(Dicentra spectabilis)*, bearded iris *(Iris* spp.*)*, and Virginia cowslip *(Mertensia virginica)*, all of which go dormant by midsummer. And think twice before dividing hellebore *(Helleborus* spp.*)*, peony *(Paeonia lactiflora)*, monkshood *(Aconitum Napellus)*, butterfly weed *(Asclepias tuberosa)*, lupine *(Lupinus* spp.), and baby's-breath *(Gypsophila* spp.). Once a decade is probably enough for these perennials, and even then, they show their initial resentment by not blooming for a year or so afterwards.

Plant List

Carnation (*Dianthus* spp.): For ordinary growing out in the garden, carnations do not demand pruning. Even so, a planting of cottage pinks (*D. plumarius*) looks neater and has a more concentrated period of repeat flowering if the plants are sheared right after blooming. And for larger blossoms on clove pink (*D. Caryophyllus*), pinch off lateral flower buds as they appear.

In the greenhouse, prune clove pink to schedule the flowers as well as to regulate the number of stems and bloom size. Young plants are commonly pinched so that they develop a few flowering stems. After those first blooms, there is a lull before blossoms again appear. The duration of the lull is influenced by available light. To spread out the production of flowers, sacrificing somewhat their total number and slowing the time to peak bloom, pinch again a month after the initial pinching. This time, pinch the tips of half the number of stems that sprouted as a result of the first going-over. Carnations also require cool temperatures for best bloom, so cut back plants from winter to early spring, or pinch them back from early spring to early summer, to delay flowering until the end of summer. As with outdoor clove pinks, remove lateral flower buds whenever you want larger flowers.

Chrysanthemum (formerly *Chrysanthemum* spp., but now also includes *Dendrathema grandiflora, Nipponanthemum nipponicum* and others): 'Mums run the gamut, from plants that are bushy mounds to those that are stately, upright, and capped by one or a few corpulent blooms. The colors and forms of flowers are equally variable. For ordinary garden culture, buy either a bushy variety or an upright, large-flowered variety, whichever you want, and just let the plant grow unfettered—pruning is not absolutely necessary. However, pruning will improve the form of either type, and is a necessity for show-quality and commercial flowers.

An important point to keep in mind, no matter how you prune, is that 'mums wait until days grow short and temperatures cool before forming flower buds. The number of shorter days needed to induce flower buds ranges from seven to fourteen weeks, depending on the variety. Low cushion 'mums need the least amount of time, while some of the large 'mums need the most. (And those of the latter that do flower very late must therefore be grown in a greenhouse or in pots that can be brought indoors in autumn.) At any rate, once a plant changes gears and enters the flowering mode, it responds differently to pruning than when it was vegetative.

To "pinch" out the growing point of a 'mum means removing only ½ in. or so at the tip of the stem. Regrowth and healing are less satisfactory when you remove any more of the shoot than that. Apply the same philosophy when taking off side shoots— rub them off while they are young.

Now, onto the details of pruning…

Out in the garden, a naturally bushy 'mum might look better if it was even more bushy. Promote bushiness by pinching out growing points when shoots are 6 in. tall. Repeat this pinching whenever new shoots grow to 6 in. Cease pinching no later that 90 days before

Pinch the growing points of chrysanthemums in spring and early summer for dense blooms in fall.

(*continued on page 187*)

Crown Bud of Chrysanthemum

Crown bud

Side shoots

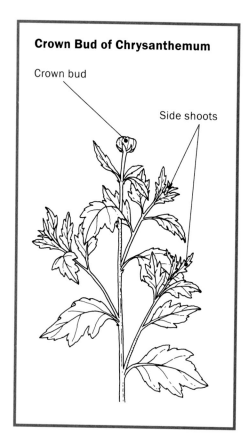

Terminal Bud Clusters of Chrysanthemum

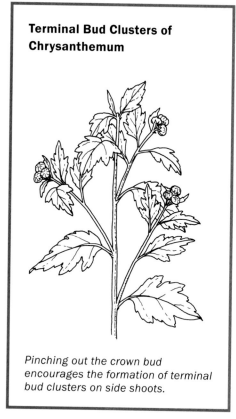

Pinching out the crown bud encourages the formation of terminal bud clusters on side shoots.

Pinching Out a Premature Crown Bud on Chrysanthemum

Crown bud

Pinch here.

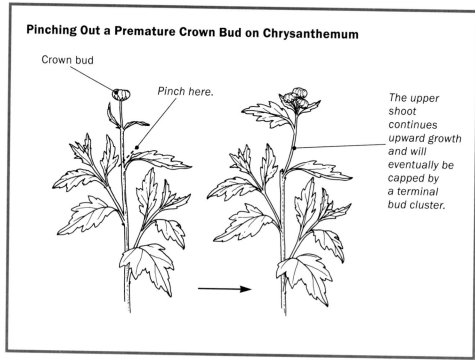

The upper shoot continues upward growth and will eventually be capped by a terminal bud cluster.

the normal bloom date (by July, in any case); that's when plants start to develop flower buds, and you don't want to remove them.

Growing 'mums for extra-large blossoms is another matter, and can be an exacting science. First choose an appropriate variety—some will not make extra-large blossoms even when the number of flower buds is reduced. Then deliberately remove all but from one to three shoots on each plant, and do not allow any branches to grow on them. Stake each shoot separately to keep it rigidly upright.

The change from vegetative to flowering phase is gradual. If you do not pinch the tip of a stem at all as days shorten, the top bud may become a "crown bud," which is a single flower bud with narrow, strappy leaves farther down the stalk, and still-vegetative shoots pushing out just below. These vegetative shoots also will be eventually capped by flowers.

If you pinch out stem tips so that crown buds do not form, nonflowering side shoots—usually three—continue upward growth. Depending on how many and how large you want your blossoms, retain one or all of these shoots. Eventually, the plant enters a full flowering phase, with the end of a shoot capped by a "terminal bud cluster," which is a cluster of flower buds. ("Terminal" in this case refers to the plant's last-ditch effort at flowering for the season.) The flowers are on long stems having normal 'mum foliage—all of which is important for a show chrysanthemum. For a large blossom from a terminal bud cluster, pinch out all but the top flower bud.

As long as a crown bud does not develop while a plant is small, either a crown bud or a terminal bud can give rise to an equally large flower. If a crown bud forms on a small plant, merely pinch it out and select one of the vegetative shoots to become an extension of the main shoot. Only a terminal bud, however, can make a "spray," which is a large flower surrounded by smaller flowers, all blooming together.

The timing of the last pinch, as well as the number of stems and flowers to allow each plant, has been carefully calculated for the best show from a number of varieties. The reason for this is the exacting requirements for time and appearance of bloom that are demanded from commercial and competition 'mum growers.

One more way to grow 'mums is as a cascading floral display. For this, you need wires or canes on which to train two stems.

(continued on page 188)

A cascade of sunny yellow 'mums.

Training Greenhouse Cucumbers

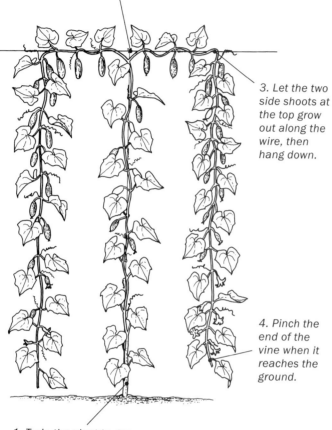

2. Pinch out the tip of the main stem just above the horizontal wire; tie the stem to the wire with string.

3. Let the two side shoots at the top grow out along the wire, then hang down.

4. Pinch the end of the vine when it reaches the ground.

1. Train the plant to grow up a vertical string or stake.

On the main stem, no fruits should be allowed on the lowest 3 ft. of vine. Elsewhere, pinch side shoots along the main stem so that each has one fruit and one leaf.

SELECTED
HERBACEOUS PLANTS
(continued)

To keep growth vigorous, initially train shoots upward at a 45° angle. Pinch side shoots completely off, or pinch out their tips when they have made three leaves. As the frame fills, gradually pull wires or canes down to a horizontal position, then further, to create a cascading effect.

Dahlia *(Dahlia* spp.): Dahlias do not demand pruning, but pruning can increase either the size or the number of flowers. On plants with naturally large blossoms, side shoots typically do not grow until the shoot tip forms a flower bud. To promote the development of side shoots, pinch out the tip of a shoot in early summer. Remove the top pair of side shoots that develops in order to spread vigor among the side shoots down along the stem. At the other extreme, you could channel energy into a single "dinnerplate" dahlia by pinching out all side shoots or lateral flower buds that form. Or, for a combination of the above treatments, pinch plants in early summer to promote branching, then disbud the resulting stems so that each develops just one flower.

Greenhouse Cucumbers *(Cucumis sativus):* If you have seen how cucumbers can sprawl in the garden, you can understand why pruning is needed to check and organize their growth in the confines of a greenhouse. To make the best use of space, always a precious commodity "under glass," train the plants upward on strings or thin stakes, then out along horizontal wires. With good growing conditions, as well as careful training and pruning, one highly productive plant can be grown in an area of about 6 square feet.

After making its first few leaves, a new plant will start producing a tendril along with each leaf. You cannot rely on the tendrils to pull the plant up, so twist the stem around the string or stake as it grows. Pinch out the tip of the main stem when it grows one leaf beyond the horizontal wire, then tie a piece of string around the stem and the wire to keep the plant from slipping downward. Pinch all side shoots that grow off the main stem back to a leaf, except for the two side shoots at the top, one of which you will guide in each direction along the top wire. After they travel along the wire for a bit, allow the ends of each of the top laterals to hang downward, then pinch their ends when they reach the ground.

Besides a tendril, you also could find a fruit at each node along the stems, especially with modern greenhouse cucumbers bearing all female flowers rather than the mix of male and female flowers borne on older varieties. Do not let any fruits form on the lower 3 ft. of the main stem. At all the remaining nodes on the plant (wherever there is a leaf), allow only a single fruit and that single leaf to remain. Pinch back any laterals or sublaterals that try to grow.

Fruits form only in new leaf axils, so the pruned plant could ultimately become bare of fruit and leaves. Before this happens, renew the plant by letting a healthy young shoot replace the main stem. Train the young shoot just as you did the old main stem, which you then cut away.

Throughout the life of the plant, adjust growth so that all the leaves are bathed in light, and balance the number of fruits with the growing conditions and the variety. For example, prune less severely if you grow an old-type cucumber with male and female flowers, because then a fruit cannot form at each node. When natural light ebbs in late autumn and winter, allow more space between the main stem and drooping laterals. You might even let two leaves grow on each lateral from the main stem and sublateral from each of the two top laterals. But pinch off any fruit that forms at the second leaf to increase the ratio of leaves to fruits.

Through this all, keep in mind that pruning is also needed to keep a plant healthy. Cut away any dead or injured growth as soon as you notice it. And while you want the maximum number of leaves to intercept whatever light is available, you also need good air circulation around those leaves to avoid diseases. This might call for occasionally snipping off a large leaf.

Go over your plants at least once a week. For plant health and ease of training and pruning, you do not want a confusion of stems—not for cucumbers in a greenhouse, at least.

Tomato side shoots form at the junction of a leaf stalk and the main stem.

Tomato *(Lycopersicon Lycopersicum):* Tomatoes are pruned when grown on stakes, and those varieties suitable for staking and pruning are so-called "indeterminate" types. These varieties form fruit clusters at intervals along their ever elongating stems, which are *indeterminately* long. "Determinate" varieties, in contrast, have stems that do not keep getting longer, because their terminal buds become flowers, then fruits (see the drawing on p. 190). Determinate varieties are not pruned because the result would be nothing more than a single short stem capped by a single cluster of fruits. Seed catalogs and packets usually specify whether a variety is indeterminate or determinate.

Growing upward rather than outward, staked indeterminate plants can be set as close as 18 in. apart to give the greatest yield of tomatoes from a given area of ground. Air

(continued on page 190)

Bearing Habit of Tomato

Indeterminate varieties
Flowers and fruits are borne along stems. The plant increases in size as any or all stems elongate.

Determinate varieties
Flowers and fruits are borne at the end of shoots. The plant increases in size by growth of the side shoots.

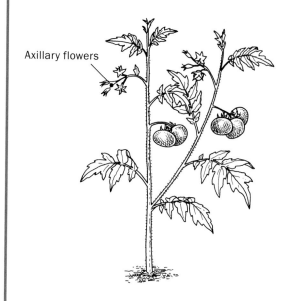

Axillary flowers

Terminal flowers

(continued)

circulating around the leaves and fruits of these upright plants reduces disease problems, and fruits held high above the ground are free from dirt, slugs, turtles, and other potential soil-level calamities. The fruits ripen earlier and are larger (though fewer) than fruits of the same variety on sprawling plants.

To avoid root damage later on, "plant" a stake next to each tomato plant when you set the plant in the ground. You will have to tie the plant to the stake, because a tomato vine lacks tendrils, holdfasts, or other means to hold itself up. Material for ties should be strong enough to hold plants up for the whole season, and bulky enough so as not to cut

into plants' stems. Torn pieces of rag or lengths of twine work well.

On indeterminate varieties, maintain a single stem by removing all side shoots right after you plant, and continuing to do so as the plant grows. Side shoots originate from buds in the leaf axils, which is where a leaf joins the stem. Tomatoes have compound leaves, so do not mistake the junction of a leaflet and a leafstalk for a leaf axil. Snap off each side shoot with your fingers, thereby avoiding the danger of transmitting diseases between plants with the blades of knives or pruning shears. Ideally, remove any shoot before it is more than 1 in. long. As you prune, occasionally step back and refocus your eyes

Left: Staked tomatoes yield cleaner and earlier fruits—and more of them, from a given area of ground.

Below: For staked indeterminate tomatoes, pinch out side shoots with your fingers to train the plants to a single central stem.

on the plant as a whole. A shoot that has made 2 ft. of growth is easily overlooked as you concentrate on small shoots just beginning to grow from leaf axils.

As the main stem grows, tie it to the stake at 12-in. to 18-in. intervals. First make a loop with tying material around the stake, and knot it tightly. Then knot the material loosely around the tomato stem.

You might want to try pinching out the tip of the single stem as soon as a few fruit clusters have set, or when the stem reaches the top of the stake. Continue to remove any new leaves or flowers that form. This pinching carries tomato pruning to the extreme, and is chancy because its success depends on the maturity of a plant's leaves and fruits. At worst, you reduce yield to a few clusters of fruit. At best, you harvest the earliest and largest tomatoes possible for that variety.

PART 3

SPECIAL PRUNING TECHNIQUES

CHAPTER ELEVEN　POLLARDING

You either like pollarding or you do not. Pollarding is not a natural look: in winter, the trunk or short scaffold limbs are terminated by a clubbed head or heads; in summer, a mass of vigorous shoots bursts wildly out of that head or heads. Pollarding is useful for lending a formal appearance to a tree (those wild shoots originate from one or just a few points, so are well contained), and for controlling the size of an otherwise large-growing tree.

Pollarding seems to have isolated but diverse appeal. You find pollarded trees lining streets in San Francisco and some European cities, as well as standing sentinel in front of homes in rural Delaware. The technique originated out of need, centuries ago in Europe, as a means of harvesting firewood without killing a tree. Regularly cutting a tree to the ground—coppicing—accomplishes the same thing on those trees that can tolerate such treatment, but sprouts growing up near ground level were prey to grazing animals.

Fast-growing deciduous trees that do not mind being cut repeatedly are ideal candidates for pollarding. Among such trees are tree-of-heaven (*Ailanthus altissima*), black locust (*Robinia Pseudoacacia*), catalpa (*Catalpa bignonioides*), chestnut (*Castanea* spp.), horse chestnut (*Aesculus Hippocastanum*), linden (*Tilia* spp.), London plane tree (*Platanus × acerifolia*), princess tree (*Paulownia tomentosa*), sycamore (*Platanus occidentalis*), and willow (*Salix* spp.). Vigorous shoots on some of these trees bring along other special effects, such as the monstrous leaves of princess tree, or the bright red bark of the 'chermesina' variety of white willow (*Salix alba*).

Nothing special needs to be done for the young tree to be pollarded except to give it a high head, with at least 5 ft. or 6 ft. of clear trunk. This high head is only for appearance's sake. While the tree is young, leave some branches on the trunk to help thicken it and to shield it from direct sunlight. But keep these branches pinched back so that they do not grow more than 1 ft. in a season, and remove them completely after a few years. For the plant that will be merely a trunk with a clubbed head, cut back the trunk in winter to the height you want for that head.

If your pollarded tree is to have stubby scaffold limbs growing off the trunk, train the tree so that these limbs are spirally arranged around the trunk, spaced 6 in. to 18 in. apart vertically, and radiating out at wide angles. Again, you are designing your tree for appearance; strength is not a concern for a tree never allowed to achieve great height or to grow limbs that are both long and thick. Once scaffold limbs develop, shorten them each winter to a point 2 ft. to 5 ft. from the trunk. Also remove any side branches growing from the scaffold limbs. The eventual size of the tree should determine what will look best as far as the spacing and length of the scaffold limbs. Do not allow the trunk to keep growing upward. Before it grows too thick or too far out of reach, lop it back to the topmost scaffold.

Once the trunk and scaffold limbs are in place, the pollarded tree needs pruning every winter, or at least every second or third winter. Pruning is easy: Just lop all young stems back to within ½ in. or so of where they began growing the previous season. Repeatedly lopping stems back to that point is what makes the knob atop the trunk or at the end of a scaffold limb.

So there you have it, a high head capped by a knobby stub, or by short scaffold limbs ending in those knobby stubs. Prune early enough in the dormant season so that you can enjoy the curious look of your pollarded tree when it is leafless. Interesting.

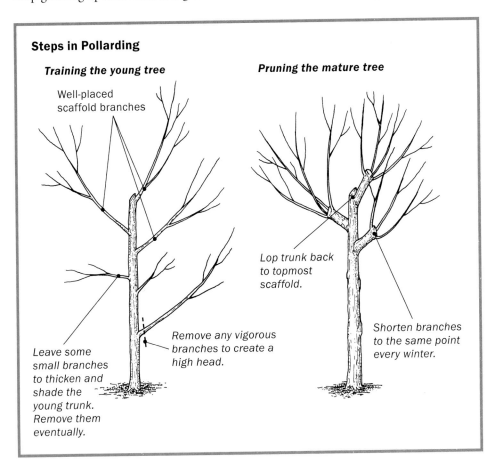

Steps in Pollarding

Training the young tree

Well-placed scaffold branches

Leave some small branches to thicken and shade the young trunk. Remove them eventually.

Remove any vigorous branches to create a high head.

Pruning the mature tree

Lop trunk back to topmost scaffold.

Shorten branches to the same point every winter.

Pleached beeches form an inviting tunnel in Williamsburg, Va.

The word "pleach" derives from the old north French word *plechier*, meaning "to braid," and this is exactly what you do when you pleach trees. You informally weave together their branches. A row of pleached trees is a two-dimensional planting, a thin, horizontal wall of greenery. Plant a row of trees on either side of a walkway, then train stems from the top of each wall over the center, and you have a shady tunnel of greenery—with fruit for the picking if the trees are, for example, apple trees. Or plant trees to enclose an area, clear their trunks of branches to "roof" height, then train a roof of greenery over this living summer house.

Choose your trees for pleaching with care. Species suitable for pleaching have strong yet flexible branches. Good choices include apple *(Malus sylvestris)*, beech *(Fagus* spp.), hornbeam *(Carpinus* spp.), linden *(Tilia* spp.), pear *(Pyrus* spp.), and sycamore *(Platanus occidentalis)*. All trees in a pleached row or "room" should be not only of the same species, but also of the same variety and of similar size, so that growth is uniform. Planting distances within the row depend on how large you are going to let the trees grow, and might range from as little as 3 ft. to as much as 10 ft. or more. Rows that stretch from north to south receive sunlight more uniformly on either side than rows that run east to west.

Although a row or a bower of pleached trees is eventually self-supporting, some sort of framework is needed to direct growth into the desired form. This support might be built of metal or wooden posts and crosspieces, or posts with horizontal wires or bamboo canes between them.

The goal in training the young planting is to force growth upward and outward. Cut plants back right after planting to stimulate vigorous regrowth of a single stem. Allow a single stem on each plant to climb upward, but periodically interrupt growth with a heading cut to promote branches, which you train horizontally in one plane. Tie the main stem and side branches to the support as growth proceeds. Even if you want a length of clear trunk from the ground up to the first branches, allow some temporary low branches to grow on the young plant to help thicken the trunk. Pinch the temporary branches back so that they never get more than about 1 ft. long, and cut them off after a few years. Completely cut back any stems growing out perpendicular to the plane of the pleached trees.

As branches from adjacent trees reach each other, informally weave them together. You could even temporarily tie them together—temporarily because the tie will eventually strangle the branches unless it decays or is removed.

Once pleached trees have filled their allotted area, they need annual pruning from top to bottom. (Keep the "top" part in mind when you plan a row of pleached trees—you'll have to reach up there for regular pruning.) Remove any vigorous upright stems growing near ground level or along branches. Thin out growth where it is too dense. This thinning gives

an airy look (if desired) to the row, and also lets light penetrate to avoid a buildup of dead, leafless wood. Cut back any unruly stems, especially those growing out perpendicular to the flat surface.

Eventually, you can remove the supporting frame. A planting of pleached trees grows sturdier with age, as the woven branches naturally graft together.

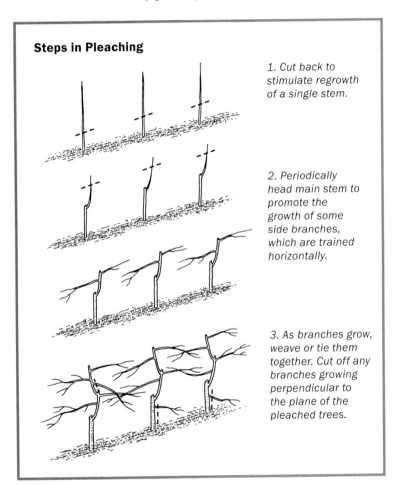

Steps in Pleaching

1. Cut back to stimulate regrowth of a single stem.

2. Periodically head main stem to promote the growth of some side branches, which are trained horizontally.

3. As branches grow, weave or tie them together. Cut off any branches growing perpendicular to the plane of the pleached trees.

A topiary requires constant attention.

gardener, and has progressed, or at least endured, to the present day. The tradition survived the Dark Ages in monastery gardens, then resurfaced in Renaissance Italy. The French and the Dutch, and occasionally the British, have been fond of topiary. In modern gardens, topiary is rare unless you count the pervasive American foundation plantings of clipped yews and junipers—derisively labelled "gumdrop" or "dot-dash" landscaping by some people—as topiary.

(Note that we are not considering here topiaries made from mesh frames filled with wet moss, then "plugged" with hens-and-chickens, or made from wire frames on which twine vining plants such as English ivy. Neither of these topiaries requires pruning for their development or maintenance.)

Only certain plants are suitable for topiary. The ideal plant is slow growing, tolerant of repeated pruning, and able to resprout from older wood. Especially for smaller topiary viewed at close range, small leaves are needed to create a surface with a crisp edge. Winter damage to a topiary tree or shrub that is years or even decades old is a disaster, so the plant also must be cold hardy for the site. If possible, select a species or variety whose natural shape approximates its intended shape: 'Brownii' yew for a sphere, 'Sentinalis' yew for a obelisk, and 'Hillii' yew for a pyramid. (Other plants, admittedly, do not exhibit such variety of form as does yew.)

Evergreens generally are used for topiary, but occasionally a deciduous

Topiary is the art of growing trees and shrubs as living sculptures—cubes, spheres, obelisks, animal shapes, even combinations of these shapes nestled side by side or piled on top of one another. The art originated in ancient Rome, where *topiarius* meant ornamental

plant such as English hawthorn (*Crataegus monogyna*) or European beech (*Fagus sylvatica*) is used. California privet (*Ligustrum ovalifolium*) also makes nice topiary, and is evergreen where winters are not too cold. A drawback to a deciduous topiary, of course, is that it is bare in winter (although beech does not shed its dead leaves until spring). Deciduous plants generally grow more exuberantly than do evergreens, so they also require more diligence to keep growth in check.

Many species of evergreens have been used for topiary. The quintessential plants for topiary are yew (*Taxus* spp.) and boxwood (*Buxus* spp.). Other suitable plants include arborvitae (*Thuja* spp.), bay laurel (*Laurus nobilis*), hemlock (*Tsuga* spp.), holly (*Ilex* spp.), holly oak (*Quercus Ilex*), Italian cypress (*Cupressus sempervirens*), juniper (*Juniperus* spp.), Leyland cypress (× *Cupressocyparis Leylandii*), *Lonicera nitida*, Monterey cypress (*Cupressus macrocarpa*), myrtle (*Myrtus communis*), Portugal laurel (*Prunus lusitanica*), and rosemary (*Rosmarinus officinalis*).

In most cases, begin shaping your plant while it is young. You could, however, carve a shape out of an old overgrown yew much as you would out of wood or stone, because yew grows so densely and sprouts so freely from old wood. Or a growing plant might suggest a form that you could then develop. You might even juxtapose two plants, or let one grow up through the other to create, for example, a pedestal on which sits a verdant animal. In any case, topiary lends itself more to

A privet 'chair.'

bold shapes than to intricate designs whose details are swallowed up between prunings. Site your topiary so that it receives good light on all sides, for dense growth throughout.

Most young topiary plants that are still in their formative stage need nothing more than frequent shearing or clipping off of the ends of stems in order to encourage dense branching. Clipping individual stems is the preferred method for plants with large leaves because shearing would mangle individual leaves. Obviously, if a stem protrudes in the direction where you want growth, leave it.

For a more complex shape, such as that representing an animal, use a frame on which to train stems. Make the frame of heavy wire and make sure that it is firmly anchored to a stake. To avoid eventually choking the stems, tie them to the frame with string that will decompose with time. As you encourage growth along the wire frame, also frequently head back side shoots to promote bushiness.

Once a topiary is fully grown and shaped, it will need pruning at least once a year, two or three times a year in some cases. Where a plant is reliably cold hardy, prune just after midsummer. By then, the spring flush of growth has ceased, and there is less chance that pruning will stimulate regrowth before the following spring. Cut freehand, or use a guide to make sure your topiary is not gradually changing shape over the years. A guide is also useful when you have matching topiaries—without the guide, you may one day look up to find that they no longer match. If you cut freehand, step back frequently to check and admire your work.

What is to be done with a neglected topiary? Severe cuts may be needed to stimulate growth within the plant. Repair a leafless hole by widening it, cutting old wood around the hole back to healthy wood. If severe cuts are needed, renovation is possible only if the plant is capable of sprouting from old, perhaps leafless, wood. Otherwise, start again with a new plant.

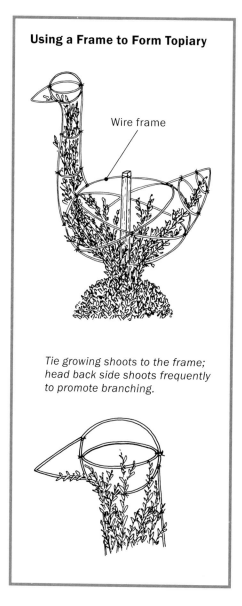

Using a Frame to Form Topiary

Wire frame

Tie growing shoots to the frame; head back side shoots frequently to promote branching.

CHAPTER FOURTEEN

STANDARDS

In the world of gardening, people are divided over how they feel about "standards." Some gardeners love them, others will have nothing to do with them. "Standard" has many meanings both in and out of horticulture, so let's first get straight which kind of "standard" we are dealing with: Here, I mean a naturally bushy plant trained to have a clear, upright stem capped by a mop of leaves. A miniature tree. I count myself among standardophiles and, if I may speak for the group, we like standards for their neatness and because they have the lollipop shape of storybook trees. "Standard" does seem like an odd word to describe such a plant until you realize that the "stand" in "standard" does indeed mean just that. ("Standard" comes from the Old English words *standan*, meaning to stand, and *ord*, meaning a place.)

A plant may set off on the road to standard-dom by several routes. One way to create a standard is to graft a bushy plant atop a straight trunk of another plant. The rootstock, then, is a plant with a naturally vigorous, upright growth habit and must of course be closely related to the plant grafted to it. A rather unique way to create an English ivy *(Hedera Helix)* standard is to use mature English ivy, an upright shrub, as a rootstock upon which you graft juvenile English ivy, a vining plant. But this is not a book about grafting, so here we will explore the ways you can make standards by pruning.

Rosemary, grown as a potted standard, provides fresh flavor and beauty all year round.

Begin, for example, with a seedling, a rooted cutting, or an established bushy plant. With the established bushy plant, start off by lopping all stems down to soil level.

From here on, the seedling, the rooted cutting, and the plant that has been lopped back can be treated in the same way. The lopped-back plant will grow faster than the others, but in any case it is important to provide excellent growing conditions for vigorous growth in developing the main stem. And you will allow only one main stem—the trunk-to-be—to develop. Set a stake in the soil and tie the growing stem to the stake every few inches. Keeping the stem upright and straight does more than just create a straight trunk. Upright growth is inherently most vigorous and naturally suppresses the growth of lower buds—just what you want in the developing standard.

Other buds will still grow, though, more or less depending on the natural bushiness of the plant. Diligently remove any shoots growing up near ground level. If you get to them while they are young, just snapping them off, they will be less inclined to regrow. Branches may also try

Steps in Creating a Standard

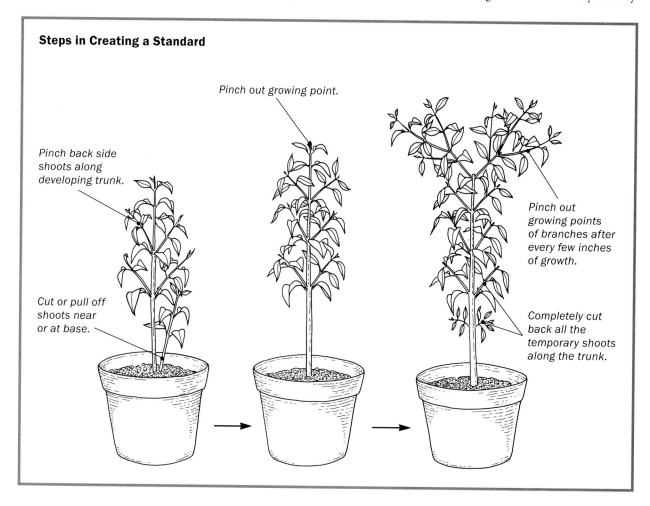

Pinch out growing point.

Pinch back side shoots along developing trunk.

Cut or pull off shoots near or at base.

Pinch out growing points of branches after every few inches of growth.

Completely cut back all the temporary shoots along the trunk.

to grow from the main stem. These branches do contribute to the total growth of the plant and thicken the developing trunk, but they also take away from the vigor of the main stem. Pinch back branches to weaken them. Some judgment is needed here. A seedling or a weak plant needs all the energy it can garner, so you might allow a couple of inches of growth on its branches. On a vigorous plant, pinch branches back to a single leaf or pair of leaves.

Once the main stem reaches full height, it is time to form the mop head. The length of the main stem is going to depend, artistically, on the density and size of the leaves, and, physiologically, on the vigor of the plant. You would have trouble getting a very long trunk on a weak-growing, weeping plant. The thin, dense leaves of my rosemary (*Rosmarinus officinalis*) look just right filling the 12-in. wide ball capping an 8-in. long trunk. (At three years old, it is indeed a trunk!) But an 18-in. mop head on a 2½-ft. long trunk is more suitable to accommodate the large, broad leaves of my potted bay laurel (*Laurus nobilis*) standard.

Begin forming the head by pinching out the growing point of the main stem. This pinch takes out the bud that made hormones that inhibited growth of lower buds. The most vigorous new branches will be those near the top of the main stem, and that's where you want them. Create a dense head, now, by pinching those branches after every few inches of growth. You also can now completely cut away any temporary branches or leaves lower down along the trunk.

Once your standard is fully grown, periodic maintenance pruning is required. Continue to snap off or cut away any shoots growing from the trunk or from ground level. As for the head of the plant, treat it just as if it were a bush. Refer elsewhere in this book for specific pruning directions for any of the many plants that can be grown as standards.

Just about any bushy plant can be trained as a standard. Upright, vigorous varieties, when they exist, are easiest to train this way. Hence, the use of 'Annabel', 'Tennessee Waltz', and 'Hidcote Beauty' for fuchsia (*Fuchsia × hybrida*) standards. On the other hand, if you want a standard with a languorous weeping head, you will have to force a weeping variety up to head height, or graft the weeping variety atop a trunk of an upright variety. (The latter method does sometimes results in an unnatural-looking juncture at the graft.) Besides fuchsia, rosemary, bay laurel, and English ivy, other plants commonly trained to standards are coleus (*Coleus × hybridus*), geranium (*Pelargonium* spp.), flowering maple (*Abutilon* spp.), heliotrope (*Heliotropium arborescens*), marguerite (*Chrysanthemum frutescens*), and verbena (*Verbena × hybrida*). You may be surprised to see in this list some plants usually grown as annuals. They can, in fact, develop woody trunks when grown as perennials, in which case they need protection from cold where winters would kill them.

For us standardophiles, artistic restraint rather than a shortage of plant candidates for treatment limits the number of standards we grow. Standards are accent plants, and too much accent becomes disturbing or ceases to be an accent at all. (But hmmm: How about forgetting about accent, and creating a forest of storybook trees?)

A bay laurel standard.

Mowing the lawn is at once the most mundane and the most unique form of pruning. Everyone does it, yet what other kind of pruning calls for cutting off only a part of the leaf blade— and thousands at a time! The growing point of a grass plant is nestled down near ground level, below the reach of mower blades, so it is able to go on making new growth.

Even though the growing point remains unscathed, mowing, like any other form of pruning, weakens a plant, so you have to strike a balance between what looks nice and what keeps the plants healthy. As a general rule, mow frequently enough to remove no more than one-third of the length of the grass blades down to a maximum acceptable height. So if you want your lawn at 2 in., mow 1 in. off when the leaves reach 3 in. Keep in mind that uniformity of cut (rather than just closeness of cut) plays a large part in making an elegantly beautiful lawn. Longer grass also needs less frequent mowing than does grass kept short, and creates shade which interferes with the germination and growth of lawn weeds such as crabgrass.

The optimum mowing height varies with the grass species and the growing conditions. Stress such as as shade or drought calls for longer grass. Also, let a newly seeded lawn grow a little longer than an established lawn. Recommended lengths, after mowing, for various types of grass are given in the chart on the facing page.

Ideally, all grass blades are dry and standing upright like soldiers when you go out to mow. By mowing down to the recommended lengths without removing more than one-third of the blades, the grass will not be so long that it is flopping over under its own weight. One advantage of a rotary mower over a reel mower is that the rotary mower's cutting blade acts like a propeller to suck the grass blades upright. Timely mowing dispenses with the need to rake up the clippings; left on the soil, they add valuable nutrients and humus. If you have been remiss in mowing, lower the grass in stages to avoid shocking it, and collect the clippings after each mowing.

As with any type of pruning, sharp cutting blades make cleaner cuts—important for plant health and appearance in the case of lawns. Reel-type mowers make the cleanest cuts, but rotary mowers can cut longer grass. No matter what type of mower you use, vary your mowing pattern each time you mow if you want to avoid the development of permanent ruts in the ground and create a uniform surface.

On the other hand, you may not want to create a perfectly uniform surface. Notice that just after you mow, the grass is a slightly different hue of green depending on the direction that the mower traveled. This effect is most dramatic when a lush lawn has been cut with a reel-type mower. In Great Britain, land of perfect lawns, lawn mavens create striped patterns in their lawns by directing their mowers back and forth across the greensward in neat parallel lines. For the British, it seems, "Regular stripes emphasize the calm and orderliness of a well-kept lawn. To a lawn fanatic the process of mowing is a pleasure in itself: the noise of the mower,

OPTIMUM MOWING HEIGHT OF GRASSES	
Plant	Height (in inches)
Bahia Grass (*Paspalum notatum*)	2.5 – 3.5
Bent Grass	
Colonial (*Agrostis tenuis*)	0.5 – 1.25
Creeping (*A. stolonifera*)	0.25 – 1.0
Bermuda Grass (*Cynodon Dactylon*)	0.25 – 1.5
Buffalo Grass (*Buchloe dactyloides*)	1.0 – 2.5
Carpet Grass (*Axonopus affinis*)	1.5 – 2.5
Centipede Grass (*Eremochloa ophiuroides*)	1.5 – 2.5
Fescue	
Chewing (*Festuca rubra* var. *commutata*)	1.5 – 3.0
Red (*F. rubra*)	2.0 – 4.0
Tall (*F. elatior*)	2.0 – 4.0
Kentucky Bluegrass (*Poa pratensis*)	1.5 – 4.0
Ryegrass	
Italian, or Annual (*Lolium multiflorum*)	1.5 – 3.5
Perennial (*L. perenne*)	1.5 – 3.5
St. Augustine Grass (*Stenotaphrum secundatum*)	2.0 – 4.0
Wheatgrass (*Agropyron* spp.)	2.0 – 4.0
Zoysia Grass (*Zoysia* spp.)	0.5 – 2.0

The British love their stripes, and perhaps you do too.

the smell of the exhaust and the oil and the warm green cuttings. For the richest green and the most pronounced stripes three-quarters of an inch is best." (Hugh Johnson, *The Principles of Gardening*, 1979). Each to his own.

For myself, I prefer a bolder effect, possible even on a less than perfect lawn, created by sculpting out two tiers of grassy growth. I like to call this "Lawn Nouveau," and I admit that the idea sprung from my lack of time and enthusiasm for mowing the lawn.

The low grass is just like any other lawn, and kept that way with a lawn-mower. The taller portions are mowed with a scythe. Clippings from the tall grass portions must be raked up after mowing or else they would leave unsightly clumps and smother regrowth. A crisp boundary between tall and low grass keeps everything neat and avoids the appearance of an unmown lawn.

Lawn Nouveau saves me time because the tall grass needs infrequent mowing, even less than once a month, and there's no rush to get it done. The "tall grass" becomes more than just grass as other plant species gradually elbow their way in. Which ones gain foothold depend on the weather and frequency of mowing. An attractive mix of Queen Anne's lace, chicory, and red clover might mingle with the grasses in a dry, sunny area, with ferns, sedges, and buttercups mixing with the grasses in a wetter portion. Design flaws are easily and quickly corrected with the help of the scythe and rake. And you can maintain or change your design at any hour you wish, without bothering your neighbors. The only sound a scythe blade makes is a

The juxtaposition of tall and short grass adds interest to the lawn.

A lawnmower carves a design for Lawn Nouveau.

The author, happily scything.

whispering swoosh, a "sound to rout the brood of cares, the sweep of the scythe in morning dew" (Alfred, Lord Tennyson, *In Memoriam*, 1850).

In addition to carving fancy designs in a lawn, tall and short grass can help define areas—"garden rooms," you might say. And rather than straight edges and 90° corners, curves in bold sweeps can carry you along, then pull you forward and push you backward, as you look upon them. These undulations are more than just imagination, for they really can change position with each mowing. Avenues of low grass cut into the tall grass invite exploration, and, like the broad sweeps, can be altered throughout the season. Such is the fluidity of Lawn Nouveau.

A bonsai planting portrays, in miniature, a natural theme—the rugged beauty of a gnarled pine on a windswept slope, the tranquility of a grove of larches, the joyousness of spring in the cascading branches of an old fruit tree bursting into bloom. To evoke such a mood, the pot must be chosen with an artistic eye; likewise for the manner in which branches are shaped and the choice of groundcover. And in addition to all this, the plant must also be kept healthy with careful attention to soils, fertilizers, watering, and the provision of winter quarters.

Pruning plays a role in creating the artistry of bonsai, and also is needed to keep a plant healthy and, of course, small. Most bonsai are created from plants that, given their way, could grow into towering trees or billowing shrubs.

You first prune a bonsai before even potting it up, beginning with the roots. Wild plants, even small wild plants, often have surprisingly far-reaching roots, and these roots must be untangled and shortened in order to fit the plant into its pot. Certain trees have taproots in addition to shallow feeder roots. The taproot must be cut off if the plant is to grow in a shallow tray.

The top of a new bonsai also might need to be cut back to bring it down to bonsai size, which is usually under 4 ft. (Bonsai are classified according to form and size, and the smallest bonsai are less than 7 in. high.) But you cannot simply

Root and shoot pruning have coaxed this Chinese elm into a diminutive size.

Bonsai (pronounced BONE-sigh) is the growing of plants, usually woody plants, in shallow trays or pots. Pruning is what makes a bonsai plant small, but pruning is only a small part of the art of bonsai. The art began in China almost 2,000 years ago, then was carried to Japan during the Kamakura period (1180-1333), where it was brought to a high state of perfection.

Shortening a Trunk to Create a Bonsai

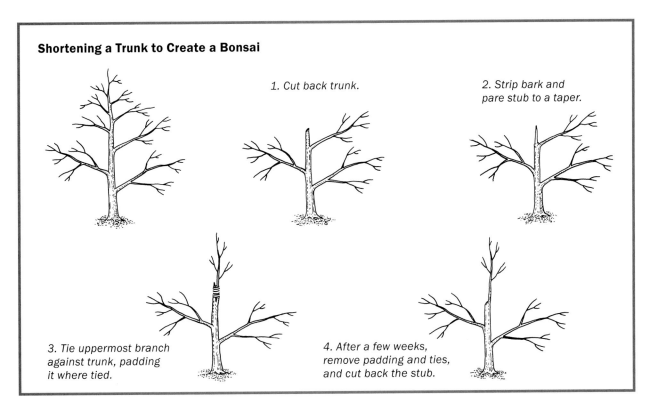

1. Cut back trunk.

2. Strip bark and pare stub to a taper.

3. Tie uppermost branch against trunk, padding it where tied.

4. After a few weeks, remove padding and ties, and cut back the stub.

lop back a stem or trunk; the plant will look like a lopped-back plant instead of an ancient tree in miniature.

To shorten a trunk, cut it back to a few inches above its desired height—no need to cut to a node, as you would with most other pruning. Trim the bark from the portion of trunk above the highest remaining node, then pare the stub to a taper. Take a branch growing from that highest node, bend it upward, and tie it right up against the tapered stub with some padding to prevent the string or wire used for tying from marring the branch. After a few weeks, when the branch can hold the upright position without assistance, remove the ties and cut back the stub, with a sloping cut, to the base of the branch that has now become the new leader—and which you will keep pruned to prevent it from growing tall.

Another way to shorten a trunk is to create a "broom" style bonsai, a trunk capped by a fan of stems (see the photo and drawing on p. 210). Begin by cutting the trunk back to where you want the branches to begin. Rather than a flat or slanted cut, leave the cut surface of the decapitated plant looking like an asymmetrical V, something like a saddle. Next, wrap rubber strips tightly around the trunk at the top to prevent it from swelling and ruining the form. Many new shoots may attempt to grow from where you cut, but rub off all but perhaps a half-dozen of them. As the shoots grow, pinch their tips to promote branching. This broom style is especially suited to the growth habits of elm and zelkova.

To create an "old" snag of wood on your young bonsai, snap off the trunk or a branch. Pull down a strip of bark from the snag as far as you want. Let the exposed wood dry out, then paint it with

A broom-style bonsai.

Creating a Broom-Style Bonsai

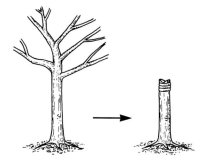

Make a saddle cut back to the desired height, then bind the trunk just below the cut with rubber strips.

Many new shoots will grow at the cut.

Rub off all but about six of the shoots, then pinch their tips to promote branching.

full-strength lime-sulfur solution three or four times every two weeks to preserve it.

Bonsai need regular pruning both above and below ground throughout their life. The frequency of pruning depends on the inherent growth rate of the particular plant, the size of the container, and the growing conditions.

Roots eventually fill the soil in the container, so root pruning is needed to make room for fresh new soil. Root-prune deciduous bonsai in early spring or late autumn, evergreen bonsai in early spring or late summer. Cut the root ball

Creating an 'Old' Snag on Bonsai

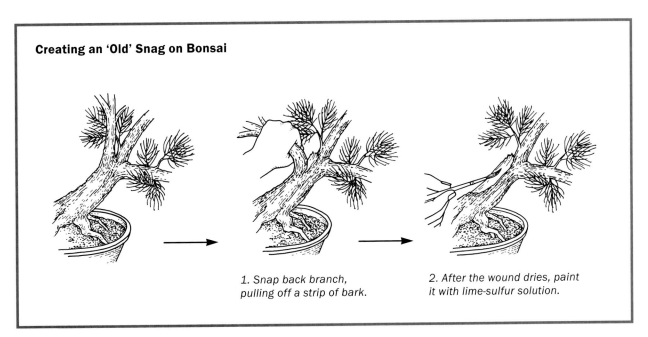

1. Snap back branch, pulling off a strip of bark.

2. After the wound dries, paint it with lime-sulfur solution.

back with a sharp knife and tease roots on the outside of the ball outward, then put the plant back in the pot, packing new soil among and around the roots.

Prune the top portion of a bonsai both while it is dormant and while it is growing to keep the plant small and to develop or maintain its form. Response to pruning is the same as for full-size plants: Pinch shoot tips to slow growth; shorten a stem where you want branches; rub off buds where growth is not wanted; pinch back "candles" of pines; pinch back expanding new growth on spruces and junipers; etc. With bonsai, though, even your fingernails might be too coarse a pruning tool. So, to avoid damaging the remaining leaves when you shorten expanding growth on spruce, for example, reach within a tuft of foliage with a pair of tweezers to tweak off all but a few new leaves.

Some bonsai benefit from having all their leaves pruned off just after they fully expand. Timed correctly, such leaf pruning forces a second flush of leaves which are smaller and hence better

proportioned to the size of the plant. You can get two seasons of development in one season with this trick, and, as an added benefit, that second flush of leaves often gives more dramatic autumn color than the first flush would have. On some trees, such as maples and elms, you can leaf-prune twice each season, as the first and second flushes of leaves fully expand. With trees such as ginkgo, beech, and oak, timing is critical for getting even a second flush of leaves. If there is any chance of injuring buds at the bases of the leaf stalks, just cut off most of each leaf with a scissors. The stalk will come off, perhaps needing some help from you, as new leaves appear.

Leaf pruning is not for every bonsai. Don't do it on evergreens or on fruiting bonsai that are bearing fruit. And leaf pruning is stressful, so avoid this practice on any tree that is weak or sick. The rigorous root and shoot pruning needed for bonsai is itself weakening, which is a good reason to take extra care in giving bonsai perfect growing conditions in every other respect.

An old snag gives this bonsai a wizened appearance.

CHAPTER SEVENTEEN

ESPALIER

A well-grown espalier
offers food and beauty.

Espalier (es-pal-YAY) is the training of a plant, usually a fruit plant, to an orderly two-dimensional form. The word is derived from the Old French *aspau*, meaning a prop, and most espaliers must, in fact, be propped up with stakes or wires. Espalier had its formal beginnings in Europe in the 16th century, when fruit trees were trained on walls to take advantage of the strip of earth and extra warmth near those walls. Strictly speaking, an espalier grown on a trellis in open ground is termed a *contre-espalier* of an *espalier-aere*. But no need to be a stickler for words. The definition of espalier is as lax as the plant is formal: The British reserve the term for a specific two-dimensional form; and some fanciful, yet well-ordered, shapes which might be called "espalier" by some gardeners, are, in fact, three-dimensional.

Why go to all the trouble of erecting a trellis and then having to pinch and snip a plant so frequently to keep it in shape? Because a well-grown espalier represents a happy commingling of art and science, resulting in a plant that pleases not only the eye, but also the palate. You apply this science artfully (or your art scientifically) by pulling exuberant stems downward to slow their growth, by cutting notches where a stem threatens to remain bare, by pruning back stems in summer to keep growth neat and fruitful—more on all of this later. The result: Every stem on a well-grown espalier is furnished throughout its length with fruits, and these fruits, bathed in abundant sunlight and air, are luscious, large, and full colored.

Despite the constant attention demanded by an espalier, caring for it is not really a great hardship. The trees never grow large, so they can be pruned, thinned, and harvested with your feet planted squarely on terra firma. And while pruning must be frequent, the cuts are small and quickly done, in many cases requiring nothing more than your thumbnail.

Espalier need not be restricted to plants bearing edible fruits. A purely ornamental espalier is in keeping with a formal setting (and so is an edible-fruited espalier). Maintenance of a purely ornamental espalier, especially when such a plant does not bear even flowers or ornamental fruit, entails nothing more than repeated clipping of wayward stems. When fruit, especially edible fruit, is a goal, however, you must carefully consider the response of the plant before you cut back stems: Are there enough leaves to nourish each fruit adequately? Will a new stem defiantly replace the one that you just cut off? Will your pruning restrict growth and keep stems furnished with fruit buds throughout their length?

Forms for an espalier

An espalier consists of one or more main stems, called leaders, which grow from the trunk. Permanent stems, called arms or ribs, may or may not arise from the leader(s). Arms usually are horizontal, or nearly so. Ribs usually refer to the herringbone pattern of stems that grow off the leaders of a fan-type espalier, which I will describe soon. Temporary stems, referred to as branches, grow directly from the leaders or, if present, arms or ribs. The trick in growing an espalier is minimizing branch growth while maximizing fruiting.

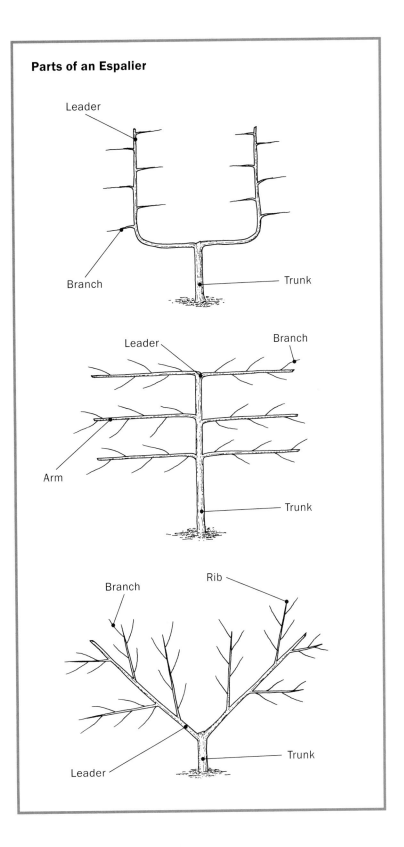

Parts of an Espalier

Leader

Branch

Trunk

Leader

Branch

Arm

Trunk

Rib

Branch

Leader

Trunk

The simplest form for an espalier is that of a single leader (which some people choose to call a "cordon" rather than an "espalier"). Vertical cordons can be set a mere 18 in. apart in a row, so they are useful, for example, for growing many varieties of apple in a small space. Or a cordon can be trained horizontally to border a path or to edge a garden.

The cordon is best suited to plants that bear fruits on short growths, called spurs, so that the cordon looks like a cordon, rather than a porcupine. Among common fruits, apples and pears, and, to a lesser extent, plums, make good cordons. To counteract the tendency to top-heavy growth due to apical dominance of a vertical leader, single

Various Forms of Espalier

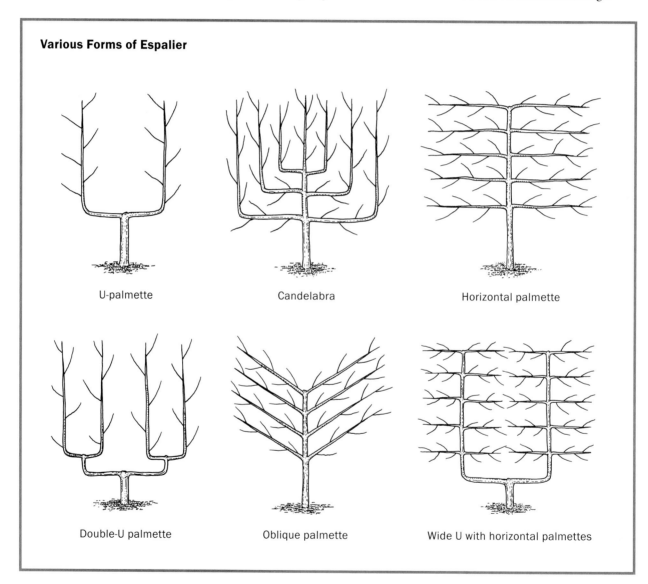

U-palmette

Candelabra

Horizontal palmette

Double-U palmette

Oblique palmette

Wide U with horizontal palmettes

cordons are commonly planted and grown at an angle, rather than vertically. This practice encourages uniform budbreak and growth up and down the cordon.

Terminate that single stem of a vertical cordon near ground level and split it into two stems, which you turn away from each other before letting them grow vertically again, and you have a U-palmette. Split those two vertical leaders of the U again and you have a double-U palmette, increasing the spread and yield from a single plant— and also changing the design, of course.

Just imagine how many variations can exist on this theme! The central stem could have two of its laterals grow out, then up, into leaders forming a wide U, then continue upward to have another two of its laterals growing out, then up, into a less wide U, and so on, candelabra fashion. Or, the central stem could grow up to the top of the plant, along the way sending out tiers of horizontal arms growing off to the left and to the right. (This latter form is what the British choose to call espalier; others call it a horizontal palmette or, if the side arms angle upward, an oblique palmette.) Or the central stem could split into a broad U with horizontal tiers of arms growing outward in two directions from each of the two leaders.

All these forms are prey to a common problem: excess growth near the tops of their upright leaders. This is the result of apical dominance, which is the tendency for the buds and shoots highest on a plant to grow most strongly. (A hormone called auxin, produced in the uppermost growing tips and buds, suppresses growth and budbreak farther down a stem.) To quote M. Gressent (*Arboriculture Fruitière*, 1869), a vertical growth "throws trouble into the whole economy of the tree and paralyzes its production and compromises the very existence of the horizontal branches." Well, not always, but those verticals do have to be watched.

Other shapes of espalier have been developed to overcome the potential hazard from vertical leaders. One popular form is the "fan," in which the

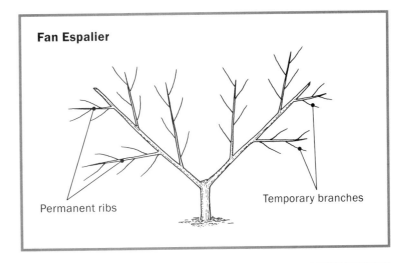

Fan Espalier

Permanent ribs

Temporary branches

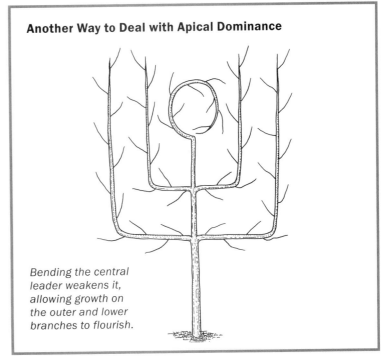

Another Way to Deal with Apical Dominance

Bending the central leader weakens it, allowing growth on the outer and lower branches to flourish.

central stem terminates low in the plant, dividing into two leaders that angle upward and outward. Off each of these leaders, above and below, grow ribs, with fruiting spurs or temporary branches growing from them. The number of ribs, and just how vertically they are allowed to grow, depend on the inherent vigor of the plant. Building up the lower and outside parts of the fan first keeps the potentially most vigorous part—that which is highest and in the center—from overtaking the rest. In other designs, the central leader is purposely weakened as it is bent around in a decorative curve, rather than allowed to grow straight upward.

Then there are espaliers composed of plants lined up and overlapping in a row. Among the most popular of such designs is the Belgian fence, a living latticework of stems. With some designs, adjacent stems graft together so that the espalier eventually becomes self-supporting.

When mature, this apple trained as a Belgian fence will become a decorative screen producing luscious fruit.

Training

Training an espalier is just like training any other plant. Use heading cuts into young wood where you want branching, and thinning cuts when you want to get rid of unwanted growth (which includes stems growing perpendicular to the plane of the espalier). The differences between training a conventional fruit plant and an espalier lie in the goals: With an espalier, you want to develop stems having near perfect symmetry and furnished with live buds throughout their length.

No matter what your design, allow sufficient space (about 12 in.) between leaders. Where you want to bend a developing leader to change its direction of growth, lessen the chance of breakage by twisting the stem slightly as you bend. Where you want a leader to divide into a Y or a U, choose for those side arms stems that are growing as nearly as possible opposite and close to each other along the leader. The plant might already have some suitably positioned stems, or you might make a heading cut just above where you want them. Because laterals originate some distance apart along any stem on plants with alternate rather than opposite leaves, arms resulting from heading back a dormant shoot on such plants will never emerge *exactly* opposite each other.

The espalier maven, however, wants perfect symmetry (even in alternate-leaved plants), and there are two ways to put arms directly across from each other. One way is merely to graft a shoot opposite an existing shoot, or a bud opposite an existing bud, where you want the arms. The other way is to cut the stem back to the level where you want it to divide, while the plant is dormant. A vigorous shoot will grow vertically from the top of that cut stem, and at the base of that shoot will be a whorl of buds close together. When the vertical shoot is about 1 ft. long, cut it back to the whorl (leaving about ¼ in. of new growth) and you should get two new shoots originating from buds within that whorl—at almost exactly the same level. Aesthetics aside, shoots originating at the same level are more likely to keep in step as they grow.

Shorten the leader or leaders of an espalier each year, while the plant is dormant. Until a leader reaches its full length, cut back one-quarter to one-half of the previous season's growth, with the more severe cuts on weaker shoots. The purpose of this annual shortening is to keep the buds along the stem active. Upon reaching full length, the leader or leaders are cut back each year to within an inch or so of the previous season's growth.

Make free use of your thumbnail to pinch the tips of growing shoots as you train an espalier. Where any shoot is trying to outgrow its brethren, maintain symmetry by pinching back its tip. Pinching back the tips (just the tips, no more) of developing leaders every foot or so also keeps buds lower on the shoot active so that you do not get blind wood, possibly reducing or even eliminating the need for dormant heading of the leader or leaders.

You will need to erect a framework—commonly of wood, wire, or metal—to support your espalier and make sure its leaders are ramrod straight and at the desired angles. (All this rigidity is more a matter of aesthetics than plant physiology.) Once you have a framework erected, tie a leader as it grows to a bamboo cane that follows the desired direction of the shoot, then tie the cane to the framework.

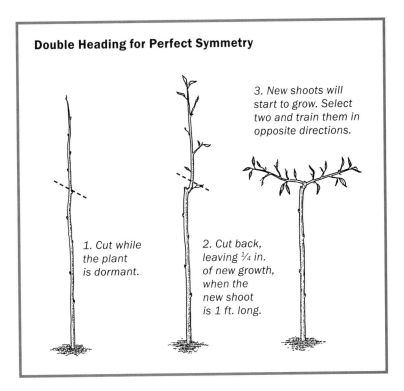

Double Heading for Perfect Symmetry

3. New shoots will start to grow. Select two and train them in opposite directions.

1. Cut while the plant is dormant.

2. Cut back, leaving ¼ in. of new growth, when the new shoot is 1 ft. long.

There are two reasons for tying a leader to the cane rather than directly to the framework. First, even though trellises are most easily constructed with horizontal and vertical members, and wires are most easily strung horizontally between end posts, the bamboo cane—with the attached leader—can be fixed at any desired angle. And second, tying a shoot to a cane rather than directly to the trellis also keeps a stem straight even if you have to raise or lower it as it grows. In this, we can befriend our old bugbear, apical dominance. For example, if your espalier will have two horizontal arms, you might want to train those arms initially at an upward angle to keep growth moving along—the more upward pointing, the faster the growth. As the arms approach full length, gradually bring them down to horizontal to slow growth. To do this, it is necessary only to untie the cane, and then, with the branch still firmly lashed to it, retie it at the desired angle.

Another way you can make use of apical dominance to build up horizontal arms while keeping growth active is to lash all but the ends of the shoots to horizontal supports. The free ends of the shoots then do what they are naturally inclined to do, turn upward, and that upward orientation keeps the growing tips vigorous. As the shoot elongates, keep tying the older portions down to the horizontal support.

Plants never follow rules exactly, and delinquent buds and shoots require special treatment. Use your knife to cut a notch just beyond a bud that needs awakening (see the photo on p. 29), or

---

Two Ways to Develop Horizontal Leaders

Leaders tied to canes and gradually lowered

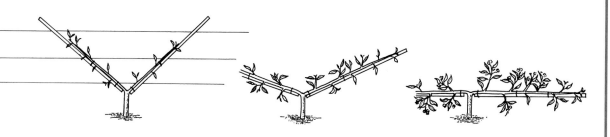

Lash the leaders to canes to keep them straight. Angle the canes upward when the leaders are young to keep growth vigorous.

As the leaders age, lower the canes to slow growth and bring the leaders into final horizontal position.

Ends left free

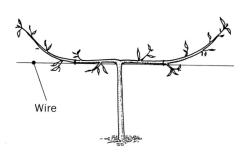

Wire

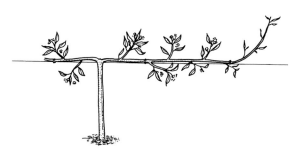

Keep tying the older portion of the leaders down, leaving the ends free to turn upward temporarily.

just below a shoot that needs restraint. A direct way to fill in a bare spot on a branch is to graft a bud, even a fruit bud, wherever it is needed. Deal with strong vertical shoots that are not wanted for extension growth either by cutting them away completely or by shortening them to a few buds, which may turn into fruit buds. But this latter pruning is the specialized pruning that is at the core of the next phase of pruning an espalier…

Maintenance pruning

Even before an espalier is fully trained, the older parts of the plant will need strict pruning to control branch growth and so maintain the neat shape of the plant—all the while avoiding sacrifice of fruit yield or quality. How pruning can help reach this goal depends on a particular plant's fruiting habit.

No matter what the plant, though, always keep shoots growing perpendicular to the plane of the espalier in check. Cut them cleanly away or pinch them back to a single leaf. And thin out branches if they become overcrowded. The stems of the perfect espalier will be solidly clothed with fruit, and if this goal is realized, make sure also to thin out some of the developing fruits. Some plants fruit on spurs, which eventually grow old and overcrowded and need to be thinned out and rejuvenated.

Now, on to some specifics, which, I caution you, must in some cases be varied to account for differences in varieties and climates.

Apple and pear espaliers

Apple and pear trees have similar growth and fruiting habits (fruits are borne on long-lived, stubby spurs) that are ideally suited for many different shapes of espalier, and made more so by the range of dwarfing rootstocks available for each of these fruits. But especially with these two fruits will you have to tailor your system of pruning to the variety and the location.

Apple 'Egremont russet' in an English garden in September.

In Lorette pruning, a half-woody shoot is cut back to the whorl of leaves at its base.

Let's start with one of the most elegant systems for pruning apple and pear espaliers, which was devised at the end of the 19th century by Louis Lorette, curator and professor of the Practical School of Agriculture at Wagonville, France. According to the Lorette system, which produces spectacular results in terms of beauty and fecundity, trees are pruned only during the growing season.

The first pruning, that of the extension growth from the tip of the leader (or tips of leaders), takes place when side shoots are about 2 in. long (the end of April in Wagonville). If a leader has not yet attained its full length, you cut back the previous season's growth by one-quarter to one-half, the lesser amount if growth was weak and the greater amount if it was strong. Shortening a developing leader keeps the lateral buds on this year-old wood active enough to prevent blind wood. The new shoot that grows from the end of a shortened leader is then allowed to grow unfettered for the whole season, thereby extending the leader. If a leader has reached its full length, cut it

back each year to where it began growing the previous season.

Pruning of branches growing off leaders begins later in the season (the middle of June in Wagonville), when they are pencil thick, about 1 ft. long, and becoming woody at their bases. Cut each branch that fits this description back to the whorl of leaves at its base, leaving a stub about ¼ in. long. Do not touch any branches that have not yet reached the proper growth maturity. Repeat this cutting back of properly mature branches at monthly intervals throughout the summer. Where regrowth has occurred following the previous pruning, also cut it back, but only if regrowth is at the proper stage of maturity. At the last pruning, in late summer, cut any immature branches back to three buds. Never shorten branches that are long, but insufficiently thick; instead, bend them over, then tie down their tips in order to furnish them with fruit buds. That's the bare bones of Lorette pruning; for more detail I refer you to *The Lorette System of Pruning* by Louis Lorette, revised edition in English published by John Lane The Bodley Head, Ltd., 1946.

Where the Lorette system works, buds at the bases of side shoots that have been cut back eventually become fruit buds hugging the leaders. And there's the rub: Lorette pruning is not effective everywhere. It seems to work where the climate is equable year round, with regular rainfall throughout summer and a long period of warmish weather in autumn. This is just the climate you find in northeastern France, but not over much of North America. My experiences in northeastern America with Lorette pruning concur with those of many others who have tried it. Variable summer rainfall, with intense sunlight, and wet autumns result too often in either rampant regrowth that is susceptible to winter injury or in dead stubs.

Across the English Channel from M. Lorette's France, the British had their own system of pruning pear and apple espaliers: the "three-bud" system. This method entails both summer and winter pruning, and also has its share of special wrinkles. In winter, the previous year's extension growth on a leader is shortened by about one-third to stimulate lateral growth for the coming season, or cut back completely if the leader is already full length. Also, at this time, young branches are cut back to three buds, and older branches are trimmed to a single stem and/or shortened to three buds beyond any fruit buds.

Subsequent pruning with the three-bud method takes place throughout the growing season. Pinch the tip of any side shoot when it has grown three leaves beyond the whorl of leaves at the base of the shoot. Shoots may also develop from older fruiting branches, and the time to pinch these shoots depends on the vigor and activity of the lower buds. If you pinch too early, those lower buds are jarred awake and grow out into shoots. But if your pinch is just right, those lower buds plump up into fat fruit buds. Close observation and the ability to predict the weather improve results, and I refer you to the previously cited edition of the Lorette book for more details.

Soon after becoming familiar with the beauty and effectiveness of the Lorette system, the British modified it to their conditions and inclinations (they weren't so keen on having to prune their trees throughout the summer). "Modified Lorette" pruning requires that the trees be pruned only twice a year. The timing of the first branch cut corresponds with that of M. Lorette's first branch cut, except that half-woody shoots are shortened to the second leaf (not counting the basal cluster of leaves), perhaps to the third leaf if growth is very strong.

The next time to cut is in winter, when you shorten regrowth from your summer cuts. If one stem grew from that two-bud stub, shorten it to two buds. If new stems grew from both those buds, shorten the one farther out to one bud and the one closer in to two buds. Either way, the branch is left with a total of three buds. The following summer, prune shoots when half woody to leave a total of three buds on any of these branches.

Other pruning methods also have proved successful for apple and pear. Pinching the tips of lateral shoots when they are half woody and about 1 ft. long, then shortening them to about 1 in. two weeks later, has quelled growth and set up fruit buds in New Zealand. In northeastern America, a similar result has been achieved by shortening any shoots longer than 1 ft. back to ¼ in. in the middle of August. This latter pruning is supplemented by winter pruning, when regrowth and all vertical sprouts are cut back. Of course, an espalier spending the bulk of the summer spiky with relatively long lateral shoots off the leaders is not particularly neat, designwise. In Australia, a technique called "twice-heading" is used to make fruiting spurs from vigorous shoots. A shoot is shortened early in the season, and then, when the resulting regrowth of two or three shoots is 3 in. to 4 in. long, a second cut is made just below where this regrowth occurs. Where summer sun is intense and hot, as in California, whether or not you can clothe a leader in fruits rather than shoots becomes a moot point, because longer shoot growth might be needed to shade and prevent sunburn of the fruits. Obviously, climate is an important factor in determining the response of apple and pear to summer pruning.

In addition to climatic influences, you also have to take varietal differences into account. For example, quite a few apple varieties—'Rome Beauty', 'Cortland', 'Bramley's Seedling', and 'Idared', to name a few—bear their fruits at the ends of thin stems rather than on spurs. To espalier such "tip-bearers," you must promote the development of these fruit-bearing stems by moderate heading of leaders during training. And you obviously cannot stub shoots or you will be cutting off fruit buds.

Espaliers of other fruits

Less elaborate systems have been devised for pruning espaliers of fruits other than apple and pear. With any of these fruits, choose a form of espalier that takes into consideration the growth and fruiting habit of the plant, and then prune to maintain lateral fruiting wood close to the leader or leaders. Below is a summary of how this has been accomplished for various fruits (again, mostly in Europe and the British Isles, where espalier has been most popular).

Apricot   Apricot trees are best trained as fans. To induce the formation of spurs, pinch out the tips of branches when they are 3 in. to 6 in. long, reserving the latter length for the more vigorous branches. The spurs are not long-lived, so periodically cut away old ones and develop replacements.

Cherry   Although sweet, tart, and duke cherries are all best trained as fans, summer-pruning tactics vary with the type of cherry. With sweet and duke cherries, pinch out the tips of side shoots when they have six leaves, then cut those shoots back to three buds in early autumn. This pruning promotes the formation of fruiting spurs. The twice-heading technique mentioned for apple and pear espaliers also has been effective (in Australia and South Africa, at least) on sweet cherry trees, with the first cut just as the cherries are coloring up, and the second cut just after harvest.

On sweet and duke cherry trees, the fruiting spurs are not long-lived, so they need periodic replacement. On tart cherry trees, thin out the branches so that they are 3 in. apart along the ribs of the fan. These branches will bear both fruits and secondary branches. Allow only one of those secondary branches, near the base of the primary branch, to grow. After harvest, cut the primary branch back to the secondary branch, which will bear fruits the following season. Eventually, any of these cherries needs to be cut back more drastically to bring fruiting wood back toward the leaders.

Currant and gooseberry   Red currant, white currant, and gooseberry can be trained as a fan, cordon, or U-palmette. Shorten branches in early July to about 5 in. During the winter, cut these shortened branches farther back, to about 2 in.

Fig   The fig—now here's a plant that does not take all that kindly to the rigidity of espalier. (Such is the temperament of a plant with Mediterranean heritage, perhaps.)

PRUNING A RED CURRANT ESPALIER

1. Summer pruning of a red currant espalier consists merely of shortening the branches in July to about 5 in.

2. In winter, further shorten the branches to about 2 in.

3. The espalier after winter pruning.

4. Dangling daintily from the branches, these red currant fruits look almost too pretty to eat.

Fan-Trained Peaches

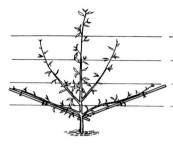

1. Train two leaders upward and outward.

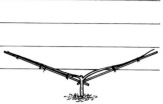

2. Just before growth begins the following season, shorten the leaders to develop permanent ribs.

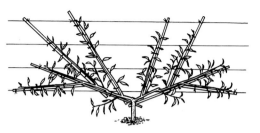

3. Train the ribs, thinning any that crowd.

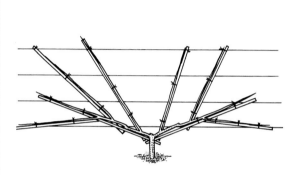

4. While the tree is dormant, shorten the ribs to induce the growth of temporary branches.

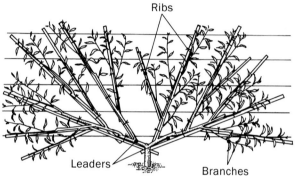

5. Remove any branches closer than 6 in. apart as growth begins. These branches are temporary, and bear fruit the following season, when they are one year old.

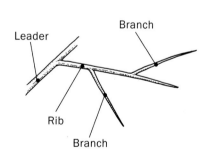

6. Before growth begins, again shorten the ribs.

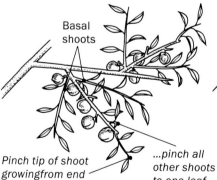

7. During the growing season, let two basal shoots grow about 18 in., then prune as shown

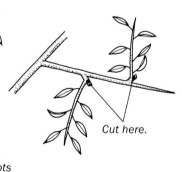

8. Right after harvest, cut each branch back to its lower basal shoot.

Nonetheless, even if the fig cannot be coerced into rigid symmetry, it can at least be kept two-dimensional, preferably as a fan. Varieties such as 'Beall', 'Flanders', 'King', 'Mission', 'Osborne', 'Pasquale', 'Tena', 'Ventura', and 'Verte', which crop on one-year-old wood, make neater espaliers than do varieties that crop mostly or only on new shoots. Manage a fan-trained fig by cutting back, in alternate years, every other fruiting branch growing from main stems to one bud. As a main stem grows old, drastically shorten it so that a young shoot can grow as a replacement; this it will do readily, reflecting the fig's naturally bushy tendency.

Peach and nectarine   Train peach or nectarine as a fan, with one-year-old stems, which bear fruit, spaced 6 in. apart and growing from the ribs. In spring, side shoots will grow from these one-year-old stems. Pinch to a single leaf all side shoots except the two at the base, and pinch back the shoot growing from the end of that one-year-old stem back to four leaves, unless there is sufficient space to let it grow freely. Depending on the space available, let those two basal shoots grow to 18 in. or less before pinching out their tips. Right after harvest, cut the one-year-old stem (which bore fruit) back to the lower basal side shoot, which will bear fruit the next season. (The other basal shoot was there only for insurance, to be left in case the lower one was damaged.)

Plum   Grow plums as fans or, less satisfactorily, as cordons. Thin branches so that they are 4 in. apart, and keep pinching them back to six leaves. After harvest, shorten the branches to three leaves.

And so we come to the close of "espalier." As you can see, it is the commonly grown fruits of Europe, the home of espalier, for which most details of training and maintaining an espalier have been devised. I repeat my earlier caution that pruning may have to be varied to suit the length of the growing season, autumn temperatures, day length, rainfall, and intensity of sunlight at any particular location. But armed with an understanding of how plants respond to pruning, as well as the fruit plants' specific growth and fruiting habits, you are now in a position to devise your own method for pruning any fruiting espalier, no matter where your plants grow.

Espalier is a fitting finale to this book, for no other aspect of plant growing requires more constant and close attention to pruning. But rest assured: All this snipping and pinching, this almost daily fussing over the plants, is rewarding work.

And the rewards of pruning are not only limited to espalier. Any pruning— whether it is to shape a rose bush, to grow a sturdy maple tree, or simply to mow a handsome lawn—is most satisfying and produces the best results when done intelligently and with attention to necessary detail.

GLOSSARY OF PRUNING TERMS

APICAL DOMINANCE
The natural tendency for strongest growth from the highest buds on a stem, along with the suppression of growth from buds or branches lower down.

BARK RIDGE
A fold of bark on the upper side of a branch near its origin.

BLIND WOOD
A portion of stem bare of either branches or flowers.

BONSAI
A plant, usually a woody plant, grown as a dwarf in a shallow pot.

BRANCH
A secondary (lateral, subordinate) shoot or stem growing off a more major shoot or stem.

BRANCH COLLAR
A swollen ring of bark on the lower side of a branch near its origin.

CANE
Usually a vague term referring to a plant stem, but in the case of grapes, a stem that made its growth the previous growing season.

CANOPY
The sum total of the branches of a tree.

CENTRAL LEADER
The central axis of a tree, growing as a continuation of the trunk and off which grow scaffold limbs. Not all trees have a single central leader.

CORDON
A woody plant grown as a single, permanent stem, or that part of a woody plant that is a single, long, permanent stem. Every year, temporary branches growing off a cordon are cut almost back to where they originated. Cordon comes from the same root as the word "cord."

CROWN
Oddly, this term can mean either the part of any plant just below the ground or the sum total of the branches—the canopy—of a tree.

DEADHEADING
Removing spent flowers from a plant to make it more tidy and prevent seed formation.

ESPALIER
A plant, usually a fruit plant, trained to an orderly two-dimensional form.

FEATHERED TREE
A young nursery-grown tree with branches.

GIRDLING
Removing a strip of bark from around the trunk or a limb of a woody plant.

HEADING CUT
A pruning cut that removes only part of a stem.

LEADER
A stem that is the main axis of a woody plant. A plant may have a single central leader or multiple leaders.

LEG
A very short length of trunk on a woody plant.

NODE
The point on a stem where a leaf was or is attached.

PINCHING
Nipping out the tip of a growing shoot with your fingernail.

PLEACHING
Informally weaving together the branches of trees to form a living wall or roof.

POLLARDING
Stubbing back all the growth of a tree each year to the same point on either the trunk or scaffold limbs, thereby creating a knobbed trunk or limb that will sprout again in the growing season.

RENOVATION
Revitalizing a plant or planting.

RINGING
Another term for girdling.

ROOT SUCKER
A shoot growing from the base of a woody plant.

SCAFFOLD LIMBS
Major branches of a woody plant.

SCORING
Making a single knife cut into and around the bark on the trunk or a limb of a woody plant.

SPUR
A naturally stubby flowering branch that grows only a fraction of an inch each year.

SHOOT
A stem in active growth.

STANDARD
This term can mean either a full-size (as opposed to a dwarf) tree, or a plant, usually one that is naturally bushy, trained to have a length of clear trunk capped by a leafy head.

STOOL
A plant periodically renewed by cutting old stems down to the ground to be replaced by new stems that grow up.

THINNING CUT
A pruning cut that removes a stem right to its origin or to a large branch.

TOPIARY
The practice of pruning a tree or a shrub to create a living sculpture.

WATERSPROUT
A very vigorous vertical shoot growing from a branch of a tree.

WHIP
A nursery-grown tree consisting of an unbranched single stem.

INDEX

CREDITS

COVERS

front, Peter Vitale
back, Susan Kahn

CHAPTER 1

p. 4, Scott Phillips
pgs. 6, 7 top, 8 left, Lee Reich
pgs. 7 bottom, 8 right, Susan Kahn
p. 9, William Talarowski/New England
    Stock Photo
p. 10, Ken Druse
p. 11 top, © Alan and Linda Detrick
p. 11 bottom, Montreal Botanic Garden,
    © Mick Hales

CHAPTER 2

pgs. 13, 16, 17, 18, 19, 20, Susan Kahn
p. 14, Lee Reich

CHAPTER 3

p. 22, Ken Druse
p. 27, Charles Kennard
p. 28, Susan Kahn
p. 29, Lee Reich

CHAPTER 4

pgs. 34, 44, Mick Hales
p. 36, Howard Rice/Garden Picture
    Library
pgs. 37 top, 53, © Alan and Linda
    Detrick
p. 37 bottom, John Glover/Garden
    Picture Library
p. 39, Susan Roth
pgs. 46, 48, 59, Susan Kahn
pgs. 49, 57, Ken Druse
pgs. 54, 67, Derek Fell
pgs. 56, 61, Lee Reich
p. 62, Charles Mann
p. 64, Michael Shedlock/New England
    Stock Photo

CHAPTER 5

p. 68, Ken Druse
pgs. 69, 70, 75, Lee Reich
pgs. 77, 78, 81, 82, Derek Fell

CHAPTER 6

pgs. 83, 91, 97, 98, 108, 109, Derek Fell
pgs. 84, 101, 104 top, Lee Reich
pgs. 87, 88, 89, 104 bottom, Susan Kahn
p. 93, Lamontagne/Garden Picture
    Library

CHAPTER 7

p. 110, Karen Bussolini
pgs. 111, 115, 117 top, Ken Druse
pgs. 113 top, 117 bottom, © Alan and
    Linda Detrick
p. 113 bottom, Derek Fell
p. 118, Susan Kahn
p. 120, Lee Reich

CHAPTER 8

pgs. 122, 137, Derek Fell
pgs. 130, 131, 133, 141, 161, 166, 167,
    170, 175, Lee Reich
pgs. 132, 135, 136, 147, 151, 153, 155,
    173, Susan Kahn
p. 142, Bruce H. Barritt
p. 145, Dodge Photography/New
    England Stock Photo
p. 149 top, W. J. Kender
p. 149 bottom, David Goldberg/David
    Goldberg Photography
p. 157, Lon J. Rombough
p. 160, David Askham/Garden Picture
    Library
p. 163, Pamela K. Pierce/David Goldberg
    Photography

CHAPTER 9

p. 177, Ken Druse
pgs. 178, 179, Susan Kahn

CHAPTER 10

p. 180, Ken Druse
p. 185, © Alan and Linda Detrick
p. 187, Karen Bussolini
pgs. 183, 189, 191, Lee Reich

CHAPTER 11

p. 192, Clive Boursnell/Garden Picture
    Library
p. 194, Marijke Heuff/Garden Picture
    Library

CHAPTER 12

p. 196, Derek Fell

CHAPTER 13

pgs. 198, 199, Ken Druse

CHAPTER 14

pgs. 201, 203, Lee Reich

CHAPTER 15

pgs. 204, 205, Ken Druse
pgs. 206, 207, Lee Reich

CHAPTER 16

p. 208, © Alan and Linda Detrick
pgs. 210, 211, Herb Gustafson

CHAPTER 17

p. 212, © Mayer/Le Scanff/Garden
    Picture Library
p. 216, Derek Fell
p. 219, John Glover/Garden Picture
    Library
p. 220, Susan Kahn
p. 223, Lee Reich

GLOSSARY

p. 227, Derek Fell

A Darkness So Bright

The heat of cooling pavement was a friendly, familiar pressure at her back as Victoria turned into the Streetside Café. Martine smiled and waved her to the usual table, vacant, as it had been every evening for the past three months. This was her place, her time: dusk at the Streetside and the sun only just below the horizon.

Joseph would sleep for another hour. Typical, he said, of one as old as he. Victoria was a rarity, even for someone whose living days were still fresh memories. As a rule, she rose half an hour before sunset. After a month of languishing about the halls of Joseph's manor, she dared the dusk and the fading day. When she returned, Joseph was waiting, ensconced in the study with a snifter in his hand. He'd smiled warmly, though, as she muttered apologies. "Have your evenings and your dying sun. Such follies are for the young with breath still fresh in their lungs. Soon enough you'll forget, and forever will begin." She was a rarity, to be sure, but the odds didn't interest her. She loved the pinprick crawl of the fading light over her skin and the giddy roller coaster fear that went with it. If the glory of the sun was denied her, then the dusk was made all the more sweet. Small price to pay.

Martine moved through the tables and customers with a waitress's special grace: smooth, unobtrusive and fully at ease. Her smile flashed, a crescent of white framed in pale skin and short, blonde hair. "The mocha, *mademoiselle?*"

Victoria smiled. Martine's accent was truly what drew her here. Victoria couldn't imagine what could convince anyone to come here, to Cincinnati, from Paris, but with Martine here, Victoria could imagine herself on the Seine, sipping mocha along a cobbled street. The coffee, too, was a part of the illusion. One small artifice Joseph had taught her. "Please," she answered, "and my friend's as well, would you?"

Martine pursed her lips at this in a look of genuine disappointment, "I am sorry, *mademoiselle*, but *Monsieur* Savage telephoned earlier. He will not be joining you this evening."

Victoria's smile never wavered, but the glow that lit it had dimmed to a glimmer. "Well, then, the mocha, for one, and Mr. Savage will just have to wish he were here." She met Martine's eyes and the smile there. "Ladies night." Martine nodded, but Victoria's mind had already wandered to what might have made Larson miss coffee tonight. *It's nothing, I'm sure.*

✛ ✛ ✛ ✛

When Victoria returned to the manor, the matter of Larson's absence was quickly put aside. Joseph stood in the foyer, straightening his tie in the bronze mirror that hung between two busts cut from Italian marble.

"Peter has chosen your gown. We must be at the Marsden promptly at eleven this evening."

A hand rose to cut off any comment before it passed her lips. "Dress. We will not be late."

She turned immediately, some visceral will pressing her to act without the faintest thought. He was so perfect, so pale and beautiful.

So cold. The thought was forgotten a moment after it dawned, and Victoria turned back down the hall toward her rooms. Peter always chose the most beautiful gowns.

✛ ✛ ✛ ✛

Draped in emerald silk, hand resting lightly on Joseph's elbow, Victoria imagined herself a vision as they passed the doorman at the Marsden Hotel. A dozen people lounged about the lobby, some seated, some reading newspapers or magazines. One couple stood at the desk arranging their room; a bellman and the concierge spoke quietly in one corner. The lobby itself was a relic of another time — the antique brass fixtures, arched ceilings and crystal chandeliers; even the sofas and chairs were designed with an eye to the earliest days of the century.

Joseph and Victoria glided through the vast room with the sharp click of heels on marble, past the concierge, past the desk, to a pair of doors nestled beneath the curve of a double staircase. Just within, behind a lectern, stood a woman impeccably dressed, though not so elegantly as her patrons.

"Mr. Bonhom. Good evening." Her smile was a picture of professional congeniality. She consulted the ledger before her and waved to a young man standing behind her. "Mr. Bonhom and Ms. Grayson will be sitting at the Lauren table." She turned back to Joseph, "Lawrence will seat you, sir. Please have a wonderful evening." Joseph nodded and followed the silent young man to a table for five where two of the place cards read *J.L. Bonhom* and *V. Hart-Grayson*. Other names decorated cards at each of the other three seats at the table, one familiar, the others not. Victoria took her seat, but Joseph, without a word to his childe, strode away from the table toward a knot of people gathered at another table.

Left to herself, Victoria scanned the room, noting faces she'd seen before, faces Joseph had named influential or important. Alan Lords stood in one corner, a trio of his associates muttering behind their hands as more guests entered. The harpy, Joseph had called him. Martin Lorry, the sheriff, stood alone, a scowl etched into his brow as he stared into his wineglass. Mr. O'Shea and Millicent, seneschal and keeper as Joseph had named them, laughed over

their own wineglasses while another knot of people huddled opposite them, the air seeming thick over their heads.

Victoria considered the room's make-up. All the Toreador were here, or as many as she'd ever seen. Joseph had the Ventrue with him, and the two he had named Tremere were coming in now. She searched the room again, noting the five or six kine finishing their dinners and preparing to leave. A waiter came to the table, smiling obsequiously as he poured: "Mr. Bonhom's own label, miss. Will you be drinking as well?"

Victoria nodded and lifted her glass to be filled, the dark fluid sharpening the tension that already lifted the hairs at the nape of her neck. She'd picked out the Brujah she knew coming in through the kitchen. The man scribbling in his folio at the table near the service door must be Mr. Lane, the only Malkavian of whom she'd been made aware. Oddly, none of the Gangrel seemed to be here, not even Gideon.

Joseph had said little of the Gangrel, but Victoria knew that they had no love for politicking. Still, though her experience had been short, there had always been at least one of them in attendance when the prince called court. Most often Gideon, Larson's sire and apparently the eldest of their Blood in the city, was the one to stand for them. From time to time, she'd seen even as many as three or four, Larson included, come to Elysium. Tonight, though, there wasn't even a hint of their presence.

Victoria scanned the room a third time. Joseph had left the company of his clansmen and strode smoothly across the room toward Mr. O'Shea, now seated at a table set only for three. As he passed Martin Lorry, the sheriff offered the barest twitch of a nod. She might have missed it if she hadn't been watching. Even now she couldn't be sure of what had been said, but she knew Joseph had spoken to Martin Lorry and Martin Lorry had agreed.

It wasn't until she saw her sire pause and lower his head that she noticed the arrival of the prince. Silence held the room suspended, wine glasses half raised, as Franklin van Wert entered and smiled to the hostess before taking his seat with Mr. O'Shea.

The last of the mortal patrons had left just moments before the prince's arrival and the serving staff were all in Millicent's palm in one way or another, so it was for the benefit of the Kindred gathering that Franklin van Wert's words carried through the room as he spoke with his seneschal.

"Mr. O'Shea, it seems our associate on the Board, Mr. Xaviar, has decided our company is not to his liking and independence is more to his tastes." Timothy O'Shea nodded, the barest of smiles crossing his lips. "I think it would be imprudent of us to retain those of his particular creed in light of this development. See that his fellows are given their papers. I believe we can afford a generous severance package for each of them as… incentive." Again, the seneschal nodded and raised a hand to beckon Mr. Lorry to the table. Words passed between the two, and the sheriff vanished through the kitchen doors.

Victoria was baffled. She'd watched all that went on, had heard the prince's proclamation, but none of it made sense. Joseph had hinted at the importance of "The Board," but he'd never said anything about a man named Xaviar. Most of those gathered had listened in stony silence, but the harpy and

his coterie had smiled openly. Joseph had stood at the seneschal's elbow throughout. Perhaps another would think him stoic, but Victoria knew better. She knew his face, his expressions, and the one he wore now was satisfaction.

Now, as Martin Lorry slipped silently through the kitchen doors and away into the night, Joseph leaned in to whisper to Mr. O'Shea, and the room awoke from the trance the prince's entrance had laid over it. The air buzzed with conversation, and while their faces appeared innocuous, even Victoria's novice ear heard the weighted tones of urgency. Something had happened and everyone knew what it was. Everyone but her.

"Your friend, yes. He wishes to see you."

The voice at her shoulder nearly made her scream, but unlife, if nothing else, had strengthened Victoria's self-control. As it was, she only lifted the wineglass to her lips and sipped at the warm vitae disguised within. Her eyes darted sharply to the windows, hoping to see some reflection of the speaker, but she saw only herself. *Nosferatu.* She spoke softly into her glass, "I don't know what you're talking about."

The voice murmured in her ear, closer now. "Mmm-mmm. Too bad. He was insistent. Yes. The Gangrel was insistent."

Its words sank in. It seemed to step away, and Victoria's control wavered. She twisted her head and rasped in her own harsh whisper, "Wait!"

The messenger returned. "Insistent, yes."

"Larson sent you?"

The voice grew closer, and she fancied that the speaking lips were almost brushing her ear. "Meet him, he says. Here." She felt something brush her lap, and a small piece of folded paper was there where none had been before. "Soon, he says. Soon." And it was gone.

The taste of fear rose in Victoria's throat and mingled with the thick flavor of blood as she scanned the room. Not a soul seemed to know she was there. Joseph had moved on from the prince's table to speak with Millicent and the Tremere. Others shuttled across the room, ferrying gossip from one camp to another, and the harpies watched all with cold, laughing eyes. Praying that all eyes were occupied, she palmed the piece of paper as carefully as she could manage and slid it into her dress.

To steady herself, she drank again from her glass, draining the vitae in one long, shuddering gulp. When she lowered the glass, he was there. She nearly dropped the goblet in surprise as she met his eyes. A man she had never met, dressed in a navy sweater, blue jeans and boots, leaned against the wall looking at her, and as their gazes crossed, he smiled, baring long white teeth. Panic washed over her. *He knows.*

Joseph saved her with a hand on her arm as a wave of inexplicable fear set her to trembling. He arched an eyebrow in concern. "Are you all right?" Victoria nodded, exerting every ounce of will to regain her composure. Satisfied, he took her elbow and turned her gently toward the kitchen. "We're leaving." Victoria nodded again and followed, the fear only a shadow as Peter pulled up in the car. The terror left confusion in its wake. There was so much she didn't know. Why was she so scared? Why, of all nights, did Larson choose this one to disappear?

Joseph offered no answers to her unspoken questions, only sat silently as Peter drove them home. In the darkness outside the car, it quietly began to rain.

✣ ✣ ✣ ✣

They slipped from the car under cover of Peter's broad, black umbrella. As they stood in the foyer, Peter shaking out the umbrella, Victoria brushing water from her gown, Joseph spoke softly. "There are matters I must attend to in the study. I will require Peter's assistance for much of the night. If there is anything you need of him, see that it is tended to now. He will not be available later." He turned to leave the foyer, but stopped as Victoria spoke for the first time since leaving Elysium, her voice barely above a whisper.

"Who was that man?"

Joseph stood with his back to her, his chin rising as he listened. "Which?"

"The one in the sweater. He came in just before we left."

The elder vampire tipped his head to one side, considering. "Tanner Banks, the prince's scourge. I want you to stay away from him."

Victoria dared to press the point, though she could tell Joseph wanted it dropped. "He looks like one of the Brujah. What does he do?"

Joseph turned, his jaw set in a line hard as marble, "He is Ventrue, and he kills." He turned to Peter and beckoned the man with a sharp gesture before turning on a heel and disappearing into the darkness of the house, his servant following after.

Victoria watched them go in silence, already planning.

✣ ✣ ✣ ✣

The street was dark, deserted, inhabited only by the hulks of abandoned cars. It had been easy enough to slip out of the house unnoticed with Joseph secreted in the study with Peter and the rest of the staff in their beds. Victoria changed from her gown to the old pea coat she'd kept from her days at the university, a pair of dark leather boots, jeans and a sweatshirt. She didn't like the idea of deceiving Joseph, but this was important. Something was going on, and somehow Larson was involved. Joseph would understand.

When she came to the place Larson's note had spoken of, she passed it by, eyes skating from side to side, searching for tails or bystanders. She circled the block, just to be safe, but apart from one old drunk snoring under a step, there was no one about. As she approached the building a second time, she noticed a sign hung over four broad garage doors. It read "We—ling Bed and Mat—s" in fading red letters. Again she stopped and scanned the street. Seeing no one, she ducked down the alley alongside the building to a door sunk deep in the shadows. The knob turned with a muted click and the door swung smoothly inward.

Inside, space yawned before her in the darkness. Carefully, Victoria followed the wall to her left, her feet pushing through piles of detritus as she made her way deeper into the old factory. The flare of a lantern suddenly blinded her, and she crouched against the wall, shielding her eyes from the light.

"Vic?" Larson's voice came with the light, heavy with the tremor of his own nerves.

"Turn it down, would you, Larson?" He turned but did nothing to dim the light. As he slipped through a broad sliding door, Victoria caught a glimpse of

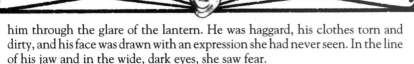

him through the glare of the lantern. He was haggard, his clothes torn and dirty, and his face was drawn with an expression she had never seen. In the line of his jaw and in the wide, dark eyes, she saw fear.

"Something happened." His voice was abrupt.

Larson paced the little office like a tiger in a too-small cage. By the light of the lantern, Victoria could see he'd been in a fight. "Slow down, Larson. What's happened?"

The Gangrel only shook his head. "We're leaving."

"Who's leaving?"

Larson Savage ran a hand through his hair, the thick auburn mane falling back from sharply pointed ears, a feature she had never noticed on him. "Me, Gideon, Lender. All of us. We gotta go."

Victoria shook her head, "I don't know what you mean. You're going where? Are you coming back? Is someone after you?"

Larson bared his teeth, "Yeah, someone's after us. Shit, everyone is after us — in this town, anyway. The prince never liked Gideon or any of us. Now he's got an excuse."

"Excuse? What are you talking about?"

The Gangrel leaned on the desk with both hands, his eyes wild. "We're leaving the Camarilla."

Victoria's face screwed itself up in a glare of disbelief, "How can you—" but Larson's expression stopped her in mid-sentence. His eyes widened, and his hair rose in a wild puff of brown. With a hiss through bared fangs, he shoved himself away from the desk, claws sprouting from his fingertips. Victoria spun and felt sharp pain lance through her chest. The stake pierced her heart, and she fell to the floor.

The light was out in a moment, but with or without it, Victoria could see nothing. Paralyzed, she lay on the floor across the desk from where Larson stood a moment ago and listened as the fight raged not a yard from her. Larson's snarls accompanied the machine-gun thump of fists driven into flesh at inhuman speeds. Had she not been immobilized, Victoria might have wept for her friend. The last thing she had seen before falling to the floor was the face of Tanner Banks.

When the little window above her exploded with light, Victoria had nearly resigned herself to death, so exchanging one blindness for another had little effect. It was the sound of an unfamiliar voice that awakened her hope.

Across the little office, what could only be the voice of Tanner Banks sounded strangely surprised. "What—?" The word became a growl of pain as the searing light burned away his sight and winked out, leaving them again in darkness.

More feet entered the room. Heavy boots pounded over the wooden floorboards. Heavy thuds followed, the sounds of blows, the falling of bodies, and finally one last wet chop and silence. Boots shuffled out, what sounded like something heavy dragging after them. Another pair of shoes entered, the steps smooth and sharp. A light flared and Victoria could see again — black leather shoes, a woman's legs and a face. A face she recognized. Martine.

The woman shook her head, tsking quietly. "*Monsieur* Bonhom will not be pleased, *mademoiselle*." She smiled, cold and inhuman. "Not pleased at all, but I am. You have done me a great service." Darkness came again as rough hands wrapped her in rough fabric. She smelled smoke for a moment, and fear drove out reason for a long time, and then there was only darkness.

✚   ✚   ✚   ✚

Victoria woke again to darkness and the smell of blood. She found the body easily enough and drank her fill before reason returned and she knew what she'd done. The body stank as it lay there dead and cold. From the light under the door, she could see it was a man, though only just. Probably not even 18. She shuddered and shrank into a corner as far from the corpse as she could get.

Hours later, or minutes – in the darkness Victoria couldn't tell the difference – the door opened and Joseph came in. Martine stood just behind him, visible over his right shoulder.

"I am very disappointed, Victoria. I had thought these whims would pass in time. I see now I was wrong to be so lenient." He straightened his tie and drew a deep breath. For the first time, Victoria saw the gestures for what they were: pure artifice. "No more forays at dusk. No more consorting with your so-called friends. You will sleep here. You will drink what you are given. You will not leave but in my company." He looked down on her, his lips curled in disgust. "I chose poorly with you, but that matter has been rectified. If you please me, you will live."

Joseph turned and walked out, but Martine stayed for a moment. She smiled. "I owe you my thanks, *mademoiselle*. Perhaps, one day, I will give it to you." With that she bared her teeth, long canines showing sharp and white in the wedge of light pouring through the door. When she left, Victoria heard the scrape of a bolt sliding home and knew she would not be getting out tonight. Tears came, and tears alone for a long time afterward. Only fear shook her from her grief as she realized she'd forgotten to breathe. An hour later, though, she decided there were more important things to think about. Eternity was a long time, and vengeance was slow in the planning.

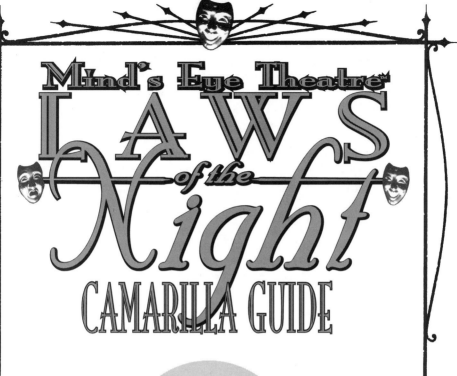

Mind's Eye Theatre™
LAWS of the Night
CAMARILLA GUIDE

CREDITS

WRITTEN BY: JASON CARL, MATTHEW HOOPER, EDWARD MACGREGOR, MIKKO RAUTALAHTI, BRETT SMITH, LAWRENCE VILES

DEVELOPED BY: CYNTHIA SUMMERS

EDITED BY: RICH RUANE

PREVIOUSLY PUBLISHED MATERIAL HAS APPEARED IN: VAMPIRE: THE MASQUERADE, THE GUIDE TO THE CAMARILLA, LAWS OF THE NIGHT REVISED

ART DIRECTION BY: AARON VOSS AND RICHARD THOMAS

ART BY: ALYSON GAUL

FRONT AND BACK COVER DESIGN: AARON VOSS

LAYOUT AND TYPESETTING BY: AARON VOSS

WHITE WOLF
GAME STUDIO

735 PARK NORTH BLVD.
SUITE 128
CLARKSTON, GA 30021
USA

Mind's Eye Theatre™
LAWS of the Night
CAMARILLA GUIDE

CONTENTS

Chapter One: Introduction

Welcome to the Final Nights

There are strange things afoot in the halls of power. Whispers of signs spoken of in the oldest texts buzz from every corner, while rumors of portents mumbled by the far-sighted become facts with each night. These are, as the Chinese might say, interesting times.

The Camarilla stands as it has for nearly six centuries, a pillar against the night. Claiming jurisdiction over every vampire across the globe, the sect has greater numbers than any other, and the reasons for membership are as varied as the Kindred themselves. For some the Camarilla means safety from enemies — the Sabbat, the Lupines, mortal hunters and other groups of Kindred. For some it means a safe place where they might continue gentler pursuits. Some belong because their sires belonged, or because they are unaware that they can belong to anything else. For the elders it is their ivory tower, and it is the default for their childer. All will agree that whatever it is to its members, the Camarilla is monolithic in its strength and purpose.

But in these nights, the monolith is beginning to show signs of strain. The change in the Malkavians has brought consternation to many. The departure of the Gangrel shook the sect nearly to its foundations. Its strongholds are assaulted on all sides by a host of enemies: the bloodthirsty Assamites; the Sabbat, who seem to have found renewed fire in these nights; and the mysterious Cathayans making incursions on the West Coast. Still the Camarilla holds fast against all comers.

Or does it?

As the power struggles grow more ferocious, as the mysteries come to pass, as the once unassailable comes under attack, will the Camarilla finally crumble? Or will it prevail, as it always has in the past — iron-willed and eternal?

What This Book Is (and Isn't)

This book details the interior of the oldest and largest sect of vampires, the Camarilla. Here stands revealed the might of the elders, the sect's secret ways and means, and the nightly business of power. On a more mundane note, here are rules for the mysterious Gargoyles, new Traits for character creation and everything a Storyteller could want to add new levels of realism and depth to her city.

This book isn't meant as a substitute for **Laws of the Night**. You'll still need that book for character creation, the lower levels of the most common Disciplines and the basic rules. This book runs on the assumption that you already own **Laws of the Night** and are at least passingly familiar with the rules of **Mind's Eye Theatre**. This book also covers only the clans of the Camarilla and their erstwhile sibling Clan Gangrel; the Sabbat and independents will find their own homes in future releases.

With that said, welcome to the halls of Elysium, where the monsters dwell.

History: Nights Gone By

The Camarilla's history, like so many other parts of the Kindred's tale, is a long and bloody one. Born in the fires of rebellious change and watered with much spilled vitae, the sect has grown since its early days as a bulwark against youthful rage and mortal hunters.

In 1381, a band of English peasants rebelled against their local lord, drawing the attention and aid of several young Kindred. Though quickly put down, the mortal rebellion left its mark on those of the Blood who took part. Frustrated in their rise to power and often suffocated under their immortal elders' iron grip, the childer of Europe kindled the beginnings of their own rebellion.

The early 1400s saw the spark that would ignite a wildfire of rebellion throughout the Kindred of Europe. A young Brujah by the name of Tyler assaulted an elder Ventrue named Hardestaadt. Inspired by this insolence, childer rose against their sires throughout the continent, clearing the avenues of power with blood and fire. War raged against the eldest of the clans. At the height of the madness, the rebels destroyed the Lasombra Antediluvian and claimed to have destroyed Tzimisce himself as well.

Bolstered by the diablerie of their elders, the rebellious youth, now called anarchs, marched through Eastern Europe, laying waste to the work of centuries. In those lands a means to break the stranglehold of the blood bond had been found, and suddenly, many neonates and ancillae were slipping leashes elders had thought secure. Eager for the opportunity to diablerize European elders, the Assamites joined the fight on the anarch side.

In 1435, Hardestaadt gathered the elders in convocation and proposed an arrangement to deal with the anarch movement. The arrangement he offered would cross blood and territorial lines to deal with the issues of the Kindred as a whole. True to form, most elders offered little more than skepticism and left for their own havens to wait out the anarch storms in the way they weathered so many trials for centuries before. A few, though, remained and joined Hardestaadt in his vision. They were the Founders, and they would lay the groundwork for the next five centuries of Kindred society.

By the middle of the 15th century, the Founders had persuaded enough elders to join their cause to put forth significant resistance to the anarch rebellion. Coteries drawn across clan lines, bound by a single purpose, gathered across the known world. With their aims finally united, the elders of Europe began to regain ground on their fractious childer. When coteries hand-picked by the Founders and their intimates finally returned with the location of the hidden Assamite fortress of Alamut, the demise of the revolt was all but assured. The war ground to a stalemate of minor skirmishing.

In 1493, the Anarch Movement agreed to parley with the Camarilla. The Convention of Thorns convened in an abbey in England, and there the anarchs accepted terms for surrender. The treaty allowed those anarchs who wished to come into the fold of the Camarilla to do so and levied punishment against the Assamites for their role. In this treaty, the Camarilla came into its own as the guiding sect of Cainite life.

Motivated by the Inquisition, which had raged across Europe in a fiery backdrop to the Anarch Revolt, the new sect deemed the long-ignored Masquerade would become the centerpiece of their order. No more would those of the Blood visibly lord their power over mortals. Instead, the Kindred would act from the shadows, enforcing the Traditions and protecting themselves from the fires of mortal wrath with a charade that would come to span the globe.

Not all anarchs accepted the Convention of Thorns. Many refused to return to the same stifling order that had caused them to rebel in the first place. They rejected the purported peace and fled to Scandinavia to nurse their wounds and grudges. When they finally re-emerged from their self-imposed exile, they had reformed into the sect that would be the Camarilla's staunchest and most bloody opposition: the Sabbat.

New World, Old War

While the Convention of Thorns ended the war, the frustrations that had started it remained. Though many elders had died in the bloody revolt, there were still far more Kindred than there were positions of power. When news came to Europe from across the sea of a whole new world for the taking, many of the most promising ancillae of the Old World packed up and went west to carve out domains of their own. Many were encouraged by their elders, who hoped that they could be rid of their troublesome childer.

Throughout the 16th century, the new-forged Sabbat fought skirmishes against the Camarilla, but the chaotic assaults were to little effect against the deeply entrenched bastions of the elders' power. With the opening of the Americas, though, a new battleground was discovered, and it would become the true crucible for Camarilla and Sabbat. The Camarilla, seeing in the Americas an opportunity to be rid of potential rivals and expand their influence, united in sending a flood of younger Kindred across the ocean aboard the colony ships of the English, Dutch and French. Similarly, the Sabbat used their minions among the Spanish and Portuguese to find footholds in the American colonies.

During this time, war between the Camarilla and Sabbat was, for the most part, a perfunctory thing. Both were more concerned with cementing their hold on the vast resources of the New World than in organizing risky, expensive offensives against the other. While rumors abound of vampiric influence on the American and French Revolutions, the effects of these on the

sects was minimal. The stalemate lasted through most of the 17th and 18th centuries; each side felt the flush of power as the Industrial Revolution flooded the cities with more and more mortals, and more and more opportunities for control. Up until the early years of the 19th century, the Camarilla concerned itself far more with capitalizing on the gains afforded them by advancing technology than on the few assaults made by the Sabbat.

The War of 1812 masked a major shift in the fortunes of the Camarilla. As the British and the Americans fought their war, the Sabbat pressed in on the Atlantic seaboard, gaining cities one at a time over the next 50 years. Flanked on the North and South by Sabbat strongholds, the Camarilla fell back again and again, finally holding on to a scant handful of cities after the attacks subsided. The East Coast has never been regained, and the fighting continues to this day. Some even say that the losses taken in the East are rising faster than ever.

In the mid-1800s, a new front opened in the war between the sects. This time, the vast tracts of the western frontier were both battleground and prize. For a long time the Camarilla teetered on the edge of disaster as the Sabbat pressed and pressed, nearly toppling the Camarilla's foothold not only in the West, but in the Americas as a whole. If not for several sudden, stunning losses and the respite they gave the faltering Camarilla, the Sabbat may well have dug in so deeply as to make it impossible to remove them. There are those that feel that without those losses, the Camarilla would have lost the Americas entirely, but those that dare suggest such a thing often find themselves speaking to silent rooms and smoldering glares.

THE LAST CENTURY

The 1900s proved ripe for upheaval among mortals and Kindred alike. As newborn social theory and political discontent rocked aging governments, the power structures of the Kindred controlling them were likewise shaken. In the chaos brought by these revolutions, many cities became primed for Sabbat incursions. When the assaults came, the Camarilla establishment often found itself struggling to bring its forces into line and frequently held onto ancient fiefdoms by the skin of its collective teeth.

In the devastation following World War I, many European Kindred tried to take control of the continent. Those that did were little more than twigs in the tide as the world plunged toward Adolf Hitler's Germany and the horror that would rise out of it. As World War II raged, some Kindred with more ambition than sense sought to turn the mortals' war to their own ends. Most did not survive. For once, those without a hold in the halls of power were luckiest, laying low and letting the storms of battle wash over them.

In the years that followed Germany's defeat, the people of America prospered, and the American Kindred along with them. In the chaos of the war, over 500 years after revolution sparked the creation of the Camarilla, the anarch movement once again reared its head. Princes on the West Coast fell as the young movement spread among the Kindred of California. But these were not the anarchs of old. Strong princes rose up to fight the tide, and, in the end, held the anarchs to their sliver of territory along the Pacific. Chicago rose as the anchor of the Camarilla in North America. Guided by Lodin's sure hand, it became a stronghold for the faithful and an example to others across the continent as cities rose overnight in a flood of immigration and urbanization.

In the latter half of the century, interest in vampires took a strange turn as subcultures embraced the image and mystique of the undead. Princes around the world saw it as an unexpected windfall, as many minor infractions could be passed off on mortal admirers, but the trend was not without its repercussions. With such increased interest, each incident became all the more memorable, and concealment became all the more crucial to survival. New technology opened ever-wider avenues to power as younger vampires took advantage of the elders' staid reliance on the old ways to carve inroads into emerging markets and industries. The tides of prosperity continue to swell as mortals flood the cities and Kindred find ever more blood to be had. The question, however, remains: how long can this last?

Omens of misfortune have plagued the Camarilla in recent years. The sect lost its one and only hold on the Far East when Hong Kong was returned to China. Younger and younger Kindred are Embracing childer of their own and with each generation, the Blood grows thinner. There are rumors of neonates whose blood is now too thin to sustain the Embrace and who can even bear the touch of sunlight. The anarchs squat on the Pacific Coast, nettling the princes of the Camarilla with their presence. More disturbingly, reports have come from Western cities of incursions by the mysterious Asian vampires. Along the Atlantic the Sabbat remains, turning back the Camarilla's attempts to recapture their long-lost cities. Only Europe remains unperturbed as the elders there

When the Convention of Thorns drew all Kindred under the auspices of the Camarilla, the Gangrel were among the seven clans who chose full membership in the sect. In the five centuries since, the Gangrel proved themselves invaluable allies, leading the fight in the war against the Sabbat. Both their combat abilities and the great wealth of intelligence gathered by the nomadic clan played decisive roles in the success of the Camarilla's efforts against their rivals.

Until recently.

Speculation abounds as to the circumstances and motives for the Gangrel defection from the Camarilla. There are as many guesses as there are mouths to voice them. Most prevalent of the rumors is that Xaviar, former justicar of the clan, entered the council chamber of the Inner Circle, spoke one sentence and left. Within a month, most of the clan had divorced themselves from the sect, though none would speak of the reasons. To be sure, many also remained, but without a justicar to defend their interests, they are vulnerable to the political machinations of those clans that retain full affiliation.

To date, the Gangrel continue steadfast in their unwillingness to explain their departure from the Camarilla. Those who ask are tersely rebuked — if they're lucky. Though now considered an independent clan, many of those who retain their claim of Camarilla membership are as welcome as ever they were. There are those who have held grudges against the shapeshifters, though, and lacking the threat of justicar retaliation leaves little reason not to make unlife hard for those that remain.

sit in their havens, long ago having learned to maintain their own control regardless of the shifting of the mortals beneath them.

The Traditions

As legend has it, Caine himself passed down the Traditions in the times of the First City to guide his childer through their unlives. To this day, they remain the bulwark of Camarilla society and are strictly upheld. It doesn't hurt that they also make good sense.

The First Tradition: The Masquerade

Thou shalt not reveal thy true nature to those not of the Blood. Doing so shall renounce thy claims of Blood.

Most Camarilla Kindred say that this is the whole of the law, and all else is incidental. Many a Methuselah has regaled a willing ear with tales of the days before the Camarilla, when the Kindred could walk abroad in the glory of their power, but times have changed. Over the past 500 years, the Kindred themselves have worked hardest at eradicating belief in vampires, squashing reports, discrediting (or eliminating) witnesses and disciplining perpetrators. The madness and slaughter that followed the Inquisition is still fresh in the memories of many elders, and the mistakes that led to it are ruthlessly punished. The penalty for breaching the Masquerade is, most often, death.

The Second Tradition: Domain

Thy domain is thy concern. All others owe thee respect while in it. None may challenge thy word in thy domain.

The world has grown a great deal smaller in the past few centuries, and the number of Kindred vying for a piece of land to call their own grows with every night. These days it's a rare Lick that holds a significant domain and isn't a prince. More often, the prince doles out portions of his own domain in payment for some favor or service and in return expects the occupant to enforce the prince's will. Those that expect autonomy in such situations, however, are in for a terrible disappointment. Recently, some more business-minded Kindred have taken to claiming dominion over certain aspects of commercial activity in a given city. Young vampires now squabble over brokerage firms and software developers instead of four blocks of prime hunting ground. Many elders, rooted in the old ways and firmly convinced of the surety of real estate, dismiss the trend as one more fantasy of youth doomed to failure. Others, though, have noticed the growing momentum of the practice and wonder at what might really be gained.

The Third Tradition: Progeny

Thou shalt sire another one with permission of thine elder. If thou createst another without thine elder's leave, both thou and thy progeny shall be slain.

Princeship bears a great many privileges, the right of creation being chief among them. Once, before princes littered the countryside and domain was free to any that could hold it, one generally sought the permission of one's sire before granting a mortal the Embrace. As centuries passed and the power of the Camarilla waxed, elder came to mean prince. These nights, Kindred vie most fervently to make their own childer, and the princes guard the right jealously.

The Fourth Tradition: Accounting

Those thou create are thine own childer. Until thy progeny shall be released, thou shalt command them in all things. Their sins are thine to endure.

Creating new vampires is a touchy thing. The changes the Blood wreaks on a mortal's body and mind are vast. The flood of power that comes with unlife can overwhelm the new vampire and provoke lapses in judgment that could threaten the entire Masquerade. So it is that those who sire new childer are charged with guiding them through the early stages of their new eternity until such time as they are aware of the risks and responsibilities their new condition has laid upon them. Until the neonate is deemed ready, her sire is responsible for her actions — *all* of her actions — and any punishment that comes as a result is laid upon sire and childe both.

Given the terrible responsibility and possible consequences of siring a childe, there are those who press the presentation of their childer earlier than might be wise. Childer found to be ignorant of the necessary protocols, whether it be through oral examination by the prince and his officers or through the actions of the childe after her release, may cause a severe punishment to be levied against her and her sire both.

The Fifth Tradition: Hospitality

Honor one another's domain. When thou comest to a foreign city thou shalt present thyself to the one who ruleth there. Without the word of acceptance, thou art nothing.

When in the company of predators, only good manners keep blood from being shed. If a Kindred crosses into the territory of another Kindred, it is customary for him to announce himself to prevent unnecessary conflict. In these days, this generally means approaching the prince of a given city and requesting his acceptance. Certainly there are those that give short shrift to this particular Tradition, the Gangrel chief among them, and in truth, if one can maintain a low enough profile while unacknowledged, the trouble incurred is negligible. In recent nights, however, princes have begun appointing particularly savvy hunters as scourges. Often granted considerable latitude in the pursuit of their duties, scourges pursue and, in some cases, destroy those who have not presented themselves to the prince. Under the aegis of preventing Sabbat incursions, the practice makes sense, but many see the scourge as a dangerous mistake waiting to happen. Many sheriffs also take umbrage at the broad clearance given the scourge, seeing it as an infringement on their own offices.

The Sixth Tradition: Destruction

Thou art forbidden to destroy another of thy kind. The right of destruction belongeth only to thine elder. Only the eldest among thee shall call the blood hunt.

As with so many of the Traditions, in earlier days the Sixth purported the right of a sire to destroy his childer. In modern nights, the prince has usurped this right. When wielded prudently, the threat of blood hunt is as effective a weapon as a prince can have. Used capriciously, it can easily lead to the downfall of a city.

In cases of a sire's destruction of her childe, the matter depends entirely on the neonate's presentation. A sire has free rein to destroy a fractious childe at any time up until the neonate's presentation to the prince. After gaining the prince's acceptance, though, the neonate becomes the property of the city and is no longer under the auspices of his sire.

The right to destroy another vampire lies solely with the prince of a city. If a vampire decides to take the right for himself and destroy another vampire, the killer can generally expect to find himself on the receiving end of a blood hunt. The power of life and death is one of a prince's most dear, and she guards it with considerable jealousy.

LEXICON

Subcultures and sects often develop their own speech patterns, inventing slang and jargon unique to their status and social situation. Vampires are no different. Though certain terms may be more prevalent in certain circles, one can generally find the following words in use, in one form or another, in all circles of Kindred society.

Allthing: A Gangrel gathering, generally held on a regional scale and called by the eldest member of the clan in the area. Smaller gatherings are called *things*.

Anarch: A vampire who has forsaken his affiliation with the Camarilla in favor of existence as an independent. Most claiming the title in the present night have been Embraced within the last hundred years.

Archon: Title given the servitors of the justicars. Most are blood bound to their justicar, speak in her name and act with her authority.

Barrens: Those areas outside the immediate environs of a city, generally considered uninhabitable by Kindred.

Blood Bond: An induced love caused by the ingestion of a particular Kindred's vitae. The bond is strong enough to inspire suicidal devotion in the recipient and is generally thought to be unbreakable.

Blood Hunt: A declaration of death levied against a criminal by the prince and often enforced by the city at large.

Camarilla: The sect of vampires espousing strict adherence to the Traditions and claiming jurisdiction over all vampires.

Chantry: A facility available to all Tremere in a city for use as haven and laboratory.

Conclave: Gathering open to the entire sect, generally called by a justicar.

Convention of Thorns: Treaty that ended the Anarch Revolt. Also, the conclave that resulted in the signing of the treaty.

Coterie: Group of vampires that generally work in concert, often crossing clan lines and rarely lasting more than a few decades.

Court: Formal assemblage of the prince and his officers most often held in Elysium. In theory, any acknowledged Kindred of the city may approach the prince at court and be heard.

Domain: Territory attributed to a particular vampire, thereby granting that vampire primary rights to hunting, influence and resources. Also, the environs deemed to be within a prince's rule.

Elysium: A site or collection of sites wherein violence and the use of Disciplines are strictly forbidden. Often places of artistic or cultural significance are designated as Elysium.

Embrace: The process of making a mortal into a vampire.

Final Death: The complete destruction of a vampire.

Ghoul: A mortal who has tasted Kindred vitae without first being drained of blood. Also, the act of creating a ghoul.

Harpy: Title given those at the center of the social pecking order. They are purveyors of rumor and innuendo and the ultimate judges of social status among the Kindred of a city.

Inner Circle: The council of elders in control of the Camarilla. The exact number and identity of those on the council are unknown.

Justicar: Title given those who carry out the will of the Inner Circle. Each clan has one justicar and each justicar serves for a period of 13 years before facing election by the Inner Circle to decide continuance or replacement. Each justicar bears considerable power in pursuit of her duties, including the right of destruction.

Keeper of Elysium: Kindred given charge of maintaining all designated Elysiums, including security and enforcement of the Traditions.

Malkavian Madness Network: The mysterious connection linking all Malkavians, supposedly through mutually altered perceptions.

Masquerade: Camarilla's strict policy of concealment denying the existence of Kindred to the mortal populace at large.

Primogen: Member of the council of elders that advise and assist the prince in the management of a city. The power held by the primogen council varies from city to city and prince to prince.

Prince: Supreme authority within a city with regard to local Camarilla matters.

Rack: Any of a series of prime hunting grounds in a city including clubs, bars and commercial districts.

Rant: A gathering of Brujah, ostensibly for purposes of determining clan policy.

Red List: List of those Kindred marked by the sect as a whole for death. Those on the list can expect to be hunted in any Camarilla city.

Scourge: Prince's officer charged with patrolling the city for outlaws and the Sabbat. Frequently, the scourge is granted the right of destruction in the pursuit of her duties.

Seneschal: The prince's second-in-command, the seneschal often deals with the routine tasks of running a city.

Sheriff: Prince's officer charged with enforcing the Traditions and the prince's proclamations.

Spawning Pools: Hidden chambers located deep in a Nosferatu warren, used for breeding and feeding bizarre animal ghouls. Many of the oldest pools house monstrous specimens of a variety of species, often grown to tremendous size.

Traditions: Six great laws said to be handed down by Caine. Together they form the core of the Camarilla's philosophy.

Vitae: Blood. Often the blood of a Kindred, though not always.

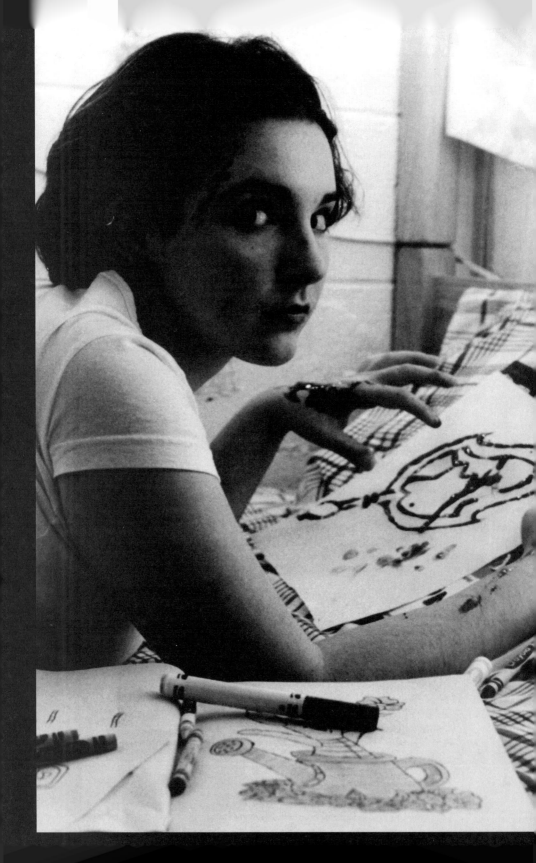

CHAPTER TWO: CHARACTER CREATION

NEW ARCHETYPES

Archetypes are the building blocks for your character's persona. In day-to-day life, people put on different Demeanors as they face the world. You behave like one sort of person at the office, another at school and maybe yet another when out partying with your friends. None of these different faces we wear are lies, exactly. But the deepest goals and motivations of a person — the innermost Nature — are rarely on display for the entire world to see. When you are building your character, you should ask yourself: What does this person truly want? What face does he show to the world in order to get it? The answers you come up with are the heart of any truly enjoyable character.

There are some Archetypes that are very common in the Camarilla. Certain clans are naturally drawn to grant these sort of people the Embrace. Likewise, Kindred in important positions within the Camarilla are always looking for servants of a certain temperament.

Idealist — You are utterly committed to some purpose greater than your own wants and needs.

Soldier — You've been given your orders, and you take pride in accomplishing them well.

Dabbler — The world is full of new things to learn, and you want to sample all of them.

Scientist — Diligent, rational examination can reveal all the secrets of the universe.

ABILITIES

There are some skills within the Camarilla that are encountered regularly. While the "Hobby/ Professional/ Expert Ability" given in **Laws of the Night** can easily cover these Abilities, it may prove helpful to use the more in-depth description of these Abilities given below. Please note that these Abilities, like any material given in this book, are to be used strictly at the option of the Storyteller.

Hunting

This skill allows you to stalk any prey, in any terrain, for any purpose. Deer hunters and Gangrel use this to bring down wild game. Most other Kindred, however, hunt a different sort of prey in the urban jungle. This skill allows them to gain their nightly sustenance without breaking the Masquerade or going hungry due to missed opportunities. This Ability gives you a retest in situations when you are attempting to refresh your Blood Pool, whether in the woods or out on the streets.

Psychology

This is a working knowledge of psychology, both in theory and in practice. You have a solid understanding of the nature of both human and Kindred minds. Given enough time and effort, you may accurately discern how a person's mind works, or how it doesn't, as the case may be. This Ability may be used to determine the given subjects' Nature or her Derangements (if any), or as a retest to gain insight into a person's motivations. Note that a separate test is needed for each piece of information. You must speak with a given subject for anywhere from 15 minutes to an hour for this skill to work — you cannot diagnose someone's insanity at a glance.

Merits and Flaws

Merits and Flaws are meant to give your character that little extra twist that sets him apart from the pack. They should always be the last step in character creation and never the main focus of a character concept . Often, new players will make the mistake of latching on to a Merit or Flaw and defining a character solely by that small detail. The end result is rarely a character that has enough depth or creativity to be worth playing for extended periods of time.

Likewise, many players will try and take as many Flaws as they can in order to buy as many points of *Generation*, Abilities or Disciplines as possible. Bear in mind that the Storyteller has every right to strip a Flaw (and its points) from a character if it isn't being played properly. Flaws are handicaps that limit the things a character can do. A Flaw that isn't a disadvantage isn't really a Flaw, and shouldn't be treated as such.

Physical

Bruiser (1 Trait Merit)

The icy stare, the cobra eyes — you've got the stone cold thug look down, and it works. You are one Trait up when comparing ties on any attempts to intimidate someone.

Friendly Face (1 Trait Merit)

Don't I know you from somewhere? You have an open, honest look about you that always seems to remind everyone of an old friend they haven't seen in years. You are one Trait up on all attempts to persuade, seduce or beguile a stranger.

Dulled Bite (2 Trait Flaw)

Your fangs never fully developed, or they never came in at all. When feeding, you need to find some other way of making the blood flow, or must win

on a Physical Challenge (in addition to any necessary to grapple your victim) in order for your bite to penetrate. A number of Caitiff and high-generation vampires manifest this Flaw.

Glowing Eyes (2 Trait Flaw)

Your eyes actually glow in the dark, not merely reflecting light like a cat's, but actually producing light. This radiation partially blinds you and, in the dark, makes you stand out like a sore thumb. Likewise, your very presence in public is a breach in the Masquerade. Only thick, wrap-around sunglasses will hide this illumination — ordinary sunglasses or contact lenses just don't cut it. You gain the following Negative Social Trait: *Bestial* and the Negative Mental Trait: *Oblivious*, neither of which can be bought off with experience points. However, you also gain the Social Trait: *Intimidating* for free. It is recommended that you wear a tag proclaiming your unusual deformity.

Permanent Fangs (2 Trait Flaw)

Your fangs do not retract, making the preservation of the Masquerade difficult at best. You must take the Negative Social Trait: *Bestial*, which cannot be bought off with experience points.

Mental

Coldly Logical (1 Trait Merit)

You have a knack for separating fact from hysteria, truth from emotion. Some may call you a cold fish, but you're too cool to care. You are one Trait up when comparing ties on any attempt to persuade you using emotion (i.e., a Social Challenge where your opponent bids Traits like *Beguiling*, *Charismatic* or *Seductive*).

Thirst for Innocence (2 Trait Flaw)

The sight of innocence of any sort arouses a terrible hunger within you. You must pass a *Self-Control* Test or else frenzy and attack the source of your hunger.

Guilt-Wracked (4 Trait Flaw)

You cannot cope with the fact that you must consume blood to survive. You must pass a *Courage* Test each and every time you attempt to feed, or else you simply cannot go through with it. This means you will often be low on blood and will easily succumb to hunger frenzies.

Supernatural

Bright Aura (1 Trait Merit)

For some reason, your aura reads as much brighter and more colorful than most Kindred's. When you are the subject of *Aura Perception*, your character appears mortal. This Merit is particularly appropriate for high-generation vampires and Caitiff.

Healing Touch (1 Trait Merit)

Normally vampires can only heal wounds left from the Kiss by licking them. With a touch, you can achieve the same effect.

Inoffensive to Animals (1 Trait Merit)

Animals generally fear and loathe the presence of the Kindred. The predator fights and the prey flees when Caine's children approach. For some reason, this does not hold true for you. Animals won't necessarily like you at first sight, but they will not automatically flee from you.

Cold Breeze (1 Trait Flaw)

A cold breeze follows you wherever you go. While this is terribly dramatic around curtains and open flames, it also proclaims your supernatural aspect to everyone around you, including mortals. You are one Trait down on any social interaction with mortals. It is recommended that you wear a tag describing this aspect of your character.

Beacon of the Unholy (2 Trait Flaw)

You radiate a palpable aura of evil. Clergy and mortals possessing True Faith are instantly aware that you are a supernatural creature of darkness and react accordingly. Likewise, you suffer the effects of True Faith when on holy ground or any place of worship.

Bound (2 Trait Flaw)

You begin the game blood bound to another player's character or Storyteller character. The knowledge that your will is not your own constantly chafes at your soul, even as you revel in your utter love for your captor. This Flaw may only be taken with the express permission of the Storyteller and, if applicable, the player whose character to whom you are bound.

Deathsight (2 Trait Flaw)

Everything appears to be dead and decaying around you. The world is a corpse, mortals are walking cadavers, and everything is in ruins. You must take the Negative Social Trait: *Callous* and the Negative Mental Trait: *Oblivious*, neither of which can be bought off with experience points. On the other hand, you are two Traits up when comparing Traits on any Social Challenge based on physical appearance (i.e., your opponent bids the Traits *Gorgeous* or *Alluring*).

Lord of the Flies (2 Trait Flaw)

Buzzing, swarming insects constantly surround you. You are one Trait down on any social or Stealth-related challenge. It is recommended that you wear a tag announcing this aspect of your character.

Master-level Influences: The Dark Heart of the City.

The most ancient Kindred of the Camarilla build power bases that are terrifying in scope. Centuries of careful planning, ghouling and scheming can produce empires. These elder vampires become the essence of the city they dwell in: Their wishes and desires shape their homes in ways that lesser Kindred can only dream of.

Surprisingly, however, very few Kindred gain influence on a national or even regional scope. Some of this is due to the fact that elder vampires are more

used to thinking in terms of city-states and towns rather than nations; the rest is because other Kindred would never stand for one of their kind obtaining that much power. Whatever the reason, Kindred tend to develop Influence in depth rather than breadth, and even the most Influential Kindred has little control over the nation he dwells in. There are always exceptions, however....

The following charts give a rough idea of the power granted Influences 6-10 in the various realms controlled by Kindred society. Bear in mind that the area of control of these Influences tend to get blurred at higher levels; someone with high levels of *Street* Influence can influence the behavior of the police and underworld without having any direct say in their activities.

Obtaining these levels of Influence requires decades, if not centuries, of hard work. Such power should only be in the hands of the most ancient and established of elders. Neonates shouldn't even be able to dream of holding such an empire in their hands.

BUREAUCRACY

A Kindred with higher level of Influence in this domain has spent decades establishing the system that shapes his city. Others may choose the mayors and aldermen of a city — you control them through the machinery of government, without which the entire city would collapse. As this power grows, you may even be able to exert your will on the regional level.

Cost	Effect
6	Initiate a major public works program (a large park or office complex)
	Completely dominate all aspects of the city's bureaucracy within a city block
	Prevent emergency services such as fire protection from responding to a major disaster
7	Stop, start or alter a state or regional program or policy
	Force an entire neighborhood to build as you see fit
	Collect taxes ($1,000)
8	Build or destroy small towns or suburbs
	Control an entire city district
	Rewrite policy on a state or regional level
9	Have a major building condemned and destroyed on short notice
	Build monuments or stadiums
10	Completely control the mayor's office
	Rebuild the city as you see fit

CHURCH

The Church is one of the most ancient bulwarks of Kindred Influence — and the most dangerous. In the World of Darkness, the Church still keeps the truth about the supernatural locked away in its oldest libraries. Kindred with high levels of *Church* Influence dare to use this power to their own ends. Most Kindred possessing level of Influence this high can still remember the foundations of some of these faiths.

Cost	Effect
6	Identify a church member with True Faith
	Stage a "miraculous" event that gains the unofficial approval of the Church
7	Excommunicate a lay member of the church
	Have a church marriage annulled or dissolved
	Find an experienced Church-associated hunter
8	Pose as a bishop or other major regional religious figure
	Nominate a member of the clergy for elevation
	Stage a "miracle" that gains official recognition by the Church
9	Create or destroy a major cathedral or temple within the city
	Exert minor influence over nationwide Church policy
	Have a member of the clergy excommunicated
10	Exert major influence over nationwide Church policy
	Discover the secrets of the modern Inquisition

FINANCE

The higher levels of *Finance* become a dizzying game for Kindred. The Cainite elders who were merchant princes during the Renaissance are in awe of the stock market, let alone the pace of electronic money transfers. In this day and age, it takes very energetic Kindred to stay on top of the financial world. Many elders delegate this power to younger Kindred. As a consequence, this is one area where ancillae can truly taste power. Elders, confident of their leash upon these upstarts, allow their childer to play — as long as they get the results they desire.

Cost	Effect
6	Obliterate all savings and credit for one individual (destroy one level of *Resources*) Control the price of a minor commodity
	Perform insider trading ($10,000)
7	Exert minor influence over local stock prices
	Purchase a minor nationwide corporation
8	Control the price of a major commodity
	Cause inflation or depression for a regional area
9	Siphon off all profits from a minor corporation ($100,000)
	Own a major nationwide corporation
	Exert major influence over local stock prices
10	Create a stock market crash Influence nationwide economic trends
	Make someone an instant millionaire ($1,000,000)

HEALTH

The modern world has more threatening things in it than Kindred. The unseen virus, the polluted air — sometimes it seems like the Earth itself has become a vampire, sucking the life out of the people. In truth, it is the Kindred who dominate this influence who make the Earth bleed for them. Ancient vampires scarcely understand why younger Kindred fear those who control the health of a city. The neonates, brought up in a world aware of the ozone layer and AIDS, know better.

Cost	Effect
6	Cause a major shortage of blood within an area
	Prevent ambulances from responding to a major disaster
7	Contaminate the entire blood supply for one mi nor hospital
	Locate samples of a minor infectious disease (influenza)
8	Cause a major shortage of one type of medicine (insulin, penicillin)
	Perform major or illegal experimentation on a large number of patients
	Shut down a small hospital permanently
9	Contaminate the blood supply for an entire city
	Shut down a major hospital permanently
	Locate samples of a major infectious disease (anthrax)
10	Shut down all medical care in a city for an entire day
	Direct genetic engineering projects

HIGH SOCIETY

This Influence tends to have younger Kindred in its upper reaches than most other spheres of Influence. Partially, this is because of the Masquerade; it's hard be a major celebrity when you only work nights. More to the point, Kindred know that their greatest strength lies in the shadows, not in the spotlight. Those Kindred who remain in this area of Influence become the purveyors of fame rather than its object. They may not be the faces the public sees in the tabloids, but they certainly choose who will appear on them.

Cost	Effect
6	Own a small but influential theater or gallery in the city
	Give someone his or her "15 minutes of fame" (create one level of Fame for one session)
7	Bring a major traveling concert or play to the city
	Destroy the career of a minor established celebrity (destroy one level of *Fame*)

8	Appoint anyone as a member of the city's elite social circles
	Make someone a minor celebrity (create one level of *Fame*)
	Become a major celebrity (grant yourself two levels of *Fame*)
	Own a large gallery or theatre in the city
9	Make someone a major celebrity (create two levels of *Fame*)
	Influence nationwide fashion trends
10	Destroy a major celebrity's career (destroy two levels of *Fame*)

I Wanna Live forever!

A great deal of the *High Society* Influence revolves around the granting or destroying the *Fame* Background. The Storyteller needs to watch this influence closely to make sure that it doesn't get abused. As a rule of thumb, if a character receives a level of *Fame* Background through the use of this Influence, the recipient must purchase the Background with earned experience as soon as possible. If the character chooses not to do so, the extra levels of Fame are automatically removed. However, the person using *High Society* Influence may choose to keep employing his Influence to grant *Fame*, essentially thrusting the character into the limelight despite his wishes. This can be a cunning trap for many Kindred...

The same rule applies to those Influences that grant *Resources*, *Allies* or other Backgrounds: The character receiving the Background must pay for it with experience as soon as possible, or the Background fades away.

| | Own the central gallery or theater within the city |
| | Create a national fashion or trend |

INDUSTRY

This is another area in which the eldest and most potent Kindred are falling behind. Most elder Kindred are familiar with a world where steel and stone are the units of power; they are unfamiliar with a place where transactions can literally move at the speed of light, and silicon is the master of the earth. As younger ancillae clamor to control this Influence, the elders look to control these eager young Kindred rather than the actual tools of industry.

Cost	Effect
6	Attract a major heavy industry to the area
	Illegally dump large amounts of toxic waste (and not get caught)

7	Siphon off company profits ($5,000)
	Eliminate or start a union in any company
8	Arrange for a major ecological disaster
	Fatally sabotage a major construction project
9	Own a major heavy industry or construction firm in the area
	Cause a major strike
10	Fatally sabotage an entire product of heavy industry or machinery
	Influence nationwide labor movements

LEGAL

At heart, many Camarilla elders are fond of law and order — at least, their versions of law and order. As a consequence, many elders at least dabble in this sphere of Influence. The truly dedicated are not interested in just manipulating the law; they want to shape it to fit their own desires. Perhaps the heavy influence of Kindred upon the law is the reason most lawyers have such poor reputations. Then again, perhaps not. Like does attract like, after all.

Cost	Effect
6	Bring any investigation short of a grand jury to a halt
	Force a guilty verdict on any misdemeanor trial
7	Appoint a state judge
	Have a lawyer disbarred
8	Successfully sue anyone for major damages (destroy one level of *Resources*)
	Force a guilty verdict on a felony trial
9	Control one of the members of the state Supreme Court
	Appoint or fire the city's District Attorney
10	Force a guilty verdict on a major or sensational felony trial
	Rewrite state or local law as you see fit

MEDIA

Controlling the media is one the most important aspects of the Masquerade. Consequently, although this field has changed as fast as anything else in the Information Age, the elders of the Camarilla have made a concerted effort to keep abreast of current developments. The Internet, however, remains a chink in the Camarilla armor — one that the ancillae are hungry to exploit.

Cost	Effect
6	Submit headline news successfully
	Cause a minor media outlet to begin an investigation
7	Destroy a minor newspaper or TV station
	Write small nationwide stories successfully

	Manufacture a major scandal (destroy one level of *Fame*)
8	Cause a major media outlet to begin an investigation
	Kill national news stories before they get off the ground
9	Broadcast fake regional stories
	Destroy a major newspaper or TV station
10	Create a fake major national news story
	Create a news blackout over an entire city

OCCULT

For obvious reasons, the occult is a subject near and dear to the Kindred in general. Influence in this area tends to provide deeper information as opposed to greater power — the more Influence a Kindred has within this realm, the closer he comes to the truth, and the fewer charlatans he has to deal with. The oldest and most powerful Kindred dominate this area.

Cost	Effect
6	Create your own Basic ritual
	Found a local cult (grant one level of *Allies* Background)
	Learn truthful lore concerning Lupines or changelings
7	Create your own Intermediate ritual
	Access major magical items
	Learn truthful lore concerning wraiths or spirits
8	Create your own Advanced ritual
	Found a regional cult (grant two levels of *Allies* Background)
	Locate and bring a specific hedge mage or medium to you
9	Access legendary magical items
	Locate and bring a specific Lupine or changeling to you
10	Locate an entire copy of the *Book of Nod* or the true lair of a Methuselah

POLICE

It is rare to find elder Kindred in the upper echelons, but those that are often quite firmly entrenched. When protected by the "blue wall," there is very little these Kindred can't accomplish. As crime-fighting moves into more high-tech spheres, however, some elders prefer to use ancillae as their pawns.

Cost	Effect

6	Control one aspect of a large city precinct (homicide, dispatch)
	Appropriate contraband or drugs from the evidence room
7	Call for SWAT raids
	Have free access to all police facilities
	Have the crime lab "lose" evidence
8	Completely control the police department of a suburb or small town
	Have people extradited across state lines
9	Have police chiefs fired
10	Complete control of a large city's police network

Political

This is another high-profile Influence that many Kindred tend to avoid at the upper levels. Although younger ancillae recognize the dizzying heights of power that such influence can bring, most Kindred prefer to work behind the scenes, appointing the leaders of men rather than serving the common good themselves.

Cost	Effect
6	Enact major legislation on the local level
	Get your candidate into a major local office (i.e., mayor of a major city)
7	Destroy the career of a major local politician
8	Get your candidate into a major federal office (i.e., senator)
	Enact minor national legislation
9	Embezzle taxpayer money ($10,000)
	Engineer a major political scandal
10	Give major support to a national political candidate
	Propose major national legislation

Street

Those who possesses a high level of this Influence own the heart and soul of their home cities. What anyone in their town knows, they know. This Influence is not broad in scope, but it is very deep. An elder who controls the streets of a city may not appear to be powerful, but those who cross him will find every hand in the city turned against them.

Cost	Effect
6	Completely dominate all aspects of a housing project or slum
	Mark a specific person who enters a downtown area for harassment
7	Locate exotic weaponry (bombs, sniper rifles)
	Start a small riot

8	Completely dominate all aspects of a downtown neighborhood
	Control a large gang
9	Locate unique or customized weaponry
	Mark a specific person who enters downtown for death
10	Completely dominate all aspects of the downtown of a major city
	Start a major citywide riot

TRANSPORTATION

This Influence still has a lot of favor within elder circles. Kindred can strangle an entire city with this influence, or they can make a community thrive. There has been substantial change in this environment over the centuries, but it has been slow enough for the elders to keep pace and maintain their hold on who enters their cities or leaves them.

Cost	Effect
6	Bar a person from entering or leaving a city via public transportation
	Attract a major transportation outlet (i.e., air port) to your city
7	Halt all public transportation and cargo shipping to a small town
	Siphon off profits from a shipping or trucking firm ($5,000)
8	Bar a specific form of cargo from entering or leaving a city
	Isolate a small town from any form of transportation (including highways)
9	Cause a major transportation disaster
	Destroy a major transportation outlet
	Completely dominate one aspect of regional transportation (airplanes, trucking, shipping)
10	Prevent anyone from leaving or entering a city via all forms of transportation (including highways)
	Bar all cargo from entering or leaving a major city

UNDERWORLD

The inception of the Mafia dates back to the Renaissance, and it's entirely likely that a Kindred thought of the idea first. Several clans of Kindred have sparred over control of the Mafia for centuries, fueling an already-volatile mix. The potential for violence, blood and easy answers to hard problems brings a never-ending stream of new investors in this ancient profession. The Camarilla has a solid foothold in the upper reaches of this Influence, but that could change at any moment. In particular, the arrival of the Eastern vampires

threatens the small grasp some Kindred have over the tongs and triads in the various Chinatowns.

Cost	Effect
6	Locate exotic weaponry (bombs, sniper rifles)
	Contract a professional hit
7	Launder money
	Supply the drug needs of a large city
8	Control the head of a small crime family
	Locate unique or custom weaponry
9	Put a price on anyone's head
	Start a mob war
10	Control the head of a large crime family
	Stage a public assassination, terrorist act or shooting spree (and get away with it)

UNIVERSITY

The quiet halls of academia are familiar to many elders. Many former monks who, when they breathed, tutored the sons of nobility seek to recreate their pasts in today's halls of higher learning. As an elder gains more and more power in this Influence, her pet campus begins to reflect her personality. The whole college becomes her personal haven, and everything on it her property.

Cost	Effect
6	Falsify a graduate degree
	Create a college class of your choice
	Discredit the head of a college department
7	Falsify a Ph.D.
	Know a contact or two with high levels of Ability or esoteric knowledge
	Discredit the dean of a college
8	Appoint the dean of a college
	Funnel university funds in your direction ($1,000)
9	Direct an entire university department to research a specific problem
	Have a research assistant attached to your service indefinitely (grant one level of *Allies*)
10	Destroy or discredit an entire college

GARGOYLES

In the earliest years of the Tremere clan, the Warlocks were assaulted on all sides. Ancient vampires, enraged at the usurpers' theft of immortality, circled the new clan like a pack of wolves. Only with strong allies could the fledgling vampires hope to survive their first nights. These allies would have to be powerful, vigilant and utterly loyal. Intimate with betrayal, the Tremere knew that any allies they found had to be beyond reproach.

The Tremere could find no such allies anywhere on Earth, so they created them. After years of experimentation, a new rite was created that would transform captive Tzmisce, Gangrel and Nosferatu into a monstrous bloodline. These new horrors had the strength, tenacity and patience of stone. They had the features of demons and the wings of nightmares. Most importantly, they were easy for the Tremere to *Dominate* into submission. These were the Gargoyles, and their existence guaranteed the survival of the young Warlock clan.

For nearly a thousand years, the Gargoyles have faithfully served their Tremere masters. In recent nights, however, something has happened, and somehow a few Gargoyles have managed to slip their leashes. They have become free creatures, unfettered by the Warlock's chains. Now the Gargoyle Clan is split into two camps. The first, called Slaves, still follow the orders of their Tremere masters. The second, who call themselves Freemen, no longer serve the Tremere, but are often without places to roost. Like Frankenstein's monster, the Gargoyles wander the earth looking for a place in a world that treats them as abominations.

Oddly, the Free Gargoyles have chosen to remain in the Camarilla. Whether this choice is due to a need for order, a desire to spite the former masters or simply force of habit is not known. But just as the Gargoyles once seemed unshakably loyal to the Tremere, the Free Gargoyles seem utterly loyal to the Camarilla as a whole. For now.

In recent years, Gargoyles have taken to embracing mortals, often by impulse or accident. They still perform the ancient rites, however, and new Gargoyles are occasionally created from Nosferatu or Tzmisce stock. Whether Embraced or created, a Gargoyle's past is lost to her once she joins the bloodline. Many Gargoyles pursue their lost identity obsessively, while others are glad for the new start.

In their own way, the Gargoyles are even more alien than the hideous Nosferatu. They are shunned by both Kindred and kine as monsters that have no ties to humanity at all, and the process of creation, which wipes away their memories, is no help. Most Gargoyles are as unruffled by this as befits their stoic natures. However, even the hard shell of a Gargoyle can crack, and many are known to secretly yearn for the touch of kindness or friendship in their lonely lives.

Most players will want to portray a Free Gargoyle. While a Slave Gargoyle can be an interesting character for a while — and an escape chronicle is always entertaining — eventually, being at the continuous beck and call of the entire Tremere clan can get boring. Slave Gargoyles are in far deeper thrall to the Tremere than any ghoul, and blind obedience rarely makes for an interesting long-term character.

Roleplaying Hints: Like the stone you embody, you possess great patience and stoicism. The Free Gargoyles won their liberty only after years of careful planning; they are not going to risk that freedom on hasty action now. You weigh and consider each action, but when planning is done, you can act with remarkable speed and decisiveness. Like a mighty train, you're slow to start, but when you're on course, slowing down is even more difficult.

Disciplines: *Fortitude, Potence, Visceratika, Flight*

Advantages: All Gargoyles automatically begin the game with the first level of *Flight* for free. In addition, the Gargoyles are natural guards, sentries and spies. As a consequence, they posses a free level of *Awareness*.

Disadvantages: Gargoyles are hideous, misshapen monsters, even more alien in nature than the Nosferatu. No Gargoyle may possess Appearance-related Social Traits such as *Alluring, Gorgeous* or *Seductive* without calling upon special powers (such as *Obfuscate*). Furthermore, all Gargoyles suffer from the Negative Traits *Repugnant* or *Bestial* whenever their true forms are apparent. These Traits may not be removed with Experience Traits or Free Traits. A Gargoyle cannot initiate any Social Challenges in his true form except for the purposes of intimidation, although he may defend against Social Challenges.

The Gargoyles have a natural weakness built into them by their Tremere masters: They easily succumb to *Dominate* and other mind-controlling effects. All Gargoyles possess the Negative Trait *Submissive* x 2 when attempting to resist *Dominate* or any other mind-controlling effects.

Bloodlines: Tremere prefer to create their Gargoyles from existing Kindred stock. The surge of competing strains of vitae and the magical effects of the transformation ritual result in wiping away almost all traces of the new Gargoyle's old memories and leaving him as a blank slate to be written upon. Free Gargoyles have taken to Embracing new members into the bloodline; the process is only somewhat gentler for them, as they still lose most of their pasts, but at least retain a vague sense of their former selves. Exact features of each Gargoyle's particular hideousness are dependent upon the combination of blood that created the Gargoyle's original ancestor, whether Tzimisce-Nosferatu, Tzimisce-Gangrel or Gangrel-Nosferatu.

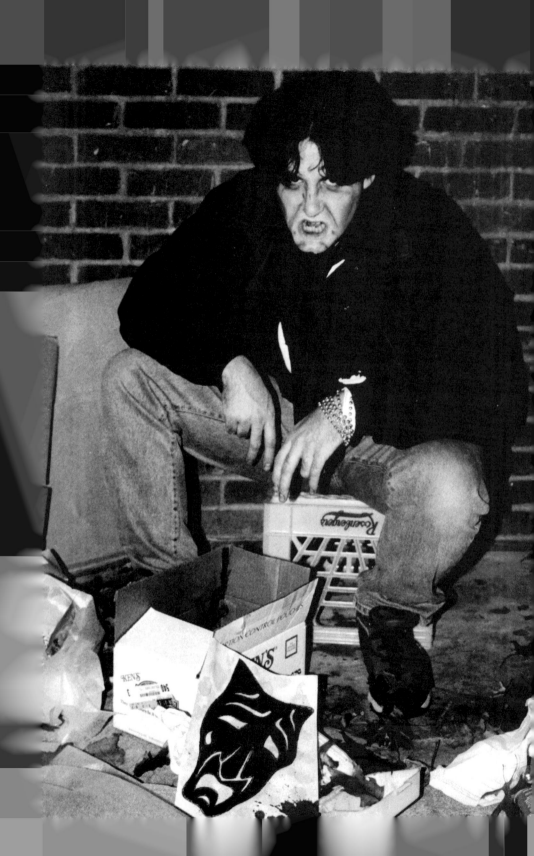

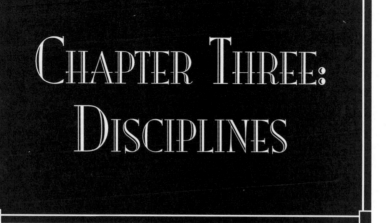

CHAPTER THREE: DISCIPLINES

When a vampire elder of suitably low generation reaches a certain power level, her command of Disciplines becomes far more powerful than that of lesser vampires. While other Kindred are limited from reaching such potential by their weaker blood, an elder can gain far more potent powers and even create powers of her own.

Any high-level powers must *always* be cleared by the Storyteller before they are allowed in the game. It cannot be stressed enough that a Storyteller who decides to let her players have such powers had best be prepared for the consequences. It's a mistake to drop such a character in the middle of the game and expect that he won't make waves — he will, and rightly so. In the hands of a player who wants to smack down those around him in order to establish his reputation, such powers can mean a quick and bloody end for the chronicle. The Storyteller is under no obligation whatsoever to accept any Disciplines of this level to her game, even if she does accept characters who have the potential to learn them. Many of the powers here also require Storyteller assistance to be properly used, and the Storyteller should prepare for that in advance.

Also, keep in mind that mastering these powers takes a long time — decades at the very least — whether that's simply the learning process or just finding a teacher. Regardless of how much experience a character might have, it is extremely unlikely that he will ever gain more than one Discipline of this level in game (unless the chronicle fast-forwards through the years between sessions). Note that a character can learn several powers from the same power level — for example, it is not impossible for a character to learn several elder-level *Obfuscate* powers if he has the experience and the time to do so.

CREATIVE INSANITY

The Disciplines that follow shouldn't be taken as the only available options; rather, they are examples of what kind of power can be achieved. It's not uncommon for an ancient vampire to have highly personalized Disciplines. Once an elder vampire has learned the five basic powers of any given Discipline, he may start creating his own. At that point, he has enough understanding of the Discipline's nature that he no longer requires a teacher. That said, having a teacher may certainly help — after all, inventing such abilities isn't quite as simple as some might think.

The Storyteller should bear in mind that this may well be an invitation to disaster — some players will invariably try to sneak some grossly overpowered stuff past the Storyteller. Storytellers should consider this official permission to mercilessly stomp such powers into the ground, and squeeze the player's nose with a particularly nasty kung fu grip until he repents his powergaming ways. It's harsh, but it's the only way.

Some Disciplines have more powers listed than others. This doesn't mean that certain Disciplines are more versatile than others — rather, it reflects the fact that certain Disciplines have better-known applications. Also, some Disciplines do not go all the way up to Methuselah level. This is because the bloodline has no known members of low enough generation to develop powers of such magnitude.

EXPERIENCE COSTS

Superior Disciplines' experience costs are as follows:

Level	Experience point cost	Generation requirement
Elder	12	8
Master	15	7
Ascendant	18	6
Methuselah	21	5

Note that the actual cost may be end up being of secondary concern to the player, as learning these powers also requires a great deal of time. The specifics are up to the Storyteller, but mastering even the Elder-level powers may take a decade or two, and mastering a Methuselah-level power can take an entire century.

Animalism

Elder Animalism

Animal Succulence

Most vampires find animal blood tasteless and less nourishing than human blood, not to mention somewhat *declassé*. Those with this power have learned to make greater use of such stuffs.

Once this power is learned, it is always in effect. Simply put, every one Blood Trait you gain from an animal counts as two. However, this doesn't mean that the natural desire for the blood of "higher" prey is in any way diminished — quite the opposite. After every third feeding from an animal, you make a Static Mental Challenge whenever you are confronted with the opportunity to feed on human or Kindred blood. If you fail, you frenzy and attempt to drain the vessel. As you accumulate feedings, you find it harder to resist the lure of finer vintage. At each additional third feeding (the sixth, ninth, etc.), you must bid three extra Traits on the challenge — for example, a vampire who has fed nine times on animal blood must bid six extra Traits on the test when she discovers an unconscious Ventrue just waiting to be fed from. Once you have frenzied and slaked your thirst, you are considered to be "starting over."

You cannot gain extra Blood Traits from any supernatural creature in animal form — this includes werecreatures, Gangrel in animal form, pooka, etc.

Shared Soul

Through the use of this power, you may probe the mind of any one animal within reach. *Shared Soul* is a somewhat difficult experience for both parties, as both are completely immersed in the thoughts and emotions of the other. With enough effort and time, both participants can gain a complete understanding of the other's mind. *Shared Soul's* primary use is in extracting memories of a specific event from the mind of an animal, but some Gangrel have been known to use this power in search of enlightenment and understanding of their own Beasts. However, too close a bond can leave both parties entangled after the sharing ends, causing the vampire to adopt behavior patterns similar to those of the animal.

To use *Shared Soul*, you must touch the intended subject, make a Mental Challenge and spend a Willpower Trait. If successful, you can now make contact with the animal's mind. For every memory you wish to read from the subject, you must make a Simple Test. For each success, you experience a memory. Failure means the contact is broken entirely and must be reestablished before attempting again.

If you wish to form a complete bond with the animal, you must spend an entire minute touching the animal and concentrating, then spend another Willpower Trait and make another Mental Challenge with the Storyteller. If successful, you can now access all of the subject's memories at will and no longer need to maintain physical contact with the subject. The Simple Test is still required, but failure merely means that you may try again next turn without penalty. The power remains active until you choose to terminate the connection.

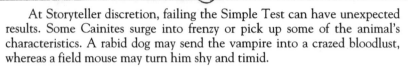

At Storyteller discretion, failing the Simple Test can have unexpected results. Some Cainites surge into frenzy or pick up some of the animal's characteristics. A rabid dog may send the vampire into a crazed bloodlust, whereas a field mouse may turn him shy and timid.

Species Speech

The power of *Feral Whispers* allows you to communicate with a single animal, but *Species Speech* goes one step beyond — it allows you to communicate with all the members of a species in your presence. It is most often used after a large group of the species has been summoned with *Beckoning*.

You must spend a Willpower Trait to establish contact with a group of animals and make a Static Social Challenge against the group. The Storyteller determines the difficulty, but most animal groups (particularly the "higher" animals) have the equivalent of 10 to 12 Traits. There is no limit to how many animals you can command with this power, but all the animals must be in your presence. You may only command one species at a time; for example, if you're in a zoo, you cannot give orders to elephants and zebras at the same time.

Apart from these differences, *Species Speech* functions like *Feral Whispers*.

Master Animalism

Conquer the Beast

Masters of *Animalism* can control animals and even gain mastery over their own Beasts, controlling them to a degree that lesser Kindred can only dream of. *Conquer the Beast* allows you to not only control your frenzies, but to enter frenzy at will. Some say that the development of this power is one of the first steps on the way to Golconda.

To frenzy at will, you make a Simple Test; on a win or tie, you plunge into a controlled frenzy. You may choose your targets as you please, but otherwise the frenzy plays itself out normally. On a failure you fall to an uncontrolled frenzy (which runs like any normal frenzy).

You may also use this power to regain your composure during an uncontrolled frenzy by making a *Self-Control* Challenge. If successful, you can regain control, but must spend a Willpower Trait every turn. While in this state, you may attempt to end the frenzy in the usual way. If you run out of Willpower Traits before the frenzy ends, you drop back into uncontrolled frenzy again.

Ascendant Animalism

Taunt the Caged Beast

This power allows you to release the Beast in others at will. With a fleeting brush against the subject, you may command your own Beast to awaken that of the subject, enraging it by threatening its spiritual territory. The victim instantly succumbs to frenzy.

To use this power, you must touch your target (Physical Challenge may be necessary on unwilling subjects), spend a Willpower Trait and then make a Social Challenge against the subject. If you win, the subject frenzies immediately. Should you lose, the frenzy falls on you instead of the subject. This power may also be used on individuals who would not ordinarily frenzy, such as normal humans.

Unchain the Beast

For most Kindred, the Beast is an abstract force of rage and bloodlust somewhere deep inside their consciousness. The elder who has mastered this power can turn that into something far more concrete. With a mere glance, you can awaken the Beast of your target, causing physical injury and excruciating agony as your victim's own violent impulses become manifest and start to tear him physically apart from within. The victim's body appears to rend itself apart, as if by invisible claws and fangs.

You make eye contact with your intended victim, then spend two Blood Traits and make a Social Challenge. With success, the victim suffers 10 minus her Humanity/Path score levels of lethal damage as her Beast attempts to claw its way out of her — for example, a victim with five levels of Humanity would suffer five health levels (10-5=5) of lethal damage. This power may be used on mortals and ghouls.

Auspex

While even conventional levels of *Auspex* grant the user amazing powers of perception, Kindred with elder levels of *Auspex* can attain a startling clarity of vision — they become capable of seeing to others' very souls and keeping an eye on events occurring in distant places while holding a pleasant conversation.

Elder Auspex

Clairvoyance

With *Clairvoyance* you can perceive distant events without the aid of *Psychic Projection*. After concentrating on a familiar person, place or object, you perceive events surrounding the subject while remaining aware of your own surroundings.

To use this power, spend a Willpower Trait and one round concentrating on a familiar subject, then make a Simple Test. With success, you may perceive everything that happens around the chosen subject. Your perspective is largely focused on your chosen subject; if you concentrated on another Kindred, your visions would follow her actions and thoughts and be unable to see around the corner to the muggers lying in wait for her. Other *Auspex* abilities may also be used to gain more information about the events that pass (provided you can win any tests they require). The power remains in effect as long as you concentrate, and you must have known your subject for at least one night to use this power.

While using *Clairvoyance*, you must bid two additional Traits for any tests to resolve events that occur in your physical surroundings as you are experiencing events in two locations simultaneously.

Prediction

With *Telepathy* you can read another's thoughts. With *Prediction*, however, you keep a channel continuously open to all those around you, a constant background buzz of surface thoughts and emotions. It is not a deep probe, nor sufficiently accurate to pick up specific thoughts, but gives clues to others' moods and attitudes, especially when in close contact with a particular subject. It is far less about true prediction and more that you sense

a thought being formed before it is spoken aloud (although the words unspoken are often far more interesting).

Any target speaking with you must truthfully answer generic questions regarding her emotional state, and describe her attitude toward the topic of discussion in generic terms. Questions like "What are you feeling at the moment regarding our discussion of Praxis seizures?" or "What's seeing your rival being so popular with your ex-lover make you feel like?" are acceptable. "Are you planning to betray me?" isn't. You may, however, choose to speculate aloud, "I dreamed today that someone was planning to betray me," and inquire about the emotional state of your listener.

Lying to a vampire with *Prediction* can be very difficult, with one's thoughts practically telegraphing the intent; all attempts to lie require a Mental Challenge, with ties going to the *Prediction* vampire. Of course, nothing prevents others from lying to you, and you need not reveal that you've picked up on their falsehoods.

If someone attempts to trick you via the use of *Subterfuge* or other similar Social Challenges, you may spend a Blood Trait and make a Mental Challenge against the other person. Success means that you're aware someone is trying to swindle you. Note that there's a difference between attempts to manipulate and outright lies — for example, leaving out certain bits of information or telling half-truths aren't the same as an outright lie.

Those with exceptionally strong Willpower (eight or more Willpower Traits, or the *Iron Will* Merit) may keep their thoughts and emotions in check to prevent others from reading them. This requires a conscious effort from them that may be detected by you. Someone who is attempting to veil her thoughts in such a manner must make a Simple Test if her concentration is disrupted (such as a surprise attack or being targeted by certain Disciplines); losing means the defender's concentration is disrupted. Note that the target must specifically know that you can read her in order to defend; a player who doesn't have the appropriate measure of Willpower but goes around claiming such a degree of constant concentration anyway can be safely classified as a stinkin' cheat.

With *Prediction*, you may not be surprised unless your concentration is on other matters, such as an attack or a debate, or your facilities are impaired (due to drugs or mental control). You can sense your enemy's intentions. This effect has a radius of 10 feet. Obviously, this offers no protection against sniping from the building across the street or other similar long-distance attacks. The Storyteller has the final word on what constitutes distraction.

MASTER AUSPEX

KARMIC SIGHT

While *Aura Perception* allows the briefest glimpses of another's spirit, *Karmic Sight* takes such abilities to a new level, allowing you to look directly into your target's very soul.

Your target must be within line of sight. Spend a Willpower Trait and make a Static Mental Challenge (difficulty equals the subject's Mental Traits). Successful use allows you to learn the character's Nature, Demeanor and whether the subject follows Humanity or another Path. You may also detect any influences on the subject's mind or soul — *Dominate, Presence* effects such as *Entrancement* or

infernal pacts. After this, you may make another Static Mental Challenge to learn the subject's Willpower and Humanity/Path scores. Finally, by making one more Static Mental Challenge, you may determine the state of your subject's karma. This is a highly abstract concept (which requires Storyteller intervention), but it will give you some idea of what kind of a person you are looking at. Regardless of highly subjective judgments of "good" and "bad," certain actions leave their marks on a soul. At the Storyteller's discretion, certain fate-related Merits and Flaws such as *Destiny* or *Dark Fate* may be detected as well.

Should you lose a test to read your subject, you risk gaining one of the subject's derangements, a Psychological/Mental/Supernatural Flaw or negative Social or Mental Traits for the duration of the session — subject's choice. If the subject has none, the Storyteller will find something appropriate. The Storyteller should always be called in to determine the end result. After losing, you must begin the process again from the ground up, including spending another point of Willpower and getting answers you already know, before you can proceed further.

Ascendant Auspex

Psychic Assault

Generally speaking, most Kindred mind tricks are subtle tools. *Psychic Assault* is anything but — it's a hammer that splits the subject's mind in half. The only indications of the attack taking place are the subject's expression of intense agony, usually accompanied by a nosebleed. Mortals killed by *Psychic Assault* appear to have died of a heart attack or aneurysm. Vampires crumble instantly to dust, regardless of their age.

To use this power, spend two Blood Traits, and either touch the victim (skin contact is not required, although a Physical Challenge may be) or establish eye contact. If you are assaulting a vampire or another supernatural creature, you must also spend a Willpower Trait. You may choose to frighten the subject, render him unconscious or kill him.

To frighten your target, make a Mental Challenge against him; if successful, the subject's mind is assaulted with horrible images. He can do nothing except clutch at his head and suffer excruciating internal pain and nightmarish thoughts for the next two turns. If your target knows who is responsible for the attack, he'll do his utmost to get away from you and avoid your company for the remainder of the evening. Should he be unable to leave, your target becomes skittish around you. He loses two temporary Willpower Traits and must bid an additional Trait whenever a challenge is called for during the rest of the night. Kindred victims need to test against Rötschreck.

To knock the subject unconscious, make two Mental Challenges against your subject (you must win both). This assault is similar but stronger than the one previously described, and your target loses consciousness. He remains unconscious for an hour, and wakes up with three health levels of lethal damage. Mortals will require medical attention, and may even die (Storyteller discretion). The victim loses two temporary Willpower Traits and a permanent Willpower Trait, and must bid two additional Traits for during the rest of the night. He may also not spend Willpower. If you succeed on only one

challenge, your target develops an unpleasant headache (treat as two levels of bashing damage), but suffers no other effects.

Should you wish to kill your target, make three Mental Challenges (in addition to the costs of invoking this power). Success on all three means a brutal death for your target as agonizing pain and terrifying images slice through his mind. Should you win fewer challenges, your target suffers as if from being frightened, as described above.

You must declare in advance what kind of effect you are attempting, and once declared, you may not change the effect. If you are attempting to render your target unconscious or kill her, and you lose on all your challenges, your subject becomes immune to *Psychic Assault* for the remainder of the night. A subject who loses his last Willpower Trait to *Psychic Assault* is rendered unconscious for the rest of the evening.

METHUSELAH AUSPEX

FALSE SLUMBER

It is commonly thought that a vampire in torpor is unable to do much of anything. In most cases, this is true, but a vampire who possesses *False Slumber* is an exception to the rule. This power allows a Methuselah's body to remain in torpor while his spirit moves about normally in his astral body.

Once this power is learned, *False Slumber* becomes active the instant you fall into torpor. Astral travel is handled as described in the rules for *Psychic Projection*. However, you may not be able to awaken physically at will; that is handled normally, as described in **Laws of the Night** p. 199.

Should your silver cord become severed in astral combat, you will become lost in the spirit realms as per normal. You also lose this *Auspex* power and half of your permanent Willpower Traits (round up), and must buy back both this power and the Willpower Traits with experience points. You spend a year and a night in torpor, during which time your soul slowly returns to your body. During this time you cannot be awakened from torpor by *any* means.

CELERITY

The previous levels of *Celerity* focused solely on speed. Those Kindred who learn superior levels of *Celerity*, however, become capable of doing far more than simply being faster than their opponents.

Note: Superior levels of *Celerity* have their own Blood Trait costs. In other words, while you can activate the five normal levels of *Celerity* by spending a single Blood Trait, you must spend additional Blood to activate the superior levels.

ELDER CELERITY

PROJECTILE

The supernatural speed of the Kindred doesn't operate by conventional physics, and thus items or weapons handled by them often have problems keeping up. For example, while the actual firing of a gun can occur in the blink of an eye, the bullet still leaves the barrel of the gun at a normal speed. A thrown rock slows down to normal speed at the instant it leaves the vampire's hand. There is no sensible explanation for this; most vampires just shrug and accept this fact. However, some of the more powerful Kindred have managed

to work their way around this — objects they throw or fire move at supernatural speeds and become truly impressive weapons.

To use this power, spend a Blood Trait and decide how many levels of *Celerity* you wish to give to the object being thrown or fired. For example, a character with six levels of *Celerity* might want to give the object three levels of *Celerity*. This would mean that the three lowest levels — both Basics and one Intermediate — would be inaccessible to the character for the remainder of the turn.

However, the attack gains one bonus Trait for every level of *Celerity* given to the object — in this example, this would mean three bonus Traits. Furthermore, bashing attacks (such as throwing a simple rock) become lethal attacks due to the incredible speed the projectile travels at. If the attack is already a lethal attack (such as a throwing knife or a bullet), it will now cause one additional health level of damage.

When you use *Projectile*, you must always announce your intention to do so as soon as it is your turn to act, and it must always be your first action — for example, actions granted by *Swiftness* or *Legerity* can be taken normally (unless said levels have been given to the object being propelled, of course), but *Projectile* must *always* be the first action on any given turn.

MASTER CELERITY

FLOWER OF DEATH

A vampire with *Flower of Death* becomes a blur of violence, striking his opponent repeatedly with incredible speed. It is not unknown for a vampire who has attained this level of *Celerity* to be so quick that his opponents are vanquished before they even know what happened.

Flower of Death costs three Blood Traits to activate. After it is activated, you gain as many extra Traits to all of your attacks as you have powers in *Celerity* for the duration of the scene. Needless to say, this makes you an extremely dangerous opponent. However, there is no damage bonus; your speed merely grants you the ability to strike faster than your foe can defend or dodge. You may use the Bomb in challenges, as per normal rules.

This power cannot be used in concert with other *Celerity* powers. *Flower of Death* can only used with hand-to-hand or melee combat — firearms, bows, thrown objects and other ranged weapons gain no bonuses if used with this power.

ASCENDANT CELERITY

ZEPHYR

One of the legendary — and rather improbable — comic book usages of superspeed is the ability to run on water or even up walls. Improbable or not, with *Zephyr*, you can easily accomplish this — ordinary obstacles cease to matter to you.

Spend a Blood Trait and a Willpower Trait. You automatically gain the ability to run on water, up walls, or even on ceilings — essentially, any relatively flat and open surface will do. You must keep on moving at all times to keep from falling off a wall or sinking into the liquid you are running on. You can easily run across most liquids, though you risk losing traction on especially slick substances like oil. A Simple Test to maintain footing may be needed (Storyteller discretion — generally once every several turns, or more often for unusually tricky surfaces

like Teflon). This power remains in effect until you stop running. If you wish to reactivate the power, you must again spend the required Traits.

With *Zephyr*, you may *always* declare Fair Escape as long as there is enough space for you to run away and you have enough Blood and Willpower Traits to activate the power, even if the threat is inches away from you. Doorways blocked by others are not a problem, as long as there is enough room for you to fit through; no one will be fast enough to grab you as you dart past. Closed windows can also be used as exits; at such speeds, you simply smash through them and hit the ground running (within reason — falling from a 10-story height will cause its own problems).

Navigating at speeds as great as this is no small feat and requires concentration. If you wish to take actions other than running, you must make a Simple Test. On a win, you may take the action normally. On a tie, you may not take the action, but may continue running. If you lose, you immediately lose control of your movement and end up smashing into whatever you were heading for. You may start moving again at the beginning of the next turn. This collision may cause bashing or even lethal damage, depending on the circumstances (Storyteller discretion).

Methuselah Celerity

Between the Ticks

A vampire who has reached this level of mastery is literally faster than the human eye can see. Other vampires — even some of those with *Auspex* — have trouble noticing her. Other beings seem almost like inanimate statues, frozen in time as she moves around them.

To use this power, spend a Blood Trait and a Willpower Trait. Everything around you instantly seems to slow down to a painful crawl. You must then spend one Blood Trait per turn to maintain this level of speed. You gain an automatically successful free attack against anyone who doesn't have at least Advanced *Celerity*. Those with Advanced *Celerity* are safe from the free attack, but you still have an extra action against them, one that is taken before the other party gets to act. You also have an extra action against other characters with Superior *Celerity*, but that action is taken after all other actions have been performed.

All attacks against you delivered at less than Advanced *Celerity* are considered to be automatic failures unless you deliberately stand still. Bullets and thrown objects can be easily dodged or even plucked out of the air (bullets fired or objects thrown with *Projectile* are handled normally). Those with Intermediate *Celerity* or Intermediate *Auspex* can perceive your movements, but only those with Advanced *Celerity* or higher may attempt to attack or stop you (unless you deliberately move slowly enough for slower characters to catch up).

For obvious reasons, you may declare Fair Escape at any time and may only be even potentially stopped by one who has an equal (or higher) level of *Celerity*.

DOMINATE

Elders who have reached Superior levels of *Dominate* become truly frightening beings, able to bend others' wills to their own effortlessly. A vampire with Superior *Dominate* may "burn through" an *Iron Willed* character's defenses as if the defender did not have the Merit in question, unless the subject

is of equal generation to the vampire attempting the *Dominate* (in which case *Iron Will* is treated normally.)

ELDER DOMINATE

CHAIN THE PSYCHE

When correctly applied, even lower levels of *Dominate* are usually enough to keep the puppets in line, but this isn't enough for some elders. With *Chain the Psyche*, the subject will experience incapacitating pain if he attempts to break free of control.

Spend a Blood Trait when you use *Dominate* on a subject. If the subject attempts to disobey implanted commands or recover lost memories, he becomes incapacitated as horrible, pulsating pain lances through his head. He will be unable to act for the next 10 minutes; it's all he can do to stay upright.

When using *Chain the Psyche*, you must decide how many attempts to resist you wish to crush and spend a Mental Trait for each — for example, to crush five attempts to resist, you must spend five Mental Traits while using *Dominate*. The Traits spent in this fashion cannot be used during the rest of the night (the expenditure of a Willpower Trait can restore all Mental Traits, as per normal). This power fades after all of the attempts to resist have been made.

Depending on the circumstances, you may wish to keep the number of Traits you spend a secret and inform the Storyteller instead, who keeps tabs on how many times the subject attempts to overcome the mental shackles.

LOYALTY

Your commands are so deeply implanted in the subject's mind that other vampires find it very difficult or even impossible to override them by using *Dominate* on their own. The name is somewhat misleading, as this power instills no particular feelings of loyalty in the subject. Reputedly the elder who developed this power felt rather strongly that loyalty should be mandatory, not voluntary. Not very surprisingly, all of his minions heartily agreed with the statement.

If another vampire attempts to use *Dominate* on the subject in a way that would cause her to act against a previously implanted command from you, the vampire attempting the *Dominate* must spend an extra Willpower Trait and bid two extra Traits while making the test.

OBEDIENCE

While *Dominate* ordinarily requires eye contact, a vampire with *Obedience* has learned to go beyond that. For her, the briefest physical contact suffices.

Instead of making eye contact, you must make skin-to-skin contact with your subject (a Physical Challenge may be necessary). You may then use *Dominate* freely. The touch doesn't need to be maintained while you give the instruction, but you can only issue one command in this fashion. If you wish to use *Dominate* on the subject again, you must touch him again.

MASTER DOMINATE

MASS MANIPULATION

Ordinarily, *Dominate* can only be used on a single target at any given time. However, a truly skilled elder can extend this power to entire groups of people, rendering her literally able to control masses.

You must declare the use of *Mass Manipulation* before you attempt the *Dominate* challenge. Spend a Willpower Trait, and make a standard *Dominate* test against the most resistant member of the target group; if he cannot be *Dominated*, then neither can those around him. If you succeed, you may then extend the effect to those around the initial target. The maximum number of additional targets is determined by halving your permanent Willpower score (round up) — for example, if you have seven permanent Willpower Traits, you may control up to four subjects, in addition to the initial target. You may choose who those subjects are, and you need only to make eye contact with the initial subject.

STILL THE MORTAL FLESH

Despite the somewhat deceiving name, this power works equally well on vampires and mortals. A vampire with this power can not only override the subject's mind, but his body as well. That may mean cutting off someone's senses or even stopping her heart. It is rumored that this power used to come more easily to Kindred in the distant past, but modern medicine has made it easier for mortals to resist this power's effects. Despite this, it is still a frightening and potent power.

To use this power, spend a Willpower Trait and make a normal Mental Challenge against the subject. If successful, you may shut off one of the subject's involuntary functions, or cause them to fluctuate erratically. Hearing,

sight, circulation, perspiration, reflex movements and similar functions are all viable targets.

A mortal whose heart is stopped will die immediately, although he may possibly be revived if he receives proper medical attention in the next few minutes. While cutting off a vampire's circulation or respiratory systems is completely ineffective, rendering her deaf or blind is quite useful.

Ascendant Dominate

Far Mastery

Essentially a refined version of *Obedience*, *Far Mastery* allows you to use *Dominate* on anyone you are familiar with whenever you please, regardless of the distance.

Spend a Willpower Trait and make a normal Mental Challenge against the target to establish contact. Once contact has been established, you may *Dominate* the subject normally as if you had established eye contact. If this power is used against another supernatural being, you must spend an additional Willpower Trait.

Methuselah Dominate

Speak Through the Blood

The famed power structures of Methusalehs didn't spring up overnight, and they certainly don't maintain themselves; indeed, these structures are such webs of deceit and intrigue that only a few can even hope to understand them, and even fewer, if any, ever see them in their entirety. To actually take charge of such an organization would be a monumental task, and while such beings' mental capacity far surpasses that of any human's, making sure that everyone stays in line and works toward the same goal can be extremely difficult. Luckily for such beings, proper application of *Speak Through the Blood* eases the task considerably: It allows a vampire to issue commands to every vampire whose lineage returns to her, regardless of whether they have even met each other. The end result is entire broods of vampires furthering agendas they are unaware of, fully believing them to be their own. New orders get accepted gradually; usually, a vampire's agenda shifts over the next decade or so to accommodate the Methuselah's wishes, and it is a very exceptional individual indeed who realizes that this change comes from an outside source.

To activate this power, spend a *permanent* Willpower Trait and make a Mental Challenge against the subject. It doesn't matter where the subject is; she may be on the other side of the planet or even on the moon — distance and location are no barriers. However, the subject must be of your own lineage. If successful, you may plant commands into the subject's mind. When combined with powers such as *Mass Manipulation*, this power can be extremely effective.

The commands must be generic, such as "Defend the Camarilla against all of its enemies and remain especially vigilant to internal threats" or "Destroy the power structure of anyone who attempts to upset Clan Tremere's power in this city." Specific orders, such as "Assassinate the prince before he makes his speech tonight" or "Bring me the head of the Nosferatu primogen" cannot be given, nor are the effects instantaneous; this power was meant for long-term planning.

Commands given in this fashion last for five years per Trait of permanent Willpower you possess. Should the power expire, the subject slowly reverts back

to her old ways. However, in many instances, the subject has built his own power base on the command, and may well continue to advance the command without noticing a difference. Still, it bears stressing that at that point she is no longer constrained by any command and may act against it (with or without knowing it).

Should a vampire reach Golconda, she becomes immune to this power. However, she remains unaware that it has been used. The rest of her lineage is still vulnerable unless they attain a similar state of enlightenment. Ghouls of affected Kindred are also affected, but to a lesser degree.

FORTITUDE

All Kindred with *Fortitude* are able withstand attacks that would cripple or kill a weaker vampire. Yet this is nothing compared to those who have mastered the truly impressive levels of *Fortitude* — they can walk through attacks that would destroy lesser Kindred.

ELDER FORTITUDE

PERSONAL ARMOR

Often, the best defense is to disarm your opponent. This is the concept *Personal Armor* is based on: any weapon used on you shatters from the impact.

With the expenditure of a Blood Trait, you can activate *Personal Armor* for the duration of the scene. Whenever you are attacked, make a Simple Test; if you succeed, all attacks against you inflict their normal damage, but if you are hit with melee weapons, the weapon shatters on impact and becomes completely unusable. If someone punches or kicks you, the attacker suffers as much damage as he inflicted on you, and the hand (or foot) he used to attack becomes unusable until that specific damage is healed — after all, it is impossible to punch someone effectively if every bone in one's hand is shattered. If someone is foolish enough to kick you, she receives the Negative Physical Trait *Lame* until the damage is healed and can only move around at a walking pace. Should someone feel adventurous enough to headbutt you, he receives double the damage he inflicted and spends the next round stunned, able to defend himself but unable to attack, as his cranium has just become a thousand small fragments of bone. Attackers who have *Fortitude* may use it to reduce the damage they might otherwise receive.

This power is somewhat useless against ranged attacks, as bullets still do damage even as they shatter. However, armor-piercing or high-caliber rounds function like normal rounds when used against you, as they shatter before they can properly pierce your defenses. Non-physical attacks, such as *Fire Bolt* or *Taste of Death* are handled normally.

Fetishes, klaives and magical weapons may be more resistant than ordinary weapons, depending on the Storyteller's ruling.

Note that you cannot be staked if you succeed in the test, as the stake shatters before it can properly pierce your heart.

MASTER FORTITUDE

SHARED STRENGTH

Powerful elders often tend to be bitter rivals, and thus mostly operate alone or with considerably weaker underlings. This is fine until the lead starts to fly, but at that point it is often preferable to the elder to have companions

who are as resistant to harm as she is. With *Shared Strength*, this becomes reality, as you can lend a portion of your resistance to others, enabling them to withstand far more injury than they can on their own.

Spend a Willpower Trait and press a drop of your vitae into the target's forehead; this leaves a mark that remains visible as long as the power is in effect. You then spend one Blood Trait per level of *Fortitude* you wish to transfer to another being — and note that if there are several targets, you must spend that many Blood Traits per target. After spending blood, make a Static Physical Challenge against the number of Blood Traits spent times three for every target. (For example, to bestow five levels of *Fortitude* on someone, you must make a Static Physical Challenge against 15 traits.) Success means your target now has as much *Fortitude* as you decided to bestow upon her for the rest of the night. In case of failure, you may retest using the *Survival* Ability; if that fails as well, the effect has failed on that particular target. You may attempt it again, provided that you have enough Willpower and Blood Traits left. Note that if the target already has *Fortitude*, only the *extra* levels you bestow count, and you only need pay Blood Traits for the levels that your target actually gains. (In other words, if a target with two existing levels of *Fortitude* is given three levels of *Fortitude* with *Shared Strength*, he will only gain a single level of *Fortitude*.)

Shared Strength may only be active once on any single target, no matter how many levels are bestowed: You can't give someone *Fortitude* one level at a time by making a lot of extremely easy challenges.

The target need not be a vampire, and normal generation limitations to how much *Fortitude* one may have don't apply. The target doesn't need to be willing to accept the benefit to receive it. For obvious reasons, you may never bestow more levels of *Fortitude* on anyone than you possess.

Ascendant Fortitude

Adamantine

Adamantine functions exactly like *Personal Armor*, except you no longer receive any damage from the weapons that shatter on your skin.

Methuselah Fortitude

Juggernaut

A vampire who attains this level of mastery is literally unstoppable, and it seems impossible to hurt him at all. It is incredible and frightening to see him in action; those few who have demonstrated this level of resistance to damage are like walking fortresses who can literally take on dozens of lesser vampires without any apparent effort. If a vampire with this power wants to go somewhere, he simply walks there — anyone on his way gets pushed out of the way or walked over. All attempts to restrain the vampire or to block his way fail automatically unless the character attempting to stop the vampire has as much *Potence* as the vampire has *Fortitude*, in which case the person attempting to stop the vampire must make a normal Physical Challenge. On a win, the vampire is forced to stop, the irresistible force having met the object that cannot be moved.

The vampire cannot walk through walls (not without suitable levels of *Potence*, anyway, although the Elder level of *Potence* is probably enough to

allow the vampire to automatically walk through most walls) or cause damage to people simply by walking at them, but no vampire or other being can stand in his way. It is up to the Storyteller to determine if characters who, for example, get crushed between the vampire and a wall suffer injury.

If two characters with *Juggernaut* meet each other, neither can move the other just by walking at him; the powers negate each other.

Whenever something inflicts damage on the vampire, the player makes a Simple Test. If the damage is aggravated, he completely ignores it on a win, and converts it to lethal on a tie. In case of lethal damage, he completely ignores the injury on a win or a tie. (Damage cannot be first tested down from aggravated to lethal, and then from lethal to bashing.) He may always use Intermediate *Fortitude* to reduce the severity of any damage that makes it through his defenses. *All* bashing damage to the vampire is completely ignored; he is simply far too resilient to care about it.

MELPOMINEE

ELDER MELPOMINEE

SHATTERING CRESCENDO

Some rare mortal singers can shatter wineglasses with their voices by finding the precise pitch at which the glass resonates. Exceptionally talented Daughters of Cacophony can go far beyond that. They are able to pitch their voices precisely enough to find the resonant frequency of virtually any object — including the bodies of humans or Kindred. Only one victim at a time can be affected by this power; everyone else in the area will hear a harmless, if unsettling, high-pitched shriek.

The subject must be within hearing range though he must not necessarily be able to hear — this power will work equally well on a deaf victim. Spend a Blood Trait and make a Mental Challenge against the victim. If you are successful, the victim suffers two health levels of aggravated damage. If you use the power against an inanimate object, it is up to the Storyteller to determine how well you succeed (and determine the number of opposing Traits for the Static Mental Challenge). Most objects (windows, normal doors, coffee machines, televisions) are easy enough to shatter with this power.

MASTER MELPOMINEE

PERSISTENT ECHO

With this power you can speak or sing to the air and leave your words there for a later listener. This may either be the next person to stand where you left your words, or a specific person you are already acquainted with. *Persistent Echo* may also be used to "suspend" other *Melpominee* powers for future listeners: a fact that makes some Kindred nervous as it is difficult to detect the usage of *Persistent Echo*.

To use this power, make a Static Social Challenge and spend a Blood Trait. You may now speak (or sing) the equivalent of one sentence; if you wish to speak longer, you must spend a Social Trait for every additional sentence. If you wish to delay another *Melpominee* power, you must spend a Willpower Trait before making the Social Challenge. The echo will stay suspended for a maximum number of nights equal to your permanent Social Traits.

You may either leave the echo audible for anyone who stands where you stood when using the power, essentially creating a repeating loop of mystical sound, or you may choose for the echo to fade after it has been heard once. If you desire, the echo may remain dormant until a specific person with whom you are familiar enters the area. If the echo can only be heard once, all traces of this power will disappear from the area once its purpose has been fulfilled.

A character who enhances her hearing with *Heightened Senses* in an area where an unactivated *Persistent Echo* was placed hears a faint murmur. If she has the *Occult* Ability, she may attempt a Static Mental Challenge against your Mental Traits; if successful, she can hear the message. If she fails, she is deafened for the rest of the night by a sudden roar of mystic static.

OBEAH

ELDER OBEAH

RENEWED VIGOR

You may now heal even the most grievous injuries with a mere touch and a moment's concentration. If life still clings to the subject — no matter how feebly — you can bring him back from death's doorstep.

To use this power, spend a Willpower Trait and touch your subject. You must remain in physical contact for a full turn, after which *all* missing health levels are restored, regardless of whether the damage is bashing, lethal or aggravated. If contact isn't maintained for the entire turn, the Willpower Trait is wasted and nothing is accomplished. You may use this power to heal yourself, even if you are Incapacitated (but not if you are in torpor, unless you have another power that allows the use of Disciplines while in torpor).

MASTER OBEAH

SAFE PASSAGE

With this power, you may pass through a group without any fear of harm. Unlike *Obfuscate*, this power doesn't make you invisible; instead, it makes you appear neutral, harmless and pleasant, and makes people respectful and helpful toward you without stopping to consider why. Anyone affected by this power will take a very dim view of those who might pursue or attempt to harm you.

You may choose to turn off this power, but otherwise it is always considered to be in effect. Those attempting to pursue you must bid an extra Trait and make a Mental Challenge against you. If you win, your pursuer loses interest and wanders off to do something else. ("What am I doing out here when I could be home watching TV? Oooh, look, a shiny thing!") If the pursuer wins, she may continue her pursuit unaffected for the remainder of the scene.

If you actively seek shelter or assistance ("Excuse me, sir, but could you tell me where I could find a place to sleep?"), you must make a Social Challenge against the subject. You gain three extra Traits for this challenge. With success the subject does his best to help you out. This only applies to seemingly harmless or innocent assistance, such as finding shelter, getting directions, or asking for advice — you cannot use this to search for guns or contraband.

The effects of this power last until the next sunrise. It affects everyone in your general area; however, it is ineffective against those who know you well. It is still quite useful against casual acquaintances and strangers, though.

ASCENDANT OBEAH

PURIFICATION

With this power, you can successfully cleanse a person, item or a location of demonic or malign spiritual presences. However, the price may be high indeed as you are pitting your very soul against the corruption you are trying to purge.

This power may only be developed or used if you have a Humanity or Path rating of 4 or higher. If the subject is willing and there is no resistance from the corrupting agent — a rare occurrence indeed — you need merely spend a Willpower Trait to purge the subject of the taint.

Most demons and their kind tend to resist such attempts, however, and thus you must engage the demon in taxing spiritual combat. You must engage in Mental Challenges against the possessing entity. The first one to acquire three more net victories than the other wins the battle. If you fail, then the *Purification* also fails. Should you lose three challenges in a row, the demon takes over your body. You may never use *Purification* on yourself, and it has no effect on the Beast or an alternate personality.

Should you win the battle, you pull the corrupting entity from the subject's body and immediately spend another Willpower Trait. You then thrust the entity into a nearby item, animal or person, trapping the demon in the selected vessel. This must be accomplished within two turns of removing the demon from the subject, and the target must be within physical reach. Otherwise the demon will go free, and is likely to locate itself a suitable vessel — such as the original subject or the person who made it so miserable.

METHUSELAH OBEAH

UNBIND THE FLESH-CLAD SOUL

Few understand the complexities of the soul as well as the Salubri do, yet most Kindred would be amazed to learn just how far this understanding goes. Some powerful Salubri elders may share that understanding with others in a rather permanent way — they may remove a willing subject's soul permanently from his body, allowing him to roam the astral plane and explore the world without the constraints of physical existence. There are those — chiefly Tremere — who warn that the Salubri may misrepresent themselves and trick others into volunteering for "release" from the concerns of flesh, while in actuality they are only using this power to trap souls in another plane of existence. Obviously, the Salubri deny this charge and tend to be rather offended by such implications.

You and your willing subject both enter a deep meditative trance for the minimum duration of an hour while you perform the ritual necessary to separate soul from flesh without damaging either. During this period you must spend twice as many Blood Traits as your subject has permanent Willpower Traits. At the end of the ritual, the subject's body slips into a coma and dies by the end of the night.

The subject's soul is removed from his body and enters the astral plane. This separation is permanent and irreversible. The game mechanics are the same as those of the *Auspex* power of *Psychic Projection*, but the subject no longer has a silver cord. If she is reduced to zero Willpower, she loses a Trait of permanent Willpower and re-forms a year and a day later at the place where her soul was separated from her body. A character reduced to zero permanent Willpower on the astral plane is destroyed forever.

This power may only be used upon mortals (except mages) and vampires who are in Golconda. The subject must have a full understanding of what the ritual entails — including its permanence and the impossibility of reversal. The body of a vampire who is unbound decays at sunrise. It is possible to drink the blood remaining in the vampire's body, but diablerie cannot be performed. Any attempt to Embrace the body of an unbound mortal automatically fails.

You may use this power on yourself, provided that you have reached Golconda.

OBFUSCATE

ELDER OBFUSCATE

CONCEAL

You may now mask inanimate objects as large as entire houses. The entire object and its contents are hidden, although as with other *Obfuscate* powers, photographs will still reveal what is hidden. While *Conceal* is in effect, passersby will walk around the object as if it were still visible, but refuse to acknowledge that they are making any kind of detour.

You must be within 30 feet of the object to be concealed, and the item must hold some personal significance. For example, you may conceal your own car or house, or even your lover's house, but not an unknown person's van. The *Conceal* power functions as *Unseen Presence* for purposes of detection.

Conceal can be used to mask a speeding car. Other drivers will subconsciously tend to steer away from the car; indeed, under the right conditions, a car hidden by *Conceal* may even clear traffic faster than an ordinary car. Should you speed, police radar still registers the speeding car, but the police officer holding the radar gun will likely believe the signal to be a glitch.

MIND BLANK

With this power, your mind is hidden the way other *Obfuscate* powers hide your body, and you may shrug off most invasive probes into your mind.

Whenever someone attempts to read or probe your mind, she must first make a Mental Challenge. Unless she wins the challenge, she cannot read your mind at all. Even if she succeeds, she must still make whatever challenge the probe requires and bid an additional Mental Trait for that challenge.

SOUL MASK

With *Soul Mask* you are now able to conceal your aura. You may display any combination of colors and shades you wish, or even make it appear as if you have no aura whatsoever. Obviously, this power is extremely useful (and dangerous) as it allows one to lie through her teeth and have her aura appear

as if she was telling the truth — or commit diablerie all week long and look squeaky clean come Sunday.

Soul Mask allows you to choose one specific kind of aura (or lack thereof) and project it at will. If you have no experience with the use of *Aura Perception*, you cannot choose an alternate aura (after all, how can you alter something if you have no idea what it should look like?). You may still choose to project no aura at all. If you wish to have multiple auras and switch between them at will, you must purchase *Soul Mask* multiple times. The fake aura is considered to be always active, and you must "switch it off" to let your real aura show through. If you purchased *Soul Mask* several times, the first aura you created is the one displayed by default.

MASTER OBFUSCATE

CACHE

While other uses of *Obfuscate* require that the user is very close to the object or person being *Obfuscated*, with *Cache* you can hide items or people so that the *Obfuscate* remains in effect even after you leave the area.

The item must be within the normal range of the *Obfuscate* power when you activate it. After that, you must spend a Willpower Trait, which activates *Cache* on top of the previously activated *Obfuscate* effect. The concealment will remain in effect as long as you stay within a distance of your permanent Mental Traits in miles. The effect will end at the next sunrise, or when the *Obfuscated* subject chooses to reveal herself, whichever comes first.

ASCENDANT OBFUSCATE

OLD FRIEND

The Nosferatu are considered by many to be able to find out just about anything, and it is certainly true that there are few who can equal them when it comes to sticking one's malformed nose where it doesn't belong. This particular power is popular among certain Nosferatu elders, who have successfully used it to squeeze secrets out of unsuspecting Kindred. *Old Friend* allows the user to probe the suspect's subconscious and take on the semblance of the individual the subject trusts more than anyone. The person being impersonated doesn't even have to be alive; the subject remembers the encounter as a dream or a ghostly visitation.

Spend a Willpower Trait and makes a Mental Challenge against the subject. On a success, the subject believes you to be an old friend, a relative or someone else he trusts. You receive three extra Traits to all *Subterfuge* tests while this power is in effect. Note that *Old Friend* only affects a single subject at a time, and onlookers will see your true features, unless you also use a *Mask of a Thousand Faces*.

This is a power that requires roleplaying from both parties, and should not be reduced to a string of *Subterfuge* tests.

METHUSELAH OBFUSCATE

CREATE NAME

While pretending to be someone else can be accomplished with lower levels of *Obfuscate*, such crude deceptions are nothing compared to *Create*

Name's effects. With *Create Name*, you may create a completely new identity. This includes appearance, speech patterns, aura and even thought processes. It is virtually impossible to see through the disguise. *Create Name* may be used to impersonate an existing person, or it may be used to create a new, fictional identity with perfect accuracy.

You must spend three hours in relative peace and silence to establish a new persona. After that, spend a permanent Willpower Trait and make a Static Mental Challenge against the Storyteller. The difficulty of this task is entirely up to the Storyteller (typical difficulties are at least 10 Traits and more for complicated personalities). The Storyteller has final word in all matters regarding this power.

Once the process is complete, you may "step in" to this new identity whenever you desire without any kind of a test. Any outside observer who doesn't have Methuselah-level *Auspex* or the equivalent sees the artificial identity and has no way of seeing through it. Your aura, Nature, Demeanor, even thoughts and Psychological Merits and Flaws, appear completely genuine, even though they have been crafted. You may have as many self-created identities as you desire, but only one of them may be "active" at any given time. To make another identity active (and the previous identity passive), you must spend a Willpower Trait and concentrate for a minute.

Besides Methuselah-level *Auspex* (Mental Challenge required), the only way to spot the personality as a fake is to notice discrepancies between the manufactured identity and the skills and abilities it should possess — for example, a character with no knowledge of *Medicine* isn't going to make a very convincing neurosurgeon if the details of his job come up. A character with enough suspicions about the identity may make a Static Social Challenge against the Storyteller to identify the fraud.

Potence

It is well-known that vampires who are learned in *Potence* are capable of clearly superhuman feats of strength, but that is nothing compared to the incredible physical prowess of those elders who have reached superior levels of the Discipline.

Elder Potence

Imprint

Some subtle applications of *Potence* exist; *Imprint* isn't one of them. While anyone with *Potence* can exert tremendous pressure on objects, a vampire with *Imprint* can literally crush steel with her bare hands. *Imprint* makes for excellent intimidation. Alternatively, it can be used to create handholds when climbing, and it goes without saying that if applied to someone's throat, the results are extremely nasty.

Spending a Blood Trait activates the power for the entire scene. You can now crush very tough objects with your hands or leave an imprint of your hands in them — for example, you will have no trouble pushing your hand into a wall or squeezing a steel pipe out of shape. If there is confusion as to whether or not the vampire can crush a certain object, the Storyteller always has final say in the matter.

If used against another vampire, the attack inflicts one additional health level of damage. Said damage is considered to be lethal.

MASTER POTENCE

EARTHSHOCK

Earthshock proves that there is more to *Potence* than just hitting something until it stops moving. With *Earthshock*, you may redirect your strength — you strike (or stomp, depending on personal preference) the ground, and the force of the blow explodes up from the ground some distance away, directly below your opponent.

To use this power, spend a Blood Trait and make a Physical Challenge against your opponent. If successful, the ground directly underneath the target explodes in a geyser of stone, rock and dirt (or, if indoors, wood, concrete and plumbing), inflicting three levels of lethal damage as sharp shards of debris rip into the target.

If used against a car, the car will be disabled unless it is specifically armored. The power may be used indoors, but the results are far more spectacular — not only will there be a gaping hole on the floor, but the resulting shower of floor materials will break nearby windows and cause other damage to the surroundings. If there is another floor or a basement below the target, she must make a Static Physical Challenge against six Traits to remain on the same floor or fall through the resulting hole. This may also happen outdoors if someone happens to be standing on directly on top of a sewer pipe, on a bridge, and so forth. A good rule of thumb is that if there is less than a foot and a half of concrete, earth or whatever, it means that there will be a large hole if *Earthshock* is used there.

The attack has a range of 10 feet per level of *Potence*, meaning that you will always have a basic range of 60 feet, if not more, as long as your target is in line of sight.

ASCENDANT POTENCE

FLICK

Subtle in use if not in effect, *Flick* is a frightening power. With *Flick* you can use the slightest of gestures to deliver truly devastating attacks. You know how to apply your full strength in the tiniest movements. You can simply snap your fingers and watch your opponent smash through the window or shrug calmly and break the bones of the unsuspecting vampire standing behind you.

You must spend one Blood Trait every time you use this power. If the target is aware of the attack, you must succeed in a normal Physical Challenge against her. However, since it is extremely hard to dodge something that you don't see coming, the target must bid three extra Traits for the challenge. If the target is unaware of the attack and there is physical contact, (for example, if you shake his hand or touch him on the shoulder in a normal social situation) no challenge need be made.

You may hit anything you can see with this power, and don't need to actually touch anyone or anything (but you must always make some kind of a gesture in the direction of the intended target). Indeed, few may realize that you're responsible for laying such waste to everything in the vicinity if you're simply standing around and making small gestures. With a win on a Static

Mental Challenge (difficulty 10 Traits, 15 if the area is dark and the character attempting the detection has no way of seeing in the dark), someone will notice the timing of your motions to the destruction.

Flick does whatever damage you would normally do in hand-to-hand combat, including all bonuses. You may also use other levels of *Potence*, such as *Earthshock*, in conjunction with *Flick*.

Methuselah Potence

Destruction

This is where pure, raw strength begins. A vampire who has reached this level of mastery can literally destroy entire buildings with her strength alone; nothing can stand in her way.

You spend three Blood Traits; for the remainder of the scene, your strength is simply monumental. If you strike something, you inflict three additional levels of lethal damage; your punches are powerful enough to pulverize bones. Where others use baseball bats or swords, you use telephone poles, pieces of concrete ripped off the walls, or even cars. Such weapons give you an additional six Traits to bid in challenges, and cause an additional two levels of lethal damage (though the Storyteller is free to modify the specifics of such weapons).

Other feats of strength are also possible, ranging from punching holes through ships' hulls to ripping cars in half and lifting entire busloads of people in the air. The Storyteller should feel free to call for Static Physical Challenges where appropriate.

Should you strike a mortal or a ghoul, they will die immediately if the strike connects — no human (or even relatively human) body can withstand such punishment. You may, of course, attempt to pull the punch.

Presence

Elder Presence

Love

The blood bond is certainly one of the most effective and traditional ways to gain control of another Kindred. However, in these enlightened days, childer are often aware of the bond and know how to avoid it, and while they can be forced into service, it's often preferable to handle the situation in a more subtle manner. *Love* is one way of accomplishing that — simply put, it has most of the benefits of the blood bond without the less-than-pleasant side effects. It's not quite as sure or lasting a method of control as the bond, but in most cases, it's efficient enough.

The subject must be in the same area and be in some sort of active social contact with you — a conversation, an exchanged look, a greeting, anything will do. Make a Social Challenge against your target. On a success, your target becomes attached to you as if he was blood bound to you for the remainder of the scene — the rules from **Laws of the Night** p. 211 apply. The same subject may be the target of this power as many times during the night as you desire; however, if any tests beyond the first one fail, the subject becomes immune to all *Presence* powers from you for the remainder of the night.

Paralyzing Glance

Elders who have reached this level of mastery may not be able to kill with a glance, but they're certainly close. This power is essentially a more developed version of *Dread Gaze*. A vampire using this on another vampire can freeze the target with mind-numbing terror.

You must make eye contact with the intended subject, then make a Social Challenge against the target; if successful, your target is reduced to a gibbering, panic-stricken wreck. The effects last for as long as you remain in the same room with your target, or until sunrise. If you leave the room or clearly abandon your target's presence (by walking to the other end of the large ballroom, for example), the subject remains paralyzed for the remainder of the scene, after which he slowly regains his senses.

If the subject's life is directly threatened (by physical assault, impending sunrise, a rampaging horde of Sabbat), he may attempt to snap out of it by making a Static Mental Challenge. If he succeeds, the paralysis ends and he may act. Should he fail, he enters a continuous state of Rötschreck for the rest of the night (which may be calmed by the usual means).

Spark of Rage

This power allows you to shorten tempers and generally raise the irritation level in the area. *Spark of Rage* causes disagreements and fights, and may well send suitably enraged vampires into frenzy.

Spend a Willpower Trait to activate this power for the remainder of the scene. All within 10 feet of you feel its effects and become increasingly hostile to others in the area. Those affected continue to be irritated and hostile even when they leave your sphere of influence, but their irritation is no longer artificially enhanced and they can calm down if they're willing and encouraged to do so. Vampires who become suitably enraged often whip themselves into frenzy. The irritation tends to be directed at others beside yourself, but if you provoke the subjects, or if there are no others present, you're the closest target for venting any ire.

Anyone influenced by this power may spend a Willpower Trait to calm down for one turn and refrain from frenzying. Those with the *Calm Hearted* Merit can spend a Willpower Trait and resist the power's effects for the next minute.

This effect should be mostly roleplayed out; applying rules to determine the degree of irritation is clumsy and inaccurate at best; each player knows when his character has reached such a degree of irritation that he snaps.

Master Presence

Cooperation

While the Camarilla is based on cooperation, it is often painfully obvious that some of its members are anything but cooperative. Old rivalries, secret ambitions and endless intrigue don't exactly breed trust and willingness to play nice with each other. An elder who has developed this power can change that in a heartbeat. It's not a perfect solution, but it does cause those it affects to try and work together. Some Ventrue maintain the opinion that the existence of this power is the only reason the Camarilla is still holding together. On the

other hand, those who voice this opinion *too* loudly tend to find themselves in situations extremely well suited to testing this theory.

The player spends a point of Willpower, which activates this power for the duration of the scene. All those in the same area with the vampire is affected by the power, and as long as it remains in effect, they are more favorably disposed toward one another and are more willing to extend trust or make cooperative plans.

These effects should always be roleplayed out; again, this is something that rules really can't govern very well. Still, there are some specific effects: All who may frenzy while this power is in effect have to make a simple test; if it is successful, the frenzy is avoided; if it fails, the vampire will have to deal with the situation as per normal rules.

ƒATHER KNOWS BEST

There is a phase in everyone's development from baby to adult where a person or persons — usually one or both of the parents — is everything to a child; a figure who knows everything and can protect the child from anything. This illusion shatters as the child grows up; in the end, we all discover that the people who once seemed so wise and capable and faultless are just human beings. However, a vampire with *Father Knows Best* can make himself seem like such a being to others and can command almost blind devotion and trust.

It costs one Blood Trait to activate *Father Knows Best*, and it will stay in effect for the entire scene unless you willfully turn it off. As long as the power is active, everyone in the same area with you admires, respects and loves you, and considers you to be a significant authority figure. Note that this doesn't mean that everyone instantly obeys you — after all, children disobey all the time. However, no one under the influence of *Father Knows Best* will ever attempt to harm you in any way and will attempt to cooperate with you. It may take a bit of coaxing, but you can talk others into doing just about anything within reason. ("Stick your head in the furnace, it won't hurt" won't work, but the equivalent of "You must tell me if you've been naughty" will.) Note that this won't regress the subjects' minds to a childlike state and treating them like children is likely to annoy the subjects.

There is a flip side to this, though. If you obviously betray another's trust or otherwise demonstrate that you are not the trustworthy figure you purported yourself to be, your children immediately resent you and refuse to cooperate. You cannot re-establish this influence for the remainder of the session without using *Forgetful Mind* to erase the incident from each person's memory. Another downside is that you may find yourself becoming an exceedingly important figure to the subjects of this power, going so far as to make it impossible for you to get away from them without them wanting to follow you around. They want to remain in your comforting presence because it feels like a safe place. Note that while the power's effects only apply as long as your subjects remain in the same area with you, they still remember the effects, and most subjects will think of them as pleasant. This may lead to some characters — especially ones who have become accustomed to your presence — becoming extremely concerned and frantic if they cannot locate you or fear that something has happened to you.

Father Knows Best is a long-term power, and you'll benefit most from it if you play your cards right, make sure your "children" are taken care of and don't abuse them. You can gain extremely loyal and devoted followers simply by spending time around them without even promising them anything. Best of all, these children will never grow out of the phase.

Ascendant Presence

Ironclad Command

Most vampires can usually resist the effects of *Presence* for brief times through an effort of will. However, some elders have developed such a force of personality that their powers of *Presence* cannot be resisted without truly heroic efforts.

This power is always in effect once it is learned. A mortal may not spend Willpower Traits to resist your *Presence* (for game purposes, "mortal" refers to ordinary human beings, not ghouls, humans who possess True Faith, hedge magicians, or other "special" folks). A supernatural being who can ordinarily resist certain *Presence* powers for one round by spending a Willpower Trait must now spend *two* Willpower Traits and make a Simple Test; on a win, they can resist the effects; on a tie or a failure, they fail to resist.

Methuselah Presence

Pulse of the City

On reaching this level of mastery, you are now capable of influencing the emotional climate of the entire region around you, up to the size of a small city. This power is always in effect; simply put, the local population reflects your emotional states. You may also project specific emotions into the minds of the residents of the area. Those who live in the area are affected much more strongly than visitors; likewise, citizens who are visiting elsewhere are still affected by the power, as are those who have very strong ties to the city.

Your emotional state is always mirrored on the local population. However, if you wish to specifically influence the local population, you decide on the emotion you wish to project and spend a Willpower Trait. You then make a Static Social Challenge. If successful, you can change the emotional climate of the city for one minute. If you wish to affect it for a longer time, you must spend additional Social Traits before making the challenge.

Vampires and other supernatural creatures are considered to be affected at one level lower — for example, while the human population will be extremely depressed for a day, the local vampires only feel like staring at a wall and thinking of sad things for an hour.

The Storyteller decides the number of opposing Traits; anywhere from 10 to 15 Traits are appropriate, depending on the size of the city. Should two Methuselahs with this power attempt to affect this area, they make the Social Challenge against each other. The Methuselah who arrived first, provided that she has spent at least six months in the area, will receive five bonus Traits to use in the challenge, as the locals have become used to her control. Such a battle for the control of the city's emotional climate will cause the local humans to become extremely frustrated, and if the situation persists, it may

even lead to riots, mass strikes or other similar outbreaks, depending on the emotions that are being broadcast by the two combatants.

This power may be used even if you are in torpor.

Trait Expenditure	Duration
One Trait	10 minutes
Two Traits	One hour
Four Traits	One day
Six Traits	One week

PROTEAN

ELDER PROTEAN

EARTH CONTROL

A character who has *Earth Melded* is normally unable to move. However, if you have mastered *Earth Control*, you can move within the earth as if you are swimming through water. This power has obvious uses both for unobtrusive travel and for nasty tricks in combat.

This power is always automatically in effect while you are *Earth Melded*. You cannot see underground, but you do gain a supernatural sense of your underground surroundings, with a range of up to 50 yards. Water, rock, cement, tree roots and other obstacles all effectively block your progress; you may only move through earth and other substances of similar consistency, such as sand or gravel. Should two or more vampires attempt to interact underground, only direct physical contact is possible. If an underground battle ensues, all participants must bid an extra Physical Trait. If an underground chase takes place, the character with higher Physical Traits wins; however, if the participants have *Celerity*, the character with the highest *Celerity* wins. (If they tie on *Celerity*, revert back to the Physical Traits; if even those tie, the Storyteller may choose to simply go to Physical Challenges.)

With this power you may surprise an unwary target, as you can rise up from the ground silently behind the target. A target who is expecting such an attack must make a Mental Challenge against you; if he wins, he is not taken by surprise.

FLESH OF MARBLE

The Gangrel have a well-deserved reputation as formidable warriors, and this power has certainly contributed to that. With *Flesh of Marble*, your skin becomes what can best be described as flexible stone. It retains its softness, muscle tone and other qualities, and appears to be, for all intents and purposes, normal skin — yet swords shatter against it and bullets ricochet off or flatten themselves against it.

Spend two Blood Traits to instantly activate *Flesh of Marble*. The effects of the power last for the remainder of the scene. While the power is active, all incoming damage is halved (round up). This applies to all physical attacks with fists, claws, swords, firearms or explosions, but not to fire, sunlight or magic. (That said, if the magical effect in question causes a physical attack, such as a

rock hurled at the character with *Movement of the Mind, Flesh of Marble* is applied normally.)

In addition to that, one health level is subtracted from all damage coming in from bashing attacks (before the damage is halved as per normal). All swords or other similar melee weapons that are used against you risk shattering unless they are exceptionally well–manufactured (Storyteller's call). The attacker must make a simple test; if he loses, the weapon shatters.

MASTER PROTEAN

RESTORE THE MORTAL VISAGE

This power allows you to restore your appearance to what it was before you were Embraced, effectively removing all of the bestial features that you have accumulated over the centuries. Perhaps not surprisingly, this power tends to divide the Gangrel into two camps. In the first camp, there are those who take an active part in politics or deal with mortals on a regular basis, and consider this power both necessary and acceptable, for obvious reasons. In the second camp are the more feral Gangrel who shun human society and have accepted the monster in them as a part of their unlives. They view this power as a disgusting defiance of the very nature of vampirism. *Restore the Mortal Visage* has only been displayed by Gangrel. Whispered rumors speak of Nosferatu elders who have studied this power and their quick, yet horrible Final Deaths when they attempted to take their mortal forms. Caine's curse is not so easily cheated.

Spend two Blood Traits and a Willpower Trait, and then make a Static Mental Challenge. If successful, all animal characteristics you have disappear completely for the duration of the scene. All Negative Social Traits caused by them also vanish for as long as the power is in effect.

SHAPE OF THE BEAST'S WRATH

This power bears some resemblance to the Tzimisce's feared *Horrid Form*, and there are indeed certain visual similarities between the two. That's where the similarities end, though, and it is a foolish vampire indeed who speaks of a connection between the two while there are any Gangrel present. With this power, you shift into a huge, monstrous form, increasing your height by half and tripling your weight. Your form changes to resemble a strange amalgamation of your own form and that of the animal you feel the closest kinship to. Wolves, rats and great cats are among the most common manifestations, but ravens, serpents, bats and even stranger beasts have been seen.

Spending two Blood Traits triggers the change. The change takes three turns, but you may quicken the process by spending Blood Traits at a cost of one Blood Trait per turn — thus, if you spend five Blood Traits, you'll transform instantly. Once transformed, you remain in this form until you choose to revert back to your normal form, or until sunrise, whichever occurs first.

You must decide which animal's characteristics you will take upon first learning this power. The form adds five Physical Traits to your statistics. You may distribute them freely, but they should reflect huge size and strength. These must also be decided upon buying the power, and cannot be changed. You may purchase this power repeatedly, which will grant you other forms.

While transformed, you inflict an additional level of aggravated damage with your fangs and claws. You also gain the equivalent of the *Auspex* power of *Heightened Senses*, with all of its advantages and drawbacks, and an additional Bruised health level.

However, there are two major drawbacks with this power. First, while using *Shape of the Beast's Wrath*, you are essentially socially crippled. Your Social Traits are decreased by five (said traits are determined upon buying the power); however, they cannot drop below one — you always have at least one Social Trait. The second problem is that you have an extremely hard time resisting the Beast and must bid two additional Traits when attempting to resist frenzy. Willpower Traits may not be used in this challenge.

SPECTRAL BODY

A powerful variation of the Advanced *Protean* power *Mist Form*, *Spectral Body* allows you to retain your physical appearance, even though you become completely insubstantial. You may walk through walls with ease and bullets, swords and fists pass through you without harm. You may even pass through the very floor you are standing on if you so wish. Although your vocal chords are no longer solid, you may still speak without hindrance.

Spend two Blood Traits. The transformation takes one turn and lasts for the rest of the night unless you decide to return to your normal form. When the power is active, you become completely insubstantial, but remain fully visible. You are unaffected by any physical attacks, and all incoming damage from fire or sunlight is treated as lethal damage. Gravity only matters to you if you so desire; you may sink through the floor or float up in the air, although you may move no faster than your normal walking speed while "flying" in this manner. While in this form, you may use any Disciplines that can be used without physical contact or a physical body. On the downside, you are completely unable to manipulate your physical environment while in this form, unless you happen to possess the *Thaumaturgy* path of *Movement of the Mind*.

ASCENDANT PROTEAN

PURIFY THE IMPALED BREAST

According to Camarilla records, very few Gangrel elders were killed during the Anarch Revolts. Many who are considered to be in the know hold the opinion that this power is the primary reason for that. With this power, you may expel foreign matter from your body with great force — even stakes through your heart may be removed in this fashion.

Spend two Blood Traits, or three if you've been incapacitated by a stake through your heart. All foreign objects—bullets, splinters, dirt, even stakes, are immediately expelled with great force. Those who are in the "line of fire" must make a Physical Challenge for every object that is expelled from your body. The challenge is made against a number of Traits equal to your *Protean* rating; if the subject loses the challenge, she is hit by the object. Each object that hits inflicts a single bashing health level of damage on those who fail the test, even if the damage comes from bullets or knives.

If you wish to leave some objects (such as prosthetic limbs) in your body, you must spend a Willpower Trait while expelling other objects. The same

applies if you want to leave an object partially embedded (for example, to leave a stake sticking out of your breastbone to fool your opponents).

Obviously, this power may be used even if you have been staked.

METHUSELAH PROTEAN

INWARD FOCUS

Unlike other *Protean* powers, this power's use is completely undetectable: It leaves no telltale visual marks that someone could notice. Indeed, its existence is only known by the handful of Gangrel Methuselahs who have managed to harness its powers. This power subtly changes the Methuselah's body into a supremely efficient construct, enhancing speed, durability and strength to truly impressive levels, even by the standards of the Kindred.

Activating this power requires three Blood Traits, and you must spend an additional Blood Trait every turn past the first to maintain it. The effects of this power are threefold.

First, you gain an extra action every turn as long as this power remains active, and you may receive another up to one additional action by spending yet another Blood Trait. (You may not spend 10 Blood Traits to gain 10 extra actions.)

Secondly, all incoming lethal and aggravated damage is halved, round up. If there is only a single health level of incoming lethal or aggravated damage (before it is halved, that is), you may make a simple test. If successful, you may ignore the damage. You automatically ignore the first two health levels of any attack that inflicts bashing damage.

Finally, your attacks inflict an additional health level of damage, whatever the damage type.

This power may be used in conjunction with all other *Protean* powers, and with *Celerity*, *Fortitude* and *Potence*. For obvious reasons, a Methuselah with this power is a terrifying opponent.

THANATOSIS

ELDER THANATOSIS

CREEPING INFECTION

Putrefaction, *Withering* and *Necrosis* are fast-working powers, and their effects can be instantly seen on the subject. *Creeping Infection* is far more insidious. You can delay the negative effects until you are well out of harm's way. Mercenary Stiffs are suspected to apply this power with a handshake upon closing the deal. Should their "partner" suddenly become less than cooperative, they have an ace up their sleeve. Then again, considering the pervasive sense of fairness and goodwill among vampires in general, perhaps that's just common sense.

You use *Putrefaction*, *Withering* or *Necrosis* as per usual, but may delay the actual effects for a number of months equal to your Physical Traits divided by three (round up). You may at any time spend a Blood Trait to activate the dormant power. If the time limit is reached without the power being used, it simply fades away with no effect.

Master Thanatosis

Dust to Dust

You gain additional benefits from your ash form of *Ashes to Ashes*. You maintain cohesion and consciousness and may even move about, albeit in a somewhat limited fashion. While the tactical advantages of being a pile of dust on the floor may not be readily apparent, clever elders have still found applications for this.

While a pile of ash, you retain full consciousness and may use any Disciplines that being a pile of dust would permit — for example, since a pile of dust has no eyes, using *Dominate* is out of the question. However, ridiculous as the thought may be, Disciplines like *Majesty* can be used, resulting in what surely must be the most impressive pile of dirt in the world — no maid would even dream of coming anywhere near it with a vacuum cleaner. You cannot be blown apart by winds, nor can you be easily separated — doing so requires a Physical Challenge, and each level of *Fortitude* or *Potence* you have counts as two extra Traits for this purpose alone. You may move around at a speed no higher than an ordinary wind could move a pile of dust around. However, you may move against the wind if you so desire. You may also "flatten" yourself, spreading your ashes so thinly that you can slip under doors or through cracks on the walls.

This power functions like *Ashes to Ashes* in all other respects.

Ascendant Thanatosis

Putrescent Servitude

While the Samedi aren't the only Kindred who have dabbled in the creation of zombies, they can claim their share of wholesome necromantic fun. Not only does this power allow them to raise the bodies of the recently dead, it can also be used to enslave mortals who are still alive. Animated corpses look the way they did when raised — pale and decaying. Mortals controlled with this power appear much the same, but they remain more intact than their already dead counterparts. Zombies created with this power are in many ways real classics — they are slow, unintelligent and can't speak. They are, however, extremely strong and resilient.

If you want to raise the dead, you must feed your blood to a recently deceased corpse (maximum time since death equals your Physical Traits divided by three, round up, in weeks). Spending two Blood Traits animates the corpse. The zombie has the same Physical Traits as it did in life. A reanimated corpse has three Mental Traits and a single Social Trait. It is capable of limited reasoning, but free thought is beyond its capacity. It cannot understand anyone but its master or an individual its master has commanded it to obey. Reanimated corpses posses both Basic levels of *Fortitude* and three extra Bruised health levels. They suffer no penalties from their wounds until their last health level, at which point they collapse in a messy heap of rotting meat and bone and cannot be reanimated again.

A reanimated corpse also "dies" at the third sunrise after its creation. This life span can be extended by feeding it more blood when it is created — one Blood Trait per extra night.

Mortals may also be affected by this power. You create a ghoul in the normal fashion by feeding the subject a Blood Trait. You then make two Mental Challenges against the subject (the *Medical* Ability can be used to retest these); if both are successful, the mortal loses all of his free will and becomes your slave. The mortal may try to break free once per night by spending a Willpower Trait and making a Mental Challenge against you; however, due to his subjugated state, he must bid three extra Traits for this challenge. If he succeeds, he regains his lost Social and Mental Traits. If he becomes blood bound to you, he may never again attempt to break free of your control. Should you perish, the subject regains his free will.

A mortal thus subjugated becomes pale and corpselike. He loses three Mental and Social Traits each, up to a minimum of one. He gains three extra Bruised health levels and takes no penalties from injuries he suffers until he reaches Incapacitated, after which he collapses. At this point, one more wound will kill him. He also gains the first level of *Potence*, as all ghouls do, and may learn other Disciplines if you're inclined to teach him.

A ghoul zombie who goes a month without vampiric blood loses all benefits of being a ghoul, as would normally occur. All effects of this power disappear and he regains his free will (although he may still be blood bound to you).

VISCERATIKA

All Gargoyles have a natural affinity for stone and earth, and this Discipline is an extension of that. The popular belief is that possession of *Visceratika* causes its user to start looking like a Gargoyle — complete with the hideously ugly, rocklike appearance and wings. The Tremere have recently released a report that states otherwise, but most Kindred don't feel like taking the risk of learning *Visceratika* and finding out that the Tremere were wrong — or lied. In any case, the point is rather moot as the Gargoyles don't feel inclined to teach one of their primary survival tools to outsiders.

No Gargoyle has ever demonstrated *Visceratika* beyond Advanced level. If higher levels of this power exist, it's either an extremely well-kept secret, or no one who has reached such a level of mastery has lived to spread his knowledge.

Retests of *Visceratika* use the *Survival* ability. *Visceratika* is bought the same way as all other clan Disciplines.

BASIC VISCERATIKA

SKIN OF THE CHAMELEON

When activated, your skin takes on the color and texture of the surrounding environment, allowing you to blend in with your surroundings. The illusion moves as you move, as long as you don't move any faster than a normal walking pace. Faster movement causes your body to become a blur of colors and textures. It offers no camouflage, but anyone trying to identify you may find it difficult. If this power is used when in flight, your skin blends in with the night sky almost perfectly. You'll still show up rather obviously against skyscrapers or other similar structures as a dark, winged humanoid shape.

When using *Skin of Chameleon*, you should cross your arms over your chest as if using *Obfuscate*, but place your hands on your shoulders to indicate the difference. You may also want to use a colored ribbon.

Spend a Blood Trait to activate this power. For the rest of the scene, anyone who wishes to detect you must succeed in a Mental Challenge. Unless the person attempting to detect you has *Auspex*, you gain four extra Traits to use in the challenge, or five Traits if you're in flight against the night sky.

SCRY THE HEARTHSTONE

Gargoyles were created to act as guardians of chantries and havens. This power allows you to maintain watch over an entire building without needing to scout around all the time. All you need do is touch the building, and you gain an innate sense of where things are located inside. Furthermore, you receive accurate information about the building's lay-out — where everything is, if there are secret passages, and so forth. You also learn the location, approximate size and physical condition of all living (and unliving) beings within.

Spend a Willpower Trait to activate this power. You may move around slowly, but maintaining the power requires constant active concentration, and you must keep touching the building (skin contact is required). The building may be as large as a multiplex theater, a parking garage or a castle, but there must a be a sizable quantity of stone or concrete in its construction.

There is a limit to how much detail you can discern; *Scry the Hearthstone* cannot be used to listen in on conversations or to see what people are holding in their hands. The Storyteller has final say on what kind of things you can detect.

You may attempt to detect *Obfuscated* Kindred within; such creatures register to your senses as something of a blur. You know there's *something* in that particular location, but you're not quite sure who or what. Challenges, if you can otherwise see someone *Obfuscated*, work as per the rules detailed under *Auspex* in **Laws of the Night** p. 137.

INTERMEDIATE VISCERATIKA

BOND WITH THE MOUNTAIN

Similar to the *Protean* power of *Earth Meld*, *Bond With the Mountain* allows you to meld with stone or concrete. However, unlike with *Earth Meld*, you don't disappear completely; the sharp-eyed may still spot a faint outline of your form. You cannot move within the substance you have bonded with unless you also possess *Flow Within the Mountain*, nor are you automatically aware of your surroundings (but you may use *Scry the Hearthstone* to be aware of events in the area, if you are Bonded with a man-made structure).

To activate the power, spend a Blood Trait and touch a suitable substance (rock, concrete, cement). Whatever you're touching must be large enough for your hulking form to fit in — a wall will do fine, but a head-sized rock will not. It takes two turns to complete the merge. Once merged, you are immune to sunlight and all aggravated damage applied against you automatically becomes lethal damage, while lethal damage becomes bashing damage. Normal bashing damage has no effect unless the attack inflicts at least two health levels of damage; anything less is

just the equivalent of beating on a stone wall. However, if you suffer three health levels of any kind of damage from a single attack, you are forcibly ejected from the wall and cannot act for an entire turn as you struggle to get your bearings.

Those wishing to spot a Gargoyle who has bonded must bid three extra Traits and make a Mental Challenge. Characters using *Auspex* do not need to bid the extra Traits.

Armor of Terra

Gargoyles are known as fearsome warriors who can defend themselves against staggering attacks. This power is largely the reason for that; combined with *Fortitude*, it allows you to withstand attacks that would reduce lesser Kindred to small piles of ash. With *Armor of Terra*, your skin becomes tough, truly rocklike and incredibly resistant to harm. Your pain threshold becomes far higher, and even fire may not hurt you (though you still retain your natural fear of it).

Armor of Terra is always active, and requires no expenditure for maintenance or activation. *Armor of Terra* subtracts one level of bashing damage after halving it normally; however, a minimum of one health level is still inflicted. Furthermore, you may convert incoming lethal damage into bashing damage by winning a Simple Test. If you are exposed to fire, you take half damage, but it is still aggravated. You'll need to make a test to resist Rötschreck.

Armor of Terra can be used with *Fortitude*; however, when used in such a fashion, it can only be used once per attack. For example, if you're under a fire attack that does aggravated damage, you may use *Armor of Terra* to try and halve the damage, and then use *Resilience* to try to convert the aggravated damage to lethal damage. But you cannot test that lethal damage down to bashing with *Armor of Terra* after that, as you've already used *Armor of Terra* on this attack. *Armor of Terra* must always be used before *Fortitude* comes into play.

Advanced Visceratika

Flow Within the Mountain

At this level of *Visceratika*, you are truly at home on stone constructs. *Flow Within the Mountain* allows you to move freely within solid rock. Obviously, while this means that you can easily enter any area in the domain you are guarding, it also has its uses as an offensive power; after all, if you can walk through the walls, gaining access to high-security areas isn't very hard. During these days of steel construction, the power isn't quite as useful as it once was, but most buildings can still be penetrated with *Flow Within the Mountain*.

To use the power, you must first use *Bond With the Mountain*. After that, spend a Blood Trait. This activates *Flow Within the Mountain* for the duration of the scene. During that time, you may move freely through solid rock or concrete. The mode of movement is similar to swimming, and you move about at a brisk walking pace.

You can also walk directly through stone walls without first using *Bond With the Mountain* by spending a Blood Trait, but the wall in question can be no thicker than two feet. You may attempt to walk through thicker walls by making a Physical Challenge, but you must bid an extra Physical Trait for every additional two feet. If you have *Potence*, each level of

Potence grants you two feet — Basic *Potence* gives two free feet, Intermediate *Potence* four, and Advanced *Potence* six. Should you have Superior *Potence*, you can move through any wall, regardless of its thickness (but must still perform the Physical Challenge). It should be noted that you can stop while within the wall, but cannot deviate from your course without using *Flow Within the Mountain*. Should you lose a challenge, you become stuck in the wall until you are chiseled out or use *Flow Within the Mountain* to escape.

Gargoyle Flight

Gargoyles may have wings, but just glancing at one makes it painfully obvious that they aren't actually supposed to be able to fly. A humanoid form with wings has all the aerodynamics of a rock, and Gargoyles' enormous weight doesn't improve things much — the heaviest Gargoyles have been reported to weigh over 800 pounds. Yet, like the bumblebee, they fly, thanks to their Tremere creators. When the Gargoyles were originally created, the Tremere used a complicated thaumaturgical ritual to make a variant of *Movement of the Mind* an essential part of all Gargoyles' being. Sadly, the Tremere scholar responsible for this met his end during the Gargoyle Revolt, and it seems that the secret of Gargoyle flight has been lost forever.

Only Gargoyles can learn *Flight*; it's their special ability, and it cannot ever be learned by others. All Gargoyles start out with Level 1 *Flight* in addition to other clan Disciplines, and can increase it with experience points as they would increase a normal clan Discipline. Note that under no circumstances can *Celerity* be used to increase flight speed.

It should be stressed that Gargoyles don't think of *Flight* as a Discipline; for them, it's merely something every Gargoyle can do — indeed, flight is as natural to them as walking is for a normal human. This is why different levels of *Flight* don't have specific names; the levels merely exist as a game mechanic to measure different degrees of skill.

If your character is flying, you should hold your arms out straight to the side, as if forming a cross. (Your group may want to agree on a different method of indicating flying characters, such as a sash of a certain color, as some characters may want to stay up in the air for quite a while, and holding your arms like that can become rather tiring.)

Basic Flight
Level 1
You cannot actually fly, but you can glide and soar as if you were hang-gliding. However, you cannot carry anything larger than your clothes and personal effects. Maximum speed equals 15 miles an hour.

Level 2
You can now attain flight under your own power, though a running takeoff is required. You can carry a maximum payload of 20 pounds. Maximum speed equals 30 miles an hour.

Intermediate Flight
Level 3

You can now take off from the very spot you're standing on if unencumbered. With a running takeoff, you can carry up to 50 pounds. Maximum speed equals 45 miles an hour.

Level 4

You can now vertically take off carrying up to 50 pounds of baggage. With a running takeoff, up to 100 pounds can be carried. Maximum speed equals 60 miles an hour.

ADVANCED FLIGHT

Level 5

You can vertically take off with up to 200 pounds. In practice, this means that it's enough to carry most Kindred — or prey. Maximum speed equals 75 miles an hour.

FLIGHT AND FAIR ESCAPE

Obviously, it's a bit hard to knock someone's teeth in if he's a quickly receding dot in the sky. While Gargoyles make fearsome warriors, they are certainly smart enough to leave if things get too hairy — and having a pair of wings is a big help.

A Gargoyle with Level 3 *Flight* can always declare Fair Escape when outdoors or next to an unobstructed window that is large enough to fit through. (The window can be closed; a Gargoyle will have no problems smashing through an ordinary window.)

A Gargoyle with at least Basic *Celerity* can declare Fair Escape with only Level 2 of *Flight* as he can achieve a speedy running takeoff.

If the Gargoyle is well above ground level (in a skyscraper, on top of a high and steep hill, in an apartment three or more floors above the ground) even a single level of *Flight* is sufficient for Fair Escape, as the Gargoyle can glide to safety.

In all cases characters with ranged attacks get to make a single attack while the Gargoyle is flying away.

Characters with an equal or higher *Flight* score may attack the escaping character normally and may continue fighting as long as they continue to pursue the escaping character.

Note that Fair Escape may also be applied indoors if the characters are in a room that is clearly large enough for someone to fly in: Large ballrooms, warehouses and similar buildings are certainly acceptable. However, the character will be easy pickings to anyone with a ranged weapon, unless the room is exceptionally large and has enough space to allow maneuvering — or a window or skylight the Gargoyle can escape through.

FLIGHT MANEUVERS

Obviously, the ability to fly comes with a tremendous tactical advantage. To represent this, Gargoyles can perform special aerial maneuvers in combat.

All maneuvers have minimum requirements of skills or Disciplines to be performed. If you can't meet those requirements, you are unable to perform the maneuver properly, and you crash if you attempt them. Maneuvers cost one Free Trait at character creation, or two experience points after character creation.

If you have not learned the maneuver but do meet the minimum requirements for the maneuver, you can still attempt to perform it, but you must bid three extra Physical Traits. If the challenge fails, you immediately crash into the ground and suffer one health level of damage, unless you have *Fortitude* or other suitable protection. Moreover, you must spend the next turn getting back to your feet, and cannot attack anyone. (You can defend yourself, but must bid an extra Physical Trait when doing so.)

Pounce

You leap at an opponent and cover a surprisingly large distance by spreading your wings. This maneuver cannot be performed in cramped places, such as tight corridors — assume that you require at least two feet of unobstructed space on both sides. However, most rooms offer enough space for you to pounce on an opponent, even if this requirement isn't strictly met. This maneuver can also be used to increase the distance you can jump normally — for example, to cross a chasm on the ground, or to leap from the roof of one building to another. In practice, this means that you can attack an opponent who is out of your normal reach. You may also pounce directly upward if need be, but cannot achieve vertical takeoff without *Flight 3*.

When pouncing, you can cover six yards of ground per level of *Flight*. A normal Physical Challenge is required.

Damage: Normal

Minimum requirements: *Flight* 1, *Brawl* 1

Swoop

You swoop down from the sky, attacking an opponent while adding your own momentum to the blow, be it with a fist or with a melee weapon, and then swoop back up. On a successful attack, you reach the safety of the sky again, and cannot be attacked except by long-range weapons. Even if the attack fails, you can get back up to safety. However, Kindred with Intermediate *Celerity* can attack you once normally when you're swooping down; Kindred with Advanced *Celerity* get two attacks. Superior *Celerity* grants one extra attack per Superior level, as characters who move with truly supernatural speed have all the time in the world to punch the attacking Gargoyle once or twice.

Targets who are covered, obscured or out of reach (underneath trees, pressed against a doorway, lying in a gutter) cannot be successfully swooped at. For obvious reasons, *Swoop* cannot be used indoors unless the room is clearly large enough for such a maneuver. Note that unlike normal attacks, you swoop down at such speed that a character with *Alacrity* or a suitable weapon cannot pre-empt the attack.

To *Swoop*, you bid an extra Physical Trait, or two Traits if your opponent is actively trying to avoid you. You then perform a normal Physical Challenge against the opponent.

Damage: One health level of bashing or lethal damage, depending on weapon used.

Minimum requirements: *Flight 2* and *Brawl 2* or *Melee 2*, depending on the attack type.

SLAM

You swoop down as before, but instead of hitting the opponent and swooping back up, you slam into your opponent at full speed. Considering a Gargoyle's enormous weight, this is an extremely serious attack. This grounds you and thus allows you to be attacked, but is likely to hurt the opponent quite a bit. Your opponent is knocked down but may attack you normally during this turn, as you aren't swooping back up. He must bid two extra Physical Traits for his next action as he struggles back to his feet. If you lose the challenge, you're still grounded, but you manage to land on your feet. Note that as this maneuver depends on your body mass: Melee weapons cannot be used in this attack.

As with *Swoop*, a character with *Alacrity* or a suitable weapon cannot preempt the attack, and targets who are well in cover (as described under *Swoop*) cannot be slammed.

You bid an extra Physical Trait, or two Traits if the opponent is actively trying to avoid him, then perform a normal Physical Challenge against the opponent.

Damage: Three health levels of bashing damage. If you have *Flight 5*, you can optionally inflict an additional health level of damage; however, if you do not have at least *Fortitude 1*, you will also suffer one health level of bashing damage. If you have *Armor of Terra*, you inflict yet another additional health level of bashing damage, cumulative with *Flight 5*. If you have *Armor of Terra*, you need no *Fortitude*: Your skin is so tough that you suffer no damage from the impact.

Minimum requirements: *Flight 2, Brawl 2*

THAUMATURGY

The following thaumaturgical paths are practiced throughout the Camarilla by the Tremere. As with all *Thaumaturgy*, the Tremere guard their secrets jealously and will not share them with outsiders.

These additional paths work as described in **Laws of the Night**. Note that a Blood Trait expenditure is always required whenever a thaumaturgical power is activated.

ELEMENTAL MASTERY

With *Elemental Mastery*, you enjoy limited control over and communion with inanimate objects. While the uninitiated may believe that the name of this path refers to the four basic elements (earth, fire, air and water), in reality this path is closer to an amalgamation of *Spirit Thaumaturgy* and the *Path of Conjuring*. *Elemental Mastery* only affects dead or inanimate objects.

BASIC ELEMENTAL MASTERY

ELEMENTAL STRENGTH

You can enhance your own physical prowess by drawing on the strength of the earth or objects around you without the need for large amounts of blood. Upon activating the power, you immediately receive three strength-related Physical Traits of your choice. You may activate this power and attack during

the same turn. These extra Traits will remain for as many turns as you have powers in *Elemental Mastery*, and you may expend a Willpower Trait to get one additional turn. This power cannot be "stacked"; the first application of it must expire before it can be used again.

Wooden Tongues

You may now talk with the spirit of an inanimate object. Sadly, as most objects are not known for their conversational skills, such discourses are likely to be extremely boring. Still, you may still get a general idea of the significant events that the object has "experienced." However, it should be kept in mind that the experiences that interest you might not be the same ones that interest a coffee maker.

You must make a Mental Challenge against the spirit in question. *Subterfuge* may be used for retests in this challenge. If successful, you may ask a question of the spirit, and the spirit may not lie. Questions like "What did the person who ran by moments ago look like?" or "Has anyone been fighting here recently?" are acceptable, but it should be kept in mind that certain concepts may be very alien to household objects. "What did they talk about?" for example is likely to confuse the spirit quite a bit. Should you fail the test, you're in for a rather inane conversation. For example, if the subject happens to be a rock reflecting on the hardness of its being, a certain amount of frustration is guaranteed.

Intermediate Elemental Mastery

Animate the Unmoving

This power allows you to cause inanimate objects to move as you will. An object cannot perform an action that would be completely inconceivable for its form — for example, a rock could not grow legs, nor could a coffee cup start playing the guitar. But a human-shaped statue could walk around; a gun might twist out of someone's hand or fire itself spontaneously, or a length of steel cable might suddenly start moving like a snake, tripping people and tying them up.

You must spend a Willpower Trait upon activating this power. You may simultaneously control up to a number of objects equal to your permanent Mental Traits divided by three (round up). Each object needs to be animated separately, and they must be in your line of sight when being animated. They remain animated as long as they are within your line of sight, or up to an hour. Simple commands to the objects may be given ("Chase that man" or "Attack anyone who comes in" are all right), but they aren't very smart and have extremely limited reasoning. (For example, "Wait for the red car" could result in an extremely confused bar stool.)

Elemental Form

You may take on the form of any inanimate object of a mass roughly equal to your own. Thus, you might assume the form of a large television or a small bed, but turning into a handgun or a van is beyond your capabilities.

Upon activation of this power, you may decide the form you wish to assume. However, you must spend a Willpower Trait if you wish to retain your senses and the ability to use Disciplines. Obviously, certain Disciplines cannot be used while in an altered form. The object functions exactly like a real object

would — for example, a television can be plugged in and turned on with no harm inflicted on you. This power lasts for the remainder of the night, although you may assume your true form at will.

ADVANCED ELEMENTAL MASTERY

SUMMON ELEMENTAL

With *Summon Elemental*, you may summon one of the traditional spirits of the elements: a salamander (fire), a sylph (air), a gnome (earth) or an undine (water). Some Tremere claim that they have managed to contact other elemental spirits, such as those of glass, electricity, blood or even atomic energy, but for the time being, such reports remain unconfirmed.

You must be near some quantity of the classical element corresponding to the spirit you wish to summon. The spirit, once summoned, may not actually follow your orders, but generally speaking, it will do what it is told. Obviously, abusing the spirit will cause the spirit to attack or refuse to cooperate.

The power level of the spirit may vary greatly, and the summoner will not know how powerful (or weak) the spirit is before it actually manifests. As a rule of thumb, all elementals have at least six of both Physical and Mental Traits; some may be far more powerful than that. All elementals have some powers related to their particular element — a fire elemental may toss fireballs, while a water elemental may be able to control water in its vicinity. The details depend on the individual spirit; they may have any combination of skills, powers and abilities the Storyteller sees fit. Moreover, all elementals have personalities; they are usually bright and not unaware of what is around them.

Once the spirit has been summoned, you must exert control over it. This is accomplished with a Static Mental Challenge against the spirit. The more powerful the spirit, the more likely it will make things as difficult as possible. If you win, the spirit obeys the caster and may consider you a superior, or at least an enlightened equal. To command the creature, spend one Mental Trait for each command you wish to give. Otherwise, the spirit will want to bargain, and spirits always want something. Should you be unable to exert control over the spirit, the elemental may think of you as an enemy and attack, or it may simply be indifferent and do as it pleases. It may choose to remain nearby or leave — spirits are unpredictable creatures, after all.

If the elemental is asked to perform a task that endangers its existence, you may enforce your will with another Mental Challenge. Success forces the creature to obey while a loss may result in a creature anxious to flee your presence or a very angry elemental, and spirit anger is an unpleasant thing.

The elemental remains in existence for as long as it is under your control. If it is unbound, it will remain for as long as it chooses — such details are best left to the Storyteller.

THE GREEN PATH

A favorite of ecologically minded Tremere, the *Green Path* concentrates on controlling and understanding nature. Anything more complex than an algae bloom can theoretically be controlled by this power, from ordinary potted plants to the sprawling vastness of the rainforest. While many Tremere

consider its practitioners to be merely eccentric tree-huggers, the *Green Path* is still as subtle and powerful as nature itself.

The *Green Path* probably originated from the Order of the Naturists, an old Druidic sect within Clan Tremere. Many practitioners are members of the order or at least mentored by one. According to Tremere history, the path is largely based on the magics formerly practiced by House Diedne, an order of mortal mages destroyed by the Tremere during the Dark Ages.

Basic Green Path

Herbal Wisdom

Merely by touching a plant, you may communicate with its spirit. The exact nature of the spirit depends largely on the plant in question — ancient trees may be extremely wise (if rather cryptic), whereas ordinary crabgrass tends to have far less insight to offer (but might still reveal the face of the last person who trod upon it).

You must touch the plant you wish to communicate with and activate the power. You may ask a single question and expect an answer, which may or may not be helpful but will always be true. To learn more details, make a Static Mental Challenge against the Storyteller; with success, the spirit will divulge more detailed information, if it can. The exact details of the answer are left to the Storyteller.

Speed the Season's Passing

With this power, you can cause a flower to grow from a seed to full bloom in mere minutes, or an entire tree to spring up overnight. Alternately, you may cause a plant to die and decay, grass to wither or stakes to crumble with but a touch.

You must touch the target plant and activate the power; the plant's growth or death, depending on your intent, will be greatly accelerated. For an almost instant effect, spend a Willpower Trait to cause a plant to spring from a seed or a tree to sprout fruit in minutes — or start decaying almost instantly. In combat, the expenditure of a Willpower Trait causes a stake or other wooden weapon to crumble into dust. However, you cannot use this power if you become staked.

Intermediate Green Path

Dance of Vines

You can now animate a mass of vegetation up to your own size, either for utilitarian or combat purposes. Vines can strangle opponents, trees may move to allow faster passage through a thick forest (and bend again to block the passage of pursuers), roots may trip unwelcome visitors, and so forth.

The target plant must be within your line of sight. You spend a Willpower Trait and concentrate on the target plant. The target must have a mass that is less than or equal to your own. The plants stay active for as many rounds equal to half your permanent Mental Traits (round down), and are under your complete control. They are considered to have Physical Traits equal to your current Willpower rating, and a *Brawl* rating one lower than your own (thus, if you only have *Brawl* 1, then the plant has no Brawl). Generally speaking, plants do two

bashing levels of damage — this can be modified, depending on the plant. They tend to be best at tripping or tying down opponents, although some enterprising Warlocks have used rowan saplings in their havens to stake unwary intruders.

Plants cannot uproot themselves and start running around: Even at their most energetic, your plants cannot walk under this power. But a tree's deep roots can extend for some distance, and who's to say how much damage 150 pounds of kudzu can do?

Verdant Haven

With this power, you may construct a shelter out of a sufficient amount of plant matter. The shelter not only provides protection from the elements, it also protects you against sunlight and attack. It also creates a mystical barrier that keeps anyone you wish to exclude from entering. A *Verdant Haven* appears as a six-foot-tall hemisphere of interlocked branches, leaves and vines with no discernible opening. Even to a casual observer, it appears to be an unnatural construction. Some claim that *Verdant Havens* have supernatural healing properties, but no Kindred who has spent time in one has reported such benefits.

You must be in a heavily vegetated area for this power to work. Upon activating this power, the *Verdant Haven* springs up around you over the course of three turns. Once the haven is sealed, anyone wishing to enter the haven without your permission must make a Mental Challenge against you — you gain two extra Traits that can be used in this challenge only. Unless the unwelcome guest wins the challenge, she cannot enter. All attacks against the haven itself are handled in the same fashion.

The haven lasts until the next sunset, or until you dispel it or leave. Sunlight does not penetrate the haven unless it has been physically breached.

Advanced Green Path

Awaken the Forest Giants

One of the most impressive applications of *Thaumaturgy* known to the Tremere, this power allows you to awaken the very trees of the forest, causing them to stretch their limbs, pull their roots out of the ground and walk with steps that make the earth shake. They are not nearly as versatile as spirits that have been summoned into existence, but their awesome strength and resilience more than makes up for that.

You must touch the tree you wish to animate, spend a Willpower Trait and concentrate on the target. You must then spend a Blood Trait for every two turns you wish the tree to remain active. (Thus, spending two Blood Traits means the tree will remain active for four turns.) Once this time expires, the tree stops moving and puts down roots wherever it is at the moment. The tree cannot be animated again for the rest of the night. While animated, the tree follows your verbal commands as well as it can. An animated tree has 10 Physical Traits plus twice as many Traits as your *Occult* rating, and a *Brawl* rating equal to your own. It is immune to bashing damage, and because of its size, all non-aggravated lethal damage is halved (round up). Its health levels depend on its size; an average tree has five or six health levels.

A tree that ceases to be animated immediately takes root wherever it is. Even if it is on concrete, its roots will punch through whatever it is standing

on at the moment until it finds earth and water underneath — thus, it is not impossible to plant a row of maples in the middle of a busy city street. Obviously, using this power to commit such an obvious breach of the Masquerade is a good way to ensure that the mistake will not be repeated.

Neptune's Might

Most vampire myths don't associate vampires with the sea, and indeed, most vampires don't feel any particular connection — the sea simply means nothing to most of them. Nevertheless, *Neptune's Might* has always had a small but devoted following among the Tremere.

Once a thaumaturge reaches the Intermediate level of *Neptune's Might*, she may choose to specialize in either salt water or fresh water. Such specialization grants her two extra Traits as appropriate when dealing with the water type of her choice, but also forces her to bid two extra Traits when dealing with the opposite. Blood is considered to be neither salty nor fresh for this purpose, and difficulties to manipulate it are unaffected. Note that this specialization is optional.

Basic Neptune's Might

Eyes of the Sea

You may look deep into a body of water and view events that have transpired in, on or around it from the water's perspective. Some practitioners of this path claim that the thaumaturge communes with the spirits of the water when using this power; some younger Kindred scoff at such claims, and others simply don't care.

You must stare deeply into a body of water when activating this power. You may see up to one day into the past. If you wish to see more, you must start making Simple Tests; with each successful test, you may gaze further back in time. Alternately, spending a Willpower Trait counts as an automatic success.

This power can only be used on standing water — lakes and puddles will do; oceans, rivers, sewers or wineglasses will not.

Prison of Water

With this dramatic power you can command a sufficiently large body of water to animate itself and imprison a subject. A significant amount of fluid is required for this power to be truly effective, although even a few gallons are sufficient to form chains of animated water. Mortals who are subjected to this power may drown if you are not careful (or if you want to kill them). The extreme pressures that can be brought to bear may even crush other vampires.

Upon activating this power, you must invest Blood Traits into the effect. Every Trait spent equals two Physical Traits for the prison. Your *Occult* rating is added to this. After that, you may form a prison of water around the subject. To break free, the subject must make a Physical Test against the Traits of the animated water. If he wins, he breaks free, breaking the animated prison and causing the water to become inanimate.

If you desire, you may crush your trapped subject, again using the prison's Physical Traits against the subject's Physical Traits. Each successful challenge results in one health level of lethal damage to the subject. You may choose to

automatically drown a mortal subject. A single prison may be used on a single subject, but you are free to invoke multiple prisons for multiple subjects.

You must always have a line of sight to both the source of water and the subject. The prison remains in existence as long as you are in the same area and maintain a line of sight to them, unless you become unconscious or fall into sleep or torpor.

If a sufficient quantity of water is not present (at least a bathtub's worth), you must bid two additional Traits when making any challenges related to *Prison of Water*.

Intermediate Neptune's Might

Blood to Water

You have now attained enough power to transmute other liquids into water. The most commonly seen form of this power is an assault: With but a touch, you may transmute the victim's blood into water. For a mortal, this is lethal, and vampires are weakened by it.

You must touch your intended victim when activating the power. You may then spend as many Mental Traits as you please; every Mental Trait counts as one Blood Trait that becomes water. For a mortal, this means death in minutes; a vampire is weakened as the vitae in his system effectively disappears. What's more, the vampire suffers wound penalties as if he were injured, even though actual injury is not inflicted. Those with at least Basic *Fortitude* are unaffected by this, but still lose the Blood Traits normally. The water evaporates out of a vampire's body at a rate of one Blood Trait per hour, but the lost blood will not return.

Liquids other than blood can be transmuted into water as well, as long as you either touch the liquid itself or the container it is in.

Flowing Wall

With this power you can command water to such an extent that you can form it into an almost impenetrable wall. You must touch the surface of a standing body of water and spend two Willpower Traits. You must then spend Mental Traits: Each Mental Trait spent in this fashion causes 10 feet of watery barrier to appear in one dimension, either in width or height. Your permanent Mental Traits are the only limit to how tall or wide a wall you can create. The wall may be placed anywhere in your line of sight and must be formed in a straight line. The wall remains in place until sunrise. It cannot be climbed, but it can be flown over.

Successful Test	Range of Effect
0	One day
1	One week
2	One month
3	One year
4	10 years

Anyone attempting to pass through the wall must make three Static Physical Challenges against your permanent Mental Traits; unless they succeed, they cannot pass through. This also applies to characters who are in astral form or in the Umbra, although those characters use their Mental Traits instead of Physical Traits.

Advanced Neptune's Might

Dehydrate

Upon reaching this level of mastery, you can directly attack both mortal and supernatural targets by removing the water from their bodies. Victims who succumb to this power leave behind hideous mummified corpses. There are other, less aggressive applications for this power, such as drying out wet clothes or evaporating puddles to keep other practitioners of this path from using them.

Make a Mental Challenge against the target's Physical Traits. If successful, you inflict three levels of lethal damage on the subject. Armor offers no protection against this attack, but it can be healed normally. Vampires lose Blood Traits instead of health levels; if the target has no more Blood Traits left, she will then lose health levels as normal. The victim must make a Static *Courage* test against the amount of health levels lost, times two; if she loses, she is overcome with agony for that turn and cannot act. Vampires who have only lost blood are not overwhelmed until they begin to lose health levels.

The Path of Corruption

The learning or even knowledge of this path is neither encouraged nor openly supported by most of the high-ranking Tremere. Those who are familiar with its intricacies hotly debate its origins. One theory holds that its secrets were originally taught to the Tremere by demons, and practicing it may bring one dangerously close to the infernal. Another states that this path is something of a relic from the days when the Tremere were still mortal wizards. The third, and to many the most disturbing, is that the path was originally learned from the Followers of Set and that knowledge of its intricacies was sold to the Tremere for an unspecified price. Obviously, this last rumor is always denied by the Tremere, which automatically makes it the favorite topic of discussion whenever the matter is brought up.

The *Path of Corruption* is path centered on influencing the psyches of other individuals. Unlike *Dominate*, it cannot be used to issue commands, nor can it be used like *Presence* to alter emotions. Instead, the powers of *Path of Corruption* slowly and subtly twist an individual's mind into a darker, more immoral state. Those who wish to engage in this must be well–versed in the darker side of human nature. Lies and deception should be second nature to the user. Accordingly, no character may have a higher rating in the *Path of Corruption* than he has in *Subterfuge*.

Using a Narrator as a proxy between the players may prevent out-of-game knowledge from influencing in-game play.

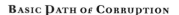

BASIC PATH OF CORRUPTION

CONTRADICT

You may interrupt a subject's thought processes, forcing the subject to reverse his current course of action. This may lead to a man shouting at his wife instead of caressing her, a police officer letting a known violent criminal go instead of arresting him, or a vampire giving into the Beast just when he had gained control at the brink of frenzy. The actual results of *Contradict* are never known in advance, but they always take the form of a more negative action than the subject had originally intended to perform.

Contradict can be used on any subject in your line of sight. You must make a Mental Challenge against the subject; if successful, the action or decision the subject is about to undertake becomes the negative, far darker opposite. The details are largely left up to the target, who must roleplay it out, although the Storyteller may intervene.

The subject gets to make a Simple Test. If he wins, he realizes that he is being influenced but doesn't know who is causing it, unless he wins a Mental Challenge against you to become aware of who attempted to influence him. If he ties on the Simple Test, he becomes vaguely aware of the fact that he is being influenced, but cannot change his course of action. If he loses, he believes that he took the twisted action of his own volition.

Contradict cannot be used in combat or to affect actions that are mainly physical or reflexive.

SUBVERT

Similar to *Contradict*, *Subvert's* effects last longer and dig deeper into the dark side of the subject's psyche. When influenced by this power, the subject acts on her own suppressed temptations, pursuing agendas that her morals or self-control would normally forbid her to follow.

You must make eye contact with the intended victim and make a Mental Challenge. If you win, the victim becomes inclined to follow a repressed, shameful desire until the effects fade. By default, the effects last for five minutes; however, if the original Mental Challenge is successful, you may make Simple Tests against the victim until you lose. The number of wins you score determines the effect's length.

The actual effects are again best left for roleplaying, although the Storyteller may intervene. The victim should follow a negative agenda for the duration of the effect — she is driven by her darker desires and moods. Psychological Flaws or Negative Traits may well come into play here. The character's Nature is also a factor in this — for example, a Loner may become violent if she is forced attend a social function. The subject does not become fixated on this new agenda to the point of stupidity, but it does influence all of her actions with varying degrees of subtlety. The expenditure of a Willpower Trait allows the character to overcome this effect for a minute.

INTERMEDIATE PATH OF CORRUPTION

DISSOCIATE

"Divide and conquer" may not be a very original tactic, but it's as effective now as it was centuries ago. The Tremere know this, and this is a powerful tool for those who wish to practice this tactic in a rather persuasive fashion. This power can break the social ties of interpersonal relationships. Even the most passionate lovers or oldest friends can be separated with this power, and more casual ties can be destroyed altogether.

Wins	Duration of Effect
0	5 minutes
One	One hour
Two	One night
Three	Three nights
Four	One week

You must touch the target and make a Mental Challenge against him. If successful, the victim's Social Traits are reduced by four (to a minimum of one) for the duration of the effect — the duration determined as with *Subvert*, above. If this power is used on a character who has participated in the Sabbat Vaulderie or similar ritual, his Vinculum rating is reduced by three for the duration of the effect.

Again, the effects of this power should be roleplayed out. The victim of this power becomes withdrawn, suspicious and emotionally distant. The expenditure of a Willpower Trait allows the character to overcome this effect for a minute or so.

ADDICTION

This power is a far nastier form of *Subvert*. *Addiction* creates just that in the victim. By exposing her to a particular sensation, situation, substance or action, you can create a powerful psychological dependency. Many Tremere ensure that their victims become addicted to substances or thrills only they can provide, thus creating a source of income and potential blackmail material.

The subject must encounter or be exposed to whatever it is that you wish to addict her to. You then touch your target and make a Mental Challenge. If successful, the target is instantly addicted to whatever it is that you have planned for her. An addicted character must get her fix on a nightly basis. For every night that she is forced to go without a fix, she must bid an additional Trait on *all* challenges she participates in — the longer she waits, the worse her condition becomes. Furthermore, if she is confronted with the object or situation of her addiction, she must make a Static *Self-Control* Challenge to keep from indulging. *Addiction* lasts for a number of weeks equal to your permanent Social Traits, divided by two (round down).

The victim may attempt to break the effects of *Addiction*. This requires that a *Self-Control* Challenge be made every night until she has accumulated more wins than the caster's rating in *Path of Corruption*. The victim may not indulge in her addiction over the time needed to accumulate the wins; if she succumbs, all accumulated wins are lost and she must start over again. If the target loses a challenge, she may try again the following night. Obviously, the longer it takes, the harder it becomes to win, as she is constantly forced to bid more and more Traits.

ADVANCED PATH OF CORRUPTION

DEPENDENCE

The final power in *Path of Corruption*, *Dependence* ties your subject's soul to your own, engendering feelings of lethargy and helplessness in her when she is not in your presence or acting to further your desires. It is no surprise that some former pawns of the Tremere speak of feelings of depression and loss they felt when they weren't in the presence of their masters.

Engage your target in conversation, then makes a Mental Challenge against the subject. If you are successful, the victim's psyche becomes subtly bonded to your own for one night per permanent Mental Trait you possess, divided by two (round down).

A bonded victim is no less likely to attack you and feels no particular affection toward you. However, she is psychologically addicted to your presence, and must bid an extra Trait in any challenges she participates in whenever she is not around you or performing tasks for you. Additionally, you gain five extra Traits when engaging her in any challenges that involve asserting your authority, whether through *Dominate*, *Presence*, *Subterfuge* or *Leadership*. Finally, she is unable to regain Willpower Traits unless she is in your presence. Again, these effects should mostly be roleplayed out.

THE PATH OF TECHNOMANCY

One of the newest and most controversial *Thaumaturgy* paths, *Technomancy* concentrates on controlling electronic devices, ranging from wristwatches to computers. The path is so new that it has yet to spread much beyond the United States, but its proponents are quickly making progress in spreading it as far as they can, stating that it is a prime example of what can be accomplished with creative applications of *Thaumaturgy* in the modern world. More conservative Tremere object to *Technomancy's* very existence, claiming that mixing magic and mortal technology borders on treason or even blasphemy. Some European regents have even banned practitioners of *Technomancy* from their chantries altogether. The Inner Council has not yet expressed any opinion on the matter, but has approved the introduction of the path into the clan's grimoires.

BASIC TECHNOMANCY

ANALYZE

Technology doesn't march on — it races. Keeping up with new innovations can be confusing at best, and many vampires find that progress rapidly leaves them behind, despite their best efforts. With *Analyze*, you can project your consciousness into a device, granting you temporary but comprehensive

understanding of its purpose, the principles of its functioning, and its means of operation. No permanent knowledge is gained; this understanding fades in a few minutes.

To use this power, you must touch the device in question. Basic knowledge (on/off and simple functions) is granted in the first turn. After that, every turn of contact with the device allows for more information, but you must spend a Mental Trait for every additional piece of information beyond the first. In the second turn, you know enough to competently operate the device. In the third turn, you have a complete understanding of the full range of the device's potential. The knowledge gained lasts for a number of minutes equal to half your Mental Traits (round down).

This power may also be used to understand new pieces of computer software. However, you must touch a computer in which the software is installed; merely holding the CD-ROM or disk will not do. You must bid an additional Mental Trait when attempting this.

BURNOUT

Burnout's only function is destruction. By causing a device's power supply to surge, you may damage or destroy the target. *Burnout* cannot be used to directly injure another individual, but destroying a pacemaker or a car's fuel injection control chip can certainly have dramatic consequences.

You must make a Static Mental Challenge. This power has a range of up to 10 times your permanent Willpower in yards, but you must bid an additional Mental Trait if you are not touching the item. Normal household appliances or desktop computers typically have three Traits, while cars or more resistant devices have six Traits. Large mainframes, passenger aircraft or other similar devices may have nine or more Traits. Devices with additional surge protection gain an additional three Traits for defense (computers well-guarded against power spikes and the like, such as banking or military mainframes, may have more at Storyteller discretion). A damaged device ceases to function and cannot be used again until it is repaired.

If you wish to destroy the target instead of merely damaging it, spend a Mental Trait and make a Simple Test; with success, the target is destroyed instead of being merely damaged. *Burnout* may also be used to destroy electronic data storage (such as disks or CD-ROMs), using the same procedure; with success, the data is destroyed beyond any hope of non-magical recovery.

INTERMEDIATE TECHNOMANCY

ENCRYPT/DECRYPT

While more conservative Tremere are often unaware of the constant struggle of governments and corporations to keep their encryption routines up-to-date, the technophilic members of the clan take great pleasure in this power as it allows them to mystically scramble a device's controls so that it only works for them. It also works on all sorts of electronic media, ranging from computer files to videotapes — files appear scrambled, the videotape displays nothing but snow and static, and so forth.

To encrypt something, you must touch the device or data container and spend a Willpower Trait. Once the power is invoked, spend Mental Traits to work the encryption; the more Traits spent, the more secure the encryption. Each level of the *Computer* Ability you possess counts as two Traits for the purposes of encryption alone. Anyone attempting to use the device or access the data without your assistance must succeed in a Static Mental Challenge against the number of Traits spent. Those who have no appropriate skills (such as *Computer, Repair, Science* or *Security*) cannot attempt the challenge at all: The device simply refuses to work. The details of the challenge are left to the Storyteller, but let common sense be your guide. You may dispel the effect at any time merely by touching the target and spending another Willpower Trait.

Encrypt/Decrypt can also be used to decrypt devices or data that have been previously encrypted with this power. The power works exactly the way it does when encrypting something, except every spent Mental Trait removes one Trait from the target, thus making using the device or accessing the data easier.

The effects of this power last for a number of weeks equal to your permanent Willpower Traits.

REMOTE ACCESS

A suitably skilled technomancer no longer needs to touch a device to operate it. This is not some form of telekinesis; instead you command the device directly with your mind. This power may be used on any electronic device in the character's line of sight. You must spend a Willpower Trait and concentrate on the target. After that, you may use the target device normally, despite the fact that you aren't actually touching it. This could mean operating a computer from afar, opening electronic locks or deactivating security systems. As long as you can see the device, you can operate it.

Remote Access remains in effect for a number of turns equal to your *Path of Technomancy* score. You must make a Simple Test for each turn after that; on a failure, the connection is broken. *Remote Access* can only be used on a single target at a time.

If the item you are operating from afar is destroyed while you are using it, you immediately take three levels of bashing damage (which is *not* halved as per normal), as the shock of having your perceptions suddenly shunted back to your body is somewhat nasty.

ADVANCED TECHNOMANCY

TELECOMMUTE

Telecommute allows you to project your consciousness into the global telecommunication network and send your mind through satellite links, fiber-optic cables and other similar devices. While thus immersed in the network, you can use any of the other *Technomancy* powers on the devices with which you make contact.

You must touch some sort of a communication device. Anything will do; it may be a cell phone, a fax machine, a computer with a modem or permanent network connection, or just an ordinary telephone. You then spend a Willpower Trait and concentrate.

The effects of *Telecommute* lasts for 10 minutes, with each level in *Computer* Ability granting an additional five minutes. This time may be extended by another 10 minutes by spending a Willpower Trait. This can be

repeated until there are no Willpower Traits left, if you so desire. The default range of *Telecommute* is 25 miles. If you wish to go further than that, you may do so by expending Mental Traits as follows:

As long as you are immersed in the network, you may apply any other *Path of Technomancy* power to any device or data you encounter. Should you become disconnected (which may occur should a part of the network your connection runs through be shut down or destroyed), you are immediately yanked back to your body and suffer five levels of bashing damage (not halved as per normal).

Should you attempt to take any actions more complicated than talking to someone while thus connected, you must bid two additional Traits for any and all challenges. It should also be noted that there are beings other than the Tremere out there in the Net, and they may well take exception to the intrusion. The Tremere who are experienced in these things know that these creatures are far more at home in this environment, and steering clear of them is often a good idea.

For obvious reasons, this power always requires Storyteller assistance.

Traits Expended	Range
0	25 miles
One	250 miles
Two	1000 miles
Four	5000 miles
Six	Anywhere in the world, including telecommunication satellites

SPIRIT MANIPULATION

Not to be confused with, or even derived from, the ancient *Path of Spirit Thaumaturgy*, *Spirit Manipulation* is actually a somewhat recent innovation for the Tremere. This path was invented to replace the old rituals created by the clan when they were still mortal wizards. Its purpose is to force spirits into situations and actions that would normally be anathema for them. *Spirit Manipulation* mimics many effects that can be created by Lupines and certain shamanic mages, but it takes a completely different approach — instead of making a sort of an agreement with the spirit in question, the thaumaturge forces the spirit into a grotesque mockery of its normal behavior. It's a dangerous practice, though; a mistake may result in the spirit's full wrath against the caster. Whenever a practitioner loses a challenge while working with a spirit, he must make a Simple Test. If he loses the test, the spirit attacks.

BASIC SPIRIT MANIPULATION

HERMETIC SIGHT

With this power you can perceive the spirit world, allowing you to gaze deeply into it, or perceive nearby spirits as a hazy overlay on the material world.

This power does not allow you to see into the lands of the dead or into the realms of the fae.

You may activate this power at will and automatically see any spirits close by. If you wish to gaze into the spirit realm itself, you must spend a Mental Trait; you may then see into the spirit realm for the duration of the scene. While looking into the spirit realm, you must bid an additional two Traits on any challenges in the physical world due to the difficulties caused by divided perceptions. You may terminate this power at any time.

Astral Cant

Most spirits don't speak English, at least not on their home turf. Some can't, but many more simply refuse to do so. With this power you can understand and communicate in the spirits' own languages.

Spending a Willpower Trait activates this power for the remainder of the scene. As long as the power is active, you may converse with spirits in their own language and understand their responses.

Intermediate Spirit Manipulation

Voice of Command

This is perhaps the most dangerous power a practitioner of *Spirit Manipulation* has at her disposal — failure here may well mean a painful death when subjected to the attack of an enraged spirit. This power allows you to give orders to a spirit, compelling it to heed your bidding whether or not it desires to do so.

To use this power, spend a Willpower Trait and make a Mental Challenge against the spirit. With success, the spirit must obey whatever command you give, as long as it doesn't endanger the spirit's well-being or conflict with its morals. By spending another Willpower Trait before making the challenge, you may force the spirit into doing something that may hurt the spirit or greatly violate its ethics. To force the spirit into a possibly suicidal action, you must make another Mental Challenge against the spirit; success means the spirit will obey, but will likely be seething with rage at this point. It should be kept in mind that spirits commanded in this manner are fully aware of the fact that they are being forced into something against their will, and they may well seek revenge at a later time. A spirit issued a command above and beyond what it was compelled to do may "agree" to the command, but never follow through, leaving its erstwhile master in a potentially fatal situation.

Entrap Ephemera

With this power, you may bind a spirit into an object. This can be done in order to imprison the spirit, but it's more often performed in order to create a fetish, an artifact that channels a portion of the spirit's power through it to affect the physical world. Fetishes created in this manner are rather fickle at best and may fail at inopportune moments, as the spirits within will do anything in their power to escape or at least thwart their captors.

The actual details of the fetish depend greatly on the details of the spirit and the item in question. For example, a spirit of pain may turn a simple whip into a terrifying weapon, whereas a spirit of sharpness may cause a sword to cut deep and cause aggravated damage. This is in no way

limited to weapons; a spirit of speed bound to a car may result in an extremely fast vehicle, and a spirit of investigation bound into a pair of binoculars may result in a spectacularly clear picture. It is impossible to provide game mechanics that will cover all of the possibilities; instead, they should be worked out with the Storyteller.

A fetish created in this fashion is activated by spending a Willpower Trait and making a Simple Test. On a loss, you must make another Simple Test. On a second loss, the fetish fails to function properly, and you must make a third Simple Test. If that test is lost as well, the physical component of the fetish will be destroyed, and the spirit will be freed.

For more information regarding fetish powers, refer to **Laws of the Wild**. The Storyteller is always the final authority in determining the powers of and mechanics of a fetish created through use of this power.

Advanced Spirit Manipulation

Duality

The height of spiritual transactions, you can now fully interact with the realm of the spirits. When you activate this power, you exist on both planes simultaneously. You can pick up objects in the material world and place them in the spirit world or vice versa. The beings and landscapes of both worlds are solid to you, and you may interact with them as you please. You can even use *Thaumaturgy* and other Disciplines in either world. Still, it's not a walk in the park — a journey such as this is not without its dangers, and a single mistake may leave you trapped in the spirit realms with no way home. Several incautious travelers have starved into torpor in the spirit realm — there is no blood to be had among the spirits, after all.

Duality may only be used while you are in the physical world. Note that while this power is in effect, you are vulnerable to attacks from both worlds. You are considered to be in the physical world, as far as basic physics and common sense are concerned — for example, if there's a road in the physical world that leads over a chasm in the spirit world, you may walk across the chasm just fine.

To activate this power, spend a Willpower Trait and make a Static Mental Challenge. If successful, you enter the spirit world without leaving the physical world. Before going further, make a Simple Test. If you lose, repeat the test — a second loss means there was a backlash and you were ripped out of the physical world and thrown into the spirit world. Whether or not there is a way back to the physical realm is up to the Storyteller.

No. of Wins	Duration of Effect
0	One turn
One	Three turns
Two	10 turns
Three	10 minutes
Four	The remainder of the scene

If the entrance was successful, and you're not trapped in the spirit realms, you now determine how long you can remain. Make Simple Tests until you lose — the number of tests won determines the duration of the effect.

After the power has been activated, you must bid two additional Traits on all challenges as long as *Duality* remains active; perceiving two realms can be distracting, making even routine tasks an exercise in concentration.

THAUMATURGICAL COUNTERMAGIC

This power is not so much a path as it is a separate Discipline. The power to resist *Thaumaturgy* can be taught independently from *Thaumaturgy*, even to those Kindred who are incapable of learning even the most basic ritual. That said, for obvious reasons, these techniques are not taught outside Clan Tremere — non-Tremere who display this ability are likely to become a topic of fatal interest for every Tremere in the area.

Thaumaturgical Countermagic is treated as a separate Discipline. You may not take this as your primary path, nor does this allow you to perform rituals. The use of this power is treated as a free action in combat. To oppose a *Thaumaturgy* power or ritual, you must have a *Thaumaturgical Countermagic* rating equal to or higher than the rating of that power or ritual — rituals higher than Advanced may never be countered with this power.

Thaumaturgical Countermagic can only be used against Tremere *Thaumaturgy* at full effectiveness. It is greatly weakened (the character will have four fewer Traits for all challenges relating to an attempt to resist the magical effects) against non-Tremere blood magic and mortal hedge magic, and is completely ineffective against other magics and powers.

Any non-Tremere character who learns this power automatically earns the Flaw *Clan Enmity (Tremere)*, receiving no free Traits for it — supposing that the Tremere know that he has this power, of course. This power cannot be taken during character creation, and it can never be spontaneously developed. It costs the same as any other non-clan Discipline to learn.

There are no names for the levels of *Thaumaturgical Countermagic*; they are simply a game mechanic that measures degree of skill.

BASIC THAUMATURGICAL COUNTERMAGIC

LEVEL 1

You may make a Mental Challenge against the caster, bidding two extra Traits. If you win, the *Thaumaturgical* power or ritual the caster is attempting fails. You may only attempt to cancel those powers that directly affect you and your garments.

LEVEL 2

The character can make a normal Mental Challenge against the caster.

INTERMEDIATE THAUMATURGICAL COUNTERMAGIC

LEVEL 3

You receive two extra Traits for the Mental Challenge against the caster. You can attempt to cancel a *Thaumaturgy* power or ritual that affects anyone or anything in physical contact with you. (Meaning while you can use this if

someone with *Flesh of Fiery Touch* is grappling you, you cannot use this to counter objects hurled with *Movement of the Mind*.)

Level 4

You receive four extra Traits for the Mental Challenge against the caster.

Advanced Thaumaturgical Countermagic

Level 5

You receive six extra Traits for the Mental Challenge against the caster. You can now attempt to cancel a power or ritual that targets anything within a radius equal to your Willpower in yards, or one that is being used or performed within that same radius.

Weather Control

Tales have long been told of wizards who could control the weather; indeed, the powers of this path are said to predate the Tremere by several centuries. This path allows for subtle weather manipulation, and at higher levels you may even command entire storms. The area affected is usually rather small (at least on a meteorological scale), no more than three or four miles in diameter, although the Storyteller may alter this as she sees fit.

Decide how you wish to change the current weather and spend a Willpower Trait. Then decide how fast you want the weather to change, spend an appropriate number of Mental Traits (see below) and makes a Static Mental Challenge against the Storyteller. If no Mental Traits are spent, the weather changes in a day.

Note that the faster you attempt to change the weather, the more taxing it will be for you. Nearly instant massive changes in local weather are considered Masquerade breaches and are guaranteed to attract unwanted mortal attention.

It should be noted *Weather Control* isn't as much about specific powers as it is about degrees of control over the local weather. Therefore the strongest weather phenomenon you can affect at any given level is listed.

Basic Weather Control

Fog

The area is filled with thick fog. Vision is impaired, and all characters engaging in challenges to spot anything by sight must bid two extra Traits unless they have Basic *Auspex* or better. Due to lack of visibility, the effective ranges of all ranged weapons are halved.

At this level, you may also call up gentle wind and produce other weather effects of a similarly mild nature. You may also increase or decrease the ambient temperature slightly, by about 10 degrees Fahrenheit.

At this level, the Mental Challenge required to alter weather is handled normally.

Rain or Snow

The effects are similar to those of *Fog* — visibility is seriously impaired. Those attempting to spot anything with normal senses must bid four extra Traits. Those with *Auspex* need only bid two extra Traits. Obviously, depending on whether it

is raining or snowing (and it cannot snow very well unless it is cold enough), things may get very wet or extremely slippery. At the very least, driving becomes a hazardous proposition. The details are left to the Storyteller.

Intermediate Weather Control

High Winds

The wind speed rises up to around 30 miles per hour, with gusts of wind up to twice that. All characters attempting ranged attacks with guns must bid two extra Traits when attacking; characters attempting to use bows or thrown objects must bid three extra Traits. You may attempt to knock people down with the winds by making a Mental Challenge against the subjects' Physical Traits, as long as they are in your line of sight and in a location that allows for such gusts of wind (outdoors or on a balcony, yes; inside a china shop, no way). This will not do any damage, but the subjects must spend the next combat turn getting back to their feet. If the characters are attempting physical feats, such as rock-climbing, or some other similarly risky activity, the consequences may be more dramatic.

Local temperature may be raised or lowered by up to 20 degrees Fahrenheit.

Storm

This power has the effects of both *Rain* and *High Winds* at the same time.

Advanced Weather Control

Lightning Strike

This attack inflicts three health levels of lethal damage on the target. You must make a Mental Challenge against the target. The target uses Physical Traits to dodge, and he must bid an additional Physical Trait while attempting to do so, as lightning strikes rather quickly. Note that unlike other *Weather*

Traits spent	Weather change
One Trait	In six hours
Two Traits	In three hours
Three Traits	In one hour
Four Traits	In 10 minutes
Five Traits	Almost instantly

Weather Control Indoors

Though *Weather Control* is certainly a powerful path, it does not lend itself very well for use indoors. While certain effects, such as temperature control, winds (provided that the room is large enough) and even fog can be attempted indoors, the Storyteller always has final say in whether or not an effect can be achieved.

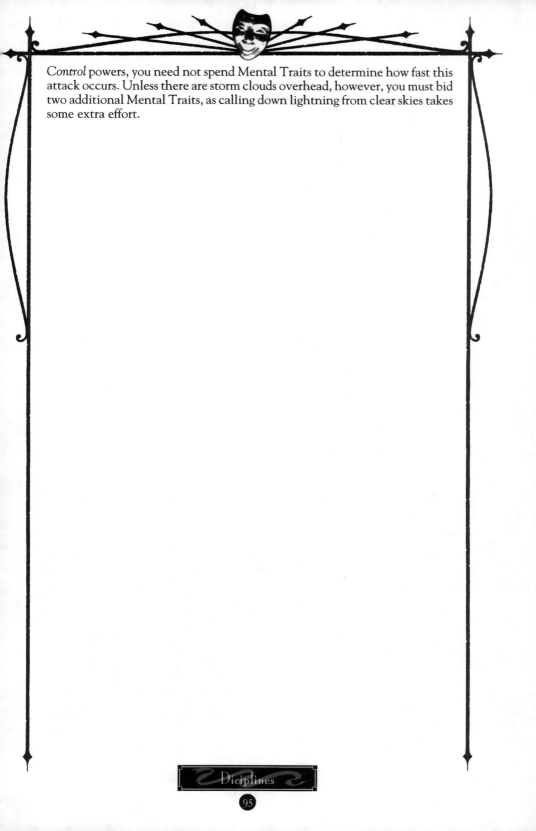

Control powers, you need not spend Mental Traits to determine how fast this attack occurs. Unless there are storm clouds overhead, however, you must bid two additional Mental Traits, as calling down lightning from clear skies takes some extra effort.

Chapter Four:
Inside Elysium

PRESENTATION

The custom of presentation is arguably the premiere tradition of modern Camarilla society. Simply put, any vampire new to a city is expected to call upon the prince, announce who he is and ask permission to stay. For newly embraced Kindred, it is their formal introduction to the creatures with which they may be spending eternity. For visiting Kindred, it is their introduction to a new city and its perils. For the prince, it is an affirmation of her power and a chance to get information. For everyone, it is a chance to size up his or her new competition.

SETTING THE STAGE

A Storyteller who knows that the night's action will feature a presentation will probably want to do a bit of planning in advance. In addition to reviewing the character of the new Kindred, she should ensure that the prince, the sire and whichever other characters will have formal roles in the presentation are aware of their duties. The seneschal can usually be counted upon to brief the parties involved, but, unless the seneschal is deliberately being lax, it is a good idea to double-check. The Storyteller may want to confer with the players of the new character and any others who would be have information about her to work out whatever background is necessary. Nosferatu and harpies often have some sort of dirt on newcomers, but they are certainly not the only ones. Previous encounters and old comrades or rivals always make good hooks for drawing new characters into the story.

If it is a childe's presentation, the prince would be expected to know about it in advance, in most cases because she gave permission for the sire to create the childe. If there is enough time, the sire should have arranged in character for this presentation during the previous session. If the presentation involves a newcomer to the city, the prince may or may not expect her presence; if the prince would not know, the player need not be forewarned. The same is true for the other players. One final complication: If the seneschal has been selectively filtering the flow of information to the prince, the Storyteller might

want to confer with him instead of the prince, following the flow of information within the domain.

Finally, remember that presentation can be an ideal mechanism for introducing new characters and new players to an existing chronicle, or even for starting a chronicle. For a new player, presentation as a childe under the direction of an experienced sire (and player) can act as an informative rite of passage that brings her into the action, introduces her to the other players and gives her a general idea of what is going on. For an experienced player, presentation sans sire can serve the same purpose, but with more of a sink-or-swim ambiance.

GIVING THE PRINCE HER DUE

The prince of the city should have a significant say in the feel of a presentation — after all, the presentation is directed at her in her court. The character of the prince will be manifest in both the general feel of the presentation and the specific details. Most princes prefer presentations to be public affairs with as many of their subjects as possible present. Others prefer to limit the attendees to only the most trusted (or powerful) Kindred in their domains. Some princes employ formal scripts that they have used for centuries — and expect all visitors to know — while others are remarkably informal. A suspicious prince may ask questions about the genealogy, motivation and history of the presentee. A cautious prince may want to ensure that the new Kindred has an ironclad understanding of the Masquerade as the prince sees it. A Malkavian prince may want to know what dreams the character had yesterday and which internal organ he thinks is the prettiest. Of course, many princes like to employ *Majesty* for this initial interview to "give the right impression." In any event, the player of the prince will probably want to ensure that she has a presentation ritual worthy of her domain, after all, this will probably give the newcomer his first taste of what unlife will be like in this city.

The Storyteller may want to work with the player to create this ceremony, to rein in any creative or formal excesses the player may introduce. For example, it is generally not acceptable for the prince to force all newcomers to drink of her blood, and the rest of the troupe does not want to sit through an hour-long ceremony that makes jury duty look interesting.

While the prince may be the most visible personage, a well-done presentation should hint at the politics and powers behind the scenes. If the prince is beholden to some other power, some hints may arise, as she needs approval for what would normally be her sole prerogative. Some princes will introduce presentees to the primogen, the sheriff and other noteworthy Kindred. Others will leave it up to the vampires in question. Some will lavish time on the new vampires while others will have more important matters to attend to. In all cases, the character of the prince and her domain should be manifest in all that occurs, foreshadowing nights to come.

PRESENTING THE CHILDE

In essence, the presentation of a childe is a straightforward affair. The sire makes the necessary arrangements with the seneschal or in some cases, the prince. Then, at the appointed time, she brings the childe in and presents him. As noted above, the prince will probably have considerable say in the form of the presentation, shaping it to reflect her philosophy of leadership. In general, the presentation

of a childe will proceed along these lines: The sire calls for the attention of the prince; the sire introduces his childe; the prince questions the childe, and the prince acknowledges the childe. Any of these stages may be modified or even omitted to suit the character of the prince, and some princes have even added other events, such as questioning the sire or testing the childe with a simple ordeal. In most cases the sire can be presumed to have seen this ritual, or possibly even partaken in it as either childe or sire, so she should know what the prince expects and have schooled her childe in the appropriate behavior.

The presentation usually begins when the seneschal informs the prince that the sire is here to present her childe. In most situations, this is merely a formality, for the prince already knows that the presentation is planned. In cases where the prince and seneschal are not on the most open of terms, the seneschal could have kept the information from the prince, hoping to cause her discomfort. Alternately, the prince might spring the event on the seneschal, implying that he is not doing the job he is supposed to. Once the sire has been announced, the presentation proper begins. Some princes expect to be thanked for having given permission for the creation of a new childe, others want the whole business over as quickly as possible so they can get back to more important matters. In any event, the sire introduces her childe to the prince, and, if the prince so desires, the rest of the court. Some sires like to take this time to press their own agendas or tout their virtues or those of their new childe, while others merely call the new Cainite up.

As any new vampire is a risk to both the Masquerade and the safety of the prince's domain, most princes like to take the time to ensure that the new Cainite understands the rules of unlife among the Camarilla. Most princes will at least ask for a recitation of the childe's lineage and the Traditions, others may give the childe an impromptu test on the etiquette of unlife. The prince may want to prepare a speech or some set of questions and tests for the occasion, to help reinforce the nature of her court and her relationship with the sire and her new childe. A prince who favors the sire may praise her and try to form the questions in such a way that the new vampire appears clever. A prince who is resentful about giving permission for the embrace may make ask difficult questions or she may ask absurdly easy ones, implying that the sire could not possibly have trained the childe well enough to handle real problems. Throughout these proceedings, the seneschal or his secretary will probably want to take notes.

Unless the childe displays gross incompetence, the prince should recognize her, conferring the Status Trait of *Acknowledged*. The prince may give a little speech, may introduce the new neonate to the rest of her court, or she may just nod and grunt. Some princes even decline to formally acknowledge the childe, making it easier to remove her should she later prove to be a nuisance. Nevertheless, from that point on, the neonate is considered a full member of the Camarilla. If things go wrong, anything can result. The prince could declare that the childe is unready for Camarilla society, sending her away unacknowledged and stripping the sire of a Status Trait for making such a mistake. She could even demand he destruction of the errant childe, precipitating a dramatic flight from Elysium. Such events are rare, though, for a prince who does so too often makes many enemies, and the harpies start to question her ability to choose deserving sires.

A childe's presentation will probably be a harrowing experience for the character. Her performance will determine the course of her entire future, including whether she will have one at all. Though in all but the most unusual cases the childe will have at least one "friendly" face, her sire's, in the audience, she should be acutely aware that if she screws up, she may not only have to face her sire's wrath, but may be ordered destroyed by the prince. A childe has at least one advantage when she undergoes presentation, though. Since a childe's performance is a reflection upon the sire, a wise sire will almost certainly brief her childe about the presentation and what to expect. She will have given the new vampire tutelage in the Six Traditions and the Masquerade. She should also have told the childe about the clans and the other Cainites of the city, with special warnings about those who are working at cross-purposes to her. The sire's player or the Storyteller may even provide a cheat-sheet with this information that the player (not the character) can reference when all the new faces, names and questions get too confusing.

While a childe's presentation should be a harrowing experience for the character, it should not be harrowing for the player — challenging, maybe, but not harrowing. After all, the character is trying to prove herself worthy of immortality; the player is there to have fun. Other players should be sensitive to this distinction and the storyteller might want to have some distraction prepared if things look like they are getting too uncomfortable.

Presenting the Newcomer

Most presentations do not involve the debut of someone's childe. According to the Fifth Tradition, the prince expects all Kindred visiting a city to present themselves. As such, it is not uncommon for a Kindred from another city to arrive in the prince's court and present himself. Such presentations have a totally different feel from those of childer. For one thing, the presentee usually has no sire to tell him which Kindred are treacherous and only rumor and hearsay as guides to the city's politics. For another, the prince and the Kindred of the city may have no idea of who this new Cainite is. He could be a diablerist on the run from justice, a Sabbat spy trying to prepare the city for invasion, an archon who has heard some disturbing rumors about one of the primogen — anything. In these last nights, a proper sense of paranoia can go a long way toward staving off the Final Death.

The actual ritual of the presentation is usually as straightforward with a stranger as it is with a childe, and usually has the unique feel of the prince's court. In most cases, once the newcomer has made his way to Elysium, he asks the seneschal to see the prince. Once he has been shown in, the newcomer introduces himself and answers any of the prince's questions. If all goes well, the prince acknowledges the newcomer, and the night goes on with one more predator added to the mix.

First, in order to be presented, the newcomer must make his way to Elysium. Most prudent Kindred learn this location before they set out to a new city. Those without the foresight (or time or resources) to learn where Elysium is will have to make a Static Mental Challenge once per night to locate it. The Storyteller may want to simply repeat the challenges till the player succeeds and say that the character has been in town that number of nights, or she may

force the player to exist outside of Elysium, subject to the vicissitudes of nightly unlife until he finds his way there. Cainites who are known to have spent time in the domain before presenting themselves are usually viewed with greater suspicion, and if the prince hears of them, she may send the sheriff or the scourge to deal with them. Other Kindred who may have information or suspicions about the newcomer may also take action of their own.

Once reaching Elysium, he waits to be introduced to the prince. Unless sequestered in some out of the way place, he will probably spend his time sizing up the locals while they look him over. It is often considered rude to speak with a Kindred before he is presented, as some princes see that as a usurpation of their prerogative. If business as usual is underway, the newcomer may learn a lot before the prince admits him.

Once the presentee has been announced, he presents himself to the prince, usually identifying himself by name, clan and whatever else he feels is necessary, and asking permission to stay in the city for however long he feels he will need. Perhaps even more so than with a childe, most princes will want to query the newcomer about their history. Unless she already knows the vampire, most princes will at least ask for the Kindred's lineage and reason for being in town. These questions can be quite serious and in depth. If the prince has reason to suspect foul play, such as if the presentee was known to have been in town for a while before presenting himself, she may ask the sheriff to continue the questioning while she attends to other matters. The prince may also ask the other Kindred of the city if any know anything about the newcomer; harpies and Nosferatu are especially apt to have heard if the newcomer has done anything spectacular. If nothing seems amiss, the sheriff will return with the newcomer and so inform the prince. Naturally, the seneschal or his secretary will probably want to take notes of all that transpires.

Unless the court can prove foul play or bring other incriminating evidence to light, the prince will probably recognize the newcomer, granting him the *Acknowledged* Status Trait. Some princes will give the newcomer information on where not to go and what not to do; some will assign the job to the seneschal, sheriff or newcomer's clan primogen. A rare few expect the newcomer to learn the rules of her domain on their own. If the prince has reason, she may turn away the newcomer. The prince may also require that a Kindred who said he would only be staying for a brief while re-present himself if he needs to stay any longer.

After the presentation, the newcomer will probably get an opportunity to meet with most of the other characters and probably hear enough innuendo and gossip to have an idea of the most obvious factions and powers that be. As for everyone else, they will probably be working on factoring the presentee into their own schemes and questioning how much of what he told them about himself was true.

SAYING NO

Even in these increasingly paranoid times, it is rare for a prince to refuse a Cainite's petition to stay in the city. Nevertheless, there are certain conditions where it is commonplace to do so. Such situations include:

- The Kindred would represent a threat to the Masquerade in the city.
- The Kindred has a history of causing trouble.

- The Kindred shows signs of supporting one of the prince's rivals.
- The domain is already overcrowded.

In such cases, the prince may grant the newcomer a couple of nights to leave her domain, or she may demand that he be gone before sunrise. Such decisions usually depend on the nature of the prince and the perceived threat of the newcomer. In extreme cases, the prince may even arrange for incarceration and destruction, but she should be cautious in exercising such measures, for it may undercut the entire tradition of presentation within her domain — an undesirable development indeed.

JUSTICE

Even among the "civilized" vampires of the Camarilla, justice can be swift and harsh. In fact, draconian is a word that is often associated with Cainite justice. Though some Kindred scholars enjoy debating the exact origins and reasons behind this ferocity, most members of the Camarilla accept that it stems from their position as secret predators. Since vampires are so predatory, they do not accept many restrictions and laws. However, since their wariness of the power of humankind compels them to operate in secret, those few laws they do accept are vital to the survival of the entire race. They cannot risk the breaking of those rules and must stop any who would do so by whatever means necessary.

Within the Camarilla, the Traditions are the fundamental laws of Kindred society. All the other rules, strictures, ordinances, etc. are merely interpretations of and elaborations on those six laws. Naturally, each Kindred has a different interpretation of the limitations the Traditions impose. Within the Camarilla, only certain opinions truly matter, however. Most vampires see the prince and the justicars as the forces of justice, the princes on the local level and the justicars throughout the entire sect. While those two groups are certainly the most visible, the real situation is more complicated: The sheriffs, primogen, princes, archons, justicars and the Inner Circle each have a significant impact on the rules of undead existence.

THE LOCAL WORLD — PRINCELY JUSTICE

"The will of the city: The will of the prince." Behind the simple words of the old saying lies a complex web of power, debt and ambition. While it is true that the prince determines the shape of justice within her domain, there are many opportunities to subvert that justice, before, during and after it reaches the prince.

The easiest way to prevent the prince from punishing a crime is to ensure that she does not learn of it in the first place. Many sheriffs and lesser Kindred are willing to cover up for other vampires if there is something in it for them. Sheriffs and Nosferatu have been renowned for their ability to accumulate and use an impressive array of prestation debts. And since charges of violating the Masquerade are often fatal, such boons are often of high value. For this reason, princes and primogen often make it a habit to monitor the prestation balance of the sheriff to ensure that he does not gain too much power behind the scenes. Scourges are rarely thought of as engaging in this behavior, not only because they are already loathed on different grounds, but also because no one values having a thin-blooded Caitiff in debt.

In most cases, once the suspect has been brought before the prince, she listens to the charges and passes judgment. In cases where a Kindred is known to have committed a crime, or at least been convincingly accused, but has avoided capture by the sheriff, a prince may opt to pass judgment in absentia. Certain princes with a flair for the dramatic may choose to hold a trial to placate the prince's subjects should they question the guilt of the accused, especially in the case of particularly celebrated or notorious Kindred. Depending on the nature of the prince and the nature of the crime, the trial may be a public one where any Kindred who wishes to attend court may observe if not participate, or it may be sequestered behind closed doors with only those the prince allows to attend. Some princes favor the Napoleonic mode of trial where they alone are entitled to ask questions, and whomever they ask had better answer quickly and completely. Other princes, usually those who have spent the majority of their existence in the United States, allow the accuser and the accused a chance to present their cases in their own words or to call upon advocates, witnesses or allies to speak on their behalf. Unless there is some other agenda involved, the word of one of the Camarilla officers typically holds more sway than that of a less illustrious vampire. In almost all cases, the courts of the Camarilla completely ignore the United States' Fifth Amendment.

Once the prince has reached a verdict, she must convey it, along with any sentence, to the court. The prince may make the pronouncement herself, or she may delegate the job to another Kindred or servant. If the verdict is guilty but the Cainite in question is not in custody, the prince may require that the Kindred of the city provide any and all aid in bringing him to justice. In the event that the sentence is destruction, the prince may order a blood hunt.

If the primogen disagree with the prince's verdict strongly enough to confront him, they may attempt to reverse his decision as described in **Laws of the Night** p. 221. Storytellers may want to handle this by secret ballot, asking each primogen privately for the number of Status Traits she is willing to devote to this cause. Once all of the Traits are allocated, the Storyteller or Narrator compares the total with the prince's permanent Status Traits and announces who is victorious.

CRIMES...

Most crimes are broken down according to the tradition they violate. While the Camarilla usually holds the First Tradition as the most important of the six, the breaking of any Tradition is a serious offense. Though princes usually determine punishment by the severity of the offense rather than which particular Tradition was broken, they like to be able to cite the Tradition that was broken as a means of establishing the legitimacy of their ruling. Seneschals and harpies often like to keep track of such things for their own reasons as well.

The First Tradition: The Masquerade

Breaches to the Masquerade can range from leaving blood-drained corpses to transforming from a fanged human into a bat in front of the audience at a rock concert. This tradition can cover any activity that could hint at the presence of vampires. Additionally, since psychic investigators, the Society of Leopold, etc. have shown interest in other mystic manifestations than the vampiric, most princes include any obviously supernatural activities even if they are not uniquely vampiric in nature. Finally, this Tradition covers the dissemination of information about the Kindred and their activities even if no demonstration is included.

The Second Tradition: Domain

Other than the Masquerade, the Second Tradition, the Tradition of Domain accounts for the most common and most varied assortment of Camarilla crimes. The reason for this is simple: The city is the prince's domain. Therefore, anything that interferes with the prince's control of the city can be depicted as a breach of the Second Tradition. Anything. Many princes have used this as a means of persecuting their rivals and enemies; almost as many have brought about their downfall by abusing this power.

Additionally, this condition passes down to the lesser domains the prince has designated throughout the city. A Cainite who interferes with the sheriff's patrol or hides some of the seneschal's notes can be charged with crimes against the Tradition of Domain as easily as someone who invades the haven of another Kindred.

The Third Tradition: Progeny

In most cases crimes against the Third Tradition are fairly straightforward: If a Kindred has sired a childe without the permission of the prince, he is guilty. Some princes have taken this one step farther and declared that the creation of ghouls also falls under this Tradition; others claim that unauthorized ghouling is a breach of the Masquerade. This debate has kept advocates entertained for almost a century.

The Fourth Tradition: Accounting

The Tradition of the Accounting is mostly used to punish Kindred who are unwise in their choice of childer. Usually the prince employs this tradition to include the sire of an offending childe in any punishments she may devise. Some princes have also employed this tradition to entrap Cainites who manage to wriggle out of charges based on the Third Tradition.

The Fifth Tradition: Hospitality

In order to properly govern her domain, the prince needs to be aware of the Kindred within. For this reason, most princes take the Tradition of Hospitality very seriously. Any Cainite new to the city who does not present himself to the prince as quickly as possible, preferably on the night that he arrives, is in violation of this Tradition. If he eventually deigns to call upon the prince or is brought in by the sheriff, it is within the prince's rights to charge him with breach of Hospitality. Ignorance of etiquette or how to contact the prince is never considered a valid defense.

The Sixth Tradition: Destruction

The Sixth Tradition is the Camarilla's answer to the Fifth Commandment: "Thou shalt not kill... without the prince's permission." This Tradition only applies to Kindred of the Camarilla whom the prince has acknowledged. The prince usually will not punish the slaying of mortals, ghouls, Sabbat and other creatures unless the murder broke one of the other Traditions. The Sixth Tradition also covers diablerie, which regularly carries the harshest of penalties.

...AND PUNISHMENTS

Camarilla justice is not as bound by jurisprudence as mortal justice. So long as she does not offend her subjects to the point of rebellion, the prince is more or less free to apply any punishment she desires. Some princes strive for

ironic justice, shaping the punishment to fit the crime; others simply select the harshest punishment they can justify, trusting that it will discourage any further offenses. In most cases, diablerie and breaches of the Masquerade are met with Final Death, preferably after slow torture.

Below is a selection of punishments in descending order of severity. There are, of course, more penalties than these as princes are known to be quite inventive in this respect.

Final Death: The criminal is beheaded, burnt or otherwise slain so that there is no hope of return.

Death/torpor: The criminal is forced into torpor, either through blood loss, injury or both.

Long-term staking: The criminal is staked through the heart and either hidden or placed on display.

Draining and exile: The criminal is almost completely drained of vitae and then driven from the city.

Exile: The criminal is driven from the city.

Blood bonding: The criminal is forced to drink the blood of another Kindred of the court over three successive nights. Most commonly, the criminal is blood bound to the prince, one or more of the primogen, or the victim of the crime.

Enforced Servitude: The criminal is forced to serve another Kindred, possibly even a ghoul.

Torture: The criminal is forced to endure some physical, psychological or social torture.

Draught of blood: The criminal is forced to drink the blood of another Kindred of the court once or twice, bringing them closer to a blood bond or bringing them into one if they have already drunk of that vampire's vitae.

Loss of station: The criminal is removed from an office in the court and loses all associated perks, perquisites and Status Traits.

Loss of property: The criminal is deprived of some possession. This can include the destruction of a childe or a ghoul.

It is also worth noting that the actual form of the punishment can vary extensively. One crime may merit death by sunlight while another may only receive death by beheading. One prince may exile a criminal by leaving him by the side of the road in the Lupine-infested countryside; another may have a blood hunt drive him from the city; another may construct a catapult to throw the criminal across the local river. Ultimately, it is the prince's choice.

CAMARILLA JUSTICE

In certain cases — usually when a prince or other powerful Cainite is accused — the situation escalates. One or more of the Camarilla's justicars may enter the picture. Such a momentous event is usually terrifying for all Cainites in the affected city, since justicars are empowered to use whatever means are necessary to protect the Camarilla and have the power to do so. In most cases, the justicar will arrive only after one of her archons investigates the situation, so the local Kindred may have a slight warning — if the archon's presence is obvious. Even then, it is possible that the archon will be able to rectify the

situation himself — a situation made easier by the near-universal desire of the vampiric populace to avoid the attention of the justicar. The sections on archons and conclaves (below) handle such events more fully.

THE BLOOD HUNT

The blood hunt — called the Lextalionis by older Cainites — is one of the nastiest weapons in the prince's arsenal: the Sixth Tradition made manifest in the streets of the city. At the command of the prince, all Kindred within her domain are granted the authority to destroy the quarry and forbidden to aid her in any manner. In certain cases, the prince may demand that her subjects actively participate in the Lextalionis, forcing the rapid and complete destruction of the heinous criminal. At least that is the theory. In fact, the city's Cainites often use the cover of the blood hunt to take care of other business as well.

THE HUE AND CRY

A prince may declare a blood hunt if some Kindred within her domain has evaded more conventional justice and the crime is grave enough. She may command the presence of all Kindred in her domain and make a public proclamation, stating the name and crimes of the subject, or she may issue the edict to the sheriff and the primogen with the expectation that they pass it along to those under their sway. From time to time, other Kindred may presume to invoke the Lextalionis, sometimes in the prince's name, sometimes in their own. This act is considered a breach of the Second Tradition. Both the instigator of the hunt and any who participate in it can expect to feel the prince's wrath. Even if the hunt was in the prince's best interests, many princes feel personally affronted that any would pretend to her powers.

The speed with which the Lextalionis is prosecuted often depends on the popular sentiment behind the prince's edict. If the primogen or other Kindred see the blood hunt as merely the persecution of one of the prince's rivals, they are far less likely to pursue it as avidly as if they believed that the subject was a threat to their own unlives or the author of some truly heinous crime. In general, Kindred will not look too askance at a prince who calls a blood hunt for a Kindred who has brought other Kindred to Final Death or committed diablerie, seriously threatened the Masquerade, conspired with the Sabbat or in other ways presented a threat to the Kindred of the city. Cainites are less concerned with Kindred who might pose a risk or inconvenience to the prince's political career and start to get paranoid when the prince begins invoking the Lextalionis over such minor matters. In such cases, they might also start looking toward the replacement of such an extreme ruler.

Another factor that shapes a blood hunt is the urgency behind it. In many cases, the prince is not so interested in the destruction of the Kindred in question as she is in his removal from her domain. Used in this fashion, a blood hunt can serve as a form of permanent exile. After all, most Cainites are inclined to avoid locations where the entire Kindred populace is authorized to destroy — and maybe even diablerize — them. At the other end of the scale, the prince may require all Kindred in her domain to actively seek to destroy the quarry. In such cases, the prince usually establishes some sort of reward for the Kindred who destroys the criminal, ranging from the criminal's possessions to the prince's favor (a Status Trait) to the station of the sheriff (who should have brought in the criminal in the first place). As an

added bonus, it has become tradition that whoever brings down the prey has tacit permission to diablerize him. A prince may explicitly forbid this, but unless she does, most of the hunters will be out for blood.

There are certain rules that apply to blood hunts, and all Kindred within the domain should know them or risk becoming the quarry of the next blood hunt. Though each prince is different and may adjust these rules as she sees fit, the following principles apply to almost all blood hunts. The first and most obvious rule

CUTTING TO THE CHASE

Storytelling a blood hunt can be incredibly complicated for it will likely involve all players at their craftiest and most active. Storytellers may want to segregate the quarry, only allowing him to communicate with the others through a designated Narrator to keep the hunters and the prey from being influenced by each other's plans.

Another area that may require special attention is the use of Influence Traits. The volatile situation may force players to use Influence in desperate ways they have not needed before. As a rule of thumb, if a player can justify it convincingly, a Narrator may let him affect an area in which she does not have Influence by allocating one more trait than would be spent by someone who did have influence in that area. If the Narrator is not convinced, she may ask that more influence be spent or simply disallow the result entirely.

Example of play: *Kascha has* Underworld *x 4 Influence, which she hopes to use to prevent Ko-Ko from escaping on a boat from pier 44. Since the Narrator feels that it would only take* Transportation *x 2 to stop the boat, he rules that Kascha needs to spend 3 of her* Underworld *influence to get the Rugsuckers to put the muscle on pier 44. If Kascha had had* Church *x 4 Influence instead, she would have been out of luck because there is no reasonable way for the local parishioners to affect Ko-Ko's boat.*

This can also apply to situations where a Kindred has the right sort of Influence, but in the wrong location or institution. A Narrator may allow a character whose Underworld Influence is tied to the East End street gangs to get them to "call in some favors" and grant him use of the talents of the Russian Mafia for the night — at the price of one or more extra Influence Traits.

In cases where two Kindred are attempting to use Influence on the same institution, the Narrator may resolve the power struggle with a challenge using the Influence Traits in question. In these cases, the Kindred trying to muscle in is still at a penalty because he is using his Influence in an unusual environment. On the other hand, if the Kindred who originally had Influence in that area is not even using a single Trait to keep an eye on his people, the interloper's pawns may be able to get in and get what they want before he even realizes that his assets are being used by another.

is that none are allowed to aid the fugitive or interfere with the hunters. The blood hunt is a matter of princely justice, not of sport or friendship. Even if the prince has not compelled universal involvement in the blood hunt, helping the criminal in any way is considered itself a crime. The second vital rule is that the Masquerade must not become a victim of the hunt. Certain Kindred find it all too easy to get caught up in the thrill of the hunt, but it is vital for them to realize that it does no good to bring down the criminal if a greater crime is committed in doing so. The third rule is that the hunt ends at the city limits. This is not so much a law as a rule of thumb; the prince will punish no one for carrying the hunt further — unless she violates another prince's domain. Taking the Lextalionis beyond city limits — as defined by the prince's control, not by lines on maps — is simply too risky. Additionally, some princes use the blood hunt as a form of permanent exile. They do not actually wish the fugitive destroyed, just out of their city. Hunters could easily fall afoul of Lupines, Sabbat packs or the quarry's confederates as they stray from their home turf. The fourth rule is that the hunt stops only with the destruction of the quarry. Even if the prince who called the hunt dies, even if later evidence exonerates the quarry, even if the quarry escapes to another city or continent, the quarry's name stays in the annals of the city and the hunt continues.

In addition to the standard rules, the prince may establish rules of her own, either for all blood hunts within her domain or on a case-by-case basis. A prince may declare that diablerie is unequivocally forbidden or that only Tremere are allowed to carry out the hunt within a three-block radius of their chantry. If she fears the quarry of being a diabolist, she may insist that the Tremere take an active role. These addenda are entirely the prerogative of the prince, but it is the duty of all Kindred within the city to be aware of them.

The blood hunt ends when the quarry has been dispatched — met his Final Death. The victor returns with whatever proof the prince has demanded and claims any prize the prince may offer. If the quarry escapes, the hunt is not considered completed. Still, should the prey escape the city — or fool the remaining Cainites into believing that he did — the blood hunt is effectively over until he shows his face again. Despite the hunt being finished for all practical purposes, it is technically still active until proof of the fugitive's death is brought back to the prince — even if it is a different prince from the one who ordered the hunt in the first place.

THE HUNTERS...

Kindred join the blood hunt in different ways, in varying degrees and with different motives. Some have a personal stake in bringing down the hunted. Others see the hunt as a license to practice their skills and a chance to experience the thrill of hunting the most dangerous of prey. Still others are looking for a way to advance themselves by demonstrating their ability, and the blood hunt is just another theatre for grandstanding. Of course some Kindred may side with the prey — or at least against the prince. There are those who are uninterested in the entire thing and just want to continue with business as usual. Finally, there are those who want to use the distraction provided by the blood hunt to cover other, shadier activities.

Those who take an active part in the blood hunt have several avenues open to them. They may physically take to the streets, rooftops, sewers or whatever in

hopes of tracking the fugitive and bringing him down. A city is a big place, though, and it is often difficult to locate a single vampire within it. Still, if the prey is not yet aware of the blood hunt, or needs to take care of certain things before he flees the city, knowledgeable or lucky Kindred may manage to catch him by heading straight for the prey's haven. Others may seek out his favorite haunts or begin patrolling the typical escape routes from the city.

Cainites who have the resources and Influence Traits may use these to aid their search. *Police, Street, Transportation* and *Underworld* Influence can be particularly useful in such situations, but depending on the moves of the prey and the ingenuity of the hunter, almost any influence may turn out useful. In most cases, the hunting Cainite will only want to use their mortal pawns to search for and inconvenience the prey. After all, if the entire architecture department vanishes on a field trip she sponsored to the old sanitarium, it is bound to have negative effects on the university's willingness to follow her advice. Nevertheless, such information can let the hunter place herself at the right place at the right time, and often that is what hunting is all about. Another use for Influences is counteracting any influence the prey may have. It is not uncommon for a hunted vampire to use the mortals under his sway to create diversion or trouble for those who are now tormenting him. While protecting against this may not be the most glorious role in the hunt, it is ideal for elders who do not feel inclined to traipse through the street looking for some pathetic fool of a neonate.

Not all of the so-called hunters will be after the prey named by the prince. Blood hunts are dangerous events and all sorts of mistakes can happen. It is not unheard of for Kindred to take advantage of the chaos to take care of business that would be too risky at other times. After all, if one of the other hunters goes missing, who is to say that the hunted did not manage to turn the tables at some point in the chase? Other, less deadly tricks include ransacking another Cainite's turf or haven under the guise of searching for the quarry, striking at a rival's herd and planting evidence or bugs for use at a later date.

Some of the city's Kindred may decide not to take an active role in the blood hunt. Under ordinary circumstances, they can get away with continuing their nightly routine, possibly warning the quarry away if they should happen to cross paths. In those cases where the prince has ordered the participation of all local Kindred, these vampires may still evade the issue by hunting in unlikely locations, using their Influence ineffectively or being so obvious that the prey could hardly fail to avoid him. This can be dangerous, for these apathetic participants run the risk of being labeled as collaborating with the quarry, and thus being thrust into an even more active role in the next blood hunt.

Finally, there will be those Kindred who are willing to go against the prince's orders and help the prey. They may do this because the prey is an ally, because they wish to humiliate the prince, because they need the chaos to last just a few nights longer for another of their schemes, or for any number of other reasons. Actively aiding the quarry can be even more difficult than hunting him. Unless the hunter and the fugitive have some previous plan for such situations, she will have to locate the prey without letting the other hunters know what she is doing and convince the prey that she is an ally. If the hunter and prey did have a plan set up for this situation, the hunter will still have to be cautious, for so close an ally is likely to be under intense scrutiny during such a hunt. An easier technique is to create diversions that draw

the attention of the other hunters. Those who would aid the hunted must be especially subtle and careful, for being caught can prove quite fatal.

...AND THE HUNTED

Being the target of a blood hunt is a terrifying, nerve-wracking experience for anyone who survives it. Though he is unlikely to encounter packs of vampires driving him through the streets — too much chance of damaging the Masquerade — he has to contend with his status as hunter reversing to that of prey. Worse, the fugitive has an idea of how powerful his pursuers are: Even now the Tremere could be tracking his movements through *Thaumaturgy*; there could be a Nosferatu across the street from him waiting to call in the Brujah, or the sheriff might have issued an APB to the police with his name and description. What can he do?

Unless the prey is suicidal or insane, his options usually take three forms: run, distract or fight back. In the long term, it is unlikely that a single Kindred can take on an entire city, so fleeing is the most likely long-term goal. Many cautious Cainites set up stashes of clothes, money and weapons in and around the city for emergencies such as this. If the Kindred is willing, he might be able to grab his stash and take the first bus to Kansas City before a strike closes the bus station down.

Sometimes the quarry has a couple of last chores to take care of, or his primary escape route is blocked. In those cases, he may try to throw his pursuers off his tail by creating distractions. Prey with Influence Traits can usually wreak enough havoc to force some of the other Kindred to devote their efforts to damage control. *Media, Police, Street, Transportation* and *Underworld* Influence can be especially helpful to the creative and desperate fugitive. Quarries often intentionally breach the Masquerade in their escape effort; after all, their pursuers are not allowed to do so and might even feel compelled to stop and patch things up. This can make things bad for the fugitive further down the road, though. Should he escape the blood hunt in his home city, he will probably want to settle down somewhere else. While a nearby prince may be willing to harbor the fugitive just to annoy her neighbor, it is unlikely that she will want to let someone who blatantly broke the Masquerade into her domain.

Finally, there comes a time when the prey must stand and fight. Clever quarries are likely to try to pick the time and place for this stand, either because he is intimately familiar with the terrain, or because he has taken the time to booby-trap it. Fleeing Gangrel have often noticed that pursuit slows down after the first Kindred encounters the punji sticks. Needless to say, a quarry stands a better chance if he can spread his pursuers apart and attack them one by one.

THE QUARRY RETURNS

From time to time, the subject of a blood hunt is constrained to return to a city in which he is hunted. Such things happen. Princes and other notable Kindred often take renewed offense at those who dare to taunt them by returning to a domain in which they are under threat of the Lextalionis. Worse, old allies may have grown distant over the time of his absence, so he should not count on their support. In most cases, the best the returning quarry can do is to lie low and try to complete whatever business has brought him back before the sheriff or the prince becomes aware of his return.

In certain cases, such as when a different prince has taken over or when new evidence has cleared the quarry of whatever transgression got him subject to the Lextalionis in the first place, the repatriate may not need to be so circumspect. It is often enough that he not flaunt his return. He should stay on his toes, though, for a tradition of pardon never made its way into Cainite justice, so he is still technically a wanted vampire. Any old rival or pack of neonates could decide to destroy him and still technically be operating within the prince's authority, so even under less hostile conditions, he would do well to be careful.

Climax or Anticlimax

Finally, either the prey will be captured and destroyed, he will be known to have escaped, or he will elude his pursuers long enough that they believe he has escaped. If there is a victorious hunter, the prince should recognize and possibly reward him. Otherwise, the prince will probably chastise her subjects for letting the prey escape, and another bogeyman will enter the city's history.

Archons

Archons are the eyes and ears of the justicars, and as such represent the first line of Camarilla justice above the level of the prince. Since princes can go bad, since traitors can move from one city to another, since some problems are hard to notice unless you can take in the big picture, the Camarilla appoints six justicars, one from each clan, to serve as sect-wide troubleshooters. And since the six justicars cannot possibly cover all the trouble there is to shoot, they employ archons. Whenever a justicar hears a rumor or gets a message about something troubling in a certain region, he sends one or more of his archons to investigate. If the archon finds that there is trouble, but nothing serious, he gives the prince or sheriff some advice on how to handle the situation and a warning that it had better be cleaned up when he returns. If he finds serious trouble, he takes care of it. If he can provide a good reason, an archon is exempt from the Sixth Tradition: He is allowed to kill with impunity. If he finds really serious trouble, he calls in his employer, one of the justicars, and matters escalate, possibly to the point of a judicial conclave. If an archon finds no trouble, he just keeps looking: No visible trouble just means that the problem is well–hidden.

Justicars may call upon archons to investigate rumors of collusion with anarchs, the Sabbat or demons; repeated or widespread failure of the Masquerade; evidence that a prince is subverting the Traditions, and any number of other problems that local princes either cannot or will not be handle. While archons may employ ghouls or younger Kindred to handle drudge work, most expect and are expected to be totally self sufficient, only contacting their patron justicars when their investigations are complete or to present regular status reports. An archon can go for weeks without contacting her employer, especially when operating under cover. This habit may have disastrous results if a justicar fails to realize that something untoward had happened to his archon.

Justicars usually select their archons from the ranks of the ancillae and younger elders — somewhere between three and six centuries old. They select Kindred of this age because they have the power and experience that comes with age, but are not yet so ossified in their ways as to be completely out of touch with the modern world. This is an important consideration since many of the problems they encounter are of modern origin. Archons almost always appear

to be incredibly competent and resourceful, blending centuries of experience in a wide range of situations with a ruthless will to get the job done. In broad terms, archons usually operate in two different modes: openly, employing shock, interrogation and intimidation; and clandestinely, employing research, subtle queries and spying. Though the typical archon can adopt whichever role he feels would be more productive, most have a preferred *modus operandi*. On those rare occasions when archons travel in teams, it is common for one archon to take on the role of public distraction while the other investigates covertly.

Regardless of which method the archon intends to employ, the first thing he usually does is research. He learns as much as he can about the city and its inhabitants from any trustworthy sources — sources whose information has usually been accurate in the past and who can be relied on not to let the subjects in question know that they have been inquired about. This information is important for several reasons: It may provide vital clues in and of itself; it gives the archon an idea of what to expect so he can recognize anomalous behavior, and it gives him an idea of what lies he should employ to make his investigation fruitful.

> • An archon receives the following two additional Status Traits: *Empowered* and *Feared*. The character can never lose these Traits permanently while remaining an archon.
>
> • When operating in an official capacity, an archon may remove a permanent Status Trait from any Kindred attempting to hinder his investigation or the sentence he has pronounced. This removal costs the archon nothing, and only a justicar can reverse it.
>
> • When operating in an official capacity, an archon can detain, interrogate or destroy any Kindred, though he will need to present evidence to his justicar to justify his actions.

MOLES

In most cases, when an archon is instructed to investigate a situation, he enters the city quietly, either avoiding the scrutiny of the prince and her court or presenting himself as some other Kindred in town on some other business. The justicars, who know that there is nothing like the arrival of an investigator to make evidence take flight, inevitably sanction this defiance of the Fifth Tradition. Usually archons adopt a disguise of some sort so they do not need to avoid the scourge or the sheriff. In most cases these Kindred represent little threat to one as skilled as an archon, but everyone get suspicious when rumors spread about the new Caitiff beating up the scourge.

Archons often present themselves as businessmen, Noddist scholars, historians or whatever other guise would allow them to nose around without arousing more suspicion than necessary. They often ask innocuous questions on a wide variety of subjects, not focusing on the matter they are investigating and being careful not to lead those they question to draw any dangerous conclusions. No Cainite is totally harmless, and all archons know that to other Kindred there is nothing more suspicious than a harmless vampire. For this reason, their covers usually suggest a threat directed far enough away that the locals feel they have nothing to worry about.

At the same time that the archon is interviewing the local Kindred, any subordinates and ghouls he may have will perform less sensitive, more time-consuming research, looking for supporting facts or suspicious trends. They may also reside in other cities, waiting to provide corroboration should anyone bother to verify the archon's cover, and then warn the archon that someone is checking up on him. As a final contingency, these deputies are sometimes told how to contact the justicar should the archon fall afoul, but most archons would rather trust their ability to get out of a tight situation than face the displeasure and embarrassment of their employer arriving for a false alarm.

SHOWMEN

Other times, archons announce their arrival with an imperious air and a list of commandments that sends every Cainite within a ten-mile radius scurrying to comply. Part bluff and part inquisition, this ploy is used when the archons feel that the threat is likely to make a mistake under pressure or when time constraints preclude an in-depth investigation. One of the more popular twists on this technique is for the archon to appear to be hunting for one criminal when he is really after another. Another trick is for the archon to create a stir and set his subordinates to snare anyone attempting to flee. The third and most common variation is to first complete a covert investigation in disguise and then make a grand entrance, displaying an uncanny understanding of the inhabitants of a city that he has presumably never visited before. In this scenario, the archon may either set his subordinates to acting as assistant interrogators, sticking their noses into any and all Kindred affairs, adding to the pressure; or he may set them to quietly watching his suspects, waiting for any false move. In the rare circumstances where he has enough deputies, he may use them both ways.

...AND JUSTICARS

There are six justicars within the Camarilla, one for each clan. Each archon reports to one of these justicars, and while archons are impressive in their own right, the abilities of the six that the Inner Circle selects to police the sect are downright terrifying. Details and official **Vampire: The Masquerade** stats for the current justicars can be found in **Children of the Night**, but the Storyteller is encouraged modify or even re-write these characters to suit her own chronicle. These Cainites possess great power and experience, which they will not hesitate to use should they feel the need to visit the story's city. And they *will* feel it is important to visit if one of their archons experiences foul play in there.

THE RED LIST

Over the years and across the world, certain Cainites have managed through infamy or treachery to arouse the hatred of the entire Camarilla. These creatures are known collectively and individually as Anathema, and in the halls of Elysia everywhere, the Red List records their names and crimes. Anyone on the Red List is effectively subject to a permanent blood hunt in any Camarilla-controlled territory. Mere membership in the Sabbat, mere diablerie, mere infernalism are not enough to condemn one to the Red List; only actions so monstrous that they are infamous even among vampires suffices for this "honor."

Two justicars must concur that the crimes of the villain are sufficiently heinous to call a conclave concerning the matter. At the conclave, the

justicars present their evidence and recite the crimes. The assembled Cainites pass judgment upon the villain. Unless someone can present a convincing reason why the accused should not be condemned, the accused is added to the Red List. The only way to get off the list is to die. The Red List is ranked according to the infamy of the convicted, not that the average Kindred stands a chance against even the lowliest Anathema.

ALASTORS

Alastors are the direct, secret servants of the Inner Council. Though they perform other duties, alastors devote most of their effort to the unremitting hunt of the Anathema. Alastors are usually secretly recruited from the ranks of the most capable archons — so secretly that to most members of the Camarilla, the alastors are little more than a rumor. The only other Kindred enlisted as alastors are those rare vampires who manage to destroy an Anathema on their own; any character who does so is immediately recruited.

In addition to those listed below, alastors also receive an astonishing array of perks, including the severance of blood bonds, training in rare Disciplines and lavish amounts of money and other resources. Each alastor receives different bonuses to compensate for agreeing to an eternal unlife hunting the most dangerous creatures known to the Camarilla. Within the rarified ranks of the alastors is another, more elite group called the Red Alastors, composed of those who have managed to destroy one of the five highest-ranked Anathema. Red Alastors are rumored to possess even greater authority and power than regular alastors.

> • A character recruited to the ranks of the alastors receives the following two additional Status Traits: *Sanctioned* and *Feared*. Short of being declared Anathema herself, the character can never lose these Traits permanently.
>
> • An alastor may remove a permanent Status Trait from any Kindred attempting to hinder her mission. This removal costs the alastor nothing.
>
> • An alastor is granted immunity to prosecution on any scale lower than a conclave.

The Trophy

The Camarilla heaps great rewards upon those who destroy its most hated enemies. Any character who kills one of the Anathema is granted all of her prey's possessions, entry into the ranks of the alastors and the Trophy. Also called "The Mark of the Beast," the Trophy is a tattoo of ink and blood that is thaumaturgically applied to the right palm. Once applied, the Trophy stays with the vampire forever, and can be detected even through gloves, though only justicars, elite archons and other Kindred in the know recognize it for what it is.

The Trophy exists for the protection of the alastor, so that an archon can tell the prince that she should not call a blood hunt on the Cainite who just decimated her city. It also exists as a precautionary measure, for alastors are prohibited from diablerizing their prey, and any alastor who breaks that

injunction or who defects from the Camarilla is a dangerous enemy who must be destroyed post haste.

ANATHEMA

It takes a special sort of vampire to be condemned to the Red List. Though creatures other than vampires occasionally make it to the Red List, it is a rare occurrence — the Red List is a Kindred institution. Each Anathema is a powerful, cunning and dangerous being, easily capable of tearing a city apart and certainly able to destroy a few foolish neonates who decide to go after it. In the past, the ranks of the Anathema have included carriers of mystical diseases, Sabbat warlords, serial diablerists, infernalists, threats to the Masquerade and other horrors that even the Kindred fear. It should go without saying that Anathema are Storyteller characters. Unless it is the central theme of the story, the Storyteller should not allow a player to control of one of these hunted pariahs.

Each Anathema is a different being with unique motivations. The only common thread among the Anathema is that the Camarilla views them as supreme threats. Storytellers should craft Anathema to suit the themes and logistics of their stories. If the story revolves around intrigue, the Anathema can add a new complication to the table. If the story focuses on the struggle against the Beast, the Anathema can represent the ultimate manifestation of the Beast run rampant. If the story centers around fate and self-determination, the Anathema could have been made what it is through forces beyond its control — or entirely of its own volition. Anathema are larger than unlife creatures that can be used to encapsulate the worst, and possibly even the best, of what it is to be Kindred.

An Anathema does not even need to make a physical appearance in a city to have his power felt. Mere rumor of the presence of one can send most Camarilla Kindred into paranoid cowardice or glory-hounding avarice, and the Trophy can be an attractive reward to those who know about it. Some characters may feel sympathy for an Anathema (especially if the Storyteller created the Anathema for just that purpose) and even try to aid it. This is a dangerous path, for the Anathema are understandably cautious and rarely gentle, even with their few allies. Even if the character survives the visit of the Anathema, odds of her surviving the subsequent encounter with the pursuing alastor are almost zero. Storytellers and players should remember that Anathema are deadly to characters and dangerous to plot lines, but what is the fun in playing if you cannot play with fire every now and then?

> • The tales and rumors of the Anathema attribute such power to them that they may be considered to have as many extra *Feared* Social Traits as the storyteller deems appropriate. Naturally, these Traits can only be used against Kindred who know what they are dealing with.

CONCLAVES

There are times when a situation requires the resources of more than just the Kindred of a given city. At those times, for those situations, the Camarilla holds conclaves. A conclave is a grand meeting of Kindred: All the Camarilla vampires who hear of it are invited to attend. Hundreds of vampires make their way to the city for the purpose of determining the solution to the problem at hand and for commingling with others of their kind. Technically, there are three kinds of conclaves: Grand conclaves are huge international affairs in response to truly momentous events. Regional conclaves concern matters in several cities or a part of a continent. Judicial conclaves are trials conducted for Cainites whose age or power puts them above princely justice. Any conclave is a rare and momentous event.

SETTING UP

Even the smaller conclaves are difficult events that strain the abilities of the Kindred hosting them. Even before word has gone out about the conclave, the hosting prince and her staff have begun the complicated and delicate process of preparation, and for weeks after, they may be forced to clean up the detritus left behind.

There must be some matter of vital importance to the Camarilla as a whole, or at least a large segment of it, to justify the trouble and expense of hosting a conclave. Justicars have called conclaves to deal with renegade princes, to discuss Camarilla policy toward the Internet, to prevent inter-clan strife and to debate how to contain the Anarch Free States.

Only justicars are allowed to call a conclave. On rare occasions, a prince whose reputation is well respected by the Inner Circle may get away with it, but it is usually safer for her to convince an archon that a situation merits this sort of attention and hope he convinces his superior. Most justicars feel that princes are too parochial in their outlook, more interested in the welfare of their domains than the Camarilla as a whole. Justicars are also unhappy about others encroaching on their authority.

Once a justicar has determined that there is a matter of sufficient gravity to warrant a conclave, he must choose the location. Most justicars prefer cities away from the epicenter of the problem so the attendees are safe from its immediate effects. Justicars may also select the site based upon the capabilities of nearby princes. Since hosting a conclave successfully brings no small amount of prestige, justicars sometimes try to give the opportunity to princes of their own clan.

The justicar usually informs the prince of the hosting city four to eight weeks in advance, but he may give less notice for particularly pressing matters. The prince is, of course, free to decline the honor, but doing so suggests that the prince is not as capable as she should be. This makes the dubious prince and her domain a likely candidate for investigation after the current crisis has been dealt with. In most cases, the prince simply accepts and redoubles her efforts to sweeping whatever problems are vexing her under the rug.

As soon as a prince learns that she is expected to host a conclave, she will probably want to summon all her trusted assistants and begin making prepa-

rations. Some princes have contingency plans in place for just such an event; others improvise. Should the justicar doubt the prince's competence, he may assign some of his archons to aid (or direct) her staff. Specifically, the justicar is expected to name the Kindred in charge of security for the conclave. If he does not choose an archon, the chosen Kindred effectively gains the rank of archon and all its privileges.

Among the many matters the prince and her staff must contend with are security, should the Sabbat or anarchs decide to mount an offensive; accommodations for the city's guests, especially the more volatile and less publicly presentable ones, and an appropriate location for the conclave itself. They must also ensure that there is an adequate source of vitae, particularly difficult given that many Ventrue are reticent about letting others learn the specifics of their rarefied needs. Some princes also take this time to clean house, shoring up alliances and taking care of those little annoyances that could embarrass them during the upcoming event.

It is impossible to keep all these preparations secret, though all princes at least make the effort. Within a few nights, the Nosferatu and any Kindred who frequent Elysium will certainly realize that something is happening. Though disseminating rumors and information about such proceedings is forbidden both for reasons of security and propriety, it usually takes less than a week for all the Kindred of the city to figure out that a conclave is coming. The information can even spread to other cities.

Most justicars announce the date and location of the conclave approximately a month in advance. Smaller conclaves may be held with less notice, but it's polite to give the invitees enough time to get their affairs in order before they are asked to travel on business. In most cases, this announcement takes place in the court of the hosting prince and travels through the Camarilla by word of mouth. All Camarilla who hear of the conclave are invited to attend, but most only show if the conclave concerns some matter of interest to them. This means that the primogen of Lisbon will probably not feel the need to attend a conclave dealing with a rash of infernalism in Detroit, though a Tremere scholar who investigated a similar event in the 18th century may feel compelled to make the trip. In certain cases, a rare independent is allowed in as well, but she will be carefully monitored. The Sabbat are more likely to be topics of conclaves than participants; it is difficult to imagine a situation where they would be invited.

Kindred may start to arrive in the city as early as a week before the conclave. Though everyone is busy, the prince is expected to allow all guests to present themselves. Justicars frown on princes refusing entry to Kindred who have come to the conclave, and Cainites still debate whether the rules of the conclave or the rules of the city pertain to those against whom blood hunts have been declared. While the prince is greeting the newcomers, the seneschal may disburse advice and instructions concerning the ways of the city. Such information may include where not to hunt, the boundaries of Elysium, where to contact a clan primogen and where hunters are known to reside. At the same time, the sheriff and his deputies try to keep tabs on the new arrivals and do what they can to verify that no enemies of the Camarilla are sneaking in amid the confusion.

The Conclave Itself

Before the appointed hour, usually midnight on the announced night, Kindred make their way to the main council chamber where the public business of the conclave takes place. All points of order and propriety in the conclave are determined according to a strange agglomeration of ancient Greek jurisprudence, European courtly etiquette and primal predatory instinct. For unchaperoned neonates, the entire experience can seem like a series of dangerous trials, from choosing the right seat to knowing when to stand or sit to knowing how to address the assembly. Naturally, the harpies are always glad to point out errors, but never willing to explain the proper course of action.

> ### Logistics, Logistics, Logistics
>
> Some players love making plans, but many players may not find arranging the minutiae of a conclave matches their idea of a good night's gaming. Fortunately, that's what lackeys and pawns are for. Preparing for a conclave often occupies a large amount of the planning Kindred's Influence: getting the convention hall's peculiar architecture past the zoning board, seeing that travel arrangements are secure and rounding up enough strays who won't be missed to make sure the vitae doesn't get stale. With the expenditure of a little Influence, experts can take care of most of this without the player needing to fret the details. Of course, even experts can make mistakes, so wise Kindred keep track of what their people are doing.

Once all the important Cainites are seated, in order of age and power, the conclave opens with the presiding justicar addressing the assembled Kindred, speaking to them about the matter at hand. From there, any attendee who has something to contribute is allowed to speak, once the justicar has recognized them. Many neonates, seated toward the back of the council chamber, find that they have trouble catching the eye of the justicar, and even when they do, there is no guarantee that any of the elders will actually listen to what they have to say. Nevertheless, this is one of the few situations where a younger vampire is guaranteed the right to speak and be heard by his elders. Discussion continues throughout the conclave under the guidance of the justicar. As the presiding officer, it is his duty to see that attention does not get diverted and that any Kindred who has something to contribute gets the chance to do so. He may limit the loquacious from speaking too long and may order the removal of any disruptive vampires from the chamber. It is his job to see that the Camarilla reaches a decision.

Traditionally, no more than eight hours of each night are relegated to business, but in most cases, the prince and her crew will try to keep the visitors within the grounds of the conclave. It is easier to watch and guard them from treachery if their movements are limited. To this end, the primogen and their clans often prepare seminars, parties and other diversions to keep the guests entertained during their stay. Some younger Kindred suspect that the true business of the conclave takes part during the recess periods, when the neonates are being distracted and the elders have retired to their own diversions.

When it is evident that the matter has been thoroughly discussed, the justicar will state that discussion is finished. He will usually then review the discussion, describe the two or three most popular courses of action and order a recess for everyone to contemplate and discuss the matter in private. Though the justicar and his archons will do their best to ensure that no coercion or skullduggery occurs during that recess, it is one of the most politically frenzied times one will ever encounter. At the end of the recess, the justicar usually re-presents the choices and calls for the vote. Every Kindred present is allowed to vote. Voting is usually done either by a show of hands or by marking the choice on paper, with the archons commonly being enlisted to tally the results. Once the votes are counted, the justicar announces the results and ritually states that this verdict represents the will of the Camarilla and all members are to adhere to its decision and to inform all others of what has transpired.

After the vote, the hosting prince usually throws a final party where the assembled Cainites celebrate their membership in the largest vampiric sect in the world. In most cases, the justicar leaves to report the results to the Inner Circle immediately after reading the verdict, though he might leave an archon or two to see that everything ends smoothly.

Afterward

After the conclave is finished, visitors are expected to depart in a timely fashion, and the sheriff will probably need to spend a good part of his time watching them and encouraging them to leave. Even with the visitors gone, it can take a month or so for the city to return to normal. The preparations for the conclave must be undone, officials must be mollified and any minor problems or breaches to the Masquerade must be taken care of before the city can return to its standard level of treachery and infighting.

Participants may find that they have gained or lost much based on their actions at the conclave. Status, respect, reputation and allies may all be affected by what a Kindred says and does, and even a neonate may earn the respect or enmity of an entire clan through her actions. Those who successfully host or command the security of a conclave can expect to gain a Status Trait in recognition of their efforts. Those who blunder can expect to pay the price, losing Status in an amount commensurate with their error and the size of the conclave — up to two Traits for smaller conclaves, possibly as many as five for the largest.

Judicial Conclaves

Justicars convene judicial conclaves for the purposes of determining the guilt or innocence of Kindred who may fall beyond the scope of princely justice. Though similar to other conclaves, judicial conclaves are far less social affairs. The justicar, often flanked by his archons, usually presides over the trial with an iron fist, discouraging any discussion that does not pertain to the guilt or innocence of the accused. In such trials, guilt is assumed, and the accused must fight to prove his innocence. Most justicars ask questions, listening to any Kindred who dares, or is ordered, to speak. Unless the justicar has reason to believe that the accused has undue influence over the domain even when incarcerated, judicial conclaves rarely involve Kindred from beyond the city.

They are meant to be quick, efficient and final. By the same note, judicial conclaves rarely last more than a handful of nights.

As with most conclaves, once the justicar feels that the available information has been revealed, he puts the verdict to a vote of all Kindred present. Nevertheless, the justicar may overrule the vote if he believes that coercion or gross corruption has been brought to bear. In such cases, justicars often favor trial by ordeal, and may Caine help the vampire who is assigned an ordeal by the Malkavian justicar.

The sentence is carried out immediately after the verdict has been reached, and the justicar departs for the next crisis soon after. The justicar may order one of his archons to stay behind to ensure that no punishment is brought to bear on any who may have testified in an unpopular manner, but they rarely stay more than a couple of nights. Such unfortunates may consider seeking other residence if they have made powerful enemies.

MEETING NEW FRIENDS

One of the possibilities for a conclave involves temporarily merging two or more troupes for the event, with one troupe hosting the conclave and the others playing the roles of visitors. While this allows the Storytellers to present a larger conclave, it creates new challenges as well. First, the Storytellers must ensure that they agree about what is going on — each troupe should be going to a conclave focusing on the same issue. The Storytellers should review the rules and go over any house rules that the other troupes have developed. The Storytellers should also try to give accurate assessments of their players and Narrators so the entire event can be shaped for the enjoyment of all. Once the Storytellers have an idea of their resources and needs, they can get down to business. In most cases, the Storytellers may want to consider the hosting troupe's Storyteller first among equals for resolving any conflicts.

PLAYING THE CROWD

Conclaves are rare, *very* rare. Even then, the smaller regional conclaves and judicial conclaves are far more common than the grand, thousand-Kindred spectacles that draw Cainites from across the globe. Even so, presenting even a small conclave can be a daunting task for a Storyteller. If the conclave is to take place in the characters' city, many of them will be active in its preparation and operation. If the Storyteller wants to show the players how things are done in a different city, she must be ready to portray an entirely new locale. Similarly, if the story focuses on a single coterie or chantry, the Storyteller will not need to cover as much ground as if her players represent all different facets of the city's Kindred. This is especially true if the troupe is so intent on a specific facet of the conclave that they experience the rest of it only peripherally. In such cases, it is possible that the Storyteller and Narrators will naturally devote most of their efforts to the central theme, but they should not let the rest of conclave go by without prodding the characters to see just how large and terrifying such an event is. Perhaps the characters need to perform some specific task at the conclave, such as swaying an elder's opinion, seeing that an artifact reaches the proper hands or handling the security. Perhaps all of the characters are elders who decide what will really happen while lesser Cainites engage in politics and socializing. Taking such a route can allow a Storyteller to portray a larger conclave with a smaller number of players.

Positions of Power

Over the centuries, the Camarilla has adopted a handful of positions or stations to see that the Kindred of a city act according to the dictates of the Traditions. In many ways, these positions define the Camarilla even as the Camarilla defines them: They offer a structured society for perpetuating the Masquerade, granting power to those who can best promote the way of the Camarilla, and punishing those who work against it.

Below are eight commonly accepted stations. However, as each Camarilla city has its unique identity, concerns and personalities, it is often prudent to adjust the ranks. One city may need a full-time general to handle the war with the Sabbat. Another may require a sort of sinecure to be created for a powerful Kindred who is not suited for the conventional roles. Usually the prince and primogen argue long and hard over the creation of these special positions. Not only does the presence of these special positions wreak havoc with the conventional balance of power and all those cunning stratagems that rely upon it, but it creates hard feelings among those who feel that the new position detracts from their power. Of course, in certain cases, that is the primary reason for the creation of the station.

Prince

The prince is often seen as the seat of all Kindred power within a city — the most powerful and cunning of vampires and the official voice of the Camarilla within the city. Certainly, the prince wields great power within his domain. In addition to whatever other powers he can claim through wits or strength, the prince traditionally possesses the right to create progeny and decide who else may do so, the right to determine the boundaries of Elysium and the right to mete out hunting grounds and place others off limits. The office also traditionally includes remarkable political power among the kine of his domain. The prince also determines the course and shape of justice among the Kindred of his domain, including declaration of blood hunts.

Yet, while the prince is almost always the strongest of the city's Kindred — at least the strongest of those who have political aspirations — he is not always the masterful figure Kindred associate with the position. In certain cases, the prince endures a nightly struggle with the primogen or other would-be usurpers. Sometimes the prince is little more than a façade, a figurehead controlled by other, more powerful Cainites, or a lesser party whom the other powers of the city have agreed upon lest one of them develop greater authority than her comrades are willing to relinquish. The power of the prince is mighty — and desirable. There is never a shortage of Kindred eager to take advantage of any weakness, or to cultivate one where it does not yet exist, in hopes of gaining the position for themselves. Few events can shake up a domain like the fall of its prince as all surviving vampires will fight and maneuver to improve their station.

The Abuse of Privilege

Sometimes a prince gets out of hand. Sometimes a player gets out of hand.

When a prince's "justice" becomes too draconian, it is only a matter of time before the other Kindred of the domain take equally extreme measures to remove him from power. This could be the central plot of a magnificent chronicle replete with unlikely alliances, clever ploys and unexpected backstabbing — if the players and Storyteller desire it. It could throw a chronicle into chaos if they do not. If it looks like the prince's justice is threatening the chronicle, the Storyteller should speak with him and determine how to keep the game enjoyable for everyone.

On the other hand, it is very, very rare for anything good to come of a player getting out of hand. If the player has resisted all attempts to get him to accommodate the rest of the troupe, the Storyteller should feel free to employ whatever means she feels are necessary to bring the situation under control. These means may be in-game, such as bringing in an archon who handily outclasses the prince to address the complaints of the city's other Kindred, or they may be out of game, such as removing the player from the chronicle. It is the Storyteller's call, but if she wants the chronicle to continue, she must do what she can to keep it enjoyable for as many as possible.

Regardless of the actual position of the prince, it is quite true that she is the focus of Camarilla power within the city. The prince — even on those occasions when she is beholden to others — is the force under which and against which all others must maneuver. A wise vampire scrutinizes the relationships between the prince and the other Kindred. These relationships are often the levers one needs to pry one's way up the ladder of Kindred society. As the arbiter of Cainite justice, all who scheme within his domain must take his temperaments, desires and goals into account. It is prudent to be able to explain any infractions one may commit as being in line with the prince's aspirations. Conversely, one should always describe one's rival's actions in the opposite light.

For his part, the prince must manage the often-conflicting goals of maintaining control of his domain and ensuring the safety of the Kindred under his control. Most princes employ their role as guardian of the Masquerade for both purposes, using the pretext of "protecting the Traditions" or "maintaining the Masquerade" for their harsher decrees.

The prince who intends to last beyond the morning must have power, a commanding presence and the ability to keep the rest of the Kindred of his domain at each other's throats instead of her own. In a social environment like the Camarilla, one should never underestimate the prince's ability to grant and remove Status Traits, for such status is power. Naturally, the prince must balance these gifts and punishments to keep the majority of her subjects grateful, or at least indebted, to her while not granting them enough power to threaten her own authority. She must use punishments to keep rivals from

becoming too potent and to discourage her subjects from disobeying her dictates. The prince need not limit herself to acting directly upon the Kindred in question. In certain cases, such as when a vampire who deserves to be commended has become too powerful for the prince's liking, she may issue an edict against one of that Cainite's rivals. Conversely, someone who has earned the prince's displeasure may find his enemies receiving the prince's largess.

Many princes are more than willing to create special posts for Kindred who catch their eye: to reward them, to keep them occupied or to vex others whose authority these new stations usurp. The demands and purposes of these posts are as varied as the needs of the princes and their domains: The past decade has seen the creation of Ambassador to the Lupines, Guardian of the City Sewers, Lord Regent of Cathayan Affairs and many others.

Of course, should these boons and chastisements prove insufficient, the prince may fall back on more extreme measures, including the blood hunt. A prince who demands such punishments had better be certain that she has the power to enforce her will though.

Seneschal

The seneschal takes on many different roles, depending on the political situation. Traditionally, the seneschal is the prince's most trusted assistant, and the Kindred who performs the prince's duties in his absence. In most cases, the seneschal is both more and less than that. Often, the seneschal is the vampire closest to the prince, the filter through which the prince may perceive his domain and the person those who would speak with the prince must convince before they are granted audience. The position of seneschal is by no means a comfortable one. Princes often use their seneschals to perform those unpleasant duties they would rather not handle themselves. Princes may also make their seneschals scapegoats, claiming that they did not give them accurate, complete or timely information. In fact, many princes see this as no more than just retribution for the times when their seneschal chose to give them incomplete information or placed the blame for some unpopular edict that was the seneschal's own creation upon the shoulders of the unknowing prince.

In many cases, the seneschal is the battleground against which the prince and primogen vie for ascendancy, and astute vampires can discern much about the political climate of a city by studying whether the prince or the primogen chose the seneschal. It is also worth noting which faction the seneschal favors — it is not always the same as the one who sponsored him. Regardless of the climate, most vampires try to curry the good will of the seneschal, for this luminary usually has the ear of all the other important Kindred in the domain. And while he may choose not to work directly against an offending Cainite, a clever seneschal can easily filter the information he puts forth so as to make the object if his ire appear a fool or a threat to the prince.

Serving as the focus for those who would speak to the prince grants the seneschal access to an impressive amount of information, and many manage to keep as well informed as their city's harpies. In certain cases, an informal rivalry may develop between the seneschal and the harpies to determine who has access to better gossip. Such competition is the bane of the seneschal, for

Inside Elysium

it is easy for other Kindred, from the Keeper of Elysium to the prince, to perceive him as in contention for their power. In general, it is only the seneschal's inside information that lets him stay one step ahead and keep his many challengers at each other's throats instead of at his. As a premiere power broker in the domain, the seneschal should keep in close contact with the Gossip (**Laws of the Night** p. 218) if the campaign has one.

Many seneschals find it useful to keep an assistant or a secretary. If he is lucky, he will be able to choose his own. Less fortunate seneschals are often "gifted" with one by the prince, one or more of the primogen, or some other powerful Kindred in the domain. Ostensibly, these Kindred are there to help the seneschal, but none are so foolish as to believe that. In truth, these assistants are almost always sponsored in hopes of gaining their patron access to some of the seneschal's information, usurping a bit of his power or as part of some other political machination. In such cases, the assistant becomes merely another front in the nightly intelligence war that marks the seneschal's existence.

Primogen

The word primogen refers to both the council of most powerful Kindred within a city and the individual Cainites that comprise it. The primogen council usually acts as both an advisory council to the prince and a check on her power. In theory, the primogen is composed of the eldest of each Camarilla clan, and the primogen of each clan is expected to protect that clan's interests within the city. Nevertheless, certain clans — usually Malkavian and Brujah, for they are often considered too volatile — may find their presence proscribed by the prince, and thus have no representation among the primogen. Additionally, some clans may have enough power in the city to command more than a single seat on the primogen council. Also, in some cases, the prince acts as his clan's representative in the primogen, in others some other vampire, often one of the prince's childer, but sometimes a rival clan member, fills that post.

The members of the primogen are usually engaged in a struggle for power with the prince and the other primogen, and daring Kindred may gain the favor of their clan primogen by performing deeds that further their power. This is a dangerous game though, for the primogen have had decades or even centuries to develop their plans and can react quite angrily to ill-informed meddlers. Naturally, it is more common for such folk to get dragged by one primogen or the other into these machinations against their will.

Most Cainites try to limit their interaction with the primogen to that of their own clan, since she is the most likely to be able to help them and interested in doing so. It might seem that a primogen could abuse her powers by repeatedly increasing the status of her clanmates, but such actions tend to result in a backlash from the other clans. Additionally, granting excessive social power to ambitious underlings can be a dangerous ploy. If Kindred are cautious around their own clan's primogen, they are doubly so around those of other clans. Unless a vampire has a reputation as a friend of the clan in question, primogen of different clans often view such creatures as little more than pawns and spies of their rivals — spies to be fed disinformation and pawns to be led astray. After all, anything that decreases the prestige of another clan

decreases the importance of that clan's primogen; and anything that reduces the power of one primogen increases the authority of the others. As senior members of their clan, primogen possess considerable power, though it is usually limited to the clan and its area of influence. Primogen rarely have official powers beyond their clan, but as they are powerful Kindred in their own right, lesser vampires tend to tread lightly in their presence.

The primogen council is usually limited to the senior members of each clan, which limits the membership to five Kindred in most cases. Nevertheless, many primogen like to maintain a lieutenant of sorts, as a means of displaying clan unity, subtly threatening the other primogen and keeping track of the sorts of tedious details that do not demand their complete attention. In Great Britain and the United States, the Primogen have adopted the term Whip to refer to these roles from their mortal legislatures. The jockeying and maneuvering among these lesser Kindred can be quite intense as the primogen like to present this as a route to prestige and power. They gloss over the fact that there is room for only one primogen in each clan, and these ancillae and neonates will only get that post by leaving for another domain or over the dead body of the current one.

HARPY

If the prince is the official face of Camarilla justice, the harpy is the de facto arbiter of vampiric propriety, culture and status. They are the undying memory of *faux pas*, innuendo, gossip, rumor and scandal — all bundled into a viciously entertaining combination of Torquemada and Miss Manners. In the world of the Camarilla, where the halls of power can often resemble an old boys' club, the harpy is as close to an equal-opportunity position as one may find. Any Kindred with the right combination of wit, maliciousness and *savoire faire* may insinuate herself into the position. Of course any pretender who tries but falls short will find that news of this particular solecism has reached the ears all but the most bucolic of domains.

Many neonates question the actual power of the harpies, claiming that all it should take is the strength to ignore their japes to render them totally impotent in the face of Kindred with *real* power. Such naïveté rarely lasts long, as all of the elder Cainites have a vested interest in the power of the harpies: It keeps conflicts within Elysium confined to the social arena, and that keeps the elder vampires that much safer. Younger vampires who underestimate the harpies' power soon learn the error of their ways — as lack of proper respect for one's elders is one of the foibles harpies most love to point out.

There is usually one primary harpy, but she may sponsor others as described in **Laws of the Night** p. 219. In addition, harpies may employ or encourage other Cainites to bring news, gossip and information their way. Such duty is doubly dangerous, for it will certainly draw the ire of those whose faults are so bought to light, and being in such close proximity to the harpies increases the chance that they will notice and broadcast their servant's faults. Nevertheless, for Kindred clever and circumspect enough to handle the demands of this situation, being a spy for the harpies can be an effective route to information, and possibly even an entry into their elite number.

THE LITTLE PEOPLE

In addition to the major stations, important Kindred often enjoy keeping personal aides, secretaries, bodyguards or whatever in attendance. As a rule, such subordinates possess no special authority unless their masters can and do grant it to them. For senior vampires, granting such powers is always a double-edged sword. One wants one's servant to have the influence to complete his assignments expediently, but one does not want him gaining enough power to become a threat. Additionally, these subordinates are often the targets of plots and even recruitment by opposing Kindred, so they must be watched carefully. Nevertheless, as the world becomes more and more complex, it has become harder for vampires from past centuries to keep apace with it all, and more of them have taken to relying on their aides to keep their interests running smoothly.

Even more than the seneschal, harpies need to keep in communication with the game's Gossip, if one is present, to record the objects of their displeasure, to verify the activities of others who are altering the status of other Kindred and — as a simulation of their network of informants — to keep them abreast of the latest developments in their chosen arena. In games where there is no Gossip and the Storyteller feels that one of the harpies is sufficiently responsible, that harpy may fulfill the role of Gossip for the game. Additionally, Storytellers will want to make sure that harpies are kept appraised of any critical gaffes the other characters may have made.

As a final note, harpy players must exercise caution to ensure that their characters direct their comments at the mistakes of the other characters, not at the players. It is all right to mock a character's choice of clothes when he attends Elysium; it is not proper to make fun of the player himself. Always keep the distinction between character and player in mind.

KEEPER OF ELYSIUM

The Keeper of Elysium has broad powers within the Camarilla, but only within certain strictly delimited boundaries. Within the confines of Elysium, the keeper has the authority to take whatever actions she feels are necessary to preserve the Masquerade and the sanctity of Elysium. Keepers are charged with the physical security of Elysium as well as the societal ramifications of what transpires there. Though such power may seem trivial in the face of the strength of the sheriff or the coercion of the harpies, Kindred know that Elysium is one of the few safe, neutral places where they can interact. As the master thereof, the keeper of Elysium possesses a particularly focused power.

If the keeper feels that a function planned for her domain would be a threat to the Masquerade or the Kindred, she is entitled to cancel it without notice even if it is already in progress. Many Cainites derive prestige, power and pleasure from events held in Elysium. Ventrue hold business dealings and entertain visiting dignitaries from distant domains. Toreador host balls and exhibits. Brujah have their raves and Tremere their discourses. And, of course, those who wish to speak with the prince must usually enter Elysium to do so. When such meetings are aborted as threats to the Masquerade, not only can it be remarkably inconvenient, but the host's image is tarnished. Additionally, the keeper is expected to control the presence of weapons within Elysium. As such, she has the right to search any Kindred who requests entrance. Such searches are rarely more than an embarrassing nuisance, but they too reduce the image of those subject to them. Additionally, one never knows what unfortunate items may turn up when one searches a vampire. Finally, some keepers have been caught spying upon certain guests, "out of concern for the Masquerade" of course. For these reasons, most Kindred try not to offend the keeper of Elysium. On the other hand, those Cainites with anarch leanings or who do not respect the tradition of Elysium often see the keeper as embodying all that they detest about Camarilla: petty, artificial tyranny, arbitrary rules and no real power to speak of.

The keeper of Elysium is one of the most public of stations. Keepers regularly interact with the primogen, the seneschal, the sheriff, any other Kindred who would have a use for a quiet neutral ground and even mortals who merely see it as another museum or library. These relationships are often professional, for example, the keeper may ask the sheriff to aid in security matters in Elysium. They can easily degenerate into rivalries, though, especially when one Cainite sees another as interfering with her duties and rights. Thus, though the station is prestigious, being keeper of Elysium is demanding, politically risky and often held only for a brief term. In some cases, the position is given to a troublemaker in the hopes that she will humiliate herself. Such cases are rare, however, for few domains can afford to have an incompetent keeper.

In addition to whatever security, catering and maintenance forces she controls, a keeper may have a significant collection of assistants. Usually keepers use ghouls, but in larger cities, lesser Kindred may fill these positions. A keeper usually wants to have at least one assistant for each separate geographical location that comprises Elysium within the city. She may also have a lieutenant in charge of security, and possibly another whose sole purpose is to act as liaison with other Kindred of note such as the seneschal and the sheriff.

SHERIFF

The sheriff is the strong arm of the Camarilla, the Cainite who ensures that even the more rebellious vampires obey the prince's orders. Though he is often seen as little more than the prince's enforcer, the predations of the Sabbat and the approach of the Final Nights have forced successful sheriffs to become more cautious, disciplined and astute. In addition to policing the local Kindred population for violations of the Masquerade — a task made more vital and dangerous by the rise of public media — the sheriff must be prepared for such crises as have been erupting in these dangerous times, up to and including being a general in an all-out war with the Sabbat.

Most Kindred are wary of the sheriff. Though princes are increasingly employing cautious, tactically savvy enforcers, Cainite folklore continues to view the sheriff as the prince's favorite thug. Since they work in different theatres of conflict, harpies and sheriffs often detest each other. Unless the sheriff has shown favoritism concerning a particular clan, the primogen are usually willing to leave him to his job while they attend to their own concerns.

Most sheriffs see the scourge's duties as encroaching on their jurisdiction, so there is rarely any love lost between the two positions. The rest of the city's Kindred usually just try to stay out of his way.

Though the prince may use the sheriff for whatever tasks he deems necessary, most sheriffs spend their time policing the Kindred community for violations of the Masquerade. Sheriffs and their deputies visit the racks and whatever hunting grounds are trendy this month to ensure that everything is suitably quiet. They listen to EMTs, the police, the local media and anybody else for rumors of suspicious happenings. Most sheriffs also keep a fair number of stool pigeons among the neonates. If they hear something, they track down the offender and drag his sorry carcass back to the prince for judgment.

Given the dangerous nature of their duties, sheriffs often take on deputies. In most cases these deputies are merely less experienced and less powerful enforcers. In certain situations the sheriff may want to have specialized deputies to handle specialized problems. Sheriffs may call for deputies who have skill fighting Lupines, experience with Sabbat tactics, rapport with anarchs or whatever expert knowledge is necessary for the protection of the domain and the execution of the prince's orders. Such specialists usually receive more respect than the sheriff's ordinary deputies do; this sometimes creates tension among the ranks. Sheriffs also employ any number of spies to bring them information about breaches in the Masquerade and about the movements of suspect Kindred. Such vampires do not count as deputies, though — they only serve the sheriff through the occasional bit of intelligence offered for some money or a minor boon.

Scourge

The scourge is charged with culling the city of undesirable vampires, specifically those created without the permission of the prince. Most of these vampires are of the 14th and 15th generation, but some are Caitiff or unrecognized childer of lower generation. Though many cities have not instituted the station of the scourge, others have, trying to stave off the "Time of Thin Blood" prophesied in the *Book of Nod*. Though some claim that the station of scourge is an ancient post dating back to the Dark Ages and resurrected in modern times, others argue that it is an entirely new creation. Regardless of the historical truth, in those cities where the scourge stalks the night, she stands as a mythic bogeyman and source of fear among those illegitimate vampires who have heard of her and among those legitimate Kindred who wonder what she might become.

In cities where one exists, most Cainites shun the scourge. Even those who perceive her existence as necessary seem troubled by her presence, perhaps worrying that the martial prowess she wields against the undesirables may one night be turned against them. For their part, most scourges shun the company of those they protect, perhaps sensing their unease, perhaps seeing them as the source of the problem that they have been called upon to correct. The few Kindred who attempt to keep the scourge fully integrated in Camarilla society are rarely appreciated by the scourge or their fellow Kindred.

On a typical night, a scourge may travel to the more dismal, less populated parts of the city, where even Nosferatu and Malkavians rarely have reason to

venture. There, she searches for signs of fugitives, such as rats and stray dogs drained of blood or street people who are more jumpy than usual. Some scourges set traps, while others hunt the Caitiff down like beasts. Some princes demand that the prey be brought back alive for questioning, in hopes of learning who is being sloppy. Others are content to see the heads or fangs of the night's take. Occasionally, sometimes based on a rumor or a tip, sometimes not, the scourge visits the city's regular Kindred, looking to see if they are harboring illegally created childer. On such occasions wise scourges are even more cautious than normal, since older vampires are far more cunning and dangerous than the untrained fledglings they normally hunt.

Unlike the other stations, the position of scourge is almost universally a solitary role. Whether out of princely fear of her violent, anti-social ways or because of the general undesirability of the position, there are few cities with more than one or where the scourge has assistants.

Keeping the Scourge Clean

A scourge can easily make a chronicle unpleasant for any troupe. The scourge ranks second to only the prince in potential for game-disrupting player abuse. Examining the theme of petty power as represented by a scourge could be a fascinating element of a chronicle if properly handled. Poorly handled, a runaway scourge could ruin the game for any players with Caitiff characters. Fortunately, there are myriad ways for a Storyteller to address this problem, ranging from the discarding of the position by the prince to an unexpected encounter, such as a young Lupine undergoing his First Change or an elder who did not feel the need to inform the prince of her presence.

The Elders of the Camarilla

What Is an Elder?

An elder is a vampire who has seen the passing of at least three centuries. Many are far older. Vampires of the Sixth, Seventh and Eighth Generation are typically considered elders. They are typically the most visible players of the Jyhad—the secret, centuries-long war waged among the Antediluvian vampires—though most elders find it preposterous that they could be the unwitting pawns of their forbearers. Sired long before the modern nights and closer to Caine's blood than their younger cousins, elders often occupy—or seize—the most prominent stations in the Camarilla sect: Many princes, primogen, archons and justicars are drawn from the elder ranks. Other elders are lone wolves, prowling just outside the acknowledged perimeter of Kindred society, watching and observing for purposes known only to them. Regardless of their visibility, younger Kindred are expected to defer to their elders and show respect for their age, though this custom is taken for granted more and more in these modern nights when the winds of change blow through every city the Camarilla still holds.

A rare few Kindred who claim the mantle of elder really don't qualify. These are the pretenders, vampires who are strong in generation but not in chronological age. Most true elders have existed far longer than any pretender, but since Kindred emphasize respect for purity of bloodline, they admit the pretenders into their society, albeit grudgingly. Pretenders normally boast a powerful sire, who may or may not be an elder herself; such vampires are honored for their lineage and not for their own merit. A few pretenders achieve their status not through the Embrace, but via a more sinister means — they steal the power of their elders through the heinous crime of diablerie.

The Ravages of Time

What happens to the typical Kindred when he reaches the age of consideration? The most obvious result is the nominal respect and status accorded to him by the younger vampires and his peers. But the passage of time itself also works distinct alterations into the mind, spirit and heart of the Kindred who survives long enough to join this august community of ancients. Sometimes subtle, other times painfully obvious, these changes affect nearly every aspect of the elder's behavior, and therefore the manner in which the elders are played.

Morality

All vampires begin to lose their connection to their lives and humanity shortly after the Embrace. It is difficult, after all, even for the most ethical and determined being to pursue the exacting ideals of human morality in the face of the nightly pressures, dangers and temptations that both surround and create Kindred society. Try as the vampire might to cling to previous ideals, she finds inevitably that love, warmth, kindness and compassion all fade slowly as the years pass. As the years become decades and the decades centuries, this disassociation from humanity becomes even more pronounced. Most elders are very close to the Beast: They feel it roiling and tearing in their gut, demanding release, and they sense it growing stronger with each casual murder or act of base cruelty they commit. Ancient elders sustain only by the most rigorous exercises in self-control. They fear that each frenzy may be their last. Those wretched souls who cross that final threshold into the ultimate ravening frenzy are disposed of like the mad dogs they resemble before they can do irreparable harm to the Camarilla's Masquerade.

In practical game terms, it is rare to encounter a true elder with a total of Morality Traits higher than 3. The number of casual murders, premeditated thefts and wanton cruelties an elder inflicts just to survive that long usually precludes any greater total. Elders on the Path of Humanity are more likely to develop *Conviction* and *Self-Control*, though the latter is often in short supply when an elder's pride is pricked or ego bruised. It is not uncommon for the Humanity of an ancient elder to have eroded to the point where she possesses only two Morality Traits. Such elders often find that only the most base cruelties and deranged pleasures can excite senses so totally jaded by centuries of stimuli that those senses might well be described as non-existent. At this point, these Kindred have difficulty relating not only to humans but to many younger Kindred as well; there is so little left within them that is recognizably human that they become a mystery to the neonates and ancillae with whom they still interact.

Appearance

A vampire's loss of Humanity is reflected not only in her behavior and psyche, but her outward appearance as well. As Humanity fades, she begins to resemble a pale, desiccated corpse — further evidence of her extreme distance from her human origins. Many elders can no longer be mistaken for human except under the most favorable (or carefully orchestrated) conditions, to the point where they cannot interact successfully with any kine who is not one of their servants. Naturally, this condition reduces the amount of contact elders may have with humans, which in turn increases their spiritual separation from them, and so the downward spiral continues toward its near-inevitable grim conclusion.

Her age and state of mind also influence the outward trappings the elder chooses to don before making a public appearance. Some elders, particularly those most insistent on maintaining both the letter and spirit of the First Tradition, play the fashion game with almost as much zeal as mortals, keeping abreast of the latest developments coming out of the European fashion houses. They retain entire staffs of ghouls who serve no purpose other than to attend to their masters' clothing and grooming. Other elders are so jaded that the entire notion of fashion palls for them; they could not care less what adorns their bodies, so long as modesty is preserved. That is not to say that the latter sort will choose clothing that risks the Masquerade, but that they are less likely to be concerned that their suit jacket or evening gown is some four decades out of date.

When deciding what your elder will wear, concentrate on the details. Unless you're extraordinarily fortunate, you probably can't afford an entire wardrobe of authentic period garb, and must make do with one or two serviceable pieces and some good accessories. The latter can suggest age and status without being elaborate: Lapel pins, brooches, rings, cigarette cases, canes, gloves, etc. can provide all the suggestion of the Old (or even Classical) World that you are likely to need. That is not to say that you should abandon the idea of looking the part to the best of your ability. LARP is even more fun when players do all that they can to create and preserve the illusion that they are indeed someone else for the evening. Try your luck at vintage clothing shops and consignment stores, and bring your friends along!

Behavior

Being something both more and less than human, all vampires are more or less monstrous. Vampire elders, however, definitely tip the scales on the "more" side of the equation. They are among the most fearful, suspicious, unfeeling and jaded beings the night has ever known, and their behavior reflects these characteristics. It is the elders who created the Camarilla and who determine its culture. The sect is ostensibly a shield designed to protect the Kindred from the horrors of a second Inquisition. But it might also be said that the Camarilla is a means of protecting the Kindred from themselves, providing a codified rationale for minimizing contact between vampires and humans, contact that becomes only more painful as the vampires age. The mental and spiritual barriers that time erects between the elders and humans is reflected in the Camarilla's Masquerade, which beyond its practical utility also provides a convenient excuse for the elders to spare themselves the acute discomfort they experience when interacting with mortals.

Playing the Part

You age, but you do not improve. Certainly your intellect, your cunning and your powers grow more vast, and if you are fortunate and clever, you may come to understand more fully the nature of your existence and environment, and the longer you survive, the more impressive these characteristics may become. But you can never grow *better*. You left that capacity far, far behind you — it belongs to the Canaille, to the mortals whom you dismiss as cattle, from whom you are now so distant in nature and thought that you might as well be an alien visitor from another planet. But that's not the worst of it. The worst of it is that you *know* it, whether you admit it to yourself or not. You're painfully aware, in the deepest recesses of what's left of your desiccated heart, that your existence is a testimony to an appalling decay of the soul that you are powerless to halt, even if you wanted to. And you don't want to, because you're an elder, and this is what enables you to survive. Even this paranoid, flavorless and dull existence is better than the Final Death.

Playing an elder character isn't easy. You can imagine what it might feel like to be a bloodsucking, animated corpse who's lived hundreds of years and lost all vestiges of human emotion, but you can't really draw from personal experience to guide you in portraying this creature. Few roleplayers have centuries of experience at their disposal with which to hone their skills at courtly intrigue, social etiquette and secret murder. But you can touch on the cornerstones of good elder portrayal: paranoia, fear, hatred and cruelty.

Fearful Passages

Your elder character isn't going to be like any other player's elder, but your character will share some similarities with others of your ilk; indeed, in many ways you will have more in common with the creatures who may prove your greatest rivals than with the incomprehensible younger generations. The ways of the past bind you together, and so does the fear that such longevity engenders. Indeed, it is fear that is your most constant companion on the long road of undeath. You might think that an elder character has little to fear from anything or anyone. After all, he has the advantages of age — higher Trait maximums, a larger Blood Pool, resistance to the formidable powers of *Dominate*, ample Willpower Traits and (if you're fortunate) more Discipline powers than the average ancillae or neonate character. But playing an elder who believes herself to be indestructible or unstoppable is the quickest way to become a dead elder. There's plenty for an elder to fear out there, and with good reason.

Change

First and foremost on your character's list of Most Feared Things is, paradoxically, something that has proven inevitable — at least so far: change. Elders may be a paranoid and jaded lot, but only those who are utterly insane fail to recognize one inescapable fact: If the fragile cords of the ancient laws and customs that bind the Camarilla together were to unravel, the elders and many Kindred with them would be plunged screaming into an eternal nightmare of chaos and bloodshed from which they might never hope to awaken. Therefore, they *must* preserve the status quo, no matter how confining, sterile or twisted it might be, so that the

Camarilla and its adherents might continue to exist. This lesson, which younger Kindred feel to be merely a reactionary foible, is actually that which has allowed many of the most ancient elders to survive long enough to see the modern nights.

Change is the one thing your character has good reason to fear more than *anything* else. Change, particularly of the abrupt and unexpected variety, unsettles all those cunning plans that your character has so painstakingly crafted over the centuries. Change disrupts the careful routines and rhythms that enable you to stave off the downward spiral into which the Beast tries to force you. So great is this fear of change that many elders go to great lengths to immunize themselves from its ravages. Unfortunately, the modern world is so complex that even a seemingly minor alteration in the local environment can be the harbinger of much greater change later. Therefore, some elders perceive *all* change to be undesirable, something to be avoided whenever possible. For them, no display of conservatism is too great if it enables them to stifle a significant change to the environment.

The fear an elder instills in other Kindred by the threat of his awesome powers is but a wan reflection of the fear of change that leaves that same elder quaking as he retires to his slumber each morning. The fear your elder character might experience at the thought of an imminent Sabbat incursion, or at the imagined sound of a diablerist's footstep in the hallway, is dwarfed by his terror that the status quo will shift once again and leave him trying desperately to understand the new paradigm before it proves his undoing. Elders who find themselves in the uncomfortable position of justifying this wholesale rejection of change to younger Kindred often point out that all one requires to understand this philosophy is the advantage of perspective. Elders need only look to the lessons of their own past for all the justification they will ever need.

Strangely, elders are less fearful of losing their unlives to the forces of change than they are of losing their power and prestige. The elder sits at the apex of the Camarilla social strata, and few are capable of divesting themselves willingly of the sweet rewards of control. It is difficult — too difficult — for them to pass on the reins of power to their younger kin, of whom they also possess a justifiable and intense fear. Consequently, elders hang on to every scrap of authority with bloody nails. They can no longer know the joys of gentler emotions, but they can still savor the darkly satisfying fruits of control, deference and obedience from those over whom they hold sway.

Discovery

Many elders recall the halcyon nights of Rome and the Dark Ages, when the eldest vampires were often in complete control of the great population centers of Europe. The elders' hand held both carrot and stick, and entire nations danced to their whims. They hunted and killed as they wished, and none dared stand against them. Then came the Inquisition, with its priests and bonfires and *auto-da-fe*, slaughtering uncounted numbers of less fortunate vampires. Consider your character's history when confronted with a decision that could potentially shift the balance of the moment away from the status quo and toward significant change: Perhaps you remember this terrible period in Cainite history only too well from personal experience. If so, you should remember how very near the

miserable, zealous Canaille came to destroying every last Cainite while armed only with crude weapons and torches. True, the Church has ceased to be the monolithic force it was in those nights, but it has not disappeared, nor has the Inquisition — a fact that should never be too far from your character's mind whenever discussion of serious change arises. Rapid change could tear great, ragged holes in the Masquerade, exposing the Kindred again to the watchful eyes of the hunters. Given that the wisest and longest-lived elders weigh the potential value of change against the threat of discovery and destruction at the hands of the kine, it is a wonder that they are not even more socially conservative.

Roleplaying this fear should prove an exercise in common sense. Decide exactly how paranoid your character is about the possibility that humans might one day discover the truth about your existence and decide to pursue you with all the modern devices and weapons at their disposal. Most elders feel their blood turn to water at the very thought of a second Inquisition sweeping across their city, and their reaction to anything that promises even the barest potential for this disaster is usually swift and harsh. Among many elders, there is no greater crime than violation of the First Tradition. Any Kindred who compromises the security of all should be punished by nothing short of the Final Death. Many also believe that this punishment should be inflicted in a manner as gruesome and horrible as can be devised — the better to demonstrate to other would-be security risks the penalty of breaching this most sacred rule. It is this very fear that often lies at the root of another hallmark of elder paranoia: fear of the modern.

TECHNOLOGY

Unless you're a pretender, you come from an age where significant technological or scientific advancement was something that happened once a century, if that. Now innovations that border on the miraculous are now a matter of course — they occur annually, monthly and sometimes *nightly*. Even as you sit in your haven and contemplate the next 20 moves in your game of political chess against your hated rival, the kine are inventing devices that can kill millions in an instant, wipe all life from the planet and leave the earth's surface boiling hot for millennia. Even the humans cannot keep abreast of their own progress with anything approaching confidence! How then can you, the product of an age in which such inventions would be considered the rankest and most vile sort of heresy, hope to comprehend the significance of each and every new development? The hard truth is that you can't, and you must increasingly turn to your inferiors for help in understanding or even utilizing the newer technologies.

This aspect of the elder character's psychology represents an inconvenience to you, the player. It's a fact that many players utilize the Internet to facilitate their roleplaying. It's a great communications tool with many applications, and it allows players and Storytellers to continue the game between actual sessions. But if the typical elder is uncomfortable with most newer forms of technology, shouldn't she be equally apprehensive about this most recent revolution in global communications? The answer is yes, she should, and not just because it's an unfamiliar tool. Encryption and safeguards notwithstanding, the Internet is a breach of the Masquerade just waiting to happen. Talk with your Storyteller about how you can address this

issue. She might allow your character to be one of the few elders who has managed to keep up with the times and for whom new technology holds no inherent fear. But in games with more than a few elder characters, this exception becomes less believable and desirable. Given the degree to which elders value their privacy and personal safety, it is simply beyond the bounds of believability for them to sit huddled at their computer terminals writing messages to one another around the globe every night. The Internet and other such devices belong to the younger generations, and if your elder utilizes such technology frequently and easily, you aren't getting the full elder experience. Consequently, try to limit the extent to which your elder character communicates via Internet: It might be less convenient for you as a player, but you'll be doing your character more justice.

Peers

They glide through the marble halls of Elysium with the same graceful ease and predator's smile that you, too, affect for the benefit of the younger Kindred — your fellow elders. Despite the fact that your character will have a great deal in common with them, don't be misled. They aren't your friends. The elders who dwell in a given city must deal with the omnipresent politics of scarcity that govern the ebb and flow of nightly urban life. There are only so many resources — kine, Influences, *Contacts*, etc. — to go around, and most of them are held in the hands of the elders. It follows then that elders must circle one another like sharks, each hoping that another will show a sign of weakness that allows her to take what another has. Each elder knows, whether she wishes to admit it or not, that one of the few ways to give her existence meaning is to claim victory over her peers. Otherwise, all the treacheries, crimes and sins she committed to achieve that victory were for nothing, and the thought of that is simply too hateful and ghastly to bear.

The Sabbat

Every elder of the Camarilla knows that the Sabbat is out there, watching and waiting for an opportunity to come howling through the night and wreak bloody havoc on the beleaguered defenses of the Camarilla. This fear is not unfounded: The vampires of the Sabbat clamor loudly for the utter destruction of the elders as one of their sect's key principles. Every loss of Camarilla territory to its enemy sends a shiver of dread through the decayed hearts of the elders, followed quickly by the heat of shame and the parching desire for revenge. Many elders project their terror of the Sabbat onto the younger generations, using their own fears to exert yet another degree of control over their progeny. The elders' desire to retake every foot of ground lost to the Sabbat, but most of them are unwilling to put themselves on the front lines of the fight, seeking instead to manipulate or even order younger Kindred into taking the brunt of the enemy's vicious attacks. With each Camarilla victory seeming more fleeting than the last, some elders even begin to harbor the secret fear that their sect is doomed and will fall to the Sabbat's seemingly limitless numbers within the foreseeable future. These elders aren't wasting any more time devising stratagems to combat the enemy and instead devote their energies into creating elaborate methods of escape and defense should the worst finally occur.

The Sum of All Fears: The Younger Generations

In your wildest dreams, you might hope that the shocking speed with which change rips across and reshapes the face of the world would drive the Kindred whimpering into the arms of the Camarilla, begging for its comfort and shelter. But while this world might seem alien and incomprehensible to you, the younger generations are quite at home here — it is, by and large, *their* world. The ancillae and neonates grew to adulthood and were Embraced amid the riotous changes that rumble through this odious world. So it is with eagerness that these younger, weaker Kindred master so easily what remains barely comprehensible to you: radio, television, fiber optics, nuclear physics, computers, Internet. Too often, you find yourself on the receiving end of an appalling hour-long lesson on the applications of one these marvels, during which time a droning neonate or ancilla attempts to instruct you in its function and operation. Sometimes you think you will go mad just from the sheer horror of it all.

It would be almost bearable, though, if it weren't so very clear that the younger have somehow fallen under the spell of humanity's most heretical notion: Technology and change are not only desirable, but necessary. Clearly, this viewpoint is evidence of a serious deficiency of character. But like a tooth that rots from within, so too does the Camarilla suffer from this pervasive disease among its junior members. Despite all the rationales, not to mention the awesome force, that the elders can bring to bear, the twin demons of democracy and freedom demand to make themselves heard throughout the halls of Elysium. It is almost as if these words are a virus that the younger Kindred contract when they feed upon the kine, a sickness that spreads further with each subsequent generation.

Consider how your elder character will react when she hears these words fall eagerly, as they will, from the lips of the younger vampires in Elysium. Does she believe them idle words, little more than the folly of youth? Or are they a chilling reminder of another time, when similar phrases were the ill-favored omen of resentment that welled up from the hearts of the younger Kindred, leading to the horror now known as the Anarch Revolt and followed by the founding of the hated Sabbat? Your character may well decide that such talk, however casual, is nothing less than another wave of resentment building against the wise and experienced guidance of her peers, and that the inevitable cries for change will quickly follow. Your character may well ask herself how long it will be before these cries for reform bring the Camarilla to its knees. Is the sect's life span measured in millennia or minutes? What can be done to stave off this rot, to shore up the crumbling walls of the sect before it collapses in on itself, burying everyone under its weight?

Fear of younger vampires reflects the elder's parallel fear of her own growing irrelevancy. As an elder ages, she grows ever more distant from the mortal world, until she reaches an age at which she no longer desires to undertake the labors that would enable her to remain relevant. Consequently, whenever an ambitious ancilla or energetic neonate embarks on a crusade or plan to reform the stale and perverse world that is Camarilla society, the elders collaborate on his destruction — or, at the very least, to thwart his plans totally. Political skullduggery, social ridicule, perverse machinations — no

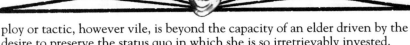

ploy or tactic, however vile, is beyond the capacity of an elder driven by the desire to preserve the status quo in which she is so irretrievably invested.

DIGNIFIED DESPERATION

Any one of the elders' many fears, taken singly, would be sufficient to produce a significant impact on their nightly behavior. Combined, they create a near paralysis that prevents many elders from committing to any course of action that is not calculated, analyzed, scrutinized and considered from a dozen different angles and weighed carefully against a myriad of possible outcomes. Consequently, the elders are relatively slow to react except in the face of clear, obvious threats, and even then they often prefer to stall for time before acting decisively. Relative to their younger relations, the elders of the Camarilla thus appear to be practically unmoving as they struggle to freeze their perverted society in place so that they need not risk parting with even a fraction of their power.

Your elder character should therefore seem, at least on the surface and in public, to face the prospect of risk with extreme reluctance. Consider carefully your character's response to any situation that threatens to upset her long-term plans or disrupt the status quo on which her power base depends. Don't be afraid to bide your time before answering questions that might lead down unwelcome paths; don't hesitate to make your persona's actions seem frustratingly conservative in the eyes of the more energetic and younger characters. Privately, of course, your character can give full vent to her emotions, particularly when dealing with younger Kindred or your own progeny, though in doing so you run the risk of being perceived as something less than dignified should word of your outbursts reach the ever-waiting ears of your peers and enemies.

STIFLING PARANOIA: THE HATE OF AGES

Fear inevitably breeds hate. We hate what we fear, and vice versa. Alone among the Kindred, elders know only too well the maddening paradox that seeps slowly into the vampire's mind after they pass a certain age. The irony of their existence is that on the one hand they enjoy nearly limitless power, but on the other they are held in the inescapable grip of paralyzing fear. This sick duality weighs heavily on their minds, and yet they prefer to face the ennui of the long centuries still to come rather than the alternative. Consequently, the elders cannot mend the wounds torn in their psyches by their own constant terrors, nor can they combat the multitude of pressures that create them. Their only recourse is to mask their boredom and horror with white-hot layers of hatred.

Elders collect grudges and nurse them with almost loving care, for these are the thoughts that sustain them when other hopes and sensations grow dim. Their memories are as long as their existences: They do not forget slights or insults, however small, and they know for a certainty that none of their peers will, either. Perversely, this capacity for hate is what enables some elders to continue on, decade after decade, century after century, when everything else that even approximates meaning has been snuffed out. No longer able to feel the gentler emotions, they cling desperately to those sensations that they can still grasp. The sharp, steely pang of hatred has enabled more than a few elders to persevere through terrible calamities and setbacks — the hot, coppery taste of vengeance yet to come is a pleasure so rarified that only an elder may truly appreciate its subtle

nuances. Hatred comes easily to elders, and so becomes a welcome companion, even a diversion, on the long and dark road down into their own personal hells.

As an elder player, don't pass up an opportunity to establish a new hatred for your character, whether it is of an individual, a place or even a point of view. Hatred can restore meaning to your character's existence when all else has been lost. Your character could suffer crushing losses that might send a lesser Kindred plummeting downward into the depths of despair, never to escape, but she clings to her hatreds the way a drowning person clings to a bit of driftwood. If your character lacks even one such hatred, you aren't getting the full elder experience. Try creating a situation so that your character is sure to gain a focus for her hate. It could be a rival, an institution or a city, but regardless it should occupy your character's waking thoughts frequently. Such emotional excesses can become the basis of some of the most challenging and memorable roleplaying experiences you'll have.

Always keep in mind two important truths about hatreds, one for your character and one for you. With every grudge your character seizes upon to sustain him in his otherwise empty existence, he grows that much more distant from his humanity, and that much more close to the Beast. Likewise, the more deeply your character feels his hatred, the more likely it is that he will act on it, and so place himself in the position of risking even more of his Humanity.

More importantly, however, remember that you are responsible for understanding that your character's hatreds are not your own. The fact that your elder character feels bitter hatred toward Justine, the Toreador whip, doesn't mean that you should feel any animosity whatsoever toward Justine's player. Indeed, if you ever catch yourself confusing the emotions your character experiences with those that *you* experience, stop playing at once and evaluate your situation. Roleplaying a hatred that helps your character stave off the crushing ennui of the passing millennia is one thing, but transferring that hatred onto real people is quite another, and it's not acceptable. Likewise, don't abuse the privilege of playing an elder character by bringing real-life grudges and problems into the game: If you have a beef with another player, it's inappropriate (not to mention poor gamesmanship) to use that as an excuse to have your character hate hers.

The bottom line: Playing an elder requires you to be even more conscientious and responsible about observing and respecting the line that separates the game from reality.

BASER PLEASURES: CRUELTY FOR CRUELTY'S SAKE

Jealousy, spite, lies and intrigue — these are the elder's meat and drink, the grease that turns the wheels of Elysium and court, and the pleasantries that divert her mind from the ghastly truth of her existence. While these characteristics permeate nearly all aspects of Kindred society, it is the elders who perpetuate them most often. Indeed, by applying them consistently and judiciously, it might be said that elders train successive generations of vampires to perpetuate these cruelties on one another and those who may be Embraced later. Younger Kindred often accept this treatment as an inevitable product of dwelling side-by-side with their less human elders, but until the neonates and ancillae also reach a similar age, they will not fully understand what drives elder vampires to these extremes of behavior.

When elders reach the point where the gentler emotions no longer have any meaning for them, when compassion and sympathy have vanished completely from their emotional landscape, they must rely on the intentional infliction of suffering to stir their aged blood. The pain of others is less important and less meaningful to them, except as a means of exciting their own dulled senses. The elder who inflicts misery on another Kindred does not care how this pain makes her victim feel; she cares only that his suffering be sufficiently powerful that she might observe it and enjoy the sensations it awakens within her jaded and decayed soul, alleviating her boredom and diverting her attention from other problems.

Elders inflict injury in this fashion almost out of habit — they feud for the sake of it rather than for any justifiable reason. This habit rises not only from the need to experience strong emotion again, but also from the stultifying boredom of nightly fare. The sheer banality of the same hatreds, grudges and fears can be a force sufficient to crush the most resilient spirit, but it must be so. All other forms of conflict are too dangerous to contemplate, given what is at stake when one reacts to a threat in a direct fashion. The ancient strictures of Elysium forbid any sort of warfare more open than the cutting remark or the petty lie, and so these are the weapons that elders turn upon one another for lack of anything more lethal. In some ways it is fortunate for all that this is the case, for imagine the disaster that would befall the Camarilla if the elders were free to give full vent to all the petty jealousies and hatreds that seethe beneath the dignified masks they wear in Elysium?

Decide how your elder character will participate in this clandestine war of intrigue. For participate she must, lest she be the target of those elders who do. Will she become the queen of rumors, spreading malicious (but untraceable) gossip of her enemies' foibles, or will she manipulate younger Kindred into taking up her causes and inflicting wounds upon her rivals? Consider your character's long-term goals and how you can use this aspect of elder behavior to further them. Want to be prince? Start that whispering campaign early, and build your network of informants so that you always have fresh — though not necessarily accurate — information at your fingertips. Want to bring a rival low? Focus on penetrating your rival's defenses to locate his weakness, and then exploit it; don't forget to discuss a mutually beneficial alliance with the other enemies of your rival. Be careful not to tip your hand or spring your traps too soon. You'll gain far more satisfaction from stalking your prey and playing with your food than devouring it whole.

Building an Elder Power Base

You are old, possibly older than the city or even nation in which you now reside. You have seen countless nights pass since your Embrace, and you stand to see countless more if you are careful and cunning. You are close to your Beast. Sometimes you think that you can actually feel its fetid breath against the back of your neck, or feel its covetous eyes burning a hole in your skull. You have struggled to remain free of the talons that tear at your gut, but you've been unable to prevent the slow, inexorable downward spiral. And you are afraid. Your fear is a paralyzing, dizzying thing. Constrained on every side by enemies and rivals and threatened by the rapidly changing mortal world, one cannot help but wonder how elders manage to maintain such a firm grip on the reins.

The answer lies in the most fundamental characteristic that defines an elder — longevity. Immortal beings who experience nightly terror for their very existence either work fervently to increase their own personal power or else they perish at the hands of the stronger. Time is the one resource that, come what may, the elders have in abundance. Elders have spent many mortal lifetimes learning how to sow the seeds of power and reap that harvest while denying the same benefits to others. The accumulation of hundreds of small but carefully orchestrated actions over the course of centuries can often more than offset a reluctance to risk potential gain on a sudden decision. True, the elders often miss opportunities to increase their power through windfall profits, but they also do not stand to lose all that they have accrued to a single toss of the dice.

STATUS

Status is one of the coins of the Kindred realm, and many elders cannot bear to be without it. The perception of strength, the favor of the harpies and the possession of unpaid debts are all trappings of power that are measured in status. Those who possess status therefore possess the ultimate currency of the night. In the rarified atmosphere of Elysium or the court, only those who hold this coin in hand can expect to enjoy the more choice benefits of Kindred society. Elders of the Toreador clan are among the most prominent adjudicators of Status, for they are possessed of the ability to judge the value of style over substance better than anyone.

Guard your Status Traits jealously. Because Status can rise and fall rapidly, it is unwise to risk even a single Temporary Status Trait on a dubious individual or cause, unless you know that you stand to gain by the outcome. Status is too precious a commodity to throw it away frivolously on questionable endeavors. If your character enjoys numerous Status Traits, it's time to start thinking about how to use them best. For example, you might suggest to the prince that only Kindred who possess a certain number of Status Traits might be allowed to gain access to Her Majesty (just make sure that you have the requisite number of Traits!), or mention to the harpies the woeful state of your rival's financial condition in order to score a hit on his own Status.

DISCIPLINES

Elders of the Sixth and Seventh Generations enjoy an additional benefit of their old age: They have the potential to increase their mastery over the supernatural powers bestowed by Caine's curse. Centuries of practice have made even passive Disciplines into deadly tools. It is ironic that many younger Kindred spend their early unlives delighting in the capabilities bestowed on them by their blood rights; by the time these Kindred reach the age of consideration, they find that their powers have become the weapon of last resort. Elders have few compunctions about using their more subtle powers, particularly *Dominate* and *Presence*, to establish their authority over the younger Cainites. But only when all other contests are ruled out or stalemated do elders turn to their Disciplines in earnest for the means of settling conflicts among themselves. To use such godlike force casually would not only be a hideous risk to the Masquerade, but it would reveal too much of the elders' true power to those who covet it. The Tremere are perhaps the clan with the most faith in the security granted by their Discipline, though other elders smile at this presumption.

Some Master Discipline powers can forever alter the course of a chronicle, destroying character concepts and eliminating plot threads with frightening speed. It is incumbent upon you, whether as the elder player or the Storyteller, to accept the responsibility that comes with access to these powers. You may find that sometimes the temptation to misuse them is nearly overwhelming, but resist: Your fellow players will thank you, and the game itself will benefit from your restraint. Exercise care and discretion when bringing these big guns to bear: Don't use a bazooka to shoot a mosquito. Kindred don't become elders by using their most powerful capabilities routinely or openly: Those who do so find themselves the target of unwanted attention, and are weeded out by their more competent and masterful peers or cannibalistic childer. If your character harbors her strength and keeps her cool, she'll gain far more in the long run than she will by crushing a pesky neonate with a swipe of her Master-level *Potence*.

Tainted Authority: Elders and Other Characters

One of the most appalling truths that any young Kindred must learn and, to a greater or lesser degree, accept is that the elders who occupy the topmost rung of Camarilla society aren't ever going to willingly step aside to allow their juniors to take their place in the driver's seat. Camarilla society functions as the classic zero-sum game: Each and every winner exists only at the expense of a loser. Elders can advance in the ranks of the Camarilla only on the backs of their rivals, but with the ancillae and neonates pushing continuously from below, even an elder who chooses to remain stationary will earn the enmity of those beneath him.

Elders thus occupy the keystone role in the Camarilla, a position that brings them into nightly contact and conflict with other Kindred. Most princes and more than a few primogen are elders. They are the visible embodiment of Camarilla society. No Kindred can afford to ignore them, not even the rebellious anarchs or the lowly Caitiff. Dealing with an elder at some point is an inevitability for nearly every member of the sect, whether they like it or not. While not every encounter with an elder need occur in the rarified atmosphere of Elysium, such interactions in a **Masquerade** game are much more likely to be of the direct, rather than the indirect, variety.

Relations with Neonates

Most elders believe that the best way to rear childer is with a generous helping of harsh discipline, coupled with constant admonitions against the evils of rebellion and a pernicious hatred of the Sabbat. They believe that in so doing they instill within their progeny the requisite attitudes and beliefs that will keep them in line. Some elders, notably the Malkavian and Nosferatu, believe that strict control only makes childer even more rebellious; they advocate less harsh treatment of neonates, and believe this will stem the flow of the youngest Camarilla vampires who reject their sires' sect in favor of the Sabbat or anarchs. Ironically, advocates of both positions may be wrong, for what most neonates want isn't better treatment, but radical changes in the very foundation and superstructure of Kindred society, something they aren't likely to achieve as long as the elders are making the rules.

RELATIONS WITH ANCILLAE

Individual ancillae wield only marginal power, but collectively they form the "middle class" on which much of the Camarilla's past achievements and future survival depend. Fortunately for older Kindred, the ancillae are as divided by clan rivalries and petty grudges as the elders themselves, making any significant organization among their ranks unlikely at best. Nevertheless, many elders fear exactly that potential, and with good reason: Most of them rose to power through secret arrangements with other ancillae. Thus, they habitually remain alert for signs of similar pacts among the rank and file, and act quickly to render them null and void, sometimes uniting briefly with other elders for the purpose, only to return to their mutual jealousies when the threat is quashed.

Elders often devote extensive time and energy exercising subtle control over ancilla pawns through a system of judicious rewards and punishments. But this sort of manipulation is a double-edged sword. The more capable the ancilla, the greater her rewards are. But the more rewards she earns, the more powerful she grows. Eventually, she grows too powerful and begins to become a source of anxiety to her elder patrons, who cannot help but fear that her ambitions will turn next toward what they possess and control. Thus, the elders make every effort to slow the pace of advancement within Camarilla society in order to prevent the ancillae from accumulating power too quickly. But even this stratagem has its drawbacks, as the ancillae inevitably chafe with frustration at the tortuously slow pace of their climb through the ranks.

INTERACTION GUIDELINES: DO'S AND DON'TS

Do cultivate the key elements of elder behavior — fear, hatred and cruelty. These are the indispensable elements of your elder disguise kit. Remember, though, that an elder keeps these emotions subdued while displaying the all-important veneer of surface calm, whether you're on the giving or receiving end of an inconvenience. No elder worthy of the title loses his cool over meaningless insults hurled by social nobodies, or engages in petty bickering with riffraff. Save your full vampiric rage for climactic scenes in which it will heighten tension, rather than unleashing every time some snot-nosed anarch punk sticks her tongue out at you.

Don't misuse your character. Demanding that every character younger than yours bend the knee or die is a gross abuse of your character's authority and role in the game. Using your character's age as a club with which to beat other players so that you can "win" is the hallmark of the abusive player. The object of the game is to have fun, and it's the object of all the players, not just you. If you can't have fun playing your elder character without being abusive, do everyone else a favor and don't play at all.

Do find reasons to interact with other characters. You're not doing yourself or anyone else any favors by hugging the dark corner for the entire game session. While it's true that your elder character may have little use for the younger members of the sect, you must recognize as a player that the game cannot proceed if the character does not make at least a token effort to approach others and be approachable. Neonates and ancillae may be annoying, but they are also useful. Does your character really want to do all her dirty work herself? Didn't think so. So persuade, charm, seduce, blackmail, intimidate and otherwise manipulate

other characters into helping you get it done. This simultaneously advances your character's goals, while helping other players get involved in the game.

Don't hog the spotlight. You aren't the only player in the game, and although elders play a key role in games set in Camarilla-controlled cities, be sure to give other players ample opportunity to shine. You'll make a lot more friends and contribute more to the chronicle by helping others to enjoy themselves than you will by demanding all the attention.

ELDERS CLAN BY CLAN

BRUJAH

The elders of this clan are something of a mystery to their juniors. To younger Brujah, it often seems as if the fires of rebellion that once burned in the breasts of their elders must have been extinguished at some point. Almost all the older members of this clan realize, eventually, that revolution for its own sake leads only to a waste of resources, and so the elder Brujah turn their attentions toward subverting and controlling the system from within. It is for this reason that many elder Brujah are consummate politicians and power-brokers, and it is why so many younger Brujah believe that their elders have sold them out to become card-carrying members of the Camarilla's "old vampire network." The truth is that younger Brujah, filled with the fire of revolt, have almost no hope of understanding their elders, whose ancient dream of a rebuilt Carthage still flickers behind their thoughtful expressions.

Elder Brujah are forced to walk an unenviable tightrope. You must somehow overcome your clan's Iconoclast image in order to be accepted and taken seriously by your elder peers, and yet by doing so you risk losing credibility among the juniors of your blood. Contemptuous pronouncements of "Upstart" might be followed by outraged cries of "Sell out!" if you aren't careful in presenting your public face to these rival factions. If you're a truly ancient Brujah — one who recalls the glories of Carthage, for instance — pay careful attention to choosing motivations that further the goals and dreams still burning brightly in the memory, if not in the heart.

MALKAVIAN

The elders of Malkav's line are among the most enigmatic, wise, insightful and dangerous Kindred to claim membership in the Camarilla. They know that only they can perceive that which is truly important, and that only if they pay attention to these signs and portents will they truly understand the riddle that is their existence. Those who refuse to see these things — that is, almost all other Kindred — earn only scant attention from the elders, who are increasingly concerned only with comprehending the ominous pattern their fractured visions reveal to them.

Embodying the elder Malkavian's enigmatic lunacy isn't a task for inexperienced players. Elder Malkavians have the benefit not only of the lunatic's insight, but the advantage of seeing the modern through the cracked lens of the past. You know only too well that the signs of imminent and radical change are everywhere to be seen, and you should consider how your behavior will reflect the truths and portents you see in the night. What is it that you hear

that you wish to relate to other Cainites, and how does what you've seen in ages before relate to what you're sensing now?

NOSFERATU

It is likely that only the elder Nosferatu, of all the clans, suspect how very costly choosing the incorrect course of action will be at this dangerous crossroads in Kindred history. Never have they felt less certain about what they should do and never quite so alone and isolated, not only from the elders of other clans but from the younger members of their own as well. Elder Nosferatu hear the stealthy approach of the legendary Nicktuku in the echo of every sound that permeates their underground lairs, while the modern world above reshapes itself a hundred times in a single year, changes spurred on by technological advancements with which even these masters of information are hard-pressed to keep pace. Many prefer to play the waiting game they know so well, hoping that the proper course of action will reveal itself if they wait and watch just a little longer.

The elder Nosferatu character finds that time is running out too fast for him to rely on his clan's customary reticence and careful neutrality to see him through what he fears may be coming. Any scrap of information, no matter how trivial it seems, may be a vital clue that will help you determine the proper course of action — you can't afford to play the same games that allowed you to gather this data slowly and carefully in the past. You fear that you're running out of time, and that if you don't get some answers you can trust very quickly, your inability to see a clear path may well doom not only yourself but your clanmates as well. Desperation isn't a characteristic of the Nosferatu, but you feel it gnawing at your gut and mind with increasing frequency.

TOREADOR

The heart of the elder Toreador must surely know the cold grip of desperation. The art forms she knew and loved in her youth are now musty relics of bygone nights, fit only to be mocked and ridiculed, or at best imitated without feeling or substance. Can art even be said to have relevance in a world where artists seem to exist only to tear down any form of expression that is not a product of their own technologically incomprehensible world? Some Toreador elders actually manage to cling to their preferred art forms despite these assaults, but even they find little solace, for the work of an artist so far removed from the emotions that originally drove her to create often loses the ability to reflect anything even remotely human, despite its technical brilliance.

Elder Toreador often lash out blindly at the younger members of their clan, even — or perhaps especially — those who display genuine artistic talent. How dare these childer attempt to set foot on the very path that you have already determined is hollow at best? Why should they know the joy of creation without the burden of pain? Some ancient Toreador seek to beguile the tedium by concocting positively Byzantine schemes of social manipulation, designed sometimes to improve their own social or political standing, and sometimes simply to inflict as much misery as possible on someone. If you have few Morality Traits, you may begin to delve into shockingly degenerate behaviors that you claim inspire you to new heights of artistry, but which in truth serve only to satisfy your growing demand for new and different pleasures.

TREMERE

Until recently, Tremere elders felt a smug self-assurance that their dominion over magic would enable them to survive whatever may be ahead for the Kindred in general, and for the Camarilla in particular. But when the Assamites somehow threw off their ancient curse, the elders' confidence faded rapidly. Now they face destruction and diablerie at the hands of their ancient enemies, and no longer do they feel safe. Despite this disaster, elder Tremere have less to fear from their juniors, thanks to the strict discipline of their clan structure.

Elder Tremere often behave in a manner that seems designed to throw their heartless nature into sharp relief. It is not that the Tremere are inherently more cruel than other Cainites, but rather that they are often better prepared to accept the inevitable price of their unliving condition. Your attitude toward your own powers will in part determine your behavior: Do you believe firmly that *Thaumaturgy* holds the key to surviving Gehenna and ruling what remains of the Kindred after it passes, or do you prefer to utilize your magical heritage in order to pursue the mysteries of the universe and ignore all that political claptrap? Is your control of the arcane arts a tool that will allow you to amass even more power, or have you yet to come to terms with your thaumaturgical abilities, making you indeed a rarity within the Tremere ranks?

VENTRUE

In these modern nights, the Ventrue feel themselves surrounded by a sea of dangers. Claiming that they bear the burden of guiding their fellow Kindred into the future, they feel the Camarilla's recent losses against the Sabbat quite sharply indeed. Yet even while they point to these setbacks as evidence that the other clans must contribute more effort to shoring up the Camarilla's defenses, the Ventrue are certain that the very Kindred they are attempting to protect are working at cross-purposes to them. Some might even be obstructing the Ventrue plans to defend the Camarilla deliberately, a concern that frustrates even the most junior bean counter in the clan's ranks.

Ventrue elder characters are the very soul of nobility. Their pride borders dangerously close to arrogance, and their desire to protect the Camarilla from the ham-handed efforts of their brethren often expresses itself as condescension. You may have been helping carry the Camarilla burden for the entirety of the sect's existence, and while you might still feel a certain *noblesse oblige,* even immortal patience grows thin. The thought that other clans might be thwarting your clan's efforts to defend the Camarilla may send you into paroxysms of rage, especially when

you compare this ingratitude to all the battles and crises the Ventrue have faced on the Camarilla's behalf. The time is coming when you feel that the clan may have no other choice but to impose order, whether the rest of the clans like it or not.

Storytelling for Elders

Ideally, you should treat elder characters in your chronicle as you would spices in a meal. They're meant to season and accentuate the main ingredients of a dish, not overpower their flavor. Elders can be easily overused, so be cautious when adding more of them to an existing chronicle. The bulk of Kindred society is comprised of neonates and ancillae. The actual number of elders in a given game can vary depending on the game's focus and scope. If you're telling a story for more than 30 characters, you're probably going to have a larger percentage of elders in the game than in a story for a dozen characters. However, the number of elders in any given game isn't as important as how well and consistently those characters are played, and how well you weave them into the tale.

Elder Moods

Elders radiate menace and embody the very essence of power. They can quiet an entire room with their inhuman attitudes and appearance; they can tip the balance of power in an entire city with a few well-chosen words. Work with the players who will play the elders in your chronicle to create the mood you desire by helping them highlight their characters' distance from Humanity. By providing them with reasons to be envious and fearful of one another, you create a mood of black paranoia as the elders begin plotting against one another. Encourage these players to involve the other characters in their schemes; this heightens the tension and invokes a mood of jealous suspicion or manic fear, depending on the lengths to which the elders go to achieve their ambitions.

Elder Themes

Elders embody myriad and often contradictory themes, most of which work very well as the central idea of a chronicle. Here are some examples:

Spoiled Love: What turns love into hate, or worse, indifference? How do Kindred cope when a love they thought was genuine turns out to be corrupt and false? Why can't Kindred maintain their hold on the finer emotions they knew in life?

Thwarted Ambition: What happens when we don't get what we want most? Who do we damage when pursuing goals that remain just out of our reach? What sorts of revenge does a heart devise when it is denied its innermost desires?

Inner Decay: Is every elder corrupt? How does their compromised integrity affect the Camarilla? Is the rot visible, or hidden like a disease that rots a tree from within? Can younger Kindred do anything to combat this problem?

Repression and Rebellion: What hope do younger Kindred have in a society where the elders cling to old glories and undeserved authority with bloody talons? What happens in a city wherein the young dare to ask this question, and are met with a backlash of furious anger from their elders?

How to Keep Elders Busy

Elders are some of the most useful plot devices in the Storyteller's toolkit. Entire plots can hang on elder characters or be driven by their actions. Unfortunately, elder characters can also wipe out an entire plot with a few ill-chosen words

or actions, often unintentionally. How do you achieve the former utility without suffering the latter disaster? First choose the right players for elder characters, and then communicate clearly and consistently with them. If you hand out elder characters to just any player, and fail to describe your expectations, you'll have no one to blame but yourself for the disaster you've unleashed on your game.

Communicate with the players while they are creating their elder characters. If there are multiple elder characters in your chronicle, do yourself and your players a favor by suggesting some threads of common history between them. If they've all been in the same city together for any length of time, they should definitely begin the game with at least one healthy rivalry per elder character, as well as an assortment of grudges, intrigues and gossip bubbling merrily away under the surface. None of these relationships or idiosyncrasies need be obvious to the other characters when the story begins — let them discover this seething cauldron of trouble naturally. Encourage elder players to create detailed character histories, and perhaps offer a bonus Freebie Trait or two for those who build useful story hooks into their backgrounds.

Describe to the elder players what sort of story you want to tell, and solicit their feedback. Don't be afraid to share your thoughts on mood and theme with them; if you trust them enough to play elder characters, you might as well trust them to collaborate with you. Get their input; ask them what they'd like their characters to do in the story, and talk about how the characters can pursue their goals actively but indirectly, so as not to turn each game into a Discipline stand-off. Encourage them to involve other characters in their machinations, and teach them how to share the main plots with other player characters rather than accruing all the story threads for themselves. Help them understand that when they foster intrigue and tension through their characters, it pays off for everyone who is playing in the game.

Disciplining Errant Elders

Most players present no problems, and they will both appreciate your efforts at telling good stories and be eager to cooperate in helping you do so. Keep a weather eye out for the player who doesn't. In games where there is only one elder, caution that player against acting petty and spiteful: This sort of behavior will annoy the other players quickly. Be alert, too, for the player who abuses his elder character's powers or authority. Powergamers can be a nuisance in any game session; a powergamer with an elder character can destroy an entire chronicle. You'll recognize these players fast: They're the ones who get a cheap ego trip at the other players' expense. There is no excuse for allowing players of this nature to ruin the game for everyone else. If you observe a player behaving in this fashion, at the very least you must take that player aside as soon as possible and explain why this sort of behavior is unacceptable. Don't be confrontational if it isn't necessary — most powergamers think that their playing style is how the game is supposed to be played — but be firm nonetheless. Your goal is to tell a story that allows all the players to have fun, and you need the support of each player in order to reach that goal. Consider carefully whether to allow the player to return to play with an elder character; if you decide to allow him to do so, continue to watch him carefully for any problematic behavior. If the player persists despite your attempts to explain the problem, then remove him from the game at the earliest possible opportunity.

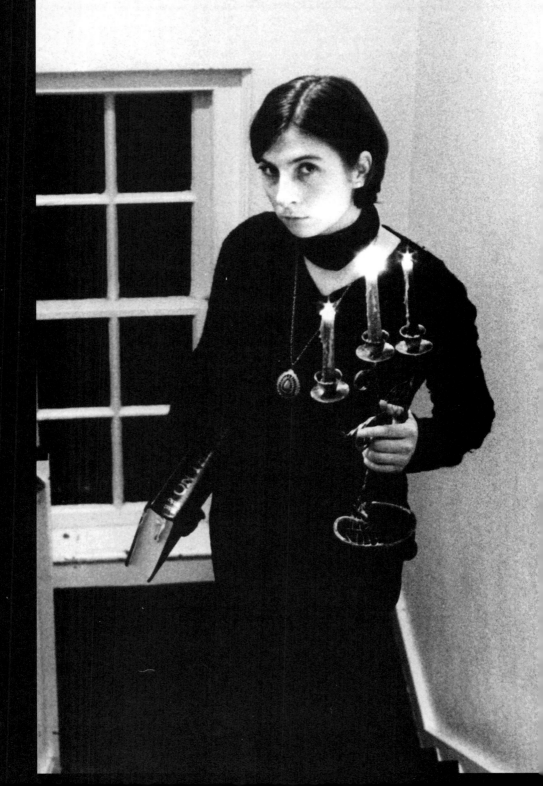

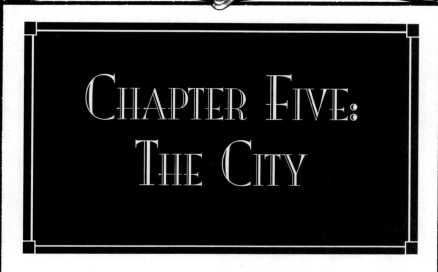

CHAPTER FIVE: THE CITY

WHERE IT ALL GOES DOWN

It is easy to overlook the importance of the city your **Masquerade** chronicle is set in. Often, it's just the place where things happen — a somewhat vague backdrop for adventures, left largely undefined except perhaps for a few details here and there.

There's much more to a city than that, though. It is a vampire's lifeline — the only thing that allows him to continue his existence. Only large gatherings of humans allow vampires to gather; after all, without blood, a vampire cannot survive. And while many vampires deem themselves to be the hidden masters of the human society, they are still quite dependent on the very society they claim to control.

This chapter is primarily intended for Storyteller use. It doesn't contain any secrets, so players can read it without feeling guilty. However, its primary use is in creating cities for **Masquerade** chronicles, and it's thus likely to be far more useful to Storytellers than it is to players. That said, reading through this chapter will probably help players think of the city where the game takes place as more than just a generic location. In addition, players will get some insight into the life of a Camarilla vampire.

IF YOU BUILD IT, THEY WILL COME

Fictional cities give you a lot of leeway; after all, you can do whatever you want, and no one can tell you that you got something wrong. However, it takes more than just coming up with a nice round number for the population and a cool Gothic name for the place to create a proper city for your **Masquerade** chronicle.

If you feel like creating a city of your own, you probably have some kind of an idea for it already. It may not be anything very definite; then again, it doesn't have to be. As long as you have a concept of what you're going for, you should be doing all right. Indeed, creating a city isn't that different from creating a character; the details may be different, but the process is much the

same — it all comes down to working up from an idea, stage by stage, bit by bit, until you reach whatever it is that you wanted. Of course, more work goes into creating an entire city than creating a single character, but when broken down, the process is very similar.

Location

First of all, you need to decide where your city is. There may be instances when you prefer to leave the actual location somewhat vague — after all, placing Gotham City or other fictional cities on a map can often be difficult at best, and doing so might even detract from the mood — it doesn't really matter where they are, as long as the place feels right. Still, even if you're going for a mood like this, it's good to come up with the approximate location of the city. Knowing where your city is can be a very important factor in deciding what your city feels like. A city located in the middle of a desert is going to be markedly different from one located on the coast — no one would ever mistake New Orleans for Las Vegas. Climate and resources can also be easily decided once you know where the city is — and from there, you can move on to what kind of industries the city has. Mining? Fishing? Tourism? It all depends on where you are.

Infrastructure

There are dozens of questions you must answer. Is there a subway system? Are there skyscrapers? Is there an airport? Is the city easy to navigate, or is it a maze of small streets and alleys? Does it have sections where ethnic groups

have settled — a Chinatown, or a Little Italy? Does it have slums? Is it modern and shiny, or old and built largely of stone?

These things define the very basics of any city — what the place looks like, how you get around. For example, all cities have extensive networks of sewers, maintenance tunnels, air shafts and whatnot, but the existence of a subway system still means happier times for the local Nosferatu. Airports and train stations are important locations — they provide means to enter and exit the city; something every cautious prince makes a point of keeping an eye on.

A Chinatown? Good news for those Tremere who look for occult lore in mysterious small shops (see **Laws of the East** for ideas about what they might find) — or certain Ventrue who tend to be picky about their meals.

Slums? Food, plain and simple. Who's going to miss a couple of bums? It may not be a gourmet meal, but it's safe feeding.

What's the industry like? What are the major imports and exports? How's the local economy doing? A poor city and a rich city can be two very different things indeed. Note that these matters may very well be two-sided — a thriving chemical industry may well improve the local overall quality of living, but it might have an adverse effect on the surrounding environment.

You shouldn't feel pressured to draw the map of the entire city (although if you happen to have the free time and the skill, go for it — your players will love you), but you should put some thought into its layout nonetheless. For example, if there are hills and a river, you should decide which neighborhoods are located on the hill and which ones by the river. Decide where the industrial areas are, what the docks are like and so forth. After all, a city is really a patchwork of many different areas; it's not a homogenous environment where everything looks the same throughout. You should also pay attention to when certain areas were constructed and how the city has expanded — there may be neighborhoods that are brand new and areas that have been around for a century or longer. These things may well be of importance to the vampiric population; if someone has lived somewhere for a hundred years but has been forced to move when the area has been rebuilt, he may not be very amused, or, in order to feel comfortable, an old vampire may have used her influence to keep a certain area from becoming too modern.

What Makes It Go?

You should also think about your city's needs a bit and see that they are taken care of. In the simplest of terms, that means that people must have food, shelter and warmth, although you can certainly make it more complicated than that if you want to. Where do the local industries' raw materials come from? Who do they sell their products to?

You don't need to go into too much detail here, but it's a good idea to think about the basics a bit. For example, is the city buying some of its required electricity from somewhere else or does it has a power source of its own? It could be that the power is coming from a local hydroelectric dam, a coal plant or perhaps a nuclear reactor. Some characters may well have an interest in these matters — an ecologically minded vampire might well want to shut down a polluting coal plant.

Population

The people who live in a city are perhaps the most important thing for a Storyteller to think about. What kind of people live there? Are they rich? Is everyone employed? Are they religious? Are they happy? A city with unhappy citizens is a city in trouble — it affects work morale, and unhappy people don't feel inclined to contribute to the city's well-being. Some Kindred may consider humans to be cattle, but even the most bullheaded vampire usually understands that even cattle must be cared for. A happy citizen is a productive citizen, and a healthy citizen is a lasting resource.

People are more than just automatons who eat, sleep, breed and work, though. They're what makes a city live. In most **Masquerade** games, completely normal, mortal humans don't play a very large part, as the player characters tend to be vampires, ghouls or other strange beings. Still, most Kindred spend most of their time interacting with the human society, even if most chronicles don't pay much attention to that. After all, that's what the Masquerade is about: hiding in plain sight. Vampires exist by feeding on real, living human beings. While all the talk of the angst and humanity of it all may not appeal to everyone, it is still something that is bound to have an impact on the characters, and you should try and make people as much a part of your city as everything else — perhaps even more so.

Authorities

Are the authorities efficient? Are there any major criminal organizations operating in the city? Who's got the political clout? Is there corruption? There's a great difference between a peaceful city where violent crime is relatively rare and a city where criminal gangs run free and fight with each other over the control of their turfs — a city where the politicians do their jobs properly and a city where politicians are on a short leash and draw fat paychecks from the people who make you offers you can't refuse. This also has a direct impact on the citizens. Joe Average prefers to live in a place where it's safe to walk the streets at night and will become displeased if he cannot do so.

Of course, criminal activities aren't the only possible problems. An economic crisis is likely to result in unhappy citizens. Without suitable funds, the city's infrastructure starts to break down, bit by bit. Public services are no longer as efficient as before. Garbage cans may be overflowing because the city can't afford proper waste disposal. Broken streetlights may not get fixed. Bureaucracy becomes slow if the people responsible for it get laid off, leaving the remaining people to handle a bigger workload, which in turn increases stress both for the overworked and the unemployed — and so forth. These are things that may easily become important factors in a chronicle if the Storyteller prepares properly. What's more, they are problems that cannot be fixed with force; it takes planning and work from the characters. While these events aren't likely to become centerpieces, they are certainly things that are likely to interest the characters quite a bit. It's largely a question of survival and quality of life for them.

These are hardly all of the important questions, of course. When was the city founded? Have there been major disasters, such as fires or earthquakes? How did they affect the Kindred population? Was there more to these disasters

than the mortal world knows? There is no master list of questions; these are all things that define what your city is like — the more detail you can come up with, the better. A good way to get a handle on these things is to look at events — especially everyday events — in your own city and ask yourself "Why are things like this? How would they be in my city?" It may seem like a lot of work to go through, and it is, but it'll pay off if it makes your players feel like they really are in a city that is more than just a shallow backdrop for adventures.

Note that it's a good idea to pay some attention to the real locations you'll be using for the game when you're designing your city. Imagination is an impressive tool, but if your fictional city has a large park, it can make your life much easier to really have access to a large park which can be used for the game. The same thing goes for everything from the climate to the generic look of the city. This is by no means a requirement, but it can make things easier if you intend to play in public locations. Of course, if you're only playing indoors, such things cease to matter and you can go wild.

HISTORY

Coming up with an extensive and detailed history for your city can be a problem. Overdo it, and you end up with a huge, boring book that no one really wants to read. Still, figuring out when your city was founded and why is a good idea, as is determining the major points in its history. Why did people want to move there and make it grow? What kind of industry did it have in the past? Who were the important people who made it all happen? Are there statues or buildings dedicated to their memory? Have there been battles in the city? Has anyone fought over the city itself?

Your city's history can be just an overview of the important events, and you can elaborate on certain things as necessary. As long as it is consistent and answers all the important questions players might have, it'll do just fine. For most games, defining the present is far more important than defining the distant past.

That said, if your chronicle deals with the past, or includes many characters who have lived in the city for a long time — perhaps for a hundred years or more — they'll need to know enough to play their roles convincingly, and that will obviously require more attention to the city's history.

It's recommended that Storytellers who face this task pay attention to real world history to see what happened in the world at any given time. Events such as the Civil War or the Great Depression or, in Europe, the World Wars and the resulting aftermath or the Inquisition (if you want to go that far into the past) have probably affected your city a great deal. In the end, it's not very difficult to do; all it requires is time, patience and a little bit of effort.

Finally, make sure that the history of your city is known to your players. How much they know should depend on what kind of characters they're playing, of course; elders are secretive beings and don't reveal their precious information easily. In any case, knowing the history helps them understand the city, and once they understand their surroundings properly, they'll have a far easier time settling into their characters comfortably. It is absolutely pointless to come up with a comprehensive and well-organized history for the city if it is never presented to the players.

Who's Doing What?

There are some organizations in any and all cities that are of supreme importance to the Kindred. Political offices, police and fire departments and the media are the first ones that come to mind, and thus you should spend time thinking about them. Unlike superficial things, such as what things look like, this is something that may have a direct impact on your game. What's more, knowing what your city is like allows you to *use* that information properly — it means that if someone uses her influence to order the local police around, you're not dealing with abstract police units, you can actually determine how that affects the rest of the city. The Kindred don't exist in a vacuum, and though they may influence the city, the city also influences them. Never forget that.

Most organizations can be defined in a few simple steps:

What does the organization do? This is simply a question of defining the organization's goals and agendas. A police department's goal is to uphold the law and catch the bad guys; a software company wants to develop software and turn a profit. Agendas may be rather simple or extremely complicated. In most cases, it's not necessary for the Storyteller to define them down to the smallest

Who's Pulling the Strings?

Vampires like to think that they are in control of the human society. At times, they are even correct; after all, if you control an influential member of a society, you can control certain areas of the society itself through that person. However, humans still have minds and concerns of their own, and vampires who forget that will find that they've bitten off more than they can chew. A city is bustling with activity; there may very well be millions and millions of people going through their lives there. While vampires may steer humans in a direction favorable to Kindred goals and use their Influence to advance their own agendas, ultimately humans may do things that damage the Kindred.

This can take many forms. It may be as simple as a Nosferatu being forced to move because his subterranean haven gets invaded by a horde of sewer workers, or it may be a Ventrue finding some of her stock losing its value because the company's CEO is making foolish decisions — or suddenly losing an important ghoul because he was shot in a mugging attempt. These things happen, and the more it feels like the characters are just a part of a bigger whole, the easier it is for the players to get into the game. Note that this doesn't mean that these should be random events; rather, they should be a logical part of the whole. A cunning vampire using her power over mortals may well be able to keep events like this from occurring at all.

details; a general understanding will do. Then again, if the organization is a major plot element, it's probably worth the trouble to get the details.

What can the organization accomplish? In other words, what kind of power and resources does it have. A police department has a great deal of authority due to their status as the local law enforcement agency, not to mention plenty of resources in the form of manpower, equipment and so forth. A huge software company has plenty of money and with money comes power — if nothing else, hiring a ravenous horde of highly paid lawyers gets you a long way. Furthermore, if their software is popular enough, they have a subtle influence over people, as changing their software also means changing the habits of the users. If nothing else, if you know the ins and outs of the software being used by everyone, you already have a potential weapon.

Who does the organization have direct influence over? A police department can disrupt most criminal operations with ease because our society grants them the authority to do so. Indeed, they may have a great deal of influence over the software company, *if* the software company commits a crime. That said, if the police department's computers run on the software company's software, the company can probably cause a lot of trouble for the department simply by releasing an extremely troublesome update for said software. Which would, of course, be illegal if done intentionally, but these things can be somewhat hazy at best....

What kind of weaknesses does the organization have? In many cases, weaknesses are something inherent to organizations — a flip side of their very nature, so to speak. While a police department has a great deal of authority while acting within the confines of the law, unless they have evidence that a crime has occurred or is occurring, they cannot legally do anything, even if they know what's going on. A software company that spreads its software everywhere and controls the market may end up in legal trouble because of that monopoly. There can be many additional weaknesses that don't follow this pattern, of course.

CONTROL

Numerous references to control and influence can be found here. Storytellers are encouraged to think about how these things are accomplished — be that through direct authority, blackmail, supernatural mind control or whatever. The Influences characters may have certainly come into play here, but instead of treating them as abstract tokens of influence, figure out exactly how the character has come by that Influence over the mortal society and how he wields it. Influences represent a certain amount of control, but it is up to the Storyteller to decide just what that means in her chronicle — is it a ghouled politician, a seat on the board of directors or a fake personality with equally fake authority?

Defining all of the major organizations in your city in this manner can take some time, but in the end you will have a good understanding of who's doing what and why. You will also know what kind of effects vampires who use their Influence will have on the big picture. Considering that in large games you may have a dozen or more powerful Kindred who use their different Influences at the same time, it's good to be able to see the big picture clearly.

Certain very important organizations exist in every city — police and fire departments, political offices, the media, power companies, schools, hospitals and so forth. They are crucial to mortal society — without them, it cannot function properly. Therefore, you should pay more attention to them; after all, they are the things that your players will be most interested in. Having a couple of cops or reporters in your back pocket can be a blessing at the time of a serious Masquerade breach. ("Nothing to see here, ma'am, you just move right along, please. You can read it in the paper tomorrow.")

However, note that micromanaging your city can quickly lead to disaster. While a certain degree of detail is fun and will improve the game, it means that you have far more work to do. A good rule of thumb is, "Is it likely that this will come up in the game?" If the answer is yes, by all means, spend time on thinking about the intricacies of the local public health services, but don't do it unless you need to. After all, chances are that you'll have plenty of other things to do, and there are only so many hours in the day.

You'll find more to this process than just defining all of these things, though. For this information to be meaningful, it must also be distributed to the players

Write down everything that you do, and everything that happens in the game. *Everything.* The importance of this can hardly be stressed enough. Just do it.

This way, when the player of that Ventrue comes to you and asks if there's any way he can try and take over the company the other character just purchased, you don't have to fidget and say something off the top of your head—you'll *know* the right answer since you have it written down. If you're following even half of the suggestions presented here, chances are that your city will be a large, complicated place that lives a life of its own, especially once the players get their hands on it. While you as the Storyteller control it, you should expect the players to change things around to better their characters' lives. Yes, this is a lot of work, but once you have it all down, you'll find that making changes to things isn't nearly as much of a hassle as you might think.

Note that it's quite all right to expect players to write reports for you. You aren't asking for novels; you're asking for simple descriptions of what they did and what happened to their characters. Even the thickest player should be able to describe these things in less that 15 minutes if he takes the time to do so in the next few days following the game while everything is still fresh in his memory. An oral report with you writing down the details does equally well. As long as you get the information, the exact method is up to you. Don't let them talk you out of it — you *need* that information to properly run the game.

properly — preferably so that they know as much about the big picture as their characters do, as determined by their character backgrounds and whatever Influence they may have. This usually comes down to simply writing the appropriate bits down and handing them to the players.... And yes, that's more work. Luckily, it'll pay off once your players get into the mood and start to use that information. While Kindred matters certainly take a lot of time and attention, most Kindred who dabble in mortal affairs take them rather seriously. If you do your groundwork well, that means that the players can actually see the effect their actions have on the city their characters live in. Just remember that you must provide them with all the relevant information for all this to work properly.

THE DARK END OF THE STREET

And last, but certainly not least, you have to think about what makes this city a part of the Camarilla and the World of Darkness and not just another normal city. After all, the game is about vampires, and while paying attention to the city itself can be important, you certainly shouldn't do so and forget all about the supernatural. If the dynamics of mortal society can be troublesome and complicated, that can be a walk in the park compared to the complicated mess a single Camarilla city can hold for its vampiric occupants.

THE CLANS

Of all the power groups in a Camarilla city, the clans are the most obvious ones. Everyone knows the exaggerated stereotypes, ranging from the artsy Toreador who goes around waving at things with his pinky pointing delicately at just the right angle, to the feral hillbilly Gangrel who has trouble spelling her name — and certainly, there's a seed of truth in all that; clan members do share common traits and characteristics and usually tend to feel varying degrees of loyalty toward each other — in many ways, a clan is similar to a family.

Clan elders tend to rule over the younger members of their clan, and their demands tend to be met with obedience. After all, doing otherwise means falling out of favor, and with falling out of favor comes all sorts of problems that most Kindred would rather avoid entirely. Besides, doing favors to an elder usually pays off — it's not just the elder who gets something out of the deal. Looking good in the eyes of a powerful Kindred tends to mean more status, influence and protection.

Therefore, clans tend to stick together. Still, it's a mistake to assume that just because someone is a member of a certain clan, she instantly shares her clanmates' agendas, goals and ideals. From the Storyteller's point of view, it is a mistake to lump all members of a certain clan into one big group and assign a certain amount of power, status and resources to them — there's usually infighting and rivalry, and even if there isn't, there's absolutely nothing that keeps a Brujah from being a poet or a Malkavian from being a quite serious and responsible scientist. The archetypes can be good for illustrating the generic nature the group in question, but they shouldn't be allowed to become rigid stereotypes. In other words, no, all Brujah do not wear leather and beat each other up, nor do all Tremere wear evil-looking cloaks and lie and cheat and backstab whenever they get the opportunity.

Furthermore, there is plenty of cooperation between the clans of the Camarilla. The "This guy is not of my clan, therefore I will not cooperate with him, but I'm sure the Camarilla will still stay united and protect me against the hordes of anarchs, Sabbat, Lupines and who knows what else out there" mode of thought is rather faulty at best, for obvious reasons. Cooperation exists partly out of necessity — the Camarilla must stay united or it will fall, and the elders realize this. They may play their own games, but very rarely do they do so at the expense of the Camarilla. Vampires who display no concern for the Camarilla's continued survival are considered security risks and rightly so, and while they may survive

the experience, it's safe to say that they make quite a number of enemies in the process. The local elders may not care about a feud between two neonates, but if said feud threatens the Camarilla, they make it their business. Indeed, many princes consider such matters direct threats to their domain and act accordingly.

The other reason for cooperation is simple — despite all the intrigue and plotting that goes on, most Kindred are mature enough to be able to form relationships with other beings. They can sit down and talk about the events of the day. They can have friends and lovers — and they *do*. Why? Because they are immortal, and immortality without entertainment gets old rather quickly. Most Kindred, all of their famed inhumanity notwithstanding, have still many basic human characteristics. If you live forever, you'll learn to enjoy a good debate. It'll be far more interesting than counting bricks or wiggling your toes. Watching a movie is a far more pleasant way of spending two hours than sitting down and scheming. "All work and no play makes Jack a dull boy," as it were.

Yes, there are those who spend their nights plotting and planning and scheming, but despite the stereotype, this certainly doesn't apply to all, or even the majority of, the Kindred. Many of them just hang out and try to make the best of their unlives. Storytellers and players alike should always keep this in mind when designing characters. It'll make for better roleplaying, and it'll make for a better game. After all, there is little drama in becoming the primogen or gaining power for its own sake — if it's the norm and the only objective of the game, who cares? A bad guy isn't a bad guy if he's no different from everyone else. Friendship loses its meaning if everyone can always be depended to backstab everyone else — as does backstabbing. The game becomes predictable and pointless. A master of intrigue rarely looks like one — no one likes to do business with someone like that; after all, why cooperate with someone if you *know* you're going to get hurt in the process?

These things should always be kept in mind. Not only do they play a major part when determining the nature of the Kindred population of your city, but they are also likely to be some of the most important things in actual gameplay. After all, in the end, most games consist of a group of vampires getting together and talking.

OTHER POWER GROUPS

The clans, powerful though they are, are hardly the only supernatural power groups in the city. Often, coteries form across clan lines. Common interests cause vampires to band together — a group of Kindred who share strong anti-Sabbat sentiments might form a secret society to battle Sabbat even during a cease-fire, or financial interests might cause a group of vampires to pool their resources to gain control of the city's economy.

Also, there may be other supernatural creatures in the city — see "Things That Go Bump In The Night" p. 164.

IMPORTANT POSITIONS

There are many important offices to be filled in any Camarilla city. The prince, the sheriff, the members of the primogen, the harpies, the keeper of Elysium — all of these positions come with quite a bit of power and influence. All of these characters will need players — some of them may be played by the Storyteller or the Narrators, but even those need good backgrounds. How did they reach their

positions? Are they comfortable where they are? Do they have any major rivals who want in their place? How long have they held their positions?

While the specifics of those are detailed elsewhere — see "Positions of Power" p. 121, it's a good idea to keep in mind that the characters are also likely to have Influence in mortal society in addition to their Camarilla duties. These positions should be treated much like any authority in the mortal world, and while the actual details depend greatly on the personality of the character holding the position, the Storyteller should probably spend some time thinking about the balance of power between these positions — both within the Camarilla and within the mortal city.

HAVENS

All but the most nomadic vampires have a haven of some kind, and said locations are considered to be the vampire's domain. Even princes — despite holding great authority in the city — tend to respect others' havens unless given good reason to violate them. After all, that pesky Tradition about respecting others' domains is still taken somewhat seriously, and while it mostly applies to princes, many feel that it also extends to personal havens. The details vary from city to city, but in most cases, in a vampire's haven, her word is law. Obviously, this doesn't mean that a vampire can kill a member of the primogen (or, indeed, anyone) in her own haven and get away with it, but it does mean that showing proper respect to a vampire while paying a visit to her home is a good idea; a good beating or loss of Status may well follow from failing to do so.

The location of a vampire's haven should always be thought out; every player should know where and what kind of a place his character lives in. Basic security (or lack of it) should be covered. After all, these details will make a great deal of difference if the vampire's haven gets invaded.

ELYSIUMS

Think about the Elysium locations carefully. While the art museums and similar locations are popular choices, they are by no means the only options. The average Elysium will be in an easily accessible location, and is likely to be well-protected. You should think about what kind of guards the Elysium has, where they're coming from (are they the keeper's personal ghouls, or merely hirelings from a mortal security firm someone has Influence in?), and whether the Elysium directly interacts with the mortal world somehow or not? (An Elysium might be located in a public building that is closed for the night, such as a library or a building that houses the city's political offices.) Is it in the middle of the city, in a public location, where the Masquerade may be far more easily breached by accident, or is it located someplace more private? What kind of entrances and exits does it have? Do the Nosferatu have tunnels there? Furthermore, as gathering places during dangerous times, they make lovely targets for the Sabbat or other enemies; after all, blowing up the place where the ruling elite is located makes for a good tactical move. Thus most Elysiums tend to be in easily defended locations.

OTHER LOCATIONS

Other important locations may include (but aren't limited to) Tremere chantries, popular clubs or restaurants patronized by vampires and the shops

of black market arms dealers. Anything that seems to suit the local vampire population's needs and desires should be thought out. The Camarilla can get organized if need be, and some cities have been known to set up safehouses for Camarilla members in case of an emergency — especially during wartime conditions. All of these things should be pre-determined (or placed in a definite location in the city if the characters decide to organize something like this during the game).

Hunting Grounds

The Kindred have established hunting grounds, and the prince of the city usually grants each clan or coterie certain areas as theirs to hunt on as they please. There are other methods of dividing up the city, ranging from simply having the strongest vampires or clans feeding where they please and the lesser vampires doing their best to stay out of their way, to the prince declaring contests or quests to establish which clans or coteries deserve to have the best hunting grounds. Some princes make an elaborate spectacle out of it all, while others toss a coin.

In most cases, groups of vampires tend to regard their hunting grounds as their territory. Passing through them is certainly permitted, unless the area happens to be headed by a particularly troublesome vampire (in which case said vampire had better be prepared to defend his territory), but making trouble on someone else's dinner table is considered bad form and may well get the culprit in trouble. Of course, the prince of the city still holds supreme power in the area — unless said prince is a particularly unimpressive weakling, in which case she's probably on her way out anyway — but the prince isn't likely to get annoyed over someone getting slapped around because he couldn't behave.

The Storyteller should pay close attention to the hunting grounds instead of just defining them randomly. The Kindred can be rather picky about their diets; therefore, hunting locations can become an important issue in the chronicle. For example, a Nosferatu may be quite happy to feed in the slums — after all, chances are that it's close to home — but the Toreador might have somewhat different opinions about looking for convenient bums when they start to feel peckish. While the prince's word is certainly law and tends to be obeyed, most princes go out of their way to make sure the inhabitants of their domains are at least relatively comfortable. After all, the Camarilla is based on cooperation, and while there's plenty of petty bickering and plotting going on, in the end it's the Camarilla against the rest of the world. It pays to keep the troops happy.

Of course, if the prince is just another player character, the player should certainly have as much input in this as she desires.

Overpopulation

An average city needs about 100,000 citizens to sustain a single vampire's existence. (For thoughts about exceptions, see "Size Does Matter," p. 167.) This number may be stretched a bit, but after a certain point, problems start to crop up. Unexplained deaths and disappearances will start to cause problems in the mortal society, and the vampires will inevitably feel the pressure and start to argue about hunting grounds and hunting rights. It's not necessarily a question of there not being enough blood to feed on (although that may be an issue as well), but rather a question of having easily accessible blood sources.

There is more to feeding than having enough people around — the people in question have to be of the type the vampires can safely feed on. After all, every time a vampire feeds is a potential Masquerade violation, and a city where vampires have to struggle to find safe sources of blood is a city where the Masquerade is just waiting to be breached.

This is merely the beginning, though, since there are other matters as well — there are only so many vampires who can pull strings in the mortal society until they start heavily stepping on each others' toes. This may not be a problem in all cities, but most vampires tend to be rather protective of their own resources, and if they are constantly being accidentally torpedoed by someone else's plans, tempers will flare. Indeed, in many cases unintentional sabotage may be considered more offensive. ("Are you saying that my plans are so poorly laid that you do not even have to *try* to ruin them?")

Even if there are no such conflicts, most vampires don't like feeling crowded or boxed in. The nature of the Camarilla makes most vampires feel somewhat uncomfortable or even threatened if there are too many vampires around. They like to have the equivalent of personal space if only because they know that if there are too many Kindred around, the prince will kick some out, and that may mean a power struggle as everyone attempts to maintain their presence in the city.

The problem is whenever there are large-scale conflicts between vampires, the Masquerade is at risk. Whatever the specifics, sooner or later a competent prince will simply clean house and toss out the vampires she considers least useful, most dangerous and easiest to get rid of in order to preserve the Masquerade and, perhaps more importantly, her own sanity.

THE HIDDEN HISTORY

You should pay special attention to supernatural events as these may very well have shaped the history of your city. If there have been vampire elders struggling for the control of the city for the past hundred years, that will undoubtedly have had an effect, directly or indirectly, on the mortal population as well as the local Kindred. If the city has been repeatedly under Sabbat attack in the past, that will certainly make the local vampires adopt a rather defensive and cautious mindset. Strangers may not get a very warm welcome and are likely to find themselves on the receiving end of some rather intensive questioning if the city has a history of infiltrators or traitors.

Pay special attention to the following things when thinking about your city's history — they're things that are likely to come up in play:

• *Why is this a Camarilla city?* "Because that's what folks want to play" is a good reason to play a Camarilla game, but doesn't hold much weight in the chronicle itself.

• *Why is the balance of power what it is?* This refers both to the Camarilla's internal balance of power and to the balance of power between the Camarilla and other supernatural groups. It may simply be a question of unsurpassed power and influence, or it may be that blackmail, dirty tricks or even open warfare are in play. Or perhaps the current balance of power is something that has just recently been achieved and has yet to stabilize.

- *What exactly have the different power groups been up to in the past?* For example, if the prince of the city has been replaced, that has probably shifted the balance of power considerably from one clan to another. More importantly, you should think about recent events and what has been accomplished — it's not like the clans just popped into existence two nights ago; chances are that they've been busy.

- *Have there been major conflicts between supernatural beings?* While such battles tend to stay hidden from the public, especially if it's an internal conflict within the Camarilla, it may very well have an indirect effect on the city, especially once the Kindred in question start to use their Influences to gain an edge against their opponents.

WHY GO THROUGH ALL THIS TROUBLE?

At this point, having read all of the above, you may be wondering why you should bother. An excellent question.

First of all, no one is expected to pick up the book and go through all of these steps one by one, in great detail, while creating a city. Rather, these ideas exist to heighten awareness of these issues and give advice and pointers on what to do when the Storyteller decides that she *does* want to create more depth and realism for her city. It's up to each individual Storyteller to use what she likes and not use what she doesn't like.

Secondly, a good background gives players the chance to play their characters properly. Instead of being vampires who convene in some generic location to plot and bicker amongst themselves for no good reason, the characters can become a part of a greater whole and occupy a particular niche within the society. Simply put, it's a roleplaying tool no different from dressing up for the part — except that it's happening inside the players' heads. Some would even argue that this is far more important than playing around with props. If the players can really feel that they are in the city and that there's far more happening around them than what they see, it will make it far easier for them to get in character and treat the city like a city instead of a shallow and meaningless backdrop.

Third: plot hooks, plain and simple. If the Storyteller wants to go beyond the basic "creepy one-eyed Tremere bastard plots to overthrow the regal and self-centered Ventrue prince" storyline, this is an excellent way to do it. It's rare for a sneaky vampire in the Camarilla to directly attack anyone, especially as that tends to be more trouble than it's worth. Why assassinate someone and risk being found out when you can just as easily capture his power base by gaining influence within the city — and do so while following the Camarilla's rules? There's an entire human society just waiting to be exploited, and if the Storyteller wants the city to become something more than just Influence Traits and the occasional Rock-Paper-Scissors test (hardly something that improves the mood), she must define it in sufficient detail for the players to get the feeling that it really works in a logical manner.

ISN'T ALL THIS WAY TOO MUCH?

No. Well, it shouldn't be. People tend to be able to absorb information relatively well. If your players aren't willing to study up on the game world you've spent all that time creating, they probably aren't very interested in the game, either.

However, always remember that it's a two-way street. While the players have the responsibility to know the rules of the game and know their characters' statistics, background and everything else that is relevant, the Storyteller has the responsibility to provide them with all of that — preferably in a format that can be easily understood. Taking the time to prepare the material is a definite requirement. If you hand them stacks of messy notes, they aren't going to be very impressed, but a document that contains all the important information will very likely do the trick. Note that a well-prepared document can be rather long and sink in just fine, whereas a short but poorly organized document may go unread.

And remember — don't overdo it. While players can be expected to read and understand information relevant to the chronicle, it's probably safe to say that most players aren't willing to memorize hundreds of pages of setting material just because you're on a roll. The exact limits differ from group to group; it's probably best to talk about this with your players beforehand so that you know where you're limits are.

THINGS THAT GO BUMP IN THE NIGHT

A Storyteller often gets the urge to throw all sorts of supernatural creatures into the mix. More often than not, the best advice here is "Think it through, and consider the possibility that this could be a very bad idea." Admittedly, this is somewhat harsh, but experience has shown that it is very easy to fill up a city with so many supernatural beings that you can't cross a street without bumping into something huge and horrifying.

This is not to say that it is impossible or wrong to use a pack of Lupines or a group of wraiths as worthy antagonists, but the "monster of the week" approach gets old very quickly. Vampires rarely interact with other supernatural creatures, and such encounters shouldn't become commonplace. If they do, you'll find your players yawning. "Oh, it's just a pack of Black Spiral Dancers. We see them all the time."

What's more, chances are that your players aren't stupid, and if it becomes obvious to them that the only reason these beings exist is to pose a threat, the game world loses much of its integrity. It's far better to keep the players wondering about what is really going on with them especially as it also gives you easy access to good plot hooks.

Rather, if you want your game to have supernatural beings in it, create a place for them from the start. Maybe the furballs like the central park or the woods outside the town, and maybe the old university holds a gathering of mortal sorcerers. The retro club downtown may serve a number of faerie customers who have a big thing for the '70s. That's all very well and good, but that means that all of these groups must have spheres of influence, agendas and weak spots, whatever they may be. Preferably, you should map them out from the very beginning of your chronicle and have them react accordingly to what the player characters might do. In most cases, what the local vampires do is of very little interest to these groups unless it threatens their existence. Most vampires' agendas tend to be so different from the others' plans that direct conflict is relatively rare. This is not to say that a suitably enraged werewolf won't call up his posse and go kick some leech butts, but in most cases it's

something that can be avoided. Your average furball won't care one bit about some vampires' internal power struggles.

Also note that just because there are such beings in your city, that doesn't mean that the player characters necessarily know about them. There is no good reason to construct the equivalent of a neon sign that says, "Here be monsters!" — it's often better that the characters find out about them by accident, if at all. Keep them guessing.

RUNNING WITH IT ALL

As you have been told repeatedly by now, you have probably realized that this is a lot of work. Depending on the nature of your chronicle, these things may or may not come up in your game. It all depends on a number of factors, such as how much time you want to spend on these matters and whether or not you want to let your players do anything in between the games (and if so, in what detail?).

Some Storytellers like to run their games both as regular tabletop roleplaying games (using the **Vampire: The Masquerade**) and as live-action games (using the **Mind's Eye Theatre**). Obviously that allows for a great deal of detail as all of the major tasks the characters undertake can be played out. The problem with this approach is that most Storytellers prefer to have lives beyond the game.

Luckily, there are other, less time-consuming options. Some Storytellers allow characters to perform certain actions between games, like do research, use Influences or make deals with other characters, but don't let them attack other characters or significantly advance the plot. Others let them do as they please — attempt to firebomb other characters' havens, travel to other cities, recruit allies, gain Influences, whatever, but draw the line at some point, saying "That's enough for now." There are many different ways to deal with this, but

the bottom line is: Let them do as much as you think is appropriate. Of course, the more realism and internal consistency you want, the more they should be allowed to do, but don't let that bog you down. Chances are that you have a real life somewhere in all of this, and you shouldn't let the game take all of your time. Burnout will ruin the game more certainly than not letting a player go over to someone's house and *Dominate* everyone there into submission.

It's also important to determine how fast (or slow) time moves. Some games span decades or even centuries, while others move forward slowly, one night at a time while in the real world months or even years pass. If you do allow characters to act between games, you should take this into account — once the period of time between games becomes months or years instead of days, the actions the characters take tend to become far more generic and the scope of the game changes. This is not a bad thing by any means, but it does require a different approach from the Storyteller.

There's No Place Like Home

You may wish to use a real city in your **Masquerade** chronicle — most likely the city where you live in. After all, that's easy enough for the players to get a feel of, and perhaps more importantly, it saves you a lot of work since the players already know the place. Furthermore, it's often fun to take the real world and rewrite it into the World of Darkness, but it takes more than a coat of black paint and a bunch of monsters to accomplish that.

A good place to start creating a Gothic-Punk version of your city is simply taking a look at its history. Chances are that there have been vampires there for a while now — for decades or even centuries. Considering that some cities in the Old World may be well over a thousand years old, that can be quite a bit of history to cover. If there have been vampires in the city, they have undoubtedly meddled in its affairs quite a bit over the years.

Note that this certainly doesn't mean that all significant events were initiated by vampires. Quite the contrary — humans are rather good at making decisions all by themselves. Still, if it has an impact on the city, it has an impact on the vampire population. Thus, the Kindred have a vested interest in keeping on top of local events, and if your city's history includes a heated political battle, it may happen to be the perfect manifestation of the power struggle of two elders — so much the better. The Kindred don't run the entire show, but they can certainly make things happen if they so desire.

In many ways, the process of converting a real city is very similar to creating a fictional city. However, there are some marked differences. Instead of coming up with organizations, you'll most likely want to take a look at the organizations in your city and use them (in addition to creating fictional ones, if you feel like it). The only way to do this accurately is research and brainwork. Note that nobody expects you to mirror everything completely; your city can and probably should be different, but it's a good idea to try and get the details right. That way the players can depend on their knowledge of the place, and that alone cuts your workload into a fraction of what it would be with a fictional city.

Size Does Matter

The size of your own city is certainly a factor, as it directly affects the vampire population. In **Mind's Eye Theatre** games the size limits are often stretched, and that's all right — after all, not everyone lives in a city populated by millions of people. However, in certain cases it becomes obvious that there are simply far more vampires in any given area than it can support.

There are three ways you can handle this:

You can stretch the limit and say that vampires can survive on smaller populations, or ignore the matter entirely. This is a simple solution, but there's a downside to this: It does mess with the game's internal logic. Depending on what kind of a chronicle you want to run, it may not be a problem at all, or it may become a huge problem. The challenge in deciding your city's Kindred-to-population ratio is to make sure it makes sense and is consistent. Otherwise the story may develop logical flaws that cause problems for the whole chronicle.

Alternatively, you can increase the size of your home town. It may well be that Smallville, Oregon only has a few hundred-thousand inhabitants (or less), but you can always pretend that it's a huge city. After all, if you can pretend that the Ventrue you're talking to actually has *Majesty* and that you can't see the Nosferatu listening in on you two just because he has his hands crossed over his chest, pretending that you live in a big city shouldn't be that hard.

The third option is to decide that there really are far more vampires in this area than usual and work out reasons why they are there and how they can survive without being detected. For example, an area with a large meat industry will produce great amounts of animal blood and no one is likely to notice if some of it ends up in the local Elysium. It's not very glamorous, but in the end, blood is blood… and blood, as we all know, is the life. Or maybe the humans do notice and take action. That should make for a different kind of a chronicle.…

Real People as Characters

When you're busy converting your city, sooner or later you're likely to get the urge to make a real person a part of your game either as a player or Storyteller character. It may be the mayor of the city, the local chief of police, a local artist — anyone who seems to fit in. It adds a lot of color and realism

MAPS

Using maps is a good idea. Buying a decent map of the city probably won't be too expensive; you may even get local tourist maps for free if you're lucky. You can easily use them to define important areas — hunting grounds, havens, Elysium — simply by marking them on the map. You'll get a much better understanding of the big picture if you can just take a look at the map and see where everything is. Suitably prepared, they can also make very good props for the game. After all, a fledgling Nosferatu may well carry a map with the most commonly used entrances and passage routes of the sewer system marked on it, or a group of elders planning the defense of the city against an upcoming Sabbat attack will certainly want to look at a map.

if a local politician becomes a part of the chronicle (after all, it nicely explains just where all of that Influence comes from). What's more, this allows you to have characters directly associated with all of those organizations you've spent so much time developing.

Still, some pitfalls do exist.

Perhaps your opinions and the players' opinions differ — you may dislike someone's politics immensely and end up making him a founding member of the Gentlemen's Club of Evil Powermongers, but the player who ends up playing him may well disagree — or vice versa. While this is probably something that can be sorted out with a simple conversation, you should always remember that the players don't necessarily agree with your views. Politics can make people touchy, and if someone believes that you're making a person she respects look bad because you dislike his politics, it's not likely to improve the game. It's a good idea to make sure that the game doesn't become anyone's personal soapbox.

Also, this is somewhat touchy ground. Let's face it, it may very well be that the person the character is based on would take offense if he finds out that he is portrayed as an immoral undead monster that sucks blood out of people, and you can't really blame him for that. Discretion is certainly advised, and you should make it clear to your players that this is a fictional character based on a real person and doesn't represent the real person. Storytellers are strongly advised to refrain from using the game as an excuse to abuse someone. It's your game, and you can do as you please, but you have been warned.

As an alternative, you can always create caricatures of people instead of using their real identities. The practice is certainly commonly used in the entertainment industry — it's a good way of making it clear to everyone what's going on, but without the risk of offending people too badly. It may not be quite as effective as using the name of a real person, but in most cases it will probably be a workable solution. Changing someone's name and background while giving her similar mannerisms and history can be just as good as the real thing — and potentially far less troublesome.

REAL-LIFE ORGANIZATIONS

The same applies to converting local organizations into whatever they are in your version of the city. You can certainly do so, and there's nothing wrong with that — quite the contrary; having the same landmarks and corporations in your game as your real city does probably enhances the mood quite a bit. Still, caution is advised. Some corporations are extremely touchy about where and how their names are being used. Again, it goes beyond the scope of this book to tell you specifically what to do about situations like this; it all comes down to the Storyteller's discretion, but it's good to pay attention to these things.

FROM THE ASHES OF THE OLD...

Certain **Masquerade** chronicles out there have been running for years now, and more often than not, sooner or later, the people running the game are going to sit down, take a look at their creation and decide that it needs an overhaul — after all, people grow. What seemed like an incredibly cool idea when you were a teenager might seem lame five years later. Perhaps the chronicle was originally founded by someone who had a quite different idea of how to go about doing things, or perhaps things have simply gotten out of control — maybe someone said "yes" when he should have said "no" a couple of times too often. These things happen. There are many chronicles that can stand to keep on chugging along just fine without intervention, but at times emergency procedures are required to keep the patient alive.

There are different levels to this — it may simply be a question of tweaking relatively small things here and there, or it may be a total overhaul that requires the brainpower equivalent of a dry dock and a huge crew of highly trained engineers and technicians. Much can be said about this, but in the end it comes down to three options: You can either subtly update your chronicle as much as is possible without changing it so much that it becomes something entirely different; you can tinker with it until you're totally satisfied with things, and accept the end result as your new chronicle, or, in some terminal cases, you can (and probably should) decide to dump it entirely and start over from scratch.

MINOR FACELIFT

Perhaps surprisingly, this option is usually the most difficult one. Updating bits and pieces here and there while attempting to keep all of the previous continuity intact can be extremely difficult — especially if there are things in the chronicle's history that you would prefer to get rid of but they are linked rather solidly to other events. Everything in the chronicle is a part of a complicated, larger whole, and if you alter one thing, that will affect everything else. You may want to just change things around as you please, but the consequences will certainly influence the whole chronicle. If the players never notice, this may not be a problem, but taking the chance is usually not advisable.

Note that you don't necessarily need to change past events in the game to fix things; at times, it may simply be enough to change things now. ("Oh, he was called back to Vienna to be briefed. I hear they have a big job for him. They're making him the regent of this chantry in Budapest or something.") If you don't like the way a current storyline is going, you can always end it right now. It may be a bit blunt and sudden, but then again, that can happen in real

life as well; it all depends on how you handle it. "What? All of this was for nothing?" may not be as epic as it could be, but it may still make for a good story when the players try to pick up the pieces after everything suddenly changes.

Messing with continuity can present serious problems, and if you don't want to deal with those, you can just tell your players, "Okay, this was really stupid in the game, and I'm not going to say that it didn't happen, but let's just sort of gloss over that and start doing things right from now on." The downside of this technique is that if it's something that happened to the characters, it's probably affected them. Requiring the players to roleplay the changes brought on by that event while ignoring the cause of the change completely may be a bad idea — or vice versa: ignoring the changes but keeping the cause isn't likely to work out much better.

In most cases, unless you know that you only need to change a couple of things, you're probably better off chucking the current continuity out the window and accepting a few big changes, as it can be almost impossible to keep everything in check while still overhauling the chronicle.

Still, if all you want is to fix relatively small things here and there, this is probably the way you want to go. Be warned that despite your original intentions, in many cases you'll end up doing something bigger as you find that the small changes just aren't enough.

Major Surgery

The second option is considerably easier — it all comes down to taking a look at what you already have and then systematically changing things around until you like what you see. However, notice that "easy" doesn't mean "effortless." It'll be a lot of work, make no mistake: Not only do you have to make all of those changes, you also have to make sure that your players know what the changes are! This means yet more writing.

There's no nice way of putting this: There are plenty of incredibly bad characters out there, ranging from stereotypical cute teddy-bear-carrying Malkavians who do silly things because they're just so darn kooky, to incredibly powerful Tremere elders who use high levels of *Thaumaturgy* to lay waste upon anyone who looks at them funny. When played badly, such characters cripple a chronicle rather effectively, and removing or fixing characters like that may be just what the game needs.

Removing and fixing bad plotlines can be more difficult. It may be that for whatever reason, there are things you want to get rid of — maybe there's a group of anarchs with a thaumaturgically modified nuclear device that will destroy all supernatural beings on the planet unless they are accepted into the Camarilla, or maybe the idea about the prince becoming obsessed with painting everything black has simply gotten old, or maybe that conference for fifth-generation Methuselahs would really screw up the game, but everything you've done this far is setting things up for that. Simply erasing these plots from existence is difficult and probably a bad idea since it means that everything that has happened this far suddenly becomes pointless and makes no sense to anyone attempting to understand the events in the game. If a certain character has been played for years with a certain set of instructions from his superiors, and said instructions suddenly change for no good reason — because a Storyteller came up with a new idea —

it's going to make the player rather displeased at best. Not only is it frustrating to have done all that work for nothing, but it's also painfully obvious to him that it's happening just because you changed your mind. It makes it impossible for the player to justify his actions to other characters, and the player will have little choice but to drop out of character and explain that he had good reasons for doing what he did until the world changed around them — hardly something that improves the game. (Note that having such a sudden change of instructions happen as a part of the game is, of course, an entirely different thing — and yes, there is a major difference there. The character is still likely to be displeased, of course, but that's another matter.)

If you do change your plans, you should try to do so gracefully so that it makes sense to the players. If at all possible, the players should never become aware that things have changed, but this may not be an option. In such cases, it's extremely important that you document the changes and make sure the players know what the new situation is like. They depend on their Storyteller to give them all the relevant information about the game world. Without that information, they are practically blind. Of course, this is a two-way street; often it is the Storyteller who finds herself blind. If there are many players and a number of games have been played, that usually means that a lot has happened, and it's very hard to remember what happened a year and a half ago without good notes.

As a last resort, if you absolutely have to, you can always say, "Look, guys, this isn't working out, so I'm going to change things, and if it really makes your life suck, let me know and we'll see what we can do." It's nowhere near a perfect solution, but it's still better than just making a decision and then running with it as if nothing had happened. That'll just annoy the players; the players won't like the other decision, either, but it'll still be better — at least you'll be leveling with them. Treating them like idiots or presuming that it's all right to make up their minds for them is a sure way to get in an argument.

In all cases, you should keep in mind that players might not be too happy with the Storyteller coming over and telling them that the chronicle has just changed radically; such changes are bound to affect their characters, and players often take a dim view of someone simply telling them what happens to their characters — and rightly so. The Storyteller does get to decide what happens, and players don't really have much choice but to accept this, but they can always vote with their feet. It's important to ensure that the players know what's going on and that the Storyteller doesn't come off as an evil dictator who warps the game just because he feels like it. After all, a successful game is a group effort.

I Think He's Gone, Doctor

The third option is something of a final solution, but a Storyteller who knows when to lay a chronicle to rest is a wise one indeed. If the players are concentrating on showing off their cool Disciplines, the major plotlines revolve around silver abominations who slaughter characters left and right while waiting for Caine to make his weekly appearance, and just thinking about the whole thing makes you cringe and fervently wish that you were somewhere else drinking beer, there is absolutely nothing wrong with calling it quits. Indeed, it's probably a good idea. There's no point in running a game that's no fun.

That said, this is hardly the only reason a chronicle should be allowed to end. Perhaps the whole thing just isn't working properly. Maybe the players who were supposed to play certain characters couldn't make it, or that great overall plot idea that looked so good on paper just didn't work out in play. Again, these things happen; assigning blame probably isn't the way to go here.

There are no valid guidelines for identifying a game that isn't working; at least none that everyone agrees on. That said, if the Storyteller is no longer enjoying the game or if the majority of players aren't satisfied with it and it looks like it wouldn't be worth the trouble of fixing everything that's broken, there are good indications that it's probably time to put an end to the chronicle.

After all, you can always start over again and learn from your previous mistakes.

The Struggle for Control

The Masquerade is perhaps the only common goal that all Kindred in the Camarilla can agree upon. Its members fight a constant battle, not only to keep the kine from witnessing vampiric activity, but also to discredit any that would try to bring forth evidence of supernatural existence. The primary weapon in this battle is the influence that the sect has developed within mortal society.

This network extends from CEOs and political officials all the way down to the gangs and the bums on the street. It can be as direct as blackmail or as subtle as misdirection. In some cases, it may be garnered through use of Disciplines or Abilities. Most often, it is bought through knowing precisely how the "machine" works and what rewards corrupted mortals desire.

Though the goal may be common, the implementation of this control is as varied as the clans and ages of the Kindred themselves. Each clan — and each individual within the clan — has its own agenda and approach toward the kine's operations. Some exert control over events that affect them. Others seek information to use as currency. Older Kindred prefer stable enterprises that have high stability and little turnover. Younger Cainites prefer innovation, which involves more risk, but promises a higher return.

Regardless of approach, such resources are coveted by Kindred with differing agendas. When this occurs, they are contested. Some of the most vicious battles fought by the Camarilla are not fought against enemies but over influence. Both sides will weave intricate plots to seize control while others stand aside to witness the maneuvering and see the outcome.

Status may be a reflection of an individual's notoriety and standing within the Camarilla, but Influence is the measure of power. The Kindred with the most sway are the ones that garner the most favor. Likewise, the ones with the most favor are rewarded with the opportunities to generate more sway. Thus, the vicious circle is created and maintained.

Running in the Shadows

Kindred in the Camarilla jockey for power and position, often at the expense of each other. Many have come to realize that the easiest way to overcome a rival is to take what is hers and make it yours. A delicate balance is created, and an intriguing dilemma. In order to be perceived as powerful,

your power must be evident. But if your power is too readily apparent, it is vulnerable to those who covet it. There is no Tradition within the Camarilla that ensures a Kindred can keep what he cannot hold.

The best way to maintain any degree of power in the Camarilla is to keep it hidden in mystery. It is hard to destroy what you cannot find. It is hard to steal what you cannot grasp. Most important, it is hard to prepare for something you cannot conceive. Within these shadows, power-bases are built and grown. The same practices that hide the truth about vampires from the mortal world are used to conceal plots and maneuvers from fellow Kindred.

Ten Tenets of Influential Enterprise: Influences from an Elder's View

- *Try to act remotely.* Many Camarilla Kindred use agents and retainers to implement their control. This serves as a stopgap for those attempting to trace the actions back to the master. It also allows for a convenient scapegoat when the prince or archon gets a little too close for comfort. A setback can easily become beneficial if the minion of one of your rivals can be your scapegoat. You may not always win, but you should never lose.

- *Maneuver with discretion.* Kindred seldom directly influence mortals in power. Such individuals are carefully monitored, often by rivals. Such scrutiny can attract conflict and attention. If the mortal's watchdogs do not interfere, the Kindred's competitors will. Indirect methods are harder to trace and to sabotage. Sometimes the best place to hide is where no one will think to look.

- *Avoid mortal contact when possible.* One way not to reveal to a mortal that he is being controlled is to not deal with the mortal at all. Accidents can erase valuable files. Itineraries can be altered at the printer. Evidence can mysteriously disappear. Objects tell no tales — to most mortals at least.

- *Be wary of strong-willed prey.* Mortals are beasts of conscience and arrogance no matter how much they may declare otherwise. When a mortal realizes he is being controlled, he will try to free himself. If he is unable to, he will become desperate. In the end, like a trapped animal, he will go to extreme lengths to be freed, even if he must harm himself or others in the process. This is far too messy for Kindred who wish to remain in the shadows.

- *Create contingencies.* A master plan should never be set in stone. It should be solid enough to be reliable and not left to chance, but it must also be flexible enough to adapt to adversity. The willow bends in the breeze that breaks mighty oaks.

- *Create redundancies.* Most matters of intrigue are maintained by departmentalizing your efforts. No single minion should factor too heavily in the success of your project. A lost piece should never cost you the game.

- *Conceal the scope of your power.* If none of your agents knows more than a piece of the overall puzzle, then no one will be able to discover the entirety by compromising one part. If you are only as strong as your weakest link, it is best if your weakest link knows only a small part of the chain. This practice was used when the Americans developed the first atomic weapons.

- *Establish a cover.* Nothing should be as it appears. Create a facade around your operations that is as different from the reality as possible. Plant rumors and false evidence supporting the charade. Pretend to fail in covering

them up so that the investigators will feel they have found your true intentions. Many times, it is easier to believe a well-told lie than a hard-to-find truth.

• *Benefit those who can support you.* Create enterprises that are more beneficial if left alone than contested. Support a strong prince by making her stronger. Do not monopolize or hoard resources; instead, control the flow. If you cut others out, they will try harder to remove you, but if the price they pay for acquiring what you have is less than that of doing the work themselves, it would be a waste of their effort. You gain more from their addictions than from their fits of withdrawal.

• *Never create that which you cannot destroy.* No vampire can withstand the united front of several Kindred — ask the Brujah. If what you control is valuable, someone will eventually seek it. If control cannot be maintained, it is better to disassemble it than to see it used against you. It takes much planning and effort to acquire someone else's domain. Frustrate them further by making it all for nothing. When there are no spoils, there is no war.

Example: *Nicolaus, the Ventrue primogen, wishes to expand his control into Underworld. Unfortunately, that Influence is currently controlled by the Brujah Prince. Nicolaus makes a proposal to the prince to open a chemical factory that could conceal the production of munitions. What Nicolaus does not mention is that this factory will also conceal the production of narcotics that Nicolaus will distribute to generate contacts. Slowly, he will sneak into a market that was closed to him.*

Example: *Joshua, a Brujah, wants to exert some control over the local police. He sends some of his female retainers to act drunk and disorderly at the bars. When the officers arrive, the women seduce them and take them into side room where the whole encounter is captured on hidden surveillance cameras. Josh will use the tapes to convince the officers to lay off the gangs he has contact with. With one plot he strengthens his hold on two areas.*

MAKING YOUR OWN BREAKS: A NEONATE'S TAKE ON INFLUENCES

• *Try the hands-on approach.* One way to control an organization is to understand how it works from the inside. By understanding the procedures and protocols, a Kindred can become aware of the loopholes that can later be exploited.

• *Take chances.* The riskier endeavors offer larger returns and are often neglected by more conservative Kindred. In addition to uncontested operation, the gamble itself can provide a rush.

• *Identify with the kine.* Getting to know how the kine feel and react can provide insight into how to best utilize them. Familiarity can also reveal the vices that would tempt kine in positions of power to benefit your operations.

• *Play on emotions.* Befriend those who seek friendship. Intimidate those who fear you. Lie to those who are easily deceived. Kine are easily swayed by their feelings.

• *Focus your efforts.* Try to avoid juggling more than you can handle. Sometimes, it is better to do one thing really well than several things adequately.

• *Cooperate with others.* Resources pooled with other Kindred of similar interests can sometimes grant access to larger schemes than one can manage on her own.

- *Market your power base.* Sometimes, other Kindred will give prestation or favors to those with influence in a certain aspect of kine society. Perhaps it is to save their time, or to conserve their efforts for larger endeavors. Deals could be made that would expand your power base.
- *It is not wise to poke a lion with a stick.* Avoid coming into conflict with those with more power than you control. Assist them if you need to; avoid them if possible. Strike only if you feel you can win.

Example: *Estacado and Sasha, both Brujah, wish to influence the local gangs. Since the gangs rely mostly on the camaraderie they have built, the Kindred are initiated into the gang. After a few months of fighting rival gang members, staging successful robberies and facing position challenges, they have built a rep for themselves within the gang. With an understanding of what motivates the members of the gang, they are able to use them when needed.*

Example: *Joseph, a Ventrue, wishes to impress the prince and decides to create a more suitable Elysium for the domain. Although he has the resources to secure the building, he knows that there is more to an Elysium than a structure. To overcome this obstacle, he agrees to assist a Toreador, in exchange for a few pieces of art, with purchasing a gallery. He further agrees to finance the upgrade of some of the Nosferatu's computer equipment in exchange for forged permits and licenses. Once he has completed the deals, he presents the complete project to the prince for approval.*

MAPPING THE CITY

Each city has a unique influential scope. Some cities are industrial centers, others are university towns. Some lie along commerce routes, others may have international airports. All these factors must be considered when deciding not only what can be accomplished with Influences but how often Kindred will come into conflict trying to in using them.

The first thing that needs to be developed is how much potential Influence exists in the city. For each of the categories, a maximum level of usable Influence Traits should be set. This level will depend on how strong the Influence category is in relation to the surrounding area. Washington, D.C. influences the politics of neighboring cities more than Muncie, Indiana. A Kindred would be able to create a higher level of influence in the former. Most towns and cities are diverse enough to allow for obtaining considerable levels of Influence. Cities of importance to states or regions would allow for exceptional levels, but are rare, and will only affect a few categories. Cities of national or international importance would allow for expansion into the highest levels that are best left to elders.

Individual limits should be placed on Influence Traits depending on what is available in the city at the start of the chronicle. If the city has little or no representation in an area of Influence, then the highest an Influence could get to is 3 or 4. A city with normal representation of an Influence would have a 5. Cities with exceptional representation may grant levels of 6 or above.

Take into account the things your city is known for and the things it may lack. Pick at least three Influences to be considered exceptional, and at least three to be lacking. The rest should be average. A small town may have *Street* 4, a college town might have *University* 5, and a state capital would have *Political* 6 or more.

The second step is to determine how accessible these Influences are. This will determine how easily Kindred can expand their control over of that Influence. It will also determine what kind of storylines will develop from the endeavors. Small town clinics are easier to infiltrate than military hospitals. Advertising agencies are easier to get into than a federal depository. Public schools are more accessible than private institutions. Overall, this ease of access provides a balance of sorts to the limited capacity. Larger metropolises allow for larger actions, but smaller cities are easier for individuals to control.

These definitions do not involve mechanics other than shaping the justifications for Experience Trait expenditures or altering the caps placed on Influence availability. It does determine what actions can be used. A small town sheriff's department might not have access to Kevlar vests. Some countries have strict gun control, and gangs may not have access to firearms. Rural areas may not have many businesses with access to higher finances.

The next step is to determine how prevalent the Influence is. How much can Kindred expand before their goals work counter to the goals of other Kindred? Mortals will only allow themselves to be pushed so many times before they become desperate and prone to irrational judgments. They will only be pulled in so many directions before they become unreliable. This places further limits on the city's Influence portfolio. A city with several universities can allow several Kindred to exert control over academics. If a city holds only one, no matter how large it is, these Kindred may come into conflict while trying to influence its operations.

Storytellers can use several systems to ensure that players understand Influence is a limited resource. It is important that they realize that roleplaying and planning, not just Experience Traits, expand Influence. Influence, more than most other Traits, encourages cooperation, but such cooperation must not encroach upon the overall themes of conspiracy and infighting that World of Darkness games rely on.

One possible system is to only allow a certain number of cumulative levels to exist in the city. Count the number of players and multiply that by a modifier based on the prevalence of the Influence. For poor Influences, the modifier would be one; for average, it would be two; for exceptional, three. Of the 15 categories, only a few should be either poor or exceptional, and they should be offset for game balance. Once all of those levels have been acquired by characters, no one can expand or develop influence in that area unless they do so at the expense of another character or by expanding the prevalence of the Influence (expending resources, markets, etc.). For instance, a state capital would have a larger pool of people involved with politics, while an industrial center with many factories would have room for several to build that Influence. Cities that are distribution centers, like Chicago or Atlanta, would have a lot of *Transportation* Influence.

Some Influence Traits should be left for the Storyteller characters. No matter how well the Kindred feel they have developed their networks, they are just a few individuals. They should never feel they know everything or can stop anything from happening. Humans often act erratically. They are prone to fits of conscience or delusions of grandeur. More often than not, they are independent, self-interested individuals who will do everything they can to

turn matters to their own benefit. Most business takes place during the day when no vampire can act. In the end, the Camarilla is only one of the Cainite factions, and they have a lot of enemies.

A City Developed: An Example

After thinking about the city and researching tourist guides, encyclopedia entries and even the Yellow Pages, Jennifer the Storyteller decides to develop an Influence portfolio for her chronicle's city.

It has a major state university and two local colleges. On the outskirts of town, there are several factories, which have not yet been affected by work going overseas. There are also a number of churches of varying faiths and sizes, and the city is in the Bible Belt. However, the city only has a small mall and very few businesses. There are no local television stations, and the local newspaper is overshadowed by the larger newspaper from another city nearby. It also has no theater and only one museum.

Jennifer decides that at the start of the chronicle, the individual limits will reflect these considerations. Levels 6 or higher in *University*, *Industrial* and *Church* can be possessed by characters (these Influences have strong, thriving bases). *Finance* capacity is at 4 (from the local banks). *Media* and *High Society* can only be at 3 (there isn't enough to anchor more unless more fine arts arrive or the newspaper gets a shot in the arm). All others can be purchased up to 5.

Next, Jennifer has to decide how available the Influence fields are. *Media* and *High Society* are rare, so for the 12 characters in the chronicle, there will only be 12 levels of Influence available. After those levels are claimed, the characters will have to roleplay expanding the market or cutting in on the levels owned by other characters. *University*, *Industrial* and *Church* are more prevalent, so there are 36 levels available. The rest of the Influences will have 24 overall levels.

Her final step is to decide the amount of influence Storyteller characters will have. At the start of the chronicle, she feels the Storyteller characters should have more Influence any individual player character. However, she decides that the levels for the individual Storyteller characters should be less than the combined totals available for the player characters to encourage political deals between characters who rely on subtle Influence over direct interaction.

In the Details

Okay. You've got the blueprint for your city all laid out. You know where the hot spots are, where the low-lifes live and where you want your plot to go. Now that you've chosen your ZIP code and built your new city, you need to take the time and figure out how to put all that into motion. A chronicle is built game by game. The techniques you use to bring your hometown to life make all the difference between building scenery and building a world. Remember, humanity is a terribly important part of a **Masquerade** game. If the ordinary humans in your town are just faceless mannequins, no one's going to get worked up over them. If you keep a few things in mind as you get your chronicle in motion, it'll be easier to keep things on track. Your players are going to push, pull, prod and occasionally blow up your new creation. Don't be afraid to let it push back.

What Do I See?

First impressions mean a lot. The way a person looks conveys a sense of style that's hard to remove. The same thing applies to the character of the city. The physical descriptions you provide your players are the most effective weapons in your arsenal for defining the style of a game. Keeping your scene descriptions consistent and thematic will go a long way toward keeping your city alive. You may well know what you want your brave new world to look like, but unless you convey that effectively to the players, you may as well not have bothered.

You'll want to start off by focusing on your game's "home base"— the locale that you start off in every night. Most Camarilla games will kick off in Elysium or the prince's court. An anarch game may not be as well-centered, but even then, characters will usually end up gathering at the same diner or courtyard every session to do their business. It's natural for people to come together at the same place regularly to hang out, whether they're mortal or Kindred.

A central point like this is a great opportunity for you to make that first impression. The more details you can give your players, the easier it'll be for them to get into the game world. This opening site is the anchor point for your chronicle. Everything in the game begins and ends here. If you use this place to define the theme and mood of your chronicle, the rest of the world will flow naturally.

If you've created your game's home city from whole cloth, then you have a lot of freedom in building your game's setting. On the other hand, you're also going to have to work harder at reminding players they aren't in the real world any more. Your best bet is to write out a page or two describing the location. Go into as much detail as you can, and remember to use all five senses in your description. The smell of a place can be just as important as how it looks. Post your description near the entry hall of your game so your players can read it before they start play. You may also wish to quickly describe the game's setting before actual play begins, just to make sure that everyone's on the same page. If there's a particularly important object or plot hook in your setting, like the prince's throne or a jukebox, you may want to put a sign near it to inform players about the relevant details of this prop.

On the other hand, if you're using your actual home city as a game setting, you may want to use a real-world location as the game's center. Again, you're probably going to have to use your imagination somewhat — while it may be possible to play a game regularly in the grand ballroom of a hotel, odds are you're going to have to find a different site most of the time. You can save yourself a lot of work by gathering background information on the "real" site. Most of the usual suspects for Elysium (museums, galleries, etc.) will happily give you source material.

On the Road

When your players do decide to leave Elysium, things get interesting. There's no way on earth that a Storyteller can anticipate all the different ideas that a group of players can throw at her. While some advance planning can help when players go out on the town, occasionally a Storyteller is just going to have to work on the fly.

First, if a group of characters decides to leave the central location of the game, make every effort to isolate them from the game's main area. Designate a specific room or corner of your game as "off site," and keep your departing characters from interacting with the main game area as much as possible. There's nothing more distracting than wandering up to another player, intent on roleplaying a conversation, only to learn that he's 10 blocks away.

When you take a group off site, always begin by giving a full description of the scene. Include as much detail as you think you can get away with — sight, sound, smell and even taste are important when creating a mood. Keep the core themes of your game in mind as you do this. Everything should match your game as a whole. While it's important to keep the scene moving, it's easier to tell when you've given too much detail as opposed to too little. Make sure that you give this description before you do anything else. Doing so helps the players to stay in character, especially if they've had to wait for you.

Be ready to give an extra level of description on demand. Many characters make a habit of using *Heightened Senses* on any strange place or thing they encounter. Players like to get some extra detail when they use a power like this. It's disappointing to examine a rusty knife for five minutes only to hear: "There doesn't seem to be anything unusual about it." That rusty knife might not have anything to do with what's going on, but players should always get something for their efforts. Again, a little advance preparation can have a big payoff. If you know ahead of time where that rusty knife has been, things get a lot easier.

If you don't have the time or creative energy to give every non-Elysium location this treatment, a "photo gallery" of sorts might be in order. Most places that characters will go can be divided up into broad categories — a church, a street, an office, etc. A day or so of wandering around your hometown with a disposable camera should provide several good snapshots of these kinds of places. Place them in a photo album, and when players go to a nearby alley, refer them to the appropriate photo. You'll be surprised at how much this can do for a chronicle. As they say, a picture is worth a thousand words. Use common sense when taking these photos, however — shooting pictures of a dangerous alley late at night is not recommended!

A Million Stories...

Making people a part of your city is one of the most important — and demanding — tasks you face as a Storyteller. How do you come up with the names and faces that make up your city? You can't be expected to come up with all the friends, enemies, and neighbors that players meet in their unlives. The players, however, can easily come up with this information for you... with a little prompting.

Encourage the players to flesh out the incidental contacts they make as they go about a typical day. Every character should have a supporting cast of friends, neighbors and enemies. Where does a character hang out to relax? In a bar? Who's the bartender? Does the character go to church? Who's the priest? Where does the character feed regularly? Is there someone he encounters there more than once? The list of possibilities is endless.

Backgrounds are also a great place to start generating names. Every time a Kindred uses her Influences, she's calling in a favor or making a bribe. Who's

giving the favor? Why are they helping the character? What are they getting out of the deal? The same thing applies to the *Contacts* background. Every contact is a snitch or a whistleblower that is helping the character for reasons all his own. Characters with *Fame* have agents, fans, and assistants. High levels of *Resources* need stockbrokers, bankers, accountants and caretakers to survive. *Herds* are an automatic source of intimate contacts for a character. A day should not go by without the character trying to get something out of a mortal.

This, of course, brings up the most intimate contact a Kindred has with a mortal: feeding. Getting blood should never be as easy as a game of Rock-Paper-Scissors. Where does the character go to hunt? Whom does she choose to feed from? Why does she choose these people? In a small game, the Storyteller may well play out a short scene with each character concerning their nightly hunt. In larger games, you may well wish to write up several "generic hunting" scenarios and let the players draw them randomly. To survive, a Kindred has to perform an act of near-rape every night. The characters — and players — should never be permitted to become blasé about this.

Don't sweat coming up with all this background material yourself. Most players will happily generate this information with little prodding. Rewarding an extra Experience Trait to players that provide this information isn't out of line — in a real sense, they're doing your work for you. If a player is truly stumped, try asking him a few leading questions to get his creative juices flowing: "Where do you feed?" "Whom do you talk to about your *Street* Influence?" Don't push too hard, and be patient. You should see some results soon.

Once these background characters are defined, don't hesitate to use them as part of the story. If someone destroys another player's Influences, she is threatening or killing the contacts that make those Influences possible. It's one thing to tell a player that her *Political* Influence has diminished from 4 to 3. It's another to tell them that Rosa, the secretary she knew at City Hall, was found dead in an alley. One is a maneuver in a game; another is a personal attack on a friend. Keep the gamespeak to a minimum. Make all the *Contacts* and Influences people, not numbers. You'll get a far more intimate, high-stakes game as a result.

Make sure that you don't use this background data arbitrarily or without taking the players into account. These people are important to the characters — they're just as much the player's extras as they are yours, in a sense. Killing one off just to make a point or further the plot is not going to go over well. At a minimum, players should be allowed to seek revenge for such things. Better still, give them just enough advance warning to let them save their friends... this time. If you don't want you players to treat mortals as pawns, you'd better avoid treating them as pawns yourself. These are people here, not stooges. If you kill one off for no good reason, players will hesitate to create more for you to abuse.

On the flip side, you should reward players who take the time to help their supporting characters out. Suppose that one character knows a cop in Internal Affairs who's having difficulty with his wife. This cop is the source of his *Police* Influence. If the character takes the time to help this cop patch up his marriage, he should be rewarded for the extra roleplay. Maybe you could give him a chance to resist a hostile takeover of his Influences if another player assaults it. The final call is up to you, but in general, players who devote time and energy to playing out their actions in the mortal world should be rewarded.

And hey — if the character engineered the cop's wife trouble in the first place, just so he could get a favor out him, then you're really getting into the spirit of things.

ACTIONS AND REACTIONS

Whenever a player starts talking to a mortal, you need to take two things into account: how human the player acts and how human the character acts. Humanity really comes into play when Kindred and ordinary mortals start interacting.

A character with low Humanity should always have a rough time of it. Humans always know something is "wrong" with such a person, even if *Obfuscate* or disguises are in place. You might dress up a serial killer in a nice suit and tie, but people will still shy away from him on the bus, no matter how much he smiles. Humans can sense Kindred the way that the deer can sense the wolf, and their first impulse should be to get away.

A character with low Humanity should never have a normal, ordinary relationship with a human. That loss should always shake a character if you can manage it. Players might not pick up on it the first time around, or even the second, but consistently giving mortal contacts an edginess when they meet a low-Humanity vampire should eventually have an effect.

Likewise, if a character has a high Humanity rating, they should be able to get along well with an ordinary person… but not perfectly. Even a Humanity 5 Kindred isn't quite kosher, and eventually, a human will notice it. Kindred have to work at being human. It doesn't come naturally anymore. Eventually, the prey will pick up the scent of the wolf again. It's only a matter of time.

So here's the setup: You've asked your players to create bunch of interesting, exciting mortals. These mortals are integral to the character's lives. However, these interesting people can never understand the characters and will always fear and hate them on some level. This may seem a little cruel.

Welcome to **Vampire**.

What are your players going to do about this dilemma? Pay close attention to what happens next. If a character treats humans like slime or gets angry with these uncomprehending mortals, take a note of it. It'll make that next meeting with those humans that much harder. Kindred can forget how to deal with a human being after a while. If a character consistently deals with mortals poorly, you might want to start making it harder for him to use his *Contacts* and *Influences*.

On the other hand, characters that work to overcome their handicap should be rewarded. The loss of Humanity is challenging, but it isn't insurmountable. Someone who spends time in the real world should find it easier to deal with human beings, maybe even gaining a little bonus in their application of Backgrounds.

That challenge to stay human should never go away, however. It's one of the foundations of the horror in this game. It's oh-so-easy to lose a grip on your Humanity. It can slip away if you don't keep an eye on it, and you may never get it back. Don't make the fight easy.

And then, of course, there are the wild cards. The innocent can see right through *Obfuscated* characters — imagine the startled look on a Nosferatu's face when a toddler comes up and asks him for help finding his mommy. True Faith has a habit of cropping up in unlikely places, even in this day and age.

And every supernatural creature can disguise herself as human in some fashion. No interaction with the human world should be seen as casual or commonplace. There's always a chance that the mortal world will surprise Kindred. Never permit the players to forget this.

LET THE TIMES WRITE YOUR CHRONICLE

The World of Darkness is essentially our own world — a darker, cockeyed version of our world, perhaps, but it's still home. Storytellers can get a lot of inspiration for the Chronicle just by reading the local newspaper on a regular basis.

With a little bit of paranoia, nearly any routine event could have a supernatural hand behind it. A robbery or fire might well be the signs of a cover-up for more sinister events. A new high-rise building or industrial park may have a Kindred owner. Any of these things can serve as the seed for a story line for a chronicle.

Sometimes, the newspaper can generate an entire story line without the Storyteller doing a thing. If a large news event happens in your area — a hurricane blowing through or a casino opening — let the players try and do things about it. Weathering a major storm becomes a great deal more difficult when Kindred can't evacuate and the blood supply leaves town. Hostile forces such as the Sabbat may choose to use the storm as cover for an invasion. On the other hand, a casino offers an opportunity for vast Influence and wealth. However, a war could erupt over the profits if too many parties get involved. Big stories like this can serve as the focus for an entire game session and impact the chronicle for a long time after things settle down.

Big events are a great way to keep the game world in motion. Even something like a convention or a political rally can generate a hive of activity among the power brokers in your game. Power doesn't just stay put in the hands of Kindred. It moves around all on its own. If a museum exhibit comes into town, Kindred might recognize some of the pieces — and want to recover their "lost" property. A politician's rise or fall on Election Day could cripple a Kindred's Influence for months. The world is always changing, despite the Camarilla's best efforts, and characters should always be scrambling to keep up.

Keeping the local paper a mainstay in the game also reminds players of another important fact — they aren't the only things happening in town. Indeed, often they aren't even the most important things in town. They certainly shouldn't be if the Masquerade is in place. The real world keeps moving past the Kindred and beyond them, no matter how much they might wish otherwise. Using stories in the game that don't begin and end with the supernatural keeps the everyday world alive behind the players as they work in the shadows.

Keep your players advised of these "real world stories" as they occur. If a particular news article grabs you as the center of a Kindred plot, copy it and give it to your players before a game begins. E-mail can be a marvelous way to keep players abreast of important actions, especially if there's a long time between games. Bear in mind that e-mail isn't always 100 percent reliable, however, and not every player may have e-mail access. It's best to give this information to players in multiple formats and at different times.

Once players get used to the notion that the Storyteller is cribbing plot lines from the newspaper, they may well decide to take action on things printed in the local news before the Storyteller officially calls notice to them. The Storyteller should pay attention to these ideas. In essence, the players are letting the Storyteller know what they want to see in the game. Even if there's too much going on in the game for the Storyteller to give the player's actions a full treatment, she should remember what the players do for later stories. Players want to feel like they are having an impact on their world. Let them do so... and suffer the consequences.

These current events supply some grand side quests and red herrings for players to investigate while you hit them with your main plot line. While it's important to have a direction for your chronicle to pursue, occasionally players simply won't want to chase the bait you're providing. In a large game, there simply may be too many people to chase down the Sabbat pack all at once. Instead of letting these players sit around Elysium waiting for the main plot to finish, they should have the opportunity to chase other stories. A good game should be like a buffet, with multiple plots and quests available for your players to sample. Many of these choices may have nothing to do with what you consider to be the true focus of your game, but that doesn't keep them from being entertaining choices in their own right. Using a resources like the local news gives you the chance to provide multiple plots at once without having to invent all the details yourself.

Of course, you may very well want to put some hints concerning the main story line into your local news as you go along. Don't be afraid to write something new as you go. After all, it's your world, and you can do with it as you see fit. Once you get the local paper established as a plot engine, anything dropped into the mix, whether generated by you or the Sunday edition, is going to keep the game going. Just try and avoid putting too much wishful thinking in there. It might be painful to see your favorite team lose the Super Bowl, but erasing that fourth-quarter touchdown for your own peace of mind is a bit much. Remember that you're running this game for your players, not for your betting pool.

HOME-GROWN INTRIGUE

Now that you have all of these busy people bustling about in your detailed town, reacting to current events, you're ready to have some fun. A dynamic environment like this allows you to create convoluted, intrigue-laden plot lines without breaking a sweat.

A good intrigue plot line is like a chain of dominos. A Kindred takes an action — he kills someone for blood. That action affects two other people — the deceased has a wife and son who can't find him. Those people affect others — the wife reports her missing husband to the police, while the son cruises the alleyways looking for his lost father. Those actions affect someone else, and on and on, until the entire system is in motion because of one simple act.

Each of these mortals your players have created can serve as a domino in your game of intrigue. Every action that your players take can serve to set the chain off. If you have a solid grip on who lives in the city and how they're related, the connections should be easy to make.

The keys to making this system work are a careful record of the actions your players take during a game and a brisk imagination. When a player does something interesting, write it down. You are writing everything that happens in the game down, aren't you? This is one of those reasons why keeping track of everything that happens in a game is so important. We'll say it again: Write everything down that happens in the game. It's important. You'll be glad you did.

The imagination comes in when you ask yourself one question: "What if?..." As you read over your notes on player's actions, keep a list of your supporting characters handy. As you look at a player's actions, ask yourself "What if this character was seen by somebody? What if someone saw her break into the abandoned warehouse? What would the witness do next? What would those actions change in turn?" Eventually, who hurt whom and who helped whom should become fairly clear, and all of your "dominoes" should be in motion.

Here's the best part of this system: Players will get things in motion all by themselves without any prompting by you. Every action that a player takes has the potential to start the domino chain, forcing Storyteller and player characters alike into motion until every life of the city touches everyone somehow.

This may be a little startling at first: You may very well feel like the game is starting to take a life of its own — *a la* Frankenstein's monster. If your players are interested in chasing a story that started three months ago with a random act, then they're busy and entertained, and you don't have to do a thing. If you really don't want a plot to keep rolling along like this, just stop helping it along. Don't ask "what ifs" about this plot and keep the number of people affected by it to a minimum. Eventually, things will die down.

But don't stop a plot just because it's not "yours" anymore. If you just drop a plot like a lead balloon, without giving any closure or hints to players, they're going to end up feeling cheated. You may be fresh out of ideas on that red herring your players are chasing, but abruptly ending things without so much as a "boo" can be a major letdown. Try redirecting this wild goose chase back into the main plotline — perhaps a minion of your main villain has been following the characters around and gets caught at an inopportune moment. Failing that, leave enough of a dangling plot thread for your characters to keep going once your batteries recharge. But the players' interest in a plot should guide you just as much as your own plans for the game. One of the great pleasures of running a **Mind's Eye Theatre** game is watching a world take shape around you without any outside help. Don't deny yourself that opportunity.

Jump in and start some intrigue yourself every once in a while and see what happens. In many games, a group of players will feel left out of the current plot. It may be that they're naturally too shy to jump in and include themselves with other players, or they may simply be too late to jump on the bandwagon. This is an ideal time to pick on one of their background characters. Give them a piece of a puzzle, or a small, personal dilemma... and then watch it spread. You should never design problems that are small enough for one person to solve — make your players ask each other for help and information. **Mind's Eye Theatre** is at its best when characters start dealing directly with each other and stop relying on the Storyteller for everything. Encourage this whenever you can.

Here are some things that you can toss into the game to keep things moving:

Offer a reward. The classic model for this sort of thing is an object that a number of players want to get a hold of. A treasure hunt like this can set off a wild web of intrigue. *The Maltese Falcon* is a classic example of a plot focusing on this sort of object. This film features enough double-crosses and scams to make your head spin — if you can encourage your players to anywhere near this level of intrigue, you'll have done well.

You shouldn't have to look hard for a good prize for your players to chase. If you have a lot of Toreador players, a piece of rare artwork will do nicely. If the Tremere are popular, offer a lost magical text or item. If you want to really draw everyone out of the woodwork, a rumor concerning a long-lost fragment of the Book of Nod will work wonders. Tailor your bait to your audience, and you'll inevitably get a response.

The prize in this hunt doesn't even have to be a physical item. An informant who knows some damning information about the prince or a fugitive from another city that has a price on his head can serve very well as a prize in this game. "Live bait" like this is a little trickier to manage, however — it tends to have ideas all it own about who will take possession of it. Keep the actions of your "bait" in mind as the player try to capture it.

No matter what the prize in the game is, don't let players obtain it easily or cheaply. Most rare artwork is tucked away very securely in museums and auctioned off at very high prices. Artifacts of magic often have… odd… guardians, and can be inherently dangerous in their own right. And a living trophy should actively defend itself from all takers. A prize like this isn't valuable if it comes cheap. Force your players to call in favors and ask others for help. Doing so lets the plot grow and the web of intrigue spread.

Be cautious about letting your prize stay in play after one of the players finally gets her hands on it, however. If it's an especially potent magic item or weapon, you may want to get rid of it after the hunt is over. One of the more amusing ways to do this is…

Threaten a punishment. A "hot potato" tossed into the game can make for a very fast paced and frenetic game of intrigue. Place something in the game that will cause all kinds of problems for its owner and watch how fast it changes hands. Objects can turn into hot potatoes with frightening speed at times: If the elder who originally owned that fascinating piece of artwork shows up, or the fragment of the Book of Nod turns out to be cursed, things can get very interesting.

While it's hard to obtain a prize, it should be very difficult to get rid of a punishment. Cursed items have a way of staying with their owners. Tossing that priceless painting into the garbage doesn't mean that the elder won't trace the piece to its new owner… and once the elder does so, he's going to ask some hard questions. Again, make players rely on each other for help to get out of trouble and watch the fun begin.

No matter what you decide to throw into the mix, keep track of who does what to whom and make sure that all the actions have consequences. With any luck, the activity your toy generates will affect characters who didn't even know it was in play.

Appendix:
For Storytellers

Inconnu, Monitors and
the Storyteller

The Ancient Ones

The Camarilla would have its constituent members believe that the two major sects of Cainites — itself and the Sabbat — are the only significant adversaries vying for supremacy of the night. But the hours of darkness do not necessarily belong to either group. Indeed, in these uncertain modern nights a growing number of vampires prefer to avoid (or reject outright) the political posturing and machinations of both groups, remaining aloof and unaligned.

Among those who would carve their own futures are beings of unimaginable antiquity and power. These individuals intentionally set themselves apart from their lesser kin, observing them from the shadows and remaining unseen by all but those to whom they wish to appear. Vampires of the Camarilla and Sabbat call them by various names, the most common being Inconnu. As the Final Nights approach, as the rumors of Gehenna arrive on ill-fated wings of omen, many eyes in both sects probe the shadows for signs of these elusive Cainites and for an indication of what role these potent Kindred will play in the unfolding drama of the Jyhad.

The Inconnu

The Inconnu are less of a sect in the accepted sense and more of a loosely affiliated community built on the principles of mutual respect and privacy. They seem to be a band of individuals that share some common interests and experiences, and yet remain at a discreet distance from each other out of respect and fear for one another's power. If there is some governing body or other rulership that leads the Inconnu, only they know about it, and they aren't talking. The few Cainites who might be willing to identify themselves as members of this

clandestine group sometimes verify these "facts," but almost never elaborate or offer more detailed information about themselves or their secretive associates.

The Monitors

Encounters between the Inconnu and other vampires are exceedingly rare at best, but the younger Kindred who do come into contact with one most likely meet their city's Monitor. For reasons and by means known only to themselves, Monitors accept the duty of observing all that transpires within a chosen city, perhaps trying to comprehend the true meanings behind the events that unfold before their watchful eyes.

Not every city has a Monitor, but those rare few that do tend to be the focus of intense Cainite activity. How these secret observers choose the cities they watch over is a mystery to everyone but themselves (the few Monitors willing to speak about themselves at all appear to have almost no discernable connections to the metropolises they inhabit), a fact that gives rise to all variety of speculations and rumors. Perhaps the most popular theory in these modern nights is that the Monitors are somehow connected with the portents that herald the advent of the Final Nights.

Storytelling Considerations

The Inconnu and Monitors hold many temptations for the unwary or inexperienced Storyteller. The thought of introducing such a tantalizing mystery into the ongoing chronicle is nearly irresistible, and with good reason: Few events in a Kindred character's existence could match an encounter with one of these ancients for sheer drama and memorability. But using these creatures in a story demands that you take special care: Mishandled contact between player characters and one of the Inconnu can plunge your otherwise smoothly run chronicle into a tailspin from which it may never recover. The primary considerations when running such a plotline are properly casting the roles, maintaining a sense of mystery and carefully using character types. The following guidelines will help you tell Inconnu and Monitor stories with confidence while leaving your ongoing chronicle intact.

Casting the Parts

Only Narrators should play characters who embody power of this magnitude. It should be obvious that only a portrayal by a Narrator — and a skilled one at that — can realize the full potential of such a being. It's inevitable that one or more players will ask for the opportunity to portray one of these creatures as a player character, but the answer must always be "No." Do yourself, your players and your chronicle a big favor and practice answering this question properly until you can do so with confidence. In fact, the only point at which you should even consider including a member of the Inconnu in your story is when you can give the role to a Narrator whom you can trust implicitly. The Narrator must be able to portray the awesome presence and barely contained power of the character believably while still adhering to your principles of interaction.

After you decide on the right Narrator for the part, involve her in creating the character she will play. Ask her to help you answer these important questions about the Inconnu persona, so that she can be confident in portraying the character as convincingly as possible:

- Where does she come from?
- What was her mortal life like?
- Who Embraced her?
- What are her most important hopes, dreams and fears?
- What tactics, strategies and schemes does she employ?
- What are her plans for the future, both hers and others?

The answers to these questions will help you decide exactly how the character behaves and how she might come to be involved in the unlives of your characters.

CHARACTER INTERACTIONS

Once you see the kind of dread and curiosity an Inconnu character can inspire, you'll be tempted to utilize one or more of them with some regularity. Resist this impulse, and employ the Inconnu and Monitors sparingly. Otherwise, you will sharply reduce their effectiveness and dilute the awe and terror they should inspire. These Kindred tend to overshadow entire chronicles with the sheer scale of their power: Their goals start to pervade all the plots and subplots if they are not used with restraint and portrayed with maturity and discretion.

Regardless of how many centuries they survive, most vampires will never meet one of the Inconnu, and even those who do often fail to realize the significance of the occasion. Most often, an Inconnu is merely an identifiable but nearly intangible presence felt in the mind rather than the senses. On those rarest of occasions when a member of the Inconnu interacts directly with a character, remember that the exchange occurs on the ancient's terms. She only meets at times and places of her own choosing, and even then, such encounters may appear to be something entirely different than what her true purpose might suggest. Strive to make these meetings as portentous and memorable as possible without revealing the exact nature of what is transpiring. Rather than reveal the character's true identity, the Narrator portraying the Inconnu should be prepared to present a false persona and use the character's powers to reinforce the disguise in the eyes and minds of those younger Kindred with whom she interacts. Before you allow a single Inconnu to appear even once in the game, even for a brief moment, establish with the Narrator playing the role the manner in which she will use the persona to evoke these feelings of fear and respect in the other characters. This need not be a flamboyant display of obvious power: Less is often more when utilizing these particular story tools.

Kindred who have never met one of these beings often imagine that they are among the most cryptic and indirect of all vampires. On the contrary, the ancients seem to have no patience for such games: They are wont to be surprisingly plain-spoken and alarmingly direct. No Monitor wishes to commit the extraordinary risk of revealing herself only to have the younger vampires with whom she wishes to converse miss the entire point she was trying to make! No matter what happens, do not allow the recipients of the Inconnu's attentions to be blasé about it — no one encounters one of these creatures and escapes unchanged, and whether that change is for good or ill is something that should plague the characters' minds for some time to come. Even the most

brash and intractable young Kindred should feel compelled to treat these ancients with the respect, even reverence, that is their due.

During the course of the interactions, younger Kindred should find it next to impossible to discern the true natures, identities and goals of these ancient beings: They should remain inscrutable in the eyes of their lessers. The Inconnu have untold centuries, even millennia, of experience and wisdom on which to draw. You can choose to stage such an encounter as a one-shot scene that isn't connected to your greater plot, or as an event that underscores the themes and moods you're incorporating into your ongoing chronicle. A member of the Inconnu might show up to deliver a warning, utter a cryptic threat, render a puzzling congratulation, conduct a subtle indoctrination or even recruit for a cause. If the encounter is between an Inconnu and a single weaker vampire, try to develop the scene in such a way that the player character is impressed with the benefits of keeping the nature of the meeting to himself. If the encounter is between an Inconnu and multiple lesser vampires, strive to give the occasion the feel of a state visit or an audience with a sovereign power rather than an informal chat.

USING THE CHARACTERS

Conflicts that include a Monitor or other member of the Inconnu must necessarily be stable enough to carry the story forward for a significant amount of time. If the story features only a single member of this mysterious sect, decrease the ancient Cainite's power so that she does not currently enjoy the full benefit of her many advantages. Perhaps she awakened only recently and requires time to restore herself to her former heights of power. Perhaps, during her convalescence, she plans to gather useful information about the Kindred of the city. If the story involves multiple ancients, the best way to achieve story stability is to make each side relatively equal in strength, at least as the story opens. A degree of parity ensures that no side will defeat the other too quickly, and instead the Inconnu must vie for pawns and allies from among the weaker Cainites of the vicinity before they can make any significant strides toward victory.

INCONNU STORIES

The Sleeper Must Awaken — A Cainite of incalculable power slumbers beneath the city. But even in her sleep, her restless mind has the ability to affect the nightly lives of the lesser vampires who populate the area. Perhaps some of the characters suffer from strange, inexplicable dreams as the result of the sleeper's slow striving toward wakefulness. And what happens when she finally awakens and emerges? Will she move among the weaker Cainites, or will she observe them clandestinely? Will she select pawns or allies from their number, or will she treat each with equal disdain or enmity? Perhaps her behavior will be so bizarre and inhuman that even the elder Cainites are at a complete loss to understand her. The mood of this story should be one of deep mystery.

Rivals to the End — The characters' home is the newest backdrop against which a pair or trio of ancients fight the latest battle in their shadow war. This conflict has raged across continents and centuries without resolution, destroying lives and unlives with equal disdain. Now, as the Final Nights loom ever closer, it threatens to engulf still more unwitting victims and devastate yet another city. The characters become the scouts, standard bearers and armies — or perhaps the chess pieces — in this latest chapter in a saga that will undoubtedly continue until

one or all of the combatants are swept from the board. Paranoia is the watchword for this tale, with a healthy dose of fear thrown in for good measure.

There Can Be Only One — Driven by rivals who are hot on his heels and thirsting for his destruction, a single ancient arrives in the characters' midst. The newcomer is battered and shaken from his ordeal and needs time to lick his wounds. Reluctant to continue running despite the power of those who hound him, he casts about for a weapon… and finds the characters conveniently at hand. He uses what little time remains to hone his unwitting allies, pitting them against foes both real and imagined but all of his own manufacture. How will the characters react when they learn that this creature has orchestrated their woes? What will happen when the pursuers finally catch up to their quarry? This is a fast-paced story that features lots of action; try to evoke a mood of excitement and escalating tension.

Portrait Gallery

Below are some basic templates and roleplaying notes for the vampires and mortals that populate Camarilla strongholds. Innocent bystanders, ghouls for cannon fodder, princes briefly glimpsed in the shadows — they're all here.

However, none of these templates will hold up under any sort of extended use. These templates exist for use as backdrops to the main action and as examples for creating more fully rounded characters. If a template starts showing up regularly, it's up to the Storyteller to build a true character sheet for this person — a cookie-cutter set of statistics just won't do.

If the players wise up to the statistics of these Narrator characters and start metagaming ("Well, we know this thug is going to be *Callous*…"), don't hesitate to doctor these templates as you see fit. Who says that this thug isn't a *Wiry, Observant* little fellow who just wants to get away and report to his boss? Occasionally throwing the players a curve ball keeps them in the game and on their toes.

Playing to Type

The difference between a good story and a great story is all in the details. It's easy to let Thug Number One become just a set of numbers so that you can roll on to the next encounter. Don't let that happen. Even ordinary thugs can be interesting people — just watch *Pulp Fiction* or *Reservoir Dogs* to see how. Every time one of your players kills that thug sent by the prince, he kills an actual human being, with hopes and dreams just as valid as his own. That's the essence of letting Humanity slip away and succumbing to the Beast.

Likewise, the second neonate on the left could just as easily be the players. Don't forget to remind them of that as the prince sends her off to execution for a *faux pas* during court. Each and every encounter is a chance to deepen the roleplaying in your chronicle. Don't let it slip by.

THE RELENTLESS JUSTICAR

Clan: Malkavian

Nature: Autocrat

Demeanor: Perfectionist

Generation: 6th

Physical Traits (16): *Athletic, Brawny, Quick x 3, Resilient x 3, Tough x 2, Steady x 3, Wiry x 3*

Social Traits (18): *Charismatic x 3, Commanding x 3, Dignified x 3, Intimidating x 6, Persuasive x 3*

Mental Traits (17): *Attentive x 3, Determined x 6, Disciplined x 2, Knowledgeable x 3, Observant x 3*

Abilities: *Athletics x 4, Brawl x 3, Dodge x 5, Firearms x 4, Intimidation x 3, Law (Kindred) x 5, Leadership x 3, Lore (Camarilla) x 5, Lore (Sabbat) x 4, Melee x 4, Politics x 4, Subterfuge x 2*

Disciplines:

Auspex: Heightened Senses, Aura Perception, Spirit's Touch, Telepathy

Celerity: Alacrity, Swiftness, Rapidity, Legerity

Dementation: Passion, The Haunting, Eyes of Chaos, Voice of Madness, Total Insanity

Fortitude: Endurance, Mettle, Resilience

Obfuscate: Cloak of Shadows, Unseen Presence, Mask of a Thousand Faces, Vanish from the Mind's Eye, Cloak the Gathering

Path: Humanity 2

Virtues: Conscience 2, Self Control 3, Courage 2

Backgrounds: *Contacts x 5, Resources x 4, Herd x 2*

Derangement: Sanguinary Animism

Status (5): *Acknowledged, Faultless, Feared, Just, Revered*

Blood: 30 (May spend 6/round)

Willpower: 16

Roleplaying Hints: You date back to the days of Rome. You have seen the birth of the Camarilla itself. There is nothing a group of neonates can do that can impress you, surprise you, upset you or even slow you down. Your derangement is something you indulge away from work. When you are performing the role of justicar, Malkav's curse never shows. When you arrive in a city, it is for only one reason — something has gone terribly, terribly wrong. Use whatever tools you have to put things right again, be they political, social or supernatural. Then leave as soon as you can. No matter how bad things are, the Kindred should fear your arrival and look forward to your departure.

THE CAREFUL ARCHON

Clan: Toreador

Nature: Judge

Demeanor: Soldier

Generation: 9th

Physical Traits (12): *Agile x 3, Quick x 3, Tough x 3, Wiry x 3*

Social Traits (11): *Charismatic x 3, Commanding x 3, Diplomatic x 2, Intimidating x 3*

Mental Traits (13): *Clever x 2, Discerning x 3, Disciplined x 3, Insightful x 3, Observant x 3*

Abilities: *Athletics x 3, Brawl x 2, Dodge x 4, Drive x 2, Firearms x 4, Investigation x 5, Law (Camarilla) x 3, Leadership x 3, Lore (Camarilla) x 4, Lore (Sabbat) x 4, Melee x 2, Politics x 3, Security x 3, Stealth x 4, Streetwise x 4, Subterfuge x 4, Survival x 2*

Disciplines:

Auspex: Heightened Senses, Aura Perception, Spirit's Touch

Celerity: Alacrity, Swiftness, Rapidity, Legerity

Fortitude: Endurance, Mettle, Resilience

Obfuscate: Cloak of Shadows, Unseen Presence

Presence: Awe, Dread Gaze, Entrancement

Path: Humanity 4

Virtues: Conscience 3, Self Control 4, Courage 5

Backgrounds: *Contacts x 3, Resources x 2*

Status (4): *Acknowledged, Esteemed, Honorable, Just*

Blood: 13 (May spend 1/round).

Willpower: 10

Roleplaying Hints: You are here to discover a secret. Somewhere, somehow, the justicar has learned that something is wrong in this town, and you are here to figure out what. Never announce yourself as an archon right away. Doing so wastes one of the best weapons in your arsenal. Use all the tools in your bag of tricks — small talk, glamour, violence, stealth — to discover the truth first. You can use all of them well, but only when you need to. You can even pose as a neonate if you have to. After you've found out what the city's dirty secret is, announce yourself and watch all the petty players run for cover as they realize how much trouble they're truly in.

THE WEARY ANARCH

Clan: Brujah

Nature: Rebel

Demeanor: Curmudgeon

Generation: 13th

Physical Traits (10): *Brawny x 2, Brutal x 2, Quick x 2, Tough x 4*

Social Traits (8): *Commanding x 2, Intimidating x 4, Magnetic x 2*

Mental Traits (9): *Cunning x 3, Determined x 3, Patient x 3, Violent (N)*

Abilities: *Brawl x 3, Dodge x 3, Drive x 3, Firearms x 3, Intimidation x 2, Leadership x 2, Lore (Anarch), Melee x 2, Security x 2, Stealth x 2, Streetwise x 4*

Disciplines:

Celerity: Alacrity, Swiftness, Rapidity

Potence: Prowess, Might, Vigor

Presence: Awe, Dread Gaze.

Path: Humanity 3
Virtues: Conscience 3, Self Control 3, Courage 4
Backgrounds: *Contacts x 3*, Influence: *Police x 1*, *Street x 3*, *Underworld x 1*, *Resources x 2*
Status (0):
Blood: 10 (May spend 1/round)
Willpower: 6
Roleplaying Hints: You've been at this a long time for an anarch, nearly 20 years. You've seen a lot of dreams die. You've still got the guts, the muscle and the cojones to make the masses see the truth and fight the system — but each night you have to work a little harder to get up and do it all over again. That's all right. You don't mind. You were strong enough to break away from the Camarilla 20 years ago. You're strong enough to stick to your guns now. You just know enough to be careful, like an old weary alley cat, ready to run and start all over again when the dream dies.

THE COMMITTED ANARCH

Clan: Brujah
Nature: Rebel
Demeanor: Visionary
Generation: 13th
Physical Traits (10): *Brawny x 3*, *Quick x 4*, *Tough x 3*
Social Traits (9): *Expressive x 3*, *Magnetic x 3*, *Persuasive x 3*
Mental Traits (8): *Cunning x 3*, *Dedicated x 3*, *Determined x 2*, *Violent (N)*
Abilities: *Brawl x 2*, *Firearms x 2*, *Leadership x 3*
Disciplines:
Celerity: Alacrity, Swiftness
Potence: Prowess
Presence: Awe
Path: Humanity 4
Virtues: Conscience 4, Self Control 3, Courage 4
Backgrounds: Influence: *Street x 2*
Status (0):
Blood: 10 (May spend 1/round)
Willpower: 6
Roleplaying Hints: You didn't let anyone back you down or tell you what to do when you were alive. Damned if you're going to let death stop you. You are a zealot for the anarch cause — you've seen the rotting shell of the Camarilla, and you know in your heart that it has to come down. You're not quite sure what being a vampire is all about yet — things like "immortality" still haven't sunk in. After 20 years you'll either be just like the Weary Anarch, or you'll be ash on the wind. But right now, you live for the moment and the cause. Give your every waking moment to making sure the Anarch movement rolls into the millennium like a freight train. There's nothing sweeter than freedom. Never let it go.

The Innocent Neonate

Clan: Toreador
Nature: Celebrant
Demeanor: Conformist
Generation: 13th
Physical Traits (8): *Lithe x 3, Nimble x 2, Quick x 3, Docile (N)*
Social Traits (10): *Expressive x 3, Gorgeous, Ingratiating x 3, Persuasive x 3*
Mental Traits (9): *Clever x 3, Creative x 3, Observant x 3*
Abilities: *Dodge x 2, Performance, Subterfuge*
Disciplines:
Auspex: Heightened Senses, Aura Perception
Presence: Awe
Path: Humanity 4
Virtues: Conscience 5, Self Control 2, Courage 1
Backgrounds: Herd, Influence: *High Society, Resources*
Status (1): *Acknowledged*
Blood: 10 (May spend 1/round)
Willpower: 3
Roleplaying Hints: Why let death stop the party? You were a pretty college kid who liked running with the wrong crowd. Well, you're really running with the wrong crowd now, and you really like it. Traditions? Whatever — all you have to do is suck up to the elders like dear old Daddy, and everything will be all right, right? You have a lot to learn before you can be considered competent at being Kindred, but your sire drummed all the rules into your head before she released you. All you have to do is enjoy yourself and stay out of trouble, and everything will be just fine. That's what you keep telling yourself, anyway....

The Bitter Ancilla

Clan: Tremere
Nature: Bravo
Demeanor: Pedagogue
Generation: 10th
Physical Traits (10): *Brutal x 3, Nimble x 3, Resilient x 3, Tireless*
Social Traits (11): *Charming x 3, Dignified x 3, Ingratiating x 3, Witty x 2*
Mental Traits (12): *Cunning x 3, Determined x 2, Knowledgeable x 3, Rational x 3*
Abilities: *Awareness x 3, Intimidation x 3, Law, Lore (Camarilla) x 2, Occult x 3, Politics x 2, Stealth x 2, Subterfuge x 2*
Disciplines:
Auspex: Heightened Senses, Aura Perception
Dominate: Command, Mesmerism
Thaumaturgy: Path of Blood: A Taste for Blood, Blood Rage
The Lure of Flames: Hand of Flame
Rituals: Communicate with Kindred Sire, Deflection of Wooden Doom, Principal Focus of Vitae Infusion

Path: Humanity 3
Virtues: Conscience 3, Self Control 2, Courage 4
Backgrounds: Influence: Occult x 3, Mentor x 3, Resources x 3
Status (2): *Acknowledged, Praised*
Blood: 10 (May spend 1/round)
Willpower: 5
Roleplaying Hints: You've figured out the trap you are in, and you don't like it at all. You're competent, and you are utterly devoted to the Camarilla and your chantry (not necessarily in that order). But because of your generation, you will never hold any meaningful position of power. You take out your rage on the neonates and apprentices under your charge — while you may say that you're merely teaching them how things work in the Camarilla, in reality you're just making yourself feel better by making them feel humiliated and worthless. And best of all, the prince still heaps meaningless praise upon you for your service to the wonderful Camarilla. Perhaps it might be worth looking into a way out....

THE FRIGHTENED ELDER

Clan: Ventrue
Nature: Penitent
Demeanor: Autocrat
Generation: 8th
Physical Traits (12): *Enduring x3, Quick x3, Tenacious x3, Tough x3*
Social Traits (14): *Charming x 3, Commanding x 2, Dignified x 3, Intimidating x 3, Magnetic x 3*
Mental Traits (13): *Alert x 3, Cunning x 3, Disciplined x 3, Knowledgeable x 3, Reflective*
Abilities: *Dodge x 2, Firearms x 2, Intimidation x 3, Law x 3, Lore (Camarilla) x 3, Politics x 4, Subterfuge x 3*
Disciplines:
Dominate: Command, Mesmerism, Forgetful Mind, Conditioning
Fortitude: Endurance, Mettle
Presence: Awe, Dread Gaze, Entrancement, Summon
Path: Humanity 3
Virtues: Conscience 3, Self Control 4, Courage 2
Backgrounds: Influence: *Finance x 4, Bureaucracy x 3, Legal x 3, Resources x 4*
Status (3): *Acknowledged, Adored, Well-Known*
Blood: 15 (May spend 3/round)
Willpower: 10
Roleplaying Hints: You had to hide a lot of bodies and do a lot of dangerous things in order to get to the top. You made it, but now you realize that you're just on the bottom of a whole new totem pole. You know the truth – about the Antediluvians and the Camarilla and the Sabbat and a few things that the rest know nothing about. Never show weakness. Never show fear. Inside, you are screaming in terror, and if anyone ever finds out, you will truly have something

to scream about. Every day is a dance between control and despair. You dare not miss a beat lest you fall into the abyss.

The Adoring Ghoul

Nature: Masochist
Demeanor: Fanatic
Physical Traits (3): *Enduring x 3*
Social Traits (5): *Charming x 2, Ingratiating x 3, Obnoxious (N)*
Mental Traits (8): *Cunning x 2, Knowledgeable x 3, Patient x 3*
Abilities: Computer, Drive, Firearms x 2, Investigation, Knowledge (Thanatology) x 2
Disciplines:
Fortitude: Endurance
Potence: Prowess
Path: Humanity 3
Virtues: Conscience 2, Self Control 4, Courage 4
Backgrounds: Influence: *Health x 2, Mentor x 2*
Blood: 3
Willpower: 2
Roleplaying Hints: Your domitor is your world. You would do anything for him. Anything. You have taken his blood and abuse for so long that you've grown to enjoy the taste. You are always by his side, waiting on him, fulfilling his every whim. You take one night at a time, one drop of blood at a time. Anything else is too much to think about, too much to ask. Just wait for the next fix of blood, the next command to give your life meaning.

The Expendable Ghoul

Nature: Conformist
Demeanor: Bravo
Physical Traits (10): *Brawny x 3, Brutal x 2, Quick x2, Tough x 3*
Social Traits (3): *Intimidating, Callous (N)*
Mental Traits (5): *Determined x 3, Disciplined x 2, Predictable (N), Violent (N)*
Abilities: *Brawl x 3, Dodge x 2, Firearms x 3, Intimidation*
Disciplines:
Potence: Prowess
Path: Humanity 3
Virtues: Conscience 2, Self Control 4, Courage 4
Backgrounds: Influence: *Street, Mentor*
Blood: 3
Willpower: 2
Roleplaying Hints: You were in a gang once. You used drugs once. Now you're in the best gang and you the best drug of all. So maybe you don't go out and party a lot anymore, it doesn't matter. You're stronger, tougher and better than you ever were before, and everyone knows that you are as bad as they come. Well, they would if they ever saw you. But it doesn't matter. You are the elite, the invincible, the best you will ever be. After all, she told you so.

The Realistic Ghoul

Nature: Survivor
Demeanor: Conformist
Physical Traits (3): *Enduring x 3*
Social Traits (7): *Ingratiating x 3, Observant x 2, Rational x 2*
Mental Traits (5): *Knowledgeable x 3, Rational, Shrewd*
Abilities: *Computer, Drive x 2, Firearms x 3, Investigation x 3, Knowledge (Thanatology) x 3, Lore (Kindred) x 2*
Disciplines:
Fortitude: Endurance
Potence: Prowess
Path: Humanity 3
Virtues: Conscience 2, Self Control 4, Courage 4
Backgrounds: Influence: *Health x 1, Street x 1, Mentor x 3*
Blood: 3
Willpower: 3
Roleplaying Hints: You've done this for a while. The blood that was your salvation and glory is now a routine part of your existence — a central one, but routine nonetheless. You don't get excited about it anymore. You've stood by your domitor through a lot, and though you have suffered terribly, you've somehow managed to get through it all in one piece. Your domitor keeps you around out of habit and maybe because he hopes your luck will rub off on him. Luck never had anything to do with it, though. It was the hunger for the blood and the will to live. That was all. You don't understand how the Kindred can underestimate that delicious power flowing through their veins. Maybe someday you'll have the will to break free and show them. Someday.

The Good Cop

Nature: Judge
Demeanor: Conformist
Physical Traits (7): *Brawny x 2, Quick x 2, Steady, Tough x 2*
Social Traits (5): *Dignified x 2, Intimidating x 2, Persuasive*
Mental Traits (3): *Observant x 2, Patient*
Abilities: *Brawl x 2, Dodge x 2, Firearms x 2, Law x 2*
Path: Humanity 4
Virtues: Conscience 4, Self Control 4, Courage 4
Backgrounds: Influence: *Police x 2, Resources x 2*
Willpower: 3
Roleplaying Hints: To protect and serve — you believe in that. The system's corrupt as hell, and it'd be easy to let this one slide. But someone has to watch out for the innocents, that someone is you. All you have is a badge, a gun and the knowledge that you are right. Be careful out there. Don't be afraid to call for backup if things look bad. Here's hoping you never find out the truth about the world you serve.

The Cocky Thug

Nature: Bravo
Demeanor: Bravo
Physical Traits (10): *Brawny x 2, Brutal x 3, Quick x 2, Tough x 2*
Social Traits (5): *Intimidating x 5, Callous (N)*
Mental Traits (3): *Determined x 2, Reflective, Violent (N)*
Abilities: *Brawl x 2, Dodge x 2, Firearms x 2, Streetwise x 2*
Path: Humanity 3
Virtues: Conscience 3, Self Control 3, Courage 4
Backgrounds: Influence: *Underworld x 1, Resources x 1*
Willpower: 2
Roleplaying Hints: Hey, you're not a bad guy. You just want something, and you're going to get it, right? Here's your gun, here's your knife, and nobody needs to get hurt if you pay attention. You're cool. You have it all under control. Maybe you're as funny, as witty and as cool as you think you are. Probably not. Who's going to argue, hey?

The Nosy Reporter

Nature: Competitor
Demeanor: Visionary
Physical Traits (3): *Quick, Steady, Tenacious*
Social Traits (9): *Charismatic x 3, Charming x 2, Dignified x 2, Persuasive x 2, Callous (N)*
Mental Traits (5): *Dedicated, Determined, Observant x 3, Shortsighted (N)*
Abilities: *Computer, Dodge, Investigation x 3*
Path: Humanity 4
Virtues: Conscience 3, Self Control 4, Courage 4
Backgrounds: Influence: *Media x 2, Resources x 2*
Willpower: 3
Roleplaying Hints: You're on the front line of the ratings war. Every night you and your crew have to find the awful tragedy of the hour — you're on the prowl for the eleven o'clock homicide, accident or fire to make those couch potatoes tune in. You have the instincts of a bloodhound when it comes to hunting down these nightly terrors, and a heart made of stone when you report them. Pack up the cameras and keep moving: there's another knifing across town. Maybe someday you'll find that big story, the conspiracy that makes it all make sense. Yeah, right. Hurry up, we're live.

The Hapless Bystander

Nature: Survivor
Demeanor: Conformist
Physical Traits (5): Energetic x 2, Quick x 2, Tough
Social Traits (6): Friendly x 2, Genial x 2, Ingratiating x 2, Naïve (N)
Mental Traits (5): Observant x 2, Patient, Rational
Abilities: Brawl, Computer, Dodge, Drive, Finance or Streetwise
Path: Humanity 4

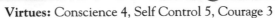

Virtues: Conscience 4, Self Control 5, Courage 3
Backgrounds: Resources x 2
Willpower: 3
Roleplaying Hints: You didn't see anything. You don't know anything. Why is he asking you? You were just minding your own business, doing what you do every day to get by, nothing special, and you didn't see anything, okay? You just want to get your paycheck, go home, watch TV and go to bed. You don't want any trouble, okay?

THE FRIGHTENED CHILD:

Nature: Child
Demeanor: Child
Physical Traits (3): *Agile, Quick, Resilient, Puny (N)*
Social Traits (3): *Friendly, Genial, Ingratiating*
Mental Traits (3): *Attentive, Clever, Creative*
Abilities: *Awareness x 3*
Path: Humanity 5
Virtues: Conscience 5, Self Control 2, Courage 3
Backgrounds: *Mentor x 2*
Willpower: 0
Roleplaying Hints: You're lost. Your daddy rushed off a while ago, and you're alone. Maybe the funny man chased him away — the one that's standing in a corner, looking at you all surprised. Maybe he's lost too. If you go and ask him nicely, he might be able to tell you where your daddy went or at least take you home. Mind your manners now, like mommy taught you, and everything will be just fine.